D1520698

JEWS AND THEIR ROMAN RIVALS

Jews and Their Roman Rivals

PAGAN ROME'S CHALLENGE TO ISRAEL

Katell Berthelot

PRINCETON UNIVERSITY PRESS

PRINCETON & OXFORD

Requests for permission to reproduce material from this work
should be sent to permissions@press.princeton.edu

Published by Princeton University Press
41 William Street, Princeton, New Jersey 08540
6 Oxford Street, Woodstock, Oxfordshire OX20 1TR

press.princeton.edu

ISBN 978-0-691-19929-0
ISBN (e-book) 978-0-691-22042-0

Library of Congress Control Number: 2021941501

British Library Cataloging-in-Publication Data is available

Editorial: Fred Appel, Jenny Tan, and James Collier
Production Editorial: Debbie Tegarden
Jacket/Cover Design: Pamela Schnitter
Production: Erin Suydam
Publicity: Kate Hensley and Kathryn Stevens

Jacket images: (top) Roman coin celebrating Roman victory against the First Jewish
Revolt (destruction of the temple in 70 CE); (bottom) Silver shekel minted by the rebels
during the Bar Kokhba Revolt of 132–135 CE. © The Trustees of the British Museum

Publication of this book has been aided by the European Research Council, under the
European Union's Seventh Framework Program (FP/2007–2013)/ERC Grant Agreement
no. 614 424.

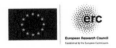

This book has been composed in Classic Miller

Printed on acid-free paper. ∞

Printed in the United States of America

10   9   8   7   6   5   4   3   2   1

CONTENTS

ILLUSTRATIONS

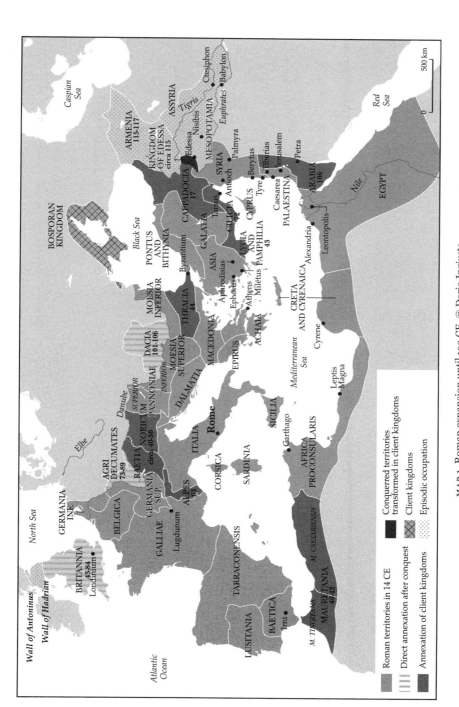

MAP 1. Roman expansion until 192 CE. © Dario Ingiusto.

Source: based on Christophe Badel, *Atlas de l'Empire romain: construction et apogée, 300 av. J.-C.–200 apr. J.-C.* (Paris: Autrement, 2012), 45.

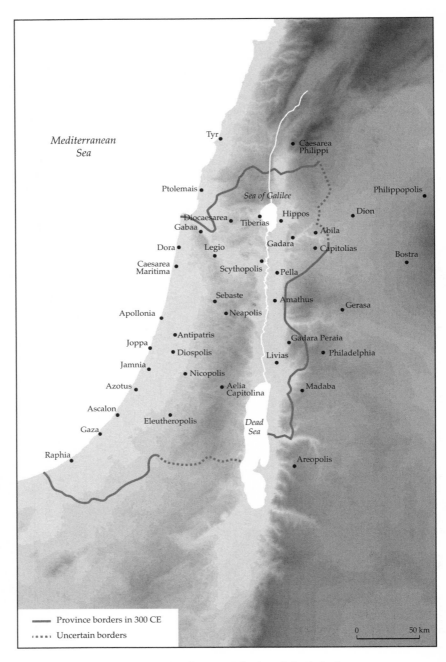

Mediterranean
Sea

Tyr

Caesarea
Philippi

Ptolemais

Sea of Galilee

Philippopolis

Diocaesarea

Hippos

Dion

Gabaa

Tiberias

Abila

Dora

Legio

Gadara

Capitolias

Bostra

Caesarea
Maritima

Scythopolis

Pella

Sebaste

Amathus

Gerasa

Apollonia

Neapolis

Antipatris

Gadara Peraia

Joppa

Diospolis

Livias

Philadelphia

Jamnia

Nicopolis

Azotus

Aelia
Capitolina

Madaba

Ascalon

Eleutheropolis

*Dead
Sea*

Gaza

Raphia

Areopolis

Province borders in 300 CE

Uncertain borders

0   50 km

MAP 2. Main cities of Roman Palestine. © Dario Ingiusto.
Source: based on Nicole Belayche, *Iudaea-Palaestina: The Pagan Cults in Roman
Palestine (Second to Fourth Century)* (Tübingen: Mohr Siebeck, 2001), 19.

ACKNOWLEDGMENTS

THIS BOOK NEVER would have seen the light without the generous support of the European Research Council, which funded the whole "Judaism and Rome" project from 2014 to 2019.[1] I thank the ERC wholeheartedly for the Consolidator grant that I was awarded, especially because it allowed me to gather both a wide network of associate scholars and a team of researchers dedicated to the project.

Among the many people who contributed to this book, directly or indirectly, by participating in "Judaism and Rome" research activities, my gratitude goes first to the members of my team: Caroline Barron, Aitor Blanco Pérez, Kimberley Fowler, Marie Roux, and Yael Wilfand. I learned a lot from each of them during the project's monthly seminars in Aix-en-Provence, and this book would have been considerably poorer were it not for our intense discussions of numerous Greek, Roman, Jewish, and Christian sources, which have directly contributed to many of the arguments that I make here. At the end of this volume, I provide a list of some important sources with links on the project's website, www.judaism-and-rome.org, but that list is far from exhaustive, and I invite the interested reader to explore the site further in order to appreciate the extent of the work that the team has performed. Alongside the researchers, I also thank the two other members of the team, Jérôme Assier and Sabrina Hanks, who efficiently handled the project's administrative and financial management.

Beyond the team, many scholars participated in this project, both through the seminars, workshops, and conferences that we organized and more generally by providing feedback and suggesting ways to refine our analyses of various sources and historical issues. Some were involved in the project since its inception in 2012, even before it had benefited from an ERC grant, and I address special thanks to these early companions: Jonathan Price (who has been a supportive and forceful coeditor of two collective volumes, in addition a most welcoming host in Jerusalem), Hervé Inglebert, Greg Woolf, Carlos Lévy, Emmanuelle Rosso, Ron Naiweld, Yair Furstenberg, Matthias Morgenstern, Gilles Dorival, Pierluigi Lanfranchi, and Peter Oakes. Special thanks are also due to Jonathan Price and Oded Irshai for organizing a wonderful workshop

1. This research has been funded by the European Research Council under the European Union's Seventh Framework Program (FP/2007-2013)/ERC Grant Agreement no. 614 424. It has been conducted within the framework of the ERC project "Judaism and Rome," under the auspices of the Centre national de la recherche scientifique (CNRS) and Aix-Marseille University, UMR 7297 TDMAM (Aix-en-Provence, France).

on languages in the Roman empire at Zikhron Yaakov in 2016; to Greg Woolf for hosting a lively seminar on *Pax Romana* at the Institute of Classical Studies in London in 2017; to Martin Goodman and Catherine Darbo-Peschanski, who helped organize the first conference on Roman law and its provincial reception, which took place in Oxford in 2015; and to Capucine Nemo-Pekelman, Natalie B. Dohrmann, and Yair Furstenberg, who helped organize the second conference on Roman law (Aix-en-Provence, 2018). I also express my deep gratitude to Capucine for introducing me to the complex field of Roman law, and to both Capucine and Natalie for coediting with me the project's final volume of proceedings, *Legal Engagement: The Reception of Roman Law and Tribunals by Jews and Other Inhabitants of the Empire* (Rome: Ecole Française de Rome, 2021). Finally, I thank Clifford Ando, Myles Lavan, and Holger Zellentin for participating in the ERC team's intensive two-day seminars and for generously sharing their knowledge with its participants.

Several people read chapters of this book and provided invaluable feedback, for which I am immensely grateful: Peter Machinist, Dominik Markl, Benedetta Rossi, Greg Woolf, Natalie B. Dohrmann, Hervé Inglebert, Sarit Kattan Gribetz, Yael Wilfand, Michal Bar-Asher Siegal, Oded Irshai, and Paula Fredricksen. They of course cannot be held responsible for any mistake remaining in this volume, nor for the opinions expressed herein.

This book greatly benefited from a scholarship granted by the Ecole Française de Rome (EFR) in the fall of 2018, for which I thank the EFR very warmly. I also offer my gratitude to the EFR and its team for hosting and impeccably organizing the project's conference on Roman power in May 2017. In addition to the EFR's library at the Palazzo Farnese, I made frequent use of the libraries of the Pontifical Biblical Institute in Rome, the Catholic Institute in Paris, and the French Biblical and Archaeological School and the National Library in Jerusalem. I am indebted to these institutions for the services they generously provided at different stages of my research.

Most important, this book would never have reached its final shape without the extremely diligent and efficient reading of Juliana Froggatt, who is simply the best linguistic editor ever and makes struggling with writing in a language that is not one's own a truly pleasant learning experience. Last but not least, I also thank Fred Appel and Jenny Tan at Princeton University Press, for their patient guidance in bringing this volume to completion.

Primary Sources

ANET	*Ancient Near Eastern Texts*
BMC	*British Museum Coinage*
CIIP	*Corpus Inscriptionum Iudaeae/Palaestinae*, edited by Walter Ameling et al. Berlin: De Gruyter, 2010–.
CIJ	*Corpus Inscriptionum Judaicarum*, edited by Jean-Baptiste Frey, 2 vols. Rome: Pontificio Istituto di archeologia cristiana, 1936–1952.
CIL	*Corpus Inscriptionum Latinarum*
CIRB	*Corpus Inscriptionum Regni Bosporani*, edited by Vasili Vasilevitch Struve et al. Leningrad: Akademia nauk SSSR, Institut istorii, 1965.
COLLATIO	*Collatio legum Mosaicarum et Romanarum*
CPJ	*Corpus Papyrorum Judaicarum*, edited by Victor Tcherikover, Alexander Fuks, and Menahem Stern, 3 vols. Cambridge: Harvard University Press, 1957–1964.
CRAI	*Comptes-Rendus de l'Académie des Inscriptions et Belles-Lettres*
C.TH.	Codex Theodosianus (Theodosian Code)
IAM	*Inscriptions antiques du Maroc*, edited by Lionel Galand et al., 3 vols. Paris: Editions du CNRS, 1966–2003.
IGLS	*Inscriptions Grecques et Latines de la Syrie*. Paris: Paul Geuthner, 1929–.
IGR / IGRR	*Inscriptiones Graecae ad Res Romanas Pertinentes*, edited by René Cagnat et al., 4 vols. Paris: Ernest Leroux, 1901–1927. Reprint: Chicago: Ares, 1975.
IJO I	*Inscriptiones Judaicae Orientis. I: Eastern Europe*, edited by David Noy, Alexander Panayotov, and Hanswulf Bloedhom. Tübingen: Mohr Siebeck, 2004.
IJO II	*Inscriptiones Judaicae Orientis. II: Kleinasien*, edited by Walter Ameling. Tübingen: Mohr Siebeck, 2004.

ILAlg   *Inscriptions Latines de l'Algérie*, edited by Stéphane
Gsell and Hans-Gerog Pflaum, 3 vols. Paris: Champion/
Alger: Société Nationale d'Edition et de Diffusion/Paris:
Académie des Inscriptions et Belles-Lettres, 1922–2003.

ILS   *Inscriptiones Latinae Selectae*, edited by
Hermann Dessau, 3 vols. Berlin: Weidmann,
1892–1916 (repr. Chicago: Ares, 1954–1979).

JIGRE   *Jewish Inscriptions of Graeco-Roman Egypt*, edited by
William Horbury and David Noy. Cambridge: CUP, 1992.

JIWE I   *Jewish Inscriptions of Western Europe, Volume 1: Italy
(excluding the City of Rome), Spain and Gaul*, edited
by David Noy. Cambridge: CUP, 1993. *JIWE* II *Jewish
Inscriptions of Western Europe, Volume 2: The City of
Rome*, edited by David Noy. Cambridge: CUP, 1995.

LIMC   *Lexicon Iconographicum Mythologiae Classicae*,
10 vols. Zürich: Artemis, 1981–2009.

LRBC   *Late Roman Bronze Coinage*

MRI   Mekhilta de-Rabbi Ishmael

NETS   *A New English Translation of the Septuagint*, edited
by Albert Pietersma and Benjamin G. Wright.
Oxford: Oxford University Press, 2007.

OGIS   *Orientis Graeci Inscriptiones Selectae*, edited by Wilhelm
Dittenberger, 2 vols. Leipzig: S. Hirzel, 1903–1905.

P. OXY.   *The Oxyrhynchus Papyri*. London: Egypt Exploration
Fund, 1898–.

RIC   *Roman Imperial Coinage*

RIC II.1   *The Roman Imperial Coinage, Volume II—Part 1,*
(REV. ED.)   *Second Fully Revised Edition, from AD 69–96, Vespasian to
Domitian*, edited by Ian A. Carradice and Theodore V.
Buttrey. London: Spink, 2007.

RPC   *Roman Provincial Coinage*

RRC   *Roman Republican Coinage*, edited by Michael H. Crawford,
2 vols. Cambridge: Cambridge University Press, 1974.

SEG   *Supplementum Epigraphicum Graecum*

Journals and Collections

AJPh	*American Journal of Philology*
ANRW	*Aufstieg und Niedergang der Römischen Welt*
BCH	*Bulletin de correspondance hellénique*
CBQ	*Catholic Biblical Quarterly*
CBR	*Currents in Biblical Research*
DHA	*Dialogues d'histoire ancienne*
HTR	*Harvard Theological Review*
IEJ	*Israel Exploration Journal*
JAJ	*Journal of Ancient Judaism*
JBL	*Journal of Biblical Literature*
JJS	*Journal of Jewish Studies*
JQR	*Jewish Quarterly Review*
JRS	*The Journal of Roman Studies*
JSIJ	*Jewish Studies, an Internet Journal*
JSJ	*Journal for the Study of Judaism*
JSOT	*Journal for the Study of the Old Testament*
JSP	*Journal for the Study of the Pseudepigrapha*
JSQ	*Jewish Studies Quarterly*
LCL	Loeb Classical Library
NTS	*New Testament Studies*
REG	*Revue des Études Grecques*
REJ	*Revue des Études Juives*
RHR	*Revue de l'Histoire des Religions*
SCI	*Scripta Classica Israelica*
ZNW	*Zeitschrift für die Neutestamentliche Wissenschaft*
ZPE	*Zeitschrift für Papyrologie und Epigraphik*

NOTE ON TRANSLATIONS

UNLESS STATED OTHERWISE, all translations of biblical passages are from the New Revised Standard Version and translations of rabbinic texts are my own.

For Greek and Latin texts, I have generally used the translations of the Loeb Classical Library (sometimes with modifications, indicated in the notes).

JEWS AND THEIR ROMAN RIVALS

Introduction

*When pagan Rome brought the ancient Hellenic and Jewish cultural life to
an end, there arose, from the ruins of the latter, a new view of the world.*

MOSES HESS, *ROME AND JERUSALEM:*
THE LAST NATIONALIST QUESTION[1]

AN ABUNDANCE OF ACADEMIC WORKS bear titles such as "Rome and Jerusalem," "Jerusalem and Rome," and "Jerusalem against Rome," followed by
various subtitles. This attests both to scholarly interest in the relationship
between Jews and the Roman empire and to the powerful *imaginaire* associated with Rome in Jewish thought and Jewish studies.[2] The tandem notions
"Rome" and "Jerusalem" have even been used metaphorically to reflect on the
realities of modern Jewry. In Moses Hess' political essay presaging modern
political Zionism, *Rome and Jerusalem: The Last Nationalist Question*, Rome
represents assimilation and emancipation in nineteenth-century Germany (or
Europe more generally), in contrast to Jewish nationalism and aspirations for
an independent state. Rome also symbolizes Christianity, which Hess criticizes

---

1. Hess' work was originally published in German, as *Rom und Jerusalem, die Letzte
Nationalitätsfrage: Briefe und Noten* (2nd edition; Leipzig: M.W. Kaufmann, 1899). It
has been translated in English under the title *Rome and Jerusalem: A Study in Jewish
Nationalism* by Meyer Waxman (New York: Bloch Pub. Co., 1918) and republished as
The Revival of Israel: Rome and Jerusalem, the Last Nationalist Question (trans. Meyer
Waxman; Lincoln: University of Nebraska Press, 1995). For the quotation, see Waxman
1918, 185–186.

2. Recent examples of such titles include Hadas-Lebel 1990, *Jérusalem contre Rome*
[English translation 2006]; Sicker 2001 (*Between Rome and Jerusalem: 300 Years of
Roman-Judaean Relations*); Goodman 2007 (*Rome and Jerusalem: The Clash of Ancient
Civilizations*); Wilker 2007 (*Für Rom und Jerusalem. Die herodianische Dynastie im 1.
Jahrhundert n.Chr.*); Mahieu 2012 (*Between Rome and Jerusalem: Herod the Great and
His Sons in Their Struggle for Recognition: A Chronological Investigation of the Period 40
BC–39 AD with a Time Setting of New Testament Events*).

as a fusion of religious and national identities.[3] Hess' book underscores how, in Jewish memory, the Roman empire—"pagan"[4] and later Christian—remained indelibly associated with the loss of political sovereignty.

From its beginnings with Pompey's victory in Judea in 63 BCE, the demise of Jewish sovereignty had a major effect on Jewish perceptions of Rome. The problem became more acute after the establishment of direct Roman rule in Judea in 6 CE and further intensified following the First Jewish Revolt against Rome (66–73 CE). This book posits, however, that the significance of the encounter between Israel and Rome extended well beyond political sovereignty. By examining Jewish sources dated to the late Hellenistic and Roman periods from the perspective of the history of ideas, this volume aims to show that engagement with the Roman empire posed a unique ideological challenge for Jews—even prior to the destruction of the Temple in 70 CE, and all the more thereafter—and had a lasting impact on Jewish self-definitions and Jewish thought.

1. Recontextualizing Israel's Encounter with the Roman Empire in the Longue Durée

Jews (or Israelites) had of course confronted imperial powers prior to the rise of Rome. The history of ancient Israel might even be characterized as a series of such encounters[5]—with, namely, the ancient Egyptian, Neo-Assyrian, Neo-Babylonian, and Persian empires, and the Hellenistic kingdoms. The impact of these encounters in shaping Jewish (or initially Israelite/Judahite) culture and thought can hardly be overestimated. As Peter Fibiger Bang and Dariusz Kołodziejczyk state in their study of universal empires, "The process of civilisation involves constant borrowing, emulation and reinterpretation of other societies," and this observation applies equally to ancient Israel.[6]

Unlike most studies of the relationship between Jews and Romans, the present volume opens with a survey of how those earlier empires affected ancient Israel and its literary production, especially the writings that now constitute the Hebrew Bible. This initial chapter aims to provide a comparative perspective that will facilitate the assessment of the novel elements in Israel's confrontation with the Roman empire.[7]

---

3. In Letter 9, Hess uses the expression "Catholic Rome," and in Letter 8 he refers to Joseph Salvador, *Paris, Rome, Jérusalem ou la question religieuse au XIXe siècle* (Paris: Michel Lévy Frères, 1860), which advocates for the universal merging of all religions.

4. Throughout this volume, I have chosen to use the term "pagan" to refer to polytheist Rome, despite the Latin Christian origins of the term and its pejorative connotations; see Brown 1999, 625.

5. For an overview of empire studies over the past two decades, see the opening of Chapter One.

6. Fibiger Bang and Kołodziejczyk 2012, 11.

7. For a similar approach, but on a more modest scale, see Baltrusch 2002.

My choice of the term "Israel" to refer to the group that experienced empire in the Neo-Assyrian, Neo-Babylonian, Persian, Seleucid, and ultimately Roman contexts may foster an artificial impression of that group's permanence and continuity. I am not denying that the Jews who lived under Roman rule in third-century CE Palestine were different from the Israelites who endured the Neo-Assyrian invasion more than a millenium earlier. Centuries of historical experiences and numerous political, social, and cultural transformations separated them. However, the transmission of collective lore and memories known from biblical writings, and the use of "Israel" as an emic term in biblical through talmudic sources enable historians to speak of Israel as a people who retained an enduring self-consciousness. Moreover, memories of Israel's encounters with the massive empires of the ancient Near East, recast and rewritten time and again, were transmitted to Jews of the Roman period. Thus, Jewish engagement with Roman imperial power did not occur in a vacuum, but rather in the context of a long tradition of reflections about empire and both Israelite and foreign kingship.

A central thesis of this monograph is that, in spite of this historical background, the Roman empire represented a qualitatively different challenge than those Israel had previously encountered. This book argues that two main factors distinguished Rome from earlier powers: the first lies in the paradoxical similarities between Roman and Jewish self-definitions; the second in Rome's policy toward the Jews from the reign of Vespasian to that of Hadrian, which could be interpreted as an attempt to eradicate the Jewish cult and replace Jerusalem with Rome. It is important to grasp that whereas Jews had previously been confronted with imperial aspirations that were enacted in the names of kings or royal dynasties, in the Romans they faced the imperialism of a people (*imperium populi Romani*), an aspect only partially moderated by the transition from the Republic to the Principate.[8] Jews and Romans were two peoples who professed that a form of divine election had endowed them with a mission that would ultimately lead to universal rule and peace. This assertion was coupled with claims by each of its superior legal system and exceptional piety. For at least some Jews, these ostensible similarities fostered a sense of competition between Israel and Rome and even a fear that the latter aimed to displace the former, which the rabbis articulated by equating Rome with Esau, Israel's twin brother and rival. As this identification can be traced to a time when Rome was still a pagan empire, it cannot be interpreted as primarily a response to Christianity.[9] The Christianization of the Roman

8. On the evolution of the term *imperium* and how it came to refer to the corporate power and hegemony of the Roman people, see Richardson 1991; Richardson 2008, 145; Edwell 2013, 41–42, 49–51.

9. On the issues raised in this paragraph, see Chapter Two. For previous scholarship on the identification of Rome with Esau/Edom, see especially Cohen 1967; Assis 2016, 175–190; Berthelot 2016; Berthelot 2017a.

empire simply made the association all the more relevant. As Daniel Weiss has argued, it was probably the linking of Christianity with the empire—which he describes as the emergence of "Christendom"—rather than the reverse, that led Jews to label Christians as "Esau."[10]

The transformation of the Roman empire from a pagan into a predominantly Christian world points us to the observation that "Rome" was in fact no more immutable than "Israel." During the six centuries covered in this study (from the second century BCE to the fourth century CE), the Roman empire underwent dramatic transformations; an awareness of these processes is key to avoiding the inadvertent imposition of an essentialist perspective. The transition from Republic to Principate in the late first century BCE and the Diocletianic reform in the late third century CE were two major institutional and ideological turning points. Other changes had more gradual trajectories. Thus, the Roman empire that Jews experienced before the First Jewish Revolt differed from that which they faced during the mid-second and early third centuries CE and from the empire as it went through the process of Christianization during the fourth century. General references to Rome, Romans, and the Roman empire should not obscure the historical transformations that occurred during these centuries.

Nonetheless, the aspects of Roman imperial ideology that were most relevant for Jews living under Roman rule remained fairly stable from the first century BCE to the fourth century CE—namely, the identification of the Roman empire with the *oikoumenē* or *orbis terrarum* (the whole world), the hoped-for eternity of Roman rule, the unique calling and virtues of the Roman people, the superiority of Roman law, and the excellence of imperial justice. By contrast, from the late first century CE onward, Jews were a defeated people, lacking both state and Temple. The significance of Roman imperial ideology evolved for them, not on account of its intrinsic transformations but because of the deterioration of their status after three failed revolts against Rome. In the wake of these Jewish defeats, the Romans destroyed the Temple in Jerusalem, appropriated Jewish *sacra*, and replaced the Jews' political and spiritual capital with a Roman colony. The ideological challenge intensified, for the God of the Jews had seemingly been defeated or, perhaps, had switched to the Roman side.[11]

When discussing the nature of the Roman empire and Roman imperialism, we may also ask whether the Jews perceived themselves as confronted with Roman or Greco-Roman domination—in other terms, whether they associated Greeks with the Roman imperial project.[12] As Aleksandr Makhlaiuk observes:

10. Weiss 2018.
11. See Chapter Two.
12. See, in particular, Veyne 2005.

In light of recent research, the Mediterranean imperial state created by Romans increasingly appears as a Graeco-Roman empire in which the power was Roman, but the culture was Greek. The role played by Greek intellectuals and urban elites in inventing and ruling the Empire is now considered as one of the decisive factors for empire building and self-consciousness of the imperial governing class in general.[13]

This important insight lends balance to previous research that paid less attention to Greco-Roman hybridity. By comparison, ancient Jewish sources convey an awareness of this hybridity: when, for example, select rabbinic texts use the figure of Alexander the Great as a stand-in for Rome or prohibit teaching Greek within the Jewish community on political (not merely cultural) grounds related to Roman rule in the East, where the primary language was Greek.[14] Other Jewish sources, however, including various passages from rabbinic literature, make a clear distinction between Greeks and Romans, especially when discussing the empires that had subjugated Israel.[15] Moreover, the equation of Rome with Esau/Edom differentiates that empire from Greece, which is instead identified with Yavan. Thus, these sources offer ample evidence that Jewish writings both connected and contrasted Rome with the Greek world.[16]

It must be stressed that, as much as Romans represented a unique challenge for Jews, Jews posed a serious challenge for Rome, particularly from the mid-first to mid-second centuries CE. Three Jewish uprisings occurred within a century (in 66–73, 115–117, and 132–135 CE, according to the conventional datings), and at least the second of these spread through various regions of the empire. No other people within the Roman empire revolted on such a large scale during the reigns of Trajan or Hadrian, broadly considered a time of great prosperity.[17] The relative scarcity of evidence for other revolts during that period does not imply that Jews were more prone to rebel than other provincial populations, nor am I suggesting a kind of Jewish exceptionalism

---

13. Aleksandr Makhlaiuk, BMCR Review of Juan Manuel Cortés Copete, Elena Muñiz Grivaljo, and Fernando Lozano Gómez (eds.), *Ruling the Greek World: Approaches to the Roman Empire in the East* (Stuttgart: Franz Steiner Verlag, 2015). See http://bmcr.brynmawr.edu/2016/2016-12-08.html.

14. See Wilfand 2020a (on Alexander); Wilfand 2017 (on the prohibition of Greek).

15. See Chapter Two, §5.

16. Concerning the problems inherent in "Greco-Roman" as a notion, see the remarks in Dohrmann and Reed 2013, 4–7. On Greek perceptions of the process of "Romanization," see Woolf 1994; Whitmarsh 2001. As Seth Schwartz notes, the fact that Greeks perceived themselves as distinct from Romans did not prevent non-Greek provincials from conflating Greeks with Rome (Schwartz 2020).

17. On revolts in the Roman empire, see Fuchs 1938; Dyson 1971; Pekáry 1987, esp. 142–143; Goodman 1991; Woolf 2011; Gambash 2015. Leaving the unreliable testimony of the *Historia Augusta* aside, during the reigns of Trajan and Hadrian the main case of uprising apart from the Jews seems to have been Mauretania, in 117 and 122 CE.

or essentialism here.[18] Neither does this evidence prove that other provincial groups were more accepting of Roman rule: fear may have fostered passivity. Nevertheless, either they did not rebel or such unrest as occurred was localized in the form of urban rioting or rural violence. The scale of the Jewish revolts remains singular, and the Roman assessment of their importance is revealed by, among other indicators, the number of legions mobilized to crush them.[19]

Furthermore, if Augustine's testimony is reliable, the renowned senator and philosopher Seneca expressed anxiety and aversion toward the spread of Jewish observances: "Meanwhile," he wrote, "the customs of this accursed race have gained such influence that they are now received throughout all the world. The vanquished have given laws to their victors."[20] While this statement sounds like rhetorical exaggeration, it may nevertheless be related to Tacitus' claim that conversion to Judaism entailed forsaking the gods of Rome, an infringement of *pietas*, and severing civic and family ties with their incumbent duties—a violation of both *pietas* and *fides*. Such sentiments may have been common among the Roman aristocracy during the first and second centuries CE. The exclamation of Rutilius Namatianus in the early fifth century—"And would that Judaea had never been subdued by Pompey's wars and Titus' military power. The infection of this plague, though excised, still creeps abroad the more: and it is their own conquerors that a conquered people keeps down (*victoresque suos natio victa premit*)"—shows that such resentments did not entirely vanish after the second century CE.[21] This is not tantamount to saying, as Erich Gruen writes with deliberate exaggeration and irony, that "the proliferation of Jews frightened pagans" or that "Jewish proselytizing panicked the officialdom and the populace."[22] Nevertheless, among certain Roman elites, Judaism became an object of deep and long-lasting hostility.[23]

18. The tendency to categorize Jews as exceptional subjects under Roman rule is exemplified by Paul Veyne's description of the Roman empire as a unified civilization, the *Romanitas*, which successfully integrated different ethnic groups, even though they retained distinct self-definitions, whereas Jews ("the Jewish theocracy") were outstanding because they maintained aspirations for "national independence" (Veyne 1980, 126).

19. See Gambash 2013, 174–177, esp. 176: "Vespasian's army was similar in scale to forces assembled for the purpose of foreign campaigns." Concerning the Bar Kokhba Revolt, see Eck 1999. On the Roman army in Judea, see also Isaac 1990, 104–107. These issues are further discussed in Chapter Two.

20. Quoted in Augustine, *The City of God* 6.11. Trans. William M. Green, LCL, 361. See also Stern 1976–1984, 1: 431–432. Cf. Horace, *Epistles* 2.1.156: "Greece, the captive, made her savage victor captive" (translation by H. Rushton Fairclough, LCL, 409).

21. Tacitus, *Hist.* 5.5.1–2; Rutilius Namatianus, *De Reditu Suo* (*A Voyage Home to Gaul*) 1.395–398, translation by J. Wight Duff and Arnold M. Duff, LCL, 799, very slightly modified.

22. Gruen 2016, 322.

23. Undeniably, some Romans praised distinct aspects of Judaism; moreover, conversions did occur. Yet ignorance and indifference prevailed. On Roman perceptions of Jews

These remarks notwithstanding, the Judeo-Roman encounter should not be reduced to sheer antagonism or viewed as a confrontation between distinct and immutable entities. Not only were the ways of being Roman and Jewish variable, but the boundaries between these peoples were fluid and individuals' identities could overlap. Beginning no later than the first century BCE, some Jews were granted Roman citizenship, thus establishing Roman Jews or Jewish Romans as a category well before 212 CE. In addition to Jews who were Roman citizens, all Jews living within the empire—namely, those who are the focus of this study [24]—were not only exposed to Roman imperialism but also participants in the empire. Jews contributed to the formation of Roman imperial culture, together with other ethnic groups. However, to describe Jews as an "organ in a large cultural organism," as Michael Satlow writes, seems to imply an overly harmonious and reciprocal relationship, insofar as every component of an organism plays an essential role in it.[25] For at least some Jews, their relationship with Rome was highly problematic and antagonistic. Jews' varying degrees of Romanness should not mask the asymmetrical balance of power between the vast majority of Jews and the empire.[26]

2. A Survey of Scholarship on "Rome and Jerusalem"

As the work of Hess quoted above indicates, "Rome" can have a variety of meanings from a Jewish viewpoint, but its significance is for obvious historical reasons strongly colored by Christianity. Since the late 1990s, numerous scholarly works have focused on how Judaism responded to the development of Christianity and interacted with this emergent religion during the early centuries of the Christian Era. The influence of Christianity on rabbinic and medieval Judaism has been hotly debated, and as a result, traditional paradigms have shifted substantially.[27]

---

and Judaism, see Feldman 1993; Schäfer 1997; Rochette 2001; Gruen 2002; Berthelot 2003; Isaac 2004; Gambash 2013; Gruen 2016.

24. The perspectives of Babylonian Jews living in the Sassanid empire are discussed in this volume solely for the sake of comparison. See §4 below.

25. Satlow 2008, 39.

26. Here, *mutatis mutandis*, I concur with Andrew Gardner's cautionary observation that "if we limit our application of postcolonial theory to attempts to describe provincial cultures as composites of fragmentary, fluid and hybrid identities, seemingly involving a fair degree of choice and subjectivity, we will fail to analyse the power relationships that create and sustain inequality" (Gardner 2013, 6). See also Rosen-Zvi 2017a, 220–221. On postcolonial theory, see §3 below.

27. See, e.g., Becker and Reed 2003; Boyarin 2004; Yuval 2006; Bar-Asher Siegal 2013; Bar-Asher Siegal 2019. Note also Sivertsev 2011, which shows how the eschatological views found in Jewish sources from late antiquity adapted motifs from Byzantine imperial ideology.

Surprisingly, the impact of pagan Rome upon Judaism did not receive similar scholarly attention until quite recently, even though it was the main power challenging Jews from the first century BCE onward.[28] Because the Christianization of Rome was a long and gradual process—the empire did not become Christian simply as an outcome of Constantine's conversion in 312 CE—pagan Rome can be dated roughly from Rome's inception until the imposition of Nicene Christianity as the sole legitimate religion of the empire by Theodosius I in 380 CE. However, the *Cambridge History of Judaism* omits the topic: volume three in this series (*The Early Roman Period*) features a chapter titled "The Legacy of Egypt in Judaism" and there are as well chapters on the sociopolitical conditions of Jews in Judea and the Diaspora, but there is not one dedicated to Jewish perceptions of Rome, Jewish responses to Rome, or the impact of the Roman empire on Jewish thought. These issues are also absent from *The Late Roman-Rabbinic Period* (volume four), although a full chapter addresses "the rabbinic response to Christianity." Yet as Natalie Dohrmann notes, until the fourth century CE, rabbinic literature offers little evidence of anti-Christian polemics:

> The preserved material gives us no reason to believe that early rabbinic identity was hardened on a "battlefield between the two competing religions" when there is scant reference to anything obviously Christian in Palestinian sources before the empire shifts in the 4th c., and even then creative exegesis is often required. Current analyses of the mid first millennium too easily elide the early centuries into a late antique narrative.[29]

In the same vein, Ra'anan Boustan notes in his review of Daniel Boyarin's *Border Lines*: "I found it especially troubling that pre-Christian Roman law, politics, and culture play so marginal a role in his account of developments in the second and third centuries."[30] An exclusive focus on Jewish-Christian relations likely has a deleterious effect on our understanding of what was at stake for Jews, including rabbis, during the first three centuries CE (even if we acknowledge that echoes of Jewish-Christian interactions may already be identified in tannaitic literature).[31]

These remarks are not meant to minimize the significance of the numerous investigations of the relationship between Rome and the Jewish people, from their first contact with the Republic, under the Hasmoneans, through the Byzantine period.[32] However, most studies of the era that preceded the Christian-

28. Dohrmann and Reed 2013, 4, 7.

29. Dohrmann 2015, 197, quoting Yuval 2011, 248.

30. Boustan 2006, 445.

31. Schremer 2009, esp. 350–351.

32. Among recent studies, see in particular Schwartz 2001; Baltrusch 2002; Eck 2007; Goodman 2007; Sivertsev 2011, on the Byzantine period; Seeman 2013, on the Hasmoneans and Rome.

ization of Rome have focused on the political, legal, and military aspects of their interactions, with little attention paid to the ideological challenge that pagan Rome posed to Judaism. It is as if Rome presented no such challenge for the Jews prior to the advent of Christianity.[33]

More precisely, the issue of Rome and Jerusalem has long been studied from one of two angles. On the one hand, many works have explored the political relationship and military conflicts between the Jews and the Romans; the conditions under which Jews lived in the Roman empire, including the "Jewish privileges" that may or may not have been granted under Roman rule; and broader Roman policies and laws that concerned Jews.[34] On the other, considerable attention has been paid to perceptions of Rome or attitudes toward Rome in Jewish literary sources, from 1 Maccabees through rabbinic literature.[35] At times, these studies risk implying that Jerusalem and Rome were, by their very essence, monolithic entities that inevitably took an oppositional stance toward each other; to a great extent, this view emanates from the Jewish sources themselves.

During the past decade, research in this field has become less focused on conflict as it has developed along two intertwined lines of inquiry. One probes the Romanness of Jews who lived in the Roman empire, including Palestinian rabbis, the other the impact of Roman values, norms, and institutions on Judaism. The latter vein relies primarily on the evidence of Jewish literary texts, but takes account also of documentary sources (inscriptions, papyri) and archaeological artifacts.

The first locates Jews in their Roman context rather than viewing them as a singular people, incomparable to any other owing to their religious characteristics. Scholars of Josephus have long considered his Roman milieu, while specialists in Philo of Alexandria or the Palestinian rabbis have only more recently taken an interest in their Roman backgrounds.[36] Especially after 212 CE, most free Jews living within the empire, rabbis included, would

---

33. On the nature of this ideological challenge, see §1 above and Chapter Two.

34. Representative examples include Juster 1914; Smallwood 1976; Rabello 1980; Linder 1987; Pucci Ben Zeev 1998; Eck 2007; Avidov 2009; Heemstra 2010.

35. Among the earliest efforts to compile all rabbinic material concerning Rome is Samuel Krauss, *Persia and Rome in the Talmud and the Midrashim*, published in 1947. In *Persia and Rome in Classical Judaism*, Jacob Neusner made a similar attempt, albeit with a different methodology, which analyzes each rabbinic composition individually (Neusner 2008). See also Herr 1970; Stemberger 1983; Hadas-Lebel 1990; Feldman 1992a; Schremer 2010; Har-Peled 2013; Morgenstern 2016; Naiweld 2016.

36. On Josephus, see, e.g., Goodman 1994b; Barclay 2000, 2007; Edmondson et al. 2005; Price 2005; Rajak 2013; Tuval 2013 (esp. ch. 4). On Philo (beyond scholarly works that focus on Philo's so-called historical treatises): Niehoff 2001, 2011, 2015, and 2018; Berthelot 2003, 2011b; Seland 2010; Hartog 2019. On the rabbis: Berkowitz 2006, ch. 6; Lapin 2012; Dohrmann and Reed 2013; Kattan Gribetz 2020, ch. 1; Furstenberg 2021. On rabbinic literature, see further the discussion below.

have been Roman citizens. On the basis of extant rabbinic writings, it has thus been argued that Palestinian Judaism represents the best-attested example of a Roman provincial culture and therefore offers historians key insights into the Roman empire.[37] In this framework, several studies explore such sociocultural issues as the Jews' use of bathhouses, their attendance at theaters and banquets, or their attitudes toward the Roman calendar and festivals.[38] Scholarly interest in the Romanness of Jews, and of Palestinian rabbis in particular, has also developed within a broader current that saw the focus shifting away from "Romanization"—a highly contested topic among archaeologists and historians of the Roman world[39]—and toward the dynamics of power relations between imperial authorities and provincials. The emphasis here is on cultural interactions and the role of local elites as partners in the management of empire,[40] and these studies rely in part on categories derived from postcolonial studies (discussed in greater detail below).[41]

The second line of inquiry examines the impact of Roman policies, laws, norms, and values on Judaism. For example, in his early writings (before he developed more nuanced views), Martin Goodman suggested that the institution of a tax collected by the *fiscus Iudaicus* (the Jewish treasury) led to an increased emphasis on religious practice in Jewish self-definition.[42] Among recent studies, Alexandria Frisch analyzes how the Roman imperial context contributed to Jewish theological thought, and theodicy in particular, and Nadav Sharon has written a monograph on the effect of Roman domination on Jewish society and the emergence of Jewish messianism from the first century BCE to the first century CE.[43]

37. See de Lange 1978; Lapin 2012; Dohrmann and Reed 2013, 2. For a different perspective, see Schwartz 2001, 162–163.

38. Rabbinic discussions of bathhouses have been studied extensively; see Jacobs 1998; Lapin 2012, 127–132, and further references there. On public spectacles, see Jacobs 2000; Weiss 2014. Jewish attendance at theaters, hippodromes, and other spaces dedicated to performances is attested by, inter alia, graffiti found in those venues; see Stern 2018. On banquets, see Baruch 2018. On calendars, festivals, and general approaches to time, see Stern 2001, 38–46; Kattan Gribetz 2016, 2020.

39. See Woolf 1997; Mattingly 1997 (esp. 7–15), and 2011; Inglebert 2005; on the subject of Romanization, the collection of articles in *Archaeological Dialogues* 21.1 (2014). This concept also appears in Jewish studies; see, for example, Regev 2010; Lapin 2012 (which uses the term "Romanization" in relation to the rabbis).

40. See Woolf 2020; already Woolf 1998, esp. 18, 30, 33–34.

41. See, for example, Mattingly 2011; Bryen 2012, which discusses "the story of how the provincials and Romans collaborated in developing a shared and vibrant legal culture" (776).

42. Goodman 1989. This idea is further developed in Heemstra 2010.

43. Frisch 2017; Sharon 2017.

The three-volume collection on the Jerusalem Talmud (Yerushalmi) and Greco-Roman culture edited by Peter Schäfer roughly twenty years ago includes several studies that address the impact of Roman values and legal norms on the rabbis, while also considering either Judeo-Roman relations or the Greco-Roman context of the Jerusalem Talmud more broadly.[44]

Christine Hayes' contributions to these volumes, for example, belong to the former category. In "The Abrogation of Torah Law: Rabbinic 'Taqqanah' and Praetorian Edict," she identifies conceptual parallels between Roman law and rabbinic law; noting, for example, that the tannaitic tolerance for *taqqanot* (rabbinic ordinances that contradict legal precedents from the Torah) is best explained by the Roman use of praetorian edicts to modify civil law. In "Genealogy, Illegitimacy, and Personal Status: The Yerushalmi in Comparative Perspective," she examines rabbinic and Roman laws on the personal status of nonaristocratic women who engaged in sexual intercourse with foreigners and slaves, and of their offspring; she concludes that the laws in both corpora were modified in the third century CE to stem the proliferation of illegitimate children, with such similarities that the likelihood of interactions between these systems cannot be dismissed.[45] More recently, Hayes has argued that the Roman use of a legal fiction to extend Roman citizenship to non-Romans for the purpose of adjudicating cases between Roman citizens and non-Romans under Roman law provided the model for the rabbis' establishment of a formal process of conversion, which is also a legal fiction that confers membership by legal means to a person who did not originally belong to the group.[46]

Scholarly reflections on the impact of Rome on ancient Judaism also owes a debt to two thought-provoking monographs by Seth Schwartz. The first volume studies the effects of Roman imperialism on Jewish society in Judea/Palestine, while the second addresses how Jews related to Roman or Greco-Roman notions of honor, euergetism, patronage, and institutionalized reciprocity.[47] In this second book, Schwartz shows that Greco-Roman social models could be simultaneously resisted and partially internalized, and he details how the rabbis devised a counter to these majority standards. My approach in the present study resembles Schwartz's, though I examine different issues.

In her study of poverty and attitudes toward the poor in rabbinic literature, Yael Wilfand also investigates the relationship between rabbinic charity and Greco-Roman euergetism, shedding further light on the dynamics of rejection and absorption analyzed by Schwartz. She shows that the Mishnah in

---

44. See Schäfer 1998, 2002a; Schäfer and Hezser 2000.

45. Hayes 1998, 2002b.

46. Hayes 2017c. See also Hayes 2015, 212–218; Hayes 2017a, 166–167. On the influence of Roman legal fictions on rabbinic legal reasoning, see Moscovitz 2003, and Chapter Five.

47. Schwartz 2001 and 2014. The second volume focuses on Ben Sira, Josephus, and rabbinic literature.

particular rejects Roman norms but simultaneously integrates some aspects of the Roman model as well. More recently, Wilfand has examined the impact of the *Pax Romana* and the cult of Pax on Jewish notions of peace, and the impact of Roman laws concerning slavery and inheritance on rabbinic discussions of converts.[48]

The volume by Beth Berkowitz on the death penalty in rabbinic texts is another significant contribution to our understanding of Rome's impact on rabbinic Judaism. In her investigation of whether Jewish exposure to Roman executions shaped rabbinic law on this subject, she affirms that "the discourse of rabbinic execution was engaged with Roman execution in both hidden and manifest ways."[49] According to Berkowitz, the rabbis responded to Roman power with ambivalence, conveying repulsion as well as attraction, competition with Roman norms alongside efforts to forge an alternative to that dominant culture.[50] A similar display of resistance and internalization is demonstrated by Sarit Kattan Gribetz in her monograph on rabbinic constructions of time and in an article by Sacha Stern which argues that the relationship between the Jewish lunar calendar and the Julian calendar involved both "a rhetoric of rejection and opposition" and "a subtle process of subversion, imitation, mimicry, and appropriation."[51]

Major studies have also addressed the relationship between Roman law and rabbinic legal thought. Natalie Dohrmann has demonstrated the impact of Roman slavery laws on the rabbinic view of manumission and of Roman literacy and legal culture on the rabbis' intellectual and religious project. In particular, she convincingly argues that rabbinic orality can be understood as a reaction against the value placed on books and writing in the Roman empire, and that the influence of Roman law on rabbinic thought is primarily evidenced not in discrete halakhic rulings but rather by the overall development of rabbinic legalism.[52] Recently she also has observed that "the most significant evidence for the impact of the Roman tribunal on early rabbinic law is the latter's near silence on the topic of arbitration," a silence that reflects rabbinic unease with restrictions on the scope of the Torah's application in the Roman imperial context.[53]

Scholars have long been interested in the potential influence of Roman law on rabbinic halakhah, albeit with a tendency to reach negative or circumspect

---

48. Wilfand 2014, 2019a, 2019b, and 2021.

49. Berkowitz 2006, 154.

50. Berkowitz 2006, 158.

51. Kattan Gribetz 2020, Chapter One; Stern 2017, 247.

52. See Dohrmann 2008, on slavery laws; Dohrmann 2015 and 2020, on orality; Dohrmann 2003 and 2013, on legalism.

53. Dohrmann 2021.

conclusions.[54] With the recent publication of various studies that affirm the influence of the Roman legal system on the rabbis, this standpoint is gradually losing ground. In addition to the contributions by Natalie Dohrmann, Christine Hayes, and Yael Wilfand outlined above, Yair Furstenberg's work is reevaluating the role of Roman law with respect to the rabbinic codification of Jewish law. He is also studying how Roman notions of citizenship influenced rabbinic definitions of affiliation with the people of Israel: he contends that the rabbis' understanding of membership, based on adherence to the law (in contrast to a strictly ethnic, genealogical definition), accords with the Roman model.[55] In a similar vein, Orit Malka and Yakir Paz have shown that certain aspects of rabbinic laws regarding captives borrow from Roman laws—and more generally, these authors argue for a profound impact of the Roman legal principles concerning citizenship on tannaitic halakhah.[56] The commonality among these studies is their emphasis on the integration of Roman legal concepts, principles, and categories into rabbinic reasoning rather than on the rabbis' adoption of specific Roman laws.[57] In these discussions, "influence" does not necessarily imply direct literary dependence;[58] rather, rabbinic familiarity with Roman legal concepts may be attributed to exposure to Roman courts and legal proceedings. Moreover, oral exchanges with Greek and Roman legal experts should not be excluded a priori as complementary sources of knowledge.[59]

Admittedly, a new scholarly consensus has not yet been reached. For example, Ishay Rosen-Zvi resists the assertion that the rabbis deliberately borrowed notions from Roman law (as distinct from being unintentionally influenced by it). He further claims that the Mishnah cannot be compared to any other literature composed in the Roman empire and that its rabbinic authors articulated a wholly original, nonnegotiable alternative to the empire.[60] Two caveats are appropriate here, however. First, as Rosen-Zvi himself would

54. Cohen 1966; Jackson 1975 and 1981; Katzoff 2003; Hezser 2007 and 2021; Rosen-Zvi 2017a and 2017b.

55. See Furstenberg 2019a, 2019b, and 2021; and his research project "Making Law under Rome: The Making of Rabbinic Halakhah within Its Legal Provincial Context," funded by the Israel Science Foundation.

56. Malka and Paz 2019 and 2021. See the discussion in Chapter Five.

57. See also Berthelot 2018b, which discusses the impact of Roman norms concerning the publication of imperial edicts and letters on rabbinic interpretations of select biblical passages that pertain to the publication of the Torah on stones upon Israel's arrival in the Promised Land (Deut 27:1–8). In this article, I emphasize that these rabbinic texts are influenced less by specific Roman practices than by general principles. The sources analyzed in this study are aggadic rather than halakhic material, but the implications are similar.

58. Contrary to Jackson 1980, 6, n. 16.

59. See Hezser 2021.

60. Rosen-Zvi 2017a and 2017b.

concede, the rabbis may have been unconscious of, and above all unwilling to admit, their integration of Roman norms. Although Seth Schwartz likewise deems the Mishnah a unique artifact within the Roman imperial context, he cautions that an analysis based solely on rabbinic resistance to Rome may be insufficient:

> We must also pay careful attention to the rabbis' embrace and even internalization of some Roman values: while they claimed, not totally incorrectly, to live outside the Roman system, and recommended such alienation to their constituents, their actual position was far more complex and interesting.[61]

Second, if the Mishnah is to be seen as a radical, quasi-utopian alternative to the Roman order, then it necessarily represents a result of Rome's impact, even if in a negative form. I consider "impact" to encompass the articulation of countermodels (more on this issue below).

This monograph thus builds on the work of other scholars who have displayed a renewed interest in the impact of Rome on Jews and Judaism. Like some of their publications, it aims to show that the encounter with Rome led at least some Jewish groups (or individuals) to redefine certain aspects of Judaism in ways that differed from the definitions operative in Jewish writings of the Hellenistic period.[62] In other words, this book is not an attempt to rethink the place of the Jews in the historiography of the Roman empire; rather, it strives to reconceptualize the role of the Roman empire in the history of Judaism. (These two intellectual endeavors are in fact complementary.) Instead of positing a clash of civilizations or a process of Romanization, this monograph approaches the Jews' encounter with Rome as an ideological challenge that ultimately contributed to shaping ancient, and even modern, Judaism in significant ways. Moreover, it argues that this Roman challenge to Israel was primarily political-religious rather than sociocultural, as I shall now briefly explain.

Whereas the encounter with the Hellenistic world posed not only a political, but also a cultural challenge that prompted Jews to develop a rich literature in Greek, which expanded into genres that included philosophy, theater—exemplified by Ezekiel's *Exagogē*—and exegetical commentaries, the encounter with Rome was of a different nature. Interestingly, hardly any known Jewish texts were composed in Latin. Some works may have been lost through a disruption in transmission, or because Christians were less interested in

---

61. Schwartz 2014, 116. On the Mishnah and rabbinic literature in general as unique literary artifacts in the Roman context, see Schwartz 2014, 113–114; Schwartz 2020.

62. As Natalie Dohrmann has persuasively argued (Dohrmann 2003 and 2013), this process is exemplified by the development of rabbinic legalism. I address this central issue in Chapter Four.

their preservation than in, for example, the oeuvres of Philo, Josephus, and earlier Jewish authors writing in Greek. However, the dearth of ancient Jewish sources in Latin is noteworthy and probably reveals that Roman culture—at least in the arts, literature, and philosophy—was not considered a major challenge to Jewish thought and culture. The Romans themselves acknowledged that, to a great extent, they had learned art and philosophy from the Greeks (though some members of the Roman elite viewed such cultural borrowings with contempt). Jews had no need to counter Roman claims of cultural superiority, because that stance was rarely expressed sensu stricto (which does not mean that Roman intellectual productions had no impact at all on certain Jews, at least at the individual level[63]). Moreover, when Jews like Philo and Josephus, following Jewish authors from the Hellenistic period, asserted that Greek wisdom stemmed at least partially from Moses, they were crediting Israel's wisdom with having indirectly inspired the Romans, via the Greeks.

The Roman challenge to Israel was first and foremost political: it was rooted in Rome's extraordinary military strength and unprecedented imperial dominion, which the Greek historian Polybius already found astonishing in the second century BCE. And insofar as military success and power were commonly thought to be gifts from the gods, or at least the result of divine support, the problem posed by Roman hegemony was not merely political but in fact political-religious. From a Jewish perspective, it cast doubt on the authority of Israel's God.[64]

Beyond the military, the Romans excelled in the realm of law, or at least so they claimed. Despite being considered one element of culture, understood as civilization, law is primarily related to the political regulation of social life. Laws, courts, and judicial proceedings are a manifestation of power[65] that corresponds to what Max Weber described as *Herrschaft*, institutionalized, legitimacy-conferring power, in contrast to *Macht*, the raw power that is closely associated with physical violence.[66] In a Roman context, law and jurisdiction, together with taxes and the army, were building blocks of the *imperium*. Moreover, as Cicero specialists in particular have argued, Roman elites cared about the legal aspects of imperial domination. Even though appeals to Roman civil law were, in principle, restricted to Roman citizens, non-Romans were not absolutely barred from accessing Roman courts and imperial justice.[67] Ultimately, the *Constitutio Antoniniana* (Caracalla's edict granting citizenship to nearly all free persons within the empire, in 212 CE) eased recourse

---

63. For an attempt to analyze the way Philo's ideas evolved following his stay in Rome and his exposure to Roman intellectual life, see Niehoff 2018.

64. On rabbinic discussions of God's power and powerlessness, see, e.g., Kraemer 1995, 179–182; Schremer 2010.

65. See Dohrmann 2015, 198: "Law is a discourse about power."

66. Weber 1972, 28–29, 122–124. See also Gotter 2008, 181.

67. On these issues, see Chapter Four.

to Roman law. This book argues that Roman imperial jurisdiction and Rome's claims regarding the quality of its laws and the efficiency of its legal system were for the Jews another facet of the Roman political-religious challenge, for such assertions defied the centrality of the Torah in their self-definition as a people and their perception of the Mosaic law as an unsurpassable legal system.

At certain times, Roman citizenship was used as an instrument of expansion and domination and was perceived as such by some provincials.[68] In particular, numerous sources testify to the Greeks' awareness that Rome granted citizenship to foreigners on an unprecedented scale, especially compared to the relative rarity of this practice in the Greek *poleis*, and that the Greeks considered this a factor in Rome's exceptional military strength. Citizenship and power are thus related notions in ancient sources, just like citizenship and law. Another argument of this monograph is that from a Jewish viewpoint, Roman policies and notions concerning citizenship were expressions of an alternative model of peoplehood, which became a component of Rome's political-religious challenge to Israel.

This study thus focuses on the interrelated notions of power, law, and citizenship and on the impact of Roman ideology and policies in these realms on Jews and Jewish thought. The book is structured as follows: Chapter One surveys the impact of previous empires on Israel, particularly from a political-religious angle. Chapter Two identifies the factors that made Rome an unprecedented challenge for Jews. Chapters Three, Four, and Five examine the impact on Jewish thought of Roman approaches to power, law, and citizenship, respectively. A brief conclusion summarizes the major findings.

Throughout this book, I analyze previously unexplored examples of the dynamics underpinning the rejection and appropriation of Roman models and present new conclusions concerning, in particular, the nature of Rome's impact on Jewish notions of law and peoplehood. This work offers the reader a synthetic analysis of vast corpuses of texts and broad issues with many ramifications. For this reason, it only occasionally provides a detailed literary analysis of a given source. Rather, it draws connections between various Jewish literary sources that are most often studied on their own—mainly Philo, Josephus, and rabbinic literature—with an interest in highlighting unexpected commonalities as well as discrepancies, either in ideological motifs or in discursive strategies. I do not posit that these materials can or should be merged into a single "Jewish response" to the challenge of the Roman empire. Even as common trends emerge, each author is distinctive; moreover, every corpus displays some level of diversity, sometimes within a single text.

Clearly, this monograph does not claim to be comprehensive. First, it neither revisits the major historical events that punctuated the relationship

---

68. See Ando 2016c. For a detailed treatment of this issue, see Lavan 2019a and Chapter Five.

between Jews and Romans, nor does it delve into the tangible effects of Roman policies on the political, social, and legal conditions of the empire's Jewish citizens and subjects (as distinct from Jewish perceptions of these conditions), since these topics have been the focus of numerous studies by other scholars. Second, as stated above, this volume does not address every aspect of the Roman empire's impact on Judaism; rather, it focuses on the political-religious challenge that Rome posed for certain Jews. Ultimately, this study suggests that, despite negative Jewish memories of the "wicked kingdom," Judaism would have taken a decidedly different path were it not for its encounter with Rome.

3. Responses to Empire: Theory, Terminology, and Method

Key terms and concepts that appear throughout this study are sometimes a matter of dispute among scholars and therefore require discussion.

Empire, Imperialism, and Imperial Ideology

The Roman empire may be classified as one of the tributary empires of antiquity, which, as Greg Woolf explains, "represented a system of political domination created by one people through the conquest and intimidation of a number of other peoples and often by the absorption of a number of earlier states."[69] Whereas the relevance of the word "empire" for the study of antiquity is rarely debated, the use of "imperialism" or "imperial ideology" in historical works on the ancient world is not universally accepted.[70] "Imperialism" generally implies a process of conquest, but not necessarily the exercise of a concerted strategy. Most fundamentally, imperialism includes "the practices, the theories and the attitudes of a dominating metropolitan centre ruling a distant territory," per the definition proposed by Edward Said and adopted by Myles Lavan.[71] In the case of Rome, however, the "territories" ruled by the metropolitan center had different statuses, so their realities were far more complex

---

69. Woolf 2015, 1.

70. The introduction to Chapter One explores the question of whether scholars can agree on a single definition for "empire." Paul Veyne has argued that the term "imperialism" should not be applied to ancient Rome, but as Greg Woolf notes, "In practice it is not feasible to dispense with the labels 'empire' and 'imperialism', as similar problems face any alternative terminology" (Woolf 2015, 1, referring to Veyne 1975; see also the reservations of Nicolet 1983). As a matter of fact, most Roman historians speak of Roman imperialism. Among numerous examples, see the two thematic issues of *Ktema* from the early 1980s "L'impérialisme romain: Histoire, idéologie, historiographie" (nos. 7 [1982] and 8 [1983]) and the recent *Companion to Roman Imperialism* (2013). On the comparison of Roman imperialism to modern imperialism and colonialism, see Ando 2016c.

71. Lavan 2013, 1, quoting Said 1993, 7.

than this definition would suggest. The important point is that Roman imperialism rested not merely on conquest and expansion, but more broadly on domination—*imperium*, the exercise of a corporate power over other nations[72]—and on the means by which domination could be secured.

Generally speaking, imperialism is not limited to military force and taxes; rather, it encompasses as well ideas, images, and imaginings. That is to say, empire and imperialism are sustained by "imperial ideology," a phrase that is frequently used by historians of the Roman empire, despite some reservations.[73] Admittedly, the term "ideology" can be misleading.[74] Especially in the Roman context, neither "imperialism" nor "imperial ideology" should be mistaken for a political program that was systematically designed from the outset. However, despite the pragmatic nature of Roman power—despite, for example, the fact that imperial decisions were often dictated by circumstances, as Fergus Millar argued in his 1977 monograph—its implementation was accompanied by ideological discourse about Roman virtues and the benefits that the empire provided for conquered peoples, claims advanced by both Roman authorities and provincial elites (for praising the Roman order served the interests of the latter).[75] Occasionally, the emperor directly participated in this discourse, as when Augustus' *Res Gestae* were engraved in stone in various cities across the empire.[76] Nonverbal modes of communication were also harnessed to spread Roman imperial ideology. Personifications of Roman virtues (such as *pietas, virtus, aequitas*) commonly appeared on the reverse side of imperial coinage, together with words that served as mottos for the empire's political and social benefits (*pax, concordia, fortuna,* and *salus,* among others).[77] Ideological messages also featured on monuments, statues, and military insignia. In addition, Roman agents and provincial leaders sponsored public performances (including games, festivals, and ceremonies associated with the imperial cult) that promoted imperial ideology, especially in urban centers.[78]

72. Some have suggested the use of the word "hegemony" instead of "imperialism," based on the choice of the Greek term *hēgemonia* to translate *imperium* in ancient Greek sources; see Edwell 2013, 40, 49–51.

73. Ando 2000; Rosso 2005; Lobur 2008. Historians working on other periods also use the phrase "imperial ideology"; in particular, see Sivertsev 2011.

74. For a critique of the Marxist concept of ideolsgy, see Ando 2000, 19–23.

75. See Noreña 2011, 16: "the specific virtues and benefits communicated by the central state on various media were frequently replicated by local aristocrats, especially in the language of honorific dedications made to the emperor." It is significant that despite the absence of systematic discourse on empire, discourse about the emperor existed. On the central role of the emperor as a figure for shaping the unity and the ideology of the empire, see Ando 2000; Tuori 2016.

76. Erskine 2010, 10.

77. Noreña 2011, Chapters Two and Three.

78. See the study of Romaia festivals in Van Nijf and van Dijk 2020. One striking example is Caius Vibius Salutaris' foundation in Ephesus in the early second century CE, which

My understanding of imperial (or royal) ideology follows Richard Fowler and Olivier Hekster, who define it as "the entire scheme or structure of public images, utterances and manifestations by which a monarchical regime depicts itself and asserts and justifies its right to rule."[79] Informed by Clifford Ando's analysis of the appropriation of imperial discourse and performances by provincial populations, which shows that "imperial ideology emerges here as the product of a complex conversation between center and periphery," Fowler and Hekster likewise emphasize that "royal ideology should be understood as a dialogue between king and subjects"—as well as, they add, their rivals and past models.[80] This approach brings into view the active participation of the subjects of imperial domination in the production of imperial ideology. Despite the intrinsic power asymmetry, subject peoples were not simply the recipients of a top-down message that was imposed on the periphery from the center. Moreover, any resistance that seeks to shift the power dynamic has an ideology of its own, as Jewish writings from the Roman period amply illustrate. Ultimately, for all parties in an imperial system, irrespective of their level of conventional power, ideology is closely intertwined with agency and self-legitimation: it serves as a tool for the acquisition, establishment, and retention of power.[81]

Analyzing Responses to Empire: Coping with Diversity
Postcolonialism, which emerged as a theory in the 1990s and has become an established field of study, has markedly influenced historians of the ancient world, including the Roman empire, in recent decades. A primary goal of this discipline, which initially focused on literary works produced in a modern, postcolonial context, is to study how the colonized, confronted with the power strategies of the colonizers, "made use of and went beyond many of those strategies in order to articulate their identity, self-worth, and empowerment."[82] In the study of ancient empires it has prompted a greater emphasis on cultural hybridity, countering, for example, assumptions of Romanization as a

---

provided the funding for ritual processions featuring statues of members of the imperial family and Roman collective entities such as the Senate and the Roman people (*I. Ephes.* 27A; Rogers 1991, 152–185 [Greek text and translation]; Rosso Caponio 2020, 144–150).

79. Fowler and Hekster 2005, 16.

80. Ando 2000, xiii; Fowler and Hekster 2005, 19.

81. See Carter 2003, 305. Eric Wolf argues that ideologies must be distinguished from ideas and ideation (which encompass "the entire range of mental constructs") because ideologies "suggest unified schemes or configurations developed to underwrite or manifest power" (Wolf 1999, 4). On the connections between ideologies and power relationships within Judean society, see Keddie 2018.

82. Sugirtharajah 2002, 11. See also Ashkroft et al. 1989, which represents a founding moment for postcolonial studies.

unidirectional process that went from "Romans" to "natives."[83] Although it is problematic to speak of "colonization" in the ancient world, phrases such as "subaltern," "hybridity," "hidden transcript," "mimicry," and, of course, "postcolonial" itself have become common in studies of ancient responses to imperial power, Roman or otherwise.[84]

The term "hidden transcript" first appeared in James C. Scott's *Domination and the Arts of Resistance: Hidden Transcripts* (1990), defined as follows:

> Every subordinate group creates, out of its ordeal, a "hidden transcript" that represents a critique of power spoken behind the back of the dominant. The powerful, for their part, also develop a hidden transcript representing the practices and claims of their rule that cannot be openly avowed. A comparison of the hidden transcript of the weak with that of the powerful and of both hidden transcripts to the public transcript of power relations offers a substantially new way of understanding resistance to domination.[85]

This resistance may seem to be characterized by informal oral communication—rumors, gossip, folktales, songs, jokes—but it is also expressed through social rituals, festivals, and artistic performances (especially theater), as well as in political acts (such as hiding crops and escaping bondage).[86] In scholarship on antiquity, the notion of "hidden transcripts" tends to overlap with that of "discursive resistance" expressed in written works. Notably, Tim Whitmarsh uses the latter concept extensively in his study of the Greek authors who are commonly identified as part of what is labeled the "Second Sophistic." They expressed their resistance to Roman domination primarily through literary means, attempting to "define an imaginary space that resists imperial control."[87]

Another key concept that originated in postcolonial studies—and the related field of subaltern studies—is "mimicry," which, according to Homi K.

---

83. See, e.g., Woolf 1997. For a critical assessment of the application of these concepts in studies of the Roman empire, especially from the perspective of archaeology, see Gardner 2013.

84. On the ways the concept of "colonization" may or may not shed light on the Hellenistic kingdoms, see, e.g., Will 1985 and Roger Bagnall's response in Bagnall 1997. For examples of the increasingly common use of postcolonial theory in analyses of the Hebrew Bible, see, inter alia, Sugirtharajah 2002; Horsley 2004 and 2008; Davidson 2011; Boer 2013; Perdue and Carter 2015; Jones 2018. On postcolonial theory in the study of ancient Judaism, see, e.g., Boyarin 1997; Barclay 2005; Berkowitz 2006; Stratton 2009; Victor 2010; Appelbaum 2010; Seland 2010; Kaden 2011; Smith-Christopher 2014; Frisch 2017 (esp. Chapter 8); Stern 2017.

85. Scott 1990, xii.

86. Moreover, resistance can include "hopes of a returning prophet, ritual aggression via witchcraft, celebration of bandit heroes and resistance martyrs," but its content is specific to each society; Scott 1990, xi.

87. Whitmarsh 2013, esp. 62, 76 (quotation on 76).

Bhabha (1994), arises from both the colonizers' search for a recognizable Other who resembles themselves (in morals and education, among other standards) and the subjects' tendency to imitate their rulers, an inclination that paradoxically emerges from a desire to be recognized as authentic. While appropriating elements of the dominant culture, the subaltern creates a discourse that is marked by hybridity or hybridization—that is, the juxtaposition of colonial and indigenous ideas. In Bhabha's view, mimicry and hybridity go hand in hand and destabilize colonial discourse by blurring the line between the languages of the colonizer and the colonized. Colonized subjects are seen to engage in a double-edged process of affiliation and resistance that goes beyond binary oppositions such as dominant/subaltern. Some scholars also use "mimicry" to refer to the subalterns' ironic imitation of dominant cultural and political models—namely, through parody of the "master," which constitutes a form of resistance.

Mimicry is not equivalent to "mimetic rivalry" or "mimetic desire," two central ideas in René Girard's work, which are predicated on the assumption that one's desire for a particular object is mediated by others' attraction to it.[88] In an article on the value and limitations of Girard's theory, Steven Weitzman argues that mimetic rivalry is useful for analyzing the relationship between Jews and Samaritans as depicted by Josephus. While describing the Samaritans as involved in a mimetic rivalry with the Jews, Josephus himself mimics the Romans' strategy of differentiating themselves from other peoples that claimed Trojan origins. Weitzman seems to use the terms "mimicry," "mimicking," "mimetic rivalry," and "mimetic struggle" interchangeably, emphasizing that they convey "an adaptive behavior, a tactic, whose motives and workings are best understood within the particular cultural habitat to which the mimic is responding."[89] This book speaks of a Jewish sense of rivalry toward the Romans, which is most clearly expressed in the identification of Rome as Esau. It uses the terms "imitation" or "mimesis," but restricts "mimicry" to instances where the adoption or imitation of Roman motifs may entail deliberate irony or parody.[90]

Because responses to empire were extremely diverse—some might prefer to characterize them as discrepant experiences of empire—no single concept or theory can adequately encapsulate them. As a result, my choice of terminology endeavors to reflect this highly nuanced range, which includes sincere ideological and political adhesion, opportunistic collaboration, adaptation, accommodation, acculturation, assimilation, imitation, mimesis, mimicry, (mimetic) rivalry, competition, the elaboration of countermodels, subversion, resistance, opposition, revolt, rebellion, and violent insurrection. An analysis of specific historical cases and sources reveals the shortcomings of clear-cut

88. See in particular *Violence and the Sacred*, originally published in French in 1972.
89. Weitzman 2009, 922.
90. See Kaden 2011, which uses the term "mimicry" in this sense in its analysis of Agrippa's speech reported in Josephus' *B.J.*

theoretical concepts, for the tangible realities are far more complex than our discursive categories. Group and individual responses to empire can be multi-faceted, comprising complementary and contradictory aspects, and they often evolve over time. Josephus perfectly illustrates this intricacy, which brings us to the specific case of Jewish experiences of Roman rule.

Jewish Responses to the Roman Empire

Jewish responses to Roman domination were manifold, ranging from revolt and harsh criticism to accommodation, imitation, collaboration, and adhe-sion.[91] By way of illustration, let us first consider Tiberius Julius Alexander, Philo's nephew, who embodied adhesion to and even identification with the Roman empire. As a Roman citizen, governor, and general, he had an out-standing career in service to the empire. Notably, he was the procurator of Judea from 46 to 48 CE—according to Josephus, during this term he ordered the crucifixion of a number of rebels (*A.J.* 20.102)—and the prefect of Egypt from 66 to 69 CE; he supported Vespasian against his rivals and contributed greatly to Titus' victory during the siege of Jerusalem in 70 CE; subsequently, he may have become the prefect of the Praetorian Guard.[92] Josephus states that Alexander did not remain faithful to the ancestral customs of the Jews (*A.J.* 20.100), and other sources that mention him hardly acknowledge that he was Jewish.[93] As far as we can tell, Tiberius Julius Alexander completely identified with Rome, as might reasonably be expected of a prominent mem-ber of the Roman elite.[94] Adhesion is further evidenced by Jews who fought in the Roman army; however, we have scant knowledge of their motivations or views on Rome.[95]

Herod the Great's integration within the empire was of quite a different type, which may be characterized as a combination of collaboration and imita-tion. Antipater, his father, was granted Roman citizenship by Julius Caesar in 47 BCE, as a reward for his military support during the latter's war in Egypt.[96] However, it is unclear whether citizenship was automatically conferred upon

91. Scholars have paid more attention to revolts than to Jewish pro-Roman positions. On the latter, see Wilker 2012.

92. See Turner 1954; Schürer 1973, 456–458; Mélèze Modrzejewski 1995, 185–190; Appelbaum 2018, 106–108.

93. Tacitus, *Hist.* 1.11.1, states that Tiberius Julius Alexandar was Egyptian. On the status of Jews in Roman Egypt, see Mélèze Modrzejewski 1995.

94. We have evidence that other Jews served in the imperial administration up to at least the fourth century CE; see Gary 2004 on Jews who held the office of *palatinus, procu-rator*, or *comes*.

95. See Oppenheimer 2005; Schoenfeld 2006; Roth 2007; Rocca 2010; and Chapter Three. According to Schürer, the Julius Alexander who was a legate under Trajan in the Parthian War, mentioned in Cassius Dio, *Roman History* 68.30.12, was probably a son or grandson of Philo's nephew (Schürer 1973, 458, n. 9).

96. Josephus, *A.J.* 14.137, 16.53.

Antipater's progeny. What is clear is that Herod was a client king of Rome who was characterized as *philorhōmaios* ("friend of the Romans"; *OGIS* 414) and *philokaisar* ("friend of Caesar" or "friend of the emperor"; *IG* II² 3441).[97] In this case, collaboration and loyalty were accompanied by imitation, as in the Augustan themes and motifs manifested in Herodian coinage and architecture and in Herod's identification with Augustus' political program.[98] However, Herod's royal ideology was twofold, referencing both Augustus and David and Solomon.[99] His renovation of the Jerusalem Temple exemplifies this dual association, linking Herod with Solomon, who constructed the First Temple, and with Augustus, whom Livy described as the "founder and restorer of all sanctuaries" (Livy, *History of Rome* 4.20.7).[100] The differences between Tiberius Julius Alexander and Herod illustrate the diverse responses and self-definitions of the Jewish elite who supported Rome and may have enjoyed Roman citizenship.[101]

At the other end of the spectrum are the Jewish revolts against Rome (to which I will return in Chapter Two). Criticism and depictions of Rome as violent, cruel, greedy, and generally malevolent appear in varying degrees and guises from 1 Maccabees and apocalyptic literature through late rabbinic works. Jewish apocalyptic texts in fact have been interpreted as resistance literature, replete with hidden transcripts (since the imperial powers they target are not explicitly mentioned).[102] Anathea Portier-Young describes them as a form of "discursive resistance against imperial hegemony and structures of domination" while acknowledging that, in select cases, these works moved beyond discursive resistance to advocate active political resistance of the sort that could spark insurrection.[103] Elsewhere, I have argued that Philo's writings also allusively criticize Rome, even though he valued some attributes of

---

97. Geiger 1997; Wilker 2005; Curran 2014. On the title *philokaisar*, which Herod may have been the first to adopt, see Suspène 2009. The title is also attested on two stone weights from Judea.

98. See Netzer 2006; Bloch 2006, which argues that some of Herod's actions should be interpreted as *imitationes Augusti* (132); Regev 2010, esp. 199–200; Jacobson 2015, which takes particular note of the presence of an aplustre—a motif typically associated with Augustus' victory at Actium—on a Herodian coin, *RPC* I.1 no. 4904. On the connections between Augustus and various aspects of Herod's rule, see also Jacobson and Kokkinos 2009.

99. Ilan 1998; Rocca 2008; Marshak 2015, 282.

100. Bloch 2006; Jacobson 2007.

101. Josephus is yet another interesting case; see Goodman 1994b.

102. For an early study of apocalyptic literature as a form of resistance, see Eddy 1961. In contrast, Jones 2011 considers that Jewish apocalyptic works produced after 70 CE do not convey a message of resistance (278).

103. Portier-Young 2011 and 2014, 145. However, she also cautions against considering resistance as a definitional function of apocalyptic literature. See also Smith-Christopher 2014; Keddie 2018; Chapter One, §4.

the empire, such as the relative peace that prevailed during the Augustan period.[104] Despite Josephus' privileged position as a Roman citizen and Vespasian's protégé after the First Jewish Revolt, his work too contains underlying criticism of Rome.[105] And obviously, many rabbinic texts fiercely condemn Rome.[106]

Nevertheless, the rabbis had an ambiguous relationship with the empire: Rabban Yohanan ben Zakkai—the renowned leader who, according to rabbinic tradition, famously escaped from Jerusalem with his followers in 70 CE to establish an academy in Yavneh—is said in rabbinic sources to have prophesied to Vespasian that he would become emperor, a prediction for which Josephus also takes credit. As Seth Schwartz notes, even though "the rabbis proclaimed their alienation from normative Roman culture in every line they wrote," the fact remains that they "were not apocalyptists: for all their show of resistance to Rome, there is an important accommodationist strain in their writings."[107] Catherine Hezser takes this position one step further:

> Rabbis lived in Romanised cities and adapted themselves to this environment. One may even argue that they profited from Romanisation and its consequences. This development allowed them to present themselves as a local intellectual elite whose functions resembled those of Roman jurists in the adjudication of (minor) civil law cases.[108]

Varied and even opposing notions such as resistance, alienation, adaptation, and accommodation are appropriate to describe the rabbis' varied strategies and attitudes vis-à-vis the Roman empire as expressed in rabbinic literature. Schwartz draws our attention to an additional point: according to him, the Mishnah compels us "to re-think the theory-driven hypothesis that resistance must take the form of mimesis, since the Mishnah is not mimetic of any Roman or Greco-Roman text or complex of ideas." More precisely, he contends that the inhabitants of the Roman empire "proved capable of significant acts of agency, that is, episodes of cultural production that were indubitably reactive or mimetic but were not simply that. They were creative too—innovative expressions of local 'great traditions.'"[109]

Building on Schwartz's observations, two points are worth reiterating. First, it would be misleading to assess Jewish responses to the Roman empire as dichotomous, characterized as collaboration versus resistance, for example,

104. Berthelot 2011b.

105. Mason 2005b. On Josephus' expectation that Rome would ultimately be subject to divine retribution, see Rajak 1991; Spilsbury 2003; Price 2005.

106. Hadas-Lebel 1990.

107. Schwartz 2014, 116.

108. Hezser 2021, 307. On the relationship between rabbis and cities, see Hezser 1997, 157–165. See also Lapin 2012.

109. Schwartz 2020, 410.

or accommodation versus opposition. Even a superficial reading of the sources confirms that there was no such either-or paradigm. Second, the adoption of Roman notions or practices should not be viewed as a passive process, a core assumption of outmoded, top-down models of Romanization. Adoption goes hand in hand with adaptation—that is, with transformation and inventiveness—since no cultural element can be transferred à l'identique from one context to another. Thus, when this book speaks of the adoption of Roman ideas by Jews in antiquity, it envisions an active and creative dynamic. Indeed, one of my purposes is to analyze the inventiveness that characterized certain Jewish responses to Roman imperial culture and policies, including the use and adaptation of Roman notions to rethink Jewish ancestral traditions.

Throughout this volume, I use the term "impact" in reference to Rome's role in the history of Judaism. A clarification is in order: in my understanding, "impact" has a wider scope than "influence." An impact serves as a trigger or catalyst, whereas an influence results from the conscious or unconscious adoption and integration, within a given system, of elements that did not originally belong to it. (Note that influence as such does not presuppose knowledge of literary traditions, as is sometimes assumed.) An impact may have an effect even absent such absorption, as in a case of sheer rejection. I therefore consider the spurning of Roman norms and the devising of countermodels to be evidence of impact. In turn, influence appears as a subcategory of impact.[110]

As Bernard Jackson rightly observes, noting that a particular institution or idea has been influenced by another cultural framework falls well short of a complete analysis of the transaction.[111] It is crucial to investigate the use and transformation of the adopted cultural notion, as well as its emergent role in the new context. The adoption and appropriation of external elements are dynamic and creative processes that can also be subversive, as when these elements are used to delegitimize the Other.

Admittedly, it is not easy to ascertain whether or how a borrowing, an influence, or, more broadly, an impact has occurred. The identification of an influence generally starts with the observation of parallels between texts, material artifacts, architectural remains, or other cultural artifacts. In a famous essay titled "Parallelomania" (1962), Samuel Sandmel rightly questioned the scholarly tendency to compile lists of (often superficial) parallels without giving sufficient attention to their context and significance. His analysis remains instructive. Scholars should recognize that similar phenomena may be the outcomes of independent developments in their respective contexts rather

110. Scholars all craft their own definitions to some extent. For example, for Jason M. Silverman, "'influence' designates the reshaping, selection, and/or interpretation of ideas, stories, characters, or doctrines from the native traditions due to interaction with another culture. This can be conscious or unconscious, positive or negative" (Silverman 2012, 34). One's adherence to clear and consistent usage is what matters most.

111. Jackson 1975, 15.

than the results of direct contact. Yet, denying the potential effects of societal and interpersonal engagement, even in asymmetric power relationships, would be equally problematic.

Michael Satlow has argued that notions such as influence, resistance, and accommodation "turn culture into static binary encounters."[112] However, it seems reasonable to contend that there is nothing inevitable about this process. Essentialist views of peoples and cultures *may* underlie the scholarly use of terms like "influence," "resistance," and "accommodation," but not necessarily. As a matter of fact, the suggestion that Jewish customs, traditions, literature, and other forms of cultural production were influenced by—and possibly contributed to—the surrounding cultures affirms a nonessentialist vision of Judaism as dynamic and evolving.

I now turn to the term "Judaism" itself, which has been the subject of repeated controversy in recent years, over both the translation of *Ioudaios* as "Jew" or "Judean" and the definition of "religion."[113] In the present study, "Judaism" is first and foremost synonymous with Jewish thought (conveyed in literary works), social norms, and customs (including rituals). "Judaism" may thus be broadly defined as the culture and way of life of the Jewish people, rooted in the Torah but potentially at variance with it. In view of this definition, the etic quality of the term "Judaism" is not intrinsically problematic, so long as it is not used in an essentialist or normative way—and this proviso applies also to the words "Jew" and "Judean," along with many others.

The greatest difficulty for the inquiry undertaken in this volume is the limited range of available sources, due to the fact that much ancient Jewish evidence is now lost. As Seth Schwartz has especially emphasized, scholars tend to extrapolate overarching narratives from discontinuous and heterogeneous data.[114] Jewish sources from antiquity are dominated by highly idiosyncratic literary artifacts—such as the books of the Maccabees, the Dead Sea Scrolls, the writings of Philo and Josephus, various apocrypha and pseudepigrapha, and the rabbinic corpus—complemented by some numismatic items, inscriptions and papyri, archaeological remains, and select Greek and Roman materials. Even when aggregated, this evidence provides only glimpses of the varied Jewish responses to the Roman empire and of how Jews redefined themselves and their traditions in that imperial context. Much need be read between the lines. Moreover, these sources allow us to speak of certain groups

112. Satlow 2008, 38.

113. Satlow 2006 and 2008; Mason 2007; Boyarin 2007 and 2009; Nongbri 2013; Barton and Boyarin 2016; Boyarin 2019 (Boyarin's argument, on "Judaism," is based on the assumption that this term refers to "religion," itself a modern notion). The bibliography on these issues is abundant. See the response to Mason and Boyarin in Schwartz (Seth) 2011; Miller 2010, 2012, and 2014; Schwartz (Daniel) 2014.

114. Schwartz 2001, 1–3.

or individuals, but not of Jews as a whole. Nevertheless, scholarly writing often makes sweeping assertions, inferring the general from the particular.

Admittedly, my own inquiry disproportionately relies on rabbinic sources. This does not depend on a conviction that these teachings were necessarily representative of Jewish thought or that they were considered authoritative by most Jews already during the first three centuries CE,[115] but rather because other than the writings of Josephus, rabbinic literature provides the best textual evidence for how a particular group of Jews responded to Roman domination. Moreover, this corpus has played a major role in shaping Judaism from late antiquity (or the early Middle Ages) through the present.[116] On the one hand, as Schwartz asserts, "the political marginality of 'rabbinic Judaism' matters profoundly both for our understanding of it and for our interpretation of rabbinic texts, not to mention for its impact on our understanding of the history of the Jews in the period of its consolidation."[117] On the other, the extent to which rabbinic teachings epitomized or shaped Jewish attitudes and religious practices during the early centuries of the Common Era is not central to this book's argument, first because all Jewish responses to Rome are of interest to me irrespective of their representativeness, and second because ultimately, the impact of rabbinic literature on Jewish thought and praxis in the *longue durée* is highly significant.

An inherent methodological problem is posed by the use of rabbinic writings to reconstruct Jewish, or at least rabbinic, responses to the Roman empire prior to its Christianization; namely, the challenge of dating this literature. On the whole, the traditions gathered in the Mishnah, Tosefta, and halakhic midrashim can be dated confidently to the period before Christianization (even if we take into account the possibility of later editorial glosses), whereas the final elaboration of other works—the Jerusalem Talmud, later midrashim such as Genesis and Leviticus Rabbah, and homiletic compositions like Pesiqta deRav Kahana—took place during the fourth and fifth centuries, in a Christian context. However, we must keep in mind that the empire's process of Christianization was a slow one, which entailed major changes alongside a great deal of continuity, and so modified rabbinic perceptions of Rome only gradually and partially. Moreover, insofar as the later collections incorporate traditions that predate the empire's Christianization, their relevance should

115. On the limits of rabbinic authority during the first centuries CE, see Goodman 1983, 101–111, 119–134; Hezser 1997; Schwartz 2001; Lapin 2012, 113–125. For a critical view of the scholarly trend that sees the rabbis as marginal during the first three centuries, see Brody 2017, and the references quoted in n. 2 in Brody's article; Miller 2017 (which responds to Schwartz 2001 and Lapin 2012 in particular). This book does not limit this question to Jews living in Roman Palestine, but looks at Jewish communities in the Roman empire as a whole.

116. See Kraemer 2013, 219–220.

117. Schwartz 2001, 2.

not be dismissed automatically because of the late timing of their completion. Each passage merits individual assessment. As Jacob Neusner has forcefully argued, attributions to particular rabbis are not a reliable way to date rabbinic traditions.[118] Yet, while these attributions should not be accepted uncritically, they are not to be discarded systematically either. In some instances they may be accurate, or at least convey memories of the historical context in which certain events and discussions took place.[119]

With respect to the Babylonian Talmud (also known as the Bavli), its Sassanian context and its redactors' interventions when engaging with Palestinian rabbinic traditions prevent us from treating it as direct testimony of the experiences of Jews who lived under the Roman empire.[120] Therefore, the Bavli is primarily referred to here in a comparative perspective, especially when it features a Babylonian version of material from a Palestinian rabbinic work, thus shedding light on that Palestinian version. As far as the Roman empire's long-term impact on Judaism is concerned, the Bavli represents a key element in the chain of transmission—given its popularity in later Judaism— but at best it offers indirect and secondary testimony of the actual experience of Jews in the empire. When discussing rabbinic sources, I will thus clearly differentiate between earlier and later works and between those of Palestinian and Babylonian provenance.

118. Neusner made this point in numerous publications; on the meaning of such attributions, see Neusner 1995. See also Green 1978.

119. See in particular Hayes 2000; Schwartz 2001, 8. See also Sysling 1996, 111–114.

120. See also Hodkin 2014.

CHAPTER ONE

Coping with Empires
before Rome

FROM ASSYRIA TO THE HELLENISTIC KINGDOMS

THE VERY NOTION of empire has been debated intensely over the past decades, giving birth to numerous comparative studies of ancient and modern empires, and to attempts at a general definition of the term.[1] Broadly speaking, there is a growing acceptance of the idea that different empires may follow different political and institutional models.[2] To give just one obvious example, at the end of the Republic, the Romans had an empire but no emperor as yet. Even though this may be considered the exception that proves the rule, it shows that an empire does not have to be a monarchy. In addition to the diversity of imperial models, increasing attention is being paid to the inner evolutions of ancient empires. Christophe Badel thus argues that what characterizes the new generation of scholars working on imperial issues is their dynamic conception of empires.[3]

Although recent works tend to refrain from proposing a theoretical definition of empire from the outset, favoring an approach based on case studies, some general conclusions can be considered accepted. Following Jane Burbank and Frederick Cooper, as well as Frédéric Hurlet and John Tolan, it is possible to argue that empires are state structures that have gathered peoples

1. See Hurlet 2008; Morris and Scheidel 2009; Burbank and Cooper 2010; Fibiger Bang and Kołodziejczyk 2012; Gehler and Rollinger 2014. Peter Fibiger Bang coordinates a comparative research program on "Tributary Empires," a presentation of which can be found at http://tec.saxo.ku.dk. Several publications deal with the comparison between ancient Rome and ancient China in particular: see Mittag and Mutschler 2008; Scheidel 2009.

2. Which themselves incorporate different social and political systems or modes of rule. See Goldstone and Haldon 2009.

3. Badel 2011, 18. Cf. Mittag and Mutschler 2008, 11.

from different ethnic backgrounds and different cultures under the same political authority, and that this pluralism sharply distinguishes them from unitary systems, such as the ancient city (*polis*) or contemporary nation-states.[4] The tension or dialectical relation between diversity and homogeneity—or, for some scholars, integration—appears as a general characteristic of empires, and studies tend to focus on the topic of diversity.

Comparing ancient empires leads to the identification of both similarities and differences. As we shall see in this chapter, several Roman imperial characteristics are not unique to Rome. For example, claims to world domination or claims of bringing order and peace to a world described as chaotic are found in several imperial contexts. It is critical to pay attention to the specific way(s) in which a given empire appropriated and expressed such claims.[5]

Comparing the ancient empires that Israel was confronted with is all the more necessary, as here we are facing phenomena of transfer, the adoption of ideological motifs (both discursive and iconographic), and political-cultural borrowings between these imperial powers. The Persians used some Assyrian and Babylonian motifs even as they imposed an ideology that was distinctly their own, based on their ethnic and linguistic particularity and the cult of Ahura Mazda.[6] The Seleucids in turn adopted Achaemenid elements. And the Romans' relationship to the Persian and Hellenistic models was highly ambiguous, involving both opposition and continuity.[7] In short, one cannot envision these empires as uninfluenced by one another.[8]

Interestingly enough, ancient authors were already reflecting on the phenomenon of the succession of empires, *translatio imperii*, and they too noted similarities and differences, even though the main purpose of these writers was neither comparison nor a precise understanding of the specific features of each empire. After the conquests of Alexander, the classical list of empires consisted of the Assyrians, the Medes, the Persians, and the Macedonians.[9] Aemilius Sura, a Roman author of the second century BCE, quoted by Velleius Paterculus at the beginning of the first century CE, thought that

4. Badel 2011, 23. See also Duverger 1980, 6; Goldstone and Haldon 2009.

5. Concerning the different meanings of "universalism," see the remarks in Badel 2011, 17–18.

6. See Weinfeld 1986, 177, and below.

7. Badel 2011, 12–13. See also Martinez-Sève 2011, on the Seleucids vis-à-vis the Persians.

8. See Fowler and Hekster 2005, 35. Cf. Mittag and Mutschler 2008, 11–12.

9. On this list and especially its use by Greek authors, see Price 2020b. The bibliography on the topic is abundant; see especially Swain 1940; Momigliano 1980; Mendels 1981; Momigliano 1982, 542–546; Alonso-Núñez 1983; Wiesehöfer 2013. The idea of the succession of the oriental empires is present in Herodotus (1.95, 130), but it was Ctesias, apparently, who first used it, in order to write a kind of universal history (see Diodorus Siculus 2.1–34).

the Assyrians were the first of all peoples to hold universal power, then the Medes, after them the Persians, then the Macedonians; then through the defeat of the two kings Philip (V of Macedon) and Antiochus (III of Syria), of Macedonian origin, not long after the overthrow of Carthage (201 BCE), supreme power passed to the Roman people.[10]

From the second century BCE, Rome therefore began to count as the fifth empire. According to later authors such as Dionysius of Halicarnassus at the beginning of the first century CE or Aelius Aristides in the second century CE, the Roman empire surpassed those of the past both in geographical extension and in duration—not to mention other aspects that had to do with its political institutions or its grants of citizenship—to the point that Rome was sometimes thought of as being the last empire, the one that would break away from the *translatio imperii* under the aegis of a changing Fortune.[11]

The Jews living in the Hellenistic and Roman periods inherited this tradition and reformulated it in different ways. For the author of the book of Daniel, the list was the Babylonians, the Medes, the Persians, and the Macedonians (Alexander and the Seleucids). Later on, Jewish authors such as Josephus and the rabbis favored a four-empire list: the Babylonians, the Medes and Persians taken together, the Macedonians, and the Romans, and some Christian authors adopted this view as well.[12]

Philo, who lived there, of course paid greater attention to Egypt than did other Jewish authors, but Egypt is generally absent from the Jewish lists, in spite of the early confrontation of Israel with Pharaonic Egypt narrated in the book of Exodus.[13] In this respect, the Jewish lists reflect the general tendency of Greek and Roman authors. Egypt represented a specific case indeed. During most of the Persian period it was under Achaemenid rule, and then it became a Hellenistic kingdom. Its absence from the classical list of empires has to do with the perspective of the Greek authors who elaborated this tradition, but it is not without some historical basis. As Christophe Badel recalls, the Egyptian (and later Ptolemaic) kingdom displayed a very high level of homogeneity in terms of territory and population, so that it fits our definition of an empire only at those times when it controlled territories farther south—Nubia—or farther north—mainly the Levant.[14] Although Late Bronze Age Egypt could certainly be

---

10. Velleius Paterculus, *Compendium of Roman History* 1.6.6, quoted in Pairman Brown 2001, 74.

11. Inglebert 2014, 252. On Roman and provincial perceptions of the future of the Roman empire, see Price and Berthelot 2020.

12. On the Jewish reception and reformulation of the classical list of empires, see Sharon 2020. On the Christian reception of both classical and Jewish lists, see Inglebert 2001, 343–364.

13. On Philo's perception of the succession of empires, see Berthelot 2020d.

14. Badel 2011, 19.

considered an empire, whose power Israel confronted because Egypt controlled Canaan during that period—as the Merenptah stela shows—and although Egypt remained an important player in Israel's history throughout the biblical and Hellenistic periods, this chapter will focus mainly on the great empires of the Middle East, up to the Seleucids, before turning to Rome in the next chapter.[15]

Strikingly enough, most Jewish lists of empires pass over in silence not only Egypt but Assyria as well, starting instead with the Babylonians. This may have to do with the fact that Northern Israel apparently did not survive as a coherent entity after the Assyrian deportation, whereas the people from Judah succeeded in preserving a certain level of self-consciousness even during the Babylonian Exile. Judean or Jewish authors of the Persian, Hellenistic, and Roman periods thus had a more "Judean" than "Israelite" memory and remembered the destruction of Jerusalem at the hands of the Babylonians much more vividly than the wiping out of the northern kingdom of Israel by the Assyrians in the eighth century BCE. In the biblical texts, however, the memory of the violent encounter between Israel and the Neo-Assyrian empire is strong, and numerous scholars consider the impact of Neo-Assyrian imperialism to be manifest in several biblical books.[16] I shall therefore start my investigation with the case of "Ashur," leaving aside other ancient Near Eastern empires, such as the kingdom of Akkad or the Hittite empire, which preceded the emergence of ancient Israel. Some scholars have argued that biblical texts record ancient Hittite traditions, such as formulas used in treatises, and a few Hittite elements may indeed have been transmitted in one way or another. On the whole, however, it is in the Neo-Assyrian imperial context that the biblical texts first allude to imperial realities and discourses in such a way that "the impact of empire" upon the literary productions of ancient Israel becomes perceptible.

Numerous scholars look at the Hebrew Bible through an "anti-imperial lens," arguing that many if not most biblical texts are inspired by a deep rejection of the different imperialisms that Israel encountered throughout its history.[17] In some prophetic books, one can also speak of a rival imperial vision, in which Israel or its God would rule over the whole world and the nations. Again, it must be emphasized that the rejection of imperial models often coincided with the selective appropriation of imperial motifs through imitation, mimicry, or parody. These processes were creative ones: not passive or servile, nor necessarily subversive.

Although some similarities between ancient Near Eastern sources and biblical texts may be explained by a common cultural background rather than

15. On what made the Seleucid kingdom an empire until the middle of the second century BCE, see Capdetrey 2008.

16. See § 1, below.

17. See Horsley 2008; Aberbach 1993; Howard-Brook 2010, for whom Israel's ethnic identity was "forged through shared resistance to empire, centered on claims of kinship, land, and religion" (205); Perdue and Carter 2015.

by the direct influence of a particular type of imperial discourse, in several cases one may nevertheless argue that a given imperial policy or ideology had a distinct impact.[18] As Judahite or Judean members of the elite were exposed to imperial documents, such as copies of treaties and imperial letters, it is probable that they had some degree of familiarity with imperial rhetoric. Still, shared literary elements must be very specific to justify the conclusion that direct borrowings took place, and the differences must be closely scrutinized as well.

Finally, a last question that must be kept in mind when dealing with biblical texts, whose redaction is generally hard to date with certainty, is whether scholars are able to distinguish among the legacies of the different empires that Israel faced, or whether one may speak only of an impact of empires in a very general way, at least up to the Hellenistic period. In a volume titled *Approaching Yehud: New Approaches to the Study of the Persian Period*, Julia O'Brien thus asks:

> Reading many of the essays in this volume left me wondering what distinguishes 'empire' in a Persian context from that of Neo-Babylonian or Neo-Assyrian contexts. How did the responses to empire in Persian texts compare with previous anti-imperial responses in the people's past?[19]

This is precisely what the next pages will explore, by looking successively at different imperial contexts and at the biblical or other Jewish sources that may be considered to respond to these empires in one way or another. Admittedly, this book can offer only a very brief and synthetic overview of the complex issues involved in Israel's encounter with the empires of the ancient Near East, and I must refer the reader to the works of biblical scholars and historians of these periods for more detailed analyses.

1. The Neo-Assyrian Empire

1.1 THE NATURE OF NEO-ASSYRIAN IMPERIALISM

From the tenth century BCE onward, a series of conquests enabled an impressive geographical expansion of the Neo-Assyrian empire (934–610 BCE). At its peak, it extended from the Zagros Mountains in the east to the Levant (including Israel and Judah) and Egypt in the west (and perhaps Cyprus as

---

18. As argued by, e.g., Smith 1996.

19. O'Brien 2007, 211. The necessity of differentiating not only between the Near Eastern imperial ideologies but also between biblical compositions or the literary strata within a given composition, which may reflect different ideologies, is emphasized in Wazana 2016: "Portraying a single royal ideology, either in the ancient Near East or in the Bible, amounts to creating an artificial 'one size fits all' pattern. The Bible, in particular, reflects various different stances towards kingship" (170).

well for a brief period), and from the Persian Gulf in the south to southeastern Anatolia in the north. Some scholars view the Neo-Assyrian empire as a revival of the Middle Assyrian empire (c. 1400–c. 1050 BCE) after a period of decline in the eleventh and the beginning of the tenth century BCE. Peter R. Bedford argues that during the first phase of the Neo-Assyrian expansion, the conquests might from the Assyrian perspective be considered "not a new act of imperialism but rather the re-establishment of control over territories in rebellion against their long-standing overlord."[20]

Originally, the Neo-Assyrian empire was a gathering of several tributary vassal states. Later, at least from the reign of Tiglath-pileser III (745–727), we observe a gradual provincialization of the conquered territories, especially in the west. The empire progressively became more centralized and unified. This was a response to the failure of the client or vassal state system, that is, to the fact that the loyalty oaths were broken and tribute left unpaid. This process was accomplished through harsh policies involving the displacement of whole groups of people.[21] According to Simo Parpola,

> The reducing of a country to a province was carried out according to a standardized procedure involving the utter destruction of the vassal's urban centers; massive deportations; rebuilding the capital in Assyrian style; the installation of an Assyrian governor; the construction of Assyrian garrisons and forts; the imposition of a uniform taxation and conscription system, imperial standards and measures, cults, and a single *lingua franca*, Aramaic. The inhabitants of the new province became Assyrian citizens; its economy was completely reorganized in line with Assyrian commercial interests; and the seat of the governor, a copy of the imperial court in miniature, became a channel through which Assyrian culture was systematically spread to the country.[22]

Some scholars claim that the Assyrians imposed no religious obligations on their vassals.[23] According to Parpola, however, such a claim is refuted by the Succession (or Vassal) Treaty of Esarhaddon (r. 681–669) (EST or VTE), in which vassals had to swear that they accepted Ashur as their god and the future king as their only lord.[24] Acceptance of Ashur as one's god was thus an aspect of the Neo-Assyrian ideology of rule. However, the recognition of Ashur's divine rule went hand in hand with political submission and loyalty to the king, and

20. Bedford 2009, 30.
21. Oded 1979; Joannès 2011, 30. For general views of how the Neo-Assyrian empire was built and functioned, see Frahm 2017; Liverani 2017a.
22. Parpola 2003, 100.
23. See Cogan 1974, 85; Liverani 2017b, 541.
24. Parpola 2003, 100 n. 4.

probably reflects the fact that the "political" and the "religious" could hardly be disentangled in the ancient world. It does not mean that the cult of Ashur was actually imposed on the populations of the Neo-Assyrian empire.

The materials documenting Neo-Assyrian imperial ideology are quite abundant. Written sources include "chronological texts, such as king lists, chronicles, and eponym lists (year-names taken from the names of officials), and royal inscriptions, such as annals, display inscriptions, votive inscriptions, and 'letters to the god' (reports on military campaigns)."[25] As most of these sources stem from the royal court, they provide useful information not only on the king's activities, but also on the ideological justifications for his conquests and on imperial ideology more broadly.

Neo-Assyrian kings claimed to have established a universal empire—a contention already made by the kings of Akkad at the end of the third millenium BCE and those of the Middle Assyrian empire at the end of the second millenium BCE.[26] It was an allegation embodied in the use of the royal title *šar kiššati*, "king of the whole (universe)."[27] As in the case of other empires, including larger ones that developed in later periods, such as the Achaemenid or the Roman, this claim was contradicted by the existence of independent political entities to the west and farther east. Yet the claim remained an important one from an ideological point of view.

Neo-Assyrian imperialism presented itself as an expression of the will of the god Ashur, which had to be made manifest to the whole world. All wars were religious insofar as they were ordered by Ashur. Assyrian expansion was thus construed in theological and moral terms: from a Neo-Assyrian perspective, it was right and proper that peoples submit to Assyrian sovereignty, and failure to do so meant resistance to Ashur's will.[28] In Mario Liverani's view, it was this expansionist dimension of the Neo-Assyrian imperial project and the ideology that sustained it that justifies speaking about an empire in the Neo-Assyrian case.[29]

Neo-Assyrian inscriptions also presented the king as a wise legislator and judge who, having an intimate relationship with Ashur, was divinely chosen to bring order and peace to the world.[30] Sennacherib (r. 705–681) is called "guardian of the right, lover of justice . . . perfect hero, mighty man, first among all princes, the powerful one who consumes the insubmissive, who strikes the

25. Bedford 2009, 31.

26. On Akkad, see Fibiger Bang and Kołodziejczyk 2012, especially 9–10. On the Middle Assyrian empire, see Pongratz-Leisten 2015.

27. See Garelli 1979, 319.

28. See Liverani 1979, 301; Oded 1992; Postgate 2007; Bedford 2009, 35, 48; Thompson 2013, 113–154.

29. Liverani 2017a.

30. See Garelli 1979, 320.

wicked with lightning."[31] The question of whether the Neo-Assyrian kings were considered divine or were merely seen as "representatives/administrators" of the gods or as something intermediate has been a matter of debate (there is no evidence that living kings were worshipped).[32] In any case, the notion of the king as a rightful judge and the empire's presentation of its own power as the force that brings peace, order, and law—and even civilization—to a world that is otherwise chaotic are recurring features of ancient empires.[33]

Yet the Neo-Assyrian inscriptions and reliefs also evoked battles, military victories, and the merciless crushing of the king's enemies, who were depicted as tortured, mutilated, impaled, or buried alive. According to Carly L. Crouch, this is particularly striking in Esarhaddon's inscriptions, especially when compared to those of Sennacherib. Esarhaddon is called "king of kings, the unsparing, who controls the insubordinate, who is clothed in terror, who is fearless in battle, the perfect hero, who is unsparing in the fight," as well as "the unsparing weapon, which utterly destroys the enemy's land," whom the gods have empowered "to rob, to plunder, to extend the border of Assyria."[34] The brutal treatment of enemies was not unique to Esarhaddon, however, and on the whole, Neo-Assyrian imperial ideology was characterized by militaristic, violent, and crudely expansionist language and visual representations.

1.2 The Legacy of Neo-Assyrian Imperialism in the Bible

The northern kingdom of Israel was destroyed by the Assyrians in 722–720 BCE, its capital Samaria demolished, and its territory transformed into a province of the empire. The kingdom of Judah, on the other hand, retained a certain level of autonomy as a vassal kingdom not fully incorporated into the Assyrian provincial system.[35] According to Parpola, Assyrian political and cultural influence gradually spread in Judah and is particularly attested in biblical and archaeological records dating to the reign of Manasseh (692–638)—for example, in locally manufactured seals and cult objects.[36]

---

31. Crouch 2009, 124, referring to Luckenbill's edition of Sennacherib's annals, 23:4–5, 23:7–9, 48:2–3, 55:2–3, 66:1–2.

32. Machinist 2006 shows how complex the picture is in the sources at hand and concludes that the king was "the primary nexus between heaven and earth" (186) but not a god sensu stricto. For Bedford (2009, 35) and Liverani (2017b, 536), Assyrian kings were not considered divine.

33. Liverani 1979, 305, 310.

34. Crouch 2009, 133–134, referring to Borger 1956, 96:19–23, 98:22, 98:34–35.

35. For a detailed summary of the main political events in the Neo-Assyrian period and the way they affected Israel and Judah, see Ackerman 2010. See also Cogan 1993, 409; Parpola 2003, 103–104.

36. Parpola 2003, 104.

As Bedford emphasizes, agreeing with many others, "The biblical texts from Israel and Judah ascribed to [*the Neo-Assyrian*] period are about our only source for the views of subjugated peoples."[37] (Interestingly enough, the situation was somewhat similar in the later context of the Roman empire: apart from the Greeks, no people subjugated by the Romans left so many written testimonies documenting its perspective on this domination as the Jews.) Bedford further claims that "texts such as First Isaiah (Isaiah 1–39), Amos, and Deuteronomy document knowledge of Assyrian literary traditions."[38] This view is actually shared by several scholars. Parpola, for example, writes: "There cannot be any doubt that, not only the king of Judah, but the ruling class of Judah as a whole was familiar with the central provisions of the treaties with Assyria, for vassal rulers were explicitly told to propagate them to their people."[39]

The Notion of a Universal God

Simo Parpola and Baruch Levine argue that the impact of Neo-Assyrian imperial ideology was felt even in the development of the Israelite or Judahite conception of the God of Israel, especially as reflected in Deuteronomy, but also in prophetic books such as First Isaiah, Amos, and Micah.[40] This is not surprising given the closely intertwined nature of political and theological notions in ancient societies and the many parallels between the conception of a deity and the representation of a king. Parpola concludes that

> in the mind of the writer of Deuteronomy 13, the God of Israel has taken the place previously occupied in the collective mind of the nation by the feared, almighty king of Assyria. [. . .] The conclusion seems inescapable that the Deuteronomic concept of God, which according to current scholarly consensus evolved in the late 7th or early 6th century B.C.E. and is basic to all later Judaism, is heavily indebted to Assyrian religion and royal ideology.[41]

In several publications, he argues that the cult of the Neo-Assyrian god Ashur influenced the development of Israelite "monotheism" (or, rather, henotheism

---

37. Bedford 2009, 32.

38. Ibid. Bedford relies on Weinfeld 1972; Machinist 1983; Paul 1991; Steymans 1995a; Otto 2002, 94–219. The dating of these biblical books is of course debated. Concerning Isaiah, see Levine 2005, 419. For a recent attempt to show that First Isaiah is to be associated with the second half of the eighth century BCE and understood as a response to Neo-Assyrian imperialism, see Aster 2017.

39. Parpola 2003, 104. See also Cogan 1974; Machinist 1983; Römer 2005, 67–106; Levine 2005, 414.

40. Parpola 2003; Levine 2005. See also Artzi 2008 (on Isa 2:2–3 and Micah 4:1–2); Flynn 2014, especially 163–166.

41. Parpola 2003, 105. See also Parpola 1997.

or monolatry—that is, the notion that the people of Israel worship only one god but do not deny that other nations have their own gods).[42] In his view, the god Ashur came to embody all deities, and this process had an impact on theological constructions in Israel as well. Focusing on universalism rather than henotheism, Richard J. Thompson has further argued that the development of a universal conception of the God of Israel was "inspired by the prestige and power of a dominant imperial, Mesopotamian god."[43]

In the context of a (proclaimed) universal empire and the threat it represented to Israel and Judah, an "enhanced God-idea" was called for, to use Levine's expression.[44] The fact that Jerusalem was not seized in 701 BCE seems to have been interpreted as a sign that the God of Israel was controlling not only the fate of his own people but also that of the Assyrians. Moreover, as we see in Isaiah 10:5–19, for example, the Assyrians were perceived as an instrument, a "rod of anger" used by God to punish Israel, an idea with parallels in Neo-Assyrian sources.[45] It was the God of Israel who granted the Assyrians their victories, not the Assyrian gods—a bold and subversive claim, but also an imitation of Neo-Assyrian discourse. In the end, God would ultimately turn against the Assyrians and chastise them as well (see, for example, Isaiah 10:5, 14:24–27). From the perspective of the biblical texts, the Assyrians' boasting about their victory over Israel was therefore pointless and foolish, because they could have accomplished nothing without the permission and support of the God of Israel. This reasoning enabled the notion that God was the sole and the ultimate power at work in history, the single deity ruling over all nations, an idea that is fundamental to the monotheistic creed that would develop later in Israel's history. Finally, it must be emphasized, as Levine says, that this evolution was based on "an important feature of response literature: Those who respond internalize; they factor-in their own ideological culture, at times inverting the propaganda of the other."[46]

God's Kingdom and Divine Kingship

According to Moshe Weinfeld, the notion of God's kingdom was also, in part, a response to Neo-Assyrian imperialism:

42. See, e.g., Parpola 1997, xiii–cviii.

43. Thompson 2013, 195.

44. Levine 2005, 411.

45. See Weinfeld 1986, 176, which quotes an inscription of Esarhaddon stating, "The great god Ashur . . . put in my hand a rod of anger (*šibirru ezzu*) to destroy the enemies, he authorized me to plunder and spoil (*ana habāti šlāli*) the land which sins . . . against Ashur." Weinfeld refers to Borger's (1956) edition, 98:30ff. See also Spieckermann 2013, 328–329.

46. Levine 2005, 422.

a similar kind of ideological resistance to imperial tyranny [as the Jewish resistance to Rome] developed in the wake of Assyrian imperialism and is clearly reflected in Israelite prophetic literature of the eighth century BCE. Isaiah the prophet, who saw the apogee of Assyrian imperialistic policy, starting with Tiglath-Pileser III and ending with Sennacherib, was the first to raise his voice against Assyrian imperialism and to predict the coming of a new divine rule which would replace Assyrian tyrannic dominion.[47]

Weinfeld refers in particular to Isaiah 10:5–15, which protests against Assyria and its crimes; 10:16–34, which foretells Assyria's destruction; and 11:1–10, which evokes the rise of the divine ruler and world salvation. He emphasizes that although the divine ruler appears in the guise of an emperor, he rules with righteousness rather than with power (Isa 11:4). God's kingdom reflects the transformation of a political empire into a spiritual or godly one, the Jerusalem Temple serving as a universal center to which all nations will come in order to receive peace (Isa 2:2–4). By contrast, "the godly nature of the kingdom as found in Isaiah 11 is not attested in Assyrian inscriptions." Weinfeld concludes that "the concept which dominates later eschatology about a new ideal kingdom built on the ruins of a former ruthless empire [in, e.g., Daniel 2:44 and 7:17–18] was actually conceived for the first time in Judah in the eighth century B.C.E. It was motivated by national feelings of oppression and subjugation to the Assyrian empire."[48]

Building on Weinfeld's analysis, Shawn Flynn argues that the author of First Isaiah opposes the notion of the warrior king personified by the Neo-Assyrian king to the model of God, the creator king.[49] Flynn does not deny that YHWH appears as a warrior in some biblical texts, but he considers that in the first part of the book of Isaiah, the destruction delivered by the God of Israel aims to establish peace, and thus God as warrior differs from the notion of the warrior king in Neo-Assyrian inscriptions, and may be understood as a deliberate response to the latter. Yet in view of Liverani's remarks on the rhetoric of Neo-Assyrian inscriptions—where destruction also aims to bring peace—this part of Isaiah could in fact be viewed as imitating Neo-Assyrian discourse.[50] Moreover, Thompson has argued that certain passages of the Deuteronomistic history describe the God of Israel as an imperial military god modeled on the image of Ashur, and just as terrifying for his enemies as the Assyrian deity.[51]

---

47. Weinfeld 1986, 170.

48. Weinfeld 1986, 182.

49. Flynn 2014, 165–169 and chap. 6.

50. Liverani 2017b, 541.

51. Thompson 2013, 223–229, 234, referring to, e.g., Deut 1:6–8, 7:4 and Josh 4:13 (for God as military commander); Deut 2:25, Josh 2:9, and 2 Sam 22:13–14 (for radiance and terror).

The Covenant between God and Israel

Since its discovery in 1955 and Donald J. Wiseman's edition in 1958, the vassal treaty that Esarhaddon, Sennacherib's son, made in 672 BCE with nine eastern vassal princes—also known as Esarhaddon's Succession Treaty, because its main aim was to secure the succession of Esarhaddon's younger son Ashurbanipal to the throne—has attracted a great deal of attention for the light it sheds on Deuteronomy, especially books 13 and 28.[52] In 2009, another exemplar of this treaty (*adē*) was discovered at Tell Tayinat (on the southern border of modern Turkey), in an unidentified temple, confirming that the Assyrians imposed the terms of this text on their western vassals—it invokes deities from the Levant in §§54 and 54B, which were damaged or missing in the tablets found in 1955 in the temple of Nabū at Nimrud (alternately, these western deities may have been omitted because this copy of the treaty was for eastern vassals).[53] Since the tablets on which this *adē* was inscribed were displayed in temples, a growing number of scholars believe that a copy was displayed in the Jerusalem Temple as well, and that Judahite scribes thus had direct knowledge of this text.[54]

Deuteronomy 28 lists the curses that will befall Israel if it does not remain faithful to God's covenant. This has no parallel in the rest of the biblical corpus, except Leviticus 26, which is formulated as direct rather than indirect speech. On the other hand, many parallels exist between the list in Deuteronomy 28 and the curses in the Vassal Treaty of Esarhaddon (henceforth VTE): they both include annihilation and/or sterility (Deut 28:20 // VTE lines 414–416), pestilence (Deut 28:21 // VTE lines 455–456), drought (Deut 28:23–24 // VTE lines 526–533), subjection to an enemy (Deut 28:25 // VTE lines 453–454), corpses left unburied (Deut 28:26 // VTE lines 425–427), skin diseases (Deut 28:27 // VTE lines 419–421), blindness (Deut 28:28f // VTE lines 422–424), lack of a savior or intercessor (Deut 28:29b // VTE lines 417–418), deprivation of property and everything held dear (Deut 28:30–34 // VTE lines 428–430), sickness (Deut 28:35 // VTE lines 461–463), and starvation (Deut 28: 38–42.53–57 // VTE lines 440–452).[55] Moreover, some of these curses follow

52. On Deut 13, see Levinson and Stackert 2012; Otto 2016, 1239–1256. On Deut 28, see Wiseman 1958; Frankena 1965; Weinfeld 1972, esp. 94–129; Steymans 1995a; Steymans 1995b; Otto 1999a, 68; Römer 2005, 74–78 (which notes that there is also an influence of Neo-Assyrian vassal treaties on Deut 6:4–7); Steymans 2013; Otto 2017, 4:1984–1990, 1994–1999, 2007–2010.

53. See Steymans 2013; Lauinger 2015 (focusing on issues of transmission).

54. See Steymans 2013.

55. Frankena 1965, 144–150. The line numbering is according to Wiseman's edition. See also Weinfeld 1972, 94–129, which argues that the curses in Deut 28:27–35 in particular must be seen as derived directly from VTE §§39–42 (lines 419–424). Moreover, Weinfeld shows that the sequence of the curses in Deuteronomy makes sense only in light of the rationale found in the VTE, in which the curses follow the organization of the Assyrian pantheon.

the same order in both the VTE and Deuteronomy. According to Rintje Frankena, "It is not only possible to discover behind the words of Deut. xxviii 28–34
the phrasing of the Assyrian parallels, but an analysis of these curses even
tells us something about the working-method of the Judaean compiler."[56] The
text in Deuteronomy, however, adds new elements not present in the Neo-
Assyrian treaties, such as the prediction of the rise of an immigrant who will
become more prosperous than the native Israelite (Deut 28:43–44); it also
drops the polytheistic aspects of the Neo-Assyrian source. Conversely, some
of the curses in the Neo-Assyrian treaty are extremely specific and are not
found in Deuteronomy. Although one could underline numerous differences
in form and content between Deuteronomy and these Neo-Assyrian vassal
treaties and loyalty oaths, the number of precise parallels remains so striking
that it strongly suggests the influence of Neo-Assyrian formulas on the elites
who were responsible for an early stage of Deuteronomy's redaction.

However, Deuteronomy remains an original work that selectively and
critically uses, and challenges, these imperial traditions.[57] The parallels imply
that from the perspective of the Judahite redactors, God takes the place of
the Assyrian king and is the true king to whom Israel must commit through
a loyalty oath. Some layers of Deuteronomy therefore convey a bold anti-
imperialism, which is all the more meaningful if one recalls that the Judahite
king Manasseh was a vassal of Esarhaddon according to the latter's annals, a
status that meant he would have had to accept the Assyrian king as his lord
and submit to both the king and the king's god, Ashur.[58] Following Eckart
Otto, one may thus speak of a subversive reception of the VTE in the Judahite
circles that produced the first edition of Deuteronomy.[59] The Neo-Assyrian
notion of a treaty (adē) gave way to the Judahite notion of a covenant (bᵉrit).[60]
In making their anti-Assyrian claim, however, the redactors of Deuteronomy
appropriated some of the ideological language of the ruling power, making it
part of Israel's tradition through a selective adaptation and an inventive transformation. As we shall see, other aspects of the book of Deuteronomy may also
be associated with the Neo-Assyrian period and its ideology.

Specific Laws of the Covenant

Several scholars, especially Moshe Weinfeld, Eckart Otto, Bernard Levinson,
and Nili Wazana, have noticed that other passages of Deuteronomy referring to specific laws may be read at least partly in light of the Neo-Assyrian

---

56. Frankena 1965, 148–149.

57. Levinson and Stackert 2012, 125.

58. Frankena 1965, 151.

59. Otto 1999a; Otto 2002. See also Levinson 2010, 342, 344. For a critical discussion
of the notion of "subversion" in this context, see Crouch 2014. ,

60. Spieckermann 2013, 332–335.

context.[61] Among these are the "canon formula" found in Deuteronomy 13:1—
"You must diligently observe everything that I command you; do not add to it
or take anything from it"—the laws regulating "apostasy" (13:2–12), the "law
of the king" (17), the laws of war (20), and the law concerning a hanged corpse
(21:22–23).

Concerning the laws of war found in Deuteronomy 20, Wazana argues that
the prohibition on destroying the fruit trees outside a city besieged by Israel
was probably inspired by Neo-Assyrian war practice and propaganda.[62] In an
inscription related to the campaign of Ashurnasirpal II (r. 883–859) against
king Ilānu and the city of Damdammusa (in the upper Tigris region) in 866
BCE, one reads:

> I took that city in hand for myself. I took the live soldiers and the heads
> to the city Amedu, his royal city, (and) built a pile of heads before his
> gates. I impaled the live soldiers on stakes around about his city. I
> fought my way inside his gate (and) cut down his orchards.[63]

Similarly, an inscription describing Tiglath-pileser III's campaign against
Mukīn-zēri of Bīt-Amūkāni in 731 BCE reads: "I killed the date-palms
throughout his land. I stripped off their fruit and filled the meadows."[64] Cutting down orchards was apparently meant to impress the besieged enemy,
push it to surrender, and thus shorten the siege. The trees, Wazana argues,
appear as "substitutes for humans in cases where the city held on or the
enemy survived the attack."[65] Neo-Assyrian reliefs depicting sieges display
razed trees, corroborating the testimony of the inscriptions. They also depict
standing trees, thus conveying the message that whereas resistance to Assyrian power brings only death and destruction, complete submission to it yields
life and fertility.

The law of Deuteronomy 20:19—"If you besiege a town for a long time,
making war against it in order to take it, you must not destroy its trees by
wielding an axe against them. Although you may take food from them, you
must not cut them down. Are trees in the field human beings that they should

61. See Weinfeld 1972; Otto 1999a; Otto 2016, 1239–1256 (on Deut 13), 1575–1576, 1581–
1605 (on Deut 20), 1659–1661 (on Deut 21:22–23); Levinson 2010, which suggests that the
authors of Deut 13 "transformed the Neo-Assyrian formula requiring exclusive loyalty to
'the word of Esarhaddon' (*abutu ša Aššur-aḫu-iddina*) into one that demanded fidelity to
'the word' (*ha-davar*) of Israel's divine overlord, Yahweh, as proclaimed by Moses" (337);
Levinson and Stackert 2012; Wazana 2008; Wazana 2012; Wazana 2016. See also Parpola
2003, 104.

62. Wazana 2008.

63. Trans. by Albert K. Grayson, in *RIMA* II, 220, iii: 105–109a, quoted in Wazana
2008, 289.

64. Trans. by Hayim Tadmor, in *Tiglath-Pileser III*, 162: 23–24, quoted in Wazana
2008, 289.

65. Wazana 2008, 289.

come under siege from you?"—is commonly dated to the reign of Josiah in Judah (c. 649–609 BCE) and understood as a measure promoting moderation and mercy in times of war. Yet Wazana suggests understanding it also as a reaction to Assyrian propaganda and notes five points of contact between these two contexts. The crucial point is that whereas the Assyrians considered cutting down fruit trees "an acceptable and ideologically significant part of siege warfare," the biblical law in Deuteronomy presents this act as divinely prohibited.[66]

The Neo-Assyrian practice of impalement, referred to in the inscription of Ashurnasirpal II quoted above, may be seen as sparking a similar reaction from the Deuteronomy redactors who lived at the end of the Neo-Assyrian period. Impalement—as well as the hanging up of the dead body after execution—was performed in public, in order that all might watch the scene, as is shown on Assyrian reliefs such as the one depicting Sennacherib's capture of Lakish in 701 BCE, found at Nineveh (Fig. 1.1).

Most important, this meant that the corpses were not buried, something the biblical texts, and Deuteronomy 21:22–23 in particular, strongly oppose. The biblical law does not prohibit the impalement of bodies as such, only their prolonged exposure and the denial of a proper burial.[67] According to Wazana, both this Deuteronomic law and the narratives found in Joshua 8:29 (the hanging of the king of Ai) and 10:26–27 (the hanging of the five kings who attacked Joshua), which she considers secondary additions, are responses to Neo-Assyrian practice and ideology. Otto rejects Wazana's analysis of the stories in the book of Joshua, arguing that the practice of impalement had to do more with a legal context than with a military one. However, Karen Radner has shown that in the Neo-Assyrian case, impalement is attested in both civil and military contexts, which makes Wazana's interpretation of the evidence from Deuteronomy and Joshua all the more convincing.[68]

On the whole, the evidence suggests that confrontation with the Neo-Assyrian practice and ideology of war led to the formulation of specific laws in Israel that were at least in part a reaction to Neo-Assyrian imperialism.

Human Kingship

Several aspects of human kingship as it is portrayed in biblical texts may be considered responses to Neo-Assyrian royal models and discourse. For example, the idea—found in 2 Samuel 7 and Psalm 2, among other places—that the legitimate king is a son of God, although not uncommon in the ancient Near East in general, may have a Neo-Assyrian origin. Otto argues that Psalm 2, in

66. Wazana 2008, 293; cf. Otto 1999b, 99–100.
67. Wazana 2012, esp. 77, 92.
68. Otto 2016, 1660; Radner 2015.

FIGURE 1.1. Neo-Assyrian reliefs from Nineveh showing
the impalement of prisoners from Lakish. The British Museum, London.
Photograph © Osama Shukir Muhammed Amin FRCP (Glasg).

which God tells the king, "You are my son, this day I have begotten you," combines Egyptian and Assyrian influences. Whereas the deity's directly addressing the king as "my son" has close parallels only in an Egyptian context, Otto
sees an Assyrian influence in the motif of the rebellion of the subject nations
and in God's promise to the king that the latter will "break them with a rod of

iron, and dash them in pieces like a potter's vessel."[69] In both the Neo-Assyrian and the biblical contexts, in contrast with the Egyptian one, the king is not divine; rather, his status as "son" of the deity is to be interpreted as a reflection of his role as mediator between the human and the divine realms. However, in Neo-Assyrian ideology a rebellion against the king is equivalent to a rebellion against the god Ashur, whereas in the Bible the prophets who oppose the kings of Israel and Judah are cast as God's spokespersons. The biblical corpus thus introduces a dissociation between the king and divine investiture that is unheard of in the Neo-Assyrian context.

The Torah has, in fact, very few laws concerning the king. Moreover, the biblical corpus gives evidence of several patently anti-monarchical traditions, such as Judges 8:23, where Gideon refuses, both himself and for his sons, to rule as king over the Israelites; Judges 9, the story of Abimelech's seizure of power and the fable of the trees, told by Jotham to teach the Israelites what is meant by bad kingship; 1 Samuel 8, which clearly states that Israel's request for a king is tantamount to a rejection of God; and 1 Samuel 10:18–19, which echoes 1 Samuel 8. These texts convey the idea that human kingship contradicts God's kingship and is merely tolerated by the God of Israel. Furthermore, as Wazana points out,

> while the royal divine image of God in the Bible (Num 23:21; Deut 33:5) remains in agreement with contemporary ancient Near Eastern notions, the anti-monarchical texts are unique, unparalleled elsewhere in the ancient Near East. These texts sever the umbilical cord connecting the human king to his divine counterpart typical of the ancient Near East and of other biblical texts.[70]

Wazana further argues that the law of the king in Deuteronomy 17:14–20, which is presented not as divinely initiated but rather as a response to a request made by Israel, is not anti-monarchical but instead reflects anti-imperial polemic. The fact that the king is forbidden to multiply wealth, horses, and women is indicative, she believes, of an imperial context rather than local kingships.[71] In her view, the law of the king was most likely a polemic against Neo-Assyrian rule, which it rejected as a threat to the covenantal relationship between God and Israel. The commandment in Deuteronomy 17:15 to appoint only a native Israelite as the king of Israel would thus be, for Wazana, a reaction to the fear of seeing Judah transformed into an Assyrian province, under direct Assyrian rule, as had been the fate of the former northern Israelite kingdom. Confronted with Neo-Assyrian political practices and imperial ideology of kingship, the redactors of Deuteronomy 17 erected an alternative kingship

---

69. Otto 2003, 343–349; see also Collins 2011b, 292.
70. Wazana 2016, 175.
71. Wazana 2016, 184–185.

model, which would undergo additional modifications in a Neo-Babylonian context.[72]

However, scholars still debate such an early dating of Deuteronomy's law of the king (even in a version that would not have included verses 18–20a). Ultimately, Deuteronomy 17:14–20 may also be read against the background of the failure of the Israelite and Judahite monarchies.[73]

On the basis of the examples discussed above, it seems reasonable to conclude that the Neo-Assyrian empire left an enduring legacy in biblical literature, especially in the first part of the book of Isaiah and the earliest redactional layers of Deuteronomy, which may go back to the seventh century BCE. It seems that several aspects of Neo-Assyrian policies and ideology were both challenged and integrated in a critical and inventive way within Israel's literary traditions, giving scholars license to assert the politico-religious impact of Neo-Assyrian imperialism not only on the history of ancient Israel, but also on the earliest layers of the Hebrew Bible.[74]

2. The Neo-Babylonian Empire

2.1 THE NATURE OF NEO-BABYLONIAN IMPERIALISM

The gradual collapse of the Neo-Assyrian empire allowed the king of Babylon Nabopolassar (r. 626–605), founder of the Neo-Babylonian empire (626–539), to seize the leading position once occupied by the Assyrians. He soon laid claim to their inheritance, in particular the western provinces that bordered the Mediterranean Sea, and Neo-Babylonian hegemony would eventually extend from the Mediterranean to the Persian Gulf and the Iranian plateau, with Babylon as its capital. From the early sixth century onward, the city was the political, cultural, and economic center of the entire ancient Near East.[75] Yet this empire was short-lived, disappearing after less than a century. Written sources on its brief history are abundant, but we lack state archives (such as are preserved for the Assyrians), and the organization of the empire therefore remains unclear.[76] The dual system of provinces under direct rule and vassal states paying tribute may have prevailed, though there is no consensus on this point. According to

72. Especially as far as the obligation to copy a scroll of the Law and to study the Law was concerned. See Wazana 2016, 189–190.

73. See, e.g., Otto 2016, 1480–1489, and Markl 2018, which both argue for a later redaction context.

74. In terms of historical experience, Frankena (1965) goes as far as to state that king Josiah initiated the so-called Deuteronomic reform—which meant going back to the Covenant with YHWH—in the wake of and in reaction to the collapse of the Neo-Assyrian empire.

75. Brinkman 1984, 1.

76. Jursa 2014, 139: ". . . no comprehensive reconstruction of the nature of Babylonian imperial control over the empire's periphery can be given."

David S. Vanderhooft, the Neo-Babylonian empire relied on the collection of tribute from client kings rather than a proper provincial administration, which now belonged to the Neo-Assyrian past.[77] Weinfeld concurs with this analysis and points out that the Neo-Babylonian empire relied on plunder and taxation instead of real wars of conquest.[78] Another distinguishing feature is that although the Babylonians did occasionally deport particular groups, such as Judeans after the fall of Jerusalem in 586 BCE, they did not follow the Neo-Assyrian policy of mixing populations in order to erase ethnic self-definitions, and allowed communities to organize themselves on an ethnic basis, as shown by the archives of Al-Yahudu (mostly dating to the Persian period).[79]

As Vanderhooft notes, there are a few differences in imperial ideology as well. Neo-Babylonian royal inscriptions tend to avoid Neo-Assyrian royal epithets that emphasize conquest and universal rule, favoring instead references to the king's building activities:

> In fact, several archaic epithets that had been common in the Babylonian tradition from early on, but which became the sine qua non of the Neo-Assyrian titulary, *šarru rabû*, "great king," *šarru dannu*, "mighty king," *šar kiššati*, "king of the universe," and *šar kibrāt erbetti*, "king of the four corners (of the earth)," are avoided by the Neo-Babylonian kings in their titulary, again with notable exceptions under Nabonidus. Furthermore, the titulary emphasizes the traditional role of the king as the caretaker of Babylon and the sanctuaries of the gods, and avoids epithets which are explicitly militaristic in tone or which lodge claims for the king's universal dominion.[80]

True, the parts of the royal inscriptions that narrate the appointing of the king by the gods occasionally contain a universalistic perspective. Nebuchadnezzar, for example, is said to have been entrusted with rule over all humankind and the four corners of the earth. Yet the emphasis is not on conquest, as in the Neo-Assyrian inscriptions.[81] Although the Neo-Babylonian kings obviously did lead wars, even wars of conquest, their ideological discourse gave greater weight to the religious role of the king, depicted as a builder or

---

77. Vanderhooft 1999, 206. Concerning the Levant, see Jursa 2014, especially the conclusion at 142.

78. Weinfeld 1986, 173. See also Jursa 2014, 124 (concerning the Levant in particular), 133–134, 137–138.

79. Around fifty tablets have been found, documents that pertain to economic activity and were made in a city called Al-Yahudu, "(the city) of Judah," of which the first ten are dated to the Neo-Babylonian period: see Pearce and Wunsch 2014; Zadok 2014; Berlejung 2017 (showing economic integration and social mobility at the end of the Neo-Babylonian and the beginning of the Persian period).

80. Vanderhooft 1999, 203–204.

81. Vanderhooft 1999, 204.

restorer of temples and a high priest.[82] According to Paul Garelli, what the Neo-Babylonian inscriptions mainly put forward is the role of the king as shepherd of his people.[83]

Another distinctive aspect of the Neo-Babylonian (or, more generally, Babylonian) ideology of rule was the king's activity as a teacher of wisdom. Following Paul-Alain Beaulieu, Michael Jursa argues that "the royal ideology of the period differed markedly from the image of, e.g., the Assyrian king: ideally, a Neo-Babylonian king wanted to be seen 'not as conqueror, administrator, or provider of social justice, but as religious leader and teacher of wisdom.'"[84] Later—once the Babylonian monarchy was no more—the scribal elite monopolized this former role of the king.[85] Interestingly enough, in Judah a parallel evolution took place.

2.2 THE LEGACY OF NEO-BABYLONIAN IMPERIALISM IN THE BIBLE

The kingdom of Judah became a vassal state of the Neo-Babylonian empire in the wake of the latter's establishment on the ruins of its Neo-Assyrian predecessor. Judah was suspected of plotting a revolt, and it was punished accordingly. The Jerusalem Temple was demolished in 587 or 586 BCE and the Judean elites deported to Babylon. Although the deportees did not become important actors at the Babylonian court—the fantasies of the book of Daniel notwithstanding—some Babylonian tablets record rations given to the exiled Judean king, Jehoiachin, at the court, and mention other exiled Judeans in different contexts.[86] The dramatic events of 587–586 BCE and the Judeans' subsequent exile and integration within the Neo-Babylonian state and culture were to have many and enduring consequences at the political, social, and religious levels and in the realm of ancient Jewish thought. The redaction of the stories of Genesis inspired by Mesopotamian mythology, the development of a theology of Zion, together with the notion of *golah*, or diaspora, were likely products of this period. The exile experience may also have contributed to the emergence of monotheism in response to the delocalization of the Judean national deity, who was now left without a temple. And this list of effects is by no means exhaustive.[87] The question, however, is whether the Neo-Babylonian ideology of rule had a specific, identifiable impact on the Judean elites, keeping in mind that in this case as well, the evidence stemming from Judah is the

82. Jursa 2014, 122, 137.
83. Garelli 1981, 2, 4, lists the nonviolent and beneficial activities of the king: building canals, suppressing corvées, restoring privileges, providing food and gifts, etc.
84. Jursa 2014, 126, quoting Beaulieu 2007, 142.
85. Beaulieu 2007, 163.
86. Cf. 2 Kings 25:27–30 and the archives of Al-Yahudu (see n. 79 above).
87. Perdue and Carter 2015, 79.

best documentation we have of ideological resistance to Neo-Babylonian pow-er.[88] As Vanderhooft emphasizes, this resistance, as expressed in the prophetic books of the Bible, was partly formulated in line with previous prophetic tradi-tions and was not shaped exclusively by the encounter with Neo-Babylonian ideas and policies. However, some texts, such as Habakkuk 1–2, may be seen as directly responding to the new context and echoing particular Neo-Babylonian ideological elements, such as the affirmation of Marduk's universal sovereignty in the *akītu* festival.[89] Beyond expressions of resistance to imperial power and its ideological justification, however, can we find an enduring legacy of Neo-Babylonian ideology in biblical thought?

The Emergence of Monotheism: Foreign Gods as Idols

Again, Deuteronomy and Isaiah are relevant sources, but the relevant chap-ters and redactional layers are now different from those discussed in the Neo-Assyrian context.[90] We should first and foremost keep in mind that the crisis of the Babylonian Exile raised the question of whether the Babylonian gods had defeated the God of Israel—whose very temple had been destroyed. This was a traditional way to understand military defeat in the ancient world. The idea put forward by the authors of the Deuteronomistic history, that it was the God of Israel who used the Babylonians to punish his people and that he was in full control of history, "prepared the way for the 'monotheistic' statements in the parts of the Deuteronomistic history that were revised and retouched last of all, in the middle of the Persian period."[91]

As far as Isaiah is concerned, Peter Machinist has argued that the so-called Second Isaiah, corresponding at least to Isaiah 40–55, documents in important ways the development of Israelite religious ideas during the Neo-Babylonian period, especially the concept of deity, and with it the concomitant characterization of foreign gods as idols. According to Machinist, the redac-tor of Second Isaiah was active during the reign of Nabonidus and may have experienced the Persian conquest at the hands of Cyrus in 539 BCE. Pointing to Isaiah 46:1–2, he hypothesizes that Deutero-Isaiah's criticism of idols is a reaction to the policy of displacing the statues of Neo-Babylonian gods under Nabonidus, who favored Sin over Marduk and his son Nabū.[92] Machinist cau-tiously concludes that one may perceive "the influence of a certain Babylonian

88. Machinist 2003, 237: "Israel and Judah have emerged as a most challenging set of cases, because they appear to offer, through the Hebrew Bible and archaeological sources, the fullest opportunity to examine this imperial impact from the side of the subjects, not simply the emperors."

89. Vanderhooft 1999, 207–208.

90. On Deuteronomy's redactional layers and their relationship to the Neo-Assyrian, Neo-Babylonian, and Persian periods, see Römer 2005.

91. Römer 2015, 217.

92. Machinist 2003, 238, 245–46, 250, 252.

Zeitgeist on the Second Isaiah—something, in short, that was not coerced or perhaps even direct, but was no less substantial and impelling for that."[93] He also rightly recalls that later texts, such as the *Prayer of Nabonidus* from Qumran (4Q242), reveal what an enduring impact Babylonian traditions pertaining to the reign of this king—such as the notion that he was cursed by the gods and struck with a skin disease—had on the cultural memory of Israel.[94] In the end, Second Isaiah used Babylonian history, traditions, and rituals as a background against which to proclaim YHWH's superiority and exclusive truth— that YHWH alone was God—and thus to challenge both the Babylonian gods and the theological basis of Babylonian kingship.[95] According to most scholars, the final redaction of Deutero-Isaiah took place during the Persian period, and the monotheistic kernels that it conveys should therefore also be read in light of the Persian context;[96] Machinist's analysis, however, shows that the original matrix of these ideas was, in important ways, the Babylonian experience.

The Election and Salvific Role of the People of Israel

Shalom Paul, focusing on chapters 40 through 48 of Isaiah, has identified phrasings that adapt the language of Neo-Babylonian royal inscriptions, especially in the matter of the king's election. Yet in Isaiah, the election is conspicuously transformed into the election not of the king, but of the people, illustrated, for example, in Isaiah 42:6—"I have created you and appointed you a covenant people, a light to the nations" (this is Paul's translation, which understands the Hebrew term *brit 'am*, literally "covenant of people," as a reversed construct meaning "people of the covenant")—and 49:8.[97] This emphasis on the people of Israel as the savior of the world, rather than its conqueror and oppressor, may be understood at least in part as a reaction against Neo-Babylonian imperial ideology, even though, admittedly, the expressions "light of all humankind" and "light of the world" were already used to characterize the king in a Neo-Assyrian context. (They are found among the royal titles of Tiglath-pileser and Esarhaddon, for example.)[98]

The idea that the people of Israel have a universal and salvific role to play would become important in later Jewish thought, albeit alongside another important notion, that of the salvation brought by the king messiah (from the word *mashiah* in Hebrew, meaning "anointed one"). This figure, who both carried on the Davidic monarchy (as its ideal heir) and acted as an anti-imperial

---

93. Machinist 2003, 254.

94. See also Beaulieu 2007, 138.

95. See Perdue and Carter 2015, 104: "This attack against the idols had the major objective of undermining the divine legitimation of Babylonian power and cultural supremacy and at the same time damaged the vitality of idol crafting in the Babylonian temples."

96. Römer 2015, 219–221.

97. Paul 2005a, 186. Alternatively, Isa 49:1–13 has also been interpreted as referring to a "servant" who is not the people as a whole but a prophet or the future messiah.

98. Paul 2005a; Paul 2012, 188–190.

force, seems to have undergone a crucial development during the Persian and Hellenistic periods (see below). Deutero-Isaiah in fact also documents the beginning of the Persian period, insofar as it pertains to Cyrus' victory.[99] As Leo Perdue—inspired by Homi K. Bhabha's discussion of ambivalence and mimicry—suggests, some passages of the book may be read as "shaped by the conflict between the desire to be the ruler (or at least the representative of the sovereign YHWH who directs history), the view of Cyrus as the new messiah, and the repulsiveness of domination."[100] This ambivalence is also expressed in the tension between Israel's role as salvific agent and that of the king messiah, who also brings about God's universal kingdom. According to some biblical traditions, the "anointed one" is none other than the people of Israel.[101]

Human Kingship

In her article on "the law of the king" in Deuteronomy 17:14–20, Wazana argues that in addition to its Neo-Assyrian layer, this text contains a redactional layer dating to the Neo-Babylonian period, which introduces new elements to the definition of the ideal Israelite king. These elements are especially found in verses 18–19, which specify that the king will "have a copy of this law [the Torah] written for him in the presence of the levitical priests," read it, and keep all the commandments therein. Wazana explains the later addition as follows:

> After the destruction of Jerusalem and the cessation of kingship, the law was adapted to the new scholarly ideal of a religious leader, relying on the Book of Torah (Deut 17:18–19). This new concept conformed to current Babylonian concepts of kingship which highlighted the religious roles of the king, and offered a new scholarly ideal.[102]

As mentioned above, the end of the Neo-Babylonian monarchy led to an increased control of religious knowledge by the Babylonian scribal elite, and a similar phenomenon can be recognized after the end of the monarchy in the kingdom of Judah. We cannot precisely date this change, which was probably gradual and happened to a great extent in the Persian period.[103]

99. Machinist 2003, 238–239. See Isa 41:2.

100. Perdue and Carter 2015, 99; Bhabha 1994.

101. See, e.g., Habakkuk 3:13, which seems to use "your messiah" as a synonym for "your people." However, this reading is not undisputed.

102. Wazana 2016, 189–190, quotation at 190. See also Machinist and Tadmor 1993, which examines criticisms of Nabonidus found in a text titled *The Verse Account*, concerning the king's pretensions to divine knowledge through revelation, contrasted with knowledge acquired through traditional study. Under this type of criticism lies a scribal model. Sources that support and praise Nabonidus, however, present the king as excelling in reading the tablets produced by the scribes (149–150).

103. Quite intense reflection on the balance of power between the king and the priests or the scribes responsible for the Torah's transmission and interpretation then took place during the Hasmonean period, as shown by some compositions found at Qumran, such as the *Temple Scroll*, and in later rabbinic texts, some of which discuss this issue in connection

All in all, the Neo-Babylonian period thus appears to have left its mark on the Bible. However, this legacy seems to a greater extent the result of actual political and military decisions made by the Neo-Babylonian kings, the experience of the Babylonian Exile, and the Israelite encounter with Babylonian culture in general (such as mythology) than a consequence of the Neo-Babylonian ideology of rule in particular. Yet, while slight, the impact of this ideology, especially on concepts of deity and kingship, is noticeable. The Persian period would bring further changes.

3. The Persian Empire

3.1 THE NATURE OF ACHAEMENID IMPERIALISM

The Persian empire was established in the wake of the conquests of Cyrus the Great (r. 559–530), which were followed by those of his son Cambyses II (r. 530–522), who extended Persian rule over Egypt. Although their follower Darius I (r. c. 522–486) was not strictly from the same lineage, since he was not a descendant of Teispes as Cyrus and Cambyses were, all the Persian kings from Cyrus to Darius III (r. 336–330) are conventionally designated "Achaemenids" after the name of Teispes' father, Achaemenes. Under Darius I the empire reached its greatest extent, stretching from Libya in the west to India in the east, and from Ethiopia in the south up to central Asia (modern Kazakhstan) in the north. The Neo-Assyrian and Neo-Babylonian empires' ideological and political center had been Mesopotamia; under the new regime, it shifted to Persia.

Pierre Briant describes the Achaemenid empire as "marked by extraordinary ethnocultural diversity and by a thriving variety of forms of local organization."[104] The administration of the empire was based on satrapies and garrisons that occasionally helped to quell revolts, but the way the satrapies functioned was far from uniform and some kinds of cultural and legal autonomy can be identified. Tribute arrangements also varied to a great extent in response to local economic situations. Beyond the diversity of the conquered peoples and the forms of rule imposed upon them, however, Briant emphasizes "the organizational dynamic of the many sorts of intervention by the central authority and the intense processes of acculturation" that characterized the Persian empire.[105]

Although there are important differences between the Achaemenids and their predecessors, to which we shall return below, it is possible to speak of a certain degree of continuity from Neo-Assyrian through Neo-Babylonian to

---

with the memory of the Hasmonean dynasty. See Fraade 2003; Berthelot 2018a, 366–371, 408–416. See also Markl 2018.

104. Briant 2002, 1.

105. Ibid. See also Goldstone and Haldon 2009, 24; Joannès 2011, esp. 39–40.

Achaemenid imperial traditions.[106] Indeed, according to Michael Jursa, the main historical role that the Neo-Babylonian empire played was that of a cultural bridge, as it "transmitted important forms of government and imperial rule that had been developed in the Assyrian empire to its Achaemenid successor (including techniques of population management, a dense communication network, as well as certain forms of taxation, organisation and army conscription)."[107] The Persian kings must be seen as having both inherited and creatively adapted previous imperial traditions, and as having opened up new avenues of imperial achievement and ideology of rule.

Scholars have demonstrated the strong impact of the Achaemenid legacy on Alexander the Great, the Seleucids, and—indirectly—the Romans. According to John Pairman Brown, Rome was even triply exposed to Persian techniques of legitimation and repression, as it took over the Punic and Hellenistic empires on the one hand and was confronted by the Parthians on the other.[108]

Local Cults and Imperial Propaganda

The main goal of the Achaemenids was to keep the territories and populations they had conquered under control. In order to achieve this goal—which they obviously shared with previous and later empires—they often appropriated local traditions and local deities. Most famously in the so-called Cyrus Cylinder, a document that refers to the Babylonian god Marduk's choice of Cyrus and imitates Babylonian (as well as Neo-Assyrian) models to legitimize the Persian king's rule over Babylonia.[109] The Cylinder mentions traditional themes such as the king's election by the Babylonian gods, his justice, his care for the welfare of the people, his activity as builder and renovator of the gods' sanctuaries, his numerous gifts to the temples and the gods, and his restoration of cities. In particular, the Cylinder emphasizes that Cyrus returned the statues of the deities that Nabonidus had displaced to their proper places in the traditional sanctuaries of Babylonia.[110] The insistence on the king's building activity and his piety may point to a Neo-Babylonian rather than a Neo-Assyrian background, but in fact the Cylinder draws on both traditions.[111]

106. Scholars who argue strongly in favor of the radical novelty of the Achaemenid ideology of rule include Root (1979; 2000) and Frei and Koch (1996).

107. Jursa 2014, 140.

108. Pairman Brown 2001, 73. According to him, the Carthaginians were exposed to Persian techniques of rule through the Persian control of the Phoenician seaboard. See also Fibiger Bang and Kołodziejczyk 2012, 12. On Roman perceptions of the Achaemenids, see Makhlaiuk 2015.

109. See *ANET* 3:315–316 and Waerzeggers 2015, 184, n. 12, for recent editions, translations, and bibliography.

110. Machinist 2003, 248.

111. On the king as builder, see also the case of Darius in Persepolis, DPa, and in Susa, DSf §§7–13; Schmitt 2009, 114, 130–133 (a palace in both cases).

It is indeed striking that, as the Cylinder testifies, the first Achaemenid rulers, Cyrus and Cambyses, enlisted the gods of the peoples they conquered in order to legitimate their rule over them and refrained from imposing their own religious beliefs and rituals.[112] This appropriation of local traditions has been interpreted as a form of religious tolerance and often opposed to the policy of the Neo-Assyrian kings. However, Amélie Kuhrt and others have shown that this interpretation is inaccurate and misleading. The Persian kings were first and foremost inspired by a "politically calculated pragmatism" that aimed to secure the loyalty of their subjects in order that they might exploit them as efficiently as possible. In fact, neither the Persians nor the Assyrians had tried to impose their cults on their subject populations, but instead mainly demanded loyalty to the ruler and his god(s). To quote Kuhrt:

> The very limited evidence at our disposal indicates that loyalty to the Persian king and empire was, metaphorically, equated with acceptance of his own prime deity, Ahuramazda. This is, in some respect, comparable to Assyrian imperial ideology, where obedience to the Assyrian ruler implied acceptance of the power of Assyria's gods, in particular Assur. But in neither case does this mean that worship of these imperial deities was ever imposed on subjects; acknowledgment of the conqueror's right to rule automatically entailed recognition of his gods' superior strength—nothing more.[113]

What is even more striking is that both the Babylonian and the Judean elites promoted the idea that their national god(s) had chosen Cyrus to defeat Nabonidus, either because the latter was a wicked king or, in the case of the Judeans, because the Babylonians had destroyed the Jerusalem Temple and oppressed the people of Israel. The support of the Babylonian elites, including the priests, for Cyrus was short-lived, however, and several revolts erupted in the wake of Cambyses' rule. These Darius I and his followers quelled without pity. Babylonian sources show that it did not take the Persian kings long to stop behaving according to the norms of Neo-Babylonian kingship: they did not indulge in building activity to any significant degree after the reign of Cyrus, lessened their financial support of the sanctuaries, and even increased fiscal pressure on priestly families and temples. Disappointment with Persian rule seems nonetheless to have been muted in Judea. Certainly the biblical traditions pertaining to the Persians are on the whole positive, recording Cyrus' role in the rebuilding of the Jerusalem Temple and calling him God's "messiah" or "anointed one" (Isa 45:1).

112. Lincoln 2007, 43.

113. Kuhrt 2007, 124. See also Herrenschmidt 1980, 90; Wiesehöfer 2009, 93; Fitzpatrick-McKinley 2016.

Persian Imperial Ideology: Universalism, Dualism, and Soteriological Mission

Achaemenid imperial ideology was clearly universalistic. Initially, however, the Persians had no adequate term to designate the political entity that emerged in the aftermath of their conquests.[114] The word *xšaça*, "kingdom," applied primarily to Persia, whereas *dahyu*, "people/land," had a local dimension and was applied to specific provinces of the empire. It was only under Darius I that the Old Persian term *bûmi*, "land," began to be used to describe the Achaemenid empire. As Briant emphasizes, from the Persian perspective, the empire-*bûmi* represented the totality of civilized lands and peoples. The Achaemenids were aware of the existence of countries (and peoples) that lay beyond their jurisdiction, but they did not view these unconquered territories as part of the civilized world; they were "relegated to nonexistence, beyond the 'parched lands' and the 'Bitter River.'"[115]

The universalistic perspective of Persian imperial ideology was also reflected in the king's claim to rule the world "from sunrise to sunset." This claim, however, was far from new: as Pairman Brown recalls, Esarhaddon had already defined his realm as extending "from the rising of the sun to the setting of the sun."[116] That the Persian claim was successfully communicated to the Achaemenids' subjects is shown by, among other witnesses, the Greek orator Aeschines, who mentions that Xerxes sent a letter to the Greeks saying that he was "lord of all mankind from sunrise to sunset" (3.132). Moreover, some biblical texts may be considered to echo—and simultaneously challenge—the Persian claim to universal rule when they declare that the name of the God of Israel is great among the nations "from the rising of the sun to its setting" (Isa 45:6; Mal 1:11; Ps 50:1, 113:3). Therefore, when, at the beginning of the first century CE, Dionysius of Halicarnassus (1.3.3) evokes the empires of the Assyrians, the Medes, the Persians, and the Macedonians and affirms that "Rome is the first and only one recorded from the beginning of time to have made the rising and setting of the sun the boundaries of its dominion," the claim and the words that express it are in fact traditional ones.[117]

A far more significant and original feature of the Achaemenids' conception of empire than its universal extent lies in the notion of paradise, *pardesu*, a word that could also refer to a piece of land in a more general way.[118] As both Bruce Lincoln and Jason M. Silverman have argued, the royal gardens that were called "paradise" stood for an ideal model of the world, or, in political

---

114. On this issue see in particular Herrenschmidt 1976; Herrenschmidt 1980; Lincoln 2007, 70.

115. Briant 2002, 179.

116. Pairman Brown 2001, 75. For the text of the VTE, in which this definition appears, see Wiseman 1958, 30 (col. i, line 8).

117. See also Chapter Two, §3.1.

118. See, e.g., Pearce and Wunsch 2014, 186, no. 53, line 2 (dated to 477 BCE).

terms, the Persian empire, which simultaneously mirrored Ahura Mazda's good creation. The cosmos created by Ahura Mazda, the king's empire, and the king's paradise were closely intertwined: they were supposed to reflect one another.[119] Certainly, royal gardens existed in the Neo-Assyrian and Neo-Babylonian contexts also, but within the Persian context they received a new ideological significance, through their close association with Ahura Mazda's creation.[120] This aspect of Achaemenid royal or imperial ideology was linked to the crucial role that the notion of creation played in Persian imperial discourse. Lincoln counts twenty-three inscriptions—70 percent (23/33) of the inscriptions containing more than two paragraphs—that begin by invoking Ahura Mazda's creative act.[121] Lincoln admits that the cosmogonic narratives are brief, stereotyped, and highly formulaic, referring generally to five acts of creation, four of which are located at the very beginning of time, whereas the fifth is located in historical time and pertains to the king.[122] However, these narratives do distinguish Achaemenid royal inscriptions from Neo-Assyrian or Neo-Babylonian ones. Moreover, "it is important to remember that Ahura Mazda is only ever associated with good and beneficial creative acts, evil being explained as independent."[123] This point leads us to examine the Achaemenids' theology of rule in a more detailed way.

The religious beliefs of the Persian kings are more clearly articulated from the time of Darius I onward than in the documents associated with Cyrus and Cambyses. In the inscription at Behistun (519 BCE), in which Darius tells how he acceded to the throne and repressed the revolts that had erupted during the first year of his reign, reference is made to the "Wise Lord" Ahura Mazda no fewer than seventy-six times, whereas none of the other deities are named.[124] Ahura Mazda is the god who has entrusted the empire to the king and confers on him his legitimacy as ruler. In addition to this "theology of election," which may be deemed traditional, there are, according to Lincoln, two other basic components of Achaemenid royal ideology: "a starkly dualistic ethics in which the opposition good/evil is aligned with that of self/other and correlated discriminatory binaries," and "a sense of soteriological mission that represents imperial aggression as salvific

119. Lincoln 2007, 78–79; Silverman 2016, 181.

120. Silverman 2016, 187.

121. Lincoln 2007, 51.

122. Lincoln 2012, 173. See, e.g., DSe §1; XEa §1; XPa §1; D2Ha §1 (Schmitt 2009, 123, 151 153, 183).

123. Lincoln 2012, 173.

124. Lincoln 2007, 44. There are inscriptions, however, that mention the other gods as protecting or supporting the king, but these deities are not named individually and are associated with Ahura Mazda: see, e.g., DPd §3; XPc §3 (Schmitt 2009, 116, 157).

action taken on behalf of divine principles, thereby recoding the empire's victims as its beneficiaries."[125]

Lincoln sees two notions as central to Persian duality: *arta* (truth) and *drauga* (lie), the latter appearing as a demonic force that inspired Darius' enemies and those of the Persian kings after him. According to Briant, these concepts are the true linchpins of the Achaemenid ideology of rule, as it is expressed in both words and images in the royal palaces at Susa and Persepolis and on the royal tomb at Naqsh-i Rustam.[126] Admittedly, the two are known mainly from Zoroastrian literature, starting with the collection known as the Avesta, which goes back to a Sassanian recension produced in late antiquity but which has not survived in any manuscripts earlier than to the fourteenth century. Because of the late date of this compilation, it is difficult to use it to reconstruct the religion of the Achaemenid dynasty, as Kuhrt cautions.[127] Yet such a reconstruction is not completely beyond reach; first, because the testimonies of Achaemenid imperial inscriptions and art and classical Greek literature provide some points of convergence with the Zoroastrian texts; and, second, because there are sections of the Avesta that, on philological grounds, appear to originate in the Achaemenid period, if not even earlier.[128] Hence, Lincoln considers that the reliefs of Darius' monument at Behistun in which the figure of Ahura Mazda is depicted at the top and the Lie below, with king Darius represented between them, may be compared to the description in the following Zoroastrian text:

> The Wise Lord is highest in omniscience and goodness. He exists for infinite time, always in the light. That light is the place of the Wise Lord. It is called "Endless Light." Omniscience and goodness exist in infinite time, as do the Wise Lord, goodness, and religion. The Evil Spirit exists in darkness, in ignorance and love of destruction, in the lowest depths. His crude love of destruction and that place of darkness are called "Endless Darkness." Between the two spirits was a space called "Air," in which the two mingle with each other. (*Greater Bundahišn* 1.1–5 [TD² MS 2.8–3.6])[129]

In addition, some of the Achaemenid inscriptions also emphasize a person's responsibility to choose between good and evil, light and darkness, and the individual fate that results from this choice. One thus reads in Darius' inscription at Naqsh-i Rustam: "The man who cooperates, him according to his cooperative action, him thus do I reward" (DNb, lines 16ff.). Moreover, from the Persians'

---

125. Lincoln 2007, 95. See also Lincoln 2012, 186.
126. Briant 2002, 138.
127. See, e.g., Kuhrt 2001, discussing Frei and Koch 1996.
128. Root 2000, 20. See also Silverman 2012, 39–75.
129. Lincoln 2007, 17–18.

perspective, people fortunate enough to be encompassed, whether voluntarily or by conquest, within the Achaemenid empire "were assisted in making the transition from lawlessness to law and from the Lie to truth."[130]

The third component of Achaemenid royal ideology, defined by Lincoln as "a sense of soteriological mission," refers to the project that the Achaemenids set for themselves: "restoring perfection on earth, as it was originally created."[131] This added a strong teleologial and eschatological dimension to Achaemenid thinking about their role as rulers, defining in Silverman's words "a teleological order, a progressive order that contributes to the end (in both senses) of the world," and "makes the Achaemenid royal theology distinctive from the elements it inherited from the Neo-Assyrian and Neo-Babylonian Empires."[132]

One may also associate this soteriological aspect with one of the most original features of Persian imperial ideology, its claimed integrative, collaborative, and peaceful dimension. In both iconography and inscriptions, one sees representations of a state of stability and consensus, in which different subjugated peoples collaborate willingly in the construction of the empire, rather than representations of victory or the crushing of the king's enemies, as seen most notably in the Neo-Assyrian context. For Margaret Cool Root, the Achaemenid empire "was arguably the first empire in world history based ideologically on the embrace of diverse peoples into an incorporated whole as a primary strategy of hegemonic acquisition and maintenance over a vast realm."[133] This ideology of collaboration, as one might call it, is reflected in the procession of peoples bearing gifts on the relief sculptures of Apadana and the "Gate of All Nations" at Persepolis, and in Darius I's foundation tablet at Susa, which describes the precious stones, woods, and other materials that every nation brought to contribute to the building of the palace[134] (Fig. 1.2).

On the reliefs of Persepolis, those who carry the throne do so easily, a depiction that Root describes as "calculated to enhance the aura of dignity and effortless, perhaps even joyous, cooperation with which these subject peoples are imbued"[135] (Fig. 1.3). Moreover, according to Root, these reliefs represent a visual incarnation of Darius' textual promise at Naqsh-i Rustam (DNb, lines 16ff.; see above). Josef Wiesehöfer nuances this vision slightly by emphasizing that "the Achaemenid 'minor arts' (e.g., glyptics) often depict nonpeaceful

---

130. Lincoln 2007, 26.

131. Lincoln 2007, xiii.

132. Silverman 2016, 189.

133. Root 2000, 19; see also Root 1979.

134. DSf §§8–13; Schmitt 2009, 131–133. See also the reliefs and inscriptions on the tombs of Artaxerxes II and III at Persepolis, which list the nations and feature them supporting the throne-platform on which the king stood: Schmitt 2009, 198–199 (A³Pb); Kuhrt 2010, 483–484.

135. Root 1979, 153.

FIGURE 1.2. Reliefs from the Apadana palace in Persepolis, showing vassals bringing gifts to the Persian king.
Photograph © Keren Su/China Span / Alamy Banque d'images.

scenes." He nevertheless concludes that the Achaemenids' royal ideology "placed more emphasis on the reciprocal relationship between royal patronage and the loyalty of the subjects" than had previous imperial ideologies.[136] In the end, scholars tend to agree that in comparison with Neo-Assyrian art and inscriptions in particular, Persian examples display a distinctive rhetoric of peace, a *pax Persica*, and that this discourse was not merely a rhetorical tool or strategy but actually reflected the Achaemenids' own view of their kingship.

3.2 ACHAEMENID IMPERIALISM IN THE BIBLE AND IN SECOND TEMPLE–PERIOD JEWISH SOURCES

As a preliminary remark, it must be emphasized that no biblical text is openly hostile to the Persians. Quite the contrary: Cyrus is credited with the decision (inspired by God) to allow the exiles to return to Yehud and rebuild the Temple (Isaiah 44:28; Ezra 1:1–4; 2 Chronicles 36:22–23). For this benevolent role in Israel's history, he is even granted the title of "anointed (or: messiah) of YHWH" (Isaiah 45:1). Given this approbation of Persian rule, at least in its

136. Wiesehöfer 2009, 93.

FIGURE 1.3. Reliefs from the Apadana palace in Persepolis, showing subject peoples
carrying the Persian king's throne.
Photograph © Keren Su/China Span / Alamy Banque d'images.

initial stage, the question arises of whether the biblical texts also attest to a
positive reception of Persian cultural and political models.

The issue of Zoroastrian or Iranian influence on Judaism has been debated
since at least the nineteenth century. Although parallelomania has often prevailed,
and in spite of the methodological problems mentioned above concerning the dating of the Zoroastrian texts, the investigation of both the Achaemenid period and
late antiquity in the field of Iranian-Jewish studies is booming—hence, the Sassanian context of the Babylonian Talmud has come under close scrutiny.[137] Numerous studies have been devoted to the impact of Persian culture, including
"Mazdean" or "Iranian"—rather than "Zoroastrian"—religion, on Deutero-
and Trito-Isaiah, as well as Ezra and Nehemiah (although some scholars now tend to date the last redaction of these books to the Hellenistic
period)[138] and the later prophets; in addition, there are several studies
of the Persian context of (parts of) Daniel, Tobit, and Esther, of the role

137. See the work of Shaul Shaked, Shai Secunda, and Geoffrey Herman in particular;
see also Elman and Secunda 2015.

138. Finkelstein 2018 dates parts of Ezra, Nehemiah, and 1 and 2 Chronicles to the
Hasmonean period, for example.

that Persian religious culture played in the development of apocalypticism and the apocalyptic genre among the Jews, and of the influence of Persian dualism on the Dead Sea Scrolls, especially the sectarian scrolls.[139] Other studies pertain to linguistic issues, such as the adoption of Persian loanwords into Hebrew or Aramaic. Finally, one should keep in mind that the theory of the succession of four empires or monarchies associated with different ages of the world, and identification of the four ages with four metals—a theory found in the book of Daniel—has been shown to have Persian origins, even if it took its final and most well-known shape in a Hellenistic context.[140]

That Judeans were exposed to Persian imperial ideology is beyond doubt. Silverman's study of the evidence for interaction between the two peoples "in the normal course of daily experience" throughout the empire concludes that "these interactions would have been official as well as accidental—both administrative and socio-economic," and would have had political, religious, and cultural aspects as well.[141] Focusing on linguistic issues, Aren Wilson-Wright has argued that there was direct contact between speakers of Old Persian and speakers of Hebrew in the Achaemenid period, beginning under Artaxerxes I.[142] Moreover, copies of the texts of the Achaemenid inscriptions were circulated in Aramaic. The text of Darius' Behistun inscription, for instance, was copied on clay and parchment for distribution throughout the empire, and an Aramaic version (DB Aram) has been found in Elephantine, where a Jewish military colony was established.[143] There is thus hardly any doubt that the ideas expressed in Achaemenid propaganda reached the elites of Judea, as well as Judeans in the various parts of the Persian empire.[144]

Further Monotheistic Developments: The Rejection of Dualism

Some scholars have argued that monotheism sensu stricto arose in the Persian context rather than immediately after the destruction of the First Temple, during the Neo-Babylonian period. The explicit claim that YHWH is the only god and that other gods do not exist is found in only a few biblical texts, which these scholars date to the Persian period. According to Thomas Römer, for example, Deuteronomy 4:39—"So acknowledge today and take to heart that the Lord is God in heaven above and on the earth beneath; there

---

139. For a short overview of the history of research in this field, see Silverman 2012, 1–8; Grenet 2013. See in particular Shaked's work, especially Shaked 1984, and the series *Irano-Judaica* published at Yad Ben Zvi.

140. Shaked 1984, 314.

141. Silverman 2011, 133, 161; see also Silverman 2012.

142. Wilson-Wright 2015.

143. Lincoln 2007, 9; Granerød 2013, 479.

144. Silverman 2012; Silverman 2016, 190; Granerød 2013.

is no other"—dates from the Persian period, which witnessed the evolution from monolatry to monotheism.[145] Moreover, in his eyes, Judean monotheism should be seen as a reflection of and response to Achaemenid universalism, "the Persian worldview according to which all nations of the world had become or were about to become parts of the universal empire."[146]

On the other hand, the idea that Judean monotheism was a reaction to "Zoroastrianism," or Mazdean religion at large, has met with skepticism.[147] The fact remains, however, that statements such as Isaiah 45:7—in which God declares, "I form light and create darkness, I make weal and create woe; I the Lord do all these things"—which are not found in older biblical traditions and remain quite marginal in the Bible as a whole, probably do reflect a rejection of Persian/Mazdean dualism. In the Achaemenid inscriptions and reliefs, Ahura Mazda is associated exclusively with light, not with darkness.[148]

Theodicy seems to have been debated within Jewish circles in the Persian period, as the book of Job—admittedly difficult to date—would seem to indicate. Although texts such as Isaiah 45:7 illustrate the rejection of dualism at the level of the deity itself, the development of angelology and demonology in Jewish texts from the Persian period onward shows that the question of the origin of evil was far from settled for all that. The appearance of the figure of the *satan* in biblical literature is difficult to date precisely, but it too may be considered a consequence of the development of monotheism in a Persian context.[149]

The Creator God

The first chapters of the book of Genesis show clearly the influence of Mesopotamian traditions, such as the flood narrative, which Genesis reformulates in critical and inventive ways. However, it has been argued that this creation account, too, is a response to dualism in Persian creation narratives, which associate light with Ahura Mazda and darkness with Angra Mainyu.[150] Unlike the Persian accounts, the beginning of Genesis stresses that it is one god who creates both light and darkness, the God of Israel (as in Isaiah 45:7).

145. Römer 2015, 218; 2005, 172.

146. Römer 2005, 175.

147. Carter 1970 argues for the association between strict monotheism and Zoroastrian influence.

148. Shaked 1984, 313–314; Elman and Secunda 2015, 424. Yet Morton Smith refers to Zoroastrian traditions that attribute to Ahura Mazda the creation of light and darkness, the good spirit, and the evil spirit (Smith 1963, 420).

149. Römer 2015, 229.

150. As Shaked 1984, 316, emphasizes, this dualism is not absolute, because there is no equality between the two; Ahura Mazda is superior insofar as he is the only one who truly exists. Yet the contrast with the description of God in Genesis remains.

As mentioned above, the late dating of the Zoroastrian sources precludes definitive conclusions. But the emphasis on YHWH as creator does seem to have roots in the Persian context.[151] Römer notes, in connection with Deuteronomy 4:32—"For ask now about former ages, long before your own, ever since the day that God created human beings on the earth . . ."—that "the idea of Yahweh as a creator god does not appear in the Assyrian and exilic layers of the Deuteronomistic History." He explains this development as a consequence of the monotheistic theology that arose in the Persian period and notes that it is accompanied, in texts such as Deuteronomy 10:14–17, by the related idea of Israel as the chosen people of this creator god, which in turn made it quite natural to maintain that the universal and only true god was none other than Israel's own national god.[152] In a comparison between the Achaemenid creation prologues found in Old Persian inscriptions and Deutero-Isaiah, Silverman even argues that "the vision of creation and form of YHWH as creator are the earliest attested instance of 'Iranian influence' on the Judaean tradition."[153] Weinfeld had already pointed out that just as the Persians considered Ahura Mazda, "who created heaven, earth, and man," to have appointed the king to rule over the territories composing the Persian empire, so Deutero-Isaiah affirmed that "I (God) made the earth and created humankind upon it; it was my hands that stretched out the heavens, and I commanded all their host; I have aroused Cyrus in righteousness, and I will make all his paths straight; he shall build my city and set my exiles free" (Isa 45:12–13).[154] It is striking that in both cases, the god who appoints the king is described as a creator god—a locution absent from Neo-Assyrian and Neo-Babylonian inscriptions. A tradition such as Isaiah 45:12–13 may thus be seen as reflecting a specifically Persian motif.[155] Interestingly enough, however, the beginning of chapter 45, which describes Cyrus as God's messiah, presents God not as the creator of the world but as the God of Israel, a particular people. So if we look at Isaiah 45 as a whole, we see that on the one hand, the redactor echoed Persian notions of the deity and of the relationship between the deity and the king; on the other hand, he maintained a particular, ethnic and "national," understanding of the deity who *elected* the king, which challenged the Persian claim designating Ahura Mazda as responsible for Cyrus' rule. Zechariah 12:1–8 similarly echoes the Old Persian creation formula in its wording while contesting the

---

151. Some of the texts referring to God as creator, such as Ps 95:5 and 96:5, are admittedly difficult to date. I thank Peter Machinist for pointing me to these biblical passages.

152. Römer 2005, 173; Römer 2015, 218.

153. Silverman 2017, 26.

154. Weinfeld 1986, 176–177.

155. See, however, Blenkinsopp 2011, which argues that Isaiah 40–48 should rather be read as a response to Babylonian ideology and the celebration of Marduk as creator and supreme god during the *akītu*–New Year festival.

political theology that it conveys, therefore challenging the Achaemenid imperial order.[156]

The notion of God as Creator has implications also for the distribution of land among human groups. As Otto notes:

> It was a central aspect of the Achaemenid ideology that the Persian imperial god Ahuramazda, the creator of the world, had given to all the nations their land with Persepolis as centre of the world. The authors of the Hexateuch refuted this idea, claiming that the world was not created by Ahuramazda but by YHWH, the god of "Israel", and so God's people in their opinion did not receive their land from the Persian imperial god but from YHWH. The authors of the Hexateuch demonstrated that for them it was the aim of creation and world-history (Gen 1–11) that "Israel" could live safely in her Promised Land.[157]

The idea that Ahura Mazda allocates territories to nations through the king—found, for example, in the Behistun inscription of Darius I—does not seem to have had a precedent in a Neo-Assyrian or Neo-Babylonian context and thus posed a new ideological challenge to the Judean elites, leading to a reinterpretation of previous traditions. Otto shows that the book of Deuteronomy underwent a redactional phase in the Achaemenid period and that chapters 2–3 in particular—which emphasize the God of Israel's role in distributing territories to Moab, Amon, etc.—are to be read in light of the redactors' wish to "resist the imperial ideology of the Achaemenids that the different peoples of the Persian empire received their territory (*gathu-*) from the Achaemenid king according to Ahuramazda's order (*arta-*)."[158]

A final issue that arises in connection with Persian creation accounts is the motif of paradise. In Hebrew, the word *pardes* (garden), of Persian origin, is found only in late biblical texts—Song of Songs 4:13, Ecclesiastes 2:5, Nehemiah 2:8—that refer neither to creation nor to paradise. However, the motif of the paradise-garden containing trees of every kind is obviously present in Genesis. Given the particular political and religious significance of the paradise-garden as the model of an ideally ordered world in Achaemenid imperial ideology, one could argue that in the Genesis account, God takes upon himself the roles of both Ahura Mazda and the Persian king or, alternately, that Adam replaces the figure of the king in the paradise-garden. In any case, what is striking is the absence of any human king in the biblical vision of paradise. This feature might have something to do with the Bible's anti-royal thread, already discussed in this chapter in connection with the Neo-Assyrian empire.

---

156. Mitchell 2014. She also points to Isa 42:5–6 as another text that echoes the Old Persian creation formula.

157. Otto 2009, 549.

158. Otto 2009, 556.

Human Kingship

Neo-Babylonian kingship was not "ethnic" in a strict sense, as the reigns of Neriglissar (560–556), of Aramean descent, and of his successor Nabonidus show. The very notion of Babylonian ethnicity is in fact problematic, as Caroline Waerzeggers insightfully points out.[159] This feature of Babylonian kingship contrasts sharply with the Achaemenid claims of belonging to a given ethnic group, and indeed to a particular lineage. In the Persian empire, ethnicity and pedigree mattered. In the Judean context, the law of Deuteronomy 17 also emphasizes the ethnic origin of the legitimate king, by requesting that he stem from "among your brothers." As we saw above, this law may have been a reaction to Neo-Assyrian rule, but it was certainly relevant in the Persian context also. Rather than a case of Persian influence on Judean notions of kingship, however, it might constitute simply an example of convergence.

The fact that Persian documents do not regard the king as divine or priestly but merely describe the royal office as a gift of Ahura Mazda is also congruent with biblical views of kingship.[160] An interesting parallel noted by Weinfeld is that both Persian inscriptions and the book of Isaiah call the king "a friend" of the god.[161] In the passages mentioned by Weinfeld, especially Isaiah 48:14, God's "friend" or "beloved" is Cyrus, who will defeat the Babylonians. It therefore makes sense to conclude that in this case we are dealing with the borrowing of a Persian motif.

The Rise of the Torah

The connection between Persian imperial rule on the one hand and the formation of the Pentateuch and the rise of the Torah to the status of the ancestral law of the Judeans (the inhabitants of the province of Yehud) on the other hand is a debated topic. According to John Collins,

> the articulation of the Judean way of life in terms of ancestral laws derived from Moses was arguably the most distinctive development in Second Temple Judaism. It was not an innovation of the Hellenistic period. Its roots must be traced at least to the Persian, and arguably to the Neo-Babylonian, period.[162]

Collins finds evidence for this development mainly in the books of Ezra and Nehemiah, commonly dated to the fifth century BCE, and further argues that "the adoption of the law of Moses as the law of Judah was a huge step in making Judaism into a religion."[163] Lester L. Grabbe writes, in a similar vein, that

159. See Waerzeggers 2015, 182–183, 203–204.
160. Lincoln 2012, 169.
161. Weinfeld 1986, 177, comparing DS 4 ("Ahura Mazda is my friend") with Isaiah 44:28, 48:14.
162. Collins 2017, 19.
163. Collins 2017, 60.

during the Persian period "it was first and foremost in the area of scripture that the seeds of later Judaism were sown."[164] The importance of the Persian context for the rise of the Torah can therefore hardly be overestimated.

The seventh chapter of Ezra—which is traditionally ascribed to the fifth or the beginning of the fourth century BCE (if the Artaxerxes alluded to is Artaxerxes II)—concerns an imperial mission conferred upon the namesake prophet by king Artaxerxes in an official letter. Ezra is to appoint "magistrates and judges to judge all the people in the province of Beyond the River who know the laws of your God, and to teach those who do not know them" (7:25), and these magistrates are to have power to punish the recalcitrant (7:26). By a literal reading of this text, the Torah of Moses, transmitted through Ezra acting as a "second Moses," would thus have become the Judeans' official law following a decision of the Persian king. Specialists of ancient Persia and many biblical scholars have rejected the theory of a "Persian imperial authorization" of the Torah that stems from this text. Yet Konrad Schmid argues that a distinction must be made between (1) the idea that the Judean laws became part of a system of local law codes integrated into imperial law—a dubious suggestion, especially in the light of the lack of evidence for Persian imperial law codes in general; and (2) the idea that Persian imperial authorities authorized certain local customs or laws in response to specific local requests. In view of the trilingual inscription of Xanthus, Schmid writes that "there is no reason to deny that at least some local laws indeed were authorized by higher authorities such as the satraps."[165] Since the letter in Ezra 7 cannot be taken as a quotation of an original document and must rather be seen as a literary fiction—though it may have been based on existing models and may in some way echo an imperial decision—we cannot know for sure what the role of the Persian authorities vis-à-vis the Torah was.[166] At the least, one may say that the fact that the central Persian government did not interfere with local norms might have encouraged local elites to codify their ancestral laws in a new way.[167]

In comparison to writings usually dated to the period of the return from exile—Haggai, Zechariah, Trito-Isaiah—which make almost no reference to the Torah, the books of Ezra and Nehemiah are Torah-centered in

164. Grabbe 2004, 360.

165. Schmid 2007, 27. See also Carr 2007 (in the same volume) and the contributions in Watts 2001, all of which deal with the question of the Persian imperial authorization of the Pentateuch.

166. Cf. Collins 2017, 53. The generosity of the king is too exaggerated in the letter for the document to be authentic.

167. See Hagedorn 2007, 64, 70–71, 76 ("The Persian presence and pressure triggers harmony and is therefore responsible for the shaping of the Pentateuch—even though Persia never officially sanctioned the process"), with further bibliography concerning the (in) authenticity of Artaxerxes' letter. On Ezra 7 and its fictitious character, see also Jones 2018.

an unprecedented way.[168] As Collins notes, "the authority of the Torah is fundamental to the reform of Ezra."[169] It is unclear, however, whether the ancestral laws identified as "the law of Moses" in Ezra and Nehemiah are in fact the Pentateuch as we know it. There are discrepancies between the laws referred to in Nehemiah and those of the Masoretic Pentateuch.[170] Moreover, the Dead Sea Scrolls have shown that textual fluidity prevailed until the Hellenistic period, and we know that there were alternatives to the Pentateuch in the formation of the canon: the Hexateuch too had advocates, and other collections or compilations may have circulated as well, of which we simply have no knowledge.[171] According to Römer, the redactors of the Pentateuch were aware that the emphasis on land and conquest in the Hexateuch could be politically subversive in the Achaemenid context, and this explains why they closed the Pentateuch with the death of Moses, before the entrance into the Promised Land.[172] In any case, the rise of the Torah as an authoritative body of laws attributed to Moses seems to characterize the Persian period.

So far, we have tackled the question of the impact of the Achaemenid empire on the role of the Torah from a historical, political, and institutional perspective. However, the Persian empire, and Persian imperial ideology in particular, may have influenced Judean notions of the Torah in yet another way; namely, from an ideological point of view. It may not be accidental that the book of Ezra refers to the law of the God of Israel as *dat*, an Aramaic term corresponding to the Persian word used to refer to the law of the king—a law formulated in accordance with the will of Ahura Mazda—in Achaemenid inscriptions written in Old Persian.[173] As Otto emphasizes, a crucial question is whether the Pentateuch constitutes a response, both positive and subversive, to Persian notions of law, including the ideological, legitimacy-conferring function of law in the Persian imperial context.[174] He answers in the affirmative, arguing that the postexilic redaction of Deuteronomy, for example, reflects such an evolution: Chapter 11 seeks to strengthen the status of the Torah and its divine origin in response to the notion, in Achaemenid imperial ideology, that the king's decrees were rooted in the law (*dāta*) of Ahura Mazda.[175] In a similar way, Yishai Kiel, who compares the role played by the figure of Moses in unifying various legal traditions—especially in the books of

168. Carr 2007, 50.

169. Collins 2017, 59. See also Römer 2005, 178–183.

170. Collins 2017, 55–56.

171. Cf. Blenkinsopp 2001, 59.

172. Römer 2005, 180–181. On the formation of the Pentateuch as a rejection of the Hexateuch, see also Otto 2005; 2009; 2013.

173. Ezra 7:12, 14, 21, 25–26; Achaemenid inscriptions: see, e.g., DB §8, DSe §3 (Schmitt 2009, 40, 124).

174. Otto 2005, 72.

175. Otto 2013, 120–121.

Ezra and Nehemiah—to that of Zarathustra, argues that "the literary reconfiguration of Ezra's mission according to Ezra-Nehemiah in terms of the consolidation and promulgation of Mosaic [Torah] can be significantly illuminated by the rhetoric that governs the king's self-perception as promoter of the 'law set down by Ahura Mazda,'" which Kiel sees as derived from the Avestan concept of divine revelation.[176]

The Development of an Apocalyptic Worldview and Literature

The development of an apocalyptic worldview and literature within Jewish circles during the Persian period is another area of debate. Without connecting them to Jewish sources, Lincoln mentions Persian texts that describe ecstatic journeys through a series of heavens and hells, which unmistakably recall Enoch's journey.[177] The traditions referred to are late, but the similarities are striking.

In the past ten years, Silverman has been the most active advocate of the theory of a Persian origin for Jewish apocalypticism, without however denying that most Jewish apocalyptic works were composed in the Hellenistic period.[178] More precisely, he argues that the development of apocalyptic literature in Second Temple Judaism was due to the adoption of a new "apocalyptic hermeneutic" that integrated ideas and methods originating in Persian culture, and he identifies several elements in Jewish apocalyptic texts that stem from a Persian context.[179] In *1 Enoch*, he sees the Watchers as modeled after Achaemenid functionaries, and the concept of astronomical solar "gates," as well as the mythological geography found in *1 Enoch* 77, as influenced by Iranian notions combined with some older Mesopotamian elements.[180] These issues cannot be discussed in detail in the framework of this book, but it seems reasonable to think that Jewish apocalypticism has a long history that reaches back into the Persian period, even though it reached its full flourishing in a Hellenistic context. Noteworthy among Silverman's arguments is what he characterizes as the teleological dimension of the Achaemenid theology of rule, which he considers a "deferred" or even "realized" eschatology: "The kings play an integral part in Ahura Mazda's plan, acting like *saošiiants* in bringing the world towards its final fulfilment, both through improvement and through foreshadowing."[181]

176. Kiel 2017, 344.

177. Lincoln 2007, 79.

178. See the nuanced discussion in Silverman 2009. See also Silverman 2016, 190.

179. Silverman 2012, 1. He defines "apocalyptic hermeneutic" as "primarily . . . a *shared interpretive framework* which interrelates apocalypticism, the apocalypses, and millenarianism" (24–25; emphasis in the original).

180. Silverman 2012, 204; Silverman 2013.

181. Silverman 2016, 188–189. The term *saošyant* comes from the Gathas, where it means something like "future benefactor" or "savior," and may have originally applied to Zarathustra himself (see Shaked 1998).

Silverman argues that the Judeans were exposed to these ideas, and that this gave rise to apocalyptic and eschatological perspectives in Jewish thought.

Eschatology and Ethics

Eschatology can be defined as people's ideas and expectations concerning the end of historical time, the fate of the cosmos and the individual at the end of days or, alternatively, at the end of one's individual life. It may thus include speculations about the final judgment of all creation by God, the survival of the soul, the resurrection of the body, hell, and paradise. The development of eschatological ideas and of apocalyptic literature in Judaism are closely intertwined but do not completely overlap, because eschatological notions can already be found in prophetic literature that does not have an apocalyptic framework. Brent Strawn has thus argued that in Isaiah 60, a passage that evokes a future age of enduring glory, peace, and prosperity and describes the nations as bringing precious gifts to Jerusalem, "the timelessness, the stateliness, the endurance of Persian imperial propaganda is [. . .] being co-opted and reapplied to Jerusalem. The *pax Persica* has become the *pax Jerusalem*."[182] Strawn's comparison is based on the reliefs and inscriptions from Persepolis, Naqsh-i Rustam, and other places associated with Achaemenid rule, and not on Zoroastrian texts. His important point is the peaceful and voluntary character of the offerings in Isaiah 60, which reflects the Achaemenid "ideology of collaboration" evoked in §3.1 above.

Other scholars, including Shaul Shaked, emphasize similarities between Zoroastrian and Jewish notions of personal eschatology, such as the fate of the soul after death and the belief in bodily resurrection, and argue for an influence of Zoroastrian ideas on Judaism.[183] In this case one may obviously object that the Zoroastrian texts are late, but it is perhaps worth keeping in mind Root's opinion, who writes:

> My own increasingly firm conviction is that the Achaemenid Persian approach to empire must reflect proto-Zoroastrian and Zoroastrian belief systems reaching back even before their settlement in western Iran. [. . .] The ethical teachings of Zoroastrianism—with its emphasis upon concepts such as truth, justice, individual responsibility, and righteousness—mesh well with what we can document of Achaemenid Persian ideology from the main official texts and from the artistic programme.[184]

182. Strawn 2007, 115.

183. Shaked 1984; 1998. See also the summary in Grabbe 2004, 364. Concerning the belief in bodily resurrection, Elledge (2017) does not favor the theory of a Persian influence, seeing it as at most one factor among others.

184. Root 2000, 20.

Shaked recognizes that the Zoroastrian sources we have are later than the Jewish texts but nevertheless emphasizes that the appearance of a full-fledged eschatology in Jewish writings dated to the second and first centuries BCE is sudden, especially given the nearly complete absence of such motifs in biblical literature, and he concludes:

> Since this was a period that followed a long Persian dominion in Palestine and an even longer period during which a substantial Jewish Diaspora had lived continuously in Mesopotamia and Persia, the emergence of a fully developed eschatology in Jewish circles, and one that displays such great resemblance to the complex of Persian ideas, cannot be a coincidence and must be explained as a result of contact between the two cultures.[185]

Insofar as the Persian culture was the dominant one, Shaked adds, the influence must have been exerted by the Persian on the Jewish culture.

In the end, many aspects of the impact of the Achaemenid empire and imperial ideology on Judaism remain difficult to assess, especially because of the dating of the Zoroastrian traditions. Yet, on the basis of Achaemenid inscriptions and iconography and Greek sources, it is possible to conclude that this impact was significant and most pronounced in the areas of monotheistic ideas, eschatological notions, and the concept of the Torah.

4. The Hellenistic Kingdoms

The two main Hellenistic kingdoms that the Jews confronted were those of the Ptolemies and the Seleucids, both characterized by scholars as multiethnic empires.[186] The Ptolemies (or Lagids) ruled Judea from 318 until roughly 200 BCE. During that period, they fought no fewer than five wars against the Seleucids over the Levant (the so-called Syrian Wars). To what extent these hostilities affected Judea in uncertain. According to Seth Schwartz, "Although coastal Palestine and Phoenicia in this century witnessed nearly constant warfare between the two dynasties, Judaea, which was a poor hill country district off the main roads and of little strategic interest, remained at peace."[187] Yet the letter of Antiochus III to Ptolemy, the *stratēgos* of Syria and Phoenicia, quoted by Josephus in book 12 of *Jewish Antiquities*, suggests that Judea and Jerusalem suffered considerably from the last, Fifth Syrian War, and they may

185. Shaked 1998, available at http://www.iranicaonline.org/articles/eschatology-i. See also Shaked 1984, esp. 321–325.

186. On the qualification of each as an "empire," as well as on their shared characteristics and numerous differences, see the forthcoming volume edited by Christelle Fischer-Bovet and Sitta von Reden.

187. Schwartz 2001, 26.

have been impacted by the previous ones also.[188] The third century BCE is also marked by the growth of Jewish communities in Egypt, beginning in the reign of Ptolemy I or Ptolemy II.[189] A vibrant Judeo-Greek culture developed, especially in Alexandria. In Judea, the first thirty years of Seleucid rule at the beginning of the second century BCE were relatively peaceful, in part due to the recognition by Antiochus III of the Judeans' right to live according to their ancestral laws (*patrioi nomoi*; see *A.J.* 12.142). The crisis associated with the Maccabees under Antiochus IV put an end to that status quo. We should remember, though, that there were also Jewish communities in other parts of the Seleucid empire—in Asia Minor and Babylonia, for example—which the crisis in Judea does not seem to have directly affected. Inner divisions weakened the Seleucids and allowed the Judeans to recover some degree of autonomy under the aegis of the Hasmonean dynasty, which lasted until the Romans took control of Syria in 64 BCE and seized Jerusalem in 63 BCE. As for Egypt, it fell fully under Roman control only after the battle of Actium in 31 BCE.

This section will focus on the impact of the Seleucid empire on Judaism. Admittedly, when dealing with Seleucid royal ideology we must keep in mind that the Hellenistic kingdoms shared certain characteristics, such as the central role of the Macedonian ethnic group and Greek culture, the development of ruler cults, and the importance of military victory for the king's legitimacy (conquest "by the spear"). Beside these commonalities, however, there were dynasty-specific aspects, for example the mixture of Hellenistic and Egyptian components in the Ptolemaic ideology of kingship, which presented the king as the son of Ammon-Re.[190] Jews were exposed to such Hellenistic royal ideologies in various places—in Egypt and in Judea, but also in Asia Minor and farther east. In view of the uncertain dating of some Jewish sources, the interaction between Jews in Judea and in Egypt, and the various experiences of power that different groups and individuals would have had over a given period, it may be difficult to isolate the impact of Seleucid as opposed to Ptolemaic royal ideology. An in-depth investigation of their respective impact on the Jews is definitively beyond the scope of the present study, but I will nevertheless try to identify some Seleucid characteristics, while admitting that certain features are those of Hellenistic kings more generally.

One final preliminary remark: during the Hellenistic period, Jews were massively exposed to Greek political culture as a whole, and not merely to

188. Josephus, *A.J.* 12.138–144, refers to considerable losses and the need to repopulate Jerusalem. On this letter, see Bickerman 1935.

189. Both the author of the Letter of Aristeas and Josephus emphasize that Ptolemy I took many Judean captives with him when he returned to Egypt after having conquered Syria, some of whom he settled in garrisons. See Let. Aris. 12–14; Josephus, *A.J.* 12.7–8.

190. On the diversity of Hellenistic royal models, as well as some unifying characteristics, see Sherwin-White and Kuhrt 1993, chap. 5; Capdetrey 2017.

royal models.[191] The Hellenistic world was a world of kings, but it also witnessed the creation of new cities and the flourishing of the *polis*.[192] Hellenistic royal models had an impact on the Hasmoneans, and to a lesser extent on Herod the Great and his successors, but at that time, and in the long run, Greek civic organization probably had greater impact on Jews and Judaism than did royal models—for example, through the creation of Jewish *politeumata* in Egypt and the participation of some Jews in the civic life of specific *poleis*. We will return to the impact of Greek models of citizenship in Chapter Five, in the discussion of Roman citizenship.

4.1 SELEUCID RULE AND ROYAL IDEOLOGY

That the Seleucid kingdom was an empire, at least during part of its history—until the reign of Antiochus IV, and maybe that of Antiochus VII—is not disputed by scholars (most of whom now also emphasize the continuities with Achaemenid rule), even though the geopolitical situation of the Seleucids, whose kingdom faced other rival kingdoms, differed in many ways from that of the Achaemenids.[193] To quote Paul Kosmin's acute formulation: "A diachronic succession of world-empires (Achaemenids to Alexander) was replaced with the synchronic coexistence of bounded kingdoms."[194]

Studies pertaining to the Seleucid kingdom have multiplied since the appearance of Susan Sherwin-White and Amélie Kuhrt's *From Samarkhand to Sardis: A New Approach to the Seleucid Empire* (1993), which inaugurated a renewal in Seleucid studies.[195] The description of the Seleucid empire (or kingdom) as stretched over too vast a territory, loosely controlled, inadequately organized and administered, and inevitably declining, is now a scholarly trope of the past. John Ma, Laurent Capdetrey, and Paul Kosmin have variously emphasized the importance of the foundation of cities with dynastic names in different parts of the empire, up to Central Asia, as a central element in the Seleucids' strategy of appropriating the space they "inherited" in the wake of Alexander's conquests. Moreover, Capdetrey has shown that beyond conquest and domination, the Seleucid kings and their administration could play a stabilizing role, both by providing for the needs of cities or *ethnē* in cases

191. The difficulty of disentagling the consequences of Seleucid domination from those of the diffusion of Hellenism in general is also noted by Martinez-Sève 2011, 99–100.

192. The theory that the *polis* was in decline during the Hellenistic period has been proved wrong. See, e.g., Gauthier 1985, and the contribution of Richard Billows in Erskine 2003, 196–215.

193. See Briant 1979 (which even argues, on p. 1414, that Alexander can be considered the last of the Achaemenid kings); Sherwin-White and Kuhrt 1993; Briant 2002; Ma 2003; Capdetrey 2007. For a criticism of the "continuity paradigm," see Strootman 2013, 76.

194. Kosmin 2014, 31.

195. See in particular Ma 2003; Capdetrey 2007; Kosmin 2014; Strootman 2014b; Chrubasik 2016.

of drought, famine, etc.—what Capdetrey calls the redistributive function of kingship—and by performing a judicial role, if only by nominating arbitrators between cities, especially in matters of territorial conflict. Capdetrey remarks that the latter aspect anticipated to a certain extent the Roman emperor's function as judge.[196] This role helps to explain the support that many cities lent to the Seleucid kings and accounts in part for the kingdom's ability to endure for at least a century and a half in a world of competing powers.

As for Seleucid royal ideology: it displays both continuities with that of the Achaemenids and features distinctly its own. A document like the Borsippa Cylinder (268 BCE), written in Akkadian and deposited in the foundations of the temple of Nabū in Borsippa when the sanctuary was rebuilt under Antiochus I's sponsorship, shows how the Seleucid king used traditional Babylonian and Achaemenid vocabulary and rhetoric to address the recently conquered populations of Mesopotamia, taking upon himself traditional titles, such as "the great king," "the mighty king," "king of the world," "king of Babylon," and "king of lands."[197] Yet, in that same document Antiochus I also emphasized his Macedonian origins. Clearly, claims to universal rule could go hand in hand with the glorification of a particular ethnic affiliation, but Kuhrt and Sherwin-White also explain the emphasis on Antiochus' Macedonian identity in the Cylinder as an imitation of the Achaemenids' affirmation of their Persian origins.[198] More generally, however, the Macedonian or Greco-Macedonian ethnic and cultural element was an important feature of all the Hellenistic kingdoms. But it did not extend to anything like a systematic exclusion of indigenous, non-Greek elites from political and administrative functions.[199] As Rolf Strootman has emphasized, the adoption by the Seleucids of part of their subjects' terminology and rituals paralleled the adoption of elements of Hellenistic court culture by local non-Greek elites, which expressed their loyalty to the king, structured their relations with the imperial center, and also played a role in local power relationships.[200] It is important to note that this process was not the result of any kind of Seleucid policy of forced "Hellenization."[201]

Strootman also argues that in spite of the division of the Hellenistic world among competing kingdoms, the Hellenistic kings shared the universalistic ideology of their Assyrian and Persian predecessors, from Alexander the Great onward—particularly in the cases of the Seleucids and the Ptolemies.[202] Alexander "claimed to have taken over from Darius the status of world ruler," by right of victory, and his followers' universalistic ambitions were reflected in "the

196. Capdetrey 2017, 35.

197. Kuhrt and Sherwin-White 1991, 76. Foundation documents were a widespread custom in ancient Mesopotamia. See also Strootman 2013; Stevens 2014.

198. Kuhrt and Sherwin-White 1991, 83.

199. Sherwin-White and Kuhrt 1993, 122–124.

200. Strootman 2013, 73.

201. Gruen 1999.

202. Strootman 2014a, 44.

ideal of limitless empire; the concept of a golden age; and the use of cosmic, in particular solar, images as expressions of universal rule."[203] Universalistic ideology was essential because the ideal of world unity was in fact the "umbrella ideology" under which the elites of the Seleucid kingdom cooperated.[204]

Another issue that deserves close examination is the role played by military victory in both the Achaemenid and the Hellenistic contexts. As numerous historians of the Hellenistic world have emphasized, military victory and conquest represented a cornerstone of Hellenistic royal legitimacy. *Doriktētos chōra* ("spear-won territory," i.e., land over which the king had legitimate sovereignty by right of victory in war) is a recurring theme in Hellenistic sources.[205] Several factors explain this emphasis on war and conquest, among them the perpetual competition between kingdoms and the consequent necessity for constantly generating revenue to maintain armies composed to a great extent of mercenaries.[206] Moreover, as Pierre Lévêque recalls, the emphasis on rights obtained "through the spear" and the charismatic aura surrounding the victor were traditional Greek cultural traits even before the Hellenistic period.[207] The imagery of the spear associated with military victory was not foreign to the Persian context either, as Briant notes, but the emphasis in Achaemenid ideology was not on military activity per se.[208] As we saw in the previous section, Achaemenid reliefs depict a peaceful and static order, in which all wealth converges on the imperial center. The Persian king is victorious, but his victories aim to protect the kingdom, and the peasants in particular, thereby preserving prosperity for all. Briant shows that Alexander did his best to conform to this Persian ideology and presented himself as the protector of the countries he was crossing in order to conquer Darius III's empire. Alexander even directed this traditional ideology of the protector-king back against Darius himself when the latter ordered crops burned to prevent Alexander's troops from finding food. In addition, Alexander claimed to benefit from the support of the Persian empire's tutelary gods.[209] As was common in the ancient Near East and the Greco-Roman worlds, the victories of the Hellenistic kings were celebrated as manifestations both of the king's merit and charisma and of the divine support he enjoyed.

Wealth was a prerequisite of kingship not merely to sustain armies but also to enable the euergetistic practices of the king that would secure his subjects' loyalty and grant him honor. An original feature of the Hellenistic kingdoms was the development of the ruler cult, mainly at the initiative of cities but in some

---

203. Ibid., 45. Strootman notes that "world empire is a main theme in Hellenistic, particularly early Ptolemaic court panegyric" (47).

204. Ibid., 56.

205. See Walbank 1984, 66; Ma 2003, 29, 33 (concerning Seleucus I).

206. Austin 1986.

207. Lévêque 1980, 111.

208. Briant 1982, 359.

209. Briant 1982, 375–380.

cases under the aegis of the king and the royal administration. In a Seleucid context, Antiochus III in particular is known to have established a public cult to himself and his ancestors. The divine honors granted to him and his family by cities were primarily an expression of gratitude for and acknowledgment of his benefactions. As Angelos Chaniotis puts it, "The *narratio* of the relevant decrees explains the cult not as recognition of superhuman, godlike achievements, but as recognition of past services," and it reflects the expectation of future gifts too.[210] Since royal euergetism manifested itself first and foremost—although not exclusively—toward cities, it makes sense that divine honors were granted primarily in a civic context. It must be emphasized that even though a distinction was made between gods and deified kings—for example, no prayers were addressed to a deceased king—the ruler cult was a new phenomenon. It paved the way to the Roman empire's imperial cult, which was anticipated, at the time of the Republic, by the divine honors and cult granted by Greek cities to Roman generals and benefactors. As far as the interaction between the Seleucids and the various populations of their kingdom is concerned, we need to keep in mind that the ruler cult was not imposed, although once it was established in a given place, the rituals had to be performed properly.

Finally, a fundamental Seleucid innovation was a new calendar system. Instead of counting time and fixing dates from the beginning of a given king's reign, with the result that a new chronological starting point was established with each new king, from the reign of Seleucus I onward time was calculated from a fixed starting point, the year 312/311 BCE, corresponding to Seleucus I's capture of Babylon. This innovation, which quickly spread throughout the kingdom and remained in use long after the Seleucid dynasty came to its end,[211] originally helped to endow the dynasty with a sense of continuity and permanence and suggested that Seleucid rule would endure forever after.[212] The Seleucid calendar can thus be seen as a political and ideological tool meant to strengthen the power of the king.

4.2 THE LEGACY OF SELEUCID IMPERIALISM IN ANCIENT JEWISH SOURCES

The question of the Seleucid legacy in Jewish sources immediately runs into the issue of the Maccabean crisis of 167–164 BCE and its aftermath, which nearly obliterates everything else.[213] This conflict between the Judeans and Antiochus IV and his successors is documented by several Jewish works dating to

---

210. Chaniotis 2003, 440.

211. See Stern 2001, 28.

212. For a detailed presentation, see Kosmin 2018, part I.

213. On the Maccabean crisis, see in particular Doran 2011; Ma 2012; Honigman 2014, 387–404.

the second century BCE—the last part of the book of Daniel and 1 and 2 Maccabees, to which we may add a few allusions in the Dead Sea Scrolls—and has resonated in Jewish memory ever since, mainly through the celebration of Hanukkah, which is based on a later, rabbinic version of the events.[214]

I would like to step back from the Maccabean crisis for a moment, however, and begin by looking at notions of human kingship, despite the fact that the issue is not exclusive to the Seleucid context. I will then examine how Seleucid practices and discourses concerning territory and time had an impact on Jewish thought and will conclude with some reflections on Jewish theology and angelology in a Hellenistic context.

Human Kingship

The impact of Hellenistic models of kingship on Judaism can be noticed at two levels. First, several Jewish works in Greek reflect on kingship—envisaged mainly as foreign royal rule—and define what constitutes a harmonious relationship between the king and the Jews, be it in Judea or in the diaspora. Second, Hellenistic models of kingship influenced the Hasmoneans, and their rule gave rise to new views of kingship among Jews. (We can identify Hellenistic influences on the Herodians too, although to a lesser extent; and they were of course also exposed to the ruling style of Augustus and his successors, itself partly based on Hellenistic models.)

Several Jewish texts of the Hellenistic period deal with Hellenistic kings and react to Hellenistic royal models. 1 Maccabees tends to present the Seleucid kings in a negative light, but the author of 2 Maccabees, while sharply condemning Antiochus IV Epiphanes, opens his account with the description of a positive model, that of the first Seleucid rulers (before the crisis under Antiochus IV): "The kings themselves used to honor the Place and aggrandize the Temple with the most outstanding gifts, just as King Seleucus of Asia used to supply out of his own revenues all the expenses incurred for the sacrificial offices."[215] A similar pattern emerges in other Jewish texts composed in Greek: a good king is a king who shows respect, and possibly admiration, for the Temple and for the Torah, bestows numerous gifts on the Jerusalem Temple and/or funds the sacrifices without interferring with them, and allows the Jews to live in accordance with their ancestral laws (a topic to which we will return below). This model is exemplified in Josephus' description of the encounter between Alexander the Great and the high priest Jaddus, a legend

---

214. The archeological excavations at Huqoq have uncovered a fifth-century CE synagogue with an impressive mosaic floor, one panel of which shows elephants involved in a battle. Karen Britt and Ra'anan Boustan have interpreted this scene as a representation of the Seleucid siege of Jerusalem by Antiochus VII. If this is correct, the mosaic represents yet another form of Jewish memory of the Hasmonean wars against the Seleucids. See Britt and Boustan 2017, 22, 62–80. See also the Huqoq excavation project's website, at http://www.huqoq.org/.

215. 2 Macc 3:2–3, trans. Daniel R. Schwartz in Schwartz 2008, 181.

with a quasi-programmatic function.[216] Conversely, a bad—"impious"—king violates the sanctuary, plunders the Temple's treasures, blasphemes against God, and deprives the Jews of the right to live according to their ancestral laws. This Hellenistic pattern later provided the prototype for descriptions of Caligula, Titus, and other bad emperors under the pens of Philo and Josephus and in rabbinic literature.

The positive model of kingship is clearly at work in the Letter of Aristeas, which was composed in Egypt probably in the second century BCE, but presents itself as written by a Greek at the court of Ptolemy II Philadelphus in the third century BCE. The king in this book shows great respect for the Jewish translators of the Torah and admires their wisdom, a sagacity obviously derived from the Torah itself. The ideal kingship evoked in the Letter is described in traditional Hellenistic terms, with the Jewish sages encouraging the king to display royal virtues such as *euergesia* and *philanthrōpia*, in a way that echoes Greek texts and papyri.[217] Yet there is also some divergence from Greek views. For example, the Letter plays down the importance of military victory and associates courage (*andreia*) in warfare with justice (*dikaiosunē*). When the king asks, "Who is it necessary to install as commanders over the armies?," the Jewish sage replies, "Those who excel in courage and justice, and those who make more of saving their men than of having victory, rashly risking life."[218] This perspective, however, may not have been shared by all Jews; the Jewish soldiers serving in Hellenistic armies certainly cared about their lives, but they probably cared about booty as well.[219]

What is even more significant is that the Letter and the other literary Jewish sources in Greek, up to Philo and Josephus, reject the notion of a deified king and Jewish participation in the ruler cult. True, we know that some Jews participated in the ruler cult and even performed priestly functions: Dositheos, son of Drymilos, for example, who became an eponymous priest of the cult of Alexander and the deified Ptolemies under Ptolemy III Euergetes I in 223/222 BCE.[220] The Jewish sources that have come down to us reflect, however, a different perspective and unanimously recommend praying for the welfare of the king and his

---

216. Josephus, *A.J.* 11.329–339.

217. Let. Aris. 205, 249, 257, 265, 290. On *philanthrōpia* as a Hellenistic royal virtue, see Berthelot 2003, 20–27.

218. Let. Aris. 281, trans. Benjamin G. Wright in Wright 2015, 411. See also Let. Aris. 199. Also noteworthy is the king's last question, "What is the greatest thing in kingship?," to which the Jewish sage answers, "To establish its subjects always in peace and to provide for justice quickly in their disputes" (Let. Aris. 291, trans. Wright 2015, 412). Of course the text reflects the perspective of the king's subjects, but whereas the sage's opinion is perfectly in line with Achaemenid imperial ideology, its dissonance with Hellenistic royal ideology is striking.

219. For Jewish soldiers in the Hellenistic armies, see Josephus, *A.J.* 12.7–8, 12.119.

220. We are able to reconstruct Dositheos' career thanks to a few papyri: see Mélèze Modrzejewski 1995, 56–61, esp. 60.

family rather than sacrificing to him. This is the perspective of literary texts, but also of synagogal inscriptions, found in Egypt from the third century BCE on, that include honorific dedications to the Ptolemies.[221]

Hellenistic models of kingship did not merely have an impact on Jewish thinking about kingship—they also impacted an indigenous Judean royal dynasty, the Hasmoneans. To summarize the issue very briefly: even before Aristobulus I (r. 104–103 BCE) and Alexander Jannaeus (r. 103–76 BCE) took the title of king, Judas Maccabee's brothers had already adopted some features of Hellenistic kingship, such as purple garments, the display of luxury at court (1 Macc 15:32), a monumental dynastic grave, vast personal estates, and various forms of euergetism.[222] John Hyrcanus (r. 134–104 BCE) and his successors are known to have used foreign mercenaries.[223] Aristobulus I was called Philhellene, and the very fact that Alexander's reign was followed by the rule of his wife, Salome Alexandra (76–67 BCE), is further evidence of Hellenistic influence. Yet another aspect of the Hasmoneans' adoption of Hellenistic and even specifically Seleucid characteristics lies in their coinage: the motif of the anchor, for example, was drawn from Seleucid coinage and seems to have symbolized not only safety but also a claim to royal legitimacy (going back to a legend surrounding the birth of Seleucus I).[224] However, the most strikingly Hellenistic characteristic of Hasmonean kingship is probably the emphasis laid on individual valor and military victory, which runs throughout 1 Maccabees. Judean priests, especially high priests, were not supposed to act as generals, for reasons of purity, certainly—but more fundamentally because, in ancient Israel, war was the business of the king, and kings were not priests. The military role of the Hasmoneans and the emphasis on their victories as a basis for their legitimacy as Israel's rulers (a doubtful legitimacy given their rather inadequate lineage) thus represent clear innovations in Judea, drawn from Hellenistic royal ideology and practice.[225] When it comes to the Herodian kings, it is still possible to speak of Hellenistic features, such as euergetism toward both Judean and Greek cities, and to point out Hellenistic motifs on coinage, such as the Seleucid anchor, which is found on coins minted under Herod the Great and his son Archelaus and again under Agrippa II.[226] But in the context of the early Roman

221. On synagogal inscriptions in Egypt, see Horbury and Noy 1992, e.g., 35–36, no. 22; Levine 2000, 82–89.

222. Greg Gardner notes that "the decree for Simon Maccabee [in 1 Macc 14] is modeled along the lines of Hellenistic-era euergetism: Simon's achievements are cast as 'benefactions,' and his powers and titles as 'rewards'" (Gardner 2007, 337).

223. Berthelot 2018a, 324–334.

224. See Jacobson 2000.

225. Seeman 2013, 368–369; Berthelot 2018a, 427–432.

226. Concerning Herod's euergetism, see *A.J.* 14.298, 15.19–20, 15.298, 15.327; Jacobson 1994; Richardson 1996, 174–196. On the anchor on Herodian coinage, see Jacobson 2000, 79–80.

empire, other aspects of Hellenistic kingship were no longer relevant: in particular, the role of military victory was minor. Two additional factors further minimized the legitimacy of the Herodians in the eyes of the Jewish populations that
they ruled: first, their status as client-kings of the Romans; and second, their
Idumean origins, which made them appear to some as "half-Jews."[227]

The Hasmoneans seem to have enjoyed some popular support, but their
rule was far from universally accepted. Josephus, who proudly claimed genealogical connections with the dynasty, relates that from John Hyrcanus onward
there were groups in Judea that opposed the Hasmoneans.[228] The Dead Sea
Scrolls are notorious for their allusive style, yet they manage to convey quite a
lot of criticism of the dynasty, especially of the Hasmoneans' claim to be both
high priests and kings—or, in the case of John Hyrcanus, a political and military leader, a high priest, and a prophet. They also criticize the Hasmoneans
for deciding to go to war on their own (without first consulting the Urim and
the Tummim, for example) and for their way of waging war, which was seen
as motivated by greed and characterized by bloodshed and impiety. In short,
the military activity of at least some of the Hasmoneans provoked antagonism
in certain circles.[229] Compositions that are not necessarily sectarian, such as
the *Temple Scroll*, also insist on limiting the power of the king, especially in
war.[230] Later rabbinic literature includes similar debates, which may go back
to this original Hasmonean context.

In parallel to concerns about distinguishing between priestly and royal
power and limiting the latter, especially as far as warfare was concerned, one
observes the development of new messianic expectations. Whereas the Rule
of the Community and the Damascus Document, compositions dated to the
second half of the second century BCE, apparently expect two messiahs, a
priestly one ("of Aaron") and a royal one ("of Israel"), other texts, such as
the first-century-BCE Psalms of Solomon, refer to a single royal messiah,
a descendant of David.[231] Messianism thus seems to develop not so much
against the model of foreign kings, Seleucid or otherwise, as against the
"native" kings who ruled Judea, first and foremost the Hasmoneans, and later
Herod.[232] Yet insofar as Hasmonean kingship was in part a Hellenistic kingship and its military dimension was central to the development of both political opposition and messianic expectations in Jewish circles, it is possible to

227. See Josephus, *A.J.* 14.403 (concerning Herod). About Agrippa I, see Schwartz
1990a, 124–126, 169–171, 219–222.

228. Josephus, *A.J.* 13.288.

229. On all these points, see Eshel 2008; Berthelot 2018a, 341–426.

230. See Fraade 2003; Berthelot 2018a, 366–371. 4Q522 9 ii is another interesting case
of a reflection on how to regulate the king's military activity.

231. See 1QS IX 10–11; CD XIX 10–11; on the Davidic messiah, 4Q252 6 V 1–5; Psalms
of Solomon 17:21–42. See Collins 2010, Chap. 3.

232. Cf. Collins 2010, 60.

argue that Jewish messianism was indirectly a response to Hellenistic models of kingship. Furthermore, this response had various aspects, including that of imitation: Jewish descriptions of the royal messiah include depictions of him as a great warrior who will defeat Israel's enemies and subjugate the nations, in line with both traditional biblical views and contemporary Hellenistic models.

Territory: Defining Israel's Relationship to the Promised Land in Legal-Historical Terms

We have seen that in the context of the Persian empire, the redactors of the Hexateuch may have articulated a protest against the idea that it was Ahura Mazda, working through the Persian king, who allocated territories to peoples. Hence the claim that YHWH created the world and gave Israel its territory, just as he gave their lands to the Edomites, the Moabites, and the Ammonites (Deut 2). In other words, we find in Deuteronomy—and elsewhere in the biblical books—a *theological* justification for Israel's possession of the Promised Land: the people of Israel received the Land of Canaan because God gave it to them, because it was God's will.

This theological argument lived on in Jewish texts of the Hellenistic period and later—as a matter of fact, it remains robust today—but from the second century BCE onward, we witness the emergence of a different way of conceptualizing the relationship between Israel and the Land, one that is legal-historical or historico-juridical in nature. Clear examples are found in the Book of Jubilees and the Genesis Apocryphon, which rewrite the story of the division of the earth among the children of Noah in such a way that the Land of Canaan is in fact originally given to Shem, Israel's ancestor. As a consequence, the Land becomes Israel's inheritance since the beginning, even before God's covenant with Abraham. This claim and this legal-historical approach were new and reflect a typically Hellenistic mode of argumentation.[233] Hellenistic kings considered their territories to be legitimately theirs by right of conquest, but also by inheritance. The claims of Antiochus III to the cities of Asia Minor and Thrace were formulated in legalistic terms. According to Polybius, Antiochus III referred to the conquest of these territories by Seleucus I and presented himself as Seleucus' heir, thus putting forward a right of inheritance.[234] John Ma aptly notes that this legalistic approach "passes over the fact that the language of property disputes is applied to acts of conquest and warfare" and thus obliterates the political dimension of the claims to ownership.[235] Yet the fact remains that the legalistic approach was extremely common in territorial disputes of the Hellenistic period, if only as a discursive strategy. In numerous territorial conflicts—between cities and between larger

---

233. For a full explanation, see Berthelot 2018a, 185–212.
234. Polybius, *Histories* 18.51.1–6.
235. Ma 1999, 32.

political entities—a legal-historical approach was used, deploying references to the past and quotes from the works of historians and poets to establish the antiquity of property rights.[236]

Jubilees and the Genesis Apocryphon might well be associated with a Seleucid context and might even indirectly echo the territorial conflict between the Judeans and the Seleucids, but their dating is uncertain. We do, however, have evidence that Jews advanced the legal-historical argument described above in a confrontation with the Seleucids, specifically in the conflict with Antiochus VII over places that the Judeans had conquered and that the king wanted to recover. In 1 Maccabees 15:33–34, Simon's response to the king is formulated as follows: "Neither have we taken a foreign land, nor (a land belonging to) others, but the inheritance of our fathers, which was held unjustly by our enemies for a certain time. But we, seizing the occasion, are clinging to the inheritance of our fathers."[237] As I have argued at length elsewhere, "the inheritance of our fathers" refers to Judea or to Judea and Samaria. What is important to note is that Simon is not talking about the divine gift of the Land to the patriarchs or to the people of Israel. Rather, he establishes the Judeans' right to their territory by arguing that it had already belonged to their ancestors and thus had been transmitted to the Judeans by inheritance—a typically Hellenistic reasoning.[238]

I add as a postscriptum that, conversely, Roman notions of land ownership seem to have had no particular impact on the way Jews conceived of their relationship to the Land of Israel. Elias Bickerman has argued that the Hellenistic world distinguished between possession and right of ownership and did not consider the continuous occupation (i.e., possession) of a territory to confer a right of ownership on the occupier; while, on the contrary, in the Roman world, the continuous occupation and exploitation of land did confer a right of ownership.[239] The explanation for Roman notions failing to influence Jewish thinking may in this case be simply that the events of 70 CE had led to the forced abandonment and confiscation of many lands in Judea, rendering the Roman argument irrelevant to the Jews.

Time, History, and Power: Foretelling the End of Empire

Several scholars see the development of Jewish apocalyptic literature, especially apocalyptic rewritings of history and visions of divine judgment and the destruction of evil, as a response to empires that came to the fore with

---

236. Berthelot 2018a, 178–182, esp. 180, n. 351.

237. Trans. George T. Zervos, NETS, 501, with slight modifications.

238. Berthelot 2018a, 161–185.

239. Bickerman 1932, 51–53; see also Ma 1999, 31; Chaniotis 2004, 190; Berthelot 2018a, 181.

particular force in the Hellenistic context.[240] Anathea Portier-Young, for example, writes: "The prophetic review of history that distinguishes the historical apocalypses embodies discursive resistance in its assertions that God governs time, that history unfolds according to God's plan, and that temporal powers are finite and transient."[241] The emphasis on *discursive* resistance is important, because it would be erroneous to see apocalyptic texts as necessarily encouraging or promoting active political resistance to foreign domination or illegitimate Jewish rulers. As Collins has emphasized, resistance can take many forms, and apocalyptic texts are often quietist—that is, they reject and condemn the present state of the world, thus making a political-religious statement, but wait for God's intervention and do not call for armed rebellion.[242] The review of history and the eschatological speculations found in several apocalypses—such as the *Animal Apocalypse* in *1 Enoch* 83–90—constitute a discourse on theodicy that continues the biblical tradition of prophesies about the fall of wicked kingdoms and arrogant kings.[243] Moreover, some apocalypses explore the issue of the origin of evil in the world. By providing explanations for evil and raising hopes for its final defeat, apocalyptic works may to some extent have helped to calm anxiety about the present, whether aroused by foreign domination or by unjust rule more generally (which could also refer to Jewish rule). Later on, in rabbinic texts, political powerlessness was juxtaposed with colorful fantasies of eschatological revenge in which the Romans were punished and destroyed. In certain cases, by envisioning the triumph of the king messiah, the restoration of Israel, and their joint dominion over the nations, some eschatological scenarios may even mimic imperial power and ideology—a point to which we will return in Chapter Three.

The development of Jewish apocalyptic and eschatological discourses in the Hellenistic period can thus be seen to some extent as a response to Hellenistic rule, even though, as Portier-Young admits, "not all apocalypses articulate a discourse or program of resistance to empire."[244] Apocalyptic texts had other functions as well. They could be inspired by exegetical or scientific concerns—the functioning of the cosmos, the natural order of creation, etc. Yet consolation and exhortation are undoubtedly primary functions of several apocalypses, not necessarily in the context of a specific crisis but as expressions of deep, abiding questions about the state of the world. In this guise apocalyptic texts may in fact be considered a type of wisdom literature.[245]

240. For a detailed review of scholarship on apocalypses and apocalypticism until 2007, see DiTommaso 2007a; 2007b.

241. Portier-Young 2014, 146, referring to Portier-Young 2011, 27.

242. Collins 2002; 2011.

243. Otzen 1990, 235, also emphasizes the connection between eschatological discourse and discursive resistance.

244. See already Eddy 1961.

245. Collins 2011a.

The development of apocalyptic discourse in response to Hellenistic rule is most clearly illustrated by the book of Daniel. In chapters 2 and 7, we find two visions that reflect both the idea of *translatio imperii* and the expectation of a final, eternal kingdom or empire, which in the book's perspective is that of the God of Israel, coming after the Babylonians, the Medes, the Persians, and the Macedonians. In Daniel 2, the king has a vision of a statue made of gold, silver, bronze, iron, and a mixture of iron and clay (Dan 2:32–33). The legs, made of iron, represent the fourth kingdom, that of the Macedonians, and Daniel explains that the statue's feet are made of both iron and clay as a symbol of division, which the protagonists try to supersede through matrimonial alliances, but in vain (Dan 2:40–43). The image plainly reflects the divisions between the Diadochi and the matrimonial strategies of the Seleucids and the Ptolemies in particular. The stone that smites the statue in the king's vision, which becomes a great mountain and fills the whole earth (Dan 2:34–35), represents God's everlasting kingdom, which will replace the divided Hellenistic kingdoms (Dan 2:44). The scheme of a succession of four kingdoms followed by the establishment of a fifth, rightful and eternal one is, in David Flusser's words, "an ideological weapon of the East against the West"—the West being Greece.[246] The expectation of the advent of the kingdom of God clearly denotes an eschatological perspective, even though the last kingdom seems to be an earthly rather than a heavenly one.

By contrast, the eschatological vision and scenario in Daniel 7 are more heavenly or cosmic. Daniel sees four great beasts coming up out of the sea and describes the fourth as different from the others, "terrifying and dreadful and exceedingly strong" (Dan 7:7). It destroys everything and has ten horns, among which emerges a little horn that is particularly arrogant (Dan 7:8). This vision is followed by a scene of judgment in which God sits on his throne, books are opened, and the fourth beast is destroyed. Then, from heaven, comes the "one like a Son of Man," to whom God gives eternal rule over all the nations (Dan 7:13–14). The political dimension of the vision is unmistakable, and there is a new dimension also, when compared to chapter 2, in the role played by the Son of Man figure, who has traditionally been identified with the king messiah.

Finally, according to a wide scholarly consensus, chapters 11 and 12 of the book of Daniel refer to the Maccabean crisis in Judea in the 160s BCE. There are allusions to Antiochus IV's failed Egyptian expedition in 168 BCE and to his subsequent policy in Jerusalem (Dan 11:32–39), and probably a hint at the notion of the resurrection of the faithful (Dan 12:2–3). This leads Portier-Young to understand the book in its final shape as a piece of "resistance literature" designed to comfort its readers and exhort them to remain steadfast and

---

246. Flusser 1972, 173. See also Swain 1940; Eddy 1961.

faithful to God's covenant, trusting in God's salvation in the present time just as Daniel and the three young men did in theirs.[247]

Kosmin has suggested reading the book of Daniel as a whole in a Seleucid context, but he argues more specifically that it represents a response to Seleucid imperial constructions of time. As mentioned above, the Seleucids created a new temporal regime, beginning with the rule of the dynasty's founder, Seleucus I, and proceeding on indefinitely in a continuous, linear count of years. This type of calendar emphasized dynastic continuity, but also facilitated breaking away from and attempting to erase the pre-Seleucid past, as well as perceiving the future as wide open, ground for a potentially boundless rule. Kosmin argues that the conception of time introduced by the Seleucids in order to unify their kingdom had a deep impact on the populations living in their realm, both in everyday life and in the broader terms of their worldview. This continuous, irreversible, and ever-accumulating temporality was challenged by some people within the empire who maintained or revived the memory of the pre-Hellenistic past and conceived of alternative time frames, often apocalyptic in nature, that chose another starting point and predicted the end of history—and hence of Seleucid domination. According to Kosmin, Jewish apocalyptic texts such as Daniel, the *Animal Apocalypse*, and the *Apocalypse of Weeks* reflect this attempt to elaborate a total and periodized history characterized by a clear sense of finitude. Therefore, as Kosmin puts it, "in some most important respects, apocalyptic eschatology was Seleucid by derivation and anti-Seleucid by consequence."[248]

Empires, Theology, and Angelology

The book of Daniel reflects the impact of the Hellenistic empires in yet other respects. Alexandria Frisch has convincingly argued that Daniel and later works based on it reveal two different understandings of empire, resulting in two different views of the deity and its role in history. In Daniel 2, the Babylonians, the Medes, the Persians, and the Macedonians are seen as succeeding one another chronologically, a phenomenon that takes place exclusively on earth.[249] The corresponding theological view, which is Deuteronomistic, is that empires are controlled by God, who lifts them up and brings them down and uses them either to punish or to rescue Israel. In Daniel 7, by contrast, the vision of the fourth beast with horns that fight each other reflects the author's perception of the Macedonians as a mixed and composite entity—a perception also partly reflected in the mixture of iron and clay in Daniel 2—which symbolizes the simultaneous presence of antagonistic powers on the world scene. Daniel 7 thus shows that the events of the Hellenistic period led to

247. Portier-Young 2011, 277–279.
248. Kosmin 2018, 185.
249. As Mario Liverani notes: "Clearly, the idea of *translatio imperii* was based on the concept that there was only one 'empire' at a time" (Liverani 2017b, 535).

a reconceptualization of empire as a power that is divided and all the more destructive for that, or, to put it differently, as multiple violent entities in constant competition for power. To explain this chaotic situation, the old theological conception of a God who uses imperial powers to advance his designs was unsatisfying. Hence the notion that behind empires lie angelic forces and that battles on earth reflect a heavenly struggle. According to Frisch, this is the background implied by Daniel's vision: the beasts are stirred up by heavenly forces that are not of God's creation; as a consequence, empires are "part of an out-of-control opposition against God."[250] In a similar vein, stories about rebellious angels, be it the Watchers in *1 Enoch* or Belial in some Dead Sea Scrolls, helped to explain why the situation was chaotic, while the promise of their ultimate defeat and judgment at the hands of God preserved the notion of a God in control of history.[251] The new perception of imperial power went together with a new etiology of evil, based on Genesis 6:1–4 and the traditions associated with it. This new etiology did not mean that God was not omnipotent, but only that he was less immanent.[252] The encounter with the Hellenistic kingdoms thus had theological consequences pertaining both to the conception of God and to the role of angelic beings in the world of human beings.

My purpose in surveying the encounter between Israel and the imperial powers of the ancient Near East has been manifold. First, by looking at the characteristics of these empires, this chapter has aimed to show that several features of Roman imperial ideology, such as universalistic claims, the notion of the emperor as a righteous judge or as divinely chosen to protect the *oikoumenē* from chaos and establish a peaceful order, and the depiction of the emperor as piously rebuilding the gods' temples in Rome and elsewhere all have a precedent in previous imperial contexts. This conclusion, however, does not rule out the possibility that these features received a new meaning in the Roman context or were perceived in a new way by Jews who lived in the Roman empire.

Second, this chapter has examined the extent to which biblical and other ancient Jewish texts reflected the Jews' encounters with various pre-Roman empires. The long redactional history of most biblical books makes it difficult to pinpoint the impact of a specific empire on any specific book. In some cases, several empires left successive marks on a given book or collection (Deuteronomy and Isaiah are cases in point). The fact that imperial ideologies

250. Frisch 2017, 116–122, quotation at 122.

251. Admittedly, the Book of the Watchers does not explicitly address the issue of the overthrow of imperial powers or kingdoms. It is the etiology of evil found in this book that is relevant to Frisch's argument.

252. Frisch 2017, esp. 216–219.

sometimes share common features, including those inherited from yet another imperial context, also contributes to the blurring of the distinctions between the impacts of various empires. In spite of these reservations, this chapter suggests that each of the empires that preceded Rome had an impact on the political and religious ideas of ancient Israel—some more significantly than others, and some more distinctly than others.

Third, this chapter has attempted to describe the nature of the impact that these empires had on Jewish thought, as it is known to us through literary productions from these periods. Four areas are particularly worth emphasizing:

1. Perhaps unsurprisingly, encounters with imperial powers had major consequences in the theological realm. Power was always conceived of as somehow connected to the gods; therefore, imperial power raised questions about the power of the God of Israel versus that of other gods. The transition from henotheism to universal monotheism owes a lot to the Neo-Babylonian and Persian contexts, whereas the rejection of dualism, the concomitant development of angelology, and the elaboration of an etiology of evil that differed markedly from the Deuteronomistic worldview were to a great extent prompted by the Jews' encounter with the Persians and their confrontation with the Hellenistic kingdoms.

2. Another logical outcome of an encounter with imperial or royal models was a growing reflection on human, and especially kingly, power. Whereas numerous biblical texts can be seen as inspired by problems raised by the Israelite or Judean kingship rather than by foreign imperial powers, others may reflect attempts to define kingship in ways that counter the imperial model by severing the connection, commonly found in the ancient Near East and in a Hellenistic context, between the king and the god(s) and by limiting the power and wealth of the king. However, in prophetic and apocalyptic texts, some descriptions of the rule of God, or that of God's messiah at the end of days, also imitate imperial features—by their triumphal tone, and by such notions a universal rule, a warrior king, and the violent crushing of enemies.

3. The development of eschatology, both collective and individual, with its corresponding sense of a determined course of history and a fixed end of time, can also be analyzed as a response to imperial contexts. According to Weinfeld, Jewish eschatological visions started to develop in response to Neo-Assyrian imperialism, as seen in First Isaiah (see §1.2 above). They developed further during the Persian and the Hellenistic periods, both in apocalyptic works and in literary works of other genres—such as 2 Maccabees, which presents the notion of individual, bodily resurrection as a direct response to the

persecution of the Seleucid king. According to Kosmin, the Seleucid imperial context was the primary catalyst for the development of the so-called historical apocalypses, such as Daniel 2 and 7 and the *Animal Apocalypse*.[253]

4. A fourth web of notions that developed partly in response to imperial contexts pertains to the covenant between God and Israel. The VTE, and probably Neo-Assyrian vassal treaties and loyalty oaths more broadly, influenced the Deuteronomic formulation of the bond between Israel and God. Later, Persian imperial discourse on the divine distribution of lands to peoples and the Seleucid way of asserting the right to conquered territories as inherited property impacted Judean conceptions of the relationship between Israel and their Land, another central aspect of the covenant.

Finally, the survey proposed in this chapter provides a background for examining precedents for various Jewish responses to Roman imperialism. For example, accommodating the ruler cult by means of sacrifices or prayers *on behalf of* the ruler rather than *to* the ruler, was a tactic already devised in the Hellenistic context. Likewise, responses to empire through apocalyptic visions with a consolatory function, such as the late first-century CE examples in 4 Ezra and 2 Baruch, share elements with previous apocalyptic works produced in the Hellenistic period. Speculations about Israel's final victory against the nations and the latter's ultimate judgment and punishment by God run from Isaiah through to the Talmud. Finally and most important, tension between the adoption or imitation of imperial features on the one hand and the rejection of imperial ideas accompanied by the elaboration of countermodels on the other is seen to have been an established dialectic in Jewish writings prior to the encounter with Rome.

Yet the encounter with Rome was also a new challenge for the Jews, and it is to this challenge that I now turn.

253. Kosmin 2018.

CHAPTER TWO

The Unique Challenge
of the Roman Empire

A RIVALRY BETWEEN TWO PEOPLES

Two peoples are in your womb: *there are two proud peoples in your womb,*
each taking pride in his world, and each in his kingdom.
 [There are] two proud peoples in your womb: Hadrian among the
nations, Solomon in Israel.

GENESIS RABBAH 63:7

UNDER THE ROMANS, the Jews lost their political independence, saw foreign
military forces occupying Judea, and were subject to taxes. It was an unhappy
situation but in the main a familiar one, very like what they had experienced
in centuries past. Admittedly, at the regional or local level we can observe specific changes at the beginning of the Roman period: in Egypt, for example,
Roman rule brought negative changes for the Jews in social and fiscal status,
with the introduction of a personal tax called the *laographia* or *capitatio*.[1]
This, however, was a consequence of the Roman redefinition of the category
of "Hellenes." It did not target the Jews as such—Egyptians too were subject
to the *capitatio*. Finally, it did not in itself represent an ideological challenge:
all in all, it was domination as usual, only more bitter.

It was in Judea that the Jews' political situation changed most significantly
during the first century BCE and the first century CE.[2] After Pompey's conquest in 63 BCE, Hyrcanus II was reestablished as high priest and ethnarch. In
37 BCE, Judea had a king again, in the person of Herod the Great, but he was
a client king of Rome, and so were his descendants. Then, in 6 CE, Judea was

1. Mélèze Modrzejewski 1995, 161–164.
2. Shatzman 1999.

taken away from Herod's brutal and incompetent son Archelaus, and made a Roman province, with a prefect—and later a procurator—at its head, under the supervision of the governor of Syria. Apart from a brief period (41–44 CE) during which Judea was again ruled by a king, Herod Agrippa I, it remained under direct Roman control until the revolt of 66 CE. After the revolt, a Roman legate governed the province of *Iudaea*. Later, after the Bar-Kokhba Revolt (132–135 CE), the name of the province was changed to Syria Palaestina. We will return to these changes in Section 4 below, which will also discuss other aspects of the Roman policies, such as the creation of the *fiscus Iudaicus*, that affected the Jews everywhere in the empire, not merely in Judea.

As we saw in the previous chapter, several ideological aspects of Roman domination—such as the claim to be establishing a universal, benevolent, and law-abiding rule, or the claim to benefit from the support of the gods—were not particularly novel either. This chapter will argue that the main reason why at least some Jews perceived the Roman empire as a unique challenge was that the city and the people associated with the name "Rome" defined themselves in ways that came surprisingly close to how Israel defined itself and the vocation of its capital city, Jerusalem. As Gerson Cohen aptly wrote: "Each considered itself divinely chosen and destined for a unique history. Each was obsessed with its glorious antiquity. Each was convinced that heaven had selected it to rule the world. Neither could accept with equanimity any challenge to its claims."[3] This chapter posits that these paradoxical similarities, together with the Roman policies toward the Jews and Jerusalem after the three Jewish revolts, led some Jews to feel that Rome was in fact trying to take Israel's place and role in God's plan for the world. In other words, it suggests that at least some Jews experienced Rome as a power that was attempting to substitute itself for Israel. It would seem that long before the Roman empire became Christian, the issue of rivalry and substitution was already a major one in the eyes of certain Jews, and that it was principally for this reason that the rabbis (and maybe other Jews as well) came to identify the Romans with Esau, Jacob's twin brother.

As the introduction to this book emphasizes, "Rome" changed over time, between the Judeans' very first encounter with it at the time of the Maccabees and the fourth century.[4] There was clearly a Roman empire even before there was a princeps or an emperor, and the empire at the time of Augustus obviously differed from the empire during the crisis of the third century, the Diocletian tetrarchy, or the reign of Constantine, not to mention under later and more thoroughly Christian emperors. We are dealing with several centuries of deep-running evolutions and transformations. Yet there were also continuities, and some motifs do recur in different contexts. In this chapter and the following ones, we will look at characteristics that prevailed from at least the first

3. Cohen 1967, 25.
4. Cf. Richardson 2008, 3–4.

century BCE to the beginning of the fourth century CE with a relative degree of continuity or recurrence, combining both transformation and permanence.

In order to assess the extent to which Jews were exposed to Roman imperial ideology and to Roman practices of empire more broadly, one needs to keep in mind that they were spread over most of the territory of the Roman empire and across several client kingdoms of Rome. For example, Jewish inscriptions from the Bosporus kingdom—whose kings claimed to be *philorhōmaioi* (friends of the Romans), like Herod—show that Jewish communities were established there in the first century CE.[5] Although Jewish presence in a given area is not always documented in a continuous way from the first century BCE to the fourth century CE—mainly because of the random nature of the evidence— literary, epigraphic, archaeological, and papyrological testimonies nevertheless document Jews and Jewish communities in Asia Minor, Syria, Arabia, Egypt, Cyrenaica, Cyprus, Greece, and Italy. The main point at this stage is that the Jews were exposed to Roman imperial power and ideology in many places and contexts all over the empire. In particular, many Jews lived in cities, where they confronted a visual landscape rich in imperial images—statues, arches, reliefs of various sorts—as well as inscriptions related in one way or another to Rome. Last but not least, from the first century BCE onward, there was an important Jewish community in Rome itself, and according to epigraphy, several syna- gogues were established in the *Urbs* from early on.[6] As the examples of Philo and Josephus (*Vita* 13–16) make clear, Jews living in the provinces also traveled to Rome on occasion and brought back vivid reports of Rome's grandiose archi- tecture and displays of power. Rabbinic literature tells of rabbis who went to Rome, and while the purpose of these stories is often didactic and consolatory, they are not necessarily without a historical basis—and when they are, they may nevertheless contain some knowledge about the city and its culture.[7] In short, there was a multitude of ways in which Jews could be exposed to Rome's power and ideology, and be impacted by them.

1. The Imperialism of a People

"Rome" stood for a city and a people, the *populus Romanus*. Admittedly, Athe- nian and Spartan "imperialism" also consisted in the imperialism of a city and a people—even though the Spartans had kings. However, these "empires" remained geographically limited, especially in comparison with the Roman

5. Gibson 1999 (for the king as *philorhōmaios*, see *CIRB* no. 74, p. 163; no. 985, p. 164; no. 1021, p. 165). On Herod and his descendants and for comparisons with other client kings, see Geiger 1997; Jacobson 2001.

6. Rutgers 1995; Levine 2000, 283–286. Some synagogues were named after prominent Roman leaders, such as Augustus and Agrippa. In contrast to the synagogue in Ostia, no remains of the Roman synagogues have been found so far.

7. See, e.g., Sifre Deuteronomy 43, ed. Finkelstein, 94.

empire. Moreover, as the Jews never had direct experience of them, they are not relevant to the present analysis. Rome was thus the first empire Israel faced that was established in the name of a people rather than that of a king or a dynasty.[8]

1.1 A JEWISH TESTIMONY FROM THE SECOND CENTURY BCE

The two most conspicuous characteristics of the Romans in the eyes of second-century BCE Jews seem to have been their invincibility—the very feature Polybius tried to explain in his *Histories*—and the fact that they had no kings. This, at least, is the testimony of 1 Maccabees 8:1–16, one of the first Jewish texts, together with 2 Maccabees, to explicitly mention the Romans.

The opening of the passage is telling: "And Judas heard the name of the Romans." The phrase "the name of the Romans" (*to onoma tōn Rhōmaiōn*), probably a translation of the Hebrew *shema' ha-Romaim*, clearly means "the reputation of the Romans."[9] Rome's fame is that of the Roman people and not that of a king or a general.[10]

The eulogy of Rome in 1 Maccabees 8 marvels at length at the Romans' exceptional strength,[11] their military victories, and the fact that they were now the main political force to be reckoned with, a force everybody feared. The text emphasizes that no king—no Greek, that is, Seleucid king in particular—was able to resist them. The author also notes in verse 3 that they conquered Spain "to gain control over the metals, the silver and the gold which was there," thus displaying his awareness that economic interests and greed motivated some of the Roman conquests. Although the author of 1 Maccabees

---

8. In a Persian context, one occasionally encounters the claim that the king associated the people with his conquests, but such a statement remains very unusual. See DPe §2: "King Darius proclaims: By the favour of Auramazda, these (are) the countries of which I took possession together with these Persian people" (Schmitt 2009, 117–118; trans. Kuhrt 2010, 486).

9. The Hebrew original may also have been *shem ha-Roma'im* (cf. Gen 6:4, 12:2) but this is less likely. *Onoma* often translates *shema'* in the Septuagint. See Abel 1949, 146; Rappaport 2004, 221; Seeman 2013, 209–210. The Hasmoneans too acquired a "name" through their heroic deeds on the battlefield (1 Macc 3:26, 5:63, 14:10). See further Chapter Three, §2.3.

10. Interestingly, *to onoma tōn Rhōmaiōn* also recalls the Latin expression *nomen Romanum*, "Roman name." In Latin texts, the most common phrase to indicate the Roman people is of course *populus Romanus*, but *nomen Romanum* also refers to the Romans as a political body, to the essence of the Roman people and their *maiestas*, to the memory of their past victories and their virtues. See Livy, *History of Rome* 4.33.5, 21.30.3, 28.28.12, 36.17.15–16; Sallust, *The War with Jugurtha* 58.3; Dupont 2005, 272–273; Baroin 2010, 174; Isaac 2017, 2–3.

11. 1 Macc 8:1 mentions twice that they are "powerful in strength," *dynatoi ischui*.

clearly wants to show the Romans—with whom Judas and the Judeans are said to have established a friendship (*philia*) and an alliance (*symmachia*)[12]—in a favorable light, he does not support the narrative according to which the Roman conquests were meant merely to defend Rome or its allies. The Romans are indeed presented as loyal to their allies and friends (1 Macc 8:1, 12–13) in keeping with the Roman insistence on *fides*;[13] but the brutality of the Roman conquests is also patent (1 Macc 8:10–11).[14]

At the end of the eulogy, the author adds a few remarks on the Roman political regime, whose relevance is not immediately clear:

> And in all this not even one of them has put on a crown nor have they wrapped themselves in purple so as to show their power by it. 15 And they built for themselves a council chamber, and every day three hundred twenty senators deliberate continuously about the multitude so that they might live in an orderly way. 16 And they trust one man to rule them each year and to govern all their land, and they all obey the one, and there is no jealousy or envy among them.[15]

This passage is clearly fraught with errors and idealization.[16] However, it is crucial evidence of how Judean elites perceived the Roman republic in the second century BCE.[17] What is particularly relevant for us at this stage is the author's astonishment at the fact that the Romans have no king, in contrast to all the previous imperial powers that the Judeans had encountered.[18] Verse 16 probably describes the election of the consuls, mistakenly affirming that there was only one elected every year.[19] The reference to the absence of envy or jealousy may have stemmed from the fact that the consuls surrendered their *imperium* at the end of each year and accepted being replaced by

12. See 1 Macc 8:17–32. On the exact nature of these diplomatic relations, see, e.g., Gruen 1984, 1:46–51; Kallet-Marx 1995, 185–186; Shatzman 1999, 62; Baltrusch 2002, 96–98; Seeman 2013, 116–119, 133; Bernhardt 2017, 364–369; Zollschan 2017, esp. Chap. 6; and Altay Coşkun's critical response to Zollschan in Coşkun 2018.

13. On this notion, see in particular Boyancé 1964.

14. See Flusser 1983 [2007], esp. 187–194; Baltrusch 2002, 88.

15. 1 Macc 8:14–16, trans. Zervos, NETS, 490.

16. See Hadas-Lebel 1990, 24–31; Rappaport 2004, 221–226; Seeman 2013, 113–119, 209–218.

17. The first book of Maccabees probably dates to the end of the second century BCE and may even have been commissioned by John Hyrcanus. Whatever the exact date of the eulogy of the Romans in chapter 8, though, we are dealing with second-century BCE Judean perceptions of Rome.

18. Baltrusch 2002, 89.

19. Clifford Ando suggests that the author of 1 Maccabees might instead have been speaking of the praetor as if he were a consul (Ando 1999, 17–18). Hervé Inglebert suggested in a private conversation that the author of 1 Maccabees or his source may have been confused by the fact that in general, only one of the two consuls was present in Rome at a time.

others, whereas Hellenistic kings murdered their opponents, including their own brothers and sisters, in order not to lose power. The bewilderment of the Judean author at a people that chose its rulers every year is quite telling. Clearly, the democratic or republican notion that a people might choose their own rulers every year was utterly foreign to Judea, despite the author's apologetic efforts to present Judas, Jonathan, and Simon as chosen not only by God but also by the Judean *dēmos*.[20]

1.2 THE *IMPERIUM* OF THE *POPULUS ROMANUS*

The first description of the Romans in Jewish literature thus focuses on Roman imperialism, and this imperialism is that of a people, not a king. Of course, the deeply ingrained Roman antipathy toward monarchy weakened with the establishment of the Principate in 27 BCE, and it would gradually fade altogether as imperial families took on greater political and religious importance in the centuries that followed. However, as Myles Lavan rightly emphasizes, "Rome had an empire long before it had an emperor and that empire continued to be seen as distinctly 'Roman' (whatever that might mean) long after the creation of the monarchy."[21] John Richardson notes that whereas a new meaning of *imperium* developed in the first and second centuries CE with reference to "the power and office of the emperor," the older meaning, expressing the corporate power of the Roman people and magistrates, endured.[22] Clifford Ando similarly points out that even with the advent of the Principate, "the notional sovereignty of the *populus Romanus* remained integral to imperial ideology and received expression in the continued holding of elections through the early third century."[23]

The testimony of Augustus' *Res Gestae*, which Andrew Erskine considers "the most forceful expression of Roman power and the ideology of empire," is telling in that respect.[24] It shows that the princeps presented his actions as subordinate to the will of the Roman people and the Senate. One of the

---

20. Chris Seeman has a different interpretation of this section. According to him, the eulogy of Rome is also a eulogy of the Hasmoneans, and the author of 1 Maccabees depicts Judas, Jonathan, and Simon as respecting Judea's "consultative traditions" in a way that is implicitly compared to Roman usage (see, e.g., 1 Macc 14:25, 27–28, 35, 41, 46). The main difference, as Seeman himself acknowledges, is that Hasmonean power was not limited to a year but rather lifelong (Seeman 2013, 215–216).

21. Lavan 2013, 1–2. On the question of *res publica restituta* under Augustus (and beyond), see Augustus, *Res Gestae* 34.1; Hurlet and Mineo 2009.

22. Richardson 2008, 178–180.

23. Ando 2000, 28. See also Béranger 1973, 209–242, 261; and now Marotta 2014; 2016.

24. Erskine 2010, 10.

inscriptions that preserves the text of the *Res Gestae*—the Latin inscription from Pisidian Antioch—opens as follows:

> Below is a copy of the achievements of the deified Augustus, by which he made the world subject to the rule of the Roman people (*imperio populi Rom(ani)*), and of the expenses which he incurred for the state and people of Rome, as inscribed upon two bronze columns which have been set up at Rome.[25]

In *Res Gestae* 26.1, we further read: "I enlarged the boundaries of all provinces of the Roman people, which had as neighbors peoples that were not subject to our rule (*hēgemonia* in Greek)."[26] The close association between Augustus and the Roman people is also apparent in the statement at §26.4 that "Cimbri and Charydes and Semnones and many other tribes of Germans sought through embassies my friendship and that of the Roman people." One may consider the references to the *populus Romanus* and the idea that the *imperium* belonged to the Roman people a mere rhetorical stance, but it was in fact more than sheer rhetoric. From both an institutional and an ideological point of view, the Principate was not a Hellenistic monarchy, even though the regime became more monarchical with the passing of time, up to late Byzantine times.[27]

This notion of the *imperium* of the Roman people is attested in a great variety of sources. Authors writing in the first and second centuries CE commonly refer to the Roman people as the master (*dominus*), conqueror (*victor, domitor, pacator*), or ruler (*princeps, imperator, moderator, arbiter*) of the whole world (*orbis terrarum*) or of all nations (*omnes gentes*).[28] Epigraphic testimonies reflect this same perspective. In the Flavian period, an inscription on the tombstone of Tiberius Plautius, the governor of Moesia, dated to 74–79 CE, states that "kings previously unknown or hostile to the Roman people he led to the bank (of the Danube), which he was guarding, to make them

25. Trans. Alison E. Cooley (Cooley 2009, 58; see p. ccii for the Latin text). Cooley's translation is based on a composite text of both Latin and Greek versions, which takes into account the inscriptions from Ancyra (Ankara), Pisidian Antioch, and Apollonia and follows the edition of the *Res Gestae Divi Augusti* produced by John Scheid (Scheid 2007). The Latin and Greek inscriptions from Ancyra have a shorter text for this passage, without the reference to the Roman people. The beginning of the inscription from Apollonia is lost. On the double meaning of *imperium*, as power or authority over something and as the territory upon which this authority is upheld, see Richardson 1991; 2008, esp. Chap. 4.

26. Cooley 2009, 91. The Latin text of §26.1 is not preserved, but the Greek inscription from Ancyra has δήμου Ῥωμαίων. In the Greek inscription from Apollonia, only the first two letters of *dēmos* (people) can be read. See also *Res Gestae* 13, 27.1, 30.1–2, 32.2.

27. On the first centuries, see the remarks on the ambivalence of the Roman imperial regime in Wallace-Hadrill 1982. See also Ando 2000, 44–45, which notes that a Hellenistic monarch *was* the state.

28. See Lavan 2013, 91–93.

honour the military standards of the Romans."[29] As in Augustus' *Res Gestae*, the victory is here presented as first and foremost that of the Roman people. Under Trajan, in 116 CE, a detachment (*vexillatio*) of the Legio III Cyrenaica in Jerusalem dedicated an object—probably a statue—to "Jupiter Optimus Maximus Sarapis, for the welfare and victory of the Emperor Nerva Trajan Caesar, the best Augustus, Germanicus Dacicus Parthicus, and of the Roman people."[30] At Dura Europos, where there was a Jewish community, a papyrus (called *Feriale Duranum*) dated to 222–227 CE was found that contains a calendar of the festivals celebrated by an auxiliary cohort of the Roman army, the *cohors XX Palmyrenorum*. This list, which mentions only Roman gods whose festivals are mainly associated with imperial anniversaries, seems to have been valid throughout the whole empire—that is, it was followed by Roman troops everywhere.[31] It starts with the record that on III Nones January, "vows are fulfilled and undertaken both for the welfare of our Lord Marcus Aurelius Severus Alexander Augustus and for the eternity of the empire (*imperium*) of the Roman people."[32] This document illustrates the persistence of the reference to the *imperium* of the Roman people, in a cultic and military context that stretches beyond the particular case of Dura Europos.

Greek inscriptions show that some *poleis* had dedicated statues and monuments to the Roman people and Roman individuals at the time of the Republic. In the imperial period, Greek cities frequently associated the emperor, the Senate, and the Roman people and addressed them jointly or made vows for their common welfare and prosperity. There are even a few cases of inscriptions celebrating the *hēgemonia* of the Romans. At Thyatira in Lydia, for example, a dedicatory inscription groups the emperor Nero, the Senate, and "the hegemony of the Romans."[33] In Ephesus, an inscription dated to 79–81 CE, recording the restoration of the wall of the Augusteum, contains vows for the health of Titus and the permanence of Roman hegemony (*diamonē tēs tōn Rōmaiōn hēgemonias*).[34] Again in Ephesus in 104 CE, Caius Vibus Salutaris, an Ephesian member of the equestrian order who was probably of Italic origin, originated a ritual procession in honor of Artemis—whom the Ephesians regarded as the founder of their city. The inscription recording its establishment

---

29. *CIL* XIV, 3608 = *ILS* 986. Trans. Robert K. Sherk in Sherk 1988, 104. See also Caroline Barron, "Tombstone of the Governor of Moesia (*CIL* XIV, 3608)," at http://judaism -and-rome.org/tombstone-governor-moesia-cil-xiv-3608.

30. *CIL* III, 13587 = *ILS* 4393.

31. Fishwick 1988.

32. P. Dura 54, col. 1, lines 2–3, available at http://papyri.info/ddbdp/rom.mil.rec;1;117. For the English translation, see Fink 1971, 428, no. 117; Beard, North, and Price 1998, 71, no. 3.5. See also Caroline Barron, "Feriale Duranum (P. Dura54)," at http://www.judaism -and-rome.org/feriale-duranum-pdura-54.

33. *IGR* IV, p. 405, no. 1195. See also *I.Eph.* 8, line 12 (86/85 BCE) (*SEG* 33.877).

34. *I.Eph.* 412, lines 3–4 (*ILS* 8797).

states that during this procession, statues of the Roman emperor (Trajan at that time), the Senate, and the Roman people (*Dēmos Rōmaiōn*) were to be paraded, respectively paired with statues of the emperor's wife, the local *boulē*, and the local *gerousia*.[35] The pedestal on which the statues of Artemis, the *Dēmos* of the Romans, and the *gerousia* of Ephesus rested when not being paraded bears a bilingual inscription that, instead of *Dēmos Rōmaiōn* (the phrase used in the text of the foundation), refers to *Rōmē Hēgemonis* (lit. "Ruler Rome") in Greek and *Urbs Romana* (the Roman City) in Latin.[36] This clearly illustrates the conceptual equivalence between the people and the city, to which we will return below. Also noteworthy is the notion of hegemony associated with Rome in the Greek text. As Emmanuelle Rosso Caponio notes, all the personifications mentioned in these inscriptions pertain to a single idea: Roman domination.[37] These examples and those mentioned in the preceding paragraphs show how widespread references to the *imperium* or the *hēgemonia* of the Roman people, alongside the emperor, were throughout the empire, including in places where Jews lived, such as important *poleis* in Asia Minor.

Literary works in Greek also convey a sense of the continued importance and sovereignty of the Roman people. At the end of the second century CE, the Greek rhetor Aelius Aristides wrote in his *Roman Oration* that the empire of the Romans was "much greater for its perfection than for the area which its boundaries encircle," because there were no areas within it that resisted or revolted against Roman rule, "nor is it merely called the land of the King, while really the land of all who are able to hold it" (§29). He meant that the Roman imperial regime differed from the Hellenistic monarchies—under which the conquered territories were labeled "land of the King"—and suggested that the empire belonged first and foremost to the Roman people. Although Aelius' statement should be considered within the context of the rhetorical strategy in his *Roman Oration*, it nonetheless clearly reflects the perception of a genuine difference between Rome and the Hellenistic kingdoms.

A similar claim is found under the pen of Herodian, who wrote a *History of the Empire* in Greek in the first half of the third century CE. In a speech addressed to the representatives of the Italian cities and attributed to the emperor Maximus (to be identified with Pupienus, who reigned with Balbinus for three months in 238, the "year of the six emperors"), Herodian writes: "The empire is not the private property of a single man but by tradition the common

35. *I.Eph.* 27 (see B, line 165, for the reference to the statue of the Roman people); text and translation in Rogers 1991, 152–185. See Rosso Caponio 2020, 144–150; see also Aitor Blanco Pérez, "The Salutaris Foundation and the Roman Representations in Ephesus," at http://judaism-and-rome.org/salutaris-foundation-and-roman-representations-ephesus.

36. *I.Eph.* 35, lines 17–18 (Greek), 7–8 (Latin); see Oliver 1941, 86–87, no. 4.

37. Rosso Caponio 2020, 151.

possession of the Roman people."[38] In the context of Maximus' discourse, this affirmation goes along with the claim that he had been elected by the Senate and the Roman people and was thus the legitimate emperor, together with Balbinus, in contrast to other pretenders. As in Aelius Aristides' *Roman Oration*, the context is highly rhetorical. It illustrates, however, the longevity of the topos that saw the empire as the common property of the Roman people (which had become nearly equivalent to the free population of the empire after 212). In the Latin panegyrics addressed to various emperors at the end of the third century CE, one also finds references to the *imperium Romanum* (in a territorial sense) and to the *potentia Romana*, which the emperor was supposed to maintain and strengthen.[39] In short, Roman supremacy—associated with the people and the city—continued to be exalted in rhetorical discourses praising the emperor, even though from the mid-third century onward, the latter was also increasingly praised as a global ruler, whose care extended to humankind as a whole.[40]

In the fourth century CE, the Augustan ideology of rule and its concomitant emphasis on the Roman people were still very much alive, or at least easily revived at the rhetorical level. According to Eusebius, Constantine had a cross added to a statue of himself, "in the most frequented part of Rome," engraved with the following legend in Latin: "By virtue of this salutary sign, which is the true test of valor, I have preserved and liberated your city from the yoke of tyranny. I have also set at liberty the Roman senate and people, and restored them to their ancient distinction and splendor."[41] Eusebius' testimony may not be fully reliable, but the reference to the freedom and past glory of the Senate and the people unmistakably recalls Augustus' *Res Gestae* and the ideology of the early Principate.[42] Latin panegyrics dated to the end of the fourth century also testify to the persistence both of the ideal of the emperor-citizen first formulated by Augustus and of references to the Roman people or Rome as a collective.[43] Admittedly, as Ando notes, "the image of the emperor as 'one among many of the same kind as himself' was ultimately supplanted

---

38. Herodian, *History of the Empire* 8.7.5, trans. C. R. Whittaker, LCL, 297.

39. *Latin Panegyrics* 2(10).7.2 (*imperium*), 2(10).8.1 and 4(8).3.3 (*potentia*); see Christol 1999, 362.

40. This is John Weisweiler's conclusion, based on honorific inscriptions dating from the mid-third to the fifth century CE (Weisweiler 2016).

41. Eusebius, *Life of Constantine* 1.40, trans. Ernest Cushing Richardson in Schaff and Wace 1904, 493. See also Eusebius, *Ecclesiastical History* 9.9.11.

42. On Augustus' use as a reference and a model by previous non-Julio-Claudian emperors, starting with Vespasian, see Rosso 2009. In the passage of Eusebius quoted above, "people" refers first and foremost to the population of the *Urbs* rather than to that of the empire as a whole.

43. See, e.g., the praise of Theodosius I composed in 389 CE, *Latin Panegyric* 12(2).12.3–6. See also Symmachus, *Relatio* 3.9–10, probably written when he was the prefect of Rome in 384–385 CE.

by a much more powerful and longer-lasting image, that of an emperor over many who were equal in their subordination to him." Nonetheless, the rhetoric of the elites "implied the priority of Rome herself as the repository of authority."[44] Emperors succeeded one another, and some lasted only a few months on the throne, but "Rome" endured—and even expanded, as the foundation of Constantinople shows.

From the end of the Republic to the fourth century CE, the *imperium* of the *populus Romanus* also received visual expression, on monumental reliefs, precious objects, and coinage, in the figure of the *Genius publicus* or *Genius populi Romani*—a personification of the Roman people and their protective double, to whom a cult was dedicated.[45] The most common representation of the *Genius populi Romani* was a young, seminude, and beardless man; his youth may have symbolized the constant renewal of Rome's strength but was meant also to distinguish this *Genius* from that of the Senate, which was generally represented as an elderly bearded man.[46] Writing at the end of the fourth century CE, Ammianus Marcellinus was still able to report that the *Genius publicus* had come to the emperor Julian in a dream—its last appearance in Roman history . . . [47]

As early as the first century BCE, coins represented the *Genius populi Romani* as a man seated on a curule chair, holding a scepter and a cornucopia, resting one foot on a globe, and crowned by Victoria, the personification or goddess of victory.[48] This was a very explicit iconographic representation of the Roman people's rule and dominion over the world[49] (Fig. 2.1).

44. Ando 2000, 46, 45.

45. See the relief of the Sebasteion of Aphrodisias showing the *Genius* of the Roman people crowning the emperor with an oak wreath (middle of the first century CE), the Arch of Titus (81 CE), the Cancelleria reliefs (dating from the period of Domitian and Nerva; see Béranger 1973, 399–410), the Arch of Trajan in Beneventum (dated to 114 CE), and the relief depicting the *adventus* of Hadrian (125–140 CE), now at the Capitoline Museums. For precious objects, see, e.g., the Boscoreale silver cup representing the triumph of Tiberius, dating from the first half of the first century CE. According to Livy, the *Genius populi Romani* became the focus of a cult in Rome as early as the end of the third century BCE (218/217 BCE, if one follows Livy, 21.62.9).

46. Kunckel 1974, 17.

47. Ammianus Marcellinus, *Res Gestae* 20.5.10.

48. See Crawford 1974, 1:409, no. 397/1, a denarius minted by P. Cornelius Lentulus Spinther in 74 BCE. See also Crawford 1974, no. 393/1a (76/75 BCE), for another clear iconographic association between the *Genius populi Romani* and worldly domination (the reverse portrays a bearded man with a scepter, a wreath, a globe, and a rudder, symbols of Roman rule *terra marique*), with the legend GPR. According to Jean Béranger, this coinage was connected to the party of the *populares*, who supported Marius (Béranger 1973, 412). On the iconography of the *Genius* of the Roman people, as well as those of the Senate and the emperor, see Kunckel 1974, esp. 15–17.

49. Nicolet 1988, 50–53. On the value of coinage as a medium for conveying ideology, see Levick 1982; Noreña 2011.

FIGURE 2.1. Reverse of a denarius representing the *Genius populi Romani* (74 BCE). *RRC* I, no. 397/1. Photograph © The Trustees of the British Museum.

On imperial coinage there are sporadic representations of the *Genius* of the Roman people, most often holding a patera and cornucopia, sometimes a scepter and cornucopia—symbols of Roman rule and of the prosperity that it was supposed to grant.[50] During the third century CE, in a context of

50. Some numismatic items represent the *Genius* but without an explicit legend, whereas others have a legend mentioning the *Genius* of the Roman people but not necessarily a representation of it. On imperial coinage, references to the *Genius* appear first in the context of the civil war of 68–69 CE: see *RIC* I, rev. ed., Civil Wars, Spain, no. 1, p. 203; Gaul, no. 79, p. 209. See further *RIC* II.1, rev. ed., Vespasian, nos. 1353–1356, p. 157 (aurei and denarii with the legend GENIVM [or GENIVS] P•R, representing the *Genius* standing left, holding a patera over an altar, and cornucopiae [no altar in 1354]); Titus, nos. 225–228, pp. 211–212 (asses with the legend GENI [or GENIO] P R, representing the *Genius* in the same way as on Vespasian's coinage); *RIC* II, Hadrian, no. 123, p. 355; no. 249, p. 369 (see also no. 574, p. 412, which does not have GENIUS P R as a legend but does represent the *Genius* standing with a foot on a globe and holding a scepter and cornucopia); *RIC* III, Antoninus Pius, nos. 70–71, p. 34; no. 661, p. 114; nos. 682–683, p. 116, all with the *Genius* of the Roman people standing and holding a scepter and a cornucopia; *RIC* IV.1, Septimius Severus, no. 26, p. 95; no. 43, p. 97, with patera and cornucopia; *RIC* V.1, Interregnum of 275 CE, nos. 1–3, p. 361; *RIC* VI, Antiochia, no. 44a, p. 618 (Diocletian), with modius on head, patera, and cornucopia; *RIC* VI, Treveri, no. 213a, p. 183 (Constantius I), with modius

political instability and constant warfare, the *Genius* of the Roman people appeared less frequently on coins, which tended to feature the *Genius* of the armies instead. With the advent of the Tetrarchy, however, the Roman people's *Genius* played an important role once again, becoming the dominant symbol on coinage from 293 CE until the reign of Constantine.[51] According to Michel Christol, this reference implied an emphasis on the victories and military successes that had made the Roman people great. Moreover, nearly all the imperial mints in the West and the East produced coins with the *Genius* of the Roman people for a period of at least ten years, in a coordinated way, as a means of underscoring the unity and the universality of the empire.[52] Constantine himself inaugurated his reign under the auspices of the *Genius* of the Roman people, which was a powerful symbol of the permanence and unity of the empire despite its changing political structure.[53] Finally, even if the *Genius* tended to disappear from post-Constantinian coinage, references to the Roman people endured, in legends such as *victoria Romanorum* (the victory of the Romans) and *gloria Romanorum* (the glory of the Romans).[54] We must keep in mind that a representation or explicit mention of the *Genius* of the Roman people was just one way among many to refer to the Roman people's might and rule.

On provincial coinage—that is, Roman coinage minted either in the provinces under Roman supervision or by provincial cities (in the latter case, generally limited to bronze issues)—references to the *Genius* of the Roman people remained rare.[55] Under Augustus, one finds a bronze issue from Italica in Spain featuring the legend GEN POP ROM on the reverse and a representation

---

on head, patera, and cornucopia; *RIC* VII, Rome, no. 276, p. 327 (Constantine I), with modius on head, globe, and cornucopia. The list is by no means exhaustive. On the bronze coinage with the *Genius populi Romani* minted under the Tetrarchy, see Christol 2001.

51. See Callu 1960; Sutherland 1963; Béranger 1973, 411–427.

52. See Christol 2001, esp. 211.

53. See *RIC* VII, London, no. 3, p. 97; nos. 30–31, p. 99; nos. 36–42, p. 100; nos. 64–67, p. 101; Rome, no. 276, p. 327 (minted in 326 CE and apparently the last example of this type of coin: see Béranger 1973, 425–426). Constantine also issued bronze coins representing the Roman people, with the inscription "POP(ulus) ROMANVS" (by then also in Constantinople) (see Brénot 1980).

54. During the reign of Julian (361–363), one still finds a nine siliqua with the words *victoria Romanorum* and a representation of Victory, with a shield inscribed VOT / XX supported by a small winged *genius* (*RIC* VIII, Antioch, nos. 207–208, p. 530; see also no. 210, p. 531, a light miliarenses with *victoria Romanorum* but without the *genius*). See also the light miliarensis with *gaudium Romanorum* and a depiction of two captives, in *RIC* VIII, Trier, nos. 151–152, p. 149 (Constantius II; Constans). The legend *gloria Romanorum* was common in the fourth century (see *RIC* VIII, pp. 234–247; no. 194, p. 265; for dozens of examples in *RIC* IX, consult index pp. 319–320).

55. On the nature of provincial coinage, see Amandry 2017, 183–190.

of the *Genius* standing with a globe at his feet.[56] This is a clear reference to Roman dominion over the world, and was a common device on Republican coinage as well. Under Nero, billon tetradrachms were minted in Alexandria, with the Greek inscription *Dēmos Rōmaiōn*, the "people of the Romans," on the reverse side, together with a representation of the *Genius* of the Roman people holding a scepter and a cornucopia.[57] At the time of the Republic, the *Dēmos* of the Romans began to receive a cult in the East, as a source of power that deserved to be honored and propitiated, like the Hellenistic kings.[58] Together with the cult of the goddess *Rhōmē* (on which see below), the cult of the *Dēmos* of the Romans was a way for the Greeks to articulate its relationship with a powerful collective entity that had no king; whereas from a Roman perspective, the cult of the *Dēmos* could be seen as the functional equivalent to the cult of the *Genius populi Romani*.[59] Other items of provincial coinage, however, refer simply to "the Romans." For example, on several silver coins issued by the imperial mint in Mesopotamia under Marcus Aurelius and Lucius Severus in the wake of their victories against the Parthians, we find on the reverse the legend Η ΝΕΙΚΗ ΡΩΜΑΙΩΝ, "the victory of the Romans."[60] Admittedly, these coins come from an imperial mint rather than from a provincial city, but the legend "the victory of the Romans" is also found on bronze issues minted by cities in Asia Minor.[61] These examples show that there were multiple ways to reference the power and rule of the Romans, besides representations of the *Genius* or the *Dēmos*.

Noteworthy in this respect is a bronze coin minted by king Agrippa I in Caesarea (37–44 CE), which features Agrippa sacrificing on a small altar on the obverse and, on the reverse, clasped hands and an oval countermark depicting a male head. The inscription on the reverse states: "Oaths of the great king

56. *RPC* I, Italica, no. 60, p. 78.

57. *RPC* I, Alexandria, nos. 5204, 5214, 5224, 5234, 5243, 5254 (*dēmos* standing with scepter and cornucopia), pp. 706–708.

58. The *dēmoi* of some Greek cities also received cults, a phenomenon described by J. Rufus Fears as "a by-product of the ruler cult" (Fears 1981, 852).

59. See Fears 1978, esp. 280–281, 286.

60. And variants thereof. See *RPC* IV (available at http://rpc.ashmus.ox.ac.uk/), Imperial Mint in Mesopotamia (Carrhae or Edessa), nos. 6494 (representing Nikē standing on a globe, holding a wreath and palm branch), 6496–6499, 6501–6502, 6859, 8525, 8631 (with the unusual representation of Iustitia/Dikaiosynē standing, holding scales and a cornucopia), 9577–9578, 10706–10707, 10746, 10748–10749, 10754. See also nos. 6495 and 8035, representing Armenia. The numbers are provisional.

61. *RPC* IV, Ephesus, nos. 1143 (minted in 161–165 CE, representing Nikē standing with a foot on a globe, inscribing a shield attached to a palm tree, with the legend ΡΩΜΑΙΩΝ ΝΕΙΚΗ ΕΦΕ C ΙΩΝ), 2671 (similar, but with the legend ΘΕΑ ΡΩΜΑΙΩΝ ΝΕΙΚΗ ΕΦΕ C ΙΩΝ); *RPC* IV, Nicaea, nos. 5542, 5979–5980, 9434 (the last example was minted in 161–169 CE and represents Nikē standing, facing forward, holding a shield and transverse trophy, with the legend ΡΩΜΑΙΩΝ ΝΙΚΗΝ ΝΙΚΑΙΕΙ C).

Agrippa for Augustus Caesar and the people (*dēmos*) of the Romans."[62] This coin is yet another example, stemming from Judea itself, of the persistence of joint references to the Roman people alongside the emperor. (It is also worth recalling the response to the Roman governor Petronius that Josephus attributes to the Judeans who tried to prevent the erection of Caligula's statue in the Jerusalem Temple: "We offer sacrifices twice every day for Caesar and the Roman people" [*B.J.* 2.197; see also *C. Ap.* 2.77].)

The dominion of the Roman people was thus proclaimed and represented visually through a great variety of media—texts, numismatic items, monuments, and other objects—from the end of the Republic down to the fourth century. Statues spoke a particularly powerful visual language, especially when they were paraded at festivals. Moreover, these references to representations of the Roman people were not merely rhetorical artifice. They expressed a real ideology, both in Roman discourse and imagery and in their provincial appropriations. No matter where Jews resided within the empire, be it Italy, Asia Minor, Judea, or elsewhere, there was hardly a place where they would not have been exposed to such representations.

1.3 ROMA: CITY, PERSONIFICATION, AND GODDESS

The Roman people was a collective entity. So was Roma, the personification of Rome, who eventually became a goddess—*thea Rhōmē* in Greek, *dea Roma* in Latin. The difference between a personification and a deity lies in the cult offered to the latter: whereas a personification can be praised in speeches and dedications of all kinds, a cult involves more: sacrifices, nonsacrificial offerings, and other honors.[63] From the second century BCE onward, Roma had a cult in the East. The cult of Roma, like that of the *Dēmos* of the Romans, at first developed in the tradition of Hellenistic ruler cults; that is, as a way, in the absence of a king, to cope with Rome's power.[64] A festival, the *Rhōmaia*, was created in honor of the goddess, with sacrifices, athletic contests, cultural competitions, and paeans sung to *Rhōmē*.[65]

In the imperial period, the cult of Roma might well have faded away, as there were now specific rulers embodying Roman power, to whom a cult could be dedicated. Nonetheless, Roma continued to receive cultic honors alongside the emperor.[66] Temples were dedicated to Roma and Octavian/Augustus as early as 29 BCE in Pergamon and Nicomedia. Herod the Great had such a temple built in Caesarea Maritima. This phenomenon was not restricted to the East,

62. Meshorer 1982, 248, no. 5a: ΟΡΚΙΑ ΒΑΣ(ΙΛΕΩΣ) ΜΕ[ΓΑΛΟΥ] ΑΓΡΙΠΑ ΠΡ[ΟΣ] ΣΕΒ[ΑΣΤΟΥ] ΚΑΙΣ[ΑΡΟΣ] Κ[ΑΙ] ΔΗΜ Ο[Υ] ΡΩΜ[ΑΙΩΝ].

63. Champeaux 2008, 86. Fears has a more complex approach to this issue: see Fears 1981.

64. Mellor 1975; 1981.

65. Mellor 1975, 165–180; van Nijf and van Dijk 2020.

66. According to Suetonius, *Augustus* 52, this was a requirement of Augustus himself.

where the cults of living rulers had been common since the Hellenistic period, but also spread to the West, where it pertained to the *Numen* or the *Genius* of the *princeps*.[67] An altar was dedicated to Roma and Augustus in Lyon in 12 BCE.[68] Temples were dedicated to Roma and Augustus in various other places as well, such as Pola (in modern Croatia, during Augustus' lifetime), Narbo (in Southern France, in 11 CE), and Leptis Magna (in Libya, between 14 and 19 CE).[69] These temples were also frequently represented on coinage, both imperial and provincial.[70] Moreover, under Hadrian, a temple to Venus and Roma was erected in Rome itself, the largest temple (or twin temples) ever built in the city, probably between 128 (when the 880th *natalis Urbis Romae*, or birthday of the city of Rome, was celebrated) and 136 or 137 CE.[71] In 307 CE it was rebuilt by Maxentius after having been damaged by a fire.[72] It was still standing when Constantius II visited Rome in 357, according to Ammianus Marcellinus (*Res Gestae* 16.10.14), and was probably closed only under Theodosius I.

The commemoration of the *natalis* was a way to celebrate not only the city but also the power that it represented, its stability and even its eternity. The papyrus from Dura Europos mentioned above, which lists the public festivals to be celebrated by the Roman army, prescribes the sacrifices to be offered to Roma on the anniversary of the city's foundation, XI Kal. May (21 April).[73] If the proposed reconstruction of the text is correct, in that context Rome is called "eternal."[74]

As we saw previously, the *Feriale Duranum* papyrus also refers to the eternity of the Roman people's *imperium*, yet another indication of how the people and the city were associated in the ideology of Rome's unique destiny. It is an association found repeatedly on coinage: for example, in Constantinople, the "new Rome," a bronze issue was minted in 327 CE that represents on the reverse Roma helmeted, standing on a shield, and holding a long scepter and

---

67. See Cassius Dio, *Rom. Hist.* 51.20.6. On the imperial cult in the East (Asia Minor), see Price 1984. On the development of the imperial cult in the West, see Fishwick 1987–2005. See also the useful clarification by Scheid 2007b, esp. 671.

68. *CIL* XIII, 1664; Fishwick 1987–2005, 1:104–105, on the coins representing the altar, with the legend ROM ET AVG. Cf. Strabo, *Geography* 4.3.2; Suetonius, *Claudius* 2.1; Cassius Dio, *Rom. Hist.* 54.32.1, which do not mention Roma.

69. Narbo: *CIL* XII, 4333; Leptis Magna: *Iscrizioni Puniche della Tripolitania* (*IPT*) 22.

70. See, e.g., *RPC* III, Cistophoric Mint in Asia, no. 1303, p. 162, a silver issue minted in 96 CE (Nerva), featuring a distyle temple, with Corinthian columns on a two-step podium and ROMA ET AVG on the architrave, within which a female figure is standing facing forward on the right, holding a cornucopia in her left hand and crowning the emperor, who stands on the left, with a scepter in his right hand.

71. Turcan 1964.

72. Aurelius Victor, *De Caesaribus* 40.26.

73. P. Dura 54, col. 2, line 5. See note 29 above. On the celebration of Rome's birthday, see also *Latin Panegyric* 2(10).1 (289 CE).

74. On the eternity of Rome—that is, of the empire—see §3.1 below.

a Victory on a globe, with the legend GLORIA RO-MANORUM, "the glory of the Romans."[75]

Roma had been a traditional motif on Republican coinage, was featured frequently on imperial coinage as well, and was still found on the reverse of many coins in the fourth century CE. This in spite of the growing importance of other cities as imperial residences.[76] Admittedly, some emperors more than others promoted her numismatic representation. For example, the Tetrarchs, who did not spend much time in Rome, did not give Roma a prominent place on their coinage. Maxentius (306–312), who, from the beginning of his reign, benefited from the support of the praetorian troops and the Senate in Rome, took the opposite course and presented himself on numerous issues as the champion of the *Urbs*. As mentioned above, he also rebuilt the temple of Venus and Roma that had been damaged by a fire.[77]

Through the centuries, Roma appeared on coinage and in reliefs and sculptures in various guises, frequently as a helmeted woman, seated (on a throne or a pile of weapons, or in front of a temple, etc.); holding or resting her foot on a globe (symbolizing universal rule); carrying a small winged Victory, a scepter, a spear, or the *palladium* (on which more below); as crowning an emperor or handing him a globe; or as being herself crowned by Victoria, next to a shield or the spoils of war.[78] On Greek coinage, which began to represent Roma around 200 BCE, she was often depicted as an Amazon, as Athena, or with a turreted crown, like the *Tychai* of Greek cities (the *tychē*, literally "fortune," of a city was both a personification and a deity).[79] This iconography also occurs

75. *RIC* VII, Constantinople, no. 17, p. 572; see also no. 23, p. 573.

76. Concerning Roma on Republican coinage, see Crawford 1974, 2:721–725. On the period running from the Tetrarchs to Constantine, see Hekster 1999.

77. See, e.g., *RIC* VI, Aquileia, no. 113, p. 325; see also the detailed commentary of Marie Roux, "Bronze Depicting the Head of Maxentius and the Emperor Together with Roma (307 CE)," at http://judaism-and-rome.org/bronze-depicting-head-maxentius-and-emperor-together -roma-307-ce. On the presence of the emperors in Rome, see the articles in "La présence impériale dans la Rome tardo-antique / Imperial Presence in Late Antique Rome," special issue, *Antiquité Tardive* 25 (2017); on Maxentius in particular, Corcoran 2017.

78. On the iconography of Roma, see Mellor 1981; Di Filippo Balestrazzi 1997 (*LIMC* VIII.1, s.v. "Roma"; *LIMC* VIII.2, 696–723, for the images), which uses the threefold classification of "Amazonian," "semi-Amazonian," and "non-Amazonian" costume (this threefold classification differs from the three types of representations found in the Sebasteion—see below).

79. Mellor 1975, 162–164. On Roman provincial coinage, see, e.g., *RPC* I, Cnossus, no. 978, p. 237 (bronze issue minted under Augustus, representing Roma wearing a tunic, standing to the left, and holding a small Victory and a transverse scepter, with RO MA in the field); *RPC* I, Magnesia ad Sipylum, no. 2459, p. 416 (bronze issue minted in 62 CE, with a turreted bust of Roma and a reference to *thea Rhōmē* in the legend); *RPC* II, Syria, no. 1910, p. 271 (an aureus minted under Vespasian: with Roma seated on two round shields, holding a long spear resting on one shield and a parazonium resting on a knee, with the legend ROMA); *RPC* II, Alexandria, no. 2508, p. 329 (minted under Domitian; Roma stands with a spear and a Victory, with the legend ΡΩΜΗ); *RPC* III, Hierapolis, no. 2350, p. 291 (minted under Trajan; Roma is helmeted and seated to the left on a cuirass

in the reliefs of the Aphrodisias Sebasteion in Asia Minor, a cultic complex dedicated to Aphrodite and the Julio-Claudian emperors (20–60 CE). There we find three types of representations: Roma standing, with a turreted crown and a spear or a scepter; Roma standing, with a Corinthian helmet, armor, a shield, and a spear—a military style that recalls statues of Mars Ultor—flanked by a kneeling barbarian captive; and Roma as an Amazon[80] (Fig. 2.2).

We shall return to the Sebasteion complex later, as several aspects of its iconography document the reception of Roman imperial ideology in a provincial context. Moreover, inscriptions indicate that a Jewish community was established in Aphrodisias in late antiquity, whose origin may go back to the Early Roman period.[81] The Jews living in Aphrodisias in the third or fourth century CE would in any case still have seen the Sebasteion with its powerful visual language. Indeed countless examples show that up to the fourth century, Roma represented a collective entity strongly associated with military victory and universal rule and was a powerful symbol of the enduring might of the Roman people.

From a Jewish perspective, the main difficulty with the representations and the cult of Roma was not so much that the latter was deified—in a polytheistic world, a new deity was not a major challenge. It was instead the politico-religious message and rituals associated with Roma that proved problematic.[82] As both a personification and a goddess, she represented Rome's exceptional might, power, and destiny, which were manifested and celebrated through images, rituals, and festivals, particularly in the East. Roma could thus be perceived as the embodiment of the challenge that the Roman empire posed to the Jews.

---

and round shield, holding Nikē on her extended right hand, a parazonium in her left, with the legend ΘΕΑ ΡΩΜΗ); *RPC* III, Antioch, no. 3568, p. 463 (minted in 100 CE; Roma is seated to the left on pile of arms, holding Nikē on her extended right hand and a parazonium in her left, which leans on a round shield); *RPC* III, Pergamum, no. 1725, p. 210 (dated to 114–116) and Stratonicea, no. 1774, p. 216 (minted under Trajan; in both cases, Roma is turreted, with the legend *thea Rhōmē*); *RPC* III, Edessa, no. 603, p. 76 (minted under Hadrian; Roma sits on a cuirass and shield, holding Nikē on her extended right hand; behind her, a turreted or helmeted figure of the city-goddess of Edessa stands to the left and crowns her); *RPC* IV, Aelia Capitolina, no. 9271 (Meshorer, Aelia Capitolina 44) (minted under Marcus Aurelius; Roma [or Minerva/Athena?], seated, holds a Victoria and a spear; in front of her seat are a cuirass and shield; legend: COLoNIAE AELIAE CAPIToLINAE); *RPC* VI, Alexandria, no. 10233 (minted under Alexander Severus, in 222 CE; Roma is seated on a throne, wearing a helmet and holding a scepter and Nikē with wreath). An original representation of Roma is found on Corinthian coinage under Commodus (184–190 CE): she advances, holding a transverse spear, carrying a trophy over her shoulder, and resting her left foot on an uncertain object; see, e.g., *RPC* IV, Corinth, no. 5198.

80. See Smith 2013, plates 56 (C 7), 80 (C 24), for the first two types; on the third, see Rosso Caponio 2020, 131–138; on the reliefs from the Sebasteion, see also Chapter Three. Other reliefs featuring Roma include the Arch of Titus (81 CE), the Antonine altar at Ephesus (169 CE), and the Arch of Galerius in Thessaloniki (298–299 CE).

81. Reynolds and Tannenbaum 1987.

82. See the discussion below of m. Avodah Zarah 3:1 and y. Avodah Zarah 3:1, 42c.

FIGURE 2.2. Relief from the Sebasteion in Aphrodisias: Roma standing.
Photograph © New York University Excavations at Aphrodisias (G. Petruccioli).

2. The "Election" of the Romans

2.1 A DIVINE SCHEME

Both the Romans and the Jews had a clear sense of a historical destiny that was both unique and the will of the gods or God. In the case of the Romans, one need only recall the words of Pliny the Elder, that Rome (and Italy more widely) had been "chosen by the providence [or: the will] of the gods (*numine deum electa*) [. . .] to become throughout the world the single fatherland (*patria*) of all the races (*gentium*)."[83]

That Rome's foundation had been willed by at least some of the gods and the city and its people destined for a unique fate received vivid expression in the myth of Aeneas, which was given particular literary prominence with the publication of Virgil's *Aeneid* (written between 29 and 19 BCE). In Book 1, lines 234–237, Venus addresses Jupiter in the following terms: "Surely it was your promise that from them [the Trojans] some time, as the years rolled on, the Romans were to arise; from them, even from Teucer's restored line, should come rulers to hold the sea and all lands beneath their sway."[84] Jupiter's response fully confirms the glorious fate that awaits Aeneas, Ascanius, and their descendants, Romulus and the whole Roman people. It is aptly encapsulated in the famous verses "For these I set no bounds in space or time; but have given empire without end" (1.278–279; see further §3.1 below).

Other poets were no less eloquent than Virgil. Tibullus, for example, also celebrated Aeneas, addressing him as

Unwearying Aeneas, brother of winged Love,
sailing with Ilium's sacred gear in exile,
now Jupiter apportions you Laurentine fields
and welcome land invites your wandering Lares.

[. . .]

Crop while you may, O bulls, the grass on the Seven Hills:
here shall be the site of a mighty city—
Rome, the name predestined for empire of the world (*Roma, tuum
    nomen terris fatale regendis*) . . . [85]

---

83. Pliny, *Natural History* 3.5.39, trans. H. Rackham, LCL, 33. On the connection between Roman piety and divine providence on behalf of Rome, see §2.3 below.

84. Virgil, *Aeneid* 1.234–237, trans. H. Rushton Fairclough (revised by G. P. Goold), LCL, 279. See also 6.851–853.

85. Tibullus, *Elegies* 2.5.39–42, 55–57, trans. Guy Lee, 3rd rev. ed. (Meksham: F. Cairns, 1990), 65.

Again we encounter the idea that Rome's destiny to rule the world goes back to the figure of Aeneas and Jupiter's decision concerning the descendants of the Trojan hero. In connection with Romulus, through whom the promise made to Aeneas would materialize, one should also note the use of the expression "people of Romulus" (*gens Romula* or *genus Romuleum*) by poets from Horace up to Prudentius at the beginning of the fifth century.[86]

The story of the mythological origins of Rome associated with Aeneas and Romulus and of Rome and the Roman's implied "election" by the gods included numerous episodes: Aeneas' flight from Troy with his father, Anchises (carried on his shoulders), and his son, Ascanius;[87] the discovery of a sow and her young, indicating that Aeneas' wanderings had come to an end and he could found his city, the ancestor of Rome; the story of Mars and Rhea Silvia; the she-wolf suckling the twins; and the foundation of Rome by Romulus. These episodes and characters were widely alluded to in literary works, and represented in reliefs, wall paintings, statues, and on coinage.[88] Paul Zanker notes that "the motif of Aeneas and his family was also widespread on finger rings, lamps, and in terra-cotta statuettes, and undoubtedly served as a token of loyalty," at least in the context of Augustus' Principate.[89]

The political use that Augustus made of his genealogy through his adoptive father, Julius Caesar, which made the princeps a descendant of Aeneas and of Venus herself, is well known. Both Aeneas and Romulus were found in Augustus' temple to Mars Ultor in Rome and on the *Ara Pacis*, the "altar of peace," in a way that highlighted "the divine providence that governed Roman history from the beginning."[90] Augustus was clearly presented as the perfect

---

86. Horace, *Odes* 4.5.1–2, *Carm. Saec.* 47; Prudentius, *Against Symmachus*, preface, 80.

87. See Virgil, *Aeneid* 2.707–725; Dionysius of Halicarnassus, *Roman Antiquities* 1.46–48.

88. On the iconography of these mythological episodes at the time of Augustus, see Zanker 1988, 201–210; Spannagel 1999, 90–131 (on the Aeneas group in the Forum of Augustus), 132–161 (on Romulus in the same Forum), 162–205 (on their respective myths and reception history), and the corresponding illustrations at the end. On the various episodes of the "Aeneas legend" on coinage, see Duncan 1948. The she-wolf with the twins was a particularly recurrent motif: see, e.g., *RIC* II.1, rev. ed., Vespasian, no. 108, p. 67, and no. 193, p. 73 (sestertii with the legend ROMA and S C in the field, representing Roma standing to the right on the seven hills, on the left the she-wolf and the twins, and on the right the river Tiber; both minted in 71 CE).

89. Conversely, the Aeneas paintings from Pompeii, which consist of a parody of Aeneas and Romulus as dog-headed apes, reveal an ironic approach to the myth in the first century CE. See Zanker 1988, 209; Kellum 1997, 173–176 (which insists that the celebratory and the amusing are mixed and that one should not read such caricatures merely in political terms).

90. Zanker 1988, 203.

embodiment of this providence at work in Roman history, as were other emperors after him.[91]

Mythological scenes associated with Rome's unique destiny were occasionally represented during the reigns of various emperors up to the fourth century CE, even though the great majority of imperial coins tended to emphasize "the charismatic claims of the emperor to rule, based on his virtues and his own achievements," rather than myths.[92] The celebration of Rome's ninth centenary, in 148 CE, under Antoninus Pius, prompted the issuing of a great number of coins (or medallions) featuring mythological scenes.[93] This was in line with Antoninus Pius' inclination to present his reign as a return of Rome's Golden Age. Christopher Howgego argues that it "was also a reflection of the Hellenization of the Antonine court: this was the time of an explosion of mythology on coinage throughout much of the Greek East."[94]

According to Thomas S. Duncan, Roman coinage shows that, in particular, the story of the she-wolf suckling Romulus and Remus was always popular.[95] In 248 CE, for the celebration of Rome's thousandth anniversary and the *ludi saeculares* (Secular Games), Philip I issued coins with the she-wolf suckling the twins.[96] At the beginning of the fourth century, Maxentius issued coins representing the she-wolf and the twins with legends referring to the "felicity of the times" (*felicitas temporum*) or the empire's eternity (*aeternitas*).[97] Particularly interesting for an assessment of the motif's impact on the Jews of Palestine, including the rabbis, is the fact that in the third century, coins from Aelia Capitolina, Caesarea, Neapolis, and Sebaste—which all had colonial status at the time—depicted the she-wolf suckling the twins.[98] On provincial coinage, this scene seems to have been much more common than that of Aeneas with Anchises and Ascanius, which is mostly restricted to certain

---

91. See, e.g., *RIC* II, Hadrian, no. 602a–b, p. 418 (mint of Rome, between 119 and 121 CE), which has the inscription PROVIDENTIA DEORUM S C on the reverse and a representation of Hadrian standing and looking left toward an eagle; no. 589a–b, p. 415.

92. Howgego 2005, 5.

93. Aeneas with Anchises and Ascanius: *RIC* III, no. 91, p. 37; no. 615, p. 109; no. 629, p. 111; the sow with the piglets: *RIC* III, no. 722, p. 119; no. 733, p. 120; the she-wolf suckling the twins: *RIC* III, nos. 94–96, p. 37; no. 603, p. 108; nos. 630–634, p. 111; nos. 648–650, p. 113; no. 718, p. 119; nos. 734–735, p. 120; Romulus: *RIC* III, no. 90, p. 37; no. 624, p. 110; no. 645, p. 112; no. 665, p. 114; no. 698, p. 117. See also the three medallions representing Aeneas analyzed in Toynbee 1925.

94. Howgego 2005, 5.

95. Duncan 1948, 20.

96. *RIC* IV.3, Philip I, nos. 15–16, p. 70 (aurei). For Rome's anniversary in 228 CE, Severus Alexander minted silver issues featuring Romulus: see *RIC* IV.2, nos. 85–86, p. 77; nos. 481–483, p. 109.

97. Cullhed 1994, 47–49, referring to *RIC* VI, Rome, no. 190, p. 375; Ostia, no. 5, p. 401; Ostia, no. 13, p. 402; Ostia, nos. 39–42, p. 404; etc.

98. Belayche 2009, 171–174. For Neapolis, see Meshorer 1985, no. 148, Trebonianus Gallus.

FIGURE 2.3. Denarius representing Hadrian on the obverse, and Roma with the
palladium on the reverse (117–138 CE).
RIC II, no. 265, p. 370. Photograph © The Trustees of the British Museum.

cities, among them Ilium (founded on the site of Troy), Apamea, and Darda-
nus. The representation of Aeneas' flight from Troy in a relief at the Aphrodisias Sebasteion was probably a way to emphasize the common connection of
Aphrodisias and Rome with Aphrodite-Venus.[99]

Another symbol of Rome's exceptional destiny strongly associated with Aeneas'
legend was the *palladium*, an archaic statue of Pallas that stood in Troy and was
said to ensure the city's safety. According to the most common version of the legend, it was stolen by Diomedes and Odysseus and eventually arrived in Rome,
where it was kept in the temple of Vesta and became a token of the city's *imperium* (*pignus imperii*), guaranteeing Rome's safety and longevity.[100] The temple
of Venus and Roma contained a statue of Roma that probably held the *palladium* (or a Victory) in her right hand.[101] On coinage too, Roma was occasionally
depicted holding the *palladium* or presenting it to the emperor[102] (Fig. 2.3).

99. Smith 2013, plate 104, also plate 102 (Anchises and Aphrodite); Jones 2001b.

100. Assenmaker 2010.

101. See Beard, Price, and North 1998, 1:257–259. See also Champeaux 2008, 92–93.

102. See, e.g., *RIC* II.1, rev. ed., Titus, nos. 166–167, p. 209 (sestertii minted in 80/81 CE,
representing Roma standing, foot on globe, and presenting the *palladium* to Titus, who is rid-
ing a horse on the left and holding a scepter); *RIC* II, Hadrian, no. 773, p. 439 (sestertius representing Roma helmeted, standing, and holding the *palladium* and a spear); no. 824, p. 444
(dupondius or as representing Roma standing, holding the *palladium* and a spear); *RIC* III,
Antoninus Pius, no. 159a, p. 45 (aureus representing Roma sitting, holding the *palladium*
and a spear, with a shield to the side); *RIC* III, Marcus Aurelius, nos. 138–140, p. 224 (denarii
with Roma seated on a shield, holding the *palladium* and a parazonium); *RIC* IV.1, Clodius
Albinus, no. 11, p. 45 (aureus representing Roma helmeted and seated on a shield, holding the
palladium and a scepter, with the legend ROMAE AETERNAE); *RIC* IV.1, Septimius Severus,
nos. 288 and 291, p. 127 (two aurei, both representing Roma seated on a shield and holding

Pierre Assenmaker notes that in the second century CE, the *palladium* was also represented on the cuirasses of imperial statues and seems to have become particularly significant under Hadrian, as a symbol of imperial sovereignty and of Rome's grandiose fate. In the fourth century, Constantine had the *palladium* transferred to Constantinople, which was thus designated as inheriting Rome's election and destiny.[103]

{⸻❧⸻}

Moshe Weinfeld has argued that while Aeneas' story has clear similarities with Greek founding myths, there are also striking parallels between Virgil's epic and the biblical narrative of Abraham.[104] Both Aeneas and Abraham were called upon to leave their homelands in order to receive a new land and give birth to a new people, who are fated ultimately to prevail over all others and rule the world. These parallels could hardly have escaped Jews exposed to Roman imperial ideology, particularly in Rome but also in the wider empire.

Yet it is the stories concerning Romulus, Remus, and the foundation of Rome that particularly caught the attention of the rabbis and were explicitly integrated into a rabbinic vision of Roman—and thus world—history. The first example comes from Sifre Deuteronomy (a third-century CE halakhic midrash), if we follow the testimony of one manuscript, MS London, and the Venetian printed edition (with slight variants); alternately, this textual tradition could result from the integration, at some point in the transmission history, of a development found in the Jerusalem Talmud, which we will examine below.[105] When evoking king Solomon's special love for his Egyptian wife, the "daughter of Pharaoh," the midrash (in the Venice edition) states:

> On the day that Solomon wed Pharaoh's daughter, Gabriel descended and stuck a reed in the sea, which raised a sandbank upon which the city of Rome would be built. And on the day when Jeroboam set up the two [golden] calves, Remus and Romulus built two cities in Rome.[106]

The reference to "two cities" is strange and is replaced by the phrase "two huts" in other versions (see below). It may reflect the idea that there was a rivalry between Romulus and Remus, each of whom wanted to found his own city. Whatever the case, a more elaborate version of this story is found in the

---

the *palladium* and a spear, the second one with the legend ROMA AETERNA); *RIC* IV.1, Caracalla, no. 167, p. 235 (aureus with Roma seated and holding the *palladium* and a spear). Over time, the *palladium* was increasingly associated with gold coinage.

103. Assenmaker 2010, 62.

104. Weinfeld 1993, 2–22.

105. On the possibility of late redactional stages of halakhic midrashim, see Stemberger 2010, 131–133.

106. Sifre Deuteronomy 52, ed. Finkelstein, 119.

Jerusalem Talmud, tractate Avodah Zarah (on "idolatry"), in the context of a discussion of a few Roman festivals: the Kalends, the Saturnalia, and one named Kratesis.[107] Because *krateō* means "to seize" and *kratēsis* can have the sense of "empowerment" or "power," the rabbis understood the Kratesis festival as a celebration of "the day on which the Romans seized power." It is unclear whether this refers to Roman victories in the East, Augustus' victory at Actium, or the accession to power of a new emperor, but the last hypothesis is the most probable.[108] At this point, the following explanation is added:

> [Kratesis] is the day on which Solomon married into [the family of] Pharaoh Necho, king of Egypt. On that day [the angel] Michael came down and thrust a reed into the sea, and pulled up muddy alluvium, and it grew to a large thicket of reeds, and this was the great city of Rome. On the day on which Jeroboam erected the two golden calves, Remus and Romulus came and built two huts in the city of Rome. On the day on which Elijah disappeared, a king was appointed in Rome: "There was no king, in Edom a deputy was king" (1 Kings 22:48).[109]

In short, the idolatrous behavior of the kings of Israel and Judah is presented by the Jerusalem Talmud as the true cause of the foundation of Rome, and Israel is thereby granted a determining factor in Rome's fate. This connection between the history of biblical Israel and the history of Rome is found elsewhere in rabbinic literature, as we shall see in the following sections and chapters. It contrasts sharply with parallel Christian attempts to correlate the two histories, which mainly consist in a chronological juxtaposition.[110]

Sarit Kattan Gribetz points to a coin minted under Antoninus Pius as a possible background to the talmudic account: on the reverse it represents the Tiber (a personification or a god) with a reed in his hand and is meant as a celebration of Rome's origins on the muddy shores of the river.[111] Instead of the Tiber, in the rabbinic rendering it is the archangel Michael who makes the

---

107. I consider the Jerusalem Talmud's final redaction, or editing, to date from the second half of the fourth century CE, following the analysis of Leib Moscovitz, who dates it to 360–370 (Moscovitz 2006, 665–667).

108. Graf 2002, 437–438; 2015, 68–69. See t. Avodah Zarah 1:3.

109. y. Avodah Zarah 1:3, 39c (according to MS Leiden, Scaliger 3), trans. Sarit Kattan Gribetz in Kattan Gribetz 2016, 66. For a discussion of the parallels in rabbinic literature and the variants, see ibid., n. 29. See also Schäfer 2002b, 341–342. On the version found in Song of Songs Rabbah 1:6, featuring Abba Kolon, see Rieger 1926; Feldman 1990–91.

110. See, e.g., Augustine, *The City of God* 18.26: "Then under Darius, king of the Persians, when the seventy years that Jeremiah the prophet had foretold were completed, the captivity was ended and liberty was restored to the Jews, in the reign of Tarquin, the seventh king of the Romans. On his expulsion the Romans themselves also began to be free from the domination of their kings" (trans. Eva M. Sanford, LCL, 457).

111. Kattan Gribetz 2016, 68–69. See *RIC* III, Antoninus Pius, nos. 642–643, p. 112 (sestertii); no. 691a, p. 116 (as), all minted in Rome in 140–144 CE.

city emerge from water, obviously at God's command and as a chastisement of Israel. The Talmud thus proposes a counternarrative to the glorious and providential history of Rome reflected in Roman and pro-Roman sources, a counterhistory that casts Rome's foundation in a negative light and severs its connection to the Roman gods.[112]

2.2 ROMAN VIRTUES

From a Roman (elite) perspective, the divine "election" of the Romans was justified by their virtues. Rome was the homeland that deserved the greatest love, according to Cicero, because "alone among all lands" it was "the home of excellence (*virtus*), imperial power (*imperium*) and good report (*dignitas*)."[113] Moreover, it was *virtus* that made Rome worthy to command other nations.[114] *Virtus* referred primarily to manliness, in the sense of physical courage and military valor.[115] It was an omnipresent characteristic of the Romans in literary accounts of their history and was perceived as having played an important role in their victories and accomplishments, especially in the time of the Republic.[116] It had a political connotation too, when it referred to great deeds performed for the sake of the state.[117]

In the ethos of the elite, *virtus* could also mean "virtue," or moral perfection, and Roman and pro-Roman sources alike characterized the Romans as "virtuous" in a more general and ethical sense, which did not conflict with the original one of manliness.[118] Dionysius of Halicarnassus, for example, wrote

112. Beyond the passage considered here, Kattan Gribetz analyzes this rabbinic discussion of Roman festivals as a kind of hidden transcript and a response to the Romans' calendar, which imposed its own, imperial construction of time, and especially its imperial festivals, on the provincials. She sees this text as reflecting both integration into the Roman world and resistance to it (Kattan Gribetz 2016, esp. 61; she refers to the notion of "counter-history" used by Amos Funkenstein on p. 64; see also Kattan Gribetz 2020, Chapter One). Rabbinic renderings of the myth of Romulus and Remus found in much later midrashim are less negative. Louis Feldman mentions that Midrash Psalms 10.6 (ed. Buber, p. 95) "refers to them [Romulus and Remus] as fatherless children who, when their mother would not raise them, were nurtured by a she-wolf summoned by God to suckle them, and who later built two huts on the site of Rome in fulfillment of the passage, 'Thou hast been the helper of the fatherless' (Ps 10:14)" (Feldman 1990–91, 242). Although the verse quoted here states that God helped Romulus and Remus, a connection with Israel's sin is lacking.

113. Cicero, *On the Making of an Orator* 1.44.196, trans. E. W. Sutton and H. Rackham, LCL, 137.

114. See Livy, 1.9.4; Lind 1972, 241, 248.

115. Laconi 1988, 13; McDonnel 2006, 12–14.

116. See, e.g., Livy, 7.6.3, telling the story of the self-sacrifice of Marcus Curtius, who contended that the supreme good for the Romans was *arma virtusque*, "arms and valor." On Romans as warriors, see further Chapter Three.

117. Galinsky 1996, 84.

118. McDonnel 2006, 385.

that "Rome from the very beginning, immediately after its founding, produced infinite examples of virtue in men whose superiors, whether for piety or for justice or for life-long self-control or for warlike valour, no city, either Greek or barbarian, has ever produced."[119] The virtues (*aretai*) he singles out here are *eusebeia* (piety), justice (*dikaiosynē*), self-control or temperance (*sōphrosynē*), and military valor (Dionysius uses a periphrase, but the corresponding virtue would be *andreia* in Greek and *virtus* in Latin). These are nearly identical with the four cardinal virtues of the Greek philosophical tradition (*phronēsis*, *andreia*, *sōphrosynē*, *dikaiosynē*), with piety replacing wisdom. Yet they are also very similar to the four virtues associated with the *clipeus virtutis*, the golden "shield of virtue" offered to Augustus by the Senate in 27 BCE, a marble copy of which was found in a sanctuary dedicated to the imperial cult in the colony of Arelate (Arles), suggesting that copies were probably sent to various cities throughout the empire.[120] The inscription on the *clipeus* mentioned *virtus, clementia, iustitia*, and *pietas*. The similarity between Dionysius' list and that of the *clipeus* shows the extent to which Dionysius was steeped in the imperial ideology of his time and illustrates as well the perception of the princeps as embodying the traditional Roman virtues.[121]

Dionysius was in fact responding to Greek authors who argued that Rome had achieved universal dominion "not through reverence for the gods and justice and every other virtue, but through some chance and the injustice of Fortune (*Tychē*), which inconsiderately showers her greatest favours upon the most undeserving"[122]—an issue already raised by Polybius.[123] At the beginning of the second century CE, Plutarch dedicated a whole treatise to the question of whether the Romans' achievements were due to Fortune (*Tychē*) or Virtue (*Aretē*) and concluded that it was the combination of both that had made Rome so great. Although *virtus* and *aretē* are not exact equivalents—as mentioned above, *virtus* could also correspond to *andreia*—the championing of the Romans' moral excellence is common to Cicero and Plutarch, with the reservation that for Plutarch, writing such a treatise may have been a mere school exercise in his early intellectual life. Yet the example of Ammianus Marcellinus shows that members of the Roman elite continued to voice these themes up to the end of the fourth century, when he still evoked Rome's destiny in terms of Virtue and Fortune:

119. Dionysius of Halicarnassus, *Rom. Ant.* 1.5.3, trans. Earnest Cary, LCL, 17–19. (We shall examine *pietas* in detail in the next section and consider justice in Chapter Four.)

120. *AE* 1952, 165, dated to 26 BCE; Augustus, *Res Gestae* 34; Galinsky 1996, 89–90. The shield appears on coins and lamps as well. See, e.g., *RIC* I, rev. ed., Augustus, Spain, no. 85a, p. 47, an aureus from 19 BCE with the *clipeus* on the reverse.

121. On the *clipeus* and the fact that the virtues it listed were also those of the *res publica* and "as such shared by all," see Galinsky 1996, 80.

122. Dionysius of Halicarnassus, *Rom. Ant.* 1.4.2, trans. Earnest Cary, LCL, 15.

123. Polybius, *Histories* 1.63.9; Ferrary 1988, 265–276, esp. 271.

At the time when Rome first began to rise into a position of world-wide splendour, destined to live so long as men shall exist, in order that she might grow to a towering stature, Virtue (*Virtus*) and Fortune (*Fortuna*), ordinarily at variance, formed a pact of eternal peace; for if either one of them had failed her, Rome had not come to complete supremacy.[124]

At the beginning of the fifth century, Augustine rejected the idea that Rome's success had to do with Fortune but echoed the view that it was the superior *virtus* (or *virtutes*) of the Romans (which enabled them to cast off most human vices, except the desire for glory) that had led God to grant them the earthly reward of a great empire.[125] From Augustine's perspective, however, this earthly reward was inferior to the heavenly rewards obtained by the Christian martyrs.

Admittedly, there were also voices, from the time of the Principate onward, which claimed that whereas the Republic had been greater than any other state in virtue and virtuous individuals, later on, wealth, luxury, and avarice had to some extent corrupted the Romans.[126] In other words, the extension of Rome's *imperium* and its subsequent increase in wealth had proved fatal to the Romans. Augustine himself thought that the Romans of his time did not live up to the model of the Republic. Yet as his writings show, the view that the Romans of old were particularly gifted with *virtus* and that this accounted for Rome's dominance nevertheless endured.

The Jewish sources that have come down to us deal with the notion of the Romans as a particularly virtuous people in various ways. One method, found in the Sibylline Oracles (book 3) and in some rabbinic texts, simply consists of rejecting this view by describing the Romans as ridden with vices. The perspectives of Philo and Josephus, whose writings were intended at least in part for a Greco-Roman audience, are more complex.[127] For example, Josephus echoes the Roman discourse on the virtues of the Romans in his rendering of Titus' speech to the rebels in book 6 of *The Judean War*.[128] However, this is not surprising, for these words are put into the mouth of a Roman general and merely demonstrate Josephus' familiarity with Roman values and imperial ideology.

124. Ammianus Marcellinus, *Res Gestae* 14.6.3, trans. J. C. Rolfe, LCL, 37.

125. Augustine, *City of God* 5.15–16; Inglebert 1996, 482–484. According to Harding 2008, for Augustine, Roman virtues were only pseudo-virtues.

126. See already Livy, *History of Rome*, praef., 11–12.

127. On Philo's non-Jewish audience for the "Exposition of the Law," see Niehoff 2011; 2018, 111–112. Josephus had a Greco-Roman audience in mind for all of his works (which does not mean that he did not hope to be read by Jews as well). See, e.g., Mason 1998; 2005a.

128. Josephus, *B.J.* 6.344–346 (Titus emphasizes his *fides*, *clementia*, and *pietas*).

A more promising avenue to explore lies in Philo and Josephus' descriptions of the Jewish people as excelling in certain virtues, a stance that might be interpreted as a response to the Roman view described above. Although such statements may appear too vague to be convincing, some specific examples are telling. In the *Embassy to Gaius* (*Legatio*), for example, Philo tells the story of how Agrippa I tried to dissuade Caligula from erecting a statue of himself in the Jerusalem Temple by reminding him of Augustus' respectful policy toward the Jews. Agrippa is said to have referred to letters sent by the princeps to "the governors in the provinces in Asia" urging them not to hinder the gatherings of the Jews or the sending of offerings to Jerusalem:

> These gatherings, he said, were not based on drunkenness and carousing to promote conspiracy and so to do grave injury to the cause of peace, but were schools of temperance (*sōphrosynē*) and justice (*dikaiosynē*) where men while practising virtue (*aretē*) subscribed the annual first-fruits to pay for the sacrifices which they offer and commissioned sacred envoys to take them to the temple in Jerusalem.[129]

In Agrippa's letter to Caligula, Philo thus has Augustus himself praise both the Jews for their virtue (*aretē*) and synagogal gatherings for teaching the Jews *sōphrosynē* and *dikaiosynē*, two cardinal virtues. The passage goes on to state that the Jews are a pious people, since they are dutiful in observing their sacred rites. Finally, the emperor himself, by showing respect for the Jews' ancestral cult and offering gifts to the Jerusalem Temple, earns praise for his piety (explicitly in §319). In short, Augustus is here depicted as offering valuable testimony not to the virtues of the Roman people but rather to the virtues of the people of Israel.

As we shall see in the next section, the emphasis on the Jews' *eusebeia* in the writings of Philo and Josephus may be also in part a response to the Roman emphasis on *pietas*. In Chapter Three we shall consider to what extent Josephus' description of the Jews' military valor and courage may be read as a response to Roman values.

2.3 ROMAN *PIETAS*

The emphasis the Romans put on their *pietas*, understood as the meticulous observance of the religious rites and the duties owed to the gods, but also to family and *patria*, is truly striking.[130] Romans boasted about their own piety like no one else in the ancient world, except for . . . the Jews! Moreover,

---

129. Philo, *Legat.* 312, trans. F. H. Colson, LCL, 157.
130. This particular piety was supposed to go back to Numa's time (Livy, 1.21.1–2). On the meaning of Roman *pietas*, see Ulrich 1930; Boyancé 1964, esp. 419; Galinsky 1996, 86–88; Scheid 2001; Scheid 2005; Manders 2012, 178.

among the Roman virtues associated with the empire's growth, *pietas* played an eminent role. Whereas military victory was commonly associated with the favor of the gods in the ancient world, the Romans differed from other peoples in believing that they benefited from divine support because of their exceptional and exemplary piety.[131]

While a Greek writer like Polybius took note of the Romans' extraordinary care for religious practice but did not see in this characteristic the decisive factor that allowed them to defeat other nations, Roman authors made this connection in no uncertain terms.[132] An inscription from the beginning of the second century BCE, the famous *IGR* IV, 1557 (*Sylloge*³ 601), which reproduces a letter sent by the Roman authorities to the Greek city of Teos in 193 BCE, shows that Romans viewed their *pietas* as the gods' motive for supporting Roman imperialism.[133] According to this document, the fact that "we (Romans) have, absolutely and consistently, placed reverence (*eusebeia*) towards the gods as of the first importance is proved by the favour we have received from them on this account."[134] In other words, the victories obtained through the favor of the gods were ultimately due to the exemplary piety (*eusebeia*) of the Romans.

In the first century BCE, Cicero also implicitly connected the military successes of Rome, the support of the gods, and the exceptional *pietas* of the Romans. In a famous passage of his speech *On the Response of the Soothsayers*, he wrote:

> Indeed, who is so witless that, when he gazes up into heaven, he fails to see that gods exist, and imagines that chance is responsible for the creation of an intelligence so transcendent that scarce can the highest artistry do justice to the immutable dispositions of the universe? Or who, once convinced that gods do exist, can fail at the same time to be convinced that it is by their power (*eorum numine*) that this great empire has been created, extended, and sustained? However good be our conceit of ourselves, conscript fathers, we have excelled neither Spain in population, nor Gaul in vigour, nor Carthage in versatility, nor Greece in art, nor indeed Italy and Latium itself in the innate sensibility characteristic of this land and its peoples; but in piety (*pietate*), in religion (*religione*), and in that special wisdom (*sapientia*) which consists in the recognition of the truth that the world is swayed and directed by the power of the gods (*deorum numine*), we have excelled every people and every nation (*omnes gentes nationesque*).[135]

---

131. Charlesworth 1943, 1; Lind 1972, 250–252. *Pace* Brunt 1978, 161.

132. Polybius, *Histories* 6.56.

133. Sherk 1969, 214–216; Errington 1980; Beard, North, and Price 1998, 350, no. 13.1a.

134. Trans. Beard, North, and Price 1998, 350; see also North 1993, 134.

135. Cicero, *On the Response of the Soothsayers* 19, trans. N. H. Watts, LCL, 339–341 (very slightly modified). See also Cicero, *On Behalf of Titus Annius Milo* 83.

Two points are worth emphasizing here. First, Cicero states that the empire of the Romans has been willed by the gods, who continue to guide it and who guarantee its existence and growth.[136] Second, he accounts for the goodwill of the gods by explaining that the Romans are the most pious people on earth, that it is *pietas*, *religio*, and a correct understanding of divine providence that constitute their superiority in comparison with other peoples. Cicero implicitly correlates Roman piety with the support granted by the gods to the Roman empire.[137] This perspective was shared by pro-Roman provincials, as the case of Dionysius of Halicarnassus shows.[138]

As mentioned in the preceding section, *pietas* was one of the four virtues listed on the *clipeus virtutis*. The inscription on the copy of this shield found in Arelate praises Augustus for his *pietas* toward the gods and the fatherland (*patria*). As Carlos Noreña points out, *pietas* was "the virtue of fulfilling one's responsibilities to anyone or anything to whom or to which one was bound in any way," and not exclusively to the gods.[139] He shows that *pietas* became one of the most important virtues displayed on Roman imperial coinage, where it referred primarily to the piety of the emperor, who was often depicted making an offering, a libation, or a sacrifice—as was also the case in reliefs.[140] Inscriptions and literary works, too, celebrated the emperor's *pietas*.[141] This emphasis, however, did not mean that *pietas* ceased to be a value commonly associated with Romans in general.[142] The *Genius* of the Roman people was often represented with a patera (a flared cup used in sacrifices), for example, a visual expression of the piety of the *populus Romanus*.[143] And coins with the legend PIETAS—ROMANA were still minted in the fourth century.[144]

136. See §2.1 above.

137. See also Horace, *Odes* 3.6.5–6; Valerius Maximus, *Memorable Doings and Sayings* 1.1.8, which also argues that the meticulous observance of religious rituals has won the Romans the benevolent support of the gods, who watch over Rome's *imperium*.

138. Dionysius of Halicarnassus, *Rom. Ant.* 1.4.2; see also §2.2 above.

139. Noreña 2011, 71.

140. On the column of Trajan, the two main virtues that are exalted are Trajan's *virtus* and *pietas*, the latter being emphasized through numerous depictions of the emperor offering sacrifices. On the Arch of Galerius (298–299 CE), this emperor's *pietas* too is emphasized, in a scene of sacrifice. Noreña points out that "*pietas* types not only communicated a core virtue of the Roman emperor, but also served as a ubiquitous reminder that the emperor was himself a proper object of *pietas* from his subjects" (Noreña 2011, 77).

141. For Antoninus Pius—the pious emperor par excellence—see, e.g., *CIL* VI, 1001; *ILAlg* 7688.

142. Pliny refers to Rome as "this city which has always shown its devotion to religion and earned through piety the gracious favour of the gods" (*Panegyricus* 74.5, trans. Betty Radice, LCL, 499).

143. Béranger 1973, 400.

144. *RIC* VIII, Trier, nos. 43, 48, 56, 65, 79, 91, pp. 143–144 (bronze issues minted between 337 and 340 CE). Pietas is shown standing and carrying an infant at her breast, a representation that could appeal to both pagans and Christians.

The notion of the Romans' piety was also linked to the figure of Aeneas, who, in the *Aeneid*, is the pious character par excellence. His reputation was based first and foremost on the fact that he was said to have rescued the Penates—the ancestral household deities of the Romans, which supposedly had Trojan origins—from destruction during the Trojan War. It was only at a later stage that Aeneas' piety was conceived of as filial *pietas* toward his father, Anchises, whom he rescued by carrying the latter on his shoulders.[145] Admittedly, as Karl Galinsky notes, not all Roman authors characterized the Trojan hero as *pius Aeneas*, and aside from Virgil the list of literary references to Aeneas' *pietas* is not very long. However, Galinsky adds that "while the *literati* might have stood aside and were reluctant to eulogize *pius Aeneas*, there is every indication that the people eagerly accepted this portrayal of the Trojan ancestor."[146] Zanker also highlights the popularity of the group comprising Aeneas, Anchises, and Ascanius as a symbol of piety, especially in the private sphere, where it featured on sarcophagi as a way to express one's *pietas* toward a deceased parent.[147] Aeneas, the putative ancestor of the Romans, thus came to symbolize both the origins and exceptional fate of Rome and the place occupied by the value of *pietas* in Roman society.[148]

⁂

Roman claims to piety certainly did not pass unnoticed by Jews, especially by the Jewish elites. Nor did derogatory attitudes toward Jewish *religio* on the Romans' part. Prominent Roman authors—such as Cicero, Quintilian, Tacitus, and Cassius Dio—testify to the fact that many Romans perceived the Jews as a superstitious people and even in some cases an impious one.[149] *Superstitio*, for the Romans, referred to incorrect and excessive religious practices, which were inappropriate and ineffective.[150] What qualified Jewish religion as "superstition" was that the Jews allegedly did not know the proper way to worship the deity and performed rituals that were ineffective. Their refusal to

---

145. Galinsky 1969, 59–61.

146. Galinsky 1969, 4.

147. Zanker 1988, 210.

148. For the association between *pietas* and Aeneas on coinage, see Duncan 1948. The characterization of Aeneas as *pius* was challenged by Christian authors: see, e.g., Lactantius, *Divine Institutions* 5.10.1–9.

149. For the Jews as superstitious, see Cicero, *Pro Flacco* 67; Quintilian, *The Orator's Education* 3.7.21 (Moses was "the author of the Jewish superstition," *Iudaicae superstitionis auctor*); Tacitus, *Hist.* 5.13.1–2; Cassius Dio, *Rom. Hist.* 37.16.2–4, 37.17.4. The sources describing the Jews as impious all postdate the first Jewish Revolt; see Fuks 1953, 157–158, and §4 below.

150. See the brief but helpful history of the notion of *superstitio* in Janssen 1979; Barton and Boyarin 2016, 33–37. *Superstitio* could have a political dimension and be perceived as "a serious offense to the Roman gods and a direct attack upon the Roman state" (Janssen 1979, 136). Judaism was sometimes viewed this way, as Tacitus' remarks in *Hist.* 5.5.1–2 show.

fight on the Sabbath, for example, was perceived as a manifestation of *super-stitio*, which had led to their defeats at the hands of Pompey in 63 BCE and of Sosius and Herod in 37 BCE.[151] In Roman sources, the Jews thus appeared as a reverse image of the Romans, who, as mentioned above, were presented as exceptional in their *pietas*—that is, religious but not superstitious.

From a Jewish perspective, the repeated claims that the Romans excelled in piety and that their empire was sustained by divine providence, added to their disparaging comments about Jewish religious practices, may have challenged the Jewish belief in the election of the people of Israel, the truly pious ones, chosen by the one, true God, whose designs the Jews understood better than the "idolaters" did. Admittedly, Roman *pietas* differs from the Hebrew *ḥessed* or *yirat YHWH*, from the Jewish practice of the mitzvot (commandments) and the keeping of the covenant. We are dealing not only with different terminology in Latin, Greek, and Hebrew but also with significant conceptual differences. Moreover, the use of the same term by different authors can be misleading: when Josephus praised Jewish *eusebeia*, this word did not mean the same thing as it did when Dionysius of Halicarnassus celebrated Roman *eusebeia*.[152] However, Romans, Greeks, and Jews shared a common world, in which many Jews were exposed to Greek and Roman views and at least some Greeks and Romans were exposed to Jewish views. As Weinfeld once suggested, Aeneas' exemplary *pietas* can to some extent be compared to the exemplary piety or obedience of Abraham.[153] Moreover, the care with which the rabbis discussed minute details of the religious obligations incumbent upon the Jews is not unlike the scrupulous attention with which the Romans fulfilled their religious rituals.

Although Philo never explicitly compares Jewish and Roman piety, it is interesting in this context to note that he presents the Jews as a particularly pious people, with the Essenes and the Therapeutae as exemplary embodiments of this general characteristic. Moreover, his exegetical comments on some biblical characters whose behavior was not above reproach reveal an apologetic concern to excuse what could appear as lack of piety. The case of Jacob is particularly illuminating. In the Bible—which does not conceal the weaknesses and shortcomings of its "heroes"—Jacob deceives his old, blind father to steal the blessing due to his brother, Esau, which leads to the younger son's dominion over the older (Gen 27). From a Roman perspective, Jacob's actions amounted to a violation of *pietas* (especially in relation to his father).

151. See in particular Cassius Dio, *Rom. Hist.* 37.16.2–4, 37.17.4, 49.22.5.

152. In the Septuagint, the expression *yirat YHWH* (fear of YHWH) found in Isa 11:2, 33:6 is translated as *eusebeia*.

153. Weinfeld 1993, 10–11, which notes several other parallels between Aeneas and Abraham (at 19: "Just as Aeneas is the first ancestor of the nation, 'the *pater*,' and not the first settler, so is Abraham 'the father'—and not, like Joshua, the conqueror and settler"). See also Cohen 1967.

Philo was aware of the problem (see in particular *QG* 4.206) and did his best to account for this behavior. In *Questions and Answers on Genesis* 4.202, in reference to Rebecca's statement in Genesis 27:13 ("Let your curse be on me, my son; only obey my word, and go, get them for me"), Philo asserts that "it is fitting [. . .] (to admire) in the son his honouring of both his parents," because

> he was drawn in opposite directions by his piety toward both, lest he seem to deceive his father and to desire (what belonged) to another, and as for his mother, lest he seem to disobey and disregard her when she addressed herself to him with supplication and importunity.[154]

Philo not only attempts to clear Jacob of every suspicion of impiety but also presents him as exceptionally pious! Furthermore, in *That Every Good Person Is Free* 57 and *On the Virtues* 209, Philo explains Esau's subjugation to Jacob on philosophical grounds, using the argument, already found in Early Stoicism, that the fool is a slave by nature and benefits from being enslaved to the wise.[155] Maren Niehoff notes that with such statements, "Philo emerges as an active participant in specifically Roman discourses" that were very much influenced by Stoicism.[156] In *That Every Good Person Is Free* 57, Philo explicitly refers to Zeno, conjecturing that he may have drawn his argument that the fool must submit himself to the wise from Moses' legislation—more specifically, from the story of Jacob and Esau in Genesis 27. Hence, Philo simultaneously exonerates Jacob and hints at the fact that some of the Stoic teachings had Jewish origins.

In Philo's eyes, *eusebeia* was the "queen" of all virtues.[157] As on the *clipeus virtutis*, piety features among the cardinal virtues in several passages of Philo's work, either as an addition to the traditional list or as a substitute for *andreia*, rather than for *phronēsis*.[158] Moreover, Philo's writings—in particular the "Exposition of the Law," probably intended for both a Jewish and a Greco-Roman audience, and the so-called historical treatises, written during or after Philo's stay in Rome—contain what may be an indirect response to the Romans' claim that the empire was a reward for their *pietas* toward the gods. In *On the Special Laws*, he presents the cult at the Jerusalem Temple and the priestly function of the whole people of Israel as sources of blessing for the universe and thus (implicitly) for the empire.[159] Similarly, in the *Embassy to Gaius* (306), Philo states that on the Day of

154. Trans. Ralph Marcus, LCL, 495–496.

155. See also *Leg.* 3.191–195.

156. Niehoff 2018, 83 (and also 85 on *Prob.* 57).

157. Philo, *Spec.* 4.135.

158. See, e.g., Philo, *Det.* 73, 143, listing *phronēsis, sōphrosynē, dikaiosynē*, and *eusebeia*. By contrast, *Det.* 18 mentions the four cardinal virtues known from Greek philosophy and adds *eusebeia*, and *Mos.* 2.216 and *Praem.* 160 have even longer lists.

159. See Philo, *Spec.* 2.167 in particular, as well as 1.97, 168, 190; *Mos.* 1.149 (on the universal priestly role of Israel); Umemoto 1994, 42–43.

Atonement, the high priest prays "according to ancestral practice for a full supply of blessings and prosperity and peace for all mankind."[160] By emphasizing the piety of the Jews who prayed and sacrificed for the welfare of all humankind, and thus of the Romans, Philo may have been suggesting that the latter's prosperity in fact depended on Jewish piety—rather than on Roman *pietas*, which from Philo's perspective was necessarily defective, since the Romans were polytheists.[161] The notion that the empire's welfare depended on the prayers and sacrifices of the Jews could have both an apologetic dimension—Jews were loyal subjects who benefited Rome—and a subversive one, namely that the empire would crumble without the Jews' prayers (i.e., the support of their God).[162]

Such an idea was of course more difficult to formulate after the Jewish revolts. The interruption of the sacrifices for the emperor at the Jerusalem Temple and the rejection of offerings made by foreigners, at the beginning of the First Jewish Revolt, were considered by the Romans—and even some of the Jews—to be impious acts.[163] *Pietas* in an imperial context referred to the cult of the gods but also meant *pietas* toward the emperor, and the Jews traditionally expressed their "political piety" through the daily sacrifices offered for the sake of the emperor at the Jerusalem Temple, as well as through dedications of buildings and other marks of honor.[164] Putting an end to the daily sacrifices for the emperor was thus an act of impiety and rebellion. Josephus perfectly understood the gravity of the Jewish rebels' decision and thus had a more difficult time than Philo in arguing for the Jews' *eusebeia*. In addition, after their defeat by Rome and erroneous interpretation of certain heavenly signs reported at length by Josephus himself, it was difficult for him to argue that the Jews excelled in understanding God's plans—even though in theory, in Josephus' eyes, biblical prophecy showed that God had granted Israel, or at least the priests versed in the Scriptures, a special knowledge of the divine design.[165] More fundamentally, the Deuteronomistic scheme that Josephus adopted to explain the Romans' victory over the Jews—the idea that God had

160. Philo, *Legat.* 306, trans. F. H. Colson, LCL, 155.

161. In his study of Philo's *Legatio*, Pieter B. Hartog also highlights "Philo's assertion that under the rule of the mad emperor Gaius, the stability and future of the Roman Empire depended on the Judaeans" (Hartog 2019, 206).

162. In the *Legatio*, Philo also suggests that the Jews, because they are spread all over the world, represent a potential threat to the Roman empire (*Legat.* 214–216). On this allusive warning, see Bilde 2009.

163. See Josephus, *B.J.* 2.414.

164. Herod's building policy is worth mentioning in this respect. Yet in areas that were not populated (mostly) by Jews, he had temples built that were dedicated to the imperial cult.

165. See Josephus, *B.J.* 6.288–315 for signs that were given to but misinterpreted by most of the Jews. Cf. Tacitus, *Hist.* 5.13.1; Suetonius, *Vespasian* 5. On Josephus' confidence in his ability to interpret signs and the fact that he even perceived himself as a new Jeremiah, see Cohen 1982; Bilde 1998, 45–55.

used the Romans as a tool to punish the sins of Israel—led him to conclude that God had indeed sided with the Romans against his own people. Finally, Josephus even admitted (maybe as a concession to his Roman audience) that the Romans could behave in a pious way in certain circumstances.[166]

However, Josephus nowhere claims that God's choice to side with the Romans was due to the latter's *eusebeia*. He asserts that it was the sinful behavior of the rebels, rather than the pious behavior of the Romans, that prompted the divine decision. Moreover, Josephus, like Philo, maintains that the Jews are an exceptionally pious people, arguing that the rebels represented only a marginal part of the whole. In *Against Apion*, in which Josephus' Roman context and audience and his attempt to present "Judaism in Roman dress" are particularly striking, he even goes so far as to imply that the Jews' piety equals, and maybe even surpasses, that of the Romans: "Above all we take pride in raising children, and make keeping the laws and preserving the traditional piety that accords with them the most essential task of our whole life."[167] As John Barclay notes, "The preservation of tradition parallels Roman conservatism in relation to *mos maiorum*, but Josephus' superlatives (the 'most essential' task of our 'whole' life) suggest a Judean superiority in this regard."[168] Moreover, Josephus highlights Jewish *eusebeia* at length in the part of *Against Apion* that deals with the Mosaic laws, arguing that the Jews' legislation is superior to that of others because Moses "did not make piety a part of virtue, but recognized and established the other [virtues] as parts of it"—the other virtues being *dikaiosynē* (justice), moderation (*sōphrosynē*), endurance (*karteria*), and "harmony (*symphonia*) among citizens in relation to one another in all matters." "For," Josephus adds, "all practices and occupations, and all speech, have reference to our piety towards God."[169] Like Philo, Josephus presents *eusebeia* as the queen of virtues, as *the* virtue to which all others are subordinate. The claim that this makes Jewish law superior to all other legislation would have rung loud and clear in a Roman environment, where both law and piety were conceived of as realms in which the Romans excelled. Josephus is implicitly challenging the Roman claim to superiority in both religion and law.

The rabbis too considered the Jews as the most, and in fact the only, truly pious people on earth and soundly rejected the notion that Roman victories

---

166. For the view that God had sided with the Romans, see Josephus, *B.J.* 5.343, 367–368, 378. For the view that the Romans were more respectful than the Judean rebels of the Jerusalem Temple and its *sacra*, see 5.334, 363.

167. Josephus, *C. Ap.* 1.60, trans. John Barclay in Barclay 2007, 43. See also *C. Ap.* 1.212; 2.146, 170–171, 181, 291, 293. It is Barclay who coined the expression "Judaism in Roman dress" (Barclay 2000).

168. Barclay 2007, 43, n. 242.

169. Josephus, *C. Ap.* 2.170–171; Barclay 2007, 266–267. See also *C. Ap.* 2.181, 187–188, 291, 293.

and rule were rewards for the Romans' piety toward the gods. Some rabbinic sources recount stories about specific Roman individuals who behaved impiously, and those dealing with Titus' victory in Jerusalem provide a particularly interesting perspective in this regard. Far from being respectful toward all the gods, including those of conquered peoples (as Roman sources and even Josephus would have it), Titus in rabbinic sources is depicted as a blasphemer who willingly desecrates the sacred space and cultic objects of the temple in Jerusalem.[170]

Hence, in the third-century midrash Sifre on Deuteronomy, Titus is said to have torn the curtains of the Holy of Holies with his sword. Moreover, he questions God's power and even his very existence. In the biblical passage on which the midrash comments, God has chastised Israel for worshipping idols and has delivered the people into the hands of their enemies. While God will ultimately save Israel, he now asks ironically: "Where are their [Israel's false] gods, the rock in which they took refuge, which ate the fat of their sacrifices and drank the wine of their libations? Let them rise up and help you! Let them be your protection!" (Deut 32:37–38). The idea expressed in these biblical verses is that Israel has abandoned the worship of the true God in favor of the illusory gods of the nations, which are nothing but powerless idols. The midrash elaborates on the words "Where are their gods?" suggesting two interpretations:

> *Then he will say: Where are their gods* [. . .] Rabbi Yehudah understands it as referring to Israel, and Rabbi Nehemiah understands it as referring to the nations of the world.
>
> R. Yehudah says: In the future Israel will say to the nations of the world: Where are your consuls [or: governors; Hebrew *hapitqim*, from the Greek *hypatikos*] and governors [or: generals; *hegmonim*, from the Greek *hēgemōn*]? *Which ate the fat of their sacrifices.* [Those] who used to give wages [*afsoniot*, from the Greek *opsōnion*] and make gifts [*donatova*, from *donativum* in Latin, pl. *donativa*] and raise salaries [*salania*, from *salarium* in Latin, pl. *salaria*]. *Let them rise up and help you.* [. . .]
>
> R. Nehemiah says: This refers to the wicked Titus (*Titus ha-rasha'*), the son of the wife of Vespasian, who entered into the Holy of Holies and tore the two curtains with a sword and said: "If He is really a god, let Him come and protest!" [*The gods*] *which ate the fat of their sacrifices* (Deut 32:38). He [Titus] said: "Moses misled them and said: Build for yourselves an altar and sacrifice burnt offerings and pour libations upon it, as it is stated [in Scripture]: *One lamb you shall offer in the*

---

170. On these rabbinic traditions, see in particular Hasan-Rokem 1993, 1998; Levinson 2003 (these works focus on the version found in Leviticus Rabbah 22).

morning, and the other lamb you shall offer at twilight (Num 28:4). *Let them rise up and help you! Let them be your protection!* (Deut 32:38)." The Holy One, blessed be He, forgives everything, [but] regarding the desecration of His name He punishes immediately.[171]

This text has a parallel in another third-century midrash, Mekhilta Deuteronomy (on the same verses),[172] and later sources attest to the tradition as well.[173] In the Mekhilta we encounter the same protagonists, R. Yehudah and R. Nehemiah, to whom the same kind of teaching is attributed, with minor variations: R. Yehudah explains the biblical question "Where are their gods?" as "Where are the auxiliary troops [or: cavalry; *alot* in Hebrew, probably from the Latin *ala*] and the legions that raised *annona* for you?" As for R. Nehemiah, he relates the verse to Titus, "who tore the two curtains with a sword, cursed and blasphemed, and said: "If He is *their God*, let Him come and stand up for His sons," thereby casting doubt on the covenantal relationship between God and Israel.

According to rabbinic tradition, both Rabbi Yehudah and Rabbi Nehemiah were disciples of Rabbi Aqiva and were active in the middle third of the second century CE—that is, in the wake of the Bar Kokhba Revolt. The Sifre states that despite the recent defeat of the Jews at the hands of Roman legions, R. Yehudah held that the day would come when Israel would be able to say to the Romans, "Where are your consuls and your governors—the leaders of your armies?"—or, in the Mekhilta version, "Where are your armies?" This implies that in the future, the Roman legions will be destroyed. Moreover, R. Yehudah's interpretation, which correlates the gods mentioned in the biblical verse with generals (in Sifre) or armies (in the Mekhilta), seems to echo (and deride) both the Romans' confidence in their military superiority and the notion that their legions owed their victories to divine support. If the Romans' armies are gone, so are their gods, whose nonexistence is thus demonstrated.

However, the midrash also considers another hermeneutical possibility: namely, that it is Israel's enemies who are posing the question "Where are your gods?" suggesting that God has abandoned Israel, is weak and powerless, or even does not exist at all. It is Titus, the destroyer of the Temple, who personifies this theological challenge addressed to Israel. The midrash attributes a provocative and derisive declaration to him: "If He is really a god, let Him come and protest!" The apparent weakness and powerlessness of the God of Israel casts doubt on his divinity, which, from a Jewish perspective, amounts

---

171. Sifre Deuteronomy 327–328, ed. Finkelstein, 378–379. On this text, see Schremer 2010, 28.

172. See Kahana 1988; 2005, 354.

173. E.g., Genesis Rabbah 10:7 (ed. Theodor and Albeck, 82–83); Leviticus Rabbah 20:5 (ed. Margulies, 458); Pesiqta de-Rav Kahana (Aḥarei Mot) 26:5 (ed. Mandelbaum, 2:392); Ecclesiastes Rabbah 8:5. See Schremer 2010, 161.

to blasphemy.[174] In connection with Deuteronomy 32:38, which follows the question "Where are their gods?" Titus further states that Moses misled the people of Israel by teaching them the divine ordinances concerning sacrifices and burnt offerings. From a biblical perspective these rituals should atone for Israel's sins and thus bring God's blessing back upon his people but, Titus suggests, they are in fact ineffectual. There are different ways to understand this passage. First, the claim that Jewish sacrificial rituals fail to produce results echoes the idea often expressed by Greek and Roman authors that the Jews are a superstitious people who have no knowledge of the rites proper to worshipping the gods. Second, one might also understand Titus' statement to mean that if Israel's sacrifices failed to prevent the Romans from gaining the upper hand, it was because the god of Israel was unable to protect his people. Finally, Titus also might be suggesting that with the Temple now fallen into Roman hands, the sacrifices can no longer be performed and thus Israel has no access to atonement, forgiveness, or salvation. The midrash's claim that God can forgive any sin—apparently implying: even if no sacrifices are performed—except the desecration of his name would be the response to such a distressing statement. In any case, R. Nehemiah's teaching ends with the idea that God will punish Titus—or, more generally, the Romans—for having desecrated his name, even though the nature of the punishment is not described.[175] His conclusion is similar to that reached by R. Yehudah: in both cases, Rome's hegemony is described as fated to come to an end, a consequence of Roman impiety and *hybris*. These early rabbinic texts were clearly challenging Roman and pro-Roman claims ascribing the empire's military victories and its power to the piety of its people and the gods' support.[176]

3. The "Vocation" of the Romans

The rivalry over "election"—again: a rivalry from the Jews' perspective, but not from the Romans'—went hand in hand with a rivalry over "vocation," broadly conceived as a universal rule that would bring peace and legal order to the world. As we saw in Chapter One, such claims were quite common in imperial contexts, even though the amount of emphasis placed on peace varied from empire to empire and could even vary from king to king. Several aspects of the Roman claim to rule the *oikoumenē* can be traced back to the empires of the ancient Near East. For example, the claim to a hegemony extending "from

174. In another midrash, Esau (who symbolizes Rome) is said to have "taunted and blasphemed" (Genesis Rabbah 63:13, ed. Theodor and Albeck, 697), recalling the expressions used in Sifre and Mekhilta Deuteronomy to describe Titus' challenge to the God of Israel. See Schremer 2010, 56.

175. The description of the punishment is found in later sources such as Leviticus Rabbah 22:3.

176. For a more systematic treatment of this issue, see Berthelot 2020b.

sunrise to sunset" is found already in Neo-Assyrian treatises.[177] What was new in the context of the Jews' encounter with Rome was (1) the successful pacification of the Mediterranean, from Augustus' Principate to the end of the second century CE, which made claims about the *pax Romana* look convincing in the eyes of many; (2) the disastrous defeats of the Jews in their wars against Rome during that same period (on which see §4 below); and (3) the association of the Romans' claims to universal and eternal rule and peace with other ideological claims, as to the Romans' piety and the superiority of their laws, for example (the latter to be explored in Chapter Four). Some Jewish texts of the Roman period may be seen as responses to these circumstances and claims.

3.1 A UNIVERSAL AND ETERNAL RULE?

Universal Rule

The idea that Roman rule was universal was to a great extent a fiction, but it was fiction fundamental to the rhetoric and ideology of empire.[178] Vitruvius and Cicero spoke of Roman dominion as if it were universal, pertaining to the whole *orbis terrarum* or to all peoples.[179] Under the Principate, we encounter the notion that the *imperium* of the city of Rome, the *Urbs*, was meant to grow and progressively coincide with the entire world, the *orbs* (or *orbis*).[180] Ovid significantly wrote: "The land of other nations has a fixed boundary, [whereas] the territory of Rome is identically that of the City and that of the world (*Romanae spatium est Urbis et orbis idem*)."[181] Bruno Rochette remarks that the joint use of these two words was not entirely new—Cicero and Cornelius Nepos occasionally paired them—but that it was in Ovid's time that these words took on such a political dimension, explained by the context of Augustus' Principate. The association of *Urbs* and *orbs* did not become very common in Roman literary sources, but it was still found in the poetry of the late Roman empire, for example under the pen of Rutilius Namatianus at the beginning of the fifth century.[182]

Rome was also variously designated as *lux orbis terrarum* (the light of the world), *caput orbis* (the head of the world), and *columen orbis* (the summit [or column] of the world).[183] The same ideology underlay some of the titles given to the emperor in inscriptions and on coinage, titles such as *pacator*,

177. See Chapter One. In a Roman context, see already Sallust, *The War with Catiline* 36.4, in the first century BCE.

178. Whitmarsh 2013, 68, referring to Nicolet 1988 (1991).

179. Vitruvius, *On Architecture* 1, praef., 1; Cicero, *On the Making of an Orator* 1.4.14; see also Brunt 1978, 168.

180. See Vogt 1960, 159.

181. Ovid, *Fasti* 2.684 (my translation).

182. Rochette 1997; Vogt 1960, 160–161.

183. See Vogt 1960, 160; Lavan 2013, 3, n. 7. For *columen orbis*, see Valerius Maximus, *Memorable Doings and Sayings* 2.8., praef.

rector, and *restitutor orbis (terrarum)* (peacemaker, governor, and restorer or savior of the world).[184] At the very beginning of the *Res Gestae*, Augustus declared that he had submitted the world (*orbis terrarum*) to the *imperium* of the Roman people. Ovid used the expression *pater orbis* (father of the world) for the Princeps, followed by Martial and Statius.[185] In an inscription dated between 14 and 29 CE, Livia is evoked as the "mother of the world," *genetrix orbis*.[186] The word *orbs/orbis* had several meanings; it was used primarily to refer to the *oikoumenē*, the "civilized" world, but it could extend further to the universal horizon of Roman dominion.[187]

From an iconographic point of view, one of the most common expressions of the Roman empire's claims to a universal reach was the globe, the visual equivalent of the expression *orbis terrarum*. As we saw in §1.2, already in the first century BCE, denarii were produced that represented the *Genius* of the Roman people with a globe, sometimes resting a foot on it.[188] We also saw that various representations of Roma featured her holding a globe or resting her foot on a globe.

In the period 31–29 BCE, Octavian was represented on the obverse of denarii that featured on the reverse a winged Victoria holding a wreath and resting her foot on a globe, together with the inscription CAESAR—DIVI F (son of the deified Caesar).[189] In other words, Roman victory was universal and was closely associated with the princeps. Another denarius from this period shows the profile of a winged Victoria on the obverse, and on the reverse, a naked man with his right foot on a globe, a scepter in his left hand, and an aplustre (an element of decoration for the stern of a ship) in his right. The man is probably to be identified with Octavian represented as Neptune, and

---

184. For inscriptions, see, e.g., *CIL* XII, 4333, side A, lines 15–16 (altar from Narbo, 12 CE; Augustus as *rector orbis terrarum*); *CIL* XIII, 9061 (Caracalla as *pacator orbis*); *CIL* VIII, 8797a (Severus Alexander as *restitutor orbis*); *CIL* III, 8031 (in 248 CE, the year of Rome's thousandth anniversary, Philip the Arab was called the "restorer of the whole world," *restituor totius orbis*, a title that was first attributed to Gordian III). For coinage, see *RIC* II, Hadrian, no. 594b, p. 416 (119–123 CE; *restitutor orbis terrarum*); *RIC* IV.1, Septimius Severus, no. 282, p. 126 (202–210 CE; *pacator orbis*); no. 287, p. 127 (*rector orbis*); nos. 288–290, p. 127 (*restitutor orbis*); *RIC* IV.1, Geta, no. 50, p. 320 (203–208 CE; *pacator orbis*); *RIC* V.1, Valerian, nos. 116–119, p. 47 (between 256 and 258 CE; *restitutor orbis*); no. 220, p. 55 (254–255 CE; with the legend RESTITVTI GENER(is) HVMANI); *RIC* V.1, Aurelian, no. 289, p. 297 (274–275 CE; *restitutor orbis*). See also Vogt 1960, 161–163.

185. See Ovid, *Ex Ponto* 2.5.75, *Fasti* 2.130; Martial 7.7.5 (*parens orbis*); Statius, *Silvae* 4.2.14–15 (*parens orbis*); Vogt 1960, 161.

186. *CIL* II, 2038.

187. Vogt 1960, 153–154.

188. See *RRC* 393/1, p. 407 (dated to 76–75 BCE, perhaps minted in Spain); 397/1, p. 409 (dated to 74 BCE, minted in Rome).

189. See *RIC* I, rev. ed., Augustus, 254a, p. 59. The mint is Italian, but the provenance is uncertain.

FIGURE 2.4. Denarius representing Victoria on the obverse, and Octavian as Neptune, with foot on globe, on the reverse (31–29 BCE).
RIC I, no. 256, p. 59. Photograph © The Trustees of the British Museum.

the image strongly evokes Roman rule *terra marique*[190] (Fig. 2.4). The same motif and ideology are found on an aureus minted by Vespasian, which speaks to the omnipresence of the Augustan model in Vespasian's attempts to acquire legitimacy for the new Flavian dynasty by presenting himself as the "spiritual" heir of Augustus.[191]

The globe remained a recurring symbol on imperial coinage. Even shaky figures who did not last long on the throne minted coins on which they appear with a globe.[192] Some changes occurred: under Antoninus Pius, Italia too was sometimes represented with a globe, meaning that Italy was associated with the city of Rome in the imperial dominion over the provinces.[193] Another common association was between Victoria and the globe, symbolizing the universal scope of Roman victories. This type of reverse continued into the fourth century.[194] Provincial coinage too represented Roman universal domination by means of a globe in association with various symbols and figures.[195]

190. *RIC* I, rev. ed., Augustus, no. 256, p. 59. Similarly, on the dynastic relief from Ravenna (dated to the reign of Claudius, 41–54 CE), Augustus is represented with his left foot on a globe.

191. *RIC* II.1, rev. ed., no. 44, p. 62; Victor A. Adda collection, no. 56, in Gambash and Gitler 2017, 202–203. See also §3.2 below, on peace.

192. See, e.g., the aureus minted in Rome by Didius Julianus in 193 CE, with the legend RECTOR ORBIS on the reverse (*RIC* IV.1, Didius Julianus, no. 3, p. 15).

193. *RIC* III, Antoninus Pius, no. 746, p. 122 (minted in Italy, not surprisingly).

194. See the numerous examples listed in *RIC* VII, p. 768.

195. See, e.g., *RPC* II, Thrace, no. 514, p. 89 (copper as minted in 80–81 CE) and no. 536, p. 90 (as minted in 82 CE), which represent an eagle facing forward, standing on a globe, on the reverse; *RPC* II, Nicaea, no. 641, p. 103 (bronze issue minted under Domitian, with an eagle on a globe); *RPC* III, Prusias ad Hypium, no. 1102, p. 134 (minted under Trajan, with an eagle standing, wings spread, on a globe); *RPC* III, Bithynia (unknown city), no. 1146,

There were of course other ways to express the universality of Roman rule in iconography. In the Aphrodisias Sebasteion, the first panel associates the goddess *Rhōmē* with *Gē*, the earth. As Emmanuelle Rosso Caponio remarks, the encounter between these two reflects the equivalence between the *orbis terrarum* and the *orbis Romanus* while signalling also the submission of the earth to *Rhōmē*.[196] Another Sebasteion panel depicts Claudius as ruler over land and sea, in a dynamic posture and heroic nudity.[197] "Land" is represented on the viewer's left, lifting a cornucopia, a symbol of prosperity and abundance, whereas "sea" features on the right, lifting a ship's rudder (Fig. 2.5). "The meaning of the composition as a whole is straightforward," as Roland Smith concludes. "Its theme is the prosperity of land and sea under imperial rule."[198]

The iconography of this panel can be linked to the notion of Roman rule *terra marique*. This idea of a rule that reaches over land and sea goes back to the Hellenistic period, when the expression was used to praise the achievements of a king or a powerful state (which need not necessarily be a maritime power).[199] As early as the second century BCE, in Lycophron's *Alexandra* and in Melinno's *Ode to Rome*, Roman rule was described as extending over land and sea.[200] Unsurprisingly, some Greek inscriptions of the imperial period also use this expression to describe Roman rule.[201] Arnaldo Momigliano has argued that while the idea of dominion over land and sea was taken over from the Hellenistic world, the idea of peace on land and at sea was characteristically Roman.[202] However, Roman sources do evoke victory and rule over land

p. 138 (minted under Trajan, with Nikē standing and holding a globe); *RPC* III, Corinth, Hadrian, nos. 187–188, p. 34 (minted under Hadrian, with a cornucopia on a globe, symbolizing the universal prosperity prevailing in the Roman empire); *RPC* III, Hadriani ad Olympum, no. 1613, p. 195 (minted under Hadrian, with Zeus seated left, holding Nikē on a globe on his extended right hand, his left resting on a scepter); *RPC* IV, Prusa, no. 4819 (minted under Commodus, 180–182 CE, with Nikē advancing on a globe and holding a wreath and a palm branch).

196. Rosso Caponio 2020, 134; see also §1.3 above.

197. Smith 2013, plate 88 (C 29, and analysis pp. 171–173).

198. Smith 2013, 172. Smith mentions that a coin minted by Laodikeia under Caracalla features the emperor with a sea figure on one side and a land figure on the other, holding a steering oar and a cornucopia, respectively; this iconography may have been inspired by that of the Sebasteion.

199. Momigliano 1942a, esp. 55.

200. See Lycophron, *Alexandra*, 1229–1230, where the Romans are described as seizing kingship over land and sea; Melinno, *Ode to Rome*, v.10. The dating of each of these works is debated.

201. See *IGR* I, 901, which refers to Augustus as "ruling over the whole earth and the whole sea," *ton pasēs gēs kai pasēs thalassēs archonta*. An inscription from Phrygia dated to 176–180 CE addresses both Marcus Aurelius and his son Commodus as "master of land and sea," *gēs kai thalassēs despotēs* (Haspels 1971, 1:333, no. 93, available at https://epigraphy .packhum.org/text/271550?hs=317–336).

202. Momigliano 1942a, 64.

FIGURE 2.5. Relief from the Sebasteion in Aphrodisias: Claudius, ruler over land and sea. Photograph © New York University Excavations at Aphrodisias (G. Petruccioli).

and sea as well. Coins minted in 56 BCE in the wake of Pompey's victories against the pirates and in Asia—including in Judea—feature on the reverse a globe surrounded by wreaths, together with an ear of corn and an aplustre, symbols of dominion over land and sea, respectively.[203] As we saw previously, Virgil's *Aeneid* refers to Jupiter's promise that from the Trojans "should come rulers, to hold the sea and all lands beneath their sway" (1.235–236).[204] From

203. *RRC* 426/4, p. 449–450 (denarius minted in Rome by Faustus Cornelius Sulla in 56 BCE); Cornwell 2017, 88–89. See also Cicero, *Pro Balbo* 16.

204. Trans. H. Rushton Fairclough (revised by G. P. Goold), LCL, 279. See also *Aeneid* 1.286–290.

Augustus on, the notion of peace on land and at sea was in fact tantamount to the establishment of Roman universal dominion.[205]

Interestingly enough, the emperor Julian made use of this theme in contrasting the fates of the Romans and the Jews in an attempt to expose the stupidity of the Christians' choice of the God of Israel over the traditional gods of Rome. "Is it better to be free continuously and during two thousand whole years to rule over the greater part of the earth and the sea, or to be enslaved and to live in obedience to the will of others?" Julian asked. The answer was not far to seek: "No man is so lacking in self-respect as to choose the latter by preference."[206] Julian's testimony is all the more significant as it is roughly contemporaneous with the redaction of the Jerusalem Talmud, which, as we shall see below, challenges this rhetoric of universal dominion.

The "universality" of the empire was in fact something less than universal. The Romans faced the Parthians (and later the Sassanids) in the East and various peoples in the North, to mention only their main adversaries during the empire's first centuries. They were aware of these very real limits, of course, but were nevertheless convinced that they had a better claim to universal rule than did the Parthians, for example.[207] As the examples cited above demonstrate, there are ample sources that document the Roman ideology and rhetoric of universality and its acceptance among provincials. The exceptional character of the Romans' claim to universal rule lay not so much in the claim itself, therefore, as in the wide recognition by provincials that it was in fact more legitimate in the case of the Romans than in previous empires.

Eternal Rule

In the *Aeneid*, Jupiter promises Venus that the descendants of Aeneas and Romulus, the Romans, will know "no bounds in space and time," will rule over an "endless empire," and will be granted "power without limit" (*imperium sine fine*), an expression with both a geographical and a temporal meaning.[208] Some voices, both Roman and Greek, claimed that Roman rule was not only universal but also eternal—or at least they expressed the hope that it would be. Admittedly, there were also skeptical voices.

---

205. Cornwell 2017. See Augustus' *Res Gestae* 3.1, 4.2, 13.1; Suetonius, *Aug.* 22. On peace, see §3.2 below.

206. Julian, *Against the Galilaeans* 218 B, trans. Wilmer C. Wright, LCL, 381.

207. On the Parthians as the other masters of the world and as rivals of the Romans, see Pairman Brown 2001, 77, which refers to Pliny the Elder, *Natural History* 5.88, Strabo 11.9.215, Pompeius Trogus (Justin) 41.1.1, and Herodian 4.10.216. The idea of the rivalry between Rome and Persia is also found in rabbinic literature: see, e.g., b. Yoma 10a—which, however, may refer to the Sassanids rather than the Parthians.

208. Virgil, *Aeneid* 1.278–279. For the translation "power without limit," see Edwell 2013, 45.

We first encounter the notion of Rome as the "eternal city," *Urbs aeterna*—and, later on, *Roma aeterna*—during Augustus' Principate.[209] The theme would continue to enjoy a prominent place for centuries, because the Roman empire was understood as having surpassed all others, and some people viewed it as destined to have no successor. It would stand, therefore, as the end stage of history.[210] The empire's eternity was expressed in various ways, as when Ammianus Marcellinus, in addition to speaking about the *Urbs aeterna*, wrote that Rome was destined to endure as long as there were human beings.[211]

From the reign of Vespasian on, imperial coinage repeatedly proclaimed the message of Rome's eternity, through either the representation of Aeternitas or an explicit legend (such as *Roma aeterna*, *Roma perpetua*, or *aeternitas imperii*).[212] A sestertius minted between October and December 70, only a few months after the destruction of the Jerusalem Temple, evokes the "eternity of the Roman people" (AETERNITAS P(opuli) R(omani)) and displays Victory advancing from the right with a palm, offering the *palladium* to Vespasian, who is standing to the left with a spear.[213] As explained above, the *palladium* symbolized the election of the city and was perceived as securing its longevity. In addition, numerous characteristics of the empire were described as "eternal," among them peace (*pax aeterna*) and victory (*victoria aeterna*).[214] References to the eternity of Rome or the empire were particularly frequent on coins minted during the reigns of Hadrian and Antoninus Pius.[215] Even during the crisis of the third century, a considerable volume of coins continued to proclaim the glory of *Roma aeterna*.[216] An inscription consisting of a dedication to

209. Ovid, *Fasti* 3.71–72; Tibullus, *Elegies* 2.5.23; Livy, 5.7.10 (see also 4.4.4). See Benoist 2005, 319–326; Isaac 2017, 35–37.

210. Inglebert 2014, 252.

211. Ammianus Marcellinus, *Res Gestae* 14.6.3. For *Urbs aeterna* in his work, see 14.6.1, 15.7.1, 16.10.14, etc.; see also Moore 1894, 36–37.

212. See Mattingly 1930, 86, nos. 423–424; *RIC* II.1, rev. ed., Vespasian, nos. 838–839, p. 119; no. 856, p. 120; nos. 866–867, p. 121 (aurei minted in 76 CE, representing Aeternitas); no. 1359, p. 157 (denarius with the legend ROMA PERPETVA and Roma standing to the left on a cuirass, with Victory and a parazonium).

213. *RIC* II.1, rev. ed., no. 32, p. 61.

214. Manders 2012, 47, 248.

215. *RIC* II, Hadrian, no. 38, p. 344 (Aeternitas standing, with legend AET•AVG•); no. 48, p. 346 (Aeternitas standing, with legend AET•AVG•); no. 81, p. 350 (Aeternitas standing); nos. 263, 263a, 265, p. 370 (legend ROMA AETERNA); no. 597, p. 417 (Aeternitas standing, with legend AETERNITAS AVGVSTI); nos. 774–775, p. 439 (ROMA AETERNA S • C •); *RIC* III, Antoninus Pius, no. 543, p. 100 (ROMAE AETERNAE S•C•); nos. 621–623, p. 110 (ROMA AETERNA S • C •); no. 664, p. 114 (ROMAE AETERNAE S•C•).

216. Manders 2012, 142. See *RIC* V.1, p. 412, and, e.g., Gallienus, no. 432, p. 102 (ROMAE AETERNAE); Aurelian, no. 142, p. 280 (minted between 270 and 275 CE, with the legend ROM[A]E AETER on the reverse); Florian, no. 22, p. 352 (ROMAE AETERNAE).

Mars and the founders of Rome, engraved under Maxentius at the beginning of the fourth century and located in the southeast corner of the Roman Forum, still celebrates Rome as *aeterna Urbs*.[217] Kenneth J. Pratt also mentions two inscriptions from the beginning of the fifth century that celebrate Rome as eternal at precisely the time when Alaric was menacing the city.[218]

The reception among provincials of the notion that Rome was to be eternal is documented mainly by inscriptions and literary sources.[219] Among the Greek writers who celebrated Rome's endurance was the poetess Melinno, who lived in the second or first century BCE and composed some particularly striking verses.[220] She wrote that to Rome alone had Fate (*Moira*) given the "royal glory of an indestructible dominion" (vv. 5–6), and again, in vv. 13–16: "Almighty time overturns everything and moulds life this way and that. It is only in your case that it does not change the favourable wind which maintains your rule."[221] Jean-Louis Ferrary rightly underlines that Melinno's choice of the term *Moira* over *Tychē* (Fortune, generally seen as unstable and unfair), was deliberate in this context; he argues that the poet's conception of empire in these verses is close to that of Virgil.[222] Later, during the first centuries CE, numerous pro-Roman Greek authors, from Dionysius of Halicarnassus to Aelius Aristides, claimed that the Roman empire distinguished itself from all previous empires not only by its geographical expanse but also by its duration.[223] Moreover, there were provincials who wished for the eternity of Roman rule, as evidenced by a graffito found on the wall of a house in Ephesus: "All-ruling Rome, let your power never vanish."[224]

217. *CIL* VI, 33856; Pratt 1965, 25. On Maxentius' care for the city of Rome, see above n. 77.

218. Pratt 1965, 30.

219. For local decrees of Greek cities describing Rome or Roman rule as eternal, see, e.g., the inscription from Cyprus published in Mitford 1960, which mentions *tēn aenaon Rhōmēn* (14 CE); the inscription of Titus Praxias' funerary foundation, which was to be protected "in the eternity of Roman rule," *tō aiōni tēs Rhōmaiōn hēgemonias* (*IGR* IV, 661 = *SEG* 13.542; 85 CE). A petition addressed to "the emperors Caesars Galerius Maximinus and Flavius Constantinus and Valerius Licinnianus Licinnius" by the cities of Lycia and Pamphylia in 312 CE requests that Christians be forced to worship the traditional gods "on behalf of your eternal and imperishable rule" (*I.Arykanda* 12, line 16, trans. Aitor Blanco Pérez in "Maximinus Daia and the Christians in Lycia-Pamphylia," at http://judaism-and -rome.org/maximinus-daia-and-christians-lycia-pamphylia).

220. Ferrary 1988, 268–271.

221. Trans. Erskine (1995, 369).

222. Ferrary 1988, 271.

223. Dionysius of Halicarnassus, *Rom. Ant.* 1.2.1, 1.3.3–5; Appian, *Roman History*, preface, §8; Aelius Aristides, *Roman Oration* 28–29, 108. See Price 2020b.

224. *SEG* 55.1204 (*I.Eph.* 599); trans. Aitor Blanco Pérez in "All-Ruling Rome, Let Your Power Never Vanish (SEG 55.1204; I.Eph. 599)," at http://judaism-and-rome.org/all-ruling -rome-let-your-power-never-vanish-seg-551204-ieph-599.

From a biblical and Jewish perspective, the destiny of Israel also had both a universal and an eternal dimension. And like Rome, its destiny was closely associated with that of a city, Jerusalem, in which all peoples were expected to gather and congregate at the end of times in order to offer their tribute to the God of Israel, or at least their praise.[225] In Jewish texts, Jerusalem sometimes appears as the center of the world, *tabur ha-aretz* or *omphalos tēs gēs*.[226] During the Second Temple period in particular, Jerusalem was conceived of as a temple city with a universal dimension and a universal vocation. When the Jews encountered the Romans, they were thus confronted by a city with a rival claim to universalism.

Some Jewish literary sources echo, critique, and even reject the Romans' ambition of universal rule, although most often they do so obliquely. A first example is found in Josephus' writings. Unsurprisingly, Josephus was familiar with the Roman notion of victory or rule over land and sea and perfectly able to use it in a traditional Roman way. Thus, when he was taken prisoner and brought to Vespasian, he foretold that the then general would become emperor, and declared: "For you, O Caesar, are not only lord over me, but over the land and the sea, and all humankind (*kai gēs kai thalattēs kai pantos anthrōpōn genous*)" (*B.J.* 3.402; my translation). Significantly, Josephus also used the expression "land and sea" in describing Israel's universal mission. In his *Jewish Antiquities* (1.282), he tells the story of the dream in which Jacob saw angels going up and down a ladder connecting heaven and earth and received a divine promise that his descendants would spread all over the world (Genesis 28:11–15, especially 14). In Josephus' formulation, Jacob's children shall fill "all that the sun beholds of land and sea." Whereas the Masoretic text speaks about spreading to the west, the east, the north, and the south, and the Septuagint about spreading to the sea, the east, the north, and the south, Josephus chooses the phrase "land and sea" (*gē kai thalassa*)—a characteristically Roman expression in his time—to refer to the world as a whole and to express the idea of the universality of Israel's presence.

Similarly, in a free paraphrase of Balaam's oracles in favor of Israel (Numbers 23–24), Josephus writes:

114 He said: "That people is happy to whom God gives the possession of myriad blessings and has granted His providence as an ally and leader for eternity. For there is no human stock [or: people] to which

225. See Isa 49:14, 22–26 (Zion's future domination over the nations), 60:3–17, 66:10–12 (the wealth of the nations will pour into the city); Jer 16:19–21; Mic 4:1–4; Zeph 3:8–9; Zech 2:14–17, 8:20–23, 14:16–19 (a plague will fall on the nations that fail to observe the Festival of Booths); Ps 22:28–29, 47 (God's universal domination over the nations), 48:1, 67:2–8, 86:9, 96:3–13, 99.

226. See Ezek 38:12; Weinfeld 1998.

you [Israelites] will not be judged superior in virtue and in zeal for the pursuits that are best and pure of wickedness; you shall bequeath these to children who are better than yourselves, since God benevolently observes you alone among humanity and provides you with the means by which you may become happier than all others under the sun. 115 Therefore, you will hold fast the land to which He Himself sent you. It will always be subject to your children, and all land and sea (*pasa hē gē kai thalassa*) will be filled with the glory surrounding them, and there will be enough of you for the world to supply every land with inhabitants from your race [or: people]. 116 Are you, therefore, amazed, O blessed army, that from a single father you have become so great? But the land of the Chananaians [or: Canaanites] will hold your present army, consisting of a few, yet know that the inhabited world lies before you as a dwelling place forever, and your multitude—as many as is the number of stars in heaven—will reside on islands and in the continent. Though they are so numerous, the Deity will not cease to grant them plenty of good things of all kinds in peace, and victory and might [or: dominion] in war (*nikēn de kai kratos en polemō*).[227]

Like Genesis 28:3–4 and 14, Balaam's oracles in Numbers 23–24 evoke both the gift of the Promised Land to Israel and the vision of the universal spread of the children of Israel to the four corners of the earth. In addition, Josephus writes that their fame or glory will fill all land and sea (meaning: the whole world). This statement cannot be found in Numbers 23–24, the passage that Josephus is paraphrasing, which merely states that Israel will multiply and become powerful (23:10, 23:24, 24:7–8). Josephus' description of Israel's fate in this passage contrasts dramatically with the situation of the Judeans at the end of the first century CE, after the defeat by Rome, and is thus highly significant. Despite the Judean loss, Josephus insists on the universal vocation and fame of the Jewish people, for in his view their destiny was not that of a defeated people but rather a glorious one. It can hardly be a coincidence that Josephus here uses the expression "land and sea" to express Israel's universal vocation, especially in connection with promises of military victory (*nikē*) and dominion (*kratos*) (§116), which are further developed in §117, a paragraph that insists on the military valor (*andreia*) of the Jews. Be it a conscious or an unconscious imitation of the Roman formulation, the use of this expression conveys the impression that Israel and Rome are rivals in universal vocation.

In rabbinic literature, we find both implicit and explicit rejections of the Roman claim of universal rule. The first example comes in Mishnah Avodah Zarah 3:1, which forbids Jews to profit from images or statues that include a

---

227. Josephus, *A.J.* 4.114–116, trans. Louis H. Feldman in Feldman 2000, 372–373.

staff, a bird, or a globe.[228] This prohibition is presented as the majority opinion among the rabbis, whereas according to Rabbi Meir (described in rabbinic
literature as a fourth-generation tanna, active after the Bar Kokhba Revolt),
all images (*tzelamim*) that are worshipped once a year are prohibited. A third
opinion is attributed to Rabban Shim'on ben Gamliel (known as a tanna of the
third generation, who survived the Bar Kokhba Revolt): any image or statue
that has something in its hand is prohibited. As the discussion of this passage
in the Jerusalem Talmud (Avodah Zarah 3:1, 42c) makes clear, the prohibition
is not merely directed against religious idolatry, but has a political dimension
as well. The Talmud identifies the staff as a scepter and the globe as a symbol
of the world and adds other items to the Mishnah's list, like a crown, a signet
ring, and a sword (items also listed in t. Avodah Zarah 6:1). As we have seen,
in Roman iconography the globe was omnipresent as a symbol of universal
dominion, and so was the scepter. The bird may have represented the eagle,
the symbol of Zeus/Jupiter, or perhaps referred to a winged Victoria. The
Talmud does not explain what the bird meant in so many words, but associates it with a biblical passage, Isaiah 10:14, that speaks of universal dominion,
clearly indicating the bird's political significance. The symbols mentioned in
the Mishnah and in the talmudic discussion of the rabbis' majority opinion as
expressed in the Mishnah could obviously evoke the emperor, but also—as we
have seen—Roma, the *Genius* of the Roman people, the personification of Victory, or Jupiter. In contrast to R. Meir, who argues that images are prohibited
insofar as they are worshipped once a year, the Mishnah's majority opinion
emphasizes not the cultic aspect but rather the political-religious significance
of the image. This opinion and its explanation in the Yerushalmi reflect the
view that Jews should not benefit from images that symbolized Roman power
and universal dominion.[229] This in itself was a political statement, but also a
theological one, because ultimately the rabbis were making a stand against
the very divinization of power.[230] As Daniel Weiss aptly notes, "The imperial
claim itself stands in sharp competition with God's proper rulership and constitutes a competing religious claim."[231]

228. On this passage, see Urbach 1959, 238–239; Belayche 2001, 126, 229, n. 76;
Schäfer 2002b, 344–345; Friedheim 2006, 290, n. 1103; Neis 2016, 95–99 (she does not
discuss the political aspect of the mishnaic text); Zellentin 2016; Weiss 2018. Holger Zellentin understands the Mishnah as focusing on the imperial cult and the Talmud as both
responding to "the broader pagan discourse on the divinity of the emperor" and addressing
the veneration of Christian emperors in particular (Zellentin 2016, 321; the idea that this
passage of tractate Avodah Zarah mainly focuses on the imperial cult comes from Urbach
1959, 238). Tosefta Avodah Zarah 6:1 adds statues that include a sword, a crown, a (seal)
ring, and a snake to the Mishnah's list.
    229. Daniel Weiss remarks that "an important element of *avodah zarah* lay in the basic
political structures and the ideology of rulership that accompanied them" (Weiss 2018, 396).
    230. See also Chapter Three.
    231. Weiss 2018, 405.

This was true in particular of the assertion of having achieved *universal* rule. After clarifying the meaning of the symbols mentioned in the Mishnah, the talmudic section brings the figure of Alexander the Great into the discussion, in connection with the globe:

> Rabbi Yonah said: Alexander Macedon wanted [or: sought] to ascend. He ascended and ascended and ascended until he saw the world as a globe and the sea as a dish [or: a bowl]. For this reason they depict him with a globe in his hand. Let him [the artist] [depict him (Alexander) with] a dish in his hand! He does not rule over the sea. But the Holy [One, blessed be He] rules over sea and land [or: the dryness], [He] saves on the sea and [He] saves on land.[232]

How the world-globe and the sea-dish relate to one another in this passage is not completely clear, but the text's main point is that whereas Alexander was represented with a globe in his hand, he was never depicted holding a dish. This remark is ironic, meant to suggest that Alexander ruled over land alone and not over the sea. As a consequence, his rule was not truly universal and was thus inferior to the rule of the God of Israel, as the next development in this talmudic section (y. Avodah Zarah 3:1, 42c) makes clear. Commenting on Psalm 146:6, which states that God has made the heaven, the earth, and the sea, Rabbi Ze'ira son of Rabbi Abbahu (a third-generation amora who, according to rabbinic tradition, moved from Babylonia to Palestine) discusses the power of human rulers in general and argues that even a *kosmokratōr* (the Talmud uses a transliteration of a Greek term that here designates the emperor) rules over only land and not the sea, whereas "the Holy One, blessed be He," rules over both land and sea.

In contrast to Christian texts, which frequently opposed the limited rule of human kings over the earth to God's dominion over both the earthly and the heavenly realms,[233] our talmudic section repeatedly refers to land and sea. This is all the more striking as R. Ze'ira's quotation from Psalm 146:6 actually includes heaven and earth. The choice of the Talmud's redactors may be significant and represent an indirect response to the Roman claim to rule *terra marique*. Moreover, as Yael Wilfand has suggested, it is possible that Palestinian rabbinic stories that tell of Alexander's desire to reach the edges of the world may likewise convey implicit criticisms of Roman expansion and

232. y. Avodah Zarah 3:1, 42c; Schäfer and Becker 1991–2001 (1995, *Synopse* IV), 273; my translation is based on MS Leiden. See also Yael Wilfand, "Jerusalem Talmud Avodah Zarah 3:1, 42c (Part One)," at http://www.judaism-and-rome.org /jerusalem-talmud-avodah-zarah-31-42c-part-one.

233. For examples of the Christian opposition between the earthly and the heavenly realm, see the anonymous *Commentary on Daniel* 4.9 (often attributed to Hippolytus); Chromatius of Aquileia, *Sermon* 32.1 (which opposes Augustus' rule on earth to Christ's rule in heaven).

greed.[234] In both Greek and Roman sources, Alexander was often compared to Roman generals or emperors and the extent of his empire to that of the Romans.[235] Augustus in particular was fascinated by him but considered that he himself had surpassed the Macedonian general, because although the latter had conquered the world, he had not been able to rule it in a lasting way.[236] Alexander was thus both a model and a rival and stood at the very heart of the Romans' reflection on their empire's universal character. The Talmud redactors' choice to refer to him in connection with the globe held by statues—which, in the world of the rabbis, were mainly Roman—was probably not accidental.

The use of the phrase "land and sea" to express universal rule or dominion may seem an unimportant detail in the history of the encounter between the Romans and the Jews, but the examples given above show that at least some Jews were acutely aware of the meaning of this expression and its part in Roman claims. Moreover, they also show that some Jews resisted these Roman claims by using this very expression not to endorse but rather to challenge the idea of Roman universal dominion.

Other Jewish texts reflect on the *length* of Roman rule. I have argued elsewhere that Philo's discourse on the rise and fall of empires implies a rejection of the idea that divine providence had set Rome apart from other peoples and dominions and would secure its rule forever. Between the lines, he suggests that the Roman empire is just one of many and would ultimately disappear, as previous empires had, whereas Israel will ultimately rise from humiliation to glory and universal hegemony. From Philo's perspective, divine providence (*pronoia*) worked only on behalf of Israel, a strong statement that stood in sharp contradiction to imperial ideology.[237]

Josephus shared this perspective to a great extent, despite the defeat in 70 CE and his repeated affirmation that God had sided with the Romans. On the basis of the retelling of Nebuchadnezzar's dream (Dan 2:34–35) in *Jewish Antiquities* 10.207–210, Paul Spilsbury has argued that he "spoke, albeit allusively and cautiously, of the future fall of the empire."[238] For Josephus, the last kingdom evoked in Daniel 2 was not Greece but Rome, and Daniel's prophecy meant that the Roman empire would ultimately perish. Moreover, when one listens closely to the words that Josephus puts in Balaam's mouth in *Antiquities* 4.127–128, it is possible to hear a warning addressed to the Romans. Josephus writes that divine providence preserves the Jews from complete

---

234. See Wilfand 2020a. The texts that she refers to are y. Avodah Zarah 3:1, 42c; y. Bava Metzi'a 2:4, 8c; Genesis Rabbah 33:1. See also Schäfer 2002b, 345, which notes in passing that Greek rule served "as a code for Roman rule."

235. Whitmarsh 2013, 69.

236. Gruen 1985, 71.

237. Berthelot 2011b.

238. Spilsbury 2002, 317.

destruction and that, after having been temporarily defeated, they will "flourish and bring fear upon those who caused injury to them."[239] This passage
may even be interpreted as betraying Josephus' hope for the resurgence of the
Judean state, at some point in the distant future. He had not given up hope
for the end of Roman hegemony and the restoration of Israel, even though he
certainly did not expect this to happen in his lifetime.[240]

Oracular and apocalyptic texts dated to the end of the first century CE—
such as the Sibylline Oracles, 2 Baruch, and 4 Ezra—as well as later rabbinic
literature convey the hope that Rome will ultimately be destroyed,[241] but
at the same time some also express great anxiety over Israel's present situation and the permanence of Roman rule. This anxiety is particularly clear in
a famous passage from the midrash Leviticus Rabbah (29:2) that interprets
Jacob's vision of the ladder with angels ascending and descending (Genesis
28:12). This midrash's final redaction dates to the fifth century CE, but it pur-
portedly reports the teachings of two third-century CE rabbis, according to
whom the angels represent "the princes of the nations," which correspond to
the empires that had oppressed Israel in the past (the background scheme
is the four empires found in Daniel 2 and 7). The angels' ascent and descent
of the ladder recalls that after a period of rising and oppressing Israel, these
empires disappeared. Yet the angel representing the Prince of Edom (Rome,
the last kingdom) does not descend, prompting Jacob to ask God, "Lord of all
the worlds, will this one never be brought down?" God's answer to Jacob is
meant to be reassuring: "Even if you see him rise to the skies, I will bring him
down."[242] Yet the anxiety emanating from this vision is perceptible.

3.2 A "MESSIANIC" VOCATION TO BRING PEACE, PROSPERITY, AND LEGAL ORDER TO THE WORLD

From at least the beginning of the Principate, the Romans presented their rule
as one that brought peace and order to the world, and from their perspective,
this order was predicated on law and not on military force alone. The passage
in Virgil's *Aeneid* in which Anchises foretells to Aeneas the fate of the people to
whom he will give birth ascribes the following mission to the Romans:

239. Josephus, *A.J.* 4.128, trans. Louis H. Feldman in Feldman 2000, 376.

240. Rajak 1991, 132; Price 2005; Berthelot 2011b, 174–175.

241. See Sib. Or. 4.130–161 (and also 3.156–161, dated from an earlier period); 2 Baruch
36.9–10, 39.5–7; 4 Ezra 11–12 (based on the identification of Rome with the fourth beast
in Daniel 7). See Sharon 2020; Noam 2020; on the Sibylline Oracles, Gruen 2020; on
4 Ezra, Stone 1990, 343–371. In rabbinic literature, see, e.g., Pesiqta de-Rav Kahana (Vayehi
beḥetzi ha-laylah) 7:11 (ed. Mandelbaum, 1:132–133). Mekhilta de-Rabbi Ishmael asserts
that the moment when "this guilty kingdom" (Rome) will come to an end is hidden from
human beings (Vayassaʿ 5, ed. Horovitz and Rabin, 171).

242. On Leviticus Rabbah 29:2, see Noam 2020.

Others, I doubt not, shall with softer mould beat out the breathing bronze, coax from the marble features to the life, plead cases with greater eloquence and with a pointer trace heaven's motions and predict the risings of the stars: you, Roman, be sure to rule peoples with authority (*regere imperio populos*) (be these your arts), to impose law on peace (*pacique imponere morem*), to spare the vanquished and to crush the proud (*parcere subiectis et debellare superbos*).[243]

These verses were not mere poetry. Ando notes that this conception of Rome's "mission" played a central role "in explaining the evolution of the empire into a 'singular and perfect coalition of its members.'"[244]

Peace (*pax*) in particular took on a new prominence and significance from the end of the first century BCE onward. It lay at the core of the Augustan ideology of rule, and it had a two-fold meaning: civil peace within Roman society on the one hand, and peace imposed on conquered territories and peoples on the other.[245] Peace was also central to the Flavian dynasty—with bitter implications for the Jews. Like Augustus, Vespasian put an end to both a civil war between political rivals and an "exterior" war—in Egypt at the time of Augustus, and in Judea under the Flavians, even though Judea was already part of the empire—and he likewise made free use of the motif of peace or pacification in his communication strategy.[246] The erection in Rome of the *Ara Pacis* by Augustus and of the *Templum Pacis* (Temple of Peace) by Vespasian illustrate the centrality of this notion for both.[247] Vespasian consciously drew on the Augustan model in other ways too: his closure of the Gates of Janus in 71 CE imitated the three closures under Augustus, which the princeps reported in his *Res Gestae*.[248] For both rulers, victory and peace were crucial elements of their legitimacy.[249]

---

243. Virgil, *Aeneid* 6.847–853, trans. H. Rushton Fairclough (revised by G. P. Goold), LCL, 593 (slightly modified). See also Chapter Four, n. 12.

244. Ando 2000, 48, quoting Gibbon 1972, 513.

245. See Weinstock 1960, esp. 45; Levi 1985, 209; Nicolet 1988, 133–134; de Souza 2008, 79–87; Noreña 2011, 127. On the connection between peace and the emperor, see also Momigliano 1942a, 64.

246. Paladini 1985, 226–227; Rosso 2005.

247. Momigliano 1942b; Weinstock 1960 (which challenges the common opinion that the altar is dedicated to Pax); Zanker 1988, 172–175. On the *Templum Pacis*, see §4 below.

248. See *Res Gestae* 13; Paladini 1985; Tuck 2016, 117–118.

249. Peace cannot be separated from the wars that led to victory and pacification. As Erich Gruen rightly emphasizes, there was no Augustan ideology of peace that would have rejected war per se, no "pacifist" ideology, to use an anachronistic term (Gruen 1985). See also de Souza 2008, 85: "The princeps was a peacemaker because he was an *imperator*." For the use of the vocabulary of pacification, see, e.g., the statue base of Augustus dedicated by the people of Baetica, designating their *provincia* as *pacata*: *CIL* VI, 31267; and Lavan 2017.

Together with victory, peace was one of the main benefits that the empire brought to its inhabitants, and one abundantly advertised on coinage, with representations of Pax (the goddess of peace) on the reverse or legends such as *Pax* and *Pax aeterna*.[250] *Pax* was first and foremost linked to the emperor (*pax Augusti*), but on occasions it was also associated with the Roman people. For example, a numismatic type minted under Nero to celebrate the peace made with Parthia in 63 CE features on the reverse a representation of the temple of Janus with closed doors, as well as the legend IANVM CLVSIT PACE P(opuli) R(omani) TERRA MARIQ(ue) PARTA, "He closed [the temple of] Janus, the peace of the Roman people having been achieved on land and at sea."[251] Sestertii minted in 71 CE, under Vespasian, show Pax standing with a branch and cornucopiae with the legend PAX P(opuli) ROMANI.[252]

Admittedly, as Greg Woolf rightly emphasizes, peace was an ideological construct. However, it was not wholly an abstraction: "The Romans' power was great, even if they did not rule the world, and the provinces were freer of war because peace had been declared than if it had not been. Imperial propagation of the image of peace contributed to sustaining it."[253] According to Ando, "There is abundant evidence that populations around the empire, particularly in the Greek East, recognized and appreciated the political and economic stability with which the imperial government endowed daily life."[254] This is particularly true of the local elites who were the first to benefit from the state of relative security and stability brought by the empire.[255] Provincial coinage featured *Eirēnē*, just as imperial coinage represented *Pax*, and bore legends celebrating peace.[256] Inscriptions also provide examples of decrees

250. Ando 2000, xii; Noreña 2011, 108, 127–132; Manders 2012, 199–205. According to Fuhrmann 2012, 89, "Anyone who handled a coin stamped *pax* or *concordia* was exposed to it." On the importance of both war and peace in Flavian coinage, see Bianco 1968, 168–172; Gambash and Gitler 2017, 71–74.

251. See *RIC* I, rev. ed., Nero, no. 50, p. 153, also nos. 51, 58, 263–267, etc. (fifty-two in total, minted mostly in Rome, with small variants in some cases, and one—no. 470—minted in Lugdunum).

252. *RIC* II.1, rev. ed., Vespasian, nos. 187–189, p. 73. See also *RIC* I, rev. ed., Civil wars, no. 4, p. 203 (denarius minted in Spain in 68–69 CE, with the legend PACI—P R on the reverse, below which clasped hands hold a winged caduceus); cf. no. 10, p. 204.

253. Woolf 1993, 190.

254. Ando 2000, 6.

255. Among Greek authors, see in particular Aelius Aristides, *Roman Oration* 64, 67–71 (Oliver 1953, 902); Plutarch, *On the Fortune of the Romans* 317b–c. See also Epictetus, *Discourses* 3.13.9.

256. Under Octavian, in 28 BCE, a cistophorus was minted in Ephesus with the legend PAX (*RIC* I, rev. ed., Augustus, no. 476, p. 79). See also, e.g., *RPC* III, region of Bithynia (unknown city), no. 1126, p. 137 (bronze issue minted under Trajan, with the legend ΕΙΡΗΝΗ ΣΕΒΑΣΤΗ); Alexandria, nos. 4379.1–2, 4380.1–2 (minted under Trajan; representing Eirēnē standing and holding a cornucopia); Alexandria, no. 5319, p. 687 (minted under Hadrian; Eirēnē standing and holding ears of corn and a caduceus, with the legend

passed by Greek cities praising the peace, concord, and prosperity brought by Rome or the emperor. At the very beginning of the first century CE, Halicarnassus thus published a decree celebrating the arrival of Augustus, which lavishly praises the princeps, whose motherland is "the divine Roma" and who is called "savior of the common race of men"; the inscription then states: "Land and sea are at peace and the cities flourish with good order, concord, and prosperity."[257] In 46 CE, after the new province of Lycia was established, its inhabitants honored the emperor Claudius as a savior for freeing them from internal strife, insecurity, and brigandage.[258] The eradication of banditry (including piracy) had been a main theme of Roman and pro-Roman discourses from the first century BCE onward, so the Lycians were expressing themselves here in a quite conventional way.[259] As to the claim that Roman rule had put an end to conflicts between Greeks, one finds a similar argument under the pen of Aelius Aristides at the end of the second century CE.[260] Another testimony stemming from the Greek East is an inscription dated to 198 CE that mentions a public festival at Nicopolis ad Istrum to celebrate "the good tidings of [the Severan] blessings, namely an oecumenical peace available for all mankind because of the defeat of the barbarians who were ever attacking the empire, and [the Severan] union in a righteous partnership."[261]

This last example testifies to the difficulties that would plague the empire during most of the third century CE, before the advent of the Tetrarchy. Despite these difficulties, which could have triggered rebellions of all sorts, in the third century many if not most provincials supported Rome, for they had come to see the empire's peace as their own, on the basis of the benefits experienced during the first and second centuries.[262] An honorific inscription dedicated to a Roman officer named Valerius Statilius Castus by the inhabitants of Termessos Minor (near Oinoanda in southern Anatolia) between 255 and 257 CE praises him for having provided "peace by land and sea."[263] Erika Manders notes that

---

ΕΙΡΗΝΗ ΣΕΒΑΣΤΗ). Alexandria also minted numerous coins featuring Eirēnē under Antoninus Pius and Marcus Aurelius, as well as under Decius.

257. For the Greek text see Hirschfeld 1916, 59–61, no. 894, lines 5–10 (PHI Halikarnassos 4); trans. Braund 1985, 59, no. 123.

258. *SEG* 51.1832 + 57.1670; Jones 2001a, 163, lines 16–20. Suetonius writes that the emperor had deprived the Lycians of their freedom "because of deadly intestine feuds" (*Claudius* 25.9.3). See the analysis of Aitor Blanco Pérez in "Honours for Claudius in the Stadiasmus Patarensis," at http://judaism-and-rome.org/honours-claudius-stadiasmus-patarensis.

259. On piracy, see Braund 1993; de Souza 1999. The opponents of Rome in the East were also conveniently labeled "bandits." See Isaac 1984; Shaw 1984; Isaac 1990, 66–67.

260. Aelius Aristides, *Roman Oration* 97, 103. See Ando 2000, 54–55.

261. *IGBulg* II, 659, lines 26–30; trans. Oliver 1989, p. 440, no. 217.

262. Ando 2000, 6.

263. *IGR* III, 481 + 1501 = *ILS* 8870, lines 11–13; trans. Aitor Blanco Pérez in "Valerius Statilius Castus, Oinoanda and the Arrival of Imperial Statues under Valerian," at

the discourse of peace continued and even gained momentum during the third century: "Apparently, at times when the *pax Romana*, and thus the Empire's unity, was threatened most, messages propagating eternal peace circulated on a large scale."[264] For Rome's thousandth anniversary, in 248, Philip I minted aurei with the legend PAX AETERNA, "eternal peace."[265]

Yet, on the other hand, Roman peace meant that any rebellion would be crushed without pity, as the paradigmatic case of Judea shows. We should not let imperial or even provincial ideology and rhetoric hide the fact that peace was first and foremost in the interest of the Romans and the provincial elites associated with Roman rule. The fact remains that "within and without the empire, Roman peace may be seen as simply a component of wider patterns of violence, a concomitant of other structures of domination."[266]

From a Jewish perspective, another problematic aspect of Rome's "mission" of peace, legal order, and universal rule was its similarity to the mission ascribed to Israel in biblical and Jewish tradition, according to which all the nations were to be blessed in Abraham and called to discover God's law, to submit to God, and finally to live in peace with one another, possibly in the messianic age to come.[267] The book of Isaiah in particular describes the eschatological peace that would follow on universal recognition of the God of Israel—"the earth will be full of the knowledge of the Lord as the waters cover the sea" (Isa 11:9)—and the restoration of the Davidic kingdom: "His authority shall grow continually, and there shall be endless peace for the throne of David and his kingdom" (Isa 9:6; verse 7 in the NRSV). Even Philo, who rarely indulged in eschatological conjecture, expected Israel and its laws to be universally acknowledged at the end of days.[268] From a Jewish perspective, then, the quasi-universal peace promised by Rome could sound like a claim that Rome was fulfilling the promises God had made to Israel. In other words, by promoting its own "messianic" age, Rome could be perceived as taking the place of Israel. The fact that the notion of *shalom* differed from the notion of *pax*—a point rightly emphasized by Martin Goodman[269]—does not undermine this argument, since Rome's claim to bring peace to the world was in any case deceitful in the eyes of most Jewish authors we know. That Rome's *pax* was not real peace from a Jewish perspective did not make the Roman or

---

http://judaism-and-rome.org/valerius-statilius-castus-oinoanda-and-arrival-imperial -statues-under-valerian.

264. Manders 2012, 203.

265. *RIC* IV.3, Philip I, nos. 40–41, p. 73 (minted in Rome).

266. Woolf 1993, 172.

267. See Gen 12:1–3; Isa 11:1–10; Isa 60; Dan 7. See also 4Q246 frag. 1, col. ii, 1–9.

268. On Philo's eschatological or messianic expectations, see *On Rewards and Punishments*, esp. §§163–171, *QE* 2.76; Goodenough 1938, 115–120; Barraclough 1984, 480–481; Borgen 1992; Scott 1995, 567–575; Borgen 1997, 261–281.

269. Goodman 2007, 324.

pro-Roman claims that Rome had brought peace to the world less problematic; on the contrary, it made them even more so.

Yet we must acknowledge that this Roman claim was perceived by Jews in various ways and prompted different types of responses, sometimes by the same author. First, Jews did not always eschew celebration of the peace and stability brought by the empire. In fact, some Jewish authors echo the Roman or pro-Roman discourse celebrating the *pax Romana*. In the *Embassy to Gaius*, for example, Philo praises the peace that prevailed during Augustus' Principate:

> This is he who not only loosed but broke the chains which had shackled and pressed so hard on the habitable world. This is he who exterminated wars both of the open kind and the covert which are brought about by the raids of brigands. This is he who cleared the sea of pirate ships and filled it with merchant vessels. This is he who reclaimed every state to liberty, who led disorder into order and brought gentle manners and harmony to all unsociable and brutish nations, who enlarged Hellas by many a new Hellas and hellenized the outside world in its most important regions, the guardian of the peace, who dispensed their dues to each and all, who did not hoard his favours but gave them to be common property, who kept nothing good and excellent hidden throughout his life.[270]

This passage has a clear rhetorical dimension: Augustus is described as a good emperor with the intent to contrast him with Caligula, the bad emperor who did not respect the rights of the Jews. Moreover, in this specific passage, Philo aims to discredit the Alexandrians by showing that they had not honored Augustus as they now sought to honor Caligula, despite the former's superiority. Finally, Philo was aware that the Roman authorities might read his work (maybe he even hoped they would), and thus had to formulate his criticism cautiously.[271] For all these reasons, his praise of Augustus should not be taken entirely at face value.[272] Nonetheless, the fact remains that Philo echoed some aspects of Roman imperial and Greek pro-Roman discourses, such as the idea that the Romans had cleared the sea of pirates and the roads of brigands.[273]

270. Philo, *Legat.* 146–147, trans. F. H. Colson, LCL, 75.

271. However, to consider the *Legatio* as aimed mainly at a Roman—or, more specifically, imperial—audience, as Goodenough 1938 argued, is not satisfactory. We should rather consider the possibility of a mixed audience (Jews and Romans), as Pieter van der Horst has suggested for *In Flaccum* (van der Horst 2003, 15–16). See also Hartog 2019, n. 87.

272. See further Berthelot 2011b. For a different perspective on this passage, see Niehoff 2001, 113–118.

273. Moreover, in this passage of the *Legatio*, Philo uses topoi that were penned by Greek authors who praised Rome. His insistence on the Hellenization of barbarian countries and peoples in the context of empire, for example, is typically Greek and not Roman. Roman imperial discourse was about peace and order, not Hellenization or civilization: see Inglebert 2005, 438–440.

For Josephus it was obviously not easy to celebrate the Flavian peace. In contrast to Philo, who passes over this point in silence, Josephus makes clear that peace is synonymous with submission to Rome.[274] However, he does his best to present Vespasian and Titus as moderate and lenient rulers who would have been ready to reach a compromise with the Judean rebels had the latter not been stubborn fanatics.[275] It is striking that Josephus describes the rebels as tyrants and *lēstai*, "bandits," a term commonly employed by pro-Roman Greek authors to qualify not only bands of robbers but also groups that opposed Rome.[276] Moreover, when Josephus speaks about the adversaries of Herod he designates them too as *lēstai*, reflecting the Herodian perspective that Herod's enemies were Rome's as well. Finally, in Josephus' account of Herod's suppression of banditry, the peace that ensues looks very much like the *pax Romana*.[277] Josephus, who composed his works in Rome for a mixed audience that included Greek, Roman and Jewish members of the elite (especially in the case of *The Judean War*), had thus absorbed a Roman or pro-Roman perspective to a great extent.[278] This perspective colors his description of the social and political troubles that occurred in Judea from the reign of Herod to the Great Revolt.

Interestingly enough, some rabbinic texts echo this praise of the benefits of the *pax Romana* and the Roman legal order. In Mishnah Avot 3:2, we thus read: "R. Hananiah [or: Hanina] the Prefect of the Priests said: Pray for the peace of the kingdom (*malkhut*), because if it were not for the fear of it, a man would have swallowed up his neighbour alive."[279] In the context of the Mishnah, "the kingdom" refers to Rome. Jews are thus encouraged to pray for the peace of the Roman empire, of which they are a part, and furthermore, the teaching attributed to R. Hananiah implies that the empire brings a certain order to a world that would otherwise be violent and chaotic.

In Genesis Rabbah, a midrash whose final redaction dates to the beginning of the fifth century CE, an even more positive opinion is attributed to Resh Laqish (a third-century CE Palestinian amora, according to rabbinic tradition), in connection with Genesis 1:31, "And God saw everything that he had made, and behold, it was very good (*we-hine tov meod*)":

274. Josephus, *B.J.* 2.340–341, 401.

275. Josephus, *B.J.* 4.58, 102, 120; 6.215–216, 344–345; etc.

276. See Josephus, *B.J.* 1.10–11 (which uses the adjective *lēstrikos*); n. 259 above.

277. Josephus, *B.J.* 1.204–205; *A.J.* 15.348.

278. Josephus seems to have composed his works both for Jews and for Greeks and Romans who had some interest in the Jews' history, traditions, and customs. See Mason 2005a, which emphasizes that Josephus' intended audience must have consisted primarily of members of the elite living in Rome. Whether and to what extent Josephus succeeded in reaching a Roman audience is a different question. See Cotton and Eck 2005a.

279. Trans. Danby 1933, 450, very slightly modified.

Resh Laqish says: *Behold, it was very good*: this is the kingdom of heaven. *And behold, it was very good*: this is the earthly kingdom. How is the earthly kingdom very good? How strange! Only because it exacts justice for the creatures [for human beings]. *I made the earth and created man/Adam/Edom upon it* (Isaiah 45:12).[280]

Resh Laqish seems to interpret the presence of the *waw* in *we-hine*—the "and" in "And behold"—as meaning that two things were declared very good: the kingdom of heaven and the earthly kingdom. The expression *malkhut ha-aretz*, literally "kingdom of the earth," can designate any worldly government, but in the Palestinian rabbinic context, this kingdom was the Roman empire. Moreover, the surprise expressed in the commentary at the possibility that the earthly kingdom might be considered good corroborates its identification with Rome rather than with some general and vague entity. In rabbinic literature, Rome was in fact frequently described as "the evil kingdom." If we understand *malkhut ha-aretz* here as designating Rome, then it is possible that Resh Laqish's use of the biblical verse Isaiah 45:12 is based not on the reading *adam—I made the earth and created man/Adam*—but rather on a different vocalization that leads to the reading *Edom*.[281] As we shall see in the last section of this chapter, in rabbinic literature "Edom" often designates Rome. The verse from Isaiah may thus be understood to mean that God created Edom—that is, the Roman empire—and established its power over the nations of the earth. According to the midrash, the explanation for such a paradoxical divine decision lies in the fact that the Roman empire "exacts justice for the creatures." In other words, it establishes a proper legal order. This passage is exceptional in rabbinic literature. Most rabbinic texts condemn the brutality and arbitrariness of Roman rule, which brought anything but security to the subject people.[282] In Chapter Four, we will examine how Jews living in the empire challenged Roman claims to have the most perfect legal system and to rule justly. This passage from Genesis Rabbah is thus all the more striking. Ultimately, it may show that it is possible to appreciate the stability and order brought by a political system that is at the same time deemed iniquitous in other respects.[283]

Alongside the partial acceptance of the idea that the *pax Romana* benefited the populations of the empire, a second type of reaction that must be taken into consideration was an insistence on describing the Jews as a very peaceful people, which is particularly obvious in Philo's and Josephus'

---

280. Genesis Rabbah 9:13, ed. Theodor and Albeck, 73–74.

281. See Albeck's commentary in the Theodor and Albeck edition, 74.

282. In Genesis Rabbah itself, see, e.g., 65:1, ed. Theodor and Albeck, 713; see also Leviticus Rabbah 13:5.

283. Cf. Weiss 2018, 417.

writings.[284] Rabbinic literature too describes Israel as peaceful, and calls the God of Israel himself "Peace."[285] As Yael Wilfand has argued, the use of the name Shalom to designate the God of Israel, which is not attested in the Bible, may have been inspired by the existence in the Greco-Roman world of a deity called Pax or Eirēnē and the ideological insistence on the *pax Romana*.[286] On the whole, this second type of reaction—be it the presentation of the people of Israel as peaceful or the fact of calling the God of Israel "Peace"—involves a certain degree of mimesis and rivalry.

A third way to deal with the challenge of Roman peace consisted of affirming that this peace was in fact due to the presence of Jews within the empire or to their prayers—and sacrifices, up to 66 CE—on behalf of it. This chapter has already referred to passages in Philo's work that point in this direction (see §2.3 above). Some rabbinic texts reflect a similar perspective. In the Jerusalem Talmud, we repeatedly encounter the idea that all the blessings that God bestows upon the world are granted only for the sake of Israel.[287] Although these passages hint at material prosperity in particular, we may surmise that in the minds of the redactors, peace was included among the blessings bestowed on the world for Israel's sake. Genesis Rabbah 66:2, which comments on Song of Songs 7:1 and the Shulammite—whose name comes from the root *sh-l-m*, meaning "peace," and who is identified with Israel—associates the latter with peace in a great variety of different ways. In particular, Israel is described as "a people through which peace will be given [to the world]."[288] This same section presents Israel as "a nation that makes peace between me [God] and my world, for without it, I would

284. Philo, *Flacc.* 48; *Legat.* 230 (the Jews are peaceful both by nature and by education). In *Legat.* 161, it is Tiberius himself who describes the Jews as peaceful. However, in other passages such as *Legat.* 202, 216–217, Philo also suggests that a lack of respect for the Jews' ancestral laws could lead to armed Jewish resistance, and constitute a threat for Rome; see Bilde 2009, 111–112. For Josephus, the people are fundamentally peaceful but are frightened by the rebels: see *B.J.* 2.302, 2.345, 3.448, 4.84, 5.53. In a highly realistic way, Josephus also mentions that the Judean elites desired peace because of their wealth (*B.J.* 2.338, 4.414).

285. See in particular Genesis Rabbah 66:2 for a close association between peace and the people of Israel.

286. Wilfand 2019a, 238.

287. See y. Shevi'it 4:3, 35b; 5:9, 36a; y. Avodah Zarah 4:9, 44b; y. Gittin 5:9, 47c.

288. Gen. Rabbah 66:2, ed. Theodor and Albeck, 745. This teaching is attributed to R. Berekhiah, who, according to rabbinic tradition, was a Palestinian amora from the fifth generation (fourth century). Contrary to Theodor and Albeck, I follow the reading of several MSS that have "through her (Israel)" (*bah*) and not "to her" (*lah*). Another way to understand *bah* is "in her (midst)," which would restrict the peace to Israel only. The midrash interprets the fourfold repetition of the word *shuvi* (return), addressed to the Shulammite, in connection with the four empires that Israel was subject to, saying that Israel entered them and went out of them in peace.

destroy my world."[289] According to this tradition, it is not only peace but the very existence of the world, and thus of the Roman empire, that depends on Israel. A few lines on, the midrash quotes a saying attributed to R. Eleazar b. Merom, which explains that the name Shulammite is given to Israel because "it safeguards [or: completes] the stability of the world, both in this world and in the world to come." The word for "stability," *istation*, derives from the Greek *station* (Latin *statio*) and refers to Roman realities, either to "the seat of the fiscal officers in the Roman provinces" (according to Marcus Jastrow) or to a military outpost, in which case it might refer to the defensive and protective aspects of peace.[290] According to the midrash, the world's true stability is not the one based on the Roman administration or army, but rather the one achieved through Israel's presence and virtuous actions. Finally, Rabbi Yehoshua of Sikhnin is reported to have said in the name of Rabbi Levi—a Palestinian amora from the end of the third or the beginning of the fourth century—that "every good that comes to the world comes only for their [the people of Israel's] sake [or: because of their merit]."[291] In all cases, the underlying idea is the same: whatever peace and prosperity the empire enjoys, it owes it all to Israel.

A fourth type of response to the *pax Romana* consisted of rejecting the Roman claim altogether and affirming that true peace would come only with the advent of the messianic era or the kingdom of God. This position can be found in the tannaitic midrash Sifre Numbers, on Numbers 6:26, "[May] the Lord lift up his face upon you, and give you peace"—the priestly blessing upon Israel. The midrash discusses the nature of this peace. A first opinion, attributed to R. Nathan—who, according to rabbinic tradition, was a third-generation tanna who lived at the time of the Bar Kokhba Revolt—states that the biblical verse refers to "the peace of the kingdom of the House of David." To support this statement, the text brings forward Isaiah 9:6, which follows the announcement that a "prince of peace" (*sar shalom*) will come: "His authority shall grow continually, and there shall be endless peace for the throne of David and his kingdom. He will establish and uphold it with justice and with righteousness from this time onward and forevermore. The zeal of the Lord of hosts will do this."[292] This biblical text could be interpreted as referring to the political and royal messiah who would be a descendant of David. In short, R. Nathan's statement means that real peace is not the peace brought

---

289. Ed. Theodor and Albeck, 745. The saying is attributed to Rabbi Samuel bar Tanḥum and Rabbi Ḥanan son of Rabbi Berekhiah of Bosra, in the name of Rabbi Idi (a fourth-generation Babylonian amora active in the first half of the fourth century, according to rabbinic tradition). There are many variants of these names in the MSS.

290. Ed. Theodor and Albeck, 746; Jastrow 1950, 55.

291. Ed. Theodor and Albeck, 746.

292. Sifre Numbers 42, ed. Kahana 2011–2015, 1:115. Further discussions of peace are found on pp. 115–119.

by Rome but only that which will stem from the coming of the messiah and the restoration of the kingdom of Israel. However, in this midrash we find other understandings of peace as well, such as the one attributed to R. Yehudah ha-Nasi—who, according to rabbinic tradition, lived at the beginning of the third century CE and was responsible for the compilation of the Mishnah. R. Yehudah affirms that the peace given by God to Israel is "the peace of Torah," a peace that derives from studying the Torah rather than from particular political circumstances or actions.[293] This passage from Sifre Numbers shows how diverse rabbinic understandings of peace were and—indirectly and implicitly—how diverse the responses to the challenge of the *pax Romana* were as well.[294]

Finally, there was a fifth category of response that went beyond discourse. It was outright revolt against the so-called Roman peace, and it is to these insurrections that we now turn.

4. The Roman Victories Over the Jews: Obliteration and Substitution

With three Jewish revolts taking place within a span of seventy years—the Great Revolt or Judean War of 66–73, the Diaspora Revolt of 115–117, and the Bar Kokhba Revolt of 132–135—the Romans' claims of bringing peace to the world rang bitterly hollow to the Jews.[295] All three revolts failed, with cumulative effects that were devastating for the Jewish people: heavy losses of Jewish lives, confiscations of land, the enslavement of a great number of Jews, the destruction of the Temple and most of Jerusalem, the partial disappearance of the scribal and priestly elites who gravitated around the Temple, the creation of the *fiscus Iudaicus*, the refounding of Jerusalem as Aelia Capitolina, and the relative emptying of the Jewish population from Judea.[296] The Diaspora Revolt, which took place mainly in Cyrenaica, Cyprus, and Egypt, also led to the

293. See further Chapter Three, §3.3.

294. On the theme of peace in Palestinian rabbinic texts, see Mekhilta de-Rabbi Ishmael, Baḥodesh (Yithro) 11 (ed. Horowitz and Rabin, 244); Sifre Zuta Numbers 6:26; Sifre Deuteronomy 199 (ed. Finkelstein, 237); Genesis Rabbah 38:6 (ed. Theodor and Albeck, 355–356); Leviticus Rabbah 9:9 (ed. Margulies, 187–195); Wilfand 2019a.

295. The precise date of the beginning of the Diaspora Revolt is debated. On the basis of papyri from Egypt, which indicate that it started in the spring of 116 (in contrast with the testimony of Eusebius, who mentions the year 115), Miriam Pucci Ben Zeev dates the Diaspora Revolt to 116–117 CE (Pucci Ben Zeev 2005, 145–156).

296. See Herr 1972, which sees the failure of the Bar Kokhba Revolt as even more devastating than the outcome of the First Revolt (116); Alon 1980, 2:648; Schwartz 2001, 15, and Part 2, which aims "to provide a description of a society that disintegrated under the impact of an imperialism sharpened by the failure of the two Palestinian revolts" (103); Schremer 2008; Schremer 2010, 42–44. For reconsiderations of the impact of the defeat of 70 CE, see Neusner 2006; Klawans 2010; Schwartz and Weiss 2012.

disappearance of most Jewish communities from those areas, at least as far as we can tell from the sources that have come down to us, which do not necessarily reflect the diversity of the situation on the ground.[297] In short, the consequences of the revolts were felt on all levels: demographic, economic, social, political, and religious.[298] Moreover, the memory of the Jewish defeats endured for quite a long time in the Roman empire. The crushing of the Great Revolt was commemorated on coinage and in monumental buildings and inscriptions in Rome, and the Jews' humiliation was perpetuated through the tax of the *fiscus Iudaicus* at least until the fourth century.[299] In the case of the Diaspora Revolt, an Oxyrrhynchite papyrus dated to 200 CE mentions an annual festival celebrating the Jews' defeat, this more than eighty years after the events themselves.[300]

The Judean War and the Diaspora Revolt involved other groups besides the Jews and the Romans, and tensions and animosity between the Jews and some of their neighbors (Syrians, Greeks, and Egyptians, among others) played important roles in sparking them.[301] Yet the fact remains that from a Roman perspective, these conflicts were not merely local: in 66 CE, the interruption of the sacrifices made for the emperor's sake at the Jerusalem Temple could be perceived only as a sign of rebellion, and in 115–117 CE, the Jews both perturbed the Roman imperial order and openly revolted against Rome, for instance by destroying buildings associated with the Roman administration or the imperial cult. Moreover, in each case, the troubles were serious enough that they forced the Romans to mobilize several legions. According to Werner Eck, up to thirteen legions, in full force or represented by *vexillationes*, were deployed to deal with the Bar Kokhba Revolt, though not necessarily all at the same time. That the situation in 132–135 was indeed difficult for the Romans, even though they faced a mere guerrilla force, is shown by the fact that Hadrian sent one of his best generals, Sextus Julius Severus, who until then had been the governor of Britain, to crush the rebels.[302] In short, the Roman authorities saw the three revolts as grave dangers.

---

297. Appian of Alexandria reports Trajan's extermination of the Jews in Egypt in *The Civil Wars* 2.90.380 (Pucci Ben Zeev 2005, 77–78). Seth Schwartz rightly cautions against hasty generalizations (Schwartz 2016, 246). It seems that a revolt also occurred in Mesopotamia, but it may not have been specifically Jewish, and its consequences for the Jews living there are unclear. Some unrest apparently occurred in Judea too at that time but did not develop into an open military conflict. On the geographical extent of the Diaspora Revolt, see Pucci Ben Zeev 2005, esp. chaps. 8 (Mesopotamia) and 9 (Judea); Horbury 2014, 190–269.

298. Schwartz 2016.

299. See below, §4.1.

300. Tcherikover and Fuks 1954–1964, 2:258–260, no. 450 (Pucci Ben Zeev 2005, 51–54).

301. On this aspect of the Judean War, see above all Mason 2014; 2016. In the case of the Diaspora Revolt, the destruction of Greek sanctuaries and monuments and the massive killing of Greeks show that the conflict was Greco-Jewish as much as Judeo-Roman.

302. Eck 1999, 81, 82–88. See Cassius Dio, *Rom. Hist.* 69.13.1–3; Millar 1964, 62, on Cassius Dio's source possibly being Hadrian's reports to the Senate.

In each case, what prompted the Jews to revolt is a complex and debated issue. In regard to the Judean War, scholars have emphasized deteriorating social and economic conditions, fiscal pressure, bad procurators, and the latter's misunderstanding of Jewish traditions, as well as ideological and social factors linked to the development of "nationalistic" movements—Zealots, Sicarii—driven by political-religious zeal for the God of Israel, whom they recognized as their only Lord.[303] Goodman has suggested that the Judean elites were at least partly responsible, as some whose position was based on wealth and connections with the Herodians tried to use the war as an opportunity to regain a legitimacy they in fact never had.[304] Steve Mason has pointed to regional factors and "profound structural problems in governing the densely multi-ethnic region of southern Syria with its scars and vestigial hostilities," together with the roles played by individuals and unforeseeable circumstances.[305] Josephus' hostility to the rebels is well known; while speaking about their motivations, he merely hints at a desire for political autonomy with a religious background—Israel being ideally subject or enslaved to no one but God alone.[306] That the rebels indeed had political-religious motivations is shown by their coinage, which featured temple vessels and legends such as "Jerusalem is holy," "Freedom of Zion," and "For the redemption of Zion."[307]

The causes of the Diaspora Revolt—or Revolts, since the singular implies that there existed a unitary movement, a point that is not proved—are probably the most difficult to reconstruct. Josephus' reference to the coming of the Sicarii to Egypt and Cyrene at the end of the Judean War sounds, retrospectively, like a warning that the seeds were sown for deterioration in these areas—even though he later mentions the eradication of these groups.[308] Victor Tcherikover, Shim'on Applebaum, and William Horbury have identified a messianic dimension of the diaspora uprising, rooted in the biblical prophecies of doom for the nations, Israel's redemption, and the ingathering of the "exiled" in the Land.[309] Although it is difficult to believe that such views were unanimously shared by diaspora Jews, the scale of the destruction and massacres in Cyrenaica, Cyprus, and Egypt, which included the demolition of roads,

---

303. See, e.g., the various approaches taken in Berlin and Overman 2002; and Popović 2011, especially the article by James MacLaren, 129–153.

304. Goodman 1987. See also Berlin 2005.

305. Mason 2014, 206.

306. See, e.g., Josephus, *B.J.* 7.410.

307. Meshorer 1982, 259–263.

308. Josephus, *B.J.* 7.410–416, 437–440; Applebaum 1979, 257; Pucci Ben Zeev 2005, 128–130.

309. Tcherikover and Fuks 1957–1964, 1:89–92; Applebaum 1979, 251–260 (which concludes: "The spirit of the movement was messianic, its aim the liquidation of the Roman régime and the setting up of a new Jewish commonwealth, whose task was to inaugurate the messianic era"); Horbury 2014, 270–277. See also Pucci Ben Zeev 2005, 130.

gives credibility to the idea that the Jews who stood up to the Greeks and the Romans in those areas did not expect to remain there but planned instead to depart for Judea.[310] Be that as it may, the Diaspora Revolt was certainly also due in part to conflicts between the Jews and their neighbors at the local level, with Roman authorities sometimes playing a role in the local dynamics.[311] Indeed, the scale of the revolts and their eruption in different regions indicates that local factors can be only part of the explanation. Even though the theory of concerted action remains speculative,[312] it is hard to escape the conclusion that the uprisings were all reactions against the Roman imperial order, which may have been caused partly by Roman misbehavior toward the Jews at the local level, of which we are not aware, but more generally by the continuous humiliation associated with the destruction of the Jerusalem Temple and the creation of the *fiscus Iudaicus*, as well as by the growing awareness that the temple would not be rebuilt as long as Roman rule endured.[313]

The Bar Kokhba Revolt was once thought to have erupted because of Hadrian's ban on circumcision, but this explanation, based on one passage in the unreliable *Historia Augusta*, has now been rightly dismissed.[314] It has become increasingly clear that Hadrian's refoundation of Jerusalem as a Roman colony was the revolt's main cause.[315] The colony, named Aelia

---

310. On the massacres of Greeks by Jews, see Cassius Dio, *Rom. Hist.* 68.32.1–3. On the destruction of roads, which may have been meant simply to prevent the movements of Roman troops, see *SEG* 9.252 (Pucci Ben Zeev 2005, 11–12, no. 11); *AE* 1951, 208 (Pucci Ben Zeev 2005, 12, no. 12).

311. For conflicts at the local level, see Pucci Ben Zeev 2005, 125, 127. For the involvement of Roman authorities, the case of Flaccus' role in Alexandria in 38 CE, long before the revolts, comes to mind immediately, but Josephus also reports Greek requests to the Romans concerning Jews after the defeat of 70 CE (see, e.g., *B.J.* 7.100–103, relating how the inhabitants of Antioch asked Titus to expel the Jews from their city).

312. Pucci Ben Zeev 2005, 263.

313. On this last aspect, see Goodman 2003, 27; Goodman 2005, 170–174; Gambash 2015, 162–163. On Jewish expectations of seeing the Jerusalem Temple rebuilt, which are particularly clear in the Tosefta, see, e.g., t. Rosh Hashanah 2:9; t. Pesahim 8:4; t. Terumot 10:15; t. Ta'anit 3:9 (MS Erfurt 4:9; see Lieberman 1955–1988, 5:1115–1116, which emphasizes the absence of this expectation in the parallels to this text); Kraemer 1995, 74–75; Shahar 2003; Klawans 2006, 199–201.

314. *Historia Augusta, Life of Hadrian* 14.2. The idea that Hadrian forbade circumcision is based on a rescript of Hadrian—found in Justinian's *Digest* 48.8.4.2, in a passage taken from book 7 of Ulpian's *On the Duties of the Proconsul*, dated to 213–217 CE—but this text deals only with castration, and if circumcision had been meant, the verb used in Latin would certainly have been *circumdere*, not *excidere* (*pace* Rabello 1995). See Boustan (Abusch) 2003, 74–80; Oppenheimer 2005c, 243–244. On the rabbinic texts discussing the issue of circumcision that have been used in support of the theory of Hadrian's ban, see Schäfer's illuminating interpretation in Schäfer 1981, 88–91 (which explains them as echoes of an inner Jewish conflict rather than a consequence of a Roman ban).

315. Weksler-Bdolah 2014; Zissu and Eshel 2016; Pucci Ben Zeev 2018; Weksler-Bdolah 2020, 51–60. According to Mor 2016, 145, the reasons for the revolt were mostly linked to

Capitolina, probably came into being in 130 CE, during the emperor's tour of the East, but it was preceded by building works undertaken in the 120s, documented by recent digs in the Old City's Cardo area. Any hopes for the Jerusalem Temple's reconstruction that remained alive at the beginning of the second century would have been dashed by Hadrian's plan.[316] Not only would this temple not be rebuilt, but pagan temples were to be erected in various parts of the city, transforming it, from a Jewish perspective, into a place of idolatry.[317] The coinage of the rebels testifies to their yearning to reconquer their city. The legend "For the freedom of Jerusalem" and representations of the façade of the Jerusalem Temple are found on silver tetradrachms from the beginning to the end of the war.[318] This revolt, too, may have had a messianic dimension, centered on its only known leader, Shim'on ben/bar Kosiba, who proclaimed himself the Prince of Israel. In any case, the so-called Bar Kokhba Revolt was directed against Rome and Roman rule in Judea and had a clear political-religious agenda.[319]

The question arises as to whether the ideological challenge that the Roman empire posed to the Jews, described in the three previous sections of this chapter, also played a role in the successive uprisings that occurred over less than a century. Could it have strengthened the conviction that Rome needed to be confronted and fought, and could it thus be one of the underlying motivations of the rebels? This hypothesis can certainly not be dismissed, but the sources at hand do not allow us to reach a firm conclusion, since apart from the coins, they hardly document the rebels' point of view. Josephus does not elaborate on the latter's understanding of the empire, and the sources associated with the Diaspora and Bar Kokhba Revolts do not shed much light on this issue either. Yet it seems reasonable to assume that the defeats and their consequences made Rome's ideological challenge all the more problematic for the Jews.

Beyond the causes and events of the revolts, which previous studies have analyzed in detail, this section will thus focus on the consequences of the defeats, which deserve particular attention, as they may have contributed to the perception by certain Jews that the Romans were rivals who threatened Israel's place and role in the world.

---

the economic burden associated with Hadrian's visit. On Hadrian's decision to found Aelia Capitolina, see Cassius Dio, *Rom. Hist.* 69.12.1–2; on the reliability of Dio's testimony, Isaac 1983. The hoard of coins found in an excavation led by Hanan Eshel in the el-Jai Cave in Nahal Mikhmash has shown that Aelia Capitolina coins began to be minted before or during the revolt, definitively dismissing the theory that the colony was founded afterward.

316. Bloom 2010 argues that some Jews may have initially misunderstood Hadrian's intentions and hoped for the rebuilding of their temple; see p. 203.

317. The issue of whether the Temple Mount was included in the urban plan of Aelia Capitolina is, in this respect, irrelevant.

318. Meshorer 1982, 264–276.

319. Linder 2006, 138.

4.1 A "GAME OF TEMPLES": FROM
JERUSALEM TO ROME AND VICE-VERSA

The destruction of the Jerusalem Temple in 70 CE deprived the Jews of their political and religious center. The expansive building works initiated by Herod and the increase in pilgrimages to Jerusalem that followed in the first century CE had made the city a prestigious focal point for Jews all over the Mediterranean (and beyond), in a way that was unprecedented. Despite the Roman administration of Judea from 6 CE onward, Jerusalem had probably never been so central as it became during the first century CE—as illustrated, for example, by Josephus' reference to the link between the city and Jews from Adiabene and from Mesopotamia more broadly.[320]

It seems that Vespasian and Titus were aware of the profound connection between the Judean War and the Jerusalem Temple.[321] Despite Josephus' claims to the contrary, the destruction of the Temple was certainly intentional.[322] At the revolt's end, in 73 CE, Vespasian also ordered the demolition of the Leontopolis sanctuary, which had been erected in the wake of the second-century BCE conflicts between Antiochus IV, the Oniads, and other priestly families in Jerusalem.[323] Josephus does not tell his readers much about this temple's role for Egyptian Jewry and gives the impression that it was politically insignificant—an unsurprising perspective from a member of a Judean priestly family who presented himself as a descendant of the Hasmoneans. In any case, Josephus describes Vespasian's decision as a measure meant to prevent a new uprising, and scholars have interpreted it as reflecting a deliberate intention to put an end to the cult of the Jewish God, who, it may be worth recalling, was never integrated in any way into the Roman pantheon.

Vespasian did not content himself with finishing off the cult of the Jewish God (meaning first and foremost putting an end to sacrifices). He also decided to create the *fiscus Iudaicus*, a special treasury for the collection of a tax of two denarii or didrachmon to be paid every year by all Jews, men and women alike, apparently from the ages of three to sixty-two for women and perhaps until death for men.[324] According to Josephus (*B.J.* 7.218), this replaced the tax of the half-shekel that Jewish men over the age of twenty used to pay annually to the Jerusalem Temple—a tax to which some of the coins minted during

---

320. Josephus, *B.J.* 2.519–520, 5.474.

321. Gambash 2015, 152–153, 158.

322. Josephus, *B.J.* 6.228; Rives 2005; Gambash 2013, 184–186.

323. Josephus, *B.J.* 7.421–436. According to Josephus' narrative, it was emptied and closed rather than destroyed.

324. See Tcherikover and Fuks 1957–1964, 2:204–208, no. 421, dated to 73 CE (Arsinoe papyrus). Apparently the tax was also due for slaves owned by Jews. On the Jewish tax, see Smallwood 1976, 371–378; Hadas-Lebel 1984b, 6; Goodman 1989; Goodman 2005; Cappelletti 2006, 100–117; Heemstra 2010.

the Great Revolt referred, together with the representation of a temple vessel on the obverse and the legend "Jerusalem the Holy" on the reverse.[325] Thus, the money that was formerly dedicated to the cult of the God of Israel was now used by Rome and served to strengthen its rule.[326]

Moreover, the money gathered in the *fiscus Iudaicus* may have contributed to the rebuilding of the Capitoline temple of Jupiter in Rome, which had burned down in 69 CE during the civil war between the Vitellians and Vespasian's partisans—leading some provincials, perhaps including the Judean rebels, to think that Rome's power was coming to an end.[327] In *B.J.* 7.218, Josephus reports that Vespasian imposed on "all Jews, wheresoever resident, a poll-tax of two drachms, to be paid annually into the Capitol (*eis to Kapetōlion*) as formerly contributed by them to the temple at Jerusalem."[328] Cassius Dio— whose treatment of the issue is known thanks to the epitome of his work by the Byzantine monk Xiphilinus—is more explicit: "From that time forth it was ordered that the Jews who continued to observe their ancestral customs should pay an annual tribute of two denarii to Jupiter Capitolinus."[329] The Capitoline temple may thus have replaced the Jerusalem Temple as the beneficiary of the tax,[330] at least in the years before the Roman state began to use this money for other purposes—since the Jews continued to pay it until at least the fourth century.[331] If this was indeed the case, then, as Seth Schwartz notes, "it is hard to imagine that this was not meant as a symbolic mark of Capitoline Jupiter's victory over the God of Israel."[332] In any event, the tax remained a symbol of the defeat of the God of Israel and of the Jews' humiliation.[333]

---

325. Meshorer 1982, 260, no. 10; 262, no. 25.

326. Goodman 2005, 170–174.

327. See Tacitus, *Hist.* 4.54, which refers to the Gauls and the misjudgment of the druids in particular. This passage bears similarities to Tacitus' description of the Jews' *superstitio* and inability to correctly decipher the omens at the beginning of the Judean War (*Hist.* 5.13.1–2).

328. Josephus, *B.J.* 7.218, trans. H. St. J. Thackeray, LCL, 567–569. Josephus' formulation "into the Capitol" (*eis to Kapetōlion*) is somewhat ambiguous: see Mason 2008, 170–171, n. 1282; Gambash 2013, 191–192.

329. Cassius Dio, *Rom. Hist.* 66.7.2, trans. Earnest Cary, LCL, 271. On the Jewish tax and the Capitoline temple, see Smallwood 1976, 374–375; Heemstra 2010, 10; Zeichmann 2015.

330. See, however, the counterarguments in Gambash 2013, 160–161.

331. According to Origen, *Epistle to Africanus* 14, the Jewish tax was still in force in the middle of the third century CE, and it seems to have been abolished only during Julian's reign in the fourth century. See Heemstra 2010, 20–21.

332. Schwartz 2016, 245.

333. For Silvia Cappelletti, "The tax [. . .] assumed a political and ideological value that, in many Jews' view, overlooked the heavy economic burden" (Cappelletti 2006, 117). On the understanding of the tax in rabbinic literature, see in particular Mekhilta de-Rabbi Ishmael, Baḥodesh (Yithro) 1 (ed. Horovitz and Rabin, 203), which presents it as a punishment for the Jews' unfaithfulness in paying the tax of the half-shekel to God; Carlebach 1975, 57.

The rebuilt Capitoline temple of Jupiter featured prominently on Flavian coinage, as a symbol of the peace, prosperity, and divine protection granted to Rome through the new dynasty. Inauspiciously enough, in 80 CE another fire broke out, but the temple was again reconstructed under Titus and Domitian.[334] The latter's coinage featured abundant representations of Jupiter's temple, and there is evidence that this coinage was used in the East as well.[335] In the eyes of the Jews and of the people in the province of Judea more generally, the widespread visual representation of the twice-rebuilt temple in Rome must have contrasted sharply with the desolate state of the sanctuary in Jerusalem. The peak of tension must have been reached with the project of erecting a temple to Jupiter in Jerusalem itself, following Hadrian's decision to have a Roman colony established there (see the next section). Before looking at the Aelia episode, however, we must first examine the displacement of the sacred vessels from Jerusalem to the empire's capital.

The Capitoline temple was where Vespasian and Titus' triumphal procession ended in 71 CE and where they offered sacrifices to the gods who had given them victory in Judea. It was in that procession that the sacred vessels from the Jerusalem Temple were exhibited, "conspicuous above all," in Josephus' words.[336] Ten years before Domitian built the triumphal Arch of Titus, whose relief includes a representation of this scene, the symbols of the cult of the Jewish god were paraded through the streets of Rome before being put in the *Templum Pacis*[337] (Fig. 2.6).

Vespasian ordered the construction of the *Templum Pacis*, or "Temple of Peace," in 71, and it was dedicated in 75.[338] As mentioned above (§3.2), this temple connected Vespasian to Augustus and his *Ara Pacis*, as did the closing of the Temple of Janus following the conquest of Judea. Yet the Temple of Peace's complex also served as a kind of museum, in which not only sacred spoils from

---

334. See *RIC* II.1, rev. ed., Titus, no. 172, p. 209 (sestertius minted in 80–81 CE).

335. *RIC* II.1, rev. ed., Domitian, no. 841, p. 329; *RPC* II.1, no. 864, p. 132 (cistophorus representing the temple of Capitoline Jupiter, with the legend CAPIT(olium) RESTIT(utum), from 82 CE). See also *RIC* II.1, rev. ed., nos. 815–816, pp. 325–326 (sestertii, 95–96 CE); Marie Roux, "Cistophorus of Domitian Representing the Temple of Capitoline Jupiter (82 CE)," at http://judaism-and-rome.org/cistophorus-domitian-representing -temple-capitoline-jupiter-82%C2%A0ce. Statius praised Domitian for restoring the temple of Jupiter (*Silvae* 1.6.85–102, 4.3.123–163).

336. Josephus, *B.J.* 7.148. See 7.153–155 for the end of the procession, the execution of Simon bar Gioras, and the sacrifices. (The triumph is described in §7.123–157, which is the most detailed description of a Roman triumph that we have: see Beard 2007.)

337. Jodi Magness (2008) argues that from the Romans' perspective, the temple vessels were meant to visually represent the aniconic God of the Jews, who was now subject to Jupiter. It seems unnecessary to push the interpretation so far: the vessels symbolized the defeat of the God of the Jews but not the god himself.

338. Cassius Dio, *Rom. Hist.* 65.15.1.

FIGURE 2.6. Reliefs on the Arch of Titus in Rome, showing the
sacred vessels from the Jerusalem Temple.
Photograph by Gunnar Bach Pedersen.
https://commons.wikimedia.org/wiki/File:Fra-titusbuen.jpg

the Jerusalem Temple but also precious objects that had once belonged to Nero
were exhibited.[339] The Temple of Peace had a library and a garden also, in
which plants from many places could be found, a symbol of what Pliny would
celebrate as the universal encounter within the empire not only of individuals
but also of landscapes and natural species from various regions—an "encounter" made possible by the Roman peace.[340] The whole complex was thus highly
ideological, celebrating peace—exterior peace in this case, rather than civil
peace—and the Roman empire's universal dimension. As Noreña emphasizes,
"The Templum Pacis was . . . a monument celebrating the pacification of foreign peoples and the power of the Roman war machine under the guidance of

339. Pliny, *Natural History* 34.84.
340. See Pliny, *Natural History* 27.1, which mentions "the boundless *maiestas* of the
Roman peace" and the fact that the gods have given the Romans to humankind as another
light, in addition to the sun.

the new Flavian dynasty," "a large-scale memorial to Roman imperialism in general and to the Flavian conquest of Judaea in particular."[341]

Indeed, Josephus' description of the Flavian triumph ends with a reference to this building, which shows quite clearly the ideological connection between the Temple of Peace and the victory in Judea, as well as the central place held by the fate of the temple vessels in his narrative:

> This [the temple] was very speedily completed and in a style surpassing all human conception. For, besides having prodigious resources of wealth on which to draw he [Vespasian] also embellished it with ancient masterpieces of painting and sculpture; indeed, into that shrine were accumulated and stored all objects for the sight of which men had once wandered over the whole world, eager to see them severally while they lay in various countries. Here, too, he laid up the vessels of gold from the temple of the Jews, on which he prided himself.[342]

Josephus' description of the Temple of Peace is somewhat similar to that of Pliny, but with a special Jewish tone and perspective. It is said to contain marvels from all over the world, which people once traveled very far to see. Among these marvels the Jerusalem Temple's vessels take their place, and Josephus clearly suggests that they are comparable to, if not even more admirable than, the most beautiful artworks produced by Greeks and Romans. He also emphasizes that Vespasian was proud to possess them. In a highly paradoxical way, the humiliation of having the vessels of the Jerusalem Temple displayed in a pagan temple in Rome becomes an opportunity to highlight the exceptional character and value of these Jewish symbols and artistic works. Yet for a Jew living in Rome at that time, the Temple of Peace must have been a constant reminder of the disaster that had befallen Jerusalem.[343]

The victory over the Judeans, so crucial to the legitimacy of the new Flavian dynasty, was in fact instrumentalized throughout the whole visual program of the Flavians.[344] In addition to the Temple of Peace, it included the construction of other monumental buildings. First, Vespasian began the construction of the Colosseum, or *Amphiteatrum Flavium*, on the site where Nero's *Domus Aurea*, or "Golden House," once stood. The first games were given under Titus in 80 CE.[345] The fact that this project was completed thanks to the spoils of the

341. Noreña 2003, 35, 38.

342. Josephus, *B.J.* 7.158–161, trans. H. St. J. Thackeray, LCL, 551–553. See Chapman 2009.

343. On the reactions of Roman Jews to the Flavian victory and policy, see, e.g., Goodman 1994b, 331–332.

344. Darwal-Smith 1996; Millar 2005; Rosso 2005; Gambash 2015, 154–156; Barron 2020. The new dynasty was also glorified by several poets: see Silius Italicus, *Punica* 3.594–629; Valerius Flaccus, *Argonautica* 1.5–17; Martial, *Epigrams* 2.2.

345. Millar 2004, 114.

Judean War was made known to the public by at least one inscription, which has been reconstituted by Geza Alföldy.[346] According to Noreña, the Colosseum can thus be considered a victory monument.[347] Second, a triumphal arch was erected in the Circus Maximus shortly before Titus' death in 81 CE, perhaps to commemorate the tenth anniversary of the triumph he had received together with his father. On this arch, a monumental inscription recalled that the Senate and people of Rome had dedicated it to Titus "because, by the orders and advice of his father he subdued (or: tamed) the Jewish people (*gentem Iudaeorum domuit*) and destroyed the city of Jerusalem, (a thing) either sought in vain by all generals, kings and peoples before him or untried entirely."[348] The claim was false even as far as Roman military operations in Judea were concerned—think only of Pompey's taking of Jerusalem. The inscription's ideological purpose is thus obvious.[349] Finally, after Titus' death, Domitian erected the famous Arch showing both the apotheosis of Titus and his triumph following his victory in Judea, probably as a way to participate in and benefit from his father's and brother's inheritance and legitimacy.[350] Coins bearing the legend IUDAEA CAPTA (or simply IUDAEA) and/or showing a captive Judean woman seated beneath a trophy or a palm tree, alone or together with a male captive, completed this program meant to inscribe the victory over Judea in a lasting way within Rome's visual landscape.[351] These coins were minted in different parts of the empire as well, including in Judea itself (the mint was in Caesarea).[352]

The "game of temples" does not end with this Flavian program, however. To the *translatio templi*, so to speak, from Jerusalem to Rome, we may add the destruction of temples by Jews in Cyrenaica during the Diaspora Revolt, known from archaeological and epigraphic evidence.[353] Applebaum notes that "the evidence of a systematic destruction of buildings, and especially of

---

346. *CIL* VI, 40454a; Alföldy 1995, 210.

347. Noreña 2003, 36; see also Millar 2005, 103, 117–119.

348. Trans. Caroline Barron in Barron 2020, 160. See also Barron, "The Arch of Titus in the Circus Maximus," at http://judaism-and-rome.org/arch-titus-circus-maximus.

349. Cf. Tacitus, *Hist.* 5.9: "Gn. Pompeius was the first of the Romans to tame (*domuit*) the Jews."

350. Östenberg 2009. See also Steven Fine's Arch of Titus Project, at https://www.yu .edu/cis/activities/arch-of-titus.

351. For a full description of the IUDAEA CAPTA types, see Cody 2003, 107–109. See also Meshorer 1982, 288–289 (coins minted in Caesarea). Edward Zarrow notes that "not until the Flavian period had an emperor sought to venerate a single exploit on his coins throughout the entirety of his reign" (Zarrow 2006, 46). He shows that "the circulation of the 'Judaea capta' type both in Rome and in Judaea suggests an ideology of Flavian domination" (ibid., 52). For an overview of Flavian coinage, see Carradice 2012.

352. Zarrow 2006, esp. 49–50, 53.

353. For a convenient summary of the destructions attested in inscriptions and papyri, see Fuks 1961, 98–99; for a detailed study of the evidence, Pucci Ben Zeev 2005.

temples, during the revolt, is clear and prominent at Cyrene and has left not inconsiderable traces at other places in Lybia, and to some extent in Alexandria and Cyprus."[354] He interprets this in light of the Jews' deep hostility to idolatry, but such an explanation is insufficient to account for their unprecedented outburst of violence against buildings that embodied both civic and religious life in the Greek cities. After all, Jews had been exposed to idolatry in Ptolemaic Egypt no less than in Roman Cyrenaica, yet no such outburst is recorded during the last three centuries BCE. Although the rejection of the Greco-Roman gods certainly played a role in the decision to destroy temples in particular, the peculiar political-religious situation of the Jews, whose traditional Temple was left ruined and desolate, must have had an influence as well.[355]

4.2 AELIA CAPITOLINA: A MINIATURE ROME

After 70 CE, the *legio X Fretensis* was permanently stationed in Jerusalem. The decision to found a Roman colony on the city's site came only later, however, under Hadrian.[356] It was unusual for a colony to be founded alongside a legionary camp.[357] Moreover, Aelia Capitolina was the last of the Roman colonies in which a new population (mainly veterans, probably of the *X Fretensis*) was settled in order to people the city, and in contrast to other colonies superimposed on existing towns, it did not take in the previous, Jewish, inhabitants.[358] Goodman thus notes: "Within Hadrian's great policy of urban reconstruction, with the foundation of many cities, Aelia Capitolina is unique in its use of the new colony not to flatter but to suppress the natives." According to him, the emperor's decision was meant from the outset to punish "a rebellious nation," by depriving the Jews of their sacred site and the possibility of rebuilding their temple.[359] For other scholars, Hadrian's intention was to prevent future rebellions and secure peace, and to achieve this goal, he attempted to transform Judea into a normalized part of the Roman world.[360]

---

354. Applebaum 1979, 259–260. See also Pucci Ben Zeev 2005, 130–132.

355. See Goodman 2004, 25–26, which notes that this explanation "is not incompatible with the argument [. . .] that the rebels had messianic aims" (n. 128).

356. For Aelia Capitolina and other Roman colonies as "miniature Romes," see Aulus Gellius, *Attic Nights* 16.13.

357. Isaac 1980–1981, 32, 49.

358. On the material remains showing the replacement of the Jewish population by a non-Jewish one, see Weksler-Bdolah and Rosenthal-Heginbottom 2014. When settlements of veterans were superimposed on existing towns, the resulting population was usually mixed (original inhabitants plus settlers): see Isaac 1980–1981, 39.

359. Goodman 2003, 23, 28–29 (quotations at 29). For Smallwood 1976, the idea that Hadrian founded Aelia "to combat resurgent Jewish nationalism" is only a possibility (434). According to Mor 2016, Hadrian's decision concerning Jerusalem was in line with his building policy in the East and was not "anti-Jewish."

360. Schäfer 1990, 295; Pucci Ben Zeev 2018, 101–102.

Whatever Hadrian's intentions, the foundation of the Roman colony of Aelia Capitolina meant that the city would now be a "normal" Roman and pagan city, with several temples to Greco-Roman gods, such as Jupiter or Venus.[361] The act of foundation itself involved performing a religious ritual, the *circumductio*, or plowing of the soil with a bull and a cow to mark out the new city's boundaries. Coins of Aelia Capitolina, some of which have been found in hoards that belonged to the rebels and were deposited in Judean desert caves, picture Hadrian himself performing the ritual, with the legend COL(onia) AEL(ia) CAPIT(olina) COND(ita).[362]

Most important among the civic cults of the colony was that of Jupiter Capitolinus, in honor of whom the colony was named (Aelia being a reference to Hadrian's *nomen gentile*, Aelius). Jupiter's temple was the colony's main sanctuary, just as its equivalent was in Rome, yet historians still debate its precise location. While several scholars, following Cassius Dio (*Roman History* 69.12.1–2), locate it at the place where the Jewish temple had stood or somewhere else on the Temple Mount, others prefer to follow the testimony of Christian authors such as Eusebius and place the temple of Jupiter where the Church of the Holy Sepulchre would later be built.[363] Nicole Belayche points to a topographical argument in favor of this second theory: the Temple Mount is not the highest point in the city, which makes the choice to build the Capitoline temple there unlikely.[364] This debate, however, is far from settled, and ideological considerations could have offset topographical ones. If the Capitoline temple to Jupiter was built on the Temple Mount, then the replacement of Israel's institutions and symbols by Roman ones would be all the more striking. But, even if Jupiter's temple was built elsewhere, its erection in the very city where the temple of the Jewish god lay in ruins was a powerful political, religious, and ideological symbol. Moreover, several sources mention that a statue of Hadrian was erected in the precinct of the former Jewish temple, complemented later on by one of Antoninus.[365]

Finally, the name of the colony, Aelia Capitolina, was in itself a reminder that Jerusalem was no more and had been supplanted by a city reproducing

361. On the Greco-Roman (and Greco-Egyptian) cults in Aelia Capitolina, see Belayche 1999 and 2001, 118–128, 154–167 in particular.

362. Meshorer 1985, 60, no. 162; Eshel 2000, 641–643. On the ritual, see Belayche 2001, 120.

363. Among those who favor locating the Capitoline temple on the Temple Mount but not necessarily at the place where the Jewish temple stood, see Kloner 2006; Newman 2014; Weksler-Bdolah 2015. For the opposing view, holding that it was built in the higher part of the city, near Golgotha, see in particular Belayche 1997; 2001, 131–154.

364. Belayche 2001, 137, referring to Vitruvius, *On Architecture* 1.7.1. Another argument against the localization of the Capitoline temple on the Temple Mount is that the emperor Julian planned to rebuild the Jewish temple where it once stood, which would not have been possible if a temple to Jupiter had been erected there (Belayche 2001, 141).

365. Belayche 2001, 140–141.

Roman institutions and sanctuaries—a "miniature Rome," to use Aulus Gellius' famous expression[366]—where Jews, from 135 onward, were forbidden to live. The change of the province's name under Hadrian, from Iudaea to Syria Palaestina, furthered what could be described as both a concrete and a symbolic obliteration of the Jews from Jerusalem and the surrounding area. As Eck remarks, even provinces where unrest was not uncommon, such as Germania, Pannonia, and Britannia, did not undergo such a renaming.[367]

In short, the Roman victories over the Jews meant not only death, slavery, and increased taxes, not only humiliation due to defeat and "stigmatization," but also the replacement of Jewish norms, institutions, and buildings by Roman ones and the substitution of Rome for Israel in the very heart of Israel's religious life, Zion-Jerusalem. The Romans' main goal was to stop the revolts and, in order to punish the Jews and prevent further insurrection, they chose to put an end to the cult of the Jewish god by not rebuilding his main sanctuary. From a Jewish perspective, however, Rome's policy could be interpreted as a deliberate attempt to substitute itself for Israel.

Jews must have resented their defeats by Rome all the more bitterly as they occurred during a period of imperial expansion and stabilization, characterized by considerable economic and urban development and the creation of new provinces, such as Arabia in 106 and Dacia in 107 (replaced by three Dacian provinces in 129). The second century CE is in fact often described as a golden century, a time of peace and prosperity during which optimism prevailed, the empire seemed unshakable, and, as we saw, discourses about the eternity of Rome and Roman peace abounded. The conjunction of (1) the Jewish defeats and their unprecedented consequences, culminating in the replacement of Jerusalem by a Roman colony, (2) the empire's prosperity, and (3) Roman ideological claims must have been extremely hard to cope with for Jews who valued their ancestral traditions. From a Jewish perspective, it could look as if Rome, the *lux orbis terrarum* ("light of the world"), had taken over Israel's role in bringing eschatological peace and prosperity to the world, as if Rome had become the fulfillment of God's promise to the Israelites.[368]

5. Rome as Israel's Twin Brother and Rival

The assimilation of Rome with Esau, Israel's twin brother—or Edom, Esau's descendant, often described as Israel's brother in biblical texts—is mainly found in rabbinic literature, even though, as we shall see, there are a few hints

---

366. Aulus Gellius, *Attic Nights* 16.13.9.
367. Eck 1999, 87–89.
368. On Israel, or Israel's messiah, as "a light for the nations," see Isa 42:6, 49:6, 60:3.

at a pre-rabbinic use of this association, going back to the first century CE.[369] It must be recognized from the outset that the identification with Esau is not the only strategy that the rabbis developed to cope with the challenge of Rome.[370] At least three can be identified that define Rome's position vis-à-vis Israel in a nutshell: (1) Rome is presented as an empire among others, whose importance is thus relativized and neutralized: in the end, Rome will disappear, as all previous empires have; (2) Rome is assimilated to Israel's twin brother, a choice that probably derives from the perception that Rome and Israel shared some features (at least on the surface) and stood in a relation of rivalry;[371] and (3) often related to the previous strategy but nevertheless distinct from it, Rome and Israel are presented as standing in a close and paradoxical relationship, especially vis-à-vis the other nations—for example, a passage from Genesis Rabbah states that Israel and Rome are the two peoples that all the other nations abhor.[372] Finally, we must also remember that the relationship between Israel and Rome is not always described as antagonistic; in some cases a path toward the reconciliation of Jacob and Esau may even be conceivable.[373]

The following section will limit itself to examining whether Palestinian rabbinic literature (especially tannaitic compositions) considered pagan Rome as merely one empire among others, with no particular significance for the rabbis, as Jacob Neusner has argued, or whether the Romans represented a special challenge.[374] The various aspects of the relation between Israel/Jacob and Rome/Esau will be explored further in the next chapters.

5.1 ROME, AN EMPIRE AMONG OTHERS?

The idea that Rome was just another empire that would ultimately vanish would not have been peculiar to the rabbis. We have seen previously that Dionysius of Halicarnassus argued against Greek historians who claimed that Rome's successes were due merely to Fortune (§2.2). Philo likewise suggested that Rome's power and achievements would pass, just as those of previous earthly empires had, but he proclaimed that Israel's glory would endure

369. On Edom as Israel's brother, see Num 20:14; Deut 23:8; Amos 1:11. For the associations between Esau, Edom, and Seir, see Gen 32:3.

370. This section deals mainly with Palestinian rabbinic sources. For an analysis of the Bavli's perspective on the special relationship between Israel and Rome, see Naiweld 2016; Bonesho 2018; Hayes 2020; Kattan Gribetz 2020, 83–85.

371. See already Cohen 1967, 25; Assis 2016, 178–179, 190; Berthelot 2016; Berthelot 2017a.

372. Gen. Rabbah 63:7, ed. Theodor and Albeck, 685. This astonishing statement leads Israel Yuval to make an interesting comment: "The preacher may have sensed a similarity between the triumphalist imperialism of Rome and the universal messianic aspirations of Judaism" (Yuval 2006, 12). However, it is not certain that from the redactor's point of view, Rome and Israel were hated for the same reasons.

373. Simon-Shoshan 2018.

374. Neusner 1996, 77–78.

forever.[375] Christian authors of the first centuries CE occasionally used the argument of *translatio imperii* and evoked the erratic nature of Fortune, or fate, as well. In his treatise *On the Vanity of Idols*, written around 247, Cyprian of Carthage thus stated that Rome had come to power as previous empires had, by chance (*sors*) alone, and through no merit of its own.[376]

Rabbinic literature too presented Rome as one empire (or "kingdom," *malkhut*) in a series. In particular, like previous Jewish authors before them, the rabbis identified Rome with the fourth kingdom of Daniel 7. This identification had various implications.[377] Let us take Mekhilta de-Rabbi Ishmael, a third-century midrash on Exodus, as a case study, looking first at MRI Baḥodesh (Yithro) 9, on Exodus 20:18, "And all the people witnessed the thunder and the lightning." In this midrash, God is said to have shown Abraham the four kingdoms that would oppress his descendants:

> For it is said: *As the sun was going down, a deep sleep fell upon Abram, and a dread, [even] a great darkness, was falling upon him* (Gen 15:12). *A dread* refers to the Babylonian Kingdom. *Darkness* refers to the kingdom of Media. *Great* refers to the Greek Kingdom. *Was falling* refers to the fourth kingdom, guilty Rome. There are some who reverse the order by saying, *Was falling* refers to the Babylonian Kingdom, as it is said: *Fallen, fallen is Babylon* (Isa 21:9). *Great* refers to the kingdom of Media, as it is said: *King Ahasuerus made great* (Esth 3:1). *Darkness* refers to the Greek Kingdom, which caused the eyes of Israel to become dark from fasting. *A dread* refers to the fourth kingdom, as it is said: *Terrifying and dreadful and exceedingly strong* (Dan 7:7).[378]

The list of empires in this passage is the one most commonly found in Jewish sources, starting with the Babylonians rather than the Assyrians. The midrash offers two interpretations of Genesis 15:12 that connect four Hebrew words in this verse to the list's four empires. The first interpretation, which is not corroborated by additional verses, associates Rome with "was falling," therefore putting the emphasis on the final destruction of this "wicked kingdom." The second interpretation, which connects the words from Genesis to the four kingdoms in reverse order, associates Rome with "a dread" and adds a biblical proof text, Daniel 7:7:

> After this [the visions of the first three beasts] I saw in the visions by night a fourth beast, terrifying and dreadful and exceedingly strong. It had great iron teeth and was devouring, breaking in pieces, and

---

375. Berthelot 2011b.

376. Cyprian, *On the Vanity of Idols* 5.

377. See Josephus, *A.J.* 10.208–210; Sharon 2020.

378. Mekhilta de-Rabbi Ishmael, Baḥodesh (Yithro) 9, ed. Horovitz and Rabin, 236; Lauterbach 2004, 2:339. The translation is mine but draws on Lauterbach's.

stamping what was left with its feet. It was different from all the beasts that preceded it, and it had ten horns.

The passage of the Mekhilta has two facets. On the one hand, the very fact that Rome is inserted into a list of four kingdoms relativizes its exceptional status, by suggesting that it is simply one kingdom among others. Yet, on the other hand, the association of Rome with Daniel 7:7 when read in full leads to the conclusion that it is particularly dreadful and differs from the previous kingdoms.

The identification of Rome with the last kingdom mentioned in Daniel 7 could in fact be read in two apparently contradictory ways: as emphasizing the fact that Rome was just one additional empire after several others or, conversely, as highlighting the uniqueness of Rome. Or, conceivably, these two interpretations could be melded into one: that although Rome represented an unprecedented challenge for Israel, it would nevertheless disappear as previous empires had done.

We encounter such a dual emphasis on both the uniqueness and the ordinary character of the Roman empire in Mekhilta de-Rabbi Ishmael, Vayehi (Beshallaḥ) 1, commenting on the end of Exodus 14:5—"(leave) our service." This midrashic passage reflects on the universal dimension of Egyptian dominion and states that "Pharaoh ruled from one end of the world to the other and had governors from one end of the world to the other, for the sake of the honor of Israel."[379] Then the midrash looks at every empire that had ruled over Israel—identifying the Medes with the Persians—and, after quoting a different biblical verse for each kingdom (which is supposed to show that each enjoyed universal dominion), concludes that "every nation or kingdom that subjugated Israel ruled from one end of the world to the other for the sake of the honor of Israel." Although five empires/kingdoms are listed (Assyria, Babylonia, Media, Greece, and Rome), Rome is nevertheless called "the fourth kingdom," which may indicate that in this context the classical Greek list of empires, featuring Rome as the fifth, was merged with the tradition identifying Daniel's fourth kingdom with Rome. The seventh chapter of the book of Daniel is quoted twice, first to prove the universal dimension of Greek rule, identified with the third beast (Dan 7:6, "[The beast had four wings of a bird on its back] and four heads; and dominion was given to it"), and second to prove the universal dimension of the Roman empire, identified with the fourth beast (Dan 7:23: "It shall devour the whole earth, and trample it down, and break it to pieces"). As we saw above, Daniel 7:7 describes the fourth beast as "terrifying and dreadful and exceedingly strong" and "different from all the beasts that preceded it." Similarly, the explanation of the vision in Daniel 7:23 states that the fourth kingdom "shall be different from all the other kingdoms."

---

379. Mekhilta de-Rabbi Ishmael, Vayehi (Beshallaḥ) 1, ed. Horovitz and Rabin, 87; Lauterbach 2004, 1:132.

This passage from the Mekhilta therefore makes a double statement (as does the previous text that we examined, but differently): on the one hand, it claims that all the kingdoms/empires that had dominated Israel were universal—an observation meant to make Israel's humiliation less painful, as its subjugation required no less than the might of a universal kingdom—and, on the other hand, it identifies Rome with Daniel's fourth beast/kingdom, which differs from all the previous ones and is more terrifying than them. In this passage, the Mekhilta thus both aligns Rome with the other kingdoms—they are all universal, so Rome is no different in that respect—and recalls Rome's difference, in connection with Daniel 7:23.

The much later midrash Leviticus Rabbah echoes the tradition of Abraham's vision of the four empires found in MRI Baḥodesh 9 but also contains new midrashic developments, identifying the four empires (from Babylonia to Rome) with various groups of four items mentioned not only in Daniel 7 but in other biblical texts as well: four rivers going out of Eden (Gen 2:10) and four prohibited animals (Lev 11:4–7).[380] A comprehensive analysis of this long midrashic section would be out of place in this chapter, but a comparison of Leviticus Rabbah and the MRI leads to the conclusion that the former emphasizes Rome's importance and uniqueness to an even greater extent than the latter. For example, Leviticus Rabbah 13:5 says that Rome is equivalent to the three previous empires taken together. The midrash links Rome's power to Isaac's prayer for Esau, and thus to the blessing of one of Israel's patriarchs, something the other empires did not receive,[381] and describes it as the last empire, which will be followed not by yet another empire but rather by the return of God's sovereignty on earth. In another passage of Leviticus Rabbah, which associates the four empires with four types of skin disease (15:9, on Lev 13:2), Rome is linked to leprosy, the worst skin disease in the Bible, with the most disastrous consequences for its victims.

This brief survey shows that Rome's listing alongside other empires in several rabbinic texts was not necessarily a mere alignment of the former with the latter. On the contrary, in several cases the juxtaposition of Rome to other kingdoms served to emphasize their differences, including Rome's particularly dreadful character. The identification of Rome with Esau/Edom, examined below, further reveals Rome's distinctiveness in the eyes of the rabbis.

5.2 ROME AS ESAU/EDOM

The identification of Rome with Esau, Jacob's twin brother, which we encounter repeatedly in rabbinic texts, is based on a paradoxical choice. In Jewish sources, the Romans were first identified with the Kittim, and thus associated

---

380. Lev. Rabbah 13:5, ed. Margulies, 281–295.
381. See also Lev. Rabbah 15:9.

with Japheth.[382] Identifying them with Esau or the Edomites would mean that they belonged instead to the line of Shem. Moreover, if one were looking for a biblical character or people that exemplified an archenemy of Israel, why not identify Rome with Babylon, another city representing an empire that had destroyed Israel's Temple?[383] Indeed, both Jewish apocalypses such as 4 Ezra and 2 Baruch, and Christian texts such as 1 Peter 5:13 and the Apocalypse of John do equate Rome with Babylon.[384] Alternatively, why not identify Rome with Amalek, who tried to destroy Israel and represents the incarnation of evil in the biblical tradition? The rabbis, however, most often chose to identify Rome with Esau, Israel's twin brother.[385]

Admittedly, references to Esau in rabbinic literature serve different purposes. He may in some cases represent an ultimate "other," with no particular historical background, so not all references to him or to Edom are to be read in connection with Rome.[386] Many, however, can be shown to be closely linked to Rome.

The identification of Rome with Esau/Edom has been explained in reference to King Herod who was a client king of Rome and whose ancestors were Idumeans (considered descendants of the Edomites).[387] However, this is not particularly convincing, especially in light of Josephus' account in *The Judean War*, according to which the Idumeans fought alongside the Judeans to protect the Jerusalem Temple from the Romans during the war of 66–70.[388] The rabbis would hardly have forgotten this remarkable display of patriotism, at least not in the late first and second centuries CE.

A different explanation relies on the numerous prophecies of Edom's doom in the Bible.[389] In addition, Cohen emphasizes the particular relevance of passages in the Lamentations of Jeremiah concerning the Edomites, in connection with the destruction of the First Temple, to understand the identification of Rome with Edom following the destruction of the Second Temple.[390]

---

382. Dan 11:30 LXX translates "Kittim" as *Rhōmaioi*; similarly, in *Pesher Habaqquq* and *Pesher Nahum*, the Kittim are to be identified with the Romans. See Brooke 1991; Eshel 2001; Sharon 2017, 171–190. For the Kittim as descendants of Japheth, see Gen 10:4.

383. Hadas-Lebel 1990, 430–435; Feldman 2004, 65.

384. On the Christian identification of Rome with Babylon, see Inglebert 2016b, 227–232.

385. For a more detailed discussion of this issue, see Assis 2016; Berthelot 2016.

386. Avemarie 1994; Bakhos 2007.

387. See Zunz 1845, 483. Most scholars working on this topic, however, have rejected this hypothesis, one notable exception being Aminoff (1981).

388. Josephus, *B.J.* 4.224, 4.229, 4.566–576, 5.248–249, 6.378–383; Appelbaum 2009; Ronen 1988, esp. 224–239.

389. See in particular the book of Obadiah, which is only twenty-one verses long but is directed exclusively at Edom; on Esau/Edom in Obadiah and other prophetic texts, see Assis 2006; Krause 2008. For the connection with Rome, see Cohen 1967, 24–25; Hadas-Lebel 1984a, esp. 377–378; Assis 2016, 177–178.

390. Cohen 1967, 24.

The explanation put forward by Neusner differs from earlier theories in claiming that prior to the fourth century CE, Rome was just a place and an empire among others, with no particular significance for the rabbis: "To invoke a modern category, Rome stood for a perfectly secular matter: a place, where things happened. Rome in no way symbolized anything beyond itself." In his view, Rome's identification with Esau was a late phenomenon, closely linked to the Christianization of the empire, because "Christian Rome posed a threat without precedent."[391] In rabbinic literature, Esau or Edom would thus refer to a Christian Rome and ultimately to Christianity itself.

Several scholars disagree with Neusner and claim that the identification of Rome with Esau/Edom occurred well before the fourth century. Israel Yuval, for instance, dates it to the first half of the second century CE.[392] Adiel Schremer has also challenged Neusner's theory, arguing that the link between Edom and Rome can already be found in tannaitic literature.[393]

The main problem with the identification of Rome with Esau/Edom in rabbinic sources is methodological: The *rabbis* who identified Rome with Edom date back to at least the third generation of tannaim in the second century CE. However, the earliest *sources* that mention their sayings, the Jerusalem Talmud and Genesis Rabbah, date from the fourth or fifth century CE. During that period, Rome progressively became Christian. Therefore, certain scholars who, like Neusner, disregard the identification of the rabbi to whom a saying is attributed and instead focus on the date of the last redaction of the work as a whole argue that one should interpret "Edom" or "Esau" as referring not to the Roman empire during the second or third century CE but rather to the Christian Roman empire or to Christianity itself.

In this debate, I tend to side with those who wish to balance Neusner's approach by considering the attribution of sayings to particular rabbis, while acknowledging that this must be done critically.[394] Moreover, some ancient sources, including tannaitic texts and not merely amoraic references to rabbis of the tannaitic period, although admittedly more allusive than later sources, tend to corroborate the view that Rome was identified with Esau or Edom from at least the third century CE, and perhaps already in the first century CE.

<hr/>

391. Neusner 1996, 77, 78.

392. Yuval 2006, 10–11. His main reference is y. Ta'anit 4:6(8), 68d, which builds on Numbers 24:17–19 (see the discussion below of Josephus' rendering of this biblical passage in *Jewish Antiquities*). Yuval follows Cohen 1967, which itself refers to Moore 1927–1930, 2:116, 329.

393. Schremer 2010, 131–134, 227, n. 61 (early examples of the identification of Rome with Edom), Chap. 6 (analysis of the impact of the empire's Christianization). On the latter, see also Stemberger 2000, which notes at 286, "At least on the surface there is no noticeable reaction to a state that has now become Christian" (see further 287–289).

394. See note 119 in the introduction.

Let us first look at a few sources dating from the first century CE: Philo, Josephus, and 4 Ezra. As we have seen, Philo repeatedly speaks about Fortune's fickleness and the corresponding *translatio imperii*: the power held by a given kingdom today will tomorrow belong to a different kingdom, and then that kingdom to yet another, and so on. In *On the Unchangeableness of God* 171–178, one of the main passages in which he tackles this issue, the discourse is in fact addressed to Edom (§166). Philo comments on Numbers 20, which tells how Israel, on its way from Egypt to Canaan, requested permission to cross through Edom's territory, but in vain. In Philo's commentary, "earthly Edom" represents a wicked or wretched person. One wonders whether "Edom," the earthly kingdom, also symbolized Rome in Philo's eyes, especially in view of the fact that in §180, he explicitly writes that the divine Logos, which distributes good fortune to cities and nations according to §176, will stop Edom and those who follow him. This passage could well have as subtext the end of Roman power, but this cannot be proved, and one runs the risk of circular reasoning. Another Philonic passage that may hint at the identification of Rome with Esau/Edom is *On the Life of Moses* 1.242, which is again based on Numbers 20 and evokes the conflict between Jacob and Esau as "renewed by the nation so many generations later"—here the behavior of Edom in Numbers 20 might also be a covert allusion to Pompey's conquest of Judea or Roman rule more generally.[395]

Josephus may likewise be making a connection between Rome and Esau/Edom in *Jewish Antiquities* 4.125, where he alludes to the oracle of Balaam in Numbers 24:17–19. The passage concerns the star that "shall come out of Jacob" and the scepter that "shall rise out of Israel." The oracle states that "Edom will become (its) possession, Seir a possession of its enemies, while Israel does valiantly. One out of Jacob shall rule, and destroy the survivors of Ir." Josephus does not quote or paraphrase the oracle but merely states that Balaam predicted great calamities for "the most distinguished cities"—a group that may have included Rome in the minds of Josephus and his readers—some of which had already happened at the time when Josephus was writing. He then adds: "From all the things that have attained the kind of end he predicted, one might draw conclusions as to what should also occur in the future."[396] Josephus may have interpreted the prophecy of Israel's victory against Edom as referring to a past event, John Hyrcanus' conquest of Idumea at the end of the second century BCE. Yet he also seems to understand it as referring to a future occurrence: the destruction of that which was Israel's enemy in his own time, namely Rome, in which case Rome would here be implicitly identified with Edom. The biblical verse's mention of "Ir," a Hebrew word than means

395. Feldman 2004, 62–63.
396. Trans. Feldman 2000, 375.

"City," might have reinforced an identification of Edom with Rome.[397] This interpretation, however, remains hypothetical, and we cannot know for sure whether Josephus had Rome in mind in this part of the *Antiquities*.

A passage from 4 Ezra also has been frequently discussed in connection with the identification of Rome with Esau. In this apocalyptic text from the end of the first century CE, the seer, "Ezra," expresses a great deal of anxiety over the fate of Israel and the punishment of the kingdom that caused the destruction of the Temple. He therefore questions the angel Uriel about the forthcoming divine judgment:

> And I answered and said, "What will be the dividing of the times? Or when will be the end of the first age and the beginning of the age that follows?"
>
> He [Uriel] said to me, "From Abraham to Abraham [or: Isaac], because from him were born Jacob and Esau, for Jacob's hand held Esau's heel from the beginning. For Esau is the end of this age, and Jacob is the beginning of the age that follows. For the end of a man is his heel, and the beginning of a man is his hand; between the heel and the hand seek for nothing else, Ezra![398]

The interpretation of the passage is disputed, but it is very probable that in this context Esau represents the Roman empire, which the kingdom of Israel would succeed immediately, without being subject to yet another foreign power's rule. This, at least, is how the author of 4 Ezra seems to have understood the affirmation in Genesis 25:26 that when the twins were born, Jacob was holding Esau's heel.

A similar idea is found in Sifre Deuteronomy 343. This midrashic section first mentions God's forthcoming punishment of Seir/Edom/Esau—which, in the midrash's context, must refer to Rome's chastisement. Then, again on the basis of Genesis 25:26, it asserts that no nation will "enter" between Esau and Jacob (that is, between Rome's dominion and Israel's future rule).[399] Moreover, in an earlier passage of Sifre Deuteronomy 343, which comments on Deuteronomy 33:2—"And he said, YHWH came from Sinai, and rose up from Seir unto them; he shined forth from Mount Paran, and he came with ten thousands of saints: from his right hand went a fiery law for them"—the midrash states:

> *And he said, YHWH came from Sinai.* When the Holy One, blessed be He, revealed himself to give the Torah to Israel, He did not reveal himself in one language only, but in four languages. *And he said, YHWH*

397. As in the Targums later on. See Nikiprowetzky 1971, 488.

398. 4 Ezra 6.7–10, trans. Stone 1990, 143–144, with commentary at 159–161.

399. Sifre Deuteronomy 343, ed. Finkelstein, 397. On the association between Seir, Edom and Esau, see below n. 401.

came from Sinai. This is the Hebrew language. *He rose up from Seir unto them.* This is the Roman language [i.e., Latin]. *He shined forth from Mount Paran.* This is the Arabic language. *He came with ten thousands of saints.* This is the Aramaic language.[400]

The passage from Deuteronomy deals with the revelation of the Torah, described as "a fiery law," at Sinai. Yet strangely enough, in addition to Sinai, the biblical verse mentions two other places, Seir and Paran. In the Bible, Mount Seir is consistently associated with Esau and Edom, whereas Mount Paran is the territory of Ishmael, considered the ancestor of the Arabs. This gives rise to the proposition that the biblical verse alludes to God's having revealed the Torah in Latin (*romi*) and in Arabic.[401] To make sense of the association between Seir and the Roman language, one must presuppose the identification of Seir/Edom with Rome (and thus of Esau with Rome, since Esau and Edom are one and the same). This is the only interpretation that can explain the text.

Since the final redaction or editing of Sifre Deuteronomy is dated to the third century CE, the passage quoted above represents a clear example of Rome's identification with Esau/Edom that predates the Christianization of the empire. Another tannaitic text that corroborates this association's origin in the tannaitic period is Mekhilta de-Rabbi Ishmael, Pisha (Bo) 14, which states that whenever Israel was exiled, God's Shekhinah (Presence) would accompany them. The text mentions exiles to Egypt, Babylon, Elam, and finally Edom, which is referred to as the last before Israel's return to their Land.[402] In the context of the MRI's composition, the Jews' last exile was to Rome after 70 CE, and thus Edom designates Rome. In a parallel passage in y. Ta'anit 1:1, 64a, an exile to Greece is added to the list after Elam (Madai), and then Israel is said to have been exiled to Rome ("Romi" in Hebrew), making Rome's identification with Edom explicit.[403]

It must be emphasized that although later works, such as Genesis Rabbah or Leviticus Rabbah, should be read within the context of their final redaction, which was clearly Christian, the fact remains that they often associate Rome/Esau/Edom with figures and events from the first three centuries CE, especially the emperors responsible for the disasters that hit the Jews during the

400. Sifre Deuteronomy 343, ed. Finkelstein, 395.

401. On Seir and Esau/Edom, see Gen 32:3, 33:14, 33:16, 36:8–9; Num 24:18; Deut 2:4; etc. On Paran and Ishmael, see Gen 21:21. On the perception of Arabs as descendants of Ishmael already during the Second Temple period, see Millar 1993b; Gruen 2009.

402. Mekhilta de-Rabbi Ishmael, Pisha (Bo) 14, ed. Horovitz and Rabin, 52 (with Isa 63:1 as biblical proof text). The midrash then considers a return to the Land of Israel, stating that the Shekhinah will also accompany Israel back to their land. I thank Yael Wilfand for drawing my attention to this passage.

403. In contrast, the parallel in b. Megillah 29a mentions only the exiles to Egypt and Babylon and the future return "from their places of exile."

first and second centuries.[404] For example, Genesis Rabbah 63:7, which comments on Genesis 25:23—God's annoucement to Rebecca that she is pregnant with twins—states that "There are two proud peoples in your womb: Hadrian among the nations, Solomon in Israel."[405] Leviticus Rabbah 13:5, which identifies the fourth river flowing from Eden with Rome/Edom, recalls that the latter destroyed the Jerusalem Temple. In both cases, Esau/Edom is thus associated with events or figures from the first or second century CE (the destruction of the Jerusalem Temple; Hadrian), and there is no allusion whatsoever to Christianity.[406] This shows that even in a later, Christian context, Esau remained first and foremost the wicked empire that had destroyed the Jerusalem Temple and replaced Jerusalem with Aelia Capitolina—in other words, "pagan" Rome.[407] As Daniel Weiss has argued, it was probably the association of Christianity with the Roman empire—that is, Christendom—that led to the identification of the Christians with Esau, and not, as Neusner thought, the Christianization of Rome that led to the association of Rome with Jacob's brother.[408]

Admittedly, clear examples of the identification of Rome with Esau/Edom are found in only a few passages of tannaitic literature. The fact that there is no commentary on Genesis among tannaitic works may partly explain this small number of occurrences. It is also possible that the identification of Rome with Esau/Edom was so bold (for the reasons given at the beginning of Section 5) that it took some time to become common. We should also keep in mind that rabbinic works dated to the fourth and fifth centuries may contain traditions going back to the tannaitic period, especially since several statements on the association of Rome with Esau/Edom are attributed to tannaitic authorities (even though, as stated above, this is not a sufficient argument in itself to establish an early dating).

The fact that Rome's identification with Esau/Edom dates from before the Christianization of the empire does not mean that it did not assume a new dimension from the fourth century onward. Christian authors too reinterpreted the Genesis stories.[409] Basing their argument on the Pauline notion that the real descendants of Abraham are those whom God elects (Romans

---

404. On Esau/Edom in Genesis Rabbah, see Morgenstern 2016; in Leviticus Rabbah, Visotzky 2003, 154–172.

405. Gen. Rabbah 63:7, ed. Theodor and Albeck, 685. In the Bavli, the two leaders are Antoninus and Rabbi, positive figures (b. A.Z. 11a).

406. See also Gen. Rabbah 63:13 (ed. Theodor and Albeck, 697), where Esau's blasphemy is associated with Titus; 65:21 (ed. Theodor and Albeck, 740), where "the hands of Esau" (Gen 27:22) are associated with Hadrian and the massacre at Betar (as in y. Ta'anit 4:6, 68d; see also b. Gittin 57b, where Hadrian is associated with the killing of Jews in Egypt).

407. See also Visotzky 2003, 171–172, which concludes that there is very little anti-Christian polemic in Leviticus Rabbah and that "at the redactive level LR also represents the thinking of earlier eras," when "the Other was undoubtedly pagan Rome."

408. Weiss 2018; Neusner 1996.

409. Cohen 1967, 31–38; Yuval 2006, 10–20.

9:6–16), some of them identified Jacob with both Christ and his followers, and Esau with Israel, the Church's older "brother." A similar typological reading associated Leah with Israel, and Rachel, Jacob's beloved one, with the Church. During the second century, these typological readings remained marginal—a few occurrences can be found in Justin's *Dialogue with Trypho* and Irenaeus' *Against Heresies*—but they began to be more common in the third, under the pen of Tertullian, Origen, and a few others.[410] In the fourth century, the typology associating Jacob with Christ followers became a recurring motif in Christian sermons and biblical commentaries. As Cohen already pointed out in his 1967 article, these Christian interpretations of Genesis must have become increasingly challenging for Jews as the empire's Christianization intensified, for "the events of the fourth century provided the Christian apologists with the necessary fuel with which to give their typology a grounding in real events."[411] Now Christians could boast that the prophecy concerning the elder brother's subjection to the younger was fulfilled.

Did the early Christian interpretation of Jacob and Esau as respectively referring to the Church and the Jewish people originate as a response to the Jewish identification of Esau/Edom with Rome? The answer is certainly negative, because second-century Christian authors did not associate Christians with the Roman empire (even though some of them taught that Christians should obey the Roman authorities).[412] Neither did Tertullian or Origen identify the Church with the empire—quite the contrary. The Christian interpretation should rather be understood as emerging from the Christians' need to cope with Israel's election, a central theme throughout the Scriptures that Christians claimed as their inheritance. In spite of persecutions (which, until Decius, were occasional and local), the Christians' major theological challenge in the first two centuries CE probably lay more in Israel's enduring existence and rejection of the Gospel than in Roman rule. The claim to be God's elect and thus the true Israel, leading to the association of the Jews with Esau, was thus an inner Christian theological issue.

---

410. In the second century, see *Epistle of Barnabas* 13 (which only indirectly hints at this typological reading); Justin, *Dialogue* 134; Irenaeus, *Against Heresies* 4.21.2–3. In the third century, see Tertullian, *Against the Jews*, chap. 1 (PL 2:597–598) (yet Tertullian continues to call the Jews "Israel"); Origen, *Hom. on Gen.* 12:3. Cohen also mentions "the Pseudo-Cyprian polemic (ca. 210–240), *De montibus Sina et Sion*" (Cohen 1967, 33). See also Yuval 2006, 12–14, which cites Thraede 1991–1994 as a more detailed study.

411. Cohen 1967, 35.

412. See Cohen 1967, 31: "the new Christian usage of Esau did not originate as a retort to the Jews, but rather as a taunt inspired by the apostle Paul's Epistle to the Romans (9:6–13), quite without regard to—or, probably, even the vaguest knowledge of—what the Rabbis were saying about their pagan Roman overlords." On Christian obedience to Roman authorities, see Romans 13:1–7; 1 Peter 2:13–14.

Neither should the identification of Rome with Esau/Edom in tannaitic writings be understood as a response to the Christian claim to be Jacob. While some tannaitic texts that insist on Israel's election may be seen as responses to both Roman and Christian assertions that God had forsaken the Jews,[413] the association of Esau/Edom with Rome is repeatedly connected to the violent events of the first and second centuries CE and the anticipation of Rome's punishment. The Christians of the first centuries were not responsible for these events and thus cannot have been targeted under the appellations "Esau" and "Edom" (except for those who were themselves Roman, and then only insofar as they were Roman). Moreover, as Cohen recalls, "At this early stage in Christian history, the Christian midrash on Esau and Jacob bore no particular sting. After all, the Christians were at this point politically no better off—in many cases, far worse off—than the Jews."[414]

In short, the Jewish identification of Rome with Esau/Edom was not originally based on the rivalry between Jews and Christians. Elie Assis has argued that the oracles against Edom in the Bible developed from the impression that Edom had replaced Israel, taking both its land and its place in God's plan, God having now chosen Edom as his people in place of Israel.[415] The identification of pagan Rome with Esau/Edom must have arisen from the same kind of fear. What did prompt it must have been the perception, from a Jewish perspective, of the paradoxical similarities between the Jews and the Romans and the sense of rivalry that grew from this perception and from the observation that Rome tended to substitute itself for Israel in both symbolic and concrete ways (as the previous sections of this chapter explain). To put it in Assis' words, "Edom was a tailor-made symbol for the Romans because they posed a threat to Israel's self-perception as the chosen nation."[416]

The implications of this identification were far-reaching. First, it was a way to symbolically allocate a place to Rome that depended on Israel, in a mental world whose center was the Jewish people. Second, the rivalry between Israel/Jacob and Rome/Esau meant that despite being a small and defeated people, Israel was nevertheless in a sense on an equal footing with Rome. Moreover, the biblical story of Jacob's supplanting of his elder and stronger brother suggested the possibility that Israel could outdo Rome. On the other hand, the identification of Rome with Israel's twin also raised the question of Israel's taking Rome's place and becoming similar to it. Both Beth Berkowitz and Christine Hayes have shown that some rabbis did indeed discuss this issue, to which we shall return in the next chapter.[417]

413. Yuval 2006, 17, reads Sifre Deuteronomy 312 (ed. Finkelstein, 353) in this light.
414. Cohen 1967, 34. *Pace* Yuval 2006, 18–19.
415. Assis 2006, 19.
416. Assis 2016, 179.
417. Berkowitz 2006, 159–165; Hayes 2020.

In the end, several factors combined to make the pagan Roman empire a unique challenge for the Jews: (1) in contrast to previous empires, Rome stood for a city and a people that could look paradoxically similar to Israel; (2) some Jews perceived a rivalry between themselves and the Romans over their respective "elections" and "vocations"; and (3) the particular historical circumstances associated with the three major conflicts that opposed the Jews and the Romans made this perceived rivalry all the more bitter, especially the fact that the Romans destroyed the Jerusalem Temple, displaced the sacred vessels, reoriented the tax associated with the temple, and refounded Jerusalem as a Roman colony. Rome could be perceived as substituting itself for Israel, something that previous empires, regardless of the devastation they brought, were not considered to have attempted.

The next question that arises is what impact, if any, the confrontation with the extraordinary power of Rome, both on the ground, on the battlefield, and at an ideological level, had on the way that Jews reflected on power.

CHAPTER THREE

The Challenge of Roman Power

Jews did not ascribe glamour to war, as Romans did.

MARTIN GOODMAN, *ROME AND JERUSALEM*[1]

AS WE SAW in the previous chapter, from the seizure of the Temple by Pompey in 63 BCE through the crushing of the Bar Kokhba revolt, Jews in both the Land of Israel and the diaspora were confronted by Roman military might, and this with particular harshness. Admittedly, power is not entirely about armed force. In *Imperial Ideology and Provincial Loyalty*, Clifford Ando has shown that Roman power, understood as the ability to exercise military coercion, does not provide an adequate explanation of the internal stability of the empire. The longevity of Rome's *imperium* resulted instead from "a slowly realized consensus regarding Rome's right to maintain social order and to establish a normative political culture."[2] Nonetheless, for some peoples, especially Jews, the encounter with Rome represented a military challenge. As the examples from 1 Maccabees and Polybius cited in Chapter Two illustrate, Rome, whose Greek name *Rhōmē* means "strength," was described as an exceptional military force by Jewish and Greek authors as early as the second century BCE. And despite significant challenges from "barbarians" in the third century CE, Rome's military power remained central to provincial perceptions

---

1. Goodman 2007, 332.

2. Ando 2000, xi. Ando's approach to power resembles Steven Lukes' definition of power as the ability to shape perceptions "in such a way that [people] accept their role in the existing order of things" (Lukes 2005, 11). For a comparison of Greek and Roman notions of power, see Gotter 2008. For a study of Roman and Jewish notions of political power, see Goodman 2007, 330–365.

of her empire throughout antiquity. This chapter will thus focus on the challenge posed to Jews by the military expression of Roman power.[3]

In the Bible, Esau is a hunter, a man characterized by his physical strength. Moreover, Isaac's blessing promises that Esau shall live by his sword (Genesis 27:40). Jewish commentators might well have seen these as fitting allusions to Roman might. Indeed, rabbinic literature links Esau's violent nature with Roman brutality against Jews, especially in the repression of the Jewish revolts. The Mekhilta de-Rabbi Ishmael connects Genesis 27:22, where Isaac says that "the hands are the hands of Esau," with Genesis 27:40, his prediction that Esau would live by his sword, to suggest that the hands of Esau will cause death.[4] The Jerusalem Talmud and Genesis Rabbah also associate these two verses, and both draw a direct connection to the Roman seizure of Bethar during the Bar Kokhba Revolt. Genesis Rabbah 65:21 recounts:

> R. Yehudah b. Ilai said: My master used to teach: *The voice is the voice of Jacob* (Gen 27:22): the voice of Jacob cries out at what *the hands, the hands of Esau* (Gen 27:22), did to him.
>
> R. Yoḥanan said: The voice (or: cry) [caused by] the emperor Hadrian who was killing eighty thousand myriads [of men] at Bethar.[5]

In R. Yehudah b. Ilai's teaching, the identification of Esau with Rome remains implicit, though it is suggested by the next interpretation, attributed to R. Yoḥanan, which associates the "voice" (presumably Jacob's) with the Jewish cries caused by the suffering that Hadrian inflicted upon the besieged Jews of Bethar. The Yerushalmi ascribes a more straightforward teaching to R. Yehudah b. Ilai: "*The voice is the voice of Jacob and the hands, the hands of Esau* (Gen 27:22): the voice of Jacob cries out at what the hands of Esau did

---

3. Chapter Four addresses Roman power as manifested in the legal realm.

4. MRI Vayehi (Beshallaḥ) 2, ed. Horovitz-Rabin, 93; Cohen 1967, 25, note 21; Schremer 2010, 125. Moreover, the Mekhilta (in the same passage) cites Gen 27:40 and Num 20:18 to prove that the Edomites/Romans "put their trust only in their sword."

5. Gen. Rabbah 65:21, ed. Theodor and Albeck, 740. According to rabbinic tradition, R. Yehudah b. Ilai was a third-generation tanna who was a disciple of R. Aqiva, whereas R. Yoḥanan was a second-generation Palestinian amora, active in the second half of the third century. On Yehudah b. Ilai and his attitude toward Rome, see Ben-Shalom 1984. R. Yehudah's master is called "Barukh," probably by mistake; see Avemarie 1994, 181. On R. Aqiva and the Bar Kokhba Revolt, see Schäfer 1980 and 2003b. Other passages in Genesis Rabbah associate Esau with an army. In relation to Genesis 32:6, which states that Esau brought four hundred men with him for his encounter with Jacob, Gen. Rabbah 75:12 (ed. Theodor and Albeck, 895) cites an anonymous teaching that interprets them as four hundred *iparkhin* (from the Greek word *hyparchos/eparchos*), meaning prefects or generals. Similarly, Gen. Rabbah 78:14 (ed. Theodor and Albeck, 934), which comments upon Gen 33:14, where Jacob addresses Esau with the words "Let my lord pass on ahead of his servant," describes Esau designating four hundred men as "my spies, my commanders [from the Latin *dux*], my generals [from the Greek *hyparchos/eparchos*], my captains [from the Greek *stratēgos*]."

to him in Bethar."[6] Esau is clearly equated with the Romans under Hadrian, whose hands murdered Jews during the Bar Kokhba Revolt. The Jerusalem Talmud then continues with R. Yoḥanan's teaching, which links the "voice" to Hadrian's massacre at Bethar. It is probably not coincidental that the biblical verse used to condemn Esau/Rome, namely Genesis 27:22, is associated with Jacob's dishonest behavior toward his father and brother. By deceiving Isaac to obtain his blessing, Jacob deprived Esau of what was legitimately his. Some exegetical effort was required to justify Jacob's actions. By associating his trick with the repression of the Bar Kokhba Revolt, the rabbinic interpretation, in a quasi-apologetic way, offered a solution to alleviate the discomfort that Genesis 27:22 might prompt.[7]

An anonymous baraita in b. Gittin 57b suggests a wider, but also more muddled, interpretation of the actions that the hands of Esau/Rome inflicted upon Jacob/Israel:

> *The voice is the voice of Jacob and the hands are the hands of Esau*: *the voice* here refers to [the cry caused by] the Emperor Hadrian[8] who killed in Alexandria of Egypt sixty myriads on sixty myriads, twice as many as went forth from Egypt. *The voice of Jacob*: this is the cry caused by the Emperor Vespasian [read: Hadrian] who killed in the city of Bethar four hundred thousand myriads, or as some say, four thousand myriads. *The hands are the hands of Esau*: this is the wicked kingdom which has destroyed our House and burnt our Temple and driven us out of our land.
>
> Another explanation is [as follows]: *The voice is the voice of Jacob*: no prayer is effective unless the seed of Jacob has a part in it. *The hands are the hands of Esau*: no war is successful unless the seed of Esau has a share in it.[9]

This Hebrew passage from the Bavli may convey a tradition from the Land of Israel; however, it includes new elements that are not present in the Yerushalmi and also articulates the relationship between events that took place during the Jewish revolts and corresponding emperors with less precision than Palestinian rabbinic writings.

The second interpretation in the baraita is of particular interest, for it suggests that the voice of Jacob and the hands of Esau embody two distinct types

---

6. y. Taʿanit 4:6(8), 68d; Schäfer and Becker 1991–2001 (2001, *Synopse* II/5–12), 261; my translation, based on MS Leiden. In MS Darmstadt 413 Rd., this teaching is attributed to R. Shimon bar Yoḥai, who transmits it in the name of R. Aqiva, in connection with Ps 137:7: "Remember, O Lord, against the Edomites, the day of Jerusalem's fall, how they said, 'Tear it down! Tear it down! Down to its foundations!'"

7. I thank Michal Bar-Asher Siegal for drawing my attention to this point.

8. Probably a mistaken reference to Trajan.

9. b. Gittin 57b, trans. Simon 1936, 266.

of power: the power of prayer characterizes Israel, whereas military power is a feature of Rome. The emphasis on spiritual power and the categorization of military power or the use of force as something foreign to Israel is a recurring theme in the Babylonian Talmud, one that even today is widely considered characteristic of classical Jewish sources.[10] Yet is this the sole perspective on Israel's power found in rabbinic literature, especially when it comes to rabbinic sources from the Land of Israel? That is, do Palestinian rabbinic sources consider physical or armed force a characteristic of the Other, something foreign to Israel? Or do they reflect a more ambivalent attitude toward military power?

This chapter's first section examines Roman, or pro-Roman claims concerning the Romans' superior strength and military skills, and how Jewish sources from within the Roman empire echo or, occasionally, challenge these discourses. The second section aims to reassess the view that Romans saw Jews as "feminine," first by investigating Jewish participation in the Roman army, and then Roman perceptions of Jewish military valor and manliness. Moreover, while concurring with Martin Goodman's assessment that "Jews did not ascribe glamour to war, as Romans did,"[11] this section argues that some Jewish literary texts written in a Roman context display a sense of rivalry with Roman bravery and military prowess. It also suggests that a number of Jewish sources, both textual and numismatic, even imitate or mimic these very Roman representations and standards. The third section of this chapter takes the opposite tack by looking at other Jewish sources produced in a Roman context that reject Roman discourses and values and propose countermodels that redefine power as the capacity to master oneself, or as an intellectual ability, or as the study of the Torah. (We shall see that these two strategies— imitation and rejection, accompanied by redefinition—in some cases coexist.) Finally, given that Roman military superiority challenged the power of not only Israel but also the God of Israel, the final part of the third section investigates whether Jewish sources attempt to reconceptualize divine power.

10. See Boyarin 1995 and 1997; Edrei 2006 (which discusses the way that Rabbi Shlomo Goren, the first chief rabbi of the Israel Defense Forces, tried to combine pragmatic military needs in the context of the modern State of Israel with the teachings of rabbinic and medieval sources. Edrei refers, e.g., to b. Megillah 3a–b and b. Sanhedrin 93b [264]). See also Walzer 2006, 153, and the quotation in n. 11 below. I return to the issue of spiritual versus military power in Section 3 below (see especially §3.3).

11. Goodman 2007, 332. Michael Walzer similarly writes: "The realism of the rabbis leads to an acceptance of the normality of war in these days, before the messianic age. But the acceptance is grim. There is no value attached to war or to warriors in rabbinic literature; biblical passages that seem to celebrate military prowess are systematically reinterpreted to prove that 'the mighty (*giborim*, also heroes) are none other than [those who are] strong in Torah'" (Walzer 2006, 153). Yet the only source that he refers to is Avot de-Rabbi Nathan, which is quite late.

1. Roman Military Power and Roman Manliness

1.1 THE CHILDREN OF MARS

According to a common version of the legend of Rome's origins, Romulus and Remus were the children of Mars, the god of war, and Rhea Silvia, the daughter of the king of Alba Lunga and a descendant of Aeneas.[12] Although the Romans did not consider themselves descendants of Romulus in the way that the Israelites identified themselves as the offspring of Jacob, the association of the Romans with Mars is so ubiquitous in Roman literature that they could reasonably be named *Martigenae*, "children of Mars."[13] These mythological origins and filiation were closely linked to the notion that, since Rome's inception, its people were destined to become an extraordinary military force. Livy remarks:

> If any people ought to be allowed to consecrate their origins and refer them to a divine source, so great is the military glory of the Roman people that when they profess that their Father and the Father of their founder was none other than Mars, the nations of the earth may well submit to this also with as good a grace as they submit to Rome's dominion (*imperium*).[14]

That is to say, the Romans' military glory justified or, at least, gave meaning to their claim of counting Mars among their ancestors. As a historian, Livy expressed reservations toward this legend but, nevertheless, echoed the widespread explanation for Rome's overwhelming military superiority.[15]

Mars was often represented on Roman coinage, although this trend was much more marked in the West than in the East, where Rome was generally associated with Aphrodite/Venus, the other divine ancestor of Romulus and Remus. On some numismatic issues, the god of war was specifically associated with the Roman people, as on *denarii* minted in Spain during the Civil War of 68–69 CE, which depict the bust of the *Genius* of the Roman people with the legend GENIO P R on the obverse side, while the reverse features Mars advancing right, naked but for a helmet and holding javelin in his right hand, with the legend MARTI VLTOR or VLTORI (Mars the Avenger)[16] (Fig 3.1). Other numismatic items occasionally feature Mars in connection with the mythic origins of Rome and the Roman people. For example, an early fourth-century

---

12. Livy, 1.3.11–4.3; cf. Dionysius of Halicarnassus, *Rom. Ant.* 1.77.

13. Silius Italicus, *Punica* 12.582; 16.532. On the poetic expression *Martia Roma*, see Ovid, *Tristia* 1.8.24; 3.7.52; Ovid, *Ex Ponto* 1.8.24; 4.9.65; Martial, *Epigrams* 5.19.5. On the Roman people's self-definitions, see Chapter Five.

14. Livy, *History of Rome*, praef., 7–8, trans. Benjamin O. Forster, LCL, 5.

15. Livy also shows a cautious approach toward this legend in 1.4.2.

16. *RIC* I (rev. ed.), Civil Wars, no. 16–19, p. 204. See also no. 20, p. 205, where Mars is depicted in military garb.

FIGURE 3.1. Denarius featuring the Genius of the Roman people on the obverse, and
Mars on the reverse (68 CE).
RIC I, no. 17, p. 204. Photograph © The Trustees of the British Museum.

argenteus, from the reign of Maxentius, depicts Mars and Victory on either
side of the she-wolf and the twins.[17]

The link between Mars and the Romans signals their reputation for
excelling in the art of war. Roman military skills and bravery in combat were
recognized and celebrated by Greek authors from early on, as attested by the
Ode to Rome, by the Greek poetess Melinno: "Certainly, out of all people you
[Rome] alone bring forth the strongest men, great warriors as they are, just
as if producing the crop of Demeter from the land."[18] Furthermore, Polybius
noted that, while every state counted *andreia* ("courage," especially in battle)
among its most cherished virtues, this was especially true of Rome.[19] For
Cicero, the glory of the Roman people (*populi Romani gloria*) had "come
down to you [Romans] from your forefathers great in everything but greatest of all in war (*in re militari*)."[20] In his *History of Rome*, Livy reports this
message attributed to the post-apotheosis Romulus, who appeared to Procu-
lus Julius:

> Go, and declare to the Romans the will of Heaven that my Rome shall
> be the capital of the world; so let them cherish the art of war (*rem*

17. *RIC* VI, Rome, no. 189, p. 375; see also *RIC* VI, Ostia, no. 11, p. 402. According to
Mats Cullhed, with the exception of *Dea Roma*, Mars was the most commonly depicted
deity on the coinage of Maxentius, even on types that were traditionally associated with
Jupiter (Cullhed 1994, 49).

18. Trans. Erskine 1995, 369 (vv. 17–20).

19. Polybius, *Hist.* 31.29.1.

20. Cicero, *On the Manilian Law* 6, trans. H. Grose Hodge, LCL, 19.

militarem), and let them know and teach their children that no human strength can resist Roman arms (*armis Romanis*).[21]

Livy later dedicated a lengthy digression to the topic of Roman military skills, arguing that, had the Romans met the armies of Alexander the Great, they would have defeated the latter due to their martial superiority, honed through centuries of practice: "Military training, handed down from the very beginning of the City, had taken on the character of a profession, built up on comprehensive principles."[22] In this section (9.17–19), he also posits that the strength of the Roman army derived from the *virtus* of its soldiers and generals. In his epitome of Livy's work, written in the second century CE, Florus reiterates this assessment.[23] As we saw in Chapter Two, Roman *virtus*, primarily understood as courage in battle and military valor, was a prominent theme in Roman literature. This characterization contrasts significantly with most descriptions of Israel that appear in Jewish writings of the Hellenistic and Roman period. Although they are not devoid of celebrations of military prowess, as we shall see in Section 2 below, in contrast to Roman sources, Jewish works do not position military bravery or skills as key elements of Israel's self-definition.

Discourse in praise of the Roman forces' valor and success in war commonly spoke a bellicose visual language, as scenes of battles and victories—replete with trophies, arms, spoils, signa, the seizing of captives or slaughtering of enemies—appeared throughout the empire on arches, columns (like those that record the triumphs of Trajan and Marcus Aurelius) and other commemorative structures (such as the monument at Nicopolis, built in 29 BCE, that celebrated Octavian's conquest in the battle of Actium), as well as on coinage and private works of art (including sarcophagi) (Fig. 3.2).

Militaristic imagery might be thought a given in imperial contexts. And indeed Neo-Assyrian reliefs, to name but one example, famously represented battle scenes, and executions or deportations of prisoners. But Persian reliefs chose a different path, primarily displaying the submission of conquered peoples and detailing their collaboratation in building the empire under the king's guidance.[24] Iain Ferris notes that under the Julio-Claudians, in Rome itself—in contrast to the provinces—battles rarely appeared on monuments, which more often conveyed prosperity and peace as their core message. A reversal of this trend began during Trajan's reign, as exemplified by the representation of armed conflict on the reliefs of the Great Trajanic Frieze and on Marcus Aurelius' column. On coinage, renderings of military trophies, spoils, weaponry, and captives were recurring motifs. Roman *capta* coins typically

21. Livy, 1.16.7, trans. B. O. Foster, LCL, 59.
22. Livy, 9.17.10, trans. B. O. Foster, LCL, 229.
23. Florus, *Epitome of the Roman History of Titus Livius*, Preface, esp. §2.
24. See Chapter One, Sections 1 and 3.

FIGURE 3.2. Battle scene on the Ludovisi Battle Sarcophagus (ca. 255 CE) (Museum Palazzo Altemps, Rome). Photograph by Jastrow. https://commons.wikimedia.org/wiki/File:Grande_Ludovisi_Altemps_Inv8574.jpg

personified a defeated people through the depiction of a captive (with the legend *Armenia capta, Iudaea capta, Germania capta* . . .), an iconography of submission that originated with the Romans.[25] There can be no question that Roman media employed martial and bellicose imagery on a large scale.

Paul Veyne has argued that these images were not always visible or given deliberate attention and therefore cannot be simply characterized as forms of "propaganda." Yet he does not deny the visual effect of monuments like Marcus Aurelius' column, and he acknowledges that such military imagery reflects ideas that originated with the people who were in power.[26] The elites, whether in monumental form or in the miniature art of coinage, cherished the image of the Romans as a brave and strong people who excelled in warfare.[27]

Historians often underscore a martial ideal of masculinity as a major element in Rome's legacy to the West, as evidenced by textual and visual representations in which Roman power often appears as brutal, "male," and even sexually aggressive. Livy's above-mentioned digression on Roman military superiority vis-à-vis Alexander the Great and his armies closes with praise for the Romans' superior strength and capacity to endure toil and the claim that, had Alexander fought against them, he would "have wished for Indians and Persians and unwarlike Asiatics, and would have owned that he had before made war upon women (*cum feminis*)."[28] Livy attributes this judgment to Alexander, king of Epirus, an uncle of Alexander the Great who was killed during the war that he waged in Italy; a similar assertion was inferred from the death of that same figure by Aulus Gellius in the second century CE.[29] Aulus Gellius describes the peoples of Asia—primarily, but not exclusively, the Persians—as "feminine," by comparison with the "masculine" Romans, an opposition that already appeared in an Athenian context.[30]

25. Methy 1992; Cody 2003, 105–113. In addition to *capta* coins stricto sensu, many issues portray barbarian captives, sometimes with the emperor standing with his foot on one of them (see, for example, *RIC* VI, Aquileia, no. 113, p. 325, a bronze issue minted by Maxentius in 307 CE).

26. Veyne 2002, 3–4. On the depiction of Dacian barbarians on monuments built under Trajan, see Ferris 2003.

27. Distinctions exist between the martial iconography found on numerous monuments and coins, and the discourse of authors such as Cicero and Pliny who celebrated the *virtus* of the Roman military but also valued peace. In his *Panegyric* of Trajan, Pliny the Younger praises a broad range of the emperor's achievements, not only his military successes. Moreover, Pliny describes Trajan as "a lover of peace" (16.1) and claims that "you [Trajan] have neither fear of war, nor any desire to cause one" (16.2) (trans. Betty Radice, LCL, 359, 361).

28. Livy, 9.19.9–11, trans. B. O. Foster, LCL, 239.

29. Aulus Gellius, *Attic Nights* 17.21.33–34: "Molossus said that he was going against the Romans as a nation of men (*quasi in andronitin*), but the Macedonian (Alexander the Great) was going against the Persians as one of women (*quasi in gynaeconitin*)" (trans. J. C. Rolfe, LCL, 283).

30. Hall 1993.

These culturally constructed categories—"masculinity" and "femininity," or "male" and "female"—are also found in Roman representations of various conquered provinces and peoples, who are repeatedly portrayed as feminine personifications on coins and reliefs.[31] And not only are they females, but depicted in postures and situations that reflect both the nature of Rome's relationship to the given province and the ideological message being conveyed. Let us consider several examples from numismatic typology: on *capta* coins, a seated province with hands tied or in a mournful pose embodies a defeated people; on *supplicatio/adoratio* types, a kneeling figure who extends her arms or offers a gift to the emperor corresponds to a provincial people that seeks to regain the favor of Rome; and, on the *fides* type, a province that is loyal to Rome is represented standing. In the last case, if the province stands beside a representative of Roman authority, she is smaller in stature.[32] In sum, a female figure which symbolizes a province is always physically dominated by the male persona that embodies Rome; that male figure's imposing form and posture in relation to the female vividly signifies the exercise of political subjugation and power.

Some scholars read sexual connotations into this imagery. In his analysis of a coin belonging to the *Iudaea capta* series, which features Judea mourning beneath a palm tree and Vespasian triumphantly standing to the left of that tree with his foot on a helmet, Jason von Ehrenkrook comments that "a large and imposing masculine representation of Rome stands over and looks down upon a small and fragile woman, Judaea. In the man's left hand is a dagger with a decidedly phallic appearance"[33] (Fig. 3.3). The "masculine representation of Rome" mentioned by von Ehrenkrook is the emperor himself, who embodies Roman power.[34] In comparison with some reliefs at the Sebasteion of Aphrodisias, to which we shall return below, this scene is quite static.[35] Nonetheless its iconography clearly conveys the disparity in physical strength between these protagonists, reflecting Rome's overwhelming control over Judea. On such coins, which were ubiquitous during the reign of Vespasian, the Judeans are symbolized by a powerless female figure. Yet we must remember that other provinces, inhabited by peoples likewise deemed "barbarian," were depicted in a similar way.

More dramatic than these numismatic portraits are certain sculptural renderings and illustrations on reliefs that show the female personification of the defeated province being physically dominated, and even trampled. The

31. Rodgers 2003.
32. Cody 2003.
33. Von Ehrenkrook 2011, 162.
34. Zarrow 2006, 45–46.
35. On the Sebasteion, see also Chapter Two.

FIGURE 3.3. Sestertius of the *Iudaea Capta* type, featuring a bust of Vespasian on the obverse, and on the reverse Vespasian with Judea seated, mourning (71 CE). *RIC* II.1 (rev. ed.), no. 167, p. 71. Photograph © The Trustees of the British Museum.

aforementioned reliefs at the Sebasteion of Aphrodisias famously exemplify this treatment, thereby illustrating the Greek reception of Roman ideological motifs. Notably, these reliefs display the Roman emperors Claudius and Nero in heroic nudity, subjugating half-naked female personifications of Britannia and Armenia, respectively[36] (Figs. 3.4, 3.5). The strength, violence, and physical—even sexual—domination that emanates from these reliefs is striking. Claudius, standing, grabs the lying Britannia by the hair and raises his (now broken) right arm in a threatening gesture. As for Nero, von Ehrenkrook colorfully writes:

> a nude Nero is holding up a slumping Armenia. The emperor towers over his victim, with his vividly muscular thighs straddling her soft naked body. Her slumped posture, juxtaposed with Nero's exaggerated muscular presence, suggests not only military subjugation but sexual conquest.[37]

To avoid a biased analysis of this evidence, we must take into account a series of statues of a different type, also displayed in the Sebasteion. They represented various *ethnē* from within (and some from beyond) the Roman empire, each standing, fully dressed, on a base that was adorned with garlands and a mask and inscribed with the name of the *ethnos*. One of the bases still reads *ethnos Ioudaiōn*, but unfortunately its statue is lost.[38] According to Smith, these *ethnē* had been "either simply defeated, or defeated and added to

36. Smith 2013, C10, plate 61 (Claudius) and C8, plate 58 (Nero).
37. Von Ehrenkrook 2011, 161.
38. Smith 1988, plate VIII, no. 5.

FIGURE 3.4. Relief from the Sebasteion in Aphrodisias: Claudius and Britannia.
Photograph © New York University Excavations at Aphrodisias (G. Petruccioli).

FIGURE 3.5. Relief from the Sebasteion in Aphrodisias: Nero and Armenia.
Photograph © New York University Excavations at Aphrodisias (G. Petruccioli).

the empire, or brought back into the empire after unwilling secession."[39] The impression they conveyed differs completely from the scenes of Claudius and Nero, more closely resembling the representations of provinces on *fides*-type coinage. Smith explains the key factor responsible for this contrast as follows: "The kind of peoples and places seen in the Sebasteion are an extension and an adjustment of the *gentes devictae*," which are multiplied because "they sum up the victories and frontier advances of a whole reign"; yet "they also suggest peaceful incorporation."[40] In this respect, we may compare these statues to the Hadrianeum reliefs in Rome (second century CE), which represented the peoples of the empire as draped women standing upright, with little "captive iconography." It is clear, then, that Roman portrayals of conquered peoples and areas varied in significant ways, and violence was not an omnipresent theme. Reliefs, sculptures, and coinage illustrated diverse aspects of the power relationship between Romans and provincials, including "peaceful" collaboration.

Moreover, the scholarly notion of the "feminization of the enemy" (or: the Other) lacks nuance.[41] First, not all enemies of Rome were depicted as such. Some barbarians, especially those along the northern *limes* in the West, such as Germans or Dacians, were perceived and portrayed as courageous and formidable. Moreover, the depiction of a province as a frail and subdued female figure was not incompatible with a description of its *ethnos* as composed of fierce warriors. As we shall see in Section 2, some *Iudaea capta* coins feature a weeping female figure of Judea alongside a muscular, male Jewish captive, who looks as if he would prove a fearsome combatant.

Second, Roma too is a female figure. This does not contradict the representation of the Romans as warlike and manly, for Roma is consistently depicted as a female warrior and thus displays several conventionally masculine traits. In Melinno's *Ode to Rome*, which reflects on the meaning of *Rhōmē* ("strength"), Roma is a daughter of Ares, the god of war, and she rides a chariot drawn by the earth and sea, who are yoked together and under her control. She is described as wearing a golden girdle, like the Amazons, who were also daughters of Ares.[42] This Amazon-like Roma commonly appears on both reliefs and coinage; and, in a Greek context, she is also depicted as the warrior-goddess Athena in yet another connection with warfare. Similarly, in the West, the vast majority of reliefs that feature Roma depict her armed and helmeted, hence a martial figure.[43]

---

39. Smith 1988, 59.

40. Smith 1988, 71.

41. See, in particular, Rodgers 2003 and von Ehrenkrook 2011.

42. *Ode to Rome*, vv. 1–2, 9–11; Erskine 1995, 369. In his much later *Roman Oration*, Aelius Aristides writes similarly about Rome-*Rhōmē*, stating that "strength is the mark of all that is hers" (§8).

43. See LIMC VIII.2, 696–723; and Rosso Caponio 2020, which shows that one representation of Roma in the Sebasteion depicts her as a female version of Mars Ultor. For a

In short, both Roma and the Romans were described in militaristic terms and, with respect to gender, were categorized as "masculine" because of their mastery of the art of war. Depictions of Rome's enemies were less consistent, and it would be an overstatement to categorize them systematically as "feminine" or "femininized." The Roman dichotomy between a feminine East and a martial West informs some of these representations, but a more nuanced view of the East is also perceptible.

1.2 JEWISH PERCEPTIONS OF ROMAN MILITARY MIGHT

At the beginning of Chapter Two, I referred to the description of the Romans in 1 Maccabees 8 to emphasize that Judeans were aware that Rome had no king. Yet 1 Maccabees 8:1–16 primarily addresses Roman victories and acts of military bravery (*andragathia*) and suggests that this people is invincible. The author is clearly impressed by the Romans' military achievements, even though he also hints at the fact that greed motivated some of their conquests (1 Macc 8:3).[44]

The notion that martial capabilities define Romans more than any other people on earth reappears in later Jewish sources. These sources are mainly literary, although select iconographic representations—such as the wall painting from Herod's palace at Herodium that may depict Octavian's victory in the naval battle at Actium—indicate that Roman military achievements could have had visual resonance in a Jewish, or at least Herodian, setting.[45]

Unsurprisingly (in view of his Roman audience in *The Judean War*), Josephus to a great extent echoes Roman views of their own military might, as for example when he reproduces statements attributed to Vespasian, Titus, and other Roman leaders.[46] In the *War*, however, the first description of Roman military qualities occurs in a passage where Josephus deviates from the subject at hand to speak in his own voice, and it closes with an affirmation that he was not writing to exalt the Romans; to the contrary, he sought to comfort the peoples that had been subjugated by them and to dissuade those that would consider rebellion as an option (*B.J.* 3.108). This lengthy digression (39 paragraphs) is quite telling: in a typical Roman trope, he writes that Rome's

---

particularly clear portrait of Roma as a martial figure, see the scene of the apotheosis of Antoninus Pius and Faustina on the base of the Antoninus column, dated to 161 CE (LIMC VIII.2, no. 221, p. 719). See also Chapter Two, §1.3.

44. On 1 Maccabees' depiction of the Romans' military exploits, see further §2.3 below.

45. This painting belongs to the permanent collection of the Israel Museum in Jerusalem. See https://commons.wikimedia.org/wiki/File:Wall_painting_from_Herodium _depicting_a_naval_battle,_it_may_represent_the_victory_of_Octavian_at_Actium,_20 -15_BC,_Israel_Museum,_Jerusalem_(15659423802).jpg

46. See, for example, *B.J.* 3.473, 475.

dominion (*hēgemonia*) is not a gift from Fortune, but rather a consequence of Roman *virtus*. Writing in Greek, he uses the term *aretē*, illustrating the fact that "in Greek culture the principal term for ideal manly behavior was not *andreia* but rather *aretē*, which from its earliest occurrences denoted many things, only one of which was physical prowess or courage."[47] Josephus' attention to the manly and, even, the military dimensions of *aretē* is demonstrated by his reference, early in this digression, to the "military organization" (*syntaxis tēs stratias*) of the Romans (*B.J.* 3.71). As in Livy, Roman superiority is ascribed to their unceasing practice of the art of warfare:[48]

> For their nation does not wait for the outbreak of war to give men their first lesson in arms; they do not sit with folded hands in peace time only to put them in motion in the hour of need. On the contrary, as though they had been born with weapons in hand, they never have a truce from training, never wait for emergencies to arise.[49]

The image of a people "born with weapons in hand" recalls the myth of the Spartoi, or "sown men," who emerged from the earth fully armed after Cadmos had sown the teeth of a dragon (the myth is about the origins of Thebes). In any case, the emphasis on continual military training is a recurring theme in the *War*, especially in Titus' speeches to his soldiers, in which he encourages them by reiterating their martial excellence relative to the Judeans' abilities.[50] Josephus also enumerates specific Roman military skills, such as expertise in building encampments and handling certain weapons; and he concludes by assessing the Romans to be nearly invincible (*B.J.* 3.106–107).

Rabbinic sources also associate Rome with warfare in quite specific ways, which occasionally reflect its reputation for having an enormous, well-trained, and well-organized army, although these echoes are articulated in less specific terms than in Josephus, and with negative connotations.[51] As two well-known passages in the Yerushalmi state, Greek is the language of poetry, whereas Latin (*romi*, "Roman") is the language of war.[52] The link between Latin and warfare may simply be rooted in the use of Latin by soldiers (even of Eastern origin), as attested by dedications and letters; however, it may also reflect the central perception of Rome as a military power.[53]

---

47. McDonnell 2006, 236.
48. See Livy, 9.17.10.
49. *B.J.* 3.72, trans. H. St. J. Thackeray, LCL, 599.
50. *B.J.* 3.475, 6.38.
51. Hadas-Lebel 1990, 216.
52. y. Megillah 1:8, 71b; y. Sotah 7:3, 21c; this passage also mentions Aramaic as the language of eulogies and Hebrew "for general speech."
53. On soldiers' use of Latin, see, e.g., the second-century CE correspondence, in Greek and Latin, between Claudius Terentianus, a soldier from Egypt, and his father Claudius Tiberianus, himself a veteran (P. Mich. VIII 467–481; Campbell 1994, 33, no. 43). See also

More specifically, the Mekhilta de-Rabbi Ishmael notes that Romans fight constantly, in a way that recalls Josephus' remarks on the strength of the Roman army. This midrash comments on "Until the going down of the sun" (Exod 17:12), in the narrative of the battle between Israel and Amalek, as follows: "Because we have learned about all the other kingdoms that they wage war only until the sixth hour of the day, whereas this guilty kingdom (*malkhut ḥayevet*) wages war from morning to evening."[54] Here the "guilty kingdom"—a nickname for Rome—is associated with Amalek, a people descended from Esau who hold a unique status in the biblical books, since Exodus 17:14 declares that God will obliterate the memory of Amalek because of that nation's cruel attack on Israel. Yet, the core message states that the Roman military is more formidable than other nations' forces.

The notion that Romans are constantly engaged in battle or military training also appears in Mekhilta de-Rabbi Ishmael, Vayehi (Beshallaḥ) 1. In this section, R. Shimon ben Gamaliel II—a tanna who, according to rabbinic tradition, was active after the Bar Kokhba Revolt—comments on "Pharaoh took six hundred picked chariots" (Exod 14:7), stating that, in contrast to the Egyptian army, which was idle, all Roman troops remain active day and night: "Come and see the wealth and the greatness of this guilty kingdom: it does not have even one *numerus* that remains idle, all of them run during both day and night."[55] The tone of this passage could be understood as an acknowledgment of Rome as a worthy enemy on the battlefield, resembling some of Josephus' comments on the Roman army. Alternatively, it may be ironic, conveying derision toward both the lax Egyptians and the frenetic Roman units.

At least once, the Jerusalem Talmud echoes the Romans' self-perception as heroic warriors, albeit sardonically. That material is found in y. Avodah Zarah 1:3 (1:2 in some editions), 39c, in a discussion on the origin of the Kalends, one of the "festivals of the gentiles (*goyim*)" listed in m. Avodah Zarah 1:3, which corresponds to the *Calendae Ianuariae*, the major festival at the beginning of the Roman year.[56] This teaching is attributed to R. Yoḥanan (mentioned at the beginning of this chapter):

---

the ostraca from Bu Njem (also known as Gholaia), a minor frontier outpost in the Libyan desert, dated to the early third century CE (Campbell 1994, 112–113, no. 181; Phang 2007). See also Adams 2003, 550–554.

54. MRI Amalek 1, ed. Horovitz and Rabin, 181, my translation (cf. Lauterbach 2004, 2:261). Cf. Mekhilta de-Rashbi 17:12, ed. Epstein and Melamed, 123.

55. Ed. Horovitz and Rabin, 89. From the second century CE onward, a *numerus* was a unit in the Roman army whose members were from a particular ethnic background and had special military skills.

56. See Schäfer 2002b, 338–341; Graf 2015, 61–68; Kattan Gribetz 2016, 78–79, Kattan Gribetz 2020, 61–63; Bonesho 2018, 82–89.

The kingdom of Egypt and the kingdom of Rome were at war with one another. They said [to each other]: "How long are we going to kill one another in battle? Come and let us make a rule that whichever kingdom will say to its chief general: 'Fall on your sword [and kill yourself],' and [whose general] will listen to that command—[that kingdom] will seize the power [over both of us] first!"

The Egyptian [general] did not listen to them.

The [general] of Rome was a certain old man with the name Januarius. He had twelve sons. They [the Romans] said to him: "If you will listen to us [and fall on your sword], we shall make your sons commanders [Latin *dux*], generals [Greek *eparchos*], and commanders in chief [Greek *stratēlatēs*]!" So he listened to them [and fell on his sword—i.e., took his own life]. That is why they call it *kalendas yanubris* [Latin *calendae Ianuarii*]. From this day on, they mourned for him: [it was a] "black day."[57]

This passage echoes accounts of the Roman army's wartime heroism and the soldiers' readiness to sacrifice themselves for the Republic that were transmitted by Roman historians, orators, poets, and philosophers.[58] In particular, it brings to mind the famous story of the Horatii and the Curiatii. According to Livy (1.24–26), while Rome and Alba were at war during the reign of Tullus Hostilius, they decided to interrupt the fighting and select three soldiers from each side as delegates for their respective forces; they would engage in a battle that would decide the outcome of the conflict, thereby sparing many lives from the two armies. Although the plots are not identical, these narratives open with the same situation and include an agreement that the camp of the defeated representative(s) will submit to the other. Moreover, they share an important motif, whereby a certain individual (or delegation) sacrifices himself (or themselves) for the common good. The famous actions of the general Marcus Atilius Regulus also exemplify the Romans' ability to sacrifice their individual interests, including their own lives, for the sake of the *patria*. During the First Punic War, after Carthage defeated the Romans, Regulus dissuaded the Senate from releasing the Carthaginian prisoners requested by that Punic city—a decision that, in his view, ran against the interests of Rome. Rather, he returned to Carthage to meet his death in a heroic demonstration of *fides*.[59] His courage was praised even by the Christian author Tertullian, who was otherwise critical toward

57. Trans. Schäfer 2002b, 340, based on MS Leiden, with slight modifications.

58. See Flusser 1956 [2009], which compares the talmudic story to the Roman practice of *devotio*. Committing suicide by falling on one's sword is also known from the Bible; see 1 Samuel 31:4–5.

59. Cicero, *On Duties* 3.26.99–29.105; Horace, *Odes* 3.5; Valerius Maximus, *Memorable Doings and Sayings* 1.1.14; Seneca, *Epistles* 98.12.

Rome.[60] Regulus' behavior sheds light on Januarius' decision in the talmudic narrative quoted above.

To better understand the stance adopted in this rabbinic story, it is worthwhile to examine Josephus' retelling of the seizure of the Antonia fortress during the siege of Jerusalem, in which he draws from Roman traditions of individual heroism and contempt for death. Titus exhorts the soldiers to launch the attack, emphasizing that Antonia is key to defeating the city, while conceding that the risk to his troops' lives is very high.[61] At one point, Sabinus, a soldier of Syrian origin, initiates the assault himself, stating that he was willingly giving his life for Titus. (Here the general substitutes for the city of Rome, which Sabinus may never have seen, as the motive for his sacrifice.) Accompanied by eleven men, Sabinus seems to succeed at first but, ultimately, he is defeated; two days later, another group of soldiers seizes the Antonia, through subterfuge rather than by force.[62] Without the slightest hint of irony, Josephus expresses admiration for Sabinus' *andreia* (§66), as if he completely embraced Roman standards of heroism.

Not so our talmudic passage, to which we must now return. First, its correlation of the responsibility for victory with the willingness of generals from the Egyptian and Roman armies to commit suicide is quite ironic. Suicide was valued as a "noble death" in Roman society, but in these circumstances, the norm would have been single combat, not suicide.[63] In addition, the refusal by the Egyptian general seems to suggest that, whereas the lives of soldiers were easily imperiled, high-ranking officers were not necessarily prepared to give their own lives to achieve victory, thus unmasking their selfishness or cowardice, or perhaps both. The Roman general, however, opts for suicide. Yet he makes this choice only after being assured that his sons will become "commanders, generals, and commanders in chief [or: military governors]." Thus, his patriotic action also demonstrates paternal concern for his sons' future status. In view of other Roman stories of honor and dedication to the Republic that prompted fathers to put their own sons to death, this description of Januarius' act in the Yerushalmi is not without irony.[64] His suicide reflects certain Roman

60. Tertullian, *Apology* 50.5.

61. Josephus, *B.J.* 6.45–53.

62. *B.J.* 6.54–69.

63. This ideal of singular combat is illustrated by the battle between the Horatii and the Curatii, and Titus Manlius Imperiosus Torquatus' fight against a giant Gaulish warrior (Livy, 7.9.8–10.14). The biblical combat between David and Goliath reflects a similar approach.

64. For Roman accounts of fathers who killed their sons to exercise military discipline or ensure Rome's victory, see again the example of Titus Manlius Imperiosus Torquatus (Livy, 8.7.1–22). Insofar as stories of heroic deeds by earlier generations of Romans had become *exempla* for rhetorical training and ethical teaching, which could be transmitted orally, it is reasonable to suppose that the rabbis could have had knowledge of them. The etymological story told in y. Avodah Zarah seems to point precisely to such an awareness of Roman legends.

standards of heroism (namely, self-sacrifice for the victory and glory of the Roman people), but his motivations are suspect. Overall this narrative has a critical feel, for it traces Roman supremacy and domination to a tragic event explicitly described as a "black day," which indicates a bad omen (the text includes a transliteration of the Greek words *hēmera melaina*, corresponding to the Latin *dies ater*). As Sarit Kattan Gribetz remarks, in Roman calendars, January 2 was marked as a *dies ater*, a detail that shows the rabbis' familiarity with that calendar.[65] By referring to this day as such, it is as if the Romans (in the Jerusalem Talmud) were acknowledging that their domination stemmed from, and perhaps consisted of, disastrous events.[66]

Both Peter Schäfer and Sarit Kattan Gribetz note that, whereas this mention of the twelve sons of Januarius probably recalls the twelve altars that were dedicated to Janus in Rome, and which were associated with the twelve months, it also evokes the twelve sons of Jacob.[67] This detail may reflect the construction of Rome as Israel's alter ego, a phenomenon that Ron Naiweld has described in Babylonian rabbinic sources, but which Palestinian sources also convey.[68] This mirroring of Israel and Rome is congruent with the identification of Rome with Esau, and the correlated notions of twinship and resemblance. Based on the parallel between the twelve sons of Januarius and the twelve sones of Jacob, Sarit Kattan Gribetz concludes that, in both the tale of Januarius and the rabbinic discussion of the Kalends that precedes it in y. Avodah Zarah, which connects the festival with Adam, "the Kalends of January has biblical resonances, imparting to the first day of the Roman year biblical overtones."[69] This analysis is founded on the presence of the number twelve in Genesis and in the talmudic narrative. Yet the mention of this number would in any case be expected in a legend whose protagonist is named after the first month of the year. Moreover, in other contexts, twelve symbolizes totality; for example, in Josephus' aforementioned account of Sabinus' attack on the Antonia, eleven soldiers follow this Roman hero, creating a force of twelve warriors (*B.J.* 6.59). Admittedly, the talmudic story mentions twelve sons, rather than a generic group of men, which increases its plausibility as a parallel with Genesis. Yet the biblical resonances that Kattan Gribetz ascribes to the Januarius episode are not striking if this talmudic passage is read on its own.[70] They actually originate in the broader rabbinic discussion of the

---

65. Kattan Gribetz 2020, 62–63.

66. Cf. Schäfer 2002b, 340; Kattan Gribetz 2020, 63.

67. Kattan Gribetz 2016, 79; Kattan Gribetz 2020, 62; see also Bonesho 2018, Chapter Three.

68. Naiweld 2016.

69. Kattan Gribetz 2020, 63.

70. In addition to the twelve sons, however, the choice of Egypt as Rome's adversary, which fits the narratives of Genesis and Exodus rather than the early history of Rome, may support Kattan Gribetz's thesis.

Kalends in this talmudic section, especially the previous passage, which links the Kalends to Adam, rather than in the episode of Januarius sensu stricto. Furthermore, the underlying allusion to the sons of Jacob in that episode may suggest a counterpoint or a contrast rather than a biblical backdrop for the establishment of the Kalends: Januarius the Roman patriarch and general may be implicitly compared with the Jewish patriarch Jacob, "a quiet man, living in tents" (Gen 25:27). This allusion to Jacob is tenuous, but if one is willing to accept it, this passage may hint at a rabbinic countermodel to Roman militarism (discussed further in Section 3, below). Similarly, for Peter Schäfer, this text articulates a contrast between the twelve sons of Januarius, who are awarded positions of military leadership as an outcome of their father's suicide, and the twelve sons of Jacob, who "have no military power and, moreover, would never urge their father to commit suicide in order to gain it!"[71] In short, y. Avodah Zarah 1:3, 39c displays familiarity with the Romans' self-perception as heroic warriors, while introducing also a touch of irony and tacitly suggesting a contrast (or even an opposition) between Rome and Israel with respect to heroism and the art of war.

Other rabbinic sources that address Roman warfare occasionally echo the cultural construction of Roman power as masculine and even sexually aggressive. Galit Hasan-Rokem and other scholars have noted that the story of Titus entering the holiest precinct of the Jerusalem Temple and slashing the curtain of the Holy of Holies with his sword resonates as a depiction of rape: the sword is seen as a phallic symbol, and the general's violent desecration of the Holy of Holies—a space that was strictly prohibited to anyone but the high priest—is compared to a man's sexual violation of a woman's body.[72] As discussed

---

71. Schäfer 2002b, 341.

72. On the association of Rome with the sword, viewed as a symbol of decapitation and thus a mode of execution rather than an instrument of war, see Dohrmann 2002; Berkowitz 2006. On the sexual connotation of this rabbinic story, especially in its late versions, see Hasan-Rokem 1993 (esp. 7) and 1998 (esp. 112–114); Yuval 2002, 54*; Belser 2014; Belser 2018, esp. Chapters 1 and 2. Yuval 2006, 46–48, argues that the tearing of the curtain in the Holy of Holies must be read against the background of Jesus' crucifixion, which according to Matt 27:51 was followed by the miraculous splitting of the temple's holy veil. (The parallel is not self-explanatory, however, as the circumstances of the curtain's tearing are completely different in the two stories, and the meaning of this act or phenomenon differs too.) Yuval posits that the versions of the narrative found in Leviticus Rabbah and the Babylonian Talmud echo the Christian legend of *Vindicta Salvatoris* (*The Avenging of the Savior*) while admitting that the question of which story came first remains open (Yuval 2006, 48). Most scholars date *Vindicta Salvatoris* to the beginning of the Middle Ages (eighth century), and there is no evidence for a tradition going back to the fourth or fifth century. In contrast, the kernel of the rabbinic story, including the depiction of Titus slashing the curtain of the Holy of Holies with his sword, is already found in two tannaitic midrashim (see n. 73 below). The evidence therefore tends to tip the scale in favor of the rabbinic tale's precedence. However, while the story as told in the tannaitic midrashim or Leviticus Rabbah does not need a Christian background to be meaningful, the later version

in Chapter Two, this episode is found in two third-century midrashim, Sifre on Deuteronomy and Mekhilta Deuteronomy, which also describe Titus as a blasphemer who reviles the God of Israel, thereby clarifying that the attack is directed against God.[73]

The sexual symbolism is made even more explicit in the retelling of this story in Leviticus Rabbah 22:3 and the Babylonian Talmud (b. Gittin 56b).[74] In these later sources, before desecrating the Holy of Holies, Titus first rapes a prostitute (*zonah*; two prostitutes in Leviticus Rabbah) on an unfurled Torah scroll upon the altar. This woman may symbolize the conquered city of Jerusalem in accordance with biblical texts (such as Isaiah 1:21 and Ezekiel 16:15–43) that blame Jerusalem's downfall on her sins.[75] Whatever her role, the motif of rape, which remained implicit in the tannaitic narrative, has become openly articulated in these later compositions. As Julia Watts Belser writes, "In this tale, a woman's violated body symbolizes and accentuates the desecration of the Temple by Roman conquerors."[76] The Temple as a metonymy or a synecdoche for Israel's incorporeal God is further highlighted in the later version by the image of the curtain starting to bleed when it is torn, giving Titus the impression that he killed God.[77] According to Galit Hasan-Rokem, Joshua Levinson, and Julia Watts Belser, this version of the story ultimately leads to a feminization or an effeminization of the divine, even though the narrative as a whole, which tells of Titus' divine punishment by means of a gnat, refutes the notion of a powerless god.[78]

---

found in b. Gittin ends with a polemical reference to Jesus (57a), according to MSS Vatican Ebr. 130, Vatican 140, and Munich 95 (see Schäfer 2007, 84–94). We must therefore differentiate the meaning of the early, tannaitic tradition from that of its Babylonian talmudic rewriting. Yet as Belser acutely remarks of b. Gittin 56b–57a, "An overemphasis on the 'polemical' interpretive frame has flattened a crucial dimension of the text: its emphasis on God's capacity to overturn imperial power" (Belser 2018, 136). I concur with Belser's assessment that this aspect is crucial to a correct understanding of the narrative. Moreover, this feature characterizes both the tannaitic and the Babylonian talmudic versions.

73. Sifre Deuteronomy 327–328 (ed. Finkelstein, 378–379); Mekhilta Deuteronomy 32:37–38. See Chapter Two, §2.3.

74. See n. 73 above. Cf. Gen. Rabbah 10:7, which offers a passing comment on Titus' desecration and eventual punishment. Another brief reference to Titus' desecration of the Holy of Holies occurs in Lev. Rabbah 20:5.

75. Cf. Hasan-Rokem 1993, 7, and 1998, 113; she points to Ezekiel 23.

76. Belser 2014, 6. See also Levinson 2003, 369.

77. This bleeding curtain recalls the sacrificial blood that the high priest would sprinkle on it during the Day of Atonement (cf. Lev 16:14–15; m. Yoma 5:4; t. Yoma 2:16). Moreover, on that day, the high priest would read a Torah scroll (m. Yoma 7:1), whereas Titus profanes a Torah scroll by raping a woman upon it. Titus' desecration of the sanctuary may thus be seen as an inversion of the priestly ritual on Yom Kippur. See Levinson 2003, 365–367, who speaks about "a grotesque reversal."

78. Hasan-Rokem 1993, 7; Levinson 2003, 369; Belser 2014, 13; Belser 2018, 47–48. On God's power and powerlessness, see §3.4 below.

Finally, how do rabbinic perceptions of Rome's military power compare with Christian views? During the first three centuries CE, certain Christian authors also condemned the brutality of Roman domination. In the late third or early fourth century (under Diocletian), Arnobius, a rhetorician from Sicca in North Africa who had converted to Christianity, wrote a treatise entitled *Against the Pagans*, which describes the Romans as a "swollen torrent" that "overthrew all nations, and swept them beneath the flood" (1.5). He presents Roman military conquests as catastrophes for which Christians could not be held responsible, seeking thus to defend Christians against the accusation that disasters were afflicting the empire because its traditional cults were being neglected due to the influence of Christianity. Notwithstanding this apologetic aspect, Arnobius' assessment of Roman conquests was largely comparable to rabbinic views of Roman military power.

The most striking feature of Christian texts, when compared with rabbinic writings, is their association of Roman power with evil spirits or Satan. In the earliest examples, the gospels depict Jesus casting off a demon who was so strong that the man whom he possessed could shatter the chains that bound him (Mark 5:2–4; Luke 8:29).[79] The evil spirit identifies himself as "Legion" (Mark 5:9; Luke 8:30) and asks Jesus not to expel him from the country (Mark 5:10); this demon, at least in Mark, is a metaphor for the occupation of the Land of Israel by the Roman army. It seems that some Jews and early Christians, in an attempt to make sense of Rome's apparent invincibility, deemed its power to be supernatural and demonic. In the Apocalypse of John, the city of Rome is described as a whore that dominates the whole world and is populated by demons (18:2). The anonymous *Commentary on Daniel*, often attributed to Hippolytus and dated to the early third century, asserts that, just as Christ summoned people from every nation and every tongue to gather them into the Church, so the Roman empire, which establishes its dominion "with the power of the satan (*kat' energeian tou satana*)," assembles the noblest men of every nation and transforms them into warriors.[80] This text comes close to describing Roman warfare as inspired by the devil. Early in the third century, Tertullian forbade Christians from serving in the Roman army, for they would be exposed to idolatrous practices and, what is more, it would be tantamount to transgressing God's law by following two masters: Christ and the emperor. He augments this dissonance by referring to the Roman army as "the camp of darkness," as distinct from "the camp of light," which is Christ's.[81] In his treatise on idolatry, Tertullian writes even more sharply: "There is no agreement

---

79. These details are absent from the parallel account in Matt 8:28–34.

80. *Commentary on Daniel* 4.9; the Greek text is available online: https://archive.org/stream/hippolytuswerko1hipp#page/n247/mode/2up. On this passage, see Inglebert 2016a, 100.

81. Tertullian, *On the Military Garland* 11.4.

between the divine and the human sacrament, the standard of Christ and the standard of the devil, the camp of light and the camp of darkness. One soul cannot be due to two masters, God and Caesar."[82] The Roman standards and the emperor's army are thus associated with darkness and the devil, making Christian participation in Roman military units unacceptable.

Admittedly, there were different Christian voices as well. Late in the first century CE, the author of 1 Clement, writing at approximately the same time as the author of Revelation, exhorted Christians to imitate the discipline of the Roman army by applying its rigor to their community life and by obeying the elders of the Church as soldiers would obey their officers.[83] More radically, the Christianization of the empire led to a re-evaluation of the Roman armies and a reconsideration of the question of Christian military service. As early as 337, the Syriac theologian Aphrahat, who lived in the Sassanian empire and wrote during the Romano-Persian wars, stated that Christ was escorting the Roman legions and would not let the empire be conquered: "His standard abounds in that place [within Rome's armies], and they are clothed in His armour, and shall not be found wanting in war." Concerning the period prior to Constantine, Aphrahat explains that it was because the Romans did not take Christ with them—although he was one of them, for he was born within the empire under Augustus—that they were unable to fully subdue the beast (a reinterpretation of Revelation 13). In his time, however, he maintains that they had become indomitable.[84]

Clearly, such an evolution in thinking about the Roman army, and Roman power more generally, could not develop in a Jewish context. Nor is the tendency to associate Roman power with supernatural, evil forces present in rabbinic writings. The rabbis seem to have consistently regarded Rome's power as part of a divine design that could be explained by Israel's sins—in accordance with the Deuteronomic worldview that emerged in the biblical period—even though this plan was sometimes perceived as unfair and Israel's punishment as excessive. This last perspective was shared by Josephus and the author of 4 Ezra, neither of whom explains Roman power or Israel's subjugation in relation to a conflict between God and an evil spiritual force.[85] Furthermore, in contrast to Christian authors, the rabbis make no mention of the possibility that a Jew might serve in the Roman army, nor do they discuss how a Jewish Roman soldier could keep the *mitzvot* while

---

82. Tertullian, *On Idolatry* 19.2, trans. Rev. S. Thelwall, in Roberts and Donaldson 1886–1905, 3:73.

83. 1 Clement 37.1–3. The author seems to combine Roman and biblical models, as the reference to "chiefs of fifty" indicates; see Exod 18:25; Deut 1:15; Jaubert 1964, 81.

84. Aphrahat, *On Wars* 24, trans. John Gwynn, in Schaff and Wace 1890, 361. On the dating of Aphrahat's work, see Barnes 1985, 128–130.

85. See Frisch 2017, 184–199, 219.

performing his duty. It was as if they found such a thing inconceivable.[86] Rabbinic sources do occasionally speak of conscription and Jews' efforts to avoid military service, however.[87]

Rabbinic silence as to Jews serving in the Roman army should not be read as reflecting the social reality of the time. In fact, some Jews *were* recruited as soldiers, and a number of them became officers. Moreover, rabbinic condemnation of Roman military power as boundless and brutal did not preclude adoption of the ideal of military bravery, entwined with a sense of rivalry, as we shall now see.

2. A Rivalry for Military Valor?

2.1 JEWS AND THE MILITARY

War was a regular experience for Israelites/Judeans in the Land of Israel. Though biblical accounts of battles can by no means be considered accurate historical descriptions, they do obliquely display a certain knowledge of warfare, occasionally ascribe value to military skills, and reflect on ideological, political, and ethical aspects of war.[88]

Moreover, we know that Judeans served as mercenaries in foreign armies at least from the Persian period onward.[89] The papyri from Elephantine document life in a Judean garrison in Egypt during the fifth century BCE, under Persian rule.[90] Josephus states that Jewish mercenaries in Egypt, during Ptolemy Philadelphus' reign, were entrusted with various citadels (*A.J.* 12.45, echoing Letter of Aristeas 35–36), and papyri attest to a Jewish military presence in various places in Hellenistic Egypt.[91] According to *Antiquities* 12.147–153, Antiochus III settled two thousand Babylonian Jewish soldiers and their families in Phrygia; he assigned them to fortresses (§149) and gave them land (§151) in an effort to stabilize that region.[92] In 1 Maccabees, Demetrius I invites Judeans to enlist in his army (1 Macc 10:36–37). Jonathan is said to have rejected that proposal, but Judean soldiers did fight alongside the Seleucids on a number of occasions, in the name of alliances between Hasmonean leaders and Seleucid sovereigns. When war broke out between Demetrius II

---

86. Schwartz 2010a, 115.

87. Oppenheimer 2005b, 183–184, referring to y. Pesahim 4:9, 32b; Gen. Rabbah 41:4 (ed. Theodor and Albeck, 409) and other parallels.

88. On war in the Bible, see, e.g., von Rad 1951; Niditch 1993; Wright 2008; Trimm 2012; Kelle, Ames, and Wright 2014. On the Hasmonean wars of conquest, see Berthelot 2018a.

89. See Wright 2011, 506–509, which argues that Judahites were already serving in foreign armies at the time of the monarchy.

90. Porten and Yardeni 1986.

91. Wright 2011, 510.

92. On the authenticity of this text, see Schalit 1960.

and the citizens of Antioch, his army included Judean soldiers dispatched by Jonathan (1 Macc 11:45–51; *A.J.* 13.137). After an alliance was formed between Antiochus VII and John Hyrcanus, their joint forces, including a Judean contingent, fought the Parthians (*A.J.* 13.249–250).

In a Roman context, we learn that military support was provided to Caesar during his campaign in Egypt by both Antipater, the father of Herod, and Hyrcanus II, who was then the high priest (*A.J.* 14.127–136).[93] In his treatment of the rule of Antipater and his sons, Josephus includes a lengthy digression about the decrees passed by the Senate concerning Hyrcanus and the Jews.[94] This section opens as follows:

> And here it seems to me necessary to make public all the honours given our nation and the alliances made with them by the Romans and their emperors in order that the other nations may not fail to recognize that both the kings of Asia and of Europe have held us in esteem and have admired our bravery (*andreia*) and loyalty (*pistis*).[95]

By "kings of Asia and Europe," Josephus means Hellenistic kings and Roman *imperatores*, from Pompey and Caesar onward. He recounts that Jews fought alongside these "kings" on various occasions and were rewarded for their military support. In particular, he highlights the Jews' *andreia* (*virtus*) and *pistis* (*fides*), two cardinal virtues of the Romans.

The military collaboration of Hyrcanus II and Antipater with Caesar and of Herod with Antony and then Augustus benefited Jews and Romans alike. Shimon Applebaum notes that in 23 BCE, M. Terentius Varro, then the legate of Syria, settled near Antioch (or maybe in the Huleh Valley of the Upper Galilee) a squadron of Jewish mounted archers who had come from Babylonia with their commander, Zamaris. In 9 BCE, that unit was entrusted to Herod to quell banditry in Trachonitis.[96] Although these archers were not technically Roman troops, they illustrate an interesting use of Jewish forces by the Romans.

Jews' participation in Roman military units, stricto sensu, is a subject of scholarly debate. In the recent *Encyclopedia of the Roman Army*, in the entry "Jews," Yann Le Bohec laconically asserts: "Sometimes enemies of Romans, always critical of Rome, never recruited in the Roman army."[97] This view is an oversimplification. Admittedly, few sources document Jews serving as Roman soldiers. Indeed, among the so-called "privileges" granted to the Jews by the Romans, Josephus in his *Jewish Antiquities* mentions Caesar's decree that no

93. Roth 2007, 417–418.
94. These decrees are discussed at length in Pucci Ben Zeev 1998.
95. *A.J.* 14.186, trans. Thackeray, LCL, 547.
96. Applebaum 1971, 181; Josephus, *A.J.* 17.23–28.
97. Le Bohec 2015, 559.

auxiliary units should be raised in Judea (*A.J.* 14.204) and cites the exemption from serving in the legions granted to Jews with Roman citizenship. He also quotes a letter by Publius Cornelius Dolabella (then governor of Syria; not Asia, as erroneously stated in *A.J.* 14.223) to the Council of Ephesus in 44 BCE, exempting Jewish Roman citizens who lived in Ephesus (or the province of Asia more broadly) from recruitment (*A.J.* 14.225–227).[98] This letter was composed at the request of Hyrcanus II, then the high priest of the Jewish people. Josephus reports that Dolabella echoed Hyrcanus' argument that the Jews' customs precluded them from serving in the Roman army; specifically, they were not allowed to bear arms or march on the Sabbath, and they followed special dietary rules (*A.J.* 14.226). These passages from Josephus have strongly influenced the scholarly view that Jews did not join the Roman army. However, as Applebaum remarks, Augustus' confirmation of Jewish rights in 2 CE does not record a general military exemption, at least according to Josephus' account in *A.J.* 16.160–166. Applebaum observes that "no obstruction existed to including Jews in the *dilectus* in provinces where they were numerous, that is, Syria, Asia, Egypt, Cyrenaica and Cyprus," the treaty with Hyrcanus II and the Herodians notwithstanding.[99]

There is in fact some evidence that Jews were recruited into the Roman army, either as individuals or, in some cases, as a group that would form a military unit.[100] First, Strabo reports that, during Augustus' rule, five hundred Jews—apparently from Egypt—participated in Aelius Gallius' military expedition in Arabia.[101] Second, Suetonius and Josephus report on an episode in 19 CE, under Tiberius, when members of "foreign cults"—especially Egyptians and Jews—were expelled from Rome. Suetonius writes that "those of the Jews who were of military age he [Tiberius] assigned to provinces of less healthy climate, ostensibly to serve in the army," whereas the others were banished from that city.[102] However, Josephus states that the Jews who were expelled were those who had refused military service to avoid violating their ancestral laws (*A.J.* 18.84). In either event, Suetonius, Josephus, and Tacitus all attest that Jews were enrolled in the army, probably in their own units, during the reign of Tiberius.[103]

---

98. Josephus refers to additional decrees which granted exemptions from military service to Jews who were Roman citizens, for example, in Delos and Sardis (*A.J.* 14.231–232).

99. Applebaum 1971, 181.

100. Applebaum 1971; Castritius 2002; Oppenheimer 2005b, 183–191; Schoenfeld 2006; Roth 2007; Rocca 2010.

101. Strabo, *Geogr.* 16.4.23.

102. Suetonius, *Tiberius* 36, trans. J. C. Rolfe, LCL, 363; Stern 1976–1984, 2:112–113. Cf. Tacitus, *Annals* 2.85.4, who adds that the Jews who were forcibly enrolled were descendants of enfranchised slaves, and that they were sent to Sardinia to suppress brigandage.

103. Rocca 2010.

We also know of individual Jews who served in the Roman military. Most famously, Tiberius Julius Alexander fought the Parthians under Corbulo and, according to Tacitus, served as one of Titus' generals during the First Jewish Revolt.[104] Another Julius Alexander, a legate (*hypostratēgos*) who served under Trajan in the Parthian war, may have been a descendant of Philo's nephew.[105] One passage in Genesis Rabbah alludes to a Jewish renegade (*meshummad*) who became a Roman officer and, ultimately, pursued two of R. Joshua's disciples during the Bar Kokhba Revolt.[106] Although this anonymous figure is certainly legendary, the story demonstrates that the rabbis considered it plausible that Jews would have served as soldiers or even officers in the Roman army.

Beyond the literary sources, inscriptions indicate Jewish participation in the Roman military as well, though generally at a later date. The most surprising of these is Aninios (Hanina), a Jewish centurion recorded in second-century Egypt, at the time of the Diaspora Revolt;[107] unfortunately, the only additional information that has come down to us about Aninios is that he had a Jewish slave named Thermauthos. A Latin inscription from Pannonia (modern Hungary), dated to the reign of Alexander Severus, refers to a certain Cosmus as both the commander of the camp (*praepositus stationis*) and the head of the synagogue at Spondilla.[108] An inscription from a fourth-century grave in Concordia, an army camp near Aquileia in Italy, mentions Flavia Optata, the wife or daughter of a soldier in the *num(erus) regi(orum) Emes(enorum) Iudeoru(m)*, the division of royal Emesene Jews.[109] A Greek funerary inscription from Jaffa mentions Thanoum son of Simonos, grandson of Benjamin the centurion (*kentēnarios*), from Parambolē in Egypt.[110] The names of Thanoum's father and grandfather, and the concluding word— *shalom*—indicate that he was Jewish. The inscription's dating is uncertain, but Thanoum's grandfather must have been active before 418 CE, when Honorius and Theodosius II banned Jews from the army (Cod. Th. 16.8.24).[111] The introduction of this law proves that, before 418, Jews had indeed served

---

104. Tacitus, *Annals* 15.28.3; Stern 1976–1984, 2:86–87. On Alexander, see Introduction, §3.

105. Cassius Dio, *Rom. Hist.* 68.30.2; this suggestion comes from Schürer 1973, 458, note 9. Schürer also mentions Tiberios Ioulios Alexandros, "commander of the *Cohors Prima Flavia* and former *eutheniarch* of the second district of Alexandria," who "erected a monument to the goddess Isis in the 21st year of Antoninus Pius" (*OGIS* 705 = *IGR* I, 1044) (ibid.). He may have belonged to the same family. See Turner 1954, 63; Applebaum 2018, 112.

106. Gen. Rabbah 82:8, ed. Theodor and Albeck, 984–985; Applebaum 1971, 182.

107. Ostrakon Edfu 159 = *CPJ* II, no. 229 (116 CE).

108. *CIJ* I, no. 677 (= *CIL* III, no. 3327).

109. *CIJ* I, no. 640; Noy 1993, 8–11, no. 6; Scharf 1997.

110. *CIJ* II, no. 920; Horbury and Noy 1992, 239–240, no. 147.

111. Linder 1987, 280–283.

in the Roman army.[112] Jewish participation is further confirmed by the *Chronicle* of Sulpicius Severus, written circa 403 CE, which notes that Jews, considered a barbarian people (*natio*), live among "us" (meaning Romans, now identified with Christians), "mixed into our armies, our cities, and our provinces."[113]

Somewhat arbitrarily, given the limited number and succinct nature of the extant sources, Jonathan Roth concludes that "Jews as often admired the Roman military, enough to join it in some cases, as they resented and opposed it."[114] That we should deduce admiration—or any other feelings—from a Jew's participation in the army is questionable; Jews' involvement may have been motivated by various reasons, such as financial considerations or, before 212 CE, interest in obtaining Roman citizenship after serving in the *auxilia*.[115] These sources do however make it quite clear that a number of Jews served in the Roman armies and continued to do so after the Jewish revolts. This is a reminder that the rabbis' perspective represented only one view, not necessarily shared by other Jews. Some of them seem to have considered a Roman military career worth pursuing, perhaps even glorious.

2.2 JEWS, WAR, AND MANLINESS: ROMAN PERSPECTIVES

When one people subjugates another, the dominant power's perspective on the subaltern, which may be internalized to a certain degree, informs the latter group's self-definition and values. Thus, before we can assess the extent to which Jewish sources reproduce or at least imitate Roman standards of manliness and conceptions of power, we must analyze Roman perspectives on Jews as soldiers and, especially, examine whether Jews were considered feminine or effeminate by the Romans—on the basis of their Eastern origins, their practice of circumcision, or for other reasons—as argued by Daniel Boyarin.[116]

Admittedly, Roman literary sources regularly associate Jews with defeat, which is less than surprising in light of the historical record. In his speech in defense of Flaccus—the governor of Asia who seized gold that the Jews of his province had sent to the Jerusalem Temple—Cicero refers to Pompey's victory in Judea in 63 BCE, and caustically concludes: "How dear [the nation of the Jews] was to the immortal gods has been shown by the fact that it has been

---

112. Oppenheimer 2005b, 188.

113. Sulpicius Severus, *Chronicle* 2.3.6. I thank Capucine Nemo-Pekelman for this reference.

114. Roth 2007, 420.

115. On military service and citizenship, see Chapter Five.

116. Boyarin 1995 and 1997.

conquered, farmed out to the tax-collectors and enslaved."[117] Cicero's aim here is to condemn the Jews' religion as a barbarian superstition, thereby justifying Flaccus' conduct. Their defeat is accordingly interpreted as a punishment from the gods, which in turn demonstrates the vacuity of their religious practices. However, despite this portrait of Judeans as "enslaved" to the Romans, nowhere in this speech does Cicero characterize Jews as weak, cowardly, incapable of waging war, or feminine. He does, in a discourse delivered to the Senate in 56 BCE, disdainfully brands Jews and Syrians as peoples that are born to be slaves.[118] In this, however, he follows the Greco-Roman convention of labelling Asian peoples as servile, admittedly a topos that classifies Jews as mediocre warriors.[119] Yet as Benjamin Isaac notes, "it is only in this one speech by Cicero that the Jews are described in such terms."[120] Moreover, Cicero's rhetoric should not be mistaken for his actual opinion of Jews, though it seems clear that he held them in low regard.[121] Isaac observes that, when Cicero refers to the contrast between "a campaign waged in Sardinia against bandits in sheepskins by a propraetor with one auxiliary cohort, and a war with the most powerful peoples and rulers in Syria carried out by a consular army," he is certainly alluding to Jews.[122]

During his sojourn in Greece in 79–77 BCE, Cicero studied rhetoric in Rhodes with Apollonius Molon, the famous rhetor from Alabanda. According to *Against Apion*, Apollonius considered Jews to be characterized by cowardice (*deilia*, the opposite of *andreia*), rashness (*tolma*), and recklessness (*aponoia*), traits that Josephus deems contradictory.[123] However, as Bezalel Bar-Kochva notes, "There is no parallel to this rebuke in any of the many surviving accusations and libels against the Jews." This conclusion is reflected in Cicero's work, which does not seem to have been strongly influenced by Apollonius Molon in this respect.[124]

---

117. Cicero, *Pro Flacco* 28.69 (dated to 59 BCE), trans. Coll Macdonald, LCL, 519; Stern 1976–1984, 1:196–201, no. 68. On the tribute that the Judeans were compelled to pay to the Romans after Pompey's victory, see Josephus, *B.J.* 1.154 and *A.J.* 14.74.

118. Cicero, *De provinciis consularibus* 5.10; Stern 1976–1984, 1:202–204, no. 70.

119. For other examples of Cicero's use of ethnic stereotypes, see Gruen 2009, 343–344. On Cicero and the Jews, see Lewy 1941–1942; Yavetz 1998, 80–82; Bernard 2000; Rochette 2001, 19–20; Isaac 2004, 454–455, 463–464, 467. By contrast, in what is probably the earliest Greek description of Jews, Hecataeus of Abdera notes that Moses made provisions for warfare and required young men to cultivate *andreia* and "endurance of every hardship" (Diodorus Siculus 40.3.6).

120. Isaac 2004, 463; see also 481.

121. According to Zvi Yavetz, "Cicero must have been influenced by some Jew-haters and Jew-baiters during his travels to Greece and Rhodes" (Yavetz 1998, 81).

122. Cicero, *De provinciis consularibus* 7.15; Isaac 2004, 464.

123. Josephus, *C. Ap.* 2.148; Barclay 2007, 252; Bar-Kochva 2010, 469–516, esp. 492–496.

124. Bar-Kochva 2010, 492.

The military support that Caesar received from Antipater, Hyrcanus, and their Judean troops, and Aelius Gallus' later decision to recruit Jews for his expedition in Arabia, indicate that at least some Roman leaders in first-century BCE Rome valued the abilities of Judean soldiers. Despite an increase in anti-Jewish sentiment among Roman authors after the First Jewish Revolt, their writings do not accuse Jews of cowardice or unmanliness.[125] To the contrary, even Tacitus notes the Jews' fierce resistance during the Judean War. Although he does not speak of their military valor, he recognizes their ability to counter assaults from Roman forces and endure severe hardships, as well as their contempt for death, which he ascribes to the Jews' *superstitio*, thus simultaneously acknowledging and denigrating their actions and attitudes.[126] In his account of the First Jewish Revolt, Cassius Dio describes the Judeans who fought during the siege of Jerusalem as skillful warriors and, concerning the final battle near the Temple, he even comments: "Though they were but a handful fighting against a far superior force, they were not conquered until a part of the temple was set on fire."[127] From Strabo to Philostratus, authors depicted the Jews as a challenge that ranged from a nuisance to a serious threat, whether during Hasmonean wars or the revolts against Rome. Their writings provide indirect testimony to the initial success achieved by Jewish military activity, despite their lack of recognition, much less praise, for the Jews' valor.[128] In the fourth century, the emperor Julian contrasted Roman victories and lasting imperial domination with the defeats endured by the Jews and their subjugation under Roman rule. He derided their martial abilities in these terms:

> Point out to me among the Hebrews a single general like Alexander or Caesar! You have no such man. And indeed, by the gods, I am well aware that I am insulting these heroes by the question, but I mentioned them because they are well known. For the generals who are inferior to them are unknown to the multitude, and yet every one of them deserves more admiration than all the generals put together whom the Jews have had.[129]

Julian is attempting to convince a Christian that it is foolish to worship the God of Israel rather than the traditional gods of Rome. Thus Christianity is

---

125. Berthelot 2003, 156–171.

126. Tacitus, *Hist.* 2.4.3, 5.5.3; Isaac 2004, 464; Barclay 2007, 250: "In light of this, Tacitus' comment on the Judeans' contempt for death (*moriendi contemptus, Hist.* 5.5.3) can only be regarded as praise."

127. Cassius Dio, *Rom. Hist.* 66.4.3–6.3, quotation from 66.6.3, trans. Earnest Cary, LCL, 269.

128. Strabo, *Geogr.* 16.2.37; Philostratus, *The Life of Apollonius of Tyana* 5.33 (these words are attributed to the Stoic philosopher Euphrates, active at the time of Vespasian).

129. Julian, *Against the Galileans* 218 B–C, trans. Wilmer C. Wright, LCL, 381–383.

FIGURE 3.6. Sestertius of the *Iudaea Capta* type, featuring Vespasian on the obverse, and a Judean captive standing alongside Judea, seated and mourning, on the reverse (71 CE). *RIC* II.1 (rev. ed.), no. 159, p. 71. Photograph © The Trustees of the British Museum.

the real target of his polemic, not Judaism. Nevertheless, the passage reveals Julian's disregard for Jews as military actors.

Despite Julian's condescending tone, his remarks also imply that Jews had generals and forces that had fought in past wars, and this without any suggestion of Jews as effeminate. Benjamin Isaac notes that "although they [the Jews] originated in the East, they are not usually accused of softness or effeminacy, unlike many other peoples from Asia Minor and Syria."[130] In the first century CE, this observation is corroborated by the iconography of Flavian coinage depicting a muscular Judean, which leaves little doubt that Jews could be perceived as real warriors (Fig. 3.6). More precisely, as Jane Cody emphasizes, "in adopting the compositional scheme and details of the republican and Augustan *capta* types, the designers intended to portray the Judean Jews as worthy enemies on the battlefield, but as uncivilised, like Gauls or Spaniards."[131]

The sources analyzed thus far do not support the notion that Romans perceived Jews as a weak, unmanly, or "feminine" people, in spite of their military defeats. Yet it has been posited that the Romans did view Jews as "feminine" on account of their practice of circumcision.[132] Although this ritual was shared, albeit with variations, by other peoples in the East—for instance, among Egyptian priests and Ethiopians—Roman writings associate circumcision primarily with Jews.[133] The practice does not appear, however, in the

130. Isaac 2004, 464.
131. Cody 2003, 110.
132. Boyarin 1997, 142.
133. Cordier 2001, 338–340.

context of "feminine" imagery. As Pierre Cordier has argued, the Romans did not categorize circumcision as a form of mutilation until the late second century (at earliest), when the legal sources witness a shift in perspective. During the first and second centuries CE, Roman authors, especially poets and satirists, often joked about the circumcized penis, while depicting Jewish men as priapic figures—quite distinct from feminized men—whose hypersexuality did not conform to Roman mores.[134] Moreover, and most importantly—given the Roman definition of masculinity in reference to sexual intercourse, which held that a "real man" would protect his body from any act of penetration or violation—the Roman authors who mocked the Jews' circumcized penis, nevertheless described them in active rather than passive roles.[135] For example, in Martial's epigrams several Jewish protagonists, often in homoerotic relationships, are presented as the active sexual partner.[136]

Thus, Daniel Boyarin's claim that Romans viewed Jews as "feminine" does not stand up to close scrutiny. Although several Roman authors criticized Jewish practices and rituals, expressed hostility toward this group for having revolted against Rome, or considered Jewish military leaders vastly inferior to Greek or Roman generals, they did not depict Jews as cowardly or unmanly, nor as unfit for war.

2.3 JEWS, WAR, AND MANLINESS: JEWISH RIVALRY WITH ROME?

What is the perspective of Jewish sources on these issues? We must first note that they generally depict Jews as highly skilled in warfare. Various texts proudly record the military achievements of biblical heroes and contemporaneous Jews, and even exalt the exploits of the God of Israel, described in Exodus 15:3 as "a man of war" (*ish milḥamah*). In the Hellenistic period, Artapanus' retelling of the story of Moses presented him as the inventor of Egyptian weaponry and a general who successfully waged war against Ethiopia, then won the Ethiopians over to his own customs.[137] Later, in a Roman context, descriptions of Jews (or Hebrews) as heroic warriors could portray them along similar lines and, whether implicitly or explicitly, as

---

134. Cordier 2001. See also Blanton 2019.

135. On Roman definitions and representations of masculinity and manliness, see, in particular, Walters 1997, who notes that, from a Roman perspective, "Not all males are men, and therefore impenetrable" (32); Williams 1999, 4 and 160–224; Gunderson 2000, 161.

136. Cordier 2001, 349–350; Roux 2017, on *Epigram* 11.94 in particular. In this epigram, Martial blames his rival, a Jew whom he calls a "circumcised poet," for sodomizing his "boy," probably his slave.

137. Artapanus' description appears in Eusebius, *Praep. Ev.* 9.27.3 and 7–10. See Borgeaud, Römer and Volokhine 2010, 3–82; Wright 2011, 513.

peers with Romans on the battlefield. These texts may, in other words, be apologetic descriptions of Jewish bravery that convey a sense of rivalry with the Romans.

Before we examine some of these passages, I would like to draw attention to the paucity of references to the *andreia* of Jews in Jewish literature written in Greek during the Hellenistic period.[138] Such references as there are occur mainly in 1 and 2 Maccabees. In 2 Maccabees 2:21 and 14:18, the words *andragatheō* and *andragathia* refer to the manliness of Judas and his men (at war), while at 6:27 the adverb *andreiōs* describes Eleazar's readiness to die, but here as a martyr rather than a fighter. In comparison, 4 Maccabees—a work of similar length that was probably composed at the end of the first century CE and deals with the issue of the Maccabean martyrs—uses *andreia*'s lexical field thirteen times.[139] The reason for these numerous references probably lies in the literary genre of this work: 4 Maccabees is a kind of philosophical sermon that, through the example of the Maccabean martyrs, aims to show that reason can master the passions, especially those opposed to the four cardinal virtues. Its insistence on courage and its Stoic overtones, however, may also have to do with its Roman cultural context. Moreover, in contrast to 2 Maccabees, 4 Maccabees concludes its description of the Judeans' martyrdom with these words:

> When the tyrant Antiochus saw the courage of their virtue and their endurance under the tortures, he proclaimed to his soldiers that they were an example for their own endurance. He made them [his soldiers] noble and courageous for fighting on foot and for siege, and [he] pillaged and conquered all his foes.[140]

While the description of the martyrs' death in 2 Maccabees 7 ends with an anticipation of the king's forthcoming judgment by God and the statement that Antiochus' cruelty did not diminish for fear of that judgment, the author of 4 Maccabees depicts the king as full of admiration for the martyrs, to the point of directing his own soldiers to take them as examples. He even suggests that Antiochus' later victories on the battlefield were owed to lessons taught the Seleucid army by the Judean martyrs. The desire to present Jews as models

---

138. Epistle of Jeremiah 58 associates *andreia* with kings. Letter of Aristeas 12 refers to Ptolemy I Soter's *andreia* in battle. Yet, as emphasized in Chapter One, the Letter plays down the importance of military victory and associates courage (*andreia*) in warfare with justice (*dikaiosunē*) and concern for soldiers' lives (§281; see also §199). Note that words associated with *andreia*'s lexical field in Jewish Hellenistic works are not necessarily related to courage in battle or before death. See, e.g., LXX Ben Sira 26:2, 28:15; cf. LXX Prov 12:4, 31:10.

139. See 4 Macc 1:4.6.11.18, 2:23, 5:23, 7:23, 15:10.23.30, 17:23–24. On the dating, see Bickerman 1945.

140. 4 Macc 17:23–24, trans. Stephen Westerholm, NETS, 540.

of *andreia*, including at war, is obvious in 4 Maccabees, whereas this purpose is absent from 2 Maccabees.

Among the Jewish works from the Hellenistic period, 1 Maccabees stands out for its insistence on the Hasmoneans' bravery and military exploits and so deserves particular attention. There is only one occurrence of the word *andreia* in this book (at 9:10),[141] but the author consistently describes Judas, his brothers, and John Hyrcanus as heroic fighters, and he uses the term *andragathiai* repeatedly to describe their military achievements.[142] These acts of bravery distinguish the Hasmoneans from their potential rivals in Judean society (see 1 Macc 5:61, 67). Moreover, as Chris Seeman remarks, the ability to perform *andragathiai* characterizes only two groups in the book, the Hasmoneans and the Romans (1 Macc 8:2).[143] Seeman further argues that the description of the Romans as quasi-invincible warriors in 1 Maccabees 8 echoes the depiction of the Hasmoneans elsewhere in the book. The Romans and the Hasmoneans are, for example, the only groups that have a "name" (*onoma*, in the sense of a reputation) for military bravery, that are called *dynatoi ischyi* ("mighty warriors"), and that inspire fear in the hearts of their enemies.[144] According to Seeman, the very raison d'être for the praise of the Romans in chapter 8 is to increase the Hasmoneans' prestige and thus to justify their rule. While the parallels identified by Seeman may occasionally pertain to the Judeans at large (or the Hasmonean troops), they are generally established only between the Romans and the Hasmonean family, making clear that the author's aim was to enhance the Hasmoneans' political legitimacy: "As the mirror of Maccabean virtue, Rome was well-qualified to authenticate Hasmonean claims."[145] Even though its description of Hasmonean bravery does not merely echo the Romans' reputation of invincibility but also builds upon biblical models (such as David),[146] the mirroring at work in 1 Maccabees is an early example of a Jewish discursive imitation of Roman features, in this case by a pro-Hasmonean author who aligned the behavior of Judea's rulers with that of the most powerful state of his time in order to increase their prestige.

---

141. When Judas faces the armies of Bacchides, which vastly outnumber the Judean army, he nevertheless refuses to order a retreat and exclaims: "Far be it from me to do this thing, to flee from them. And if our time has drawn near, let us die with courage (*andreia*) for the sake of our brothers, and let us leave no accusation against our honor (*doxa*)" (1 Macc 9:10, trans. George Zervos, NETS, 491).

142. 1 Macc 5:56, 9:22, 10:15, 16:23.

143. Seeman 2013, 210. Polybius often uses both the verb *andragatheō* and the noun *andragathia* in referring to the Romans' military achievements (Assan-Dhôte and Fine 2014, 104–105).

144. Seeman 2013, 209–211.

145. Seeman 2013, 211 (see also 216).

146. Berthelot 2018a, 109–118.

Rome's impact on Jewish discourses about courage in war and military achievements is also manifest in the frequency with which Jewish texts in Greek from the Roman period use the lexical field of *andreia*, often in the context of war or a noble death.[147] Moreover, they tend to focus on the bravery and military skills of biblical characters to a much greater extent than previous Jewish authors had. Let us look, for instance, at Philo's recasting of Genesis 14—where Abraham wages a war against King Chedorlaomer and three other kings allied to him, who had attacked the king of Sodom together with four other kings, and taken Abraham's nephew Lot prisoner.[148] Philo first comments on its literal meaning, emphasizing that "the man of worth was not merely peaceable and a lover of justice but courageous (*andreios*) and warlike (*polemikos*), not for the sake of warring, for he was not quarrelsome (*dyseris*) or cantankerous (*philoneikos*), but to secure peace for the future, the peace which the opponents were destroying."[149] From §236 onward, Philo offers an allegorical interpretation of this biblical episode, identifying the two groups of kings as the four passions and the five physical senses, respectively.[150] Before that transition, however, Philo reports Abraham's military exploits, adding details to Genesis 14 that are meant to extol this patriarch's achievements. The kings whom Abraham fights— Chedorlaomer and his allies—are described as rulers over the eastern half of the inhabited world, on both sides of the Euphrates (*Abr.* 226). They are further characterized as invincible (*amachos*, *Abr.* 231). The biblical text presents Abraham's victory as an extraordinary one, for he countered four armies with his cadre of 318 servants. Genesis 14:15 specifies that they launched a surprise night-time assault. Philo builds on the biblical narrative, adding: "Nor did he stay his hand until he had completely slaughtered the opposing army with their kings as well and left them lying in front of the camp."[151] Whereas Genesis 14:15 suggests that these kings and their troops fled after Abraham's victorious attack, Philo states that the four kings and their armies were wiped out. Abraham's prowess as a warrior is thus exalted beyond the biblical account, a choice which may reveal that Philo is

147. On Philo and Josephus, see below. Wisdom of Solomon 8:15 mentions courage in war once, as a characteristic of the king who will rely on divine wisdom (Solomon is supposed to be the speaker), while listing *andreia* as one of the four cardinal virtues at 8:7. On 4 Maccabees, see above.

148. On the place of military episodes in the lives of the biblical patriarchs against the background of ancient Near Eastern literature, see Muffs 1982; on the redaction history of Gen 14, and its early rewritings in Jubilees and the Genesis Apocryphon, see Berner 2015.

149. Philo, *Abr.* 225, trans. F. H. Colson, LCL, 111.

150. See also *Ebr.* 105.

151. *Abr.* 234, trans. F. H. Colson, LCL, 115.

here adopting Roman standards of military heroism, whether consciously or inadvertently.[152]

Another compelling feature of Philo's interpretation of this passage from Genesis 14 is his portrayal of Sodom as a rebellious town or people, in contrast to the other provinces in the kings' empires: "Now the other nations continued to be free from sedition, obeying the orders of the kings, and paying their taxes without demur. Only the country of the Sodomites, before it was consumed by fire, began to undermine this peaceful condition by a long-standing plan of revolt."[153] For a Roman audience, this description would have cast the Sodomites in a negative light. While we cannot know whether Philo formulated the remark deliberately or had merely internalized Roman imperial rhetoric on revolts, being aware of Roman norms helps us to contextualize some aspects of Philo's rewriting of Abraham's life.

Josephus' treatment of the episode from Genesis 14 differs from Philo's in several ways.[154] First, he identifies Chedorlaomer and his allies as Assyrian, as if this story were set during the time of the kingdoms of Israel and Judah. Second, the Sodomites appear as friendly neighbors of Abraham, not as a rebellious people (§176). Third, Josephus ascribes the success of Abraham's night-time attack to some of the Assyrians having been drunk, thus offering a plausible explanation for his unlikeky victory. Fourth, staying closer than Philo to the biblical narrative, Josephus writes that Abraham pursued the enemy as far as the country of the Damascenes (§178), without stating that he slaughtered them. Josephus praises Abraham's military valor, but not to the extent that Philo does—the comparison of their respective accounts further highlights Philo's exaggeration.

Nevertheless, Josephus' overall tendency in *Antiquities* is to describe biblical Hebrews/Israelites as formidable adversaries. Much like Artapanus, Josephus depicts Moses as the conqueror of Ethiopia (*A.J.* 2.238–253) and draws an idealized military portrait of Moses as *stratēgos*.[155] Josephus does not engage the lexicon of *andreia* in his description of Abraham or Moses, but he introduces this term when he writes that, during the period of the judges, the Israelites "returned to their former polity, entrusting supreme judicial authority to him who in battle and in bravery (*andreia*) had proved himself the best."[156]

---

152. See also Birnbaum 2015, which does not discuss Philo's Roman context. On the dating of *On the Life of Abraham*, see Niehoff 2018, 7–8, which argues that it was written after Philo's stay in Rome in 38–41 CE.

153. *Abr.* 226, trans. F. H. Colson, LCL, 111.

154. *A.J.* 1.171–178.

155. See Feldman 1992b; Damgaard 2008; Petitfils 2014 (which insists on the importance of Josephus' Flavian context and reads his depiction of Moses' actions in light of the Romans' discourse of their own exemplarity).

156. *A.J.* 6.85, trans. H. St. J. Thackeray and Ralph Marcus, LCL, 209.

This passage reads like a Romanized version of the Book of Judges, since that biblical text does not predicate selection as a judge upon wartime courage; rather, faithfulness to God's covenant with Israel is the deciding qualification. Moreover, in the biblical narrative, God, not the people, chooses judges.

From the period of the judges onward, *andreia* recurs as an essential quality in Josephus' descriptions of biblical political and military leaders: Ehud (*A.J.* 5.188), Saul (*A.J.* 6.80, 346–348), David (*A.J.* 6.167, 196, 200; 7.390), Uriah (*A.J.* 7.138), Abimelech (*A.J.* 7.142), Jehoshaphat (*A.J.* 8.315), as well as Judas Maccabee (*A.J.* 12.284, 339) and his brother Jonathan (*A.J.* 13.43, 45, 195) are all depicted as *andreioi*. Louis Feldman noted long ago that "in a number of additions to the biblical narrative, [Josephus] stresses the military prowess and courage of the Jews."[157] This emphasis probably derives from the prominent role played by *virtus/andreia* in the Roman world in which Josephus lived, and to the fact that he addressed a Roman audience (composed of both Jews and non-Jews).

Beyond this general inclination to accentuate the military valor and bravery of biblical characters, some passages in *Antiquities* may be seen to reflect Josephus' Roman context and audience more specifically—especially those related to the troops of David, whose personal *andreia* Josephus praises repeatedly. For instance, based on 2 Samuel 23, Josephus asserts that David's soldiers were all fearless, and that thirty-eight of them were exceptionally renowned. Then he adds that "of these I shall relate the exploits of only five, for they will serve to make clear the heroic virtues of the rest, being powerful enough to subdue countries and conquer great nations."[158] Yet this biblical chapter, whose main subject is warfare against the Philistines, does not claim Israelite conquests against major nations. To put it bluntly, Josephus' insistence on the military ability and the power of David's men seems exaggerated, in a manner that resonates with Roman imperial ideology.[159]

Rabbinic literature also elaborates on biblical examples of Israel's military valor. In a comment on Numbers 27:17, where Moses asks God to provide a leader who will marshal Israel in combat, the midrash Sifre Numbers (third

---

157. Feldman 1993, 222.

158. *A.J.* 7.307; this text conveys an implicit reference to 2 Sam 23:39, which includes the number "thirty-seven."

159. Another passage associated with David's men that resonates with Roman values is *A.J.* 7.12, where Josephus recounts the battle that took place after Saul's death between the army of Saul's general, Abner, and Joab, the commander-in-chief of David's troops (2 Sam 2:12–17). While the biblical text simply states, "Abner said to Joab: 'Let the young men come forward and have a contest before us.' Joab said, 'Let them come forward,'" Josephus comments that Abner and Joab sought to know which of their men were the most courageous. This emphasis on military bravery (*andreia*) is probably a result of Josephus' immersion in Roman values and, by extension, his conscious or latent desire to suggest that Jews were no less heroic than Romans.

century CE) explains the phrase "who shall go out before them" to mean a military officer who marches at the head of his army and is the first to face the enemy. Illustrations include Moses, Joshua, and Pinhas, whose courage is praised by comparison with the "others" (*aḥerin*, referring to non-Jewish kings or generals), who directed their armies forward and followed them, thus eschewing danger.[160] Significantly, Moses is portrayed as a valiant general going to war although, in the Bible, he is never directly involved in battle (even in Exodus 17, the war against Amalek).

Whereas this passage refers to "others" without mentioning a specific nation, another passage in Sifre Numbers explicitly compares the military valor of Rome and Israel. It comments on "While Israel was staying at Shittim"—the opening phrase of Numbers 25, a chapter that describes Israel being seduced by Moabite women—and connects this episode to Israel's prior victory against the kings Sihon and Og in Numbers 21:21–35, affirming that Israel was corrupted by the spoils of those earlier wars. The brief digression that follows contrasts the territories conquered by Israel and by Rome:

> They [Israel] came and waged war with Sihon and Og. They [Sihon and Og] fell into their hands, and they [Israel] took everything that belonged to them. This kingdom [Rome] boasts and vaunts, [yet] it has only four cities (*medinot*) that are eligible for kingship. These are Akhia, Alexandria, Kartikani [Carthage], and Antiochia. But to those [the kingdoms defeated by Israel—namely, Sihon and Og] belonged sixty cities ('*ir*) and all of them were eligible for kingship, as it is written: [*At that time we captured all his towns; there was no citadel that we did not take from them:*] *sixty towns, the whole region of Argob, the kingdom of Og in Bashan* (Deut 3:4).[161]

As Menahem Kahana notes, the comparison between Rome's four *medinot* and the sixty '*arim* (although they are sixty, the midrash uses the singular form '*ir*) shows that cities are being discussed in both cases. However, Akhia seems to designate Achaia, in the northern Peloponnese, which became a Roman province in 27 BCE.[162] Kahana explains that "eligible for kingship" probably indicates a large city that was prominent enough to host an imperial residence. This list, however, has no historical basis. Moreover, whereas Alexandria and Antioch qualify as important cities in the Roman Empire, Carthage is probably mentioned because of this Punic city's status as Rome's adversary in the third- and second-century BCE. In fact, these four cities may stand for

160. Sifre Numbers 139, ed. Kahana 2011–2015, 1:65 [סה]. The biblical proof texts quoted in this midrash are: Numbers 21:34 (for Moses), Joshua 5:13 (for Joshua), and Numbers 31:6 (for Pinhas).

161. Sifre Numbers 131, ed. Kahana 2011–2015, 1:53 [נג]. See Yael Wilfand, "Sifre Numbers 131," http://www.judaism-and-rome.org/sifre-numbers-131.

162. Jastrow 1950, 63; Kahana 2011–2015, 4:1093, notes 75 and 76.

the four main kingdoms or empires that Rome defeated in the second and first centuries BCE, when it acquired most of its territory: (1) Achaia for the Macedonians—Philip V, whom Rome defeated in the battle of Cynoscephalae in 197 BCE, was originally allied with the Achaean League; (2) Antioch for the Seleucids—Rome defeated Antiochus III at Magnesia ad Sipylum in 189 BCE and drove Antiochus IV from Egypt in 168 BCE; (3) Carthage—which the Romans destroyed in 146 BCE—for the Carthaginians; and (4) Alexandria for the Ptolemies—whose last queen, Cleopatra, Octavian defeated in 31 BCE. If this were the background for the claim in Sifre Numbers that Rome boasted about having these four major cities in its dominion, they would symbolize the four decisive victories or stages that led to the establishment of Rome's "universal" empire. In any case, this midrash seeks to underscore Israel's military superiority, by recalling its seizure of two kingdoms that together had no fewer than sixty important cities, not a mere four, and thus openly conveys a sense of rivalry between Israel and Rome.[163]

So far we have shown that Jewish authors in a Roman context referred to Israel's martial bravery in biblical sources to show—either implicitly or explicitly—that their nation was as praiseworthy as Rome, or even more so. Now the question arises: What did they say about the military valor of the Jews who lived in the Roman Empire?

Josephus' praise for Jews who served various armies as mercenaries during the Hellenistic and early Roman periods has already been mentioned.[164] His *Judean War* also celebrates the military skills and quasi-invincibility of Herod the Great, thereby suggesting that the latter compared favorably with the Romans.[165] In Josephus' own time, however, Jewish military activity—at least among Judean Jews—primarily consisted of armed conflict with Rome. Unsurprisingly, his description of the Judean rebels' skills and valor is markedly ambiguous. On the one hand, he refrains from presenting the rebels, and especially their leaders, as heroes who display *andreia*. Because they had chosen a path that Josephus repeatedly condemned, he could not glorify their deeds; thus, he stressed their recklessness (*tolma*) rather than their courage.[166] On the other hand, Josephus could not minimize the rebels' resistance

---

163. The characterization of Rome as "boasting and vaunting" is also found in the fifth-century midrash Leviticus Rabbah (7:6), a passage which focuses on theodicy and Rome's future punishment.

164. See *A.J.* 14.186, and above, §2.1.

165. See *B.J.* 1.429–430; Hezser, forthcoming.

166. See, for example, Josephus' description of Simon bar Giora in *B.J.* 4.503–504. He is strong and audacious rather than brave and logically (from Josephus' perspective) joins a band of brigands (*lēstai*). John Barclay notes that "a common trope in Josephus' *War* is the contrast between Judean recklessness in warfare and the Roman characteristics of experience, control, and discipline: see, e.g., *War* 3.152–53, 475–79; 4.424–25; 5.285 (a rare exception); cf. 3.14–15, 209–12. At one point Josephus indicates that this is the typical

or the reality of their challenge to the Romans during the siege of Jerusalem. His patriotic pride as a Judean and the nature of Flavian propaganda—which grounded the political legitimacy of this new dynasty on the outcome of the war in Judea—prevented him from relativizing the Flavians' victory.[167] Josephus thus astutely ascribes to Titus some statements that indirectly praise the Judeans' valor. Admittedly, in his speech prior to the assault against the Antonia (*B.J.* 6.34–53), Titus clearly extols Rome's military superiority and, like Cicero, refers to Jews as a people that is used to being enslaved, implying that they are not capable warriors. Titus' point is that Roman soldiers would be ashamed if they failed to defeat such an enemy:

> It would indeed be disgraceful that Jews, to whom defeat brings no serious discredit since they have learnt to be slaves, should, in order to end their servitude, scorn death and constantly charge into our midst, not from any hope of victory, but for the sheer display of bravery (*andreia*); and yet that you, masters of well nigh every land and sea, to whom not to conquer is disgrace, should never once venture into the enemy's ranks, but should wait for famine and fortune to bring them down, sitting idle with weapons such as these, and that though at a little hazard you have it in your power to achieve everything.[168]

This passage is replete with Roman stereotypes and ideological motifs, most prominently a reference to Roman domination over land and sea (analyzed in Chapter Two). Despite its scornful tone toward Jews, the speech nevertheless indirectly praises their courage. In contrast to the Roman soldiers, who do not dare to launch an expedition against the Antonia, these Jews risk their lives, not for the sake of victory—since their situation is already desperate— but as an expression of *andreia*. Josephus displayed political savvy in having Titus acknowledge the military bravery exhibited by the Jewish rebels. First, he protected himself against potential accusations of sympathy toward enemies of Rome. Second, he depicted the head of the Roman army praising Jewish courage in battle despite typical Roman prejudices against Jews: a splendid response to anti-Jewish accusations, such as those formulated by Apollonius Molon.

One of the few rabbinic narratives about the Bar Kokhba Revolt also mentions the recognition of Jewish military abilities by a Roman leader. Rabbinic accounts of this revolt are ambiguous but, on the whole, their depictions of its

---

Roman perception of 'barbarians' (*War* 4.45–47)" (Barclay 2007, 252). Josephus seems to have embraced this Roman perspective to some extent.

167. What kind of glory would there be in a victory against a weak and unworthy enemy? See *B.J.* 1.7–8 in particular.

168. *B.J.* 6.42–44, trans. H. St. J. Thackeray, LCL, 389.

leader tend to be negative.[169] Yet one aspect of the story of the fall of Bethar suggests a "rivalry of bravery" much like the passage from Josephus' *Judean War* discussed above. In y. Ta'anit 4:6, 68d–69b and Lamentations Rabbah 2:4, Bethar falls to the Romans because of a fit of rage during which Bar Kokhba murdered R. Eleazar ha-Modai, who had been interceding for the city. Without the prayers of that righteous rabbi, Bethar is immediately seized and Bar Kokhba killed. When his head is presented to Hadrian, the emperor asks: "Who killed him?" The man who plotted to have R. Eleazar ha-Modai murdered claims to have killed Bar Kokhba, but Hadrian then asks to see his corpse. When Bar Kokhba's body is brought in front of the emperor, Hadrian discovers that he was bitten by a snake and, thus, killed by God—who sent the snake—rather than by a man. The emperor then exclaims: "If God did not kill him, who could have killed him?" and applies to him the biblical verse "Unless their Rock had sold them and their Lord had given them up!" (Deut 32:30).[170] Hadrian's reaction signifies that Bar Kokhba was such an exceptional combatant that no human being could have defeated him. Like the Romans (as a collective rather than as individuals), he was invincible. Only God could decree the end of Bar Kokhba's life.

As in Josephus' account of the seizing of the Antonia, in this rabbinic tradition, praise for military valor demonstrated by Jews—specifically, the leader of their revolt—comes from the Roman commander-in-chief. The fact that the redactors of these rabbinic texts put such comments in Hadrian's mouth reveals their longing that the greatness of the Jews be recognized by their enemies; and this is a pattern that appears elsewhere in rabbinic literature, where gentiles acknowledge the perfection of the Torah or the overall superiority of Israel.[171] It might be interpreted as evidence of the rabbis' need to compensate for the mockery and humiliation that Israel endured from non-Jews, as well as an indication that they felt a sense of rivalry with gentiles, especially the Romans—which led them to claim that their defeat by Rome was not caused by a lack of bravery.

2.4 JEWISH MIMESIS AND MIMICRY
OF ROMAN POWER

Some of the examples cited in the preceding section display a certain degree of mimesis vis-à-vis Roman power. Rivalry and imitation can actually go hand in hand, as René Girard has pointed out.[172] Even after a defeat, the vanquished

169. See, in particular, Reinhartz 1989; Schäfer 2003b, 7; Novenson 2009 (specifically on R. Aqiva's statement about Bar Kochba).

170. Trans. Schäfer 2003b, 6. See y. Ta'anit 4:6, 68d–69a; Schäfer and Becker 1991–2001 (2001, *Synopse* II/5–12), 262.

171. See Chapter Four.

172. See Introduction.

may consciously or unintentionally mimic the victor to symbolically compensate for their defeat, because imperial subjects who face overwhelming political domination are inevitably exposed to the ruling culture and its models.

Concerning Jewish imitation of Roman discourses, representations, and social practices that relate to power and military valor, let us first examine depictions of the enemy as feminine. Presenting an individual or collective foe as effeminate was a strategy that Roman orators and authors regularly employed to undermine various Eastern peoples (as discussed previously) or opponents within Roman society, such as political "tyrants." Jason von Ehrenkrook has shown that Josephus' description of John of Gishala, his rival in the Galilee early in the revolt, who later joined the rebels in Jerusalem, was influenced by these Roman cultural categories. In *War* 4.560–562, the Judean rebels under John's command, now under siege in Jerusalem, are portrayed in these terms:

> With an insatiable lust for loot, they ransacked the houses of the wealthy; the murder of men and the violation of women were their sport; they caroused on their spoils, with blood to wash them down, and from mere satiety unscrupulously indulged in effeminate practices (*enethēlypathoun*), plaiting their hair and attiring themselves in women's apparel, drenching themselves with perfumes and painting their eyelids to enhance their beauty. And not only did they imitate the dress, but also the passions of women, devising in their excess of lasciviousness unlawful pleasures and wallowing as in a brothel in the city, which they polluted from end to end with their foul deeds.[173]

Josephus portrays the rebels and, by implication, their leader as "effeminate objects of sexual penetration."[174] This feminizing depiction of Josephus' personal adversaries, who were also enemies of the empire, may have resulted from a semi-conscious adoption of Roman discourse and gender constructions, which were not at odds with Jewish notions. However, Josephus also seems to have had a deliberate strategy. As von Ehrenkrook emphasizes, through this imagery, "Josephus underscores just how alike Judaeans and Romans really were. Both were afflicted with a decadent and effeminate tyrant—Nero in Rome and John in Galilee/Judaea."[175] Indeed, Josephus often presents Jews and Romans with similar features and as having more commonalities than the events of 66–73 CE would indicate (at least from a Roman perspective). The depiction that von Ehrenkrook analyzes is part of this strategy.[176]

173. *B.J.* 4.560–562, trans. H. St. J. Thackeray, LCL, 167.
174. Von Ehrenkrook 2011, 146.
175. Von Ehrenkrook 2011, 162–163.
176. For other aspects of this strategy, see Goodman 1994b, 334–335; Haaland 1999; Barclay 2000 and 2007, 362–369.

By contrast, Genesis Rabbah describes Esau—who symbolizes the Romans—as effeminate and as having adopted a passive sexual role, thus rendering himself unmanly by Roman standards. Commenting on Genesis 25:27, "Esau was a skilful hunter, a man of the field," the midrash—speaking through R. Hiyya bar Abba, a third-generation amora from Palestine (late third century)—states that "He made himself free to all like a field," meaning that he was sexually available to all, as if he were ownerless property that had been found in a field. In the midrash, this teaching prompts Israel to cry out to God: "Master of all the worlds, is it not enough that we have been enslaved to the seventy nations? Must we also be enslaved to this one [Esau/Rome], who is penetrated like a woman?"[177] God reassures Israel by promising that Esau will pay for his crimes in a manner that matches his degrading behavior, citing Jeremiah 49:22, "The heart of the warriors of Edom on that day shall be like the heart of a woman in labour." Based on a "measure for measure" principle, as punishment for Esau's unmanly sexual conduct, the soldiers of Esau/Rome will become as weak and fearful as women were alleged to be from Roman and rabbinic perspectives. The literal meaning of the biblical text does not cast Esau in such a light, and it is paradoxical for him to be depicted as unmanly on the basis of a verse that portrays his strength and ability for battle.[178] This passage of Genesis Rabbah shows how the rabbis adopted Roman standards to cast the Romans themselves in negative light, thus employing a subversive strategy of reversal. Presenting Esau/Rome as unmanly clearly entailed a dimension of irony. Yet Israel's outraged response in Genesis Rabbah implies that Israel and Rome held a common view of men who take a passive role in homosexual relations. Here, mimicking Roman standards to ridicule Rome goes along with an internalization of these same standards.[179] However, this phenomenon is an outcome not simply of political domination but also of the fact that Roman and rabbinic understandings of manliness partially overlapped. As Michael Satlow has argued, the rabbis defined manliness as self-control or self-restraint, which involved mastery over one's body. Being penetrated by another person contradicted this ideal.[180]

177. Gen. Rabbah 63:10, ed. Theodor and Albeck, 693.

178. This midrashic interpretation is based on the term "field," which makes a connection to Deut 22:25–27 (a passage that addresses the case of a virgin who was raped in a field) through a *gezerah shavah* (the association of two unrelated verses that share a particular word or expression), and thereby links Esau with rape. Alternately, in Gen. Rabbah 63:12, Esau is depicted as having raped a young woman in a field rather than surrendering himself to sexual assault.

179. See Berkowitz 2012, 88 for a similar analysis of Sifra.

180. Satlow 1996. In some cases, however, the rabbinic and Roman definitions of masculinity are less congruent. In Gen. Rabbah 30:8 (ed. Theodor and Albeck, 275), Mordekhai is depicted suckling his infant niece Esther, because he could not find a wet nurse for her. I thank Yael Wilfand for drawing my attention to this passage.

Another possible instance of mimesis of Roman norms appears in Josephus' *Antiquities*, which describes Israel settling in the Land after its initial conquest under Joshua. By his account, a neglect of military training and the softening of Israelite mores followed:

> Thereafter the Israelites relaxed the struggle against their enemies and devoted themselves to the soil and to labours thereon. And as their riches increased, under the mastery of luxury and voluptuousness, they recked little of the order of their constitution and no longer hearkened diligently to its laws.[181]

The underlying biblical text in the Book of Judges only says:

> Then the Israelites did what was evil in the sight of the Lord and worshipped the Baals; and they abandoned the Lord, the God of their ancestors, who had brought them out of the land of Egypt; they followed other gods, from among the gods of the peoples who were all around them, and bowed down to them; and they provoked the Lord to anger. (Judges 2:11–12)

Whereas this biblical passage emphasizes idolatry and betrayal of the covenant with God, namely religious observance, Josephus highlights the corrupting effects of wealth on Israel's ancestral customs and political life. Paradoxically, in this text, Josephus accuses Israel of decadence in a way that recalls Cato the Elder's criticism of the Roman lifestyle of his time—which led this Roman senator and censor to advocate stringent laws against luxury and defend a traditional, modest lifestyle. This passage stands out within *Antiquities*. As noted previously, in this work Josephus generally emphasizes the manliness of Israelite leaders and soldiers. However, his focus on both Israelite military exploits and the risk that success, and the resultant increase in wealth, could imperil traditional values suggests a rather fundamental similarity between Israelites and Romans. As in his description of John of Gishala, the mimesis of Roman cultural patterns here is certainly intentional.

The imitation of Roman discourses, representations, and social practices related to manliness and war took many forms. In the wake of the Judean War, the coinage of Agrippa II appropriated iconographic representations of Roman victory and power, thus emulating visual rather than verbal language. The coinage of Philip and Agrippa I, Herod's son and grandson respectively, had already incorporated Roman motifs: portraits of the emperors, and the image of two clasped hands, symbolizing *concordia*.[182] However, the imitation or adoption of Roman motifs pertaining to Roman victories had new significance on coins minted under Agrippa II. In 74/75 CE, Agrippa issued coins

181. *A.J.* 5.132, trans. H. St. J. Thackeray and Ralph Marcus, LCL, 61–63.
182. Meshorer 1982, Agrippa I, no. 5 (mint of Caesarea), p. 248.

with a portrait of laureated, draped, and cuirassed Titus on the obverse, and Nikē holding a wreath and a palm branch on the reverse.[183] Many other issues followed, with Titus or Domitian on the obverse, and Nikē in various poses on the reverse.[184] Ya'akov Meshorer has suggested that these coins should not be interpreted as referring specifically to the Flavian victory in Judea, since the appearance of Nikē on Roman coinage need not denote a particular victory.[185] He claims further that only one issue of coins minted in 89/90 CE, which shows Titus and Nikē writing on a shield, can be linked confidently to the twentieth-anniversary commemoration of Judea's defeat.[186] However, Meshorer's arguments concerning other issues featuring Titus are not convincing. Since the victory in Judea was fundamental to the legitimacy of the Flavian dynasty, the coins minted by Agrippa that picture Titus and Nikē would hardly have been viewed by the inhabitants of that province as anything other than a commemoration of Titus' victory over the Jews. In any case, Agrippa II's coinage celebrated Roman military victories in typical Roman fashion. It was only expected that client kings would salute Roman victories, but Agrippa's coinage unmistakably declares the degree to which he shared the Roman perspective on these events, at least officially.

As the last Judean king, Agrippa II had no successors whose policies could reflect Roman political practices. However, Bar Kokhba (or: Kosiba), also known as the "prince" (*nasi*) of Israel, and the Jewish patriarchs offer points of comparison. Bar Kokhba seems to have been a merciless, authoritarian leader, but the scant information about his brief rule offers no clues to indisputable Roman influence.[187] As for the Jewish patriarchs, who exercised a considerable authority over Jews from the third century onward, not only in Palestine but across the empire, the extent to which they imitated features of Roman governance is a relevant question, but here too the evidence is scanty.[188] Origen, writing in the third century, states in his *Epistle to Julius Africanus* that

> even now, under Roman rule, when the Jews pay the didrachma in
> tax, the Ethnarch [referring to the Patriarch] acts as the authority for

183. Meshorer 1982, Agrippa II, no. 9, p. 251.

184. Meshorer 1982, Agrippa II, no. 10, 10a, p. 251 (on these coins, Titus is only laureated); no. 15, p. 252 (78/79 CE); no. 32 and 32a, p. 254–255 (86/87 CE); no. 40, p. 256 (87/88 CE); no. 45, 45a, 45b, 46, p. 257 (89/90 CE). Other coins from 74/75 CE depict a laureated bust of Domitian on the obverse, and Nikē standing and writing on a shield on the reverse (no. 11, 11a, 11b, 11c, p. 251); see also no. 13 and 13a, p. 252 (75/76 CE); no. 19, p. 253 (79/80 CE); no. 22 and 24, p. 253 (84/85 CE); no. 27, p. 254 (85/86 CE); no. 42 and 42a, p. 256 (87/88 CE); no. 48, 48a, 48b, p. 257 (from 89/90 CE); no. 54, 54a, 55, p. 258 (from 95/96 CE).

185. Meshorer 1982, 76.

186. Meshorer 1982, Agrippa II, no. 46, p. 257, and the discussion on 76–78, 89.

187. On Bar Kokhba, see, in particular, Schäfer 2003b.

188. On the Jewish patriarchate, see Levine 1979; Goodman 1992; Jacobs 1995; Schwartz 1999; Stern 2003; Appelbaum 2012.

the Jews, and, as it were with the connivence of the Emperor, he is in no way different from a king over his people. For cases are tried surreptitiously according to the [Jewish] law, and people are even condemned to death, albeit not entirely openly, but certainly not without the knowledge of the Emperor.[189]

Although Origen's testimony should be taken with caution, it cannot be wholly without basis. It primarily pertains to jurisdiction and Jewish tribunals, to which we shall return in Chapter Four. However, Origen's statement on the good relationship between the patriarch and the emperor, which is also noted in rabbinic sources, is relevant for the present discussion.

Several passages from the Jerusalem Talmud depict the patriarch Rabbi Judah Nesiah (mid-third century CE, according to rabbinic tradition) hiring foreign mercenaries as bodyguards. These soldiers are described as Goths or Germans, two groups that served in the Roman army at that time.[190] (Other rabbinic texts, such as the fifth-century homiletical work Pesiqta de-Rav Kahana, lament that the Roman army is now composed of Goths and other "barbarian" peoples.)[191] The Jerusalem Talmud reports on a conflict between Rabbi Judah Nesiah and R. Shimon ben Laqish (Resh Laqish), that arose when the latter said: "A ruler/patriarch (*nasi*) who sinned, they punish him with lashes by the decision of a court of three judges."[192] Rabbi Judah Nesiah considered this a personal insult and sent his guards (Goths) to arrest Resh Laqish, who managed to escape.[193] In this story, the patriarch shows himself unable to tolerate criticism, and his response resembles the violence of Roman rule. The historicity of this passage from the Yerushalmi is of course questionable, and such talmudic stories should not be used to draw straightforward historical conclusions. Nevertheless, this passage does indicate how the redactors of the Talmud imagined Rabbi Judah Nesiah's exercise of power. It suggests that, in their eyes, the patriarch could share certain characteristics with the Roman emperor, and that Jewish (patriarchal) and Roman approaches to authority did not always diverge as much as might be expected.

Some Jewish sources also articulate imitations of Roman military practices—including the organization of troops, tactics, and weaponry—at least at the level

---

189. Origen, *Ep. ad Africanum* 14 (*PG* XI, cols. 82–84), trans. Oppenheimer 2005a, 176.

190. See y. Horayot 3:1, 47a, and its parallel in y. Sanhedrin 2:1, 19d; y. Shabbat 6:10, 8c (which attributes a German bodyguard to R. Judah Nesiah). According to y. Betzah 1:5, 60c, Rabbi Abbahu, head of the *beit midrash* in Caesarea, also hired Goths as bodyguards. According to Sokoloff 2017, 113, these people were primarily servants.

191. PRK (Ha-Ḥodesh ha-zeh) 5:7, ed. Mandelbaum, 1:89–90. For a more logical reading, the word "Kuthi" (Samaritan) in this passage should probably be corrected as "Gothi." See Krauss 1947, 179–180, and n. 38; Hadas-Lebel 1990, 218.

192. Based on y. Sanhedrin 2:1, 19d.

193. On the unusual spelling of the word "Goths," see Jastrow 1950, 228; Sokoloff 2017, 113.

of literary representations. Jean Duhaime has compared the *War Scroll* from Qumran to Greco-Roman tactical treatises, such as those by Asclepiodotus and Arrian (although, admittedly, Arrian wrote much later), and demonstrated the similarities between these works, which could indicate that the authors of the Qumran scroll might have had some familiarity with Greco-Roman military tactics.[194] Although the literary kernel of the *War Scroll* originates in the Hasmonean period and a Seleucid context, its final redaction dates to the period when Judea was occupied by Rome.[195] While the author(s) responsible for the final stage of this text probably did not have access to Greco-Roman tactical treatises, they could observe the Roman army in Judea. The *War Scroll* details the eschatological war between the sons of light and the sons of darkness, and displays a number of unique features that distinguish it from Greco-Roman treatises, such as the involvement of angels and evil spirits in what appears to be a cosmic battle, and an emphasis on the role of priests.[196] Given its sectarian and utopian character, the scroll's incorporation and imitation of Greco-Roman tactics is particularly striking. It reveals mimesis at work among imperial subjects, even in a group that is thought to have been highly secluded.

By contrast, it is to be expected that Josephus would display familiarity with Roman military tactics and organization. Moreover, in his case, the imitation of Roman military models may not have been limited to literary representation. Josephus claims that, at the beginning of the revolt, he organized and trained the Judean army in Galilee according to Roman protocols:

> After that, since he [Josephus] realized that the unbeatable strength of the Romans had come about in particular through prompt obedience and exercise with weapons, on the one hand he abandoned the instruction, followed by practice; on the other hand, seeing that the [Romans'] promptness to obey arose from the number of their commanders, he divided his army in a more Roman way (*rhōmaikōteron*) and appointed more officers. He created distinctions among the soldiers and subordinated them to decurions, centurions, and then tribunes, and above these, commanders in charge of bulkier divisions.[197]

John Pairman Brown notes that Josephus may have overstated the Roman character of the reorganization, and he identifies a Maccabean pattern in Josephus' description.[198] This passage also recalls Jethro's advice for Moses to appoint officials over each group of one thousand, one hundred, fifty, and

194. Duhaime 1988, esp. 148.

195. On the importance of the Roman context for understanding the final redactional stage of 1QM, see Schultz 2009, 401–402.

196. Duhaime 1988, 141–142; Schultz 2009, 343–352. The liturgical aspect of the *War Scroll* was initially emphasized by Jean Carmignac (1955, xii).

197. *B.J.* 2.577–578, trans. Mason 2008, 390–391.

198. Pairman Brown 2001, 93.

ten (Exod 18:13–22). As Steve Mason observes, Josephus' paraphrase of this biblical material "transforms Moses' move into a military reorganization, with the officers' ranks expanded to match Roman positions."[199] The most striking aspect of this section from *War*, however, is Josephus' overt declaration that he imitated a Roman model. That is to say, that imitation was the best strategy for dealing with the Romans.

The God of Israel is sometimes Romanized too, being portrayed in the attire of a Roman emperor or general at war. Particularly striking is the passage in Pesiqta de-Rav Kahana 7:11 that depicts the ten plagues against the Egyptians (Exod 7:15–12:33) as if God were conducting a Roman siege. This text is replete with Greek and Latin military vocabulary:

R. Levi bar Zechariah in the name of R. Berekhiah: "[It was] with the tactics (*taxis*) of kings/emperors [that] God came against them.

First, he shut their water supply, then he brought shouters against them, then he shot arrows, then he brought legions [*legionot*, from Latin *legio*] against them, then he brought against them reprisals [*drolēmsia*, i.e. *androlēpsia*, seizing hostages], then he poured burning oil [*naft*, from Greek and Latin *naphta*] on them, then he threw stones [with a] catapult [*aveney balistra*, from Latin *ballista*] against them, then he established conquerors over them, then he put them in prison [*be-palqiyot*, from Greek *phylakē*], then he took out their greatest figure and killed him.

[Here are the proof texts from Scripture:]

First he shut their water supply: *He turned their river into blood* (Ps 78:44).

Then he brought shouters against them: [This refers to the] frogs [Exod 8:5–6]. [. . .]

Then he shot arrows: [This refers to the] lice [Exod 8:12–13].

Then he brought legions: [This refers to the] flies [Exod 8:24].

Then he gave them reprisals: *A very heavy plague* (Exod 9:3).

Then he poured burning oil upon them: [This refers to the] boils [Exod 9:9–10].

Then he threw stones [with a] catapult against them: [This refers to the] hail [Exod 9:22–23].

Then he established against them conquerors: [This refers to the] locusts [Exod 10:12–15].

Then he put them in prison: [This refers to the] darkness [Exod 10:21–23].

Then he took out their greatest figure and killed him: [This refers to the] killing of the firstborn [Exod 11:4–6, 12:29].[200]

199. Mason 2008, 391, note 3468, in reference to *A.J.* 3.71–72.
200. PRK (Vayehi beḥetzi ha-laylah) 7:11, ed. Mandelbaum, 1:132. See Krauss 1947, 242–243, which indicates parallels in later midrashim.

The notion that God besieged Egypt is unusual, to say the least. Some of the pairings between the plagues and military operations are quite intuitive, such as darkness (Exod 10:21–23) and prison, or hail (Exod 9:22–23) and stones from catapults, even though the latter association requires more imagination. Interpreting the locusts that devour crops as a reference to "conquerors" (*kovshim*), probably the governors and tax collectors imposed on subjugated populations, also makes sense. However, the overarching correlation between the ten plagues described in Exodus and the actions undertaken during a military siege, including the execution of the enemy leader—which could allude to the public killing in Rome that would mark the completion of a triumph—seems quite far-fetched. Rather than trying to provide an exegetical interpretation of Exodus 7:15–12:33, the author of this tradition is applying the model of Roman siege warfare as fully as possible to the Exodus narrative, in a remarkable show of midrashic virtuosity.

Yet why should God behave like a Roman general or emperor? The answer may lie in the next section of this midrash, which foretells God's judgment against Rome: each plague that afflicted the Egyptians anticipates an aspect of God's impending chastisement of Rome. This whole passage thus combines imitation of the Roman art of warfare, by no less a personage than God, with the foretelling of Rome's destruction, suggesting that God will ultimately take up the Romans' own tactics to destroy their empire. The text can thus be read as both a revenge fantasy and a parody of Roman military power, that is, a deliberately ironic imitation of Roman features.[201]

Through these examples, we see that mimesis encompasses different forms and meanings. Its manifestations range from the imitation of Roman numismatic representations of victory on Agrippa II's coinage and Josephus' claim to have organized the Jewish army in Galilee according to Roman models, to the rabbinic depiction of a Jewish patriarch employing Gothic and German soldiers just as the Roman emperor does and the portrayal of the God of Israel as an expert military strategist who deploys Roman tactics in siege warfare. Mimesis can also signal the adoption of Roman norms and values for use against the (Roman) enemy, in a strategy of reversal, as the depiction of Esau in Genesis Rabbah illustrates.

The underlying question raised by these examples is: to what extent does mimesis lead to resemblance and, ultimately, to the blurring of distinctions

---

201. Occasionally, rabbinic texts cast God's eschatological punishment of the nations in violent and bloody terms. Sifre Deuteronomy 332, for example, relies heavily on biblical verses that depict God slaughtering the nations. One such verse is Isaiah 34:6, which mentions Edom and thus supports the midrashic interpretation that God's retribution is specifically directed against Rome. See further Stratton 2009, which analyzes the use of the lexicon of the arena in rabbinic descriptions of the eschatological judgment and highlights similar combinations of revenge fantasy and mimicry, or at least mimesis, as in Pesiqta de-Rav Kahana 7:11.

between the one who imitates and the one being imitated? Even mimicry and parody, which involve irony and thus imply a critical distance, do simultaneously create similarity. The rabbis seem to have anticipated that, by imitating Roman practices and adopting Roman values, Israel might inadvertently transform itself in its twin brother Esau/Rome, thereby losing its true self. Beth Berkowitz has identified this dynamic in rabbinic discussions of capital punishment, the paradigmatic expression of legal, officially sanctioned violence. Whereas the rabbis recognized decapitation as the least painful means of execution, R. Yehudah nevertheless maintained that Jews should reject this practice as "the way of the kingdom," namely the preferred Roman method of capital punishment (for *honestiores*) (t. Sanhedrin 9:11). R. Yehudah's position reflects a concern lest Israel become like Rome, specifically in terms of violence and the use of force.[202] In short, mimesis and even mimicry are not without risk. The lines can be blurred and the mimic become more similar to the Other than was intended.

Yet some ancient Jewish sources also transmit voices that openly criticize Roman power and propose countermodels by positing alternative approaches to strength, manliness, and power. As we turn to these texts, we will consider the extent to which they represent inversions of Roman norms, articulate alternative models that may have existed in the Greco-Roman world, or present truly innovative insights.

3. Jewish Criticism and Redefinitions of Bravery, Manliness, and Power

Let us begin this discussion of Jewish redefinitions of bravery, manliness, and power by considering Daniel Boyarin's analysis of the relationship between R. Yoḥanan and Resh Laqish in b. Bava Metziʿa 84a. Despite its reliance on a Babylonian source, its relevance for the present discussion will rapidly become clear.[203] Boyarin argues that the rabbis characterized Roman men as violent and hyper-masculine, whereas they envisioned themselves as feminized, effectively accepting Roman stereotypes of Jews while recasting femininity and feminization and, thereby, forging a new definition of masculinity and

202. Berkowitz 2006, Chapter Six, esp. 159–165; for a different approach, see Lorberbaum 2015, 124–134. In some rabbinic texts, this danger even extends to the God of Israel; see Stratton 2009, 75–76, on Genesis Rabbah 22:9, which suggests that God may be compared to a "blood-thirsty emperor" (75). Christine Hayes has shown that, in b. Avodah Zarah 2a–3b, where God judges all nations at the end of times, he is depicted as a tyrant who cruelly mocks his creatures, again revealing the rabbis' anxiety lest Israel and their God become similar to the wicked kingdom that they are charged to defeat (Hayes 2020, 455–463).

203. Boyarin 1997, Chapter Three. See also Boyarin 1995 for an earlier discussion of this talmudic text.

manliness. Boyarin further contends that this creative move by subalterns in an imperial context ultimately fostered the ideal of the *yeshivah bokhur*, who is fully immersed in talmudic study and whose manliness differs markedly from the archetype of the Christian knight and, later, the Western soldier.

When it comes to the Roman period, several assumptions in Boyarin's thesis merit revision. First, as discussed in the preceding section, Romans did not view Jews as feminine or effeminate. Therefore, the claim that rabbis would have internalized this stereotype is unfounded. It would seem that Boyarin has read a medieval phenomenon into the Roman period. (In the Middle Ages, some Christians even believed that, as a punishment for Christ's death, Jewish men had menstrual cycles, as women do.[204]) Furthermore, Boyarin's understanding of Roman standards could do with greater nuance. His systematic association of Roman masculinity with weapons, for example, is inaccurate.[205]

Second, the question arises of whether rabbinic literature from the Land of Israel comes at this issue from the same perspective that Boyarin identifies in Babylonian texts. The descriptions of Resh Laqish in both corpora seem to exemplify a divergence in their orientations; indeed, Boyarin himself remarks that certain Palestinian rabbinic sources depict this sage exercising force against his opponents even after having entered the rabbinic study house (these texts are detailed below). Therefore, the Resh Laqish that we discover in Palestinian texts does not neatly fit the model of Jewish masculinity that Boyarin derives from Babylonian texts. On the other hand, some rabbinic sources from the Land of Israel draw a contrast between studying Torah and military activity, thus reinforcing Boyarin's assertion. He rightly cites Genesis Rabbah 63:10—which stresses the contrast between Esau as a man of the field and hunter, and Jacob as a man of the tents in Genesis 25:27—as a case in point.[206] In biblical texts, the tent is the locus for women and domestic life, whereas hunting is traditionally associated with men. Thus, starting with the biblical text, Jacob is linked to the female realm, a point that is enhanced by his closeness to Rebecca, and contrasts with Isaac's fondness for Esau.[207] In its interpretation of Genesis 25:27, Genesis Rabbah equates the tent with the *beit midrash*, the rabbinic study house. Thus the study of Torah stands in contrast to hunting and, by extension, war, for Isaac's blessing foretells that Esau will live by his sword (Gen 27:40). For Boyarin, this midrashic text gives expression to a new Jewish countermodel that directly refutes the Roman norm of masculinity by favoring

204. Resnick 2000; Marienberg 2003, 56–61.

205. Boyarin 1997, 142.

206. Boyarin 1997, 144.

207. This reading of the biblical text does not imply that rabbinic literature associates Jewish women exclusively with the household's private space. On this issue, see Baker 2002, who argues that "in a number of rabbinic constructions, a house is not where a woman/wife is, but rather a house is, in part, who and what she is" (35).

intellectual activity over the art of war and elevating powerlessness and suffering, even to the point of martyrdom, over physical strength.

This countermodel has been described as diasporic not only by Boyarin in his study of Babylonian rabbinic sources, but also by Daniel Schwartz in relation to Hellenistic Jewish sources, such as 2 Maccabees.[208] The diasporic origin of 2 Maccabees remains debated[209] but, in any case, the praise for martyrs and the role of their suffering for the redemption of the people of Israel in that book differs meaningfully from the praise expressed in 1 Maccabees for the battles waged by Judas and his brothers. Although the martyrs' suffering and the heroic deeds of Judas are also recognized in 1 and 2 Maccabees, respectively, the actions that are considered essential to saving Israel clearly differ in these two books.[210]

The contrasting messages in the books of the Maccabees further complicate our investigation: do the focus on "passivity" and Torah study and the distancing from the art of war in rabbinic sources constitute a reaction against a Roman model whose definitions of manliness and virtue center on courage in battle or, do these factors instead mark the continuation of a diasporic trend that can be traced to the Hellenistic period? Or might these be interrelated phenomena? The books of Maccabees indicate that the rejection of "militarism" may reflect an intra-Jewish debate and an attempt to suppress Jewish models that take a more favorable view of military activity, such as the Maccabees in the Hellenistic period and, in the Roman period, the Zealots or Bar Kokhba. Especially in a Palestinian setting, discussions of the use of armed force and the place of military valor were probably not mere articulations of a Jewish self-definition distinct from Roman standards, but were again part of an intra-Jewish debate. With this caveat in mind, we can now turn to Jewish definitions of bravery, manliness, and power formulated in a Roman context.

3.1 REDEFINING COURAGE AS SELF-CONTROL AND THE ABILITY TO FACE SUFFERING AND DEATH

As we saw in Chapter Two, from at least the first century BCE onward, *virtus* was applied not only to courage in warfare but to moral virtue more broadly, much like *aretē* in Greek. Likewise, in philosophical writings—particularly by the Stoics—courage was not exclusive to military settings, for this virtue also

---

208. Boyarin 1995; Schwartz 2008, who characterizes 2 Maccabees as "an expression of diasporan Judaism of the Hellenistic age" (VIII).

209. Most scholars agree that 2 Maccabees originated in the diaspora; see Schwartz 2008, 45–51; Doran 2012, 16–17. However, Sylvie Honigman asserts that this work was redacted in Judea (Honigman 2014, 65–94, 184–185).

210. Berthelot 2006; Berthelot 2018a, 76–77, 131–132. For a detailed study of martyrdom in 2 Maccabees, see Van Henten 1997.

related to self-control and the ability to endure suffering and face death.[211] In such cases, courage amounted to power, but it was power over oneself (*enkrateia*).[212]

This understanding of courage is found frequently in Jewish writings of the Roman period. In Mishnah Avot 4:1, in a saying attributed to Shimon ben Zoma—according to rabbinic tradition, a second-generation tanna active in the early second century CE—we read: "Who is a hero (*gibbor*)? [or: Who is mighty?] The one who overcomes [lit.: conquers (*kovesh*)] his [evil] inclination (*yetzer*)."[213] This statement is followed by a quotation from Proverbs 16:32 which suggests that this teaching specifically speaks of anger, thereby equating courage and strength with self-control.[214]

The ability to endure suffering and face death is the ultimate manifestation of self-control and thus of courage. According to both Philo and Josephus, this type of courage characterizes Jews in general, for they are willing to die rather than transgress their ancestral laws. In *On the Embassy to Gaius*, Philo recalls how Jews turned to Petronius, then the governor of Syria, upon hearing that Caligula planned to erect a statue of himself in the Jerusalem Temple. They implored him as follows:

> We are unarmed as you see, though some accuse us of having come as enemies in war, yet the parts which nature has assigned to each of us for defence, our hands, we have put away where they can do nothing and present our bodies as an easy target for the missiles of those who wish to kill us. [. . .] [we] have prostrated ourselves before Gaius in doing so to you, that you and he may either save us all from ruin or send us all to perish in utter destruction.[215]

From §233 onward, the elders explain that Jews would rather perish than witness the desecration of the sanctuary, with vivid descriptions of how they might die. This plea stresses their powerlessness and preparedness for death, not anger and threats of revolt.[216] Similarly, Josephus emphasizes again and again the Jews' willingness to die for the sake of their laws, especially in

---

211. See, e.g., Epictetus, *Discourses* 4.12–15, a passage that speaks of poverty, deprivation of office, exile, and death.

212. A similar idea is found in Letter of Aristeas 222, which states that the most powerful type of rule (*archē*) is the capacity to master oneself and not get carried away by impulses.

213. MS Kaufmann.

214. On the Greco-Roman context of Tractate Avot, see Tropper 2004, esp. 136–188.

215. *Legat.* 229–230, trans. F. H. Colson, LCL, 119–121.

216. Catherine Hezser notes that "In advocating non-violent resistance and self-restraint rather than violent anger, Philo represents a philosophical tradition reminiscent of Stoicism" (Hezser 2013, 235).

Against Apion.[217] He even states proudly that Jews "face death on behalf of the laws more courageously than everyone else."[218]

Steven Weitzman asserts that Josephus' emphasis on the Jews' contempt for death for the sake of their ancestral laws has a distinctly Roman flavor.[219] Courage as the ability to face death bravely, including by suicide, was indeed a common theme in Roman literature, most notably in Roman Stoic writings. In Epistle 24 to Lucilius, Seneca thus praises the courage of Cato the Elder, for despising death and choosing to commit suicide, while conceding that this example might have become overused.[220] As John Barclay notes, "There is nothing originally Roman about this virtue [contempt for death], but it is notably prominent in Roman moral discourse."[221]

However, it seems that praise for the Jews' readiness to die for the Torah has strong roots in the Maccabean period. As the example of Eleazar in 2 Maccabees 6:27–28 shows, this readiness to give one's life for the law could be associated with the Greek concept of a "noble death," as exemplified by Socrates.[222] It is therefore difficult to consider the emphasis on dying rather than fighting for the law as a trope that developed in a Roman context. Josephus' interest in highlighting the compatibility of Jewish and Roman values is clear, but his statements concerning the Jews' loyalty to their ancestral traditions do not come as news. They are quite familiar to us from earlier Jewish literature, such as 2 Maccabees. By comparison, rabbinic traditions on the martyrdom of various figures—Pappus and Julianus, Miriam bat Tanhum and her seven sons, R. Aqiva, R. Hanina ben Teradion—have a different emphasis, encapsulated by Daniel Boyarin as "dying for God" rather than "dying for the Law."[223] These traditions generally appear in late sources, dating to the fourth century at the earliest. It seems probable that here Christian martyrdom narratives—including traditions about the Maccabees—played a role in

---

217. *C. Ap.* 1.42–43, 190–191, 212; 2.146, 219–234, 272, 294. See Barclay 2007, 32, note 175. For a full list of episodes of "noble death" in Josephus' works (a suicide whose motivations range from killing an enemy or escaping slavery, to dying for the Law or remaining faithful to God's covenant), see van Henten 1999, 137–139.

218. *C. Ap.* 2.234, trans. Barclay 2007, 304. On Josephus' view of martyrdom, see van Henten 1999; Rajak 2001, 124–126; Rajak 2012; Klawans 2016.

219. Weitzman 2009, 930.

220. *Epistle* 24.6: "Oh, say you, those stories have been droned to death in all the schools; pretty soon, when you reach the topic 'On Despising Death,' you will be telling me about Cato" (trans. Richard M. Gummere, LCL, 169).

221. Barclay 2007, 366.

222. Rajak 2001, 120–122; Van Henten and Avemarie 2002, 28–30. This type of noble death must be distinguished from those of Homeric heroes, whose physical integrity was essential to their characterization as heroes. By contrast, Maccabean martyrs were mutilated and thereby disfigured (Baslez 2007, 150–157).

223. Boyarin 1999, 96, which refers to Rajak 2001.

shaping the rabbinic accounts. If so, we are witnessing a new phenomenon, one prompted by the rabbis' exposure to Christian discourses and festivals.[224]

In the interest of balance, it is significant that Philo and Josephus not only speak of dying for piety and the law but also occasionally advocate fighting for them, as the Maccabees did. In his treatment of the punitive expedition against the Midianites who led Israel astray (Numbers 31), Philo places these words in the mouth of Moses:

> The contest before you is not to win dominion (*archē*), nor to appropriate the possessions of others, which is the sole or principal object of other wars, but to defend piety and holiness, from which our kinsfolk and friends have been perverted by the enemies who have indirectly caused their victims to perish miserably.[225]

The Midianite women had lured Israelite men to worship foreign idols, and thus to foresake God's law. Here the defense of "piety (*eusebeia*) and holiness (*hosiotēs*)" is tantamount to faithfulness to the Law and the Covenant. By presenting these as the defining principles of a just war, Philo draws a stark contrast with wars that are motivated by more conventional goals, such as seizing power or booty. In this passage, there is no shift from killing to being killed (for the sake of Torah). Philo also recounts the story of the war against Midian in the section of *On the Virtues* that discusses courage in warfare and, again, he claims that this war was waged to uphold *eusebeia*, and that God joined the fight as an ally of Israel (*Virt.* 34–50). Killing enemies in a war that was conducted to restore faithfulness to the Covenant therefore qualifies as an act of courage.

A similar redefinition of the purpose of war is articulated by Josephus who, in *Against Apion* 2.272, contrasts Jews' readiness to fight for the preservation of their ancestral laws with wars that are waged to conquer new lands, which he deems expressions of greed (*pleonexia*). This passage may be implicitly criticizing Roman territorial expansion. Josephus also draws a contrast between the Spartans, whose endurance and contempt for death are motivated by gain—they aimed "to conquer everyone against whom they went to war"—and the Jews, who have no less fortitude but dedicate themselves to the noble goal of keeping their ancestral laws.[226] This remark may also be read as indirect criticism of Roman military conquests. John Barclay comments on *Against Apion* 2.272 that "both Romans (Cicero, *Resp.* 1.27) and Judeans (Philo, *Mos.* 1.307) were keen to disavow [the motive of aggrandizement] in the case of their own warfare."[227] However, what Cicero in fact says is that

---

224. Boyarin 1999, esp. 93–97; Van Henten and Avemarie 2002, 132–173; Kalmin 2003; Lapin 2021.

225. Philo, *Mos.* 1.307, trans. F. H. Colson, LCL, 437.

226. *C. Ap.* 2.230, trans. Barclay 2007, 303.

227. Barclay 2007, 323, note 1090.

military commands and consulships must be "undertaken from a sense of duty and not sought for profit or glory."[228] He addresses individual motivations, not the goals of the Roman people as a whole. Therefore, redefining the collective goal of warfare as faithfulness to ancestral traditions, rather than defense or the conquest of new territories, seems to be a distinctly Jewish argument, which was initially expressed in 1 Maccabees but gained renewed prominence in a Roman context.[229]

In short, neither the definition of *courage* as the ability to die for the law nor the other option that emphasized fighting for the law originated as a response to the Roman valorization of *virtus*, be it at the level of discourse or that of practice. Rather, they represent a reactivation of responses to imperial power that emerged in a Seleucid context.

3.2 REDEFINING POWER IN RELATION TO THE VIRTUOUS MIND

Philo often redefines power in relation to the virtuous mind, as exemplified by the sage, whom he contrasts with the king, whose power is embodied in his army. Philo opposes those who seek external gain, such as wealth and authority acquired by military means, to those who cherish virtue and wisdom, the true goods. In *On the Life of Abraham*, while commenting on Abraham and Lot on the literal level, Philo notes that for the sake of peace, Abraham invited Lot to choose the land that he wished to settle, despite having more men and the ability to impose his will on his nephew (*Abr.* 214–215, based on Genesis 13). Philo then ponders:

> And yet who else would give way in any single point to the weaker if he were the stronger? Who, when he could conquer, would be willing to be defeated and not avail himself of his power? He alone took for his ideal not the exercise of strength (*rhōmē*) and self-aggrandizement (*pleonexia*) but a life free from strife and so far as lay with him of tranquillity, and thereby he showed himself the most admirable of men.[230]

Abraham is characterized by his reluctance to exert his authority by claiming the best lands. Like Israel—in their war with the Midianites, as described in *Mos.* 1.307 and Josephus' *Against Apion* 2.272 (see above)—the Hebrew patriarch is free of greed (*pleonexia*). It is difficult to read *On the Life of Abraham* 216 without hearing implicit criticism of Roman imperialism. Philo's

---

228. Cicero, *De re publica* 1.27, trans. Clinton W. Keyes, LCL, 49.

229. For a discussion of Simon's response to Antiochus VII in 1 Maccabees 15:33–35—a passage that rejects wars of conquest by contrasting them with holding on to ancestral territory, not with defending ancestral traditions—see Berthelot 2018a, 161–185.

230. *Abr.* 216, trans. F. H. Colson, LCL, 107.

association of *pleonexia* with *rhōmē* ("strength," but also "Rome") increases the plausibility that this passage alludes to Roman military conquests.

Philo continues by reflecting on how Abraham and Lot differ from one another:

> 220 Each of the two characters possesses what we may call flocks and herds. The devotee of things external has silver, gold, raiment, all the materials of wealth and the means for procuring them, and again arms, engines, triremes, cavalry, infantry and naval forces, the foundations of sovereignty which produce security of power. The lover of moral excellence has the principles of each separate virtue and the truths discovered by wisdom itself. 221 Now those who preside and have charge over each of these two are, as it were, herdsmen of cattle. The externals are cared for by lovers of wealth or glory, the would-be generals and all who hanker for power over multitudes, the things of the soul by lovers of moral excellence and virtue, who prefer the genuine goods to the spurious and not the spurious to the genuine. 222 So there is a natural conflict between them since they have no common principle but are for ever jangling and quarrelling about the most important thing in life, and that is the decision what are the true goods.[231]

Abraham embodies the "lover of moral excellence," the sage who nurtures the true goods: virtue and wisdom. By contrast, Lot personifies those who pursue wealth and conventional power through the use of "arms, engines, triremes, cavalry, infantry and naval forces," military equipment that the Romans possessed in greater quantities than any other nation in Philo's time. It seems reasonable to suppose that Abraham stands for Israel and Lot, implicitly, for Rome.

Philo's work contains other insinuations critical of Roman hegemony and the fact that it was secured by military force. As discussed in Chapter Two, the leitmotif "over land and sea" was regularly used by Roman and pro-Roman authors to describe the wide expanse of Rome's influence—theirs was rule over land and sea, victory over land and sea, peace over land and sea, and so on. The notion was also expressed in iconographic representations, such as those at the Sebasteion of Aphrodisias. Philo's use of this expression with respect to conquest and rapacity is certainly not coincidental; for instance, he denounces the greed and unrestrained bids for honor that lead men "to the furthest boundaries of land and sea."[232] Philo contrasts the wordly desires of these men with the mind (*nous*) of the sage, which can reach "not only as far as the bounds of land and sea but of air and sky also" and even exceeds those and aims "at apprehending if possible the nature of God, which, beyond the bare fact that He is,

---

231. *Abr.* 220–222, trans. F. H. Colson, LCL, 109.
232. *Post.* 116; cf. *Agr.* 23–24.

is inapprehensible."[233] Through this lens, the mind of the God-oriented human being is more far-reaching than Roman power.

Moreover, Philo explains that the true king is not one with dominion over land and sea but the sage who serves God:

> For it belongs to great leaders (*megalōn hēgemonōn*) to search for and accomplish wisdom, not leaders who have subdued sea and land with arms (*ouchi tōn hoplois gēn kai thalattan hypēgmenōn*), but those who through the powers of the soul (*psychēs dynamesi*) have conquered the medley and confusion of the multitude which beset it.[234]

Here Philo defines great or true *hēgemonia* in relation to the soul; it differs from the hegemony of political rulers with armies at their command. Despite the generic nature of Philo's remark, in his context it must primarily refer to Roman emperors and generals, especially as the reference to *hēgemonia* over land and sea so clearly echoes contemporary Roman discourse.

In a similar vein, in his treatment of Genesis 23:5–6, where the Hittites call Abraham "a king (or prince) from God," Philo writes that "no one of the foolish (is) a king, even though he should be master of all the land and sea, but only the wise and God-loving man, even if he is without the equipment and resources through which many obtain power with violence and force."[235] Again, genuine kingship is framed in philosophical and spiritual terms, as a counter to an earthly and military reign that strongly evokes Roman imperial rule and its claim to hegemony over land and sea.[236] Here Philo explicitly states that power (*kratos*) over land and sea is insufficient to confer the title "king" on a fool. He may have had Caligula in mind.

Philo clearly embraces the Stoic notion that the sage is a king, in fact the only real king.[237] This principle complements the idea that mastery over oneself (*enkrateia*) is a necessary condition for kingship.[238] For the Stoics, as for most Hellenistic philosophical schools, it was the philosopher who best embodied the power of self-control through his independence from wealth and worldly authority. The identification of true goods with virtue and wisdom

---

233. *Det.* 89, trans. F. H. Colson and G. H. Whitaker, LCL, 263 (slightly modified).

234. *Ebr.* 113, trans. F. H. Colson and G. H. Whitaker, LCL, 379. See also *Her.* 7; *Mos.* 1.155; *QG* 4.76.

235. *QG* 4.76, trans. Ralph Marcus, LCL, 354. On Abraham as a king in Philo, see Sandmel 1971, 178–179, n. 348.

236. See also *Her.* 6–7. For Philo, political and military hegemony over land and sea lacked intrinsic value and compared poorly with the true power of the sage, the servant of God. Elsewhere Philo speaks of the spiritual and eternal kingship of Israel, which he compares to a lily (see Berthelot 2011b).

237. Long 1993; Winston 1995, 815; Uusimäki 2018, 5–7. For Philo, Moses is the ideal king; see More 2012.

238. Cf. m. Avot 4:1; see also section 3.4 below.

rather than external possessions was another principle firmly rooted in Stoic thought. However, for the Stoics, sages were rare among human beings: Chrysippus considered the Stoic sage to be equal in virtue to Zeus.[239] In Philo's eyes, it was instead various figures in the history of Israel—most prominently, Moses—who could most accurately be termed sages. Yet Philo defined their wisdom in reference to their knowledge of God and their personal piety or holiness.[240] God is the one who bestows upon the sage "the power (*kratos*) that no other power (*archē*) can dispute."[241] That is to say, while Philo's reframing of power as the prerogative of the sage is derived from Stoic ethical teachings, it differs from Stoicism by associating that human model not only with rationality, but with God himself.[242] Finally, Philo's redefinition also has an underlying political dimension, insofar as it minimizes the importance of Rome's power, which is being contrasted with the authority of the God-oriented soul.

3.3 REDEFINING STRENGTH AS TORAH AND TORAH STUDY

While Philo locates real power with the sage who seeks virtue and wisdom, in rabbinic literature, true strength is associated with Torah and Torah study. Here too power is conceptualized through intellectual discipline, but with a different focus.

The link between Torah and strength initially appears in early rabbinic sources, namely halakhic midrashim. The Mekhilta de-Rabbi Ishmael comments on the words "The Lord is my strength (*'oz*) and my might (*zimrah*)" (Exod 15:2) as follows: "*My strength* (*'oz*): There is no 'my strength' except for Torah, as it is said: *The Lord gives strength* (*'oz*) *to his people* (Ps 29:11)."[243] Since God's central gift to Israel is the law at Sinai, this verse from Psalm 29 is read as a reference to Torah. Sifre Deuteronomy 343 comments almost identically on Psalm 29:11, saying: "There is no strength except for Torah."[244] This interpretation appears in a discussion of the verse "The Lord came from

239. Long 1993, referring to Long and Sedley 1987, 380, frag. 61 J. See also Epictetus 2.19.26–27; Diogenes Laertius 7.119.

240. *Sobr.* 57; *Post.* 128; *Mutat.* 153.

241. *Sobr.* 57, my translation.

242. By comparison, Wisdom of Solomon characterizes a sage's wisdom as a divine gift (Wis 9:6), without elaborating on his power. The sage is embodied by Solomon, a king who is transformed into a sage, rather than the reverse. See Uusimäki 2018, 17. On kingship in Wisdom of Solomon, see also More 2012.

243. MRI Shirah (Beshallaḥ) 3, ed. Horovitz and Rabin, 126. This midrash continues with additional interpretations of "my strength," including in relation to kingship.

244. Ed. Finkelstein, 398.

Sinai . . ." (Deut 33:2).[245] The midrash first associates Deuteronomy 33:2 with Psalm 29:3, "The voice of the Lord is over the waters; [the God of glory thunders, the Lord, over mighty waters]," to assert that the voice of God at Sinai frightened the entire world. The nations are said to have approached the prophet Balaam to inquire what was happening, and whether the world would be destroyed. Balaam reassures them by explaining that "The Lord gives strength to his people" signals that he is giving the Torah (at Sinai). Another proof text is then adduced, "With him are strength and wisdom" (Job 12:16). Both strength and wisdom, which are first and foremost divine attributes, become identified with the Torah itself. Torah is then linked with peace, as illustrated in Psalm 29:11, which reads in full: "The Lord gives strength to his people, the Lord blesses his people with peace." In their exchange with Balaam, the nations respond to his explanation by quoting the end of Psalm 29:11.

Psalm 29:11 recurs in a passage from Sifre Numbers suggesting that true peace differs from the *pax Romana*, which was secured with military force. In its commentary on the final verse of the priestly blessing, "(May) the Lord lift up his face upon you, and give you peace" (Numbers 6:26), Sifre Numbers lists various interpretations of the phrase "and give you peace." Those attributed to R. Nathan and R. Yehudah ha-Nasi deserve special attention:

> R. Nathan says: This is the peace of the kingdom [or kingship] of the House of David, as it is said: *His authority shall grow continually, and there shall be endless peace [for the throne of David and his kingdom. He will establish and uphold it with justice and with righteousness from this time onwards and for evermore. The zeal of the Lord of hosts will do this]* (Isa 9:6).
>
> Rabbi [Yehudah ha-Nasi] says: This is the peace of Torah, as it is said: *The Lord gives strength to his people, [the Lord blesses his people with peace]* (Ps 29:11).[246]

Rabbi Nathan, who, according to rabbinic tradition, was a fourth-generation tanna and contemporary of Rabbi (with whom he is often depicted debating),[247] understands this blessing as a reference to the peace associated with the coming of the Messiah, the descendant of David, to whom Isaiah 9:6 is thought to allude. This peace has a political dimension: it implies the demise of the Roman empire and the restoration of the Davidic monarchy.[248] It was probably the kind of peace that rebels in the First Jewish Revolt

245. As we saw in Chapter Two, this midrash also interprets this verse from Deuteronomy to indicate that the Torah was given in four languages, including Latin (*romi*).
246. Sifre Numbers 42, ed. Kahana 2011–2015, 1:115.
247. Bacher 1889, 437–452; Strack and Stemberger 1996, 80.
248. Wilfand 2019a, 230.

and the Bar Kokhba Revolt anticipated. Rabbi offers a completely different perspective.[249] He understands the peace mentioned in Numbers 6:26 to be the peace of Torah. His teaching is based on Psalm 29:11 which, as we have seen, views both peace and strength as divine gifts. Rabbi's teaching presupposes the identification of strength with Torah, as in Sifre Deuteronomy 343. He then infers from the juxtaposition of strength/Torah with peace in Psalm 29:11, that peace will come to Israel through Torah study. In contrast to R. Nathan's teaching, Rabbi's position might be considered "accommodationist." He seems to reject the idea that Numbers 6:26 refers to a messianic peace. Yet his interpretation could just as easily be seen as a rejection of a literal reading of Psalm 29:11 that would equate peace with strength, traditionally understood as physical or military superiority. This section of Sifre Numbers may be contrasting the *pax Romana*, with its reliance on physical strength and military power, with Israel's peace, which is founded on Torah, i.e. spiritual strength.

The conviction that studying Torah confers strength and peace upon Israel is common in Orthodox Jewish circles even today. The name of a still active radical ultra-orthodox group, Neturey Karta ("Guardians of the city" in Aramaic), reflects the notion that scholars who study and teach Torah are the true guardians of the cities that they inhabit. This idea goes back to the Jerusalem Talmud:

[I:1 A] R. Shimon b. Yoḥai taught: "If you see towns that have been uprooted from their location in the Land of Israel, you should know that the inhabitants did not pay the salary of the scribes (*soferim*) and teachers (*meshanim*) [who worked there]."

[B] What is the scriptural basis for that statement?

[C] *Why is the land ruined and laid waste like a wilderness, so that no one passes through? And the Lord says: Because they have forsaken my law* (Torati) *which I set before them* (Jer 9:11–12 [NRSV 9:12–13]).

[I:2 A] R. Yudan the Patriarch sent R. Hiyya, R. Assi, and R. Ammi to travel among the towns of the Land of Israel to establish for them scribes [or: Bible teachers] and teachers [of the Oral Law].[250] They came to one place and found neither a scribe nor a teacher. They said to the people: "Bring us the guardians of the town (*netorey karta*)." The people brought them the guardians of the town (*santorey karta*).

[B] They said to them: "[Do you think] these are the guardians of the town (*netorey karta*)? They are none other than the destroyers of the town (*ḥarovey karta*)."

[C] They said to them, "And who are the guardians of the town (*netorey karta*)?"

249. On Rabbi (Yehudah ha-Nasi), see Oppenheimer 2017.

250. According to Sokoloff, in this context, *safar* means a "Bible teacher" or "school-teacher," and *matnayyan*, a "teacher of the Oral Law" (Sokoloff 2017, 434 and 374).

[D] They said to them, "The scribes and teachers."

[E] That is in line with what is written: *Unless the Lord builds the house,* [*those who build it labor in vain. Unless the Lord watches over the city, the watchman stays awake in vain*] (Ps 127:1).[251]

Jacob Neusner translates the expression *santorey karta* at the end of section I:2 A, as "the citizens of senatorial class in the town." This translation is based on the phonetic proximity between the Aramaic term *santer,* "guardian" or "watchman," and the Latin word *senator,* and the notion that a city's elite ensured its safety.[252] Yet the verb *sinter* means not only "to guard," but also "to bear a grudge"; hence *santer* signifies "guardsman," whereas *santurey* or *santuraya* can be translated as "hidden hatred" or "grudge."[253] The Talmud's use of the phrase *santorey karta* ("hidden hatred of the town"), in contrast to *netorey karta* ("guardians of the town"), introduces a wordplay that underscores the difference between two groups: the city's actual guardians versus those who merely appear to secure its welfare. This pun lays the groundwork for the teaching attributed to R. Hiyya, R. Assi, and R. Ammi—all third-century Palestinian amoraim, roughly contemporaneous with Diocletian, according to rabbinic tradition—who state that the designated guardians of the city are in fact the agents of its ruin, *harovey karta,* due to their neglect of Torah study and teaching. The absence of Torah teachers in this town demonstrates that God's law is not a priority for its elites, who are thus responsible for its impending doom, as foretold by Jeremiah 9:11–12.[254]

To a certain extent, the Torah may also be seen as a weapon. In Genesis 3:24, God places cherubim with swords that are "flaming and turning to guard the way to the tree of life" at the entrance of the Garden of Eden. In its commentary on this verse, Genesis Rabbah 21:9 depicts Adam pondering the future of the children of Israel. He wonders who will protect them from this fiery sword, which is identified with the furnace of the Day of Judgment, described in Malachi 3:19. Rav Huna[255] explains this as the "sword of circumcision"

---

251. y. Hagigah 1:7, 76c; Schäfer and Becker 1991–2001 (2001, *Synopse* II/5–12), 316; trans. Jacob Neusner, in Neusner 1983–1994, 20:31 (slightly modified). See also the parallel versions in Lamentations Rabbah 2:1; Pesiqta de-Rav Kahana (Eikhah) 15:5, ed. Mandelbaum, 1:253.

252. Another example of *santer* rendered as "senator" or "senate" appears in the Soncino translation of Genesis Rabbah 67:8 (ed. Theodor and Albeck, 763), which describes Esau's hatred for Jacob (Gen 27:41). See the discussion in Kattan Gribetz 2020, 63–64.

253. Jastrow 1950, 1006.

254. The above-mentioned talmudic story about Bethar (y. Ta'anit 4:6, 68d–69b; Lamentations Rabbah 2:4), which ascribes that city's ability to withstand a siege to R. Eleazar ha-Modai's prayers, conveys a similar message. Upon that righteous rabbi's death, Bethar fell to Hadrian. In this case, rather than study sensu stricto, it was prayer that protected the city, yet these efficacious prayers came from a Torah scholar.

255. A fifth-generation Babylonian tanna, according to rabbinic tradition; here he speaks in the name of R. Abba (maybe R. Abba bar Zabdai).

(*ḥerev milah*) that will save Israel, in accordance with Joshua 5:2 ("At that time the Lord said to Joshua: Make flint knives [or: swords] and circumcise the Israelites a second time"). However, the sages' majority opinion views this as the salvific "sword of Torah" (*ḥerev Torah*), in relation to Psalm 149:6–7, "[Let the high praises of God be in their throats, and a] two-edged sword (*ḥerev pifiyot*) in their hands, [to execute vengeance on the nations . . .]."[256] This understanding of *ḥerev pifiyot* as a reference to the Torah is probably based on the etymology of *pifiyot*, which is related to *peh* ("mouth") and, thus, to speech. It also derives from the first part of Psalm 149:6: a weapon that consists of speech could refer either to prayer, as implied by the first portion of this verse, or to words of Torah.[257] Ultimately, Genesis Rabbah interprets Psalm 149:6 as an assertion that praise and Torah are Israel's arms against the nations.

In Pesiqta de-Rav Kahana, R. Samuel bar Nahman—a Palestinian amora from the third generation (late third century)—teaches that words of Torah have been compared to a weapon (*zayin*) because they serve the needs of whoever "works with them" (i.e., dedicates himself to study Torah), just as a weapon serves its owner.[258] As in Genesis Rabbah 21:9, Psalm 149:6 is cited as the proof text, followed by a discussion of the term *pifiyot*. R. Yehudah (probably R. Yehudah b. Ilai) explains *pifiyot* as a reference to the two Torahs: one written and one oral (the biblical text and rabbinic traditions, respectively), once more drawing a connection between Torah and a weapon (*ḥerev*). R. Nehemiah (known in rabbinic tradition as a contemporary of R. Yehudah) counters that *pifiyot* refers to the "two-edged" nature of a sword (*ḥerev*), as do modern translators, yet he adds that this sword "gives life in this world and in the world to come." Therefore, he too identifies the double-edged sword in Psalm 149:6 with Torah.[259]

Another aspect of the image of Torah as a weapon, albeit with ambiguous connotations, is related to the fact that the study of Torah in a *beit midrash* can resemble a conflict, and even warfare, where words may kill.[260] This is apparent in b. Bava Metziʿa 84a, the text that Daniel Boyarin presents as a case study in the innovative rabbinic model of masculinity: R. Yoḥanan invites Resh Laqish to abandon his previous life, which depended on physical force

---

256. Gen. Rabbah 21:9, ed. Theodor and Albeck, 204.

257. See also b. Berakhot 5a. Philo interprets the "sword" (*ḥerev, machaira*) in Numbers 22:29 as "the power of words" (*dynamis logōn*) (*Cher.* 32), as already noted in Theodor and Albeck, 204.

258. PRK (BaḤodesh haShlishi) 12:5, ed. Mandelbaum, 1:207.

259. See also Song of Songs Rabbah 1:2, pisqah 5, where the "two-edged sword," *ḥerev pifiyot*, is identified with the Torah, which gives life in both this world and the world to come, thus on two "sides."

260. On the atmosphere of violence in the study house in a Babylonian context, see Rubenstein 2003, 54–55.

and weaponry, in order to embrace a life of study.[261] He succinctly proposes "Your strength for the Torah," thus urging Resh Laqish to exchange physical and military might for the study of the law. R. Yoḥanan indirectly suggests that the Torah is the real source of a man's strength. When Resh Laqish enters the river, he leaves his spear on the shore, and he cannot retrieve it after arriving on the other side.[262] This story suggests that he experienced a kind of conversion and that, henceforth, he will be armed with words alone.[263]

Yet the remainder of this story demonstrates that Torah study is as dangerous as warfare. Resh Laqish marries R. Yoḥanan's sister and becomes a great Torah scholar. One day, these two sages—who have become closely associated, not only as brothers-in-law, but also through their relationship as *ḥavruta* partners[264]—have a halakhic dispute over the impurity of weapons. Alluding to Resh Laqish's past as a bandit, R. Yoḥanan comments: "A robber is an expert in robbery," an ironic and humiliating statement that runs counter to rabbinic teachings which prohibit recalling someone's past wrongdoings.[265] Resh Laqish angrily replies: "How have you benefited me? There [when I was among outlaws] they called me 'Rabbi' and here [in the *beit midrash*] they call me 'Rabbi'!"[266] Resh Laqish's answer reflects a critical stance toward the world of rabbinic study. By making a parallel between his former and current companions, Resh Laqish suggests that intellectual exchange in the study house is no less violent than armed robbery. R. Yoḥanan's caustic remark leads Resh Laqish to contract a fatal illness; while mourning the death of his study partner, R. Yoḥanan falls sick with longing, and his life too is abruptly cut short. As Daniel Boyarin aptly notes, in this narrative, initially "the valor of war-making is replaced by the valor of Torah study, metaphorically realized as a sort of battle," but as the text also suggests:

> Perhaps our vocal combat is not so different from theirs [the Romans'] after all. They kill with the spear, but we kill with the voice. The renunciation of the weapon turns out to be merely the substitute of the vocal weapon for the physical one. In this reading of the narrative, it essays

261. On this famous story, see, e.g., Kalmin 1999, 1–5; Hevroni 2008; Kosman 2010; Zalkah 2013; Rosen-Zvi 2013. The story is only indirectly echoed in the Jerusalem Talmud, y. Megillah 1:11 (72b).

262. See Fraenkel 1981, 73–77, esp. 76.

263. For a comparative approach to rabbinic and Christian stories of repentant robbers, which examines the story of Resh Laqish in light of Christian examples, see Bar-Asher Siegal 2015.

264. Boyarin 2015, 526.

265. See m. Avot 3:12; and the case of R. Eliezer in b. Bava Metzi'a 58b–59b; Kalmin 1999, 3.

266. For a complete translation of this passage, see Boyarin 1997, 127–128; Kalmin 1999, 1–2.

a far-reaching critique of the implicit violence of the institutionalized male competitiveness in Torah study.[267]

According to this reading, Torah study as the rabbinic alternative to the Roman model of war-making is quite ambiguous, for its oppositional stance incorporates mimesis.[268]

Ishay Rosen-Zvi has also underscored this confrontational component of Torah study, this time in tannaitic sources elaborated within a Roman setting. Drawing on Boyarin's work without wholly accepting his analysis, Rosen-Zvi writes:

> The sages substituted the external Roman world with that of the *beit midrash*, but while doing so they adopted its deeply agonistic ethos. While Boyarin sees the retiring from politics to the private spaces as a "symbolic enactment of femaleness," it seems here that the retreat from the world of political power was accompanied by its profound imitation. The Roman soldier, the *hoplite*, is brought into the *beit midrash* itself; not with his weapons, to be sure, but with all his agonistic ethos and rules of warfare. The Dyadic Wars are replaced by the wars of Torah, but they remain wars just the same.[269]

This mention of the Dyadic Wars refers to Tosefta Miqvaot 7:11, a halakhic discussion between R. Aqiva (and secondarily R. Shimon b. Nanas) and R. Yose ha-Gelili (and secondarily R. Tarfon), all third-generation tannaim from the second century CE, who debate whether a cow that drank water for purification and was then slaughtered within twenty-four hours is pure or impure.[270] With a decisive argument that receives the support of thirty-two elders who declare the cow pure, the less experienced R. Yose defeats the great R. Aqiva. Rabbi Tarfon then allegorically likens this halakhic battle to Daniel 8:4–7, a text that describes the wars between Alexander's successors, the Diadochs, who are symbolized by beasts. R. Aqiva is associated with the ram (v. 4), whereas R. Yose is identified with the goat that has "a conspicuous horn between his eyes" (v. 5; this horn symbolizes R. Yose's halakhic argument). In Daniel 8, the he-goat defeats the ram, and this passage concludes that "there was no one who could rescue the ram from his power" (v. 7), which R. Tarfon interprets as the elders who concurred with R. Yose. In short, this halakhic contest is seen as analogous to the wars waged between the generals of Alexander the Great after his death. This passage from the Tosefta, redacted in third-century Palestine, long before

267. Boyarin 1997, 135 and 147. Other rabbinic texts speak of words having the power to kill, in connection with the lethal potential of gossip; see, e.g., y. Peah 1:1, 16a.

268. For a similar analysis of the rabbis' appropriation of the agonistic language of games in the arena, see Levinson 2003, 357–358.

269. Rosen-Zvi 2013, 14.

270. t. Miqvaot 7:11, ed. Zuckermandel, 660–666, trans. Rosen-Zvi 2013, 12–13.

the completion of the Babylonian Talmud, shows that some rabbis in the Land of Israel viewed intellectual debates in the *beit midrash* through a military lens. Although martial conceptualizations of verbal combat in the study house may be more numerous in the Babylonian Talmud, such imagery occurs in Palestinian rabbinic texts as well.

Thus far, our discussion of an agonistic, quasi-military ethos in the *beit midrash* has primarily involved discourse (sometimes with fatal consequences); however, there are also sources that describe rabbis engaging in physical combat. This subject returns our attention to Resh Laqish, who is often presented as a former gladiator in scholarly literature.[271] Several Palestinian sources suggest that Resh Laqish, far from having completely abandoned the use of arms, was prepared to exercise force when necessary, as to defend fellow Jews, and especially rabbis, against bandits. These depictions of Resh Laqish appear in a passage from the Jerusalem Talmud, y. Terumot 8:11, 46b, which discusses a tannaitic ruling that, in a situation where non-Jews attack Jews and request that one Jew be surrendered in exchange for the safety of the rest of the group, such an offer should be rejected, unless the negotiation concerns a Jew who has committed a crime. This scenario is illustrated by the biblical example of Sheba son of Bichri, who had been condemned to death by David and was delivered to David's men by the inhabitants of Abel of Beth-maacah (2 Samuel 20:15, 21–22).[272] Resh Laqish accepted this decision only for persons who had been condemned to death, such as Sheba son of Bichri, whereas R. Yoḥanan advocated surrendering the requested individual to save the other Jews in all cases.

Up to this point, this talmudic unit is in Hebrew; several anecdotes follow in Aramaic, including two about Resh Laqish. The first relates an incident when R. Assi—a Babylonian amora who, according to rabbinic tradition, came to Palestine to study with R. Yoḥanan—was captured.[273]

> R. Yonathan said: "Let the corpse be wrapped in its sheet [or: shroud; meaning: there is nothing that can be done for him]." R. Shimon ben Laqish said: "Before I kill or am killed, I will go and save him by strength [or: argument (*ḥayyala*)]." He went and persuaded [those who were holding R. Assi] and they gave him to him. He said to them: "Come to the elder [R. Yoḥanan] and he will pray for you [meaning: he will bless you for returning R. Assi unharmed]." They came to R. Yoḥanan. He said to them: "What you were planning in your heart to

---

271. Bacher 1892, 342–344; Brettler and Poliakov 1990; Boyarin 1997, 128, note 3, and 135; Rosen-Zvi 2013, 10. This assessment is mainly based on b. Gittin 47a; however, b. Bava Metziʻa 84a presents this sage as a *listes* (*lēstēs* in Greek), a thief or outlaw.

272. See also t. Terumot 7:20; cf. m. Terumot 8:12.

273. This text mentions that he was seized in a *safsufa*, understood as a "riot" in Jastrow 1950, 1015, and as an "act of treachery" in Sokoloff 2017, 432.

do to him will happen to you." They had not arrived at Palmyra before all of them were gone [taken into captivity; or: had died].[274]

This section then tells how R. Ammi and R. Samuel attempted to rescue Zeir bar Hanina, who had been kidnapped and brought to the court of Queen Zenobiah in Palmyra. In this case, however, the rabbis are depicted as powerless and their colleague is rescued by miraculous means. By contrast, in the previous narrative, Resh Laqish succeeds in rescuing R. Assi by his own means, which include a willingness to employ lethal force and endanger his own life to save a fellow rabbi. The Palestinian Aramaic word *ḥayyala* is variously translated as "strength," "army," "multitude" or "argument"; in this passage, it could mean either "strength" or "argument," for Resh Laqish indeed persuades the kidnappers peacefully.[275] Interestingly, *ḥayyala* denotes "strength" in b. Bava Metziʿa 84a when R. Yoḥanan tells Resh Laqish: "Your strength for Torah." In y. Terumot, Resh Laqish has become a Torah scholar and is capable of engaging language instead of force, but he has also retained physical strength as an asset rather than rejecting it entirely and acknowledges violence as an option, as illustrated by the phrase "Before I kill or am killed . . ." Ultimately, Resh Laqish chooses persuasion and devises a ruse to punish the kidnappers. After securing the release of R. Assi, he dispatches the captors to be blessed by R. Yoḥanan. The blessing, however, turns out to be a curse, which is enacted soon after. Resh Laqish therefore appears as quite a multifaceted character.

The second anecdote involving Resh Laqish unequivocally underscores his physical strength and bravery. In this instance, R. Yoḥanan's property has been stolen by robbers; this material loss affects him so deeply that Resh Laqish decides to intervene on his behalf by pursuing the robbers on his own. Upon seeing him approach, the thieves immediately start to negotiate with him, seemingly from fear. They offer to return half of R. Yoḥanan's belongings, but Resh Laqish rejects their proposal, saying, "By your lives, I am taking the whole property back," which he does. In contrast to the prior narrative, here Resh Laqish neither negotiates nor relies on trickery. Apparently, his exceptional strength convinced the robbers to restore R. Yoḥanan's possessions. Acting as a rabbinic Robin Hood, Resh Laqish exercises his physical courage and ability to fight to defend fellow sages. Significantly, unlike other rabbinic texts such as b. Bava Metziʿa 84a, this narrative does not redefine strength as knowledge or study of Torah.

274. y. Terumot 8:11, 46b (in Maʾagarim); 8:10 in Schäfer and Becker 1991–2001 (1992, *Synopse* I/6–11), 116; my translation, based on MS Leiden and, for the last sentence, on Jastrow 1950, 104. The term *apiphasros* (MS Leiden), or *apisphasron* (MS Vaticanus), is spelled differently in other manuscripts and, thus, is difficult to identify. According to Sokoloff 2017, 504, one should read *prosodos* ("path" in Greek) and understand: "By the time they reached the curved path, they had all died."

275. Sokoloff 2017, 202–203.

This analysis requires one more observation, albeit a tentative one: if the end of the first passage involving Resh Laqish is indeed a reference to Palmyra (which is not certain), then both this story and the following one, which features R. Ammi and R. Samuel, associate kidnappers with the realm of Queen Zenobia, who, with her son Vaballathus, revolted against Rome. In 270–272 CE, they brought most of the Roman East under their dominion, an operation that culminated with the annexation of Egypt. In y. Terumot, the groups that abducted R. Assi and Zeir bar Hanina, respectively, would thus be associated with a kingdom that was famous for its successful campaign against Rome. It hardly seems random that the people who posed a threat to rabbis (or, perhaps, Jews in general) were identified as enemies of Rome. However far-fetched these talmudic stories appear, they may have been informed by events that took place during the reign of Aurelian and thus reflect the position that taking up arms against Rome's enemies was a wiser move than acting against the Roman empire, a course that had proved disastrous in the past. Yet this hypothesis cannot be based solely on the example of Resh Laqish; therefore, a more systematic investigation of Palestinian rabbinic sources is required.

In closing, this analysis of the redefinition of strength in relation to the Torah makes clear the diversity of positions conveyed in Palestinian rabbinic literature. On the one hand, a tendency to view Torah study as preferable to military training and the practice of warfare is indeed present in Palestinian rabbinic sources (and not only in later Babylonian ones). On the other hand, they do not condemn or altogether devalue the use of strength. The Mishnah and Tosefta also occasionally discuss the rules of warfare, particularly in the case of an optional war (*milḥemet reshut*), meaning an offensive that aims to expand Israel's territory, in contrast to wars waged defensively or ordained by God.[276] Admittedly, these rules remained theoretical while the Mishnah and the Tosefta were being composed.[277] Moreover, according to Günter Stemberger, tannaitic texts tend to view wars led by Jews as a phenomenon of the past or an eschatological scenario rather than a possibility in the present.[278] However, these works plainly indicate that the rabbis did not in principle oppose the use of force. Thus, the ethos of the Palestinian rabbis proves itself multifaceted, like the figure of Resh Laqish, who is depicted both as a learned rabbi who acknowledges the spiritual power of R. Yoḥanan and as a capable fighter who could defend and rescue his rabbinic peers.

276. See, e.g., m. Sanhedrin 1:5, 2:4; m. Sotah 8:7; t. Sotah 7:24; m. Eruvin 1:10; t. Eruvin 2:6, 3:7; t. Megillah 3:25; and also y. Shabbat 1:7, 4a; y. Sotah 8:7, 23a; y. Sanhedrin 1:5, 19b; 2:4, 20b; Berthelot 2018a, 368–369. See also Walzer 2006, which argues that the rabbis "write about the wars that the Jews should or should not, can or cannot, will or will not fight and about the internal decision-making process and rules of conduct relevant to those wars" but not about the actual wars waged by the nations that surrounded them (150).

277. They are also undeveloped; Edrei 2006, 257.

278. Stemberger 2005, 138–139.

3.4 "THE LORD IS A MAN OF WAR":
REDEFINING GOD'S POWER?

After enduring multiple defeats at the hands of Rome, some Jews must have come to question the power and, in some cases, the very existence of God.[279] Tannaitic literature occasionally echoes such doubts although, predominantely, it affirms the permanence and steadiness of God's authority, as does Josephus. Adiel Schremer notes that in several tannaitic midrashim,

> the rabbis emphasize that God's strength is still "with Him": He exists and is still full of His power. The rabbis felt a need to express loudly God's efficacy because it had been questioned as a consequence of the destruction of Jerusalem and the Temple, and as a result of Jews' defeat in the Bar Kokhba rebellion. These events were taken by many to imply not only Israel's failure but God's, too.[280]

Schremer especially refers to Mekhilta de-Rabbi Ishmael, Shirah 4 (ed. Horovitz and Rabin, 129–130) and the parallel in Mekhilta de-Rabbi Shimon bar Yoḥai on Exodus 15:3 (ed. Epstein and Melamed, 81–82).[281] Additionally, Sifre Deuteronomy 327–328 on Deuteronomy 32:37, a midrashic text that foretells the destruction of the Roman legions, exemplifies the tendency to reaffirm God's might.[282] Another noteworthy passage, Sifre Deuteronomy 192 on Deuteronomy 20:3, states that Israel should not be fearful on the eve of battle, for the nations of the world "come with the victory (*nitzaḥon*) of flesh and blood, while you come with the victory of the Lord (*ha-Maqom*)."[283] Not only is God depicted as powerful, but his capacity as a warrior far exceeds that of kings of flesh and blood, including Roman emperors. Confronted by both Roman victories and the divinization of imperial power, the rabbis asserted that God retained his might and that true power belonged to him alone.

The opposition between divine and human power is manifest in the account of Bar Kokhba's death in y. Taʻanit 68d–69a and its parallel in Lamentations Rabbah 2:4. As related above, upon seeing Bar Kokhba's corpse and recognizing that his death was caused by a snake bite—and thus that he had been killed by God rather than by the Samaritan who claimed to have defeated him—Hadrian exclaims: "If God did not kill him, who could have killed him?" and applies this biblical verse to Bar Kokhba: "Unless their Rock had sold them and their Lord had given them up!" (Deut 32:30).[284] I have

---

279. Schremer 2008 and 2010, 25–48.

280. Schremer 2010, 35.

281. Schremer 2010, 165, note 48. He also mentions Sifra, Emor, parashah 9.5 (on p. 30).

282. See ed. Finkelstein, 378, and Chapter Two.

283. Ed. Finkelstein, 233.

284. Trans. Schäfer 2003b, 6. See also Reinhartz 1989, 183–184.

emphasized above that Hadrian's sentence was an indirect acknowledgment of Bar Kokhba's exceptional military valor. Yet his remark also signifies that the God of Israel is the arbiter of life and death, victory and defeat, not the Roman emperor or his army. This story thus asserts God's might and superiority over Roman forces, through words that are ironically ascribed to the Roman emperor himself.

A similar statement appears in a narrative that shares several elements with the tale of Bar Kokhba's death, in Sifre Deuteronomy 322 on the verse: "They are a nation void of sense; there is no understanding in them" (Deut 32:28). The midrash presents two interpretations of this verse: the first, attributed to R. Yehudah (b. Ilai), states that "a nation void of sense" applies to Israel, for they have forsaken the Torah; the second, attributed to R. Nehemiah, identifies the "nation void of sense" as the nations of the world, who have forsaken the seven commandments that God gave to them.[285] Both of these sages interpret the second part of Deuteronomy 32:28 in light of Deuteronomy 32:30, positing that, if Israel was militarily weak before the nations, this was a sign that "their Rock had sold them and their Lord had given them up" (Deut 32:30). Yet, according to R. Nehemiah, the nations admit that this situation will be reversed in the days of the Messiah. He then presents a tale related to the Bar-Kokhba revolt: a *decurio* (*diqurion* in Hebrew) on horseback was pursuing a Jew with the intention of killing him but, as he was on the verge of seizing him, the Jew was bitten by a poisonous snake. Before dying, he exclaimed (addressing the *decurio* and speaking of Romans more broadly, as the plural verb indicates): "You will not hope to say: '[The Jews] have been delivered into our hands because we are great warriors (*gibborim*). Unless their Rock had sold them[, the Lord had given them up]* (Deut 32:30)."[286] That is to say, this Jew tells the Roman that God alone determines whether Jews shall be defeated; military skill and bravery confer ostensible power upon the Romans, but real power resides with God.

Another means of reasserting divine power in rabbinic literature is the portrayal of God as a warrior, a device that can be traced to various biblical texts.[287] Commenting on Exodus 15:3—"The Lord is a man of war (*ish milḥamah*), the Lord is his name"—the Mekhilta de-Rabbi Ishmael reports a teaching attributed to R. Yehudah which illustrates God as "a man of war" through biblical verses that present him in military attire: with a sword (Ps 45:4), in a coat of mail and helmet (Isa 59:17), with a spear (Hab 3:11; Ps 35:3), with bow and arrows (Hab 3:9; 2 Sam 22:15), and with shield and buckler

285. On the seven Noahide commandments, see Chapter Four, §4.3.

286. Sifre Deuteronomy 322, ed. Finkelstein, 372. In the manuscripts, this passage is transmitted with numerous minor variations and additions, but they do not affect its meaning.

287. See, e.g., Exod 15:3; 1 Sam 1:3, 11; 17:45. Many additional biblical verses describe God as "Lord of armies" (*YHWH tzevaot*, usually translated as "Lord of hosts").

(Ps 91:4; Ps 35:2); and, as a horseman (Ps 18:11). Ultimately, however, this midrash states: "I might understand that he needs one of these measures (*middot*), therefore Scripture says: *The Lord is a man of war, the Lord is his name*. It is by [means of] his name that he fights and he has no need of any of these measures." Later in this passage, the Mekhilta restates this point:

> *The Lord is his Name*. It is by [means of] his name that he fights and he has no need of any of these measures. And so David says: *You come to me with sword and spear and javelin; but I come to you in the name of the Lord of hosts, [the God of the armies of Israel, whom you have defied]* (1 Sam 17:45). And it is written: *Some take pride in chariots, and some in horses, but our pride is in the name of the Lord our God* (Ps 20:8). And [of] Asa it also says: *Asa cried to the Lord his God: [O Lord, there is no difference for you between helping the mighty and the weak. Help us, O Lord our God, for we rely on you, and in your name we have come against this multitude]* (2 Chron 14:10).[288]

Thus, the characterization of God as a "man of war" in Exodus 15:3 leads to an examination of the biblical verses that describe God as bearing arms, like a soldier. Yet, this midrash concludes by differentiating divine power from human force, for God does not depend on weaponry. The claim that God's name is the ultimate military asset is derived from the biblical phrase "the Lord (YHWH) is his name." This assertion is then supported by quotations from several verses that include the phrase "the name of the Lord" and contrast it with human forces.

Rabbinic texts also portray God as a general or king/emperor commanding an army, but, in these instances too, the comparison primarily emphasizes the differences between God and human leaders.[289] For example, whereas a human monarch on the verge of waging war dismisses the nations that approach him with their needs, God hears the prayers of all creatures. Whereas a human ruler struggles to provide food for his army, God feeds the whole world.[290] There are some cases, however, where the parable (*mashal*) does not seem to draw a contrast. In Sifre Numbers 82—on the description of the ark of the covenant preceding Israel in the wilderness to locate a resting-place for them (Num 10:33)—the ark is identified as the Shekhinah (the divine presence), which is compared to an *atikaesar* or "pro-Caesar." This title is modeled on "proconsul," and means "vice-emperor";[291] it may have developed during

---

288. MRI Shirah (Beshallaḥ) 4, ed. Horovitz and Rabin, 129 and 131; translation based on Lauterbach 2004, 188, 191. On this passage and other rabbinic texts dealing with God as warrior, see Perani 2005; Stemberger 2005.

289. Alan Appelbaum argues that, in most third-century parables, the king does not symbolize God; rather, his actions are compared to God's own (Appelbaum 2010, 98–99).

290. MRI Shirah (Beshallaḥ) 4, ed. Horovitz and Rabin, 130–131; Mekhilta de-Rashbi 15:3, ed. Epstein and Melamed, 82.

291. Jastrow 1950, 84; Appelbaum 2010, 62.

the period of the Tetrarchy, but it may also reference earlier eras of Roman history when two figures shared imperial power, as under Marcus Aurelius and Lucius Verus in 161–169 CE. In the midrash, the *atikaesar* and the Shekhinah go before the Roman army and the children of Israel, respectively, in search of a suitable encampment. They parallel rather than contrast with each other. However, as Menahem Kahana points out, Sifre Numbers implicitly signals that the conduct of this *atikaesar* is unusual, underscoring how the Shekhinah and, by extension, God differ from a human emperor or vice-emperor.[292]

Thus far, the references to God's power in the Palestinian rabbinic texts detailed here have reflected biblical patterns and ideas, with only occasional elements that reveal influence from the Roman context. It is reasonable to ask whether this context informed the rabbis' conceptualization of divine power. That is to say, do we observe a shift in perspectives on God's might from biblical and Second Temple traditions to rabbinic discourse?

It is possible to see such an evolution in the paradoxical claim articulated in texts such as y. Berakhot 7:3, 11c: namely, that God's power resides in his ability to remain silent following the destruction of his Temple. Yet, as we shall see, this claim appears in conjunction with questions concerning the powerlessness of God, a concern that was not wholly new but one that seems to have received greater prominence during the Roman period.

The idea that God sometimes chooses to be silent is not without a biblical basis. Moreover, several mentions of God's silence appear alongside affirmations of God's might and actions as a warrior. In Zephaniah 3:17, for example, the prophet announces to Jerusalem that God is in her midst as "a warrior who gives victory" and as one who remains silent in his love for her. This positive connotation of silence is utterly lacking in rabbinic references to God's silence in the wake of Israel's defeats by the Romans. Hence the Mekhilta de-Rabbi Ishmael interprets Exodus 15:11—"Who is like you, O Lord, among the gods?"—as follows:

> *Who is like you, O Lord, among the gods (elim).* Who is like you among the strong ones (*alamim*) and who is like you in the wonders (*nissim*) and mighty deeds (*gevurot*) which you performed for us at the sea, as it is said: *Awesome deeds by the Red Sea* (Ps 106:22); *He rebuked the Red Sea, and it became dry* (Ps 106:9). *Who is like you, O Lord, among the gods (elim)* [or: *ilem*, lit.: mute]. Who is like you among the silent ones (*ilemim*), O Lord, who is like you who, though seeing the insult heaped upon your children, nevertheless keeps silent. As it is said: *For a long time I have held my peace, I have kept silent and restrained myself; now I will cry out like a woman in labour, I will gasp and pant* (Isa 42:14).[293]

292. For the text: ed. Kahana 2011–2015, 1:200; commentary at 3:554–556.

293. MRI Shirah (Beshallaḥ) 8, ed. Horovitz and Rabin, 142; translation based on Lauterbach 2004, 1:204. The Babylonian Talmud (b. Gittin 56b) briefly echoes this teaching and attributes it to the school of R. Ishmael. See n. 295 below.

This midrash offers two interpretations, enabled by the defective spelling of the word *elim*, "gods," written אלם (*alef-lamed-mem*) in Exodus 15:11. The term is first read in relation to the root *alam*, "to be strong," and thus, as an affirmation that God's strength cannot be compared to any other, which is congruent with the Mekhilta passages detailed above. The second interpretation is based on a reading of אלם as *ilem*, "mute," and understands this verse as a reference to God's silence; Isaiah 42:14 is quoted as further evidence that God sometimes keeps silent before his adversaries. Yet Isaiah 42:13 describes God as a "man of wars" (*ish milḥamot*) who shouts aloud and displays his might (*gevurah*) to his enemies. Hence, the Mekhilta's depiction of God, as both a mighty warrior and a silent presence in front of his enemies, seems to echo the two-fold description of YHWH in Isaiah 42:13–14. In his discussion of God's silence in the Mekhilta, Adiel Schremer aptly notes: "In its context, this interpretation is clearly presented as God's praise: God's greatness is expressed in His ability to restrain Himself and remain 'mute,' despite what He sees that happens to His children," an idea that must be understood as a response to the supposition that God's lack of reaction following Roman victories is indicative of powerlessness. Schremer further remarks that "What makes the rabbinic response so cunning is the fact that it uses a major Roman value, that of 'self-restraint,' in order to subvert the supremacy of Rome itself."[294]

In the Mekhilta, as in the Bible, God may reveal himself to Israel as a God of might or as a God of silence; however, silence may troublingly resemble powerlessness, the opposite of might. By contrast, in the Jerusalem Talmud, it is God's silence itself that becomes the manifestation of his power:

> R. Pinhas said: Moses fixed the form of prayer: *The great* (gadol), *mighty* (gibbor) *and awesome* (nora) *God* (Deut 10:17).
>
> Jeremiah said: *The great and mighty God* (Jer 32:18), but he did not say "awesome." Why did he call him "mighty?" Because it is fitting to call "mighty" [one] who [is able to] see the destruction of his Temple and keep silent. And why did he not call him "awesome"? Because "awesome" refers only to the Temple, as it is said, *Awesome is God in his sanctuary* (Ps 68:35).
>
> Daniel said: *The great and awesome God* (Dan 9:4), but he did not say "mighty." [When] his sons are surrendered with chains around the neck (*qolarin*, from the Latin *collare*, "collar"), where is his might? And why did he call him "awesome"? It is fitting to call him "awesome" because of the awesome deeds he performed [to save] us in the fiery furnace.[295]

294. Schremer 2010, 31.

295. y. Berakhot 7:3, 11c (Ma'agarim); 7:4 in Schäfer and Becker 1991 [*Synopse* I/1–2], 192; my translation is based on MS Leiden. See also the parallel in y. Megillah 3:6, 74c. Compare with b. Gittin 56b, mentioned in §1.2 above, which describes Titus profaning the Holy of Holies by tearing the curtain at its entrance and making it bleed. The Bavli

This talmudic text puts forward the idea that God is called mighty (*gibbor*) because he is able to remain silent after witnessing the demise of his Temple. As in the Mekhilta, this passage emphasizes God's self-control. Yet here it becomes an expression of might (*gevurah*), a quality that is generally associated with military power. This paradoxical declaration is somewhat comparable to Shimon ben Zoma's teaching in Mishnah Avot 4:1 that a real *gibbor* "overcomes his [evil] inclination (*yetzer*)," based on Proverbs 16:32, "One who is slow to anger is better than the mighty, and one whose temper is controlled than one who captures a city."[296] I do not claim that God is seen as having to control an evil *yetzer*, simply that the Yerushalmi and the Mishnah apply the ideal of personal discipline to both God and the sage. Moreover, the quotation from Proverbs indicates that this mishnaic teaching focuses on anger, an emotion ascribed to God in various biblical texts. Furthermore, Proverbs 16:32 contrasts one who shows self-restraint with one who seizes a city, an image that evokes God silently witnessing the conquest of Jerusalem and the destruction of the Temple, and Titus' hubris.[297] Although these two teachings are not exactly parallel, they share common motifs. As mentioned above, self-control was crucial to rabbinic understandings of manliness and the rabbis' definition of the sage.[298] Some rabbis seem to have deemed self-restraint to be a divine quality as well. While there was a solid Greco-Roman background to the idea that a human being's courage or strength might lie in a capacity for self-control (see §3.1 above), the claim that God's power might consist, at times, in silence and self-restraint was truly original. It represents another dimension of the rabbis' redefinition of power—in this case, divine power—in a Roman context.

The quotation from Daniel 9:4, however, offers a different perspective. On the basis of this verse, the talmudic discussion ascribes the absence of the term "mighty" to Roman control over Israel: *gevurah* cannot be attributed to God while his children, Israel, are dominated by the Romans. This association with Rome is suggested by the use of the term *qolar*, derived from Latin, for the instrument that enchains Israel. Although the word "awesome" appears in

---

attributes a teaching to Abba Ḥanin (a third-generation tanna, according to rabbinic tradition) which interprets Psalm 89:9—"Who is strong like you, O Lord?"—to mean: "Who is like you, mighty in self-restraint, that you hear the blasphemies and insults of that wicked man and stay silent?" As in y. Berakhot 7:3(4), 11c, Abba Ḥanin suggests that the power of God resides in his silence and self-restraint. In the Bavli, this *sugya* continues with a teaching attributed to R. Ishmael: "*Who is like you among the gods* (elim)? (Exod 15:11) Who is like you among the silent ones (*ilemim*)?" This interpretation is similar to the reading from MRI Shirah (Beshallaḥ) 8, examined above. On b. Gittin 56b, see further Besler 2014, 13.

296. See §3.1 above. On *yetzer ha-raʿ* in rabbinic literature, see Rosen-Zvi 2011 (on m. Avot 4:1, see 29–30).

297. In addition to the sources referred to in n. 295 above, see the discussion of Titus' desecration of the Temple and the Holy of Holies in the previous section of this chapter, and in Chapter Two, §2.3.

298. Satlow 1996.

Daniel 9:4, read here in association with God's rescue of the three young men condemned to die in a Babylonian furnace, this passage raises the possibility that God lacks *gevurah*, an alternative understanding of God's silence and inaction in the face of Roman victories over Israel. The Jerusalem Talmud thus explores different theological interpretations of Israel's defeats at the hands of Rome.

Tractate Berakhot, which addresses blessings and prayers, actually discusses the issue of whether God is powerful or powerless in several places. In y. Berakhot 9:1, 12d, a section that evokes God's wonders or miracles (*nissim*) for Israel, Rav—who, according to rabbinic tradition, was a Babylonian amora from the first half of the third century who had recently returned to Babylonia from the Land of Israel—reportedly interpreted Job 37:23—"We have been unable to reach [or: find] the Almighty, great in strength (*koaḥ*), judgment and in abundance of justice; he will not respond"—to signify: "We have not found the strength (*koaḥ*) and power (or: might, *gevurah*) of the Holy One, blessed be he."[299] The plain meaning of Job 37:23 is that God is "great in power" (or: strength, *koaḥ*) and in justice, despite not answering human beings, which is to say, notwithstanding his silence. In this talmudic unit, however, Rav seems to suggest that humans cannot experience God's power, a proposition that could cast doubt on the existence of divine might. Adiel Schremer comments that Rav's reading should be seen "as a bold statement that does not hesitate to express in the most unequivocal manner the claims regarding God's lack of power. Such a bold and honest declaration indicates that the crisis was deep indeed."[300] As in Job, what Rav appears to be referring to here is God's silence; but unlike Job, what he questions is God's ability to act forcefully against Israel's enemies and not divine justice. These texts address different divine attributes.[301]

Other interpretations of Rav's teaching are also possible. According to both Jacob Neusner and Heinrich W. Guggenheimer, this passage states that human beings cannot find adequate words to describe God's power, which is infinite.[302] However, this reading presupposes a reconstitution of a text that is

299. y. Berakhot 9:1, 12d; Schäfer and Becker 1991–2001 (1991, *Synopse* I/1–2), 218; my translation is based on MS Leiden. See also Pesiqta de-Rav Kahana (Ki Tisa) 2:10, ed. Mandelbaum, 1:34, which mentions only "his strength," and comments as follows: "The Lord does not come with burdensome [laws to be imposed] upon Israel" (see Jastrow 1950, 552). Here divine strength is understood as a form of coercion that could be exercised against Israel.

300. Schremer 2010, 32.

301. On rabbinic questionings of theodicy, see, e.g., Stratton 2009, 75–76 (on Gen. Rabbah 22:9); Gregerman 2016 (which focuses on the Midrash on Lamentations, and analyzes how this work charges God with disobedience to biblical Law); Hayes 2020 (on b. Avodah Zarah 2a–3b).

302. Tzvee Zahavy's translation in the English translation of the Jerusalem Talmud edited by Jacob Neusner says: "[The verse implies] we cannot find [adequate words to

not backed by its actual wording. These scholars may have been influenced by the continuation of this talmudic discussion, which cites another verse from Job: "Should he [God] be told that I want to speak? Did anyone ever wish to be swallowed up?" (Job 37:20). This verse speaks of Job's hesitation to address the Almighty directly, given the unjust fate that God has brought upon him. R. Abbahu teaches in the name of R. Yoḥanan:

> If a man comes to tell the strengths (*gevurot*) of the Holy One blessed be He, he is swallowed up [or: destroyed] from the world. R. Samuel bar Nahman said: *Who can utter the mighty deeds* (gevurot*) of the Lord?* (Ps 106:2). For example, I and my companions.[303] R. Abun said: *Who can utter the mighty deeds of the Lord?* Jacob of Kefar Naburaia translated [or: explained] in Tyre [the verse]: *Silence* (dumiah*) is praise* (tehillah*) *for you, O God in Zion* (Ps 65:2) [as]: The essence of all [praise] is silence. As regarding a priceless pearl: everyone who [attempts to] praise it, [in reality he] diminishes it [its beauty, or value].[304]

R. Yoḥanan's statement can be understood to mean that humans cannot adequately praise God's mighty deeds and, thus, may be "swallowed up" as a consequence of their profane words. According to Jacob of Kefar Naburaia, described in rabbinic tradition as a fourth-century Palestinian amora, silence is a more fitting form of praise than language. With the phrase "The essence of all [praise] is silence," the text switches from Hebrew to Aramaic, which probably indicates that this is Jacob's explanation in Aramaic of Psalm 65:2. This teaching reinforces R. Yoḥanan's previous statement, namely, that silence is the most suitable form of praise that humans can offer in response to God's mighty deeds. In the context of the talmudic discussion that starts with Rav's comment, this position, which stems from an exegesis of Job 37:20 that presents silence as a prudent option in light of God's seemingly erratic behavior, may reasonably be read as a response to Rav's teaching. In other words, it is better to remain silent on the subject of God's *gevurot* than to suggest that God lacks power, that his strength (*koaḥ*) and might (*gevurah*) "cannot be found."

Let us conclude this brief overview of the theme of God's power and powerlessness in Tractate Berakhot by noting one more opinion on God's reaction, or lack thereof, to the destruction of his Temple. A discussion of the blessings to be recited upon experiencing a variety of meteorological phenomena

---

describe] God's power and might" (Neusner 1983–1994, 1:307). For Heinrich W. Guggenheimer, Rav's statement means "It is too much for finite man" (Guggenheimer 1999, 604, note 17).

303. Cf. Zahavy's translation: "['Who is better at prayer,' asked the Psalmist,] 'than me or my associates?'" (Neusner 1983–1994, 1:307). Yet this text could also refer to R. Samuel bar Nahman and his rabbinic circle.

304. y. Berakhot 9:1, 12d; Schäfer and Becker 1991–2001 (1991, *Synopse* I/1–2), 218–220; my translation is based on MS Leiden. Cf. Guggenheimer 1999, 603.

prescribes the recitation of "Blessed be He whose strength (*koah*) fills the worlds" for storms and thunderbolts, as well as meteors and earthquakes. The text explains the latter as follows:

> When the Holy One, blessed be He, looks down on the theaters and circuses that sit secure, serene, and peaceful, whereas his Temple [lies] destroyed, he [looks upon] his world threatening to destroy it [and therefore the earth trembles]. In this regard, Scripture says: *The Lord will roar from on high, and from his holy habitation utter his voice* (Jer 25:30). [He will roar] because of [the destruction of] his Temple [lit.: his ornament].[305]

In this instance, God does not remain silent in the face of his ruined sanctuary: to the contrary, he "roars" and "utters his voice" in anger. However, since earthquakes afflict Jews and non-Jews indiscriminately, they are hardly an adequate divine response to the devastation wrought by the Romans. Ultimately, the question of God's apparent passivity and powerlessness remains unresolved.

⊰⸱⸱⸱⊱

Catherine Hezser has rightly argued that Jewish texts from the Second Temple and rabbinic period cannot be broadly characterized as "non-violent," "pacifist," or opposed to war.[306] Given the three revolts initiated by Jews within a century, it would admittedly be difficult to argue that Jews in general tended to avoid armed conflict. A number of Roman, Greek, and Jewish sources highlight fierce resistance by Jewish rebels, and, more broadly, Roman authors do not depict the Jews as an effeminate Eastern people. Moreover, albeit on the basis of documentation that is limited and unevenly distributed across centuries, scholars now agree that some Jews were enrolled in or associated with the Roman army, individually or as special units, from the first century BCE until the early fifth century CE. Therefore Jews experienced Roman military power both as opponents and as participants, from outside and from within.

The works of Philo, Josephus, and the rabbis convey a great deal of ambivalence toward Roman military power and the Roman emphasis on bravery (*virtus/andreia*). These Jewish texts occasionally acknowledge and even express admiration for Roman might and valor, yet in other instances those Roman traits are minimized or derided. Certain passages betray a sense of rivalry with Rome with regard to courage in combat and military expertise, while others—and, at times, the same ones—mimic Roman discourses, representations, or practices. Far from presenting the Jews as rejecting the use of force and

---

305. y. Berakhot 9:2, 13c; Schäfer and Becker 1991–2001 (1991, *Synopse* I/1–2), 232; my translation, based on MS Leiden.

306. Hezser 2013.

the art of war, a portion of this literature highlights the military achievements of Israel's ancestors or contemporaneous Jewish figures, such as Bar Kokhba (despite his critical portrayal in rabbinic texts). In rabbinic literature, God too is sometimes portrayed as a Roman general or emperor fighting against his enemies, with details that evoke Roman practices. Yet at the same time, God is often contrasted with these Roman models. Rivalry and mimicry raise the possibility that Israel might become like Rome in the exercise of power and force and thus prompt the question of how to preserve Israel's distinctiveness.

On the other hand, various literary sources examined here attempt to formulate a response or a countermodel to Roman military power and, thus, to redefine human and divine power, as well as bravery. Some of these redefinitions, such as conceiving of courage as the ability to face death unflinchingly and power as the capacity to master oneself, were not unique to Jews, for they were common in the Greco-Roman world, especially among those conversant with philosophy. Philo draws from such philosophical concepts in his descriptions of the sage as one who is truly strong and qualified for kingship, though he also makes clear that this power is cultivated by orienting the mind and the soul toward God. Moreover, Philo often contrasts this form of power with military domination over land and sea, which may have been an allusion to Roman imperial rule. In another likely polemic against Rome, Philo depicts Abraham (and implicitly Israel) shunning conquest and self-aggrandizement. He legitimates only wars that are waged in the name of justice or faithfulness to the Covenant. Josephus adopts this same line of argument, particularly in *Against Apion*, where he affirms that Jews do not aim to conquer other nations' territory; rather they aspire simply to live by their ancestral laws, a goal that justifies war when it is thwarted. Nonetheless, Josephus generally seems to be less inclined than Philo to redefine power and courage, and he stays closer to conventional views, such as understanding *andreia* as bravery in combat. In rabbinic texts, we encounter the claim that the Torah, or its study, is Israel's true source of power—namely, another way (when compared to Philo) to redefine power as an intellectual ability that derives from engagement with a divine gift. Yet this redefinition did not eliminate more conventional discussions of warfare and Torah commandments related to battle. One of the most striking redefinitions of power in rabbinic literature is the conception of God's might as the ability to remain mute after witnessing the destruction of his Temple, articulated in the Jerusalem Talmud. The identification of power with silence goes beyond the biblical and rabbinic juxtaposition of might with silence as two potent yet distinct manifestations of God. However, this provocative and paradoxical assertion remains marginal alongside the numerous rabbinic passages that reflect on God's apparent powerlessness or reaffirm God's might in a more traditional way, already attested in biblical responses to the destruction of the First Temple.

Overall, the sources examined in this chapter demonstrate that the attribution of spiritual power to Israel and military power to Rome—as illustrated by the quotation from b. Gittin 57b, discussed in the introduction to this chapter—is but one approach taken in Jewish texts produced in a Roman context. Far from expressing a systematic rejection of military power and the use of force, this literature actually conveys different types of responses (individually or in combinations): criticism, rivalry, imitation, subversion, rejection, and attempts to reframe human and divine power to distance them from Roman norms. Some of these responses display considerable continuity with biblical reactions to the empires of the ancient Near East. Certain biblical passages already defined Israel's strength in spiritual terms while affirming God's ultimate power over the nations (see, e.g., Zechariah 4:6, Psalm 33:16–20). However, the insistence of some of the sources examined here on the Jews' bravery in war goes beyond similar statements in biblical texts and, in all likelihood, is to be understood in light of the valorization of the military in a Roman context and as a way to cope with Jewish defeats at the hands of Rome.[307]

307. A similar insistence on bravery is found in 1 Maccabees in a Hellenistic context. Yet in that book, courage in war generally characterizes the Hasmoneans rather than the Jews as a whole, because military success was key to the dynasty's legitimacy. See Section 2.3 above.

CHAPTER FOUR

The Challenge of Roman Law and Jurisdiction

Rome, *"mother of arms and laws"* (armorum legumque parens)

CLAUDIAN, *ON STILICHO'S CONSULSHIP* 3.136

"And what other great nation has statutes and ordinances as just as this entire law that I am setting before you today?"

DEUTERONOMY 4:8

ROMAN POWER was not simply about the military—it also took a judicial form. As Clifford Ando has amply demonstrated, the imperial administrative and judicial system played an important role in the consensual adhesion to Roman rule of provincial populations.[1] One of the factors that made Roman law and jurisdiction particularly challenging for the Jews, beyond its intrinsic connection with Roman rule, was the Romans' claim that their laws were far superior to those of other peoples, including the Greeks, and obviously the Jews. Beyond this ideological claim, there was in fact a Roman specificity. As Ando points out,

> No other legal tradition of the ancient Mediterranean—save in complex respects Jewish law in the Roman period—develops any remotely similar practices that we might denominate a theory of autonomous law, or traditions of statutory interpretation, or rules of precedent, or institutions of legal education and practices of jurisprudence.[2]

The reference to Jewish law is significant. Boaz Cohen once wrote that Romans and Jews were "the two most legally minded peoples of antiquity," and this

---

1. Ando 2000.
2. Ando 2018, 668.

similarity must have been striking to some ancient Jews as well.[3] Cohen dealt at length in his scholarship with the question of the relationship between Roman and Jewish law—by which he meant rabbinic halakhah rather than biblical law—comparing them on specific legal issues and pointing out some common features. He also emphasized a striking contrast:

> The Romans were the only people of antiquity who disentangled completely their civil law from all their religious precepts in historical times. Perhaps the Roman theory about the origin of their law is not unconnected with this phenomenon. The belief in the divine inspiration of the Law, which was current among most ancient peoples, was confined by the Romans to ritual prescriptions, known as *Fas*, whereas the changeable rules regulating intercourse between individuals in society, termed *lex*, were regarded as human institutions. *Fas lex divina ius lex humana est.*
> The Jews did not make this distinction.[4]

As a matter of fact, the Romans were unique in developing law as an independent field of knowledge and technical competence, distinct from religious precepts. However, the nonreligious character of Roman law—at least in the imperial period—did not mean that it could not be perceived by at least some Jews as a competitor to Jewish law. The Jews who lived in the framework of the Roman empire, and indeed as Roman citizens after 212 CE, in many ways confronted Roman laws and courts. This fact raises the question of the attitude of the Jews—especially the rabbis, who claimed to be legal experts—toward the Roman legal system, how they negotiated its claims and justified (or not) submission to it.

Before we go any further, a methodological clarification is in order: we need to distinguish between what the rabbis *said* Jews should do or refrain from doing and what they *did* when they elaborated their halakhic rulings, possibly borrowing foreign concepts (without acknowledging it) to develop their legal thinking—and thus undergoing a process of conscious or unconscious acculturation.[5] The fact that some rabbis drew a distinction and even a sharp opposition between the laws of the nations and those of Israel does not necessarily reflect their practice as legal experts and arbitrators. Moreover, the ideological discourse of opposition is not the only one found in rabbinic literature, as we shall see.

The purpose of this chapter is first to expound on the nature of the challenge that the Roman legal system, in both its ideological and its practical aspects, presented for the Jews. It will then tackle the similarities between Roman and rabbinic laws and the question of the integration of Roman legal

3. Cohen 1966, 1:123.
4. Cohen 1944, 422–423; see also Hezser 2007, 151–152.
5. See Schwartz 2010a, 116.

rulings or reasoning within rabbinic halakhah before turning to the ideological discourses of Jews living in the Roman period concerning Israel's law and the laws of other peoples. The bulk of the chapter is dedicated to an analysis of the evidence documenting a sense of rivalry between Jews and Romans around the question of law and jurisdiction, with special attention to the dialectic between opposition and imitation already highlighted in previous chapters. Building upon Christine Hayes' recent work on rabbinic notions of law, this chapter also looks at the rabbinic trend toward rejecting universalist views of the Torah through the prism of the rivalry between Israel and Rome.

1. The Nature of the Challenge

1.1 THE IDEOLOGICAL DIMENSION OF THE CHALLENGE

According to some Roman literary traditions, the inspiration for the Twelve Tables came from the Greeks, particularly from the Athenian lawgiver Solon.[6] However, most Romans (at least among the elites) tended to perceive the Roman legal system as an original corpus that displayed the particular genius of the Roman people.[7] This perspective is exemplified in Cicero's *On the Making of an Orator*:

> Though the whole world grumble, I will speak my mind: it seems to me, I solemnly declare, that, if anyone looks to the origins and sources of the laws, the small manual of the Twelve Tables by itself surpasses the libraries of all the philosophers, in weight of authority and wealth of usefulness alike. [. . .] Wisdom as perfect went to the establishment of her [Rome's] laws, as to the acquisition of the vast might of her empire (*imperium*). You will win from legal studies this further joy and delight, that you will most readily understand how far our ancestors surpassed in practical wisdom the men of other nations, if you will compare our own laws with those of Lycurgus, Draco and Solon, among the foreigners. For it is incredible how disordered (*inconditum*), and wellnigh absurd (*ridiculum*), is all national law (*ius civile*) other than our own.[8]

According to Cicero, it is precisely in comparison with the legislation of the most prestigious Greek cities, Sparta and Athens, that Roman laws distinguish themselves by their superior wisdom. In this passage, even the work of famous Greek

---

6. Cicero, *On Laws* 2.59, 2.64; Livy, 3.31.8, 3.32.6, 3.33.5. There is still an echo of such traditions in Symmachus, *Epist.* 3.11.3.

7. Rome did indeed have "a culture and a knowledge that was not Greek," as Natalie Dohrmann and Annette Yoshiko Reed aptly write (Dohrmann and Reed 2013, 5).

8. Cicero, *On the Making of an Orator* 1.44.195–197, trans. E. W. Sutton and H. Rackham, LCL, 137.

lawgivers such as Lycurgus and Solon is deemed "disordered" and "absurd." As to barbarian laws, Cicero had little interest in them.[9] Most important, in *On the Making of an Orator* he suggests that Rome's *imperium* coincided with its legal wisdom: as a consequence, it was beneficial for the peoples conquered by Rome to live under its sway. Rhetoric and ideology were not the only aspects of Cicero's thought on provincial laws, however, and when practical legal and political issues were at stake, he was able to display a much more positive attitude, as the speeches against Verres show.[10] On the other hand, pride in the intrinsic genius of the Roman laws was not merely a rhetorical stance suited to orators' speeches. Jill Harries notes that "well into the imperial period, Roman legal writers prided themselves on the separateness of 'their' *ius civile*. In his explanation of the Roman *ius civile*, [the jurist] Gaius was at pains to point out that certain revered institutions and legal practices were unique to the Romans."[11]

Another important ideological claim was that the Roman empire provided access to jurisdiction and justice to the peoples who lived under its dominion, starting from the idea that Rome brought laws where there had been none before.[12] Even though Roman jurists were clearly aware of the legal systems of non-Roman peoples—considering that each *civitas* had its own laws (*ius civile*), while all nations shared common laws (*ius gentium*)[13]—the assertion that the Romans brought legal order to numerous areas and peoples can be found under the pen of various authors up to the 5th century CE. Writing under Augustus and Tiberius, Velleius Paterculus described the Germans, after their defeat at the hands of Quintilius Varus, as distracting the latter from his military duties

> by feigning a series of made-up lawsuits, now summoning each other to disputes, now giving thanks that Roman justice (*ea Romana iustitia*) was settling them and that their savagery was being rendered mild by this unknown and novel discipline and that quarrels that were customarily settled by arms were now being settled by law (*et solita armis discerni iure terminarentur*).[14]

9. Lévy 2021.

10. The rhetorical dimension of these speeches must also be taken into account. See Dubouloz 2021.

11. Harries 2013, 47. These legal practices included *patria potestas*, *manus*, and certain forms of purchase and sale.

12. According to H. Rushton Fairclough's translation of the *Aeneid* (revised by G. P. Goold) in the LCL (p. 593), Virgil claimed that the Romans were a people destined to bring legal order to the *oikoumenē* ("to crown peace with justice" [6.852]). Yet *mos*, here translated as "justice," can also mean "habit" or "morality," and Nicholas Horsfall, for example, favors the translation "to set the force of habit upon peace" (Horsfall 2013, 1:59, 2:585).

13. On *ius civile* and *ius gentium*, see Gaius, *Inst.* 1.1.

14. Velleius Paterculus, *Compendium of Roman History* 2.118.1, trans. Clifford Ando in Ando 2016b, 288. Cf. Cassius Dio, *Rom. Hist.* 56.18.1–2, which does not mention a trick by the Germans.

In this passage, Velleius attributes to the Germans a perception and understanding of the Romans' ideological claim to be initiating barbarians into judicial proceedings and legal relationships. What is even more striking is that he also grants the Germans the ability to manipulate this claim to their own ends, since the lawsuits were in fact a trick to defeat Varus.

The idea of Rome as bringing law to conquered nations was still very present among the Roman elites in the fourth century CE and at the beginning of the fifth. According to Ammianus Marcellinus, two elements stood out in Rome's glorious past: it had "humbled the proud necks of savage nations" and "made laws, the everlasting foundations and moorings of liberty."[15] Although Rome's role in introducing legal order to savage nations is suggested only by the juxtaposition of these two actions statements, it is probably the underlying meaning of the text, which recalls Virgil's famous verses in the *Aeneid*: "You, Roman, be sure to rule peoples with authority (be these your arts), to impose law on peace, to spare the vanquished and to crush the proud."[16]

At the beginning of the fifth century, Rutilius Namatianus wrote in his poem addressed to Roma:

> You have made from distinct and separate nations (*gentes*) a single fatherland: it has benefited those who knew not laws, to be captured by your conquering sway; and by giving to the conquered a share in your law, you have made a city of what was once a world (*dumque offers victis proprii consortia iuris, urbem fecisti quod prius orbis erat*).[17]

Echoing the pun between *urbs* (city) and *orbs* (world) already found under the pen of Ovid (*Fasti* 2.684), Rutilius, who wrote long after the *Constitutio Antoniniana*, claimed that the empire was like a city ruled by common laws, which had brought civilization to the barbarian nations "who knew not laws."

The *Roman Oration* of Aelius Aristides reflects a similar perspective, demonstrating both the prevalence of such ideas before 212 CE and the fact that Greek elites reproduced Roman discourses:

> There is no need whatsoever now to write a book of travels and to enumerate the laws which each country uses. Rather you yourselves [Romans] have become universal guides for all; you threw wide all the gates of the civilized world and gave those who so wished the opportunity to see for themselves; you assigned common laws for all and you put an end to the previous conditions which were amusing to describe

---

15. Ammianus Marcellinus, *Res Gestae* 14.6.5, trans. J. C. Rolfe, LCL, 37.

16. *Aeneid* 6.851–853, trans. H. Rushton Fairclough, rev. G. P. Goold, LCL, 593 (slightly modified; see n. 12 above for alternative translations). In particular, the phrase *superbas cervices* (proud necks) in Ammianus' text recalls the *superbi* (proud [ones]) in Virgil.

17. Rutilius Namatianus, *De reditu suo* 1.63–66, trans. Ando 2000, 49.

but which, if one looked at them from the standpoint of reason, were intolerable.[18]

It is remarkable that a Greek author should minimize the importance of the civic laws of Greek *poleis* to such an extent and see the Roman empire as united by common laws already in the second century CE. This statement should not be taken literally, however, but rather understood in light of the *Oration*'s literary genre—panegyric—and of Aristides' personal situation: he was a Greek but also a Roman citizen and delivered this speech in Rome (probably in 154/155 CE).

Some Christian authors echoed this Roman discourse as well, but the first such testimonies date after 212. In 238, despite the occasional persecutions of Christians that still occurred in the empire, Gregory Thaumaturgus wrote in his *Address of Thanksgiving to Origen*:

> Another branch of learning occupies my mind completely, and the mouth binds the tongue if I should desire to make any speech, however brief, with the voice of the Greeks. I refer to those admirable laws by which the affairs of all men subjected to the power [*archē*] of the Romans are now directed, and which are neither composed nor learnt without difficulty. And these are wise and exact in themselves, and manifold and admirable, and, in a word, most thoroughly Grecian [*Hellēnikōtatoi*]; and they are expressed and committed to us in the Roman tongue, which is a wonderful and magnificent sort of language, and one very aptly conformable to royal authority, but still difficult to me.[19]

Gregory came from a wealthy pagan family and converted to Christianity as an adult. Originally from Neocaesarea in Pontus, he spent some time in Berytus, a major center for the study of Roman law in the third century. In this letter, he discloses both his identification with the Greek language and culture in which he was born and his admiration for Roman laws, which he studied in Latin. The latter are described as wise (*sophoi*), precise (*akribeis*), and manifold (*poikiloi*) in particular. Gregory thus seems to have been seduced by the intellectual complexity and intricacy of Roman law. His perspective was that of an educated Greek man rather than an ordinary Christian and contrasts sharply with the viewpoint of the texts known as the acts of the martyrs, which describe confrontations between governors and Christians in a judicial context.[20]

---

18. Aelius Aristides, *Roman Oration*, §102, trans. Oliver 1953, 906.

19. Gregory Thaumaturgus, *Address of Thanksgiving to Origen* 1, trans. Rev. S. D. F. Salmond, in Roberts, Donaldson, and Coxe 1886, 21 (slightly modified). See also Mélèze Modrzejewski 1971; Lepelley 2002, 841–842; Kimberley Fowler, "Gregory Thaumaturgus, *Address of Thanksgiving to Origen* I," at http://judaism-and-rome.org/gregory -thaumaturgus-address-thanksgiving-origen-i.

20. On martyrdom literature, see inter alia Bryen 2014.

In the fourth and fifth centuries, Christian authors echoed Roman praises of the empire's legal system to an even greater extent, and in a traditional Roman way. Prudentius, for example, places great emphasis on Rome's role in bringing law and justice to the nations it has conquered.[21] As Albrecht Dihle remarks, however, for Prudentius, "Christianity makes [Roman citizens] the representatives of civilisation against the Barbarian world," enabling Rome to "exercise its cultural mission."[22] Prudentius' perspective therefore represents a Christianized version of Rutilius' view described above.

{⦚⦚⦚⦚⦚⦚}

Such admiration for the "civilizing role" of Roman law is hardly to be found in Jewish sources, not even in Josephus. The most explicit Jewish testimony about the merits of imperial justice is found in Philo, but only in *Against Flaccus* and *On the Embassy to Gaius*, which rhetorically praise "good" governors and emperors in order to better condemn Flaccus and Caligula.[23] Most conspicuous is Philo's evocation of the trials that awaited bad governors when they came back to Rome after oppressing provincial populations:

> On these occasions the emperors showed themselves impartial judges; they listened equally to both the accuser and the defender, making it a rule to condemn no one offhand without a trial, and awarded what they thought to be just, influenced neither by hostility nor favour but by what actually was the truth.[24]

It is the emperor's role as supreme guarantor of justice that Philo emphasizes here. By contrast, nowhere does he praise Roman laws as such. He does not seem to have been impressed by the intellectual achievements of the Roman jurists of his time, or perhaps he simply did not have access to their works. In his commentary on the Mosaic law, Philo refers only to famous Greek lawgivers, such as Solon and Lycurgus.[25] Josephus' strategy in *Against Apion* is similar: in his defense of Mosaic law, he never compares Jewish and Roman laws explicitly, and he emphasizes the superiority of Jewish laws only vis-à-vis those produced by Greek lawgivers.[26]

In rabbinic literature, we find only a few rare hints at the legal order established by the Romans. The first two examples have already been mentioned

---

21. Prudentius, *Against Symmachus* 1.455–466 (around 402–403 CE).

22. Dihle 1994, 586.

23. Philo, *Flacc.* 105–107; *Legat.* 8.

24. Philo, *Flacc.* 106, trans. F. H. Colson, LCL, 361.

25. Philo, *Opif.* 104–105; *Spec.* 3.22; *Prob.* 47. See also Martens 2003. Philo knew about the Roman legal principle of *patria potestas*; see *Legat.* 28 (an explicit reference), *Spec.* 2.231–233 (where Philo may be implicitly contrasting biblical and Roman laws), and Niehoff 2018, 160.

26. See in particular Josephus, *C. Ap.* 2.154; see also § 3 below.

in Chapter Two. In Mishnah Avot 3:2, R. Hananiah is reported to have taught, "Pray for the peace of the kingdom [*malkhut*], because if it were not for the fear of it, a man would have swallowed up his neighbour alive."[27] In the context of the Mishnah, "the kingdom" is the Roman empire, which thus appears as bringing political and legal order to the peoples it has conquered. In Genesis Rabbah 9:13, the connection with the Roman legal system is more explicit. Commenting upon Genesis 1:31 ("And God saw everything that he had made, and behold, it was very good"), Resh Laqish explains that God declared "the earthly kingdom"—to be identified with Rome in this context—"very good" because "it exacts justice [*dikion*, from the Greek *dikē*] for the creatures [i.e., human beings]."[28]

Another passage of Genesis Rabbah, pertaining to Abraham's pleading for Sodom in Genesis 18:25, reports two teachings of R. Yudan (Yehudah) bar Shimon (a fourth-generation Palestinian amora, according to rabbinic tradition) which present Abraham as urging God to behave justly—which in the context of Genesis 18 means not condemning the innocent together with the guilty—and as using Roman examples to illustrate his point. First, Abraham argues that God has to judge in an equitable manner because no human being can appeal his judgment, in contrast to a human judge. The argument's Roman background is apparent in the remark that "in the case of a human [judge], an appeal can be made from the commander [Latin *dux*] to the prefect [Greek *eparchos*] and from the prefect to the military governor [Greek *stratēlatēs*]." In R. Yehudah's second teaching, the reference to Rome is even more explicit. Abraham tells God: "When you wanted to judge your world, you entrusted it to the hands of two [judges], such as Remus and Romulus, so that each would hinder what the other requested."[29] The underlying idea is that if two persons are appointed as judges, equity and mercy have a better chance to prevail than if there is only one person in charge of the sentence. Abraham uses an implicit a fortiori argument to convince God that since he has no fellow judge who could object to his decisions, they must be all the more equitable. The reference to Remus and Romulus in this context is counterintuitive: in Roman sources, far from being a model of cooperation and balance, the two brothers fight each other and the latter kills the former. The reason for mentioning them must therefore lie in a conscious or unconscious association between the Roman legal system, vaguely connected to the origins of the city of Rome, and the ideal of justice.

On the whole, however, rabbinic texts reflect a clear rejection of Rome's claim of bringing legal order to the *oikoumenē*. Another passage of Genesis Rabbah depicts Rome as an "evil kingdom" that "steals and oppresses while pretending to be administering justice" (by erecting a *bemah*, a platform for the

---

27. Trans. Danby 1933, 450 (slightly modified).
28. Genesis Rabbah 9:13, ed. Theodor and Albeck, 73–74.
29. Genesis Rabbah 49:9, ed. Theodor and Albeck, 510–511. See de Lange 1978, 275.

tribunal).[30] In a similar vein, another fifth-century midrash, Leviticus Rabbah, identifies Rome with the pig, an animal that seems to be pure but is not:

> Just as the pig when it lies down puts forth its hooves [one of the criteria for a mammal to be considered pure, or kosher] as if to say, "See that I am pure," so too does this wicked kingdom [Rome] boast as it commits violence and robbery while looking as if it were establishing a tribunal [bemah]. This may be compared to a governor in Caesarea who was sentencing to death the thieves, adulterers, and sorcerers. He said to [one of] his counsellors [speaking about himself]: "This man did these three [things] in one night."[31]

These passages sharply criticize Roman courts and legal actors, which pretend to exercise justice but in fact hide their criminal behavior behind the appearance of legality and so offer a mere parody of justice.[32]

In addition, in earlier rabbinic works we encounter a rejection of the way that capital punishment was staged. Mishnah Avodah Zarah 7:1 forbids Jews to take part in the construction of any basilica, gradus (platform), stadium, or tribunal (bemah), implying that the places where Roman legal activities were performed were places of bloodshed and that executions of people were staged as a spectacle.[33] As a matter of fact, in the Roman empire, convicted criminals of low status were often killed in the arena, whether through damnatio ad bestias (being torn by wild beasts), burning, or crucifixion.[34] According to Donald J. Kyle, the ritualization of penal sanctions in the form of public spectacle aimed to reinforce political and social cohesion.[35] The rabbis condemned the cruelty involved in these modes of punishment, just as Christians did, but both groups occasionally envisioned divine retribution against their oppressors in a similar way.[36]

---

30. Genesis Rabbah 65:1, ed. Theodor and Albeck, 713.

31. Leviticus Rabbah 13:5, ed. Margulies, 291–292.

32. On the way Roman courts (identified with Esau) were perceived as forcing people into confessing crimes they had not committed, see Gen. Rabbah 37:2, 63:10. On the negative depiction of Roman courts and trials and the perception of Roman judges as cruel and corrupted, see Lieberman 1944, 24–26; Aminoff 1981, 3:285; Goodman 1983, 166; Hadas-Lebel 1990, 356–357.

33. Lieberman 1944, 13; Sperber 1984, 76–78; Vismara 1991; Hayes 1995; Kyle 1998, 53, 55; Lapin 2012, 130.

34. Garnsey 1970, 104.

35. Kyle 1998, 265–266.

36. Kyle notes that "Christians sought and even delighted in revenge against their persecutors along remarkably Roman lines of vengeance and punishment, and later Christian methods of punishing heretics owe much to Roman legal precursors" (Kyle 1998, 268). Stratton 2009 highlights allusions to the Roman arena in rabbinic descriptions of God's eschatological judgment, arguing that "these references constitute forms of colonial mimicry, which ambivalently appropriate Roman symbols of power for their own self fashioning" (45).

1.2 THE CONCRETE DIMENSION OF THE CHALLENGE

The Romans did not attempt to impose their laws on the populations they had conquered. As John Richardson notes,

> The history of the development of Roman law in the provinces is not one of systematic exportation of one pattern of law to replace others, undertaken by an imperial power anxious to impose uniformity on its subjects. Still less does it seem to be the adoption by non-Romans of a set of laws seen as intrinsically superior to their own.[37]

As a matter of principle, decisions on matter of penal law were the privilege of imperial authorities, while in the realm of private law, local rules continued to apply and local courts to pass sentences.[38] Yet one must differentiate between the western and the eastern parts of the empire. Whereas Roman law spread rapidly in the West, where legal written traditions were apparently not well developed, in the East it coexisted with ancient legal traditions of various kinds. In the eastern empire, many different legal statuses existed: in free cities, for example, citizens continued to use their own laws and courts. There were also *poleis* that were placed under the governor's judicial power, with a division of jurisdiction between Roman and local civic authorities.[39] The Greek *poleis* in Egypt were an interesting exception: from the beginning of the Roman period, they were deprived of autonomous jurisdictional institutions. Notwithstanding this particular case, Gaius' statement that each people has its own *ius civile* (*Inst.* 1.1) primarily applied to the Greek *poleis*, which were considered *civitates*. Yet the East also had *gentes* and *nationes* living in cities and villages that the Romans did not consider civic entities. These groups could have written as well as unwritten laws, local courts, and other modes of social regulation—through a council of elders, for example.[40] But whatever their exact status and legal tradition, it is certain that the provincial communities, through administrative and legal mechanisms of various sorts, came increasingly in contact with Roman law and were progressively impacted by it.[41]

Already at the time of the Republic, when Roman *ius civile* was in principle restricted to Roman citizens, *peregrini* could and did have access to

---

37. Richardson 2015, 56. See also Fournier 2010, 593–595.

38. Concerning the permanence of local courts, Egypt is an exception. As José Luis Alonso notes, "In Egypt, this survival of the local legal traditions did not result from the preservation of autonomous peregrine courts. As far as our sources let us see, in fact, there was in the province no alternative to the Roman jurisdiction" (Alonso 2016, 352).

39. Lintott 1993, 54–65, 129–148.

40. Concerning the contrast, from a Roman perspective, between *civitates* and *gentes*, as well as their respective laws, see Mélèze Modrzejewski 2014, 244–248. On the various statuses of individuals and communities within the empire, see Jacques and Scheid 1990, 209–289.

41. Ando 2000, 117–130, 363–364.

Roman civil law in certain cases, because Roman jurists created legal fictions that made it possible to assimilate *peregrini* to Roman citizens. Roman civil law therefore became "an instrument of empire" from very early on.[42]

Furthermore, from Augustus onward a reorganization of the system made access to Roman courts possible not only on the basis of Roman citizenship or through a legal fiction, but also because of the nature of the case—for example, in financial disputes that involved a considerable sum.[43] Anna Dolganov argues that the comparison of Roman legal sources with papyrological evidence for Roman jurisdiction in Egypt makes clear that in certain cases, before 212, "Roman rules and remedies were dispensed by Roman courts to provincials regardless of their civic status."[44] Moreover, provincials were aware of this possibility. In 186 CE, a woman named Dionysia, certainly helped by legal advisers, brought a lawsuit against her father, Chaeremon, who wanted to cancel her marriage on the basis of local legal traditions. She won the case by referring to previous Roman judgments, based on Roman legal norms rather than "the laws of the Egyptians" (which in this case referred to Greek legal norms rather than Egyptian ones, according to Joseph Mélèze Modrzejewski).[45]

That provincials who were not Roman citizens knew about Roman legal forms, sentences, and venues is also shown by the archives of Babatha, a Jewish woman living near the Dead Sea in the province of Arabia in the first half of the second century CE. Her personal documents included three Greek copies of the *formula* of the Roman *actio tutelae* (concerning the duties of the guardian of a child under wardship), which she apparently intended to use, or was advised to use, in a lawsuit at the Roman governor's court.[46]

Ari Bryen notes that "the ideology of the Roman legal system in the provinces was that fundamentally it was a system which could be accessible to all free individuals."[47] The reality on the ground was of course more complex, with access to the governor and other Roman officials depending on one's social status, personal connections, and wealth.[48] However, provincials of various backgrounds and statuses did indeed turn to Roman jurisdictions. Governors regularly toured their provinces to judge cases brought to them by provincials,

---

42. Ando 2011, ix (quotation), 6–11; Ando 2016b, 286–288.

43. Fournier 2010; Hurlet 2011, 132–133; Hurlet 2019, 125–127.

44. Dolganov 2019, 47.

45. P. Oxy. II, 237; Mélèze Modrzejewski 2014, 259–262. On Dionysia's case, see also Kreuzsaler and Urbanik 2008, 130–142; Bryen 2017. On the role of legal advisers and access to official documents in the provinces more broadly, see Kantor 2009, 262–263.

46. P. Yadin 28–30; Cotton 1993; Harries 2010, 95–98; Czajowski 2017, 93–105.

47. Bryen 2008, 200 (and 183).

48. Financial aspects mattered; see Harries 2010, 98: "The choice of courts and adjudicators, therefore, was a wide one—wider perhaps for those with money who could afford the pressures of possibly long drawn-out litigation in the Roman courts."

and a papyrus from 209 CE records that in Egypt, the Roman prefect Subatianus Aquila had to deal with more than 1,800 petitions from the Arsinoite nome during a single *conventus*.[49] The governors' assizes functioned as venues where legal rituals were performed and the notion of Roman law and justice became highly visible.[50] In the end, as Bryen further comments,

> one of the most immediate consequences of Roman rule was that, despite the professed desire of the Romans to preserve local laws and institutions, there was an increasing number of venues and jurisdictions in which cases could be judged, and a tendency for provincials of varying status to try to access venues monopolized by Roman power (such as the governor's assizes) to handle their complaints.[51]

In addition, as both Fergus Millar and Kaius Tuori have emphasized, another important aspect of the provincials' experience of the Roman legal system resided in appeals to the emperor, made in the conviction that the emperor was the supreme source of justice and that all could, at least in theory, appeal to him.[52] Imperial rescripts strengthened this conviction, as they showed that even commoners or small village communities could receive a response from the emperor. Some inscriptions document imperial visits that gave provincials exceptional opportunities to present their pleas.[53] Access to Roman jurisdiction was thus an important aspect not only of Roman imperial ideology but also of Roman imperial policy.

Already before 212 CE, the corollary of the spreading of Roman law and jurisdiction was thus their use by provincials, in a context of legal pluralism or multilegalism.[54] Some provincials turned to Roman courts rather than to local tribunals, from the start or in order to appeal a sentence passed at the local level. Litigation provided an opportunity to assess the respective values of the legal solutions offered by the different systems. Caroline Humfress has described this phenomenon as "forum shopping."[55]

Jill Harries rightly emphasizes that such use of the Roman legal system was not tantamount to political support for Rome.[56] In most cases opportun-

---

49. P. Yale 1.61; Humfress 2011, 39.

50. Ando 2000, 375–377, 408–410.

51. Bryen 2012, 775. On the ways that Roman law and legal actors coped with the provinces, forming a unified yet multilayered legal system, see Ando 2011, 19–36.

52. Millar 1977, 507–516; Tuori 2016; see also Ando 2000, 362–364; Edmonson 2015. On appeals to the emperor, see Aelius Aristides, *Roman Oration* 65, and the anecdote concerning Hadrian reported in Cassius Dio, *Rom. Hist.* 69.6.3.

53. Blanco-Pérez 2021.

54. Fournier 2010, Part III; Humfress 2013b and forthcoming; Ando 2016b.

55. Humfress 2013a. In other cases, provincials had to appear at Roman courts against their will—for example, those who were the subjects of criminal prosecution.

56. Harries 2010, 98.

ism motivated the choice of legal venue, as each person tried to find the legal framework that would best serve his or her needs. A lot of negotiation ensued, involving legal experts with good knowledge of both Roman and local law, and as a consequence, hybrid forms of law emerged. Through judicial practice, imperial authorities tended de facto to integrate some elements of local law into the provincial legal system, while interpreting these local norms in the light of Roman norms.[57] Provincials who turned to imperial authorities also tended to present their case, even when it was based on local laws, in the light of Roman legal principles that would appeal to Roman officials. (Dionysia's suit against her father mentioned above is telling in this respect.) Recent scholarly works underscore the role of provincials in legal doings. Far from being passive recipients of the Roman legal system, provincials are now seen to have played an active role in adapting to it, using Roman law to their own advantage when possible.[58] Bryen even defines the legal history of the Roman provinces as "the story of how the provincials and Romans collaborated in developing a shared and vibrant legal culture."[59]

In her book on the Babatha and Salome Komaise archives from the Judean desert, Kimberley Czajkowski acutely writes:

> Provincials [. . .] did not think in terms of 'systems' and picking between them, they thought in terms of authorities [. . .]: how to appeal to them, how to gain their favour and thus win their help with enforcement, or how to harness certain concepts of authority to lend weight to their documents and transactions.[60]

This remark draws our attention to the importance of authority at the juncture between the political and the legal. What is law without enforcement? In other words, even though local actors had their strategies and sometimes succeeded in using Roman jurisdiction in their own interests, we should not forget the power discrepancy underlying the encounter between the Roman legal system and the provincials, their laws, and their local instances of jurisdiction.

Caracalla's edict of 212 CE granting citizenship to nearly all the free inhabitants of the empire introduced a significant change to the lives of provincials: they were now of full legal status and could have Roman law applied to their cases.[61] This capacity, however, was not equivalent to an obligation. According to Caroline Humfress, "In reality, no state act obliged Roman citizens to use

57. See Dolganov 2019, 59: "The 'laws of the Egyptians' were manifestly interpreted by Roman administrators and legal practitioners through the lens of Roman legal concepts." See also the remarks of Ando 2016b, 290–291.

58. See Harries 2010, 98; Bryen 2012; Humfress 2013b; Czajkowski 2017.

59. Bryen 2012, 776.

60. Czajkowski 2017, 200.

61. Ando 2011, 27: "the landscape of actual legal relations remained fully as heterogenous as before, but the participants [in] those relations now had full and undeniable

Roman private law. Citizenship should be understood rather as an enabling mechanism offering access to the juridical procedures and remedies of the society at different levels."[62] Moreover, the change of individual status (from noncitizen to citizen) did not necessarily modify the status of communities, so at a local level local legislation usually remained in force.[63] In other words, the *Constitutio Antoniniana* did not eradicate local laws and jurisdictions.[64] Mélèze Modrzejewski has argued that local laws were integrated into the Roman legal system as "customary law," whose authority was inferior to that of classical Roman law but still very real.[65] He shows, however, that these provincial customs were sometimes rejected by Roman judges as contrary to Roman norms and then became illegal. For example, marriages between siblings and half-siblings were common in Egypt but prohibited by Roman law; after 212, probably as a consequence of the *Constitutio Antoniniana*, brother-sister marriages disappear from Egyptian documents.[66] In general, however, Roman judicial authorities tended toward leniency, flexibility, and accommodation. Over time, provincial customs sometimes even influenced Roman law, as shown by cases involving the right of women to be legal guardians and to adopt.[67] Imperial rescripts show instances of imperial law absorbing elements of local laws by adopting the local legal solutions advocated by litigants.

Although the *Constitutio Antoniniana* did not eradicate local legal norms, some scholars observe that there was a progressive erosion of local jurisdictions from the third century CE onward.[68] Claude Lepelley even writes of a radical leveling of law in the Roman world that began under Diocletian. The process took centuries, however, and may have finished only in Justinian's time.[69] Yet at the end of the third century or the beginning of the fourth, Menander of Laodicea noted that there was no more point in praising a city for its laws, "since we conduct public affairs by the common laws of

---

standing before the law in Roman courts." On the *Constitutio Antoniniana*, see also Chapter Five below.

62. Humfress 2013b, 80; see also Humfress 2011, 37.

63. Jacques and Scheid 1990, 235, 237, 281, 284; Carrié 2005, 274–275. See, e.g., the case of Aphrodisias, including Gordian III's rescript from 243 on its legal autonomy: Reynolds 1982, 136; Lepelley 2002, 843–844.

64. Contra Mitteis 1891 in particular.

65. Mélèze Modrzejewski 1970 and 2014; Nemo-Pekelman 2010, 64–66. José Luis Alonso contends that even before 212, Roman jurists and other legal actors recognized local customs as law, on the basis of the authority granted to tradition. He points to the lack of theoretical thought about custom among Roman jurists as an indication that the category of "customary law" was not available until at least the third century CE (Alonso 2016). For a perspective more focused on jurisprudence, see Humfress 2011.

66. Keenan, Manning, and Yiftach-Firanko 2014, 176–177.

67. Mélèze Modrzejewski 2014, 327–342.

68. Lepelley 2002; Fournier 2010, 10, 595.

69. Bryen 2012, 811.

the Romans." He then added: "Customs (*ēthē*) however vary from city to city, and form an appropriate basis of encomium."[70] Yet the exact nature of these customs, and their relationship to law, remains unclear. Another literary testimony probably to be dated to the third century, the Syriac *Book of the Laws of the Countries*, describes the Romans as divesting the inhabitants of 'Arab (in Osrhoene, an area turned into a Roman province in 216 CE) of their legal traditions and imposing their own laws. However, Nathanael Andrade notes that the corresponding passage in Rufinus' Latin translation of the *Clementine Recognitions*—whose literary relationship to the Syriac *Book of the Laws of the Countries* is not yet fully clarified—"departs from the testimony of the Syriac *Book* entirely" and "represents the Romans as benignly steering people to adopt their laws." Moreover, "it also depicts the peoples of the Roman empire as willingly submitting to Roman customs after the initial fact of conquest, with the result that diverse peoples characterized by their unique customs had adopted *ius Romanum*."[71]

These literary sources reflect the ideological perspectives of their authors, not the complex and varied reality on the ground, which are known to us from the papyri. On the whole, it nevertheless can be argued that from 212 onward, local laws became more tightly integrated into the imperial legal system, while the inhabitants of the provinces (most of whom had become formal Roman citizens) increasingly used Roman laws and legal procedures.[72] In themselves, these trends were not new, but they probably intensified at that time as a consequence of the wider access to imperial jurisdiction granted by the *Constitutio Antoniniana*.[73]

In view of this general judicial situation in the provinces of the Roman empire both before and after 212, let us now focus on the case of the Jews. The papyrological evidence from Egypt, the documents from the Judean desert, the New Testament, and rabbinic literature indicate that Jews turned to Roman authorities to settle some conflicts, just as other provincials did.[74] This phenomenon was apparently of special concern to the rabbis, who considered themselves experts in the Torah and placed the study and observance of the *mitzvot* at the core of Jewish life. They must have been keenly aware that no legal system can endure without actually being put into practice, and

---

70. Menander of Laodicea, *Treatise* 1.3.363, lines 11–14; trans. Russell and Wilson 1981, 67. See also Humfress 2011, 23; 2013b, 73.

71. Andrade 2020, 369, referring to *Clem. Recog.* 9.27.6–7.

72. Mélèze Modrzejewski 1970, esp. 368, and 2014, esp. 311–313; Coriat 1997, 410–415; Riggsby 2010, 221; Keenan, Manning, and Yiftach-Firanko 2014, 175–182 (on family law in Egypt).

73. On the way the *Constitutio Antoniniana* impacted various populations living within the empire, especially from a legal perspective, and facilitated the *ius civile*'s penetration of the provinces, see Mathisen 2006, 1014–1016; Ando 2016a, 23.

74. See, e.g., Cotton 2002; Tropper 2004, 190–191; Czajkowski 2017.

that it was thus a matter of survival for Jewish law to continue to be applied in one way or another. The first task, however, was to define what precisely comprised Jewish law. As Kimberley Czajkowski notes, "Jews could conduct their legal business exactly as gentiles could, and we should not expect or demand that they use—explicitly or implicitly—'Jewish law' in their business at all times. Indeed, what that term even means in this context is hugely problematic."[75] Different kinds of usages were considered normative by different groups of Jews. In the diaspora in particular, customs at variance with biblical law were in fairly wide use.[76] And Jewish papyri from Egypt occasionally mention as *patrioi nomoi* (ancestral laws) rules that correspond to laws in force in the Ptolemaic kingdom.[77] Local Jewish communities could thus diverge in the understandings of what traditional law was. Defining Jewish law and safegarding its implementation in the lives of at least some Jews was thus of crucial importance if it was to survive at all in the imperial legal context.[78]

Moreover, for the rabbis the application of Jewish law was also an issue of power, as their legitimacy and authority over fellow Jews stemmed at least in part from their legal knowledge and ability to settle disputes.[79] In Roman Palestine, we may assume that Jews had access to (depending on the nature of the case) arbitration by various intermediaries; city or village courts, which may have been Jewish—but not necessarily rabbinic—in places where the population was predominantly Jewish; and the governor's assizes (complemented by access to lower officials).[80] Hannah Cotton has observed that the Greek documents in the Babatha archives from the Judean desert mention only the governor's court, whereas the documents in Aramaic mention no court at all.[81] On the other hand, rabbinic literature repeatedly refers to local courts, and as Cotton writes in another publication, "It would be absurd to claim that the Roman government took it upon itself to deal with all civil cases in the province of Judaea/Syria Palaestina."[82] These local courts, however, may have been

---

75. Czajkowski 2017, 204.

76. Mélèze Modrzejewski 1995, 112–119 (concerning Jews in Egypt in the Hellenistic period); Mélèze Modrzejewski 2011, 255–260 (on a divorce at the beginning of the Roman period; see *CPJ* II, no. 144 = *BGU* IV 1102).

77. See P. Polit. Iud. 9, line 29, from Herakleopolis (132 BCE); Cowey and Maresh 2001, 103–111, at 105; Honigman 2003, 97. P. Polit. Iud. 9 also refers to an "ancestral oath" (*patrios horkos*) (1.8), and a similar notion appears in no. 3, line 29 and no. 12, line 10.

78. Daube 1944, 359, thus emphasizes the importance of the rabbinic creation of a code of private law in the Roman context.

79. Hezser 1997, 450–466.

80. Cf. Linder 2006, 135–136.

81. Cotton 2002, 19. See also Cotton and Eck 2005b.

82. Cotton 1999, 231.

"no more than forms of private arbitration, not backed by [. . .] the Roman authorities."[83]

The extent to which the rabbis exercised judicial power over their fellow Jews has been and remains a matter of debate, although few scholars today would go so far as to attribute full judicial power to them.[84] It is in fact crucial to distinguish between the period of the tannaim, up to roughly 212, and the period of the third and fourth centuries, post–*Constitutio Antoniniana*. Martin Goodman has argued that during the tannaitic period at least, rabbis were at best arbitrators, and that it is impossible to speak of a conflict between rabbinic and Roman jurisdictions at that time.[85] The tensions alluded to in rabbinic sources pertain to local (Jewish but non-rabbinic) village and city courts.[86] During the third and fourth centuries, however, the rabbis may have enjoyed a more significant role, maybe thanks to the support of the patriarchs.[87]

To understand the roles of the rabbis as judges, arbitrators, or advisers, it is necessary to look at the nature of the cases in which they were involved. Admittedly, rabbinic texts cannot be taken at face value, as if they conveyed a straightforward account of what was happening in Palestinian cities and villages. However, they do provide some information on both the activity of the rabbis in settling disputes between Jews and the limits of the former's power.

Most of the issues discussed in rabbinic literature would have been of no concern to imperial authorities.[88] This is vividly illustrated in a passage from the Book of Acts in the New Testament, even though it pertains to an earlier period and a different context. During Paul's stay in Corinth, his Jewish adversaries brought him to the Roman proconsul of Achaia, Gallio, and accused him of "persuading people to worship God in ways that are contrary to the law." But the proconsul was indifferent:

83. Cotton 2002, 20.

84. The degree of influence enjoyed by the rabbis among their fellow Jews, on the one hand, and their judicial power, on the other, may be considered two distinct but correlated issues. The trend in recent scholarship has been to recognize that the rabbis' influence was minimal during the tannaitic period and slowly grew from the third century onward. Whether they ever enjoyed real judicial power, however, is difficult to state. See Chajes 1899; Goodman 1983; Hezser 1997; Cohen 1999b; Schwartz 2001, esp. 120; Oppenheimer 2005a; Linder 2006, 136; Lapin 2010 and 2012; Dohrmann 2013, 64; Brody 2017; Hayes 2017d, 77–78; Furstenberg 2018.

85. Whatever the actual extent of the rabbis' jurisdiction, the fact remains that *from their perspective*, Roman law could conflict with the laws of the Torah. On the sense of rivalry between Jewish and Roman law and jurisdiction in rabbinic literature, see § 3 below.

86. Goodman 1983, 155–171. See also Hezser 1997, 475–480.

87. On the relations between the rabbis and the patriarchs, and the connections of both to Roman officials, see Jacobs 1995, 124–205; Hezser 1997, 405–449.

88. Harries 2010, 91.

14 Just as Paul was about to speak, Gallio said to the Jews, "If it were a matter of crime or serious villainy, I would be justified in accepting the complaint of you Jews; 15 but since it is a matter of questions about words and names and your own law, see to it yourselves; I do not wish to be a judge of these matters." 16 And he dismissed them from the tribunal. 17 Then all of them seized Sosthenes, the official of the synagogue, and beat him in front of the tribunal. But Gallio paid no attention to any of these things.[89]

Only a criminal case or a very serious financial one would have justified the intervention of the proconsul, in line with Roman policy in the provinces during the first century CE. (The fact that Paul was a Roman citizen could have motivated Gallio to intervene, but in this episode Paul does not seem to have mentioned his status.) More generally, it seems that the Romans considered many aspects of Jewish law as internal Jewish affairs. There is evidence in late imperial legal compilations that this view persisted up to that date.[90]

As for rabbinic literature, Hayim Lapin has analyzed 197 cases adjudicated by rabbis in Palestinian rabbinic sources.[91] This survey shows that in the tannaitic period, most issues settled by rabbis related to purity, vows, and other halakhic matters that they interpreted in a particular way. Only 33 percent of the cases had to do with issues of property or family. Lapin argues that "tannaitic cases may thus serve as an index of critical areas of rabbinic piety at a particular moment, rather than rabbis' reach to outsiders." Moreover, it seems that the plaintiffs were agreeable to the religious views of the rabbis and that "even at the level of implied claimants, the cases judged presuppose voluntary arbitration."[92] By contrast, cases brought to amoraic sages show an evolution: Issues of property and status double in comparison to the tannaitic period, representing nearly 77 percent of the cases heard by the Palestinian amoraim. Only three cases deal with purity concerns. Lapin concludes:

> Rabbis claimed to and may well have expanded their activity and their reach in the third and fourth centuries. We have no direct way of measuring how far rabbinic influence extended, but the expansion of property and related issues in rabbinic judging may well be an index of the

89. See Acts 18:12–17.

90. See C.Th. 16.8.8 (17 April 392), concerning a lawsuit by Jews whom the patriarch had excommunicated. The imperial decision was to not interfere. See Linder 1987, 186–187, no. 20; Harries 2010, 92. Matrimonial issues, however, were not considered a purely internal affair: an imperial constitution dated to December 30, 393 (C.Iust. 1.9.7), forbids Jews to marry "according to their law," maybe an allusion to polygamy. See Linder 1987, 191–193, no. 22; Nemo-Pekelman 2010, 60–64; Nemo-Pekelman 2014.

91. See also a previous study of this kind: Cohen 1999b, 962–969, 980–987.

92. Lapin 2010, 263–265.

weakness of the Roman imperial state and the practical necessity, even institutionalization, of arbitration by its subjects.[93]

The question remains of whether institutionalized arbitration amounted to full judicial power. The problem with arbitration is that it relies on the voluntary commitment of the litigants and lacks the means to enforce the arbitrator's decision. Seth Schwartz emphasizes that "no one was compelled to accept rabbinic judgment. The rabbis could threaten, plead, and cajole but could not subpoena or impose a sentence. Only the Roman governor and his agents had such authority."[94] Rabbinic literature itself suggests that enforcement was problematic. A passage in the Mishnah declares that a bill of divorce given under compulsion by a Roman court—literally "gentiles"—is not valid unless it enforces the sentence of a Jewish (that is, rabbinic) court.[95] This ambiguous position reveals that rabbinic decisions, even in matters of civil law pertaining to personal status, might require the intervention of a Roman tribunal for their enforcement. The latter could also overturn a sentence passed by the rabbis. The Jerusalem Talmud tells the story of a woman called Tamar, who was sentenced to an unspecified punishment by what seems to have been a Galilean rabbinic court and appealed the decision to the governor of the province.[96] This greatly upset the rabbis, who turned to Rabbi Abbahu (the head of the Jewish community in Caesarea, who had connections with Roman officials) to plead their case before the governor.[97] Again, this story, no matter whether

93. Lapin 2010, 272. Cf. Schwartz 2001, 120: "The Palestinian Talmud itself, interested though it is in playing up rabbinic authority, never describes the rabbis as possessing jurisdiction in the technical sense." Harries 2010, 91: "In Roman terms, therefore, rabbis were 'arbitrators' of small disputes and therefore of no concern to the ruling power." On arbitration in rabbinic writings, see Dohrmann 2003 and 2021.

94. Schwartz 2001, 120. For the opposite perspective, at least concerning the third and fourth centuries, see Nemo-Pekelman 2014. The Theodosian Code (C.Th. 2.1.10, dated to 3 February 398; Linder 1987, 204–211, no. 28) specifies that in civil cases and by formal agreement (*compromissum*) between the parties, resort could be made to Jewish judges or patriarchs "as if before arbitrators." Jill Harries comments: "A crucial difference between patriarchal jurisdiction in the fourth century, as envisaged in this law, and the rabbinic arbitration model suggested above was that at that time the patriarchs could summon the Roman authorities to enforce their decisions, 'as if such arbitration had been assigned by the decision of a (Roman) judge'. But this enhanced patriarchal jurisdiction was short-lived: after the patriarch Gamaliel had fallen foul of the Roman authorities in 415 CE, his powers of jurisdiction were removed along with his honorary Roman rank (C.Th. 16.8.22), and by 429 CE the patriarchate was no more (C.Th. 16.8.29)" (Harries 2010, 92). In C.Iust. 1.9.8, which repeats the principle formulated in C.Th. 2.1.10, there is no reference to the patriarchs any more, only to "the Jews" (meaning Jewish arbitrators).

95. m. Gittin 9:8; cf. t. Yevamot 12:13; see Section 3 below.

96. y. Megillah 3:2 (3:1 in Ma'agarim), 74a. See Oppenheimer 2005a, 179; Harries 2010, 92; Lapin 2010, 273.

97. On R. Abbahu, see Lapin 2010, 273; Niehoff 2019. Niehoff notes that actually, according to the talmudic narrative, Rabbi Abbahu did not turn to the governor, and

fanciful or real, affords insight into the jurisdictional hierarchy. As Lapin aptly notes, it reveals the precariousness and rather informal nature of rabbinic jurisdiction.[98]

Roman law and tribunals thus represented both an ideological and a practical challenge for ancient Jews, particularly for the rabbis. Although rabbinic literature sharply criticizes Roman judicial power, the fact that the rabbis aimed to exercise jurisdiction in at least some respects led them to elaborate strategies of accommodation.[99] Indeed, recent research shows that the rabbis even appropriated certain Roman legal principles, and that the empire's legal culture thus left an enduring legacy in rabbinic legal thinking, as we shall now see.

2. Rabbinic and Roman Law: A Partly Shared Legal Culture?

The question of the relationship between Roman and rabbinic law, including whether the former influenced the latter—or, to formulate it differently, whether rabbinic halakhah adopted and transformed some aspects of Roman legal culture—has been debated since at least the beginning of the nineteenth century.[100] Until recently most scholars cautiously rejected the idea that Roman law influenced rabbinic halakhah, at either the level of the principles and tools associated with legal reasoning or in the laws themselves.[101] Boaz Cohen, for example, was ready to consider the possibility of Roman law's influence on rabbinic legal thinking (as well as the reverse scenario, Jewish influence on Roman law) but warned:

> Before presupposing influence, we should first endeavor to eliminate every possibility of independent parallel development by finding out whether or not, similar economic, social, political or ethical factors and

---

instead tried to bribe Tamar's lawyers (304–305). In view of this text and other rabbinic traditions involving R. Abbahu, Niehoff convincingly argues that he was in fact "a prominent negotiator of Halacha and Roman law" (307) and that he adopted some Roman legal principles, such as "the Roman notion of betrothal as a separate, preliminary act, which does not yet imply any marital obligations" (310).

98. Lapin 2010, 273.

99. See in particular Furstenberg 2018.

100. For the history of research in this field, see Cohen 1944, 269–280; Hezser 2003a, 1–13. Among the main contributors are Alexander Gulak (the first to take into account the legal papyri from Egypt), Boaz Cohen, David Daube, Reuven Yaron, and Bernard Jackson. For recent work by a new generation of scholars, see the discussion below.

101. See in particular Jackson 1975, 22; Katzoff 2003, 286: "I have not yet seen a single convincing argument for any particular instance of reception of Roman law into Jewish law"; Hezser 2003a, 13; Hezser 2007. In the past, the legitimacy and the utility of the comparison were questioned, but this is hardly the case anymore; see Cohen 1944, 409–410.

motives did not supervene to precipitate the same rule. It is further necessary to establish by a historical study of the origin and development of the law, whether the given rule under consideration, is a logical development of its earlier phase, and is in keeping with its spirit and purpose, or whether it represents such a novelty and departure as to excite suspicion of being an alien intrusion.[102]

Admittedly, some similarities between Roman and rabbinic laws are very general in nature and may indeed be explained as parallel responses to comparable needs in Roman and Jewish societies or as parallel developments stemming from a common legal-cultural background that combined Near Eastern, Greek, and Roman elements.[103] Catherine Hezser has repeatedly emphasized this point in her publications on Roman and rabbinic law.[104] For example, she argues that because slaves were considered to be both chattel and human beings not only in both the Roman and the rabbinic legal systems but also in other cultural contexts, this convergence does not need to be explained as influence of the Roman legal worldview on the Jewish one.[105] She also argues that it may be difficult, especially from the third century CE onward, to determine the precise origin of a given legal rule or idea, since by then it was part of a common legal culture.[106] This raises the question of intent. That the rabbis adopted Roman legal principles nearly unconsciously, by a kind of osmosis, seems a rather doubtful scenario, in view of the elevated self-consciousness involved in the rabbinic project of codifying and developing Jewish law. Particularly in cases where the Roman and rabbinic legal corpora share a specificity that is not found in Greek or Near Eastern legal traditions, it is difficult to rule out Roman influence on the rabbis—or, to use less contentious phrasing, the possibility that rabbis adopted Roman notions and adapted them to their own legal system.

Without denying the importance of Greek and Near Eastern elements in the legal culture of Rome's eastern provinces, the fact remains that Roman law—available in Latin, and maybe also in Greek translations—was the dominant system at the time of the elaboration of the Mishnah and the Tosefta. It is a power relationship difficult to overlook. Legal anthropologists have noted the tendency of minority groups to adopt features of the dominant legal system, emphasizing that appropriation goes together with adaptation and

102. Cohen 1944, 416–417.

103. See Tropper 2004, 194 (and also 196), which speaks of a "shared socio-political and intellectual climate"; Simon-Shoshan 2012, 81–82. On the impact of Hellenistic law on rabbinic law, see in particular Gulak 1935; Yaron 1960 (which completely rejects the hypothesis of Roman influence on rabbinic inheritance law).

104. Hezser 1998; 2003a, 10–11; 2007, 144.

105. Hezser 2007, 153.

106. Hezser 2021, 304–305.

transformation.[107] This observation should not be dismissed in the case of the rabbis simply because their project differed in significant ways from that of the Roman jurists—or worse, because of some kind of cultural essentialism. The very fact of Roman jurisdiction in Judea/Palestine makes it reasonable to assume a certain degree of knowledge of Roman law and procedures among Jews, as already exemplified in documents from the Judean desert dating to the beginning of the second century CE.[108] Bernard Jackson acutely remarks that this point is relevant "to the problem of Roman influence on the *content* of Jewish law," whereas the pressure that Roman jurisdiction may have exerted on those responsible for the development of Jewish law—because of its power of attraction for Jews and its ability to override the Jewish courts—"is likely to prove significant primarily as one of the factors influencing its *form*."[109] One should therefore expect to find Roman influence in both content and form.

Hezser understands "influence" as involving direct knowledge of written sources and characterizes the search for such cases of literary influence as "positivistic."[110] However, this is a matter of definition, and, as the general introduction to this book emphasizes, it is possible to conceive of influence differently, as a phenomenon that involves not only written documents but also oral exchange and social interaction, especially in business and legal matters pertaining to daily life, such as property issues, land lease, and sale contracts. In a recent article, Hezser does take into account these kinds of exchange, as well as the possibility that wealthy Jews, including the patriarchs, used Greek legal advisers familiar with Roman law. While still refraining from using the terms "influence" and "impact" (which she finds imprecise) and from supposing that the rabbis had direct knowledge of Roman written legal codes, she writes that "we should reckon with various degrees of knowledge and adaptation of Roman law among Jews in Roman Palestine," and she acknowledges that "rabbis may have adapted and integrated Roman legal rules," among other strategies.[111]

In several of her studies, Hezser has in fact highlighted numerous suggestive similarities between Roman and rabbinic law, between the legal worldviews of the two systems, and between the roles of Roman jurists and rabbis in their respective societies.[112] In the recent article mentioned above,

---

107. See, e.g., the special issue of the *Journal of Legal Pluralism* (n°53–54, 2006) on *Dynamics of Change and Continuity in Plural Legal Orders*, edited by Franz and Keebet von Benda-Beckmann. They also note that transformation processes are not uni-directional (9).

108. See, e.g., Czajkowski 2015. On the diffusion in the East of knowledge of Roman law already at the end of the first century CE, see Jones 2007. See also Tropper 2004, 191, 207.

109. Jackson 1981, 159.

110. Hezser 2003a, 5, 10–11; 2021, 303–304.

111. Hezser 2021, 311.

112. Hezser 1998, 2003b, 2007, and 2021. See also Tropper 2004, 189–207 (on tractate Avot and Roman legal culture).

she provides examples of the rabbis' knowledge and adoption of Roman legal principles in business matters. First, she considers the case of shipping law governing jettison—that is, the rules that applied when merchandise had to be thrown overboard during a tempest to keep the ship and its passengers safe. According to the *Digest* (14.2.1–2), what had been lost for the benefit of all had to be made up by the contribution of all, but the amount of the loss had to be proportional to the value of the property belonging to and rescued by each passenger—the value of the lives of freemen not included. Tosefta Bava Metziʻa 7:14 seems to echo this ruling, stating that in such circumstances "they reckon [the damage to be paid] in accordance with the load [the value of the shipped goods]" but not in accordance with (the value of) the lives of the passengers. The Tosefta adds that "they do not differ from the custom of the ship (*minhag ha-sfinah*)," which may be an allusion to Roman usage, which the rabbis would have known through hearsay and practice. In any case, there is no rule concerning shipping and jettison in biblical or Jewish legal traditions of the Second Temple period. Hezser perceptively notes that the presentation of this ruling in y. Bava Qamma 6:4, 5c, which specifies that each passenger will have to pay in proportion to the value (*mamon*) of his or her share of the goods that were saved, is more precise than the wording of the Tosefta and may indicate a greater familiarity with Roman law among the rabbis at the time of the elaboration of the Yerushalmi.[113]

The second example that Hezser brings forward concerns the legal notion of *peculium*, the amount of money granted by a father or a master to a son under his *patria potestas* or to a slave, which the latter could use relatively freely, "to develop independent business activity in the interest of the family group and its head."[114] Although the term *peculium* is not found in rabbinic literature, the Tosefta here again seems to echo the Roman ruling: "The son who does business with what belongs to his father, and likewise the slave who does business with what belongs to his master, behold, they [the proceeds] belong to the father; behold, they belong to the master" (t. Bava Qamma 11:2).[115] Biblical law and Jewish legal texts of the Second Temple period never consider such a possibility, nor do they draw a parallel between the case of a son and that of a slave. Therefore, it seems that once more the Tosefta testifies to the adoption of a Roman legal tool. Yet, as in the preceding example, it does not display detailed knowledge of the complexity of Roman law.

Hezser believes the adoption of Roman legal principles by the rabbis to be less likely in the private sphere, while conceding that "even in family law and the law of personal status, adjustments to Roman law are possible."[116] As an

113. Hezser 2021, 314. Translation of the Tosefta by Hezser.
114. Berger 1991, 624.
115. Translation by Hezser in Hezser 2021, 315.
116. Hezser 2021, 312.

example of rabbinic "resistance" to Roman family law, she considers the issue of married women's right to manage their own property. In Roman law, marriages could be *in* or *cum manu*, which meant that the husband had full control over his wife's property, or *sine manu*, in which case the wife retained the right to use her goods as she wished.[117] From the end of the first century BCE, the tendency among Roman citizens was clearly toward marriages *sine manu*. Rabbinic law, by contrast, maintained the principle that it was the husband who controlled his wife's property, while garanteeing, through the *ketubbah*, the woman's rights in the event of divorce. In this case, the rabbinic rulings clearly differed from contemporary Roman norms. A Roman perspective likely would deem the rabbis' position conservative and old-fashioned. From 212 CE onward, free Jewish women—those able to enter into a *conubium*, or, in Jewish terms, *qiddushin*—were Roman citizens and thus able to contract a marriage according to Roman law, even though a citizen woman's ability to choose a husband must have been limited to those of high social standing. The possibility that Jewish women could turn to a Roman court after 212 to have Roman law applied to a marriage initially contracted according to rabbinic norms is not to be discounted either. In any event, it seems likely that the *Constitutio Antoniniana* increased concern among the rabbis over Roman laws pertaining to family and personal status, which were now relevant to all Jews who had received Roman citizenship.

Several studies have in fact found in rabbinic literature instances of the adoption and adaptation of Roman legal principles in the realms of family law and personal status.[118] One of the most famous is m. Qiddushin 3:12, which discusses the status of children born from four types of unions: (1) if the marriage is valid and sinless, the child is granted the status of the father; (2) if the marriage is valid but sinful—that is, it does not respect the prohibitions found in Jewish law, for example concerning the union of a high priest and a divorcée—the child is granted the status of the parent who is considered inferior (for instance, an Israelite is inferior to a priest, and a *mamzer*, a "bastard," is inferior to an Israelite); (3) if the mother is unable to contract a legal marriage with the father but can contract a legal marriage with other men, the child is a *mamzer*; (4) if the mother is unable to contract a legal marriage with either the father or other men, the child is granted her status.[119] According to the Mishnah, the last category refers to children born of the union between an Israelite man and a gentile or a slave; such a child would be considered a slave

117. Treggiari 1991, 16–36.
118. In addition to the example of m. Qiddushin 3:12 below, see Furstenberg 2019b (pertaining to social and legal aspects of the divorce procedure). See also Niehoff 2019 on R. Abbahu's understanding of the *symphon*, which "echoes Roman notions of betrothal" (309); and Milgram 2019 on tannaitic inheritance laws (esp. 34, Chapter 1, 202–217).
119. Cohen 1946–1947; Cohen 1999a, 263–307; Hayes 2002a, 182, 184; Hayes 2002b; Katzoff 2003; Hezser 2005, 197–201; Furstenberg 2019a, 183–186.

if the mother is a slave, and a non-Jew if the mother is a free gentile, because from the perspective of the rabbis, non-Jews were not able to contract a legal marriage in the Jewish sense. This raises questions concerning the child born of the union between an Israelite woman and a slave, who in theory should be considered a *mamzer* if the woman is able to contract a legal marriage with another man but an Israelite if she is not. This paradoxical application of the mishnaic ruling sparked quite a lot of debate among the rabbis.[120] In the end, the matrilineal principle prevailed in such cases, leading to the general rule that a child born of a Jewish mother and a non-Jewish father (freeman or slave) receives the mother's status.[121] One finds similar principles in Roman law, such as the notion that in the framework of a legal marriage the children have the status of the father, whereas in the absence of such a legal framework they receive the mother's status.[122] The *Lex Minicia*, of uncertain date but known to Gaius, later introduced a change declaring that the child born of a Roman mother and a peregrine father inherited his father's inferior status; after 212 CE, however, the implications of this restriction would have been minimal, as most free persons within the empire were by then Roman citizens. Most important, in Roman law as in the Mishnah, the overarching principle is that of legal capacity for marriage (*conubium, qiddushin*).[123]

On the basis of these similarities, Shaye Cohen has hypothesized that the appearance of the matrilineal principle in rabbinic Judaism was the result of the rabbis' adoption of Roman legal principles (although he gives consideration to other explanations as well).[124] Ranon Katzoff resists Cohen's suggestion because of the difference in substance between Roman and rabbinic laws.[125] But, as Yair Furstenberg argues, the main point that they have in common is their overarching principle of classification—which rests on the legal capacity of the parents—and if "the rabbis are not copying Roman legal practice but rather adopting Roman legal categories," the differences in the details of the laws become "negligible."[126]

Several additional cases of rabbis adopting Roman legal principles pertain to the realm of personal status, and especially "civic" status. It appears that

120. See, e.g., the anonymous opinion in t. Qiddushin 4:16, that the child of an Israelite woman and a gentile or a slave is a *mamzer*, and y. Qiddushin 3:12, 64c (3:14 in Schäfer and Becker 1991–2001 [1998, *Synopse* III], 418), which also records this opinion. See also Hezser 2003b, 147–148.

121. The emergence of the matrilineal principle in Judaism is a complex topic that is still debated nowadays. See, e.g., S. Cohen 1992, 25–26; Cohen 1999a, 263–307; Cohen 2005, 141–142.

122. *Tituli ex corpore Ulpiani* 5.3–8; cf. Gaius, *Inst.* 1.55–92.

123. Furstenberg 2019a, 184.

124. Cohen 1999a, 306.

125. Katzoff 2003.

126. Furstenberg 2019a, 185, note 7.

the rabbis to some extent conceived of membership in the people of Israel in terms of "citizenship" (I shall return to this issue at length in Chapter Five). Natalie Dohrmann has analyzed the similarities between rabbinic thinking about the manumission of slaves, which involves their accession not only to freedom but also to full participation in the community of Israel as Jews (albeit with the inferior status of freedman or freedwoman), and Roman laws concerning the manumission of slaves by Roman citizens, which allowed the slaves to become citizens themselves on the day of their manumission, provided it followed certain rules (though as *liberti* they remained second-class citizens). The connection between manumission and citizenship or membership—not to mention the status of freedperson itself—does not exist in pre-rabbinic Jewish law, and so reflects the absorption of Roman models by the rabbis.[127] In a similar vein, Yael Wilfand has compared Roman and rabbinic laws pertaining to the transmission of inheritance to the children of new citizens (converts, in a Jewish context) and shown that the way rabbinic halakhah severs the connection between a father to his children on the day that he converts—that is, on the day that he becomes a new "citizen" within the people of Israel—has parallels in Roman law (Gaius, *Institutes* 1.93–94, 3.19–20). She concludes that here as well, "The parallels between these two legal frameworks are too strong to be mere coincidence, especially since this subject has no biblical antecedent."[128] Another example is found in laws pertaining to captives. Orit Malka and Yakir Paz have dedicated two articles to this issue, specifically concerning the obligations of a husband toward his captive wife on the one hand and the property of prisoners held by enemies on the other. They argue that some rabbinic texts illustrate not merely a superficial borrowing of Roman rules but, more significantly, the adoption of the legal rationale underlying the Roman laws of captivity.[129] As stated above, it is tempting to consider the impact of Roman law on the rabbinic elaboration of *halakhot* relating to personal status—be it that of children, slaves, converts, or captives—as a partial consequence of the *Constitutio Antoniniana*: that is, of the change of status of the free Jews living within the empire, who became Roman citizens and were thus more exposed to Roman legal norms and definitions.[130] In some cases, however, Roman norms may have impacted rabbinic legal constructions even before Caracalla's edict.

127. Dohrmann 2008. Hezser already suggested a parallel between the status of the manumitted slave in a Roman context and that of the freedman in a Jewish context, but only in passing (Hezser 2003b, 134 [as a hypothesis]; Hezser 2005, 26, 28). On this issue, see also Chapter Five.

128. Wilfand 2021, 360.

129. Malka and Paz 2019 and 2021. According to Roman law, a captured person ceased to be a citizen, which implied the dissolution of all legal bonds, at least until his or her return from captivity. See further Chapter Five.

130. Some rabbinic texts on these issues might be seen as attempts to accommodate Jewish law to Roman legal definitions; see Furstenberg 2018 and 2021.

Finally, Leib Moscovitz's study of the use of legal fiction in Roman and rabbinic law offers another fascinating example of how rabbinic thinking integrated some aspects of Roman legal reasoning. He notes that "the shared and frequent use of fictions in Roman and rabbinic law is far more significant than the differences" between them and adds:

> Various scholars have pointed out that other ancient legal systems, such as ancient Near Eastern law, Greek and Hellenistic law, and pre-rabbinic Jewish law, are largely or totally devoid of legal fictions, in sharp contrast to Roman law and rabbinic law. The question accordingly arises: Why is legal fiction first (seriously) attested in Roman and rabbinic law? I cannot offer a conclusive answer to this question, although it seems almost impossible to believe that it is mere coincidence that fictions first developed prominently among the Romans and the Jews—"the two most legally minded peoples of Antiquity," in Boaz Cohen's famous words.[131]

Moscovitz cautiously refrains from speaking about an influence of Roman legal thinking on the rabbis. However, in view of the absence of legal fictions in pre-rabbinic Jewish law and the central role they played in Roman law from early on, it is methodologically sound to assume that the rabbis learned of and adopted this tool during their encounter with Roman law.[132] In Chapter Five we shall come back to this issue by examining the way the rabbis used a specific Roman legal fiction in relation to converts.

When one looks at the cumulative evidence, it is hard to reject the conclusion that the rabbis knew about and took inspiration from certain Roman legal principles, even though they never acknowledged such borrowings explicitly and probably encountered these legal notions in daily interactions or experiences at courts rather than through direct access to Roman legal texts.

Rabbinic literature can in fact be described as both idiosyncratic and very much in tune with Roman legal thinking. Some scholars choose to emphasize the idiosyncrasy—arguing that the Mishnah stands out starkly among provincial literary productions[133]—whereas others focus on the commonalities with Roman legal culture.[134] It is important, however, to take both aspects into account simultaneously, to point out the similarities but also to note the differences (indeed, this is the very essence of a comparative approach).

Nobody would deny that rabbinic literature, even if restricted to halakhah alone, differs sharply from Roman legal texts, in both content (including all kinds of cultic and purity laws, for example) and form (rabbinic discussions

---

131. Moscovitz 2003, 131, referring to Cohen 1966, 1:123.
132. On legal fictions in Roman law, see Ando 2011, chap 1.
133. Rosen-Zvi 2017b; Schwartz 2020.
134. Furstenberg 2018 and 2021.

of legal issues include anecdotes, moral teachings, and theological consider-ations that are not found in Roman legal codes). Rabbinic law is partly rooted in biblical texts and to some extent continues previous hermeneutical debates attested in documents of the Second Temple period, such as the legal texts from Qumran.[135] Scholars have become increasingly aware also of the central role played by conflicts of legal interpretation in the emergence of "sectarian-ism" in Second Temple Judean society. The rabbis' exegetical and legal activity undoubtedly originated in such a Jewish context.

Yet at the same time, the rabbinic project as a whole was novel. In Second Temple literature, one finds hardly anything like the legal codification embod-ied in the Mishnah and the Tosefta. In his treatise *On the Special Laws*, Philo classifies the commandments of the Mosaic law under the ten headings of the Decalogue, but his description hardly resembles the casuistic reasoning of the Roman jurists or the rabbis. The expansion of the realm of the law, the multiplication of rulings, and their extremely detailed character are striking in rabbinic halakhah. As Moshe Halbertal argues, law becomes an end to itself here: the rabbis ultimately build a portable sanctuary made of laws as an alter-native to the destroyed temple.[136] Dohrmann concludes that "rabbinic liter-ature represents a break from Jewish precedent precisely in its legality" and that this "in turn may tell us something about Romanization."[137] Furstenberg also identifies a "turn to law" in rabbinic texts but understands it as the result of the imposition of a foreign legal system, which catalyzed the transformation of local practices into a coherent and stable whole.[138]

In fact, scholars have interpreted rabbinic legalism in diverging ways. The phenomenon raises numerous questions: Was the creation of rabbinic hal-akhah a utopian project, or was it meant to enable Jewish law's application as customary law, especially in a post-212 context? Was it inward looking or an attempt at integration into Roman provincial law? Was it counterimperial, or does it show signs of accommodating the empire? Alternatively, does rabbinic halakhah embrace and express these divergent trends and perspectives all at once? If one answers this last question affirmatively, is this phenomenon to be explained as a consequence of the rabbis' diversity of opinions or as the result of a diachronic evolution from one model to another, from utopia to accommodation?

Some scholars argue that the rabbinic project was utopian to a large extent and represented a form of resistance to imperial domination, creating a fantasy

135. On the legal texts from Qumran, see in particular Shemesh 2009; Noam 2010; Fraade 2011a.

136. Halbertal 2013, 23. See also Hayes 2017d, 78. According to Brandes 2019, however, the Mishnah functioned primarily as an anthology of tannaitic literature, and it was only at a later stage that it was seen as an authoritative and binding legal code.

137. Dohrmann 2013, 63–64.

138. Furstenberg 2021, 276. See also Daube 1944.

of Jewish power that was both a response and an alternative to empire.[139] This view tends to be corroborated by several facts: rabbinic texts do not explicitly refer to Roman law, rabbinic teachings remained oral for a long time, this literature was composed in Hebrew and Aramaic in an elliptical style, and it dealt in great detail with cultic and purity issues that were impossible to put into practice after the destruction of the Temple.[140]

There are also scholars who defend the idea that rabbinic law represents an attempt to adapt to Roman jurisdiction, especially after 212 CE, when local laws became part of the Roman legal system in a more effective way. Jonathan S. Milgram thus writes in relation to tannaitic inheritance laws: "The rabbis ultimate desire may have also been to legislate, therefore, a law consonant with the legal idiom of their time and place."[141] Furstenberg goes one step further and argues that the rabbis tried to function as legal intermediaries between the Roman authorities and the Jews. He suggests that they acted like indigenous elites in modern colonial contexts and sees the Romans' incentivizing of the codification and alignment with Roman norms of the provincials' customary law as comparable to similar pressure put on natives in modern colonial situations. This would explain rabbinic attempts to make Jewish law conform to Roman standards in legal principles and reasoning, at least to a certain extent. According to Furstenberg, "the very formation of a local system of civil law was a direct result of the provincial situation, and it was intended to offer a viable option under Roman jurisdiction."[142] Rabbinic legalism was not a merely utopian project but instead a concrete attempt to transform Jewish legal traditions into a comprehensive legal system befitting the imperial legal landscape.

While some issues remain a matter of debate and further research needs to be done, it is clear nowadays that the rabbinic stance toward Roman jurisdiction cannot be reduced to resistance and opposition. It entailed a great deal of adoption and imitation as well, together with adaptation and creative reformulation. Moreover, individual rabbis held different positions.[143] Yet at the level of rabbinic discourse, it is the rhetoric of opposition that comes most clearly to the fore. I now turn to a closer examination of this rhetoric and what it reveals about self-representation and self-definition.

---

139. Lapin 2012; Rosen-Zvi 2017a and b; Schwartz 2020; Naiweld 2021. Dohrmann shares this view to a certain extent, yet she also emphasizes the ambivalence of the rabbinic position, the fact that the rabbis internalized some Roman norms and models while resisting them (see Dohrmann 2008, 2013, 2015, and 2021).

140. See, e.g., Dohrmann 2015, 199–200: "How did the rabbis think they fit into this world of ever encroaching imperial law, even as they were building a sprawling legal cosmos of their own? It is clear that on the whole, rabbinic laws simply ignore Roman law, implicitly allowing it no jurisdiction."

141. Milgram 2019, 217.

142. Furstenberg 2021, 271.

143. Niehoff 2019, esp. 312–313.

3. A Rivalry of Legal Systems: The Torah versus Roman Jurisdiction

Keeping in mind the historical, political, and legal context of the Jews as described in the preceding sections, we can now look at how Jewish works from the Roman period conceptualized opposition between Israel's Torah and the laws of the nations and what this may teach us about the Jews' potential sense of rivalry with the Romans in the legal realm. Let me emphasize again that this analysis does not undermine the possibility that in practice, the rabbis developed an accommodationist approach to Roman law and courts. Ideological discourses and sociopolitical strategies may differ, and individuals as well as groups may articulate differing and even contradictory views and goals. In order to understand the Jews'—and especially the rabbis'—stances toward Roman jurisdiction, we must assess as many aspects of their discourse and self-representation as possible. As far as rabbinic literature is concerned, the coexistence of a selective integration of Roman legal reasoning on the one hand and discourses of resistance and opposition on the other also has to do with the nature of the texts one looks at: whereas halakhic texts dealing with concrete legal issues may tacitly display a readiness to integrate Roman legal concepts, aggadic texts are less inclined to do so and tend to present an oppositional stance. This division, however, is neither rigid nor systematic, and, as we saw in the previous chapters, opposition does not preclude imitation. In some cases the former may even prompt the latter.[144]

To illustrate this point on aggadah and provide a first illustration within rabbinic literature of the sense of rivalry between Israel and Rome in the legal realm, let us consider the example of the midrash Genesis Rabbah. At least two passages put forward the idea that Jacob and Esau, respectively symbolizing Israel and Rome, both have their own laws and that these legal traditions represent an aspect of their rivalry.[145] The first one deals with Genesis 27:40, Isaac's blessing for Esau: "By your sword you shall live, and you shall serve your brother; but when you break loose, you shall break his yoke from your neck." The midrash comments:

> *And you shall serve your brother.* R. Huna said: "If [Jacob] deserves it, you will serve (*ta'avod*) him; if not, you will destroy (*teabbed*) [him]. *But when you break loose (tarid), [you shall break his yoke from your neck]*. He told him: "You have your own fairs (or: markets, *yeridim*), and he has his own fairs (*yeridim*); you have your own laws (or: customs, *nimosot*, from Greek *nomos*), and he has his own laws (*nimosot*)." R. Yose b. Ḥalafta said: "If you see your brother Jacob breaking

---

144. David Daube offers an example of this in the legal realm (Daube 1944, 365).
145. On Esau/Edom in Genesis Rabbah, see Morgenstern 2016.

the yoke of Torah from his neck, decree upon him persecutions [i.e., attempts at destruction], and you [will] rule over him."[146]

According to this passage, both R. Huna and R. Yose ben Ḥalafta present Esau/Rome as the agent of God's punishment of Israel if the latter does not remain faithful to the covenant and the Torah.[147] From this perspective, the "persecutions" (*shmad*, lit. "destruction," a term used in rabbinic literature in connection with the Bar Kokhba revolt in particular) are the consequence of Israel's negligence vis-à-vis the Torah's commandments, an interpretation that fits into the traditional Deuteronomistic explanation of the catastrophes that Israel experienced throughout its history. What is unusual is the affirmation, attributed to R. Huna, fictionally presented as addressing Esau, that "you have your own fairs and he [Jacob] has his own fairs; you have your own laws and he has his own laws." The first part of this statement puns on the similarity between the verb *tarid* ("to break loose, to err," from the root *r-w-d*), found in Genesis 27:40, and the word *yarid* (fair, market). The midrash then adds that Jacob and Esau—Israel and Rome—also both have their own *nimosot*, their own laws or customs, implying that they are distinct: Rome has its own laws, which somehow parallel and compete with those of Israel.[148] The following teaching by R. Yose shows that the underlying argument is that Israel should stick to their own laws (the Torah) and refrain from adopting those of Rome. Doing the latter would amount to rejecting the yoke of the Torah and would allow the Romans to punish Israel and rule over them. The curious expression "when you break loose" in Genesis 27:40 thus seems to be interpreted as an allusion to the particular ways of Esau/Rome, including its legal system, and to represent the main danger that threatens Israel (that it might adopt Esau/Rome's laws and in consequence fall under the domination of Esau).

Another passage from Genesis Rabbah that sheds light on the rabbinic perspective of a rivalry of legal systems between Israel and Rome relates to the interpretation of Genesis 25:22, the fight of the twin brothers in their mother's womb:

> The children struggled together (vayitrotzatzu) within her. [Discussion between] R. Yoḥanan and Resh Laqish. R. Yoḥanan said: "This one (*zeh*) runs [or: ran] to kill this one, and this one runs [or: ran] to kill this one." R. Shimeon ben Laqish said: "This one annuls (*mattir*) the commandments (*tzivuyim*) of this one, and this one annuls the commandments of this one."[149]

146. Gen. Rabbah 67:7, ed. Theodor and Albeck, 762–763.

147. According to rabbinic tradition, R. Yose ben Ḥalafta was a third-generation tanna; R. Huna may have been a fifth-generation tanna (beginning of the third century) or a fourth-generation amora (first half of the fourth century) who is said to have immigrated from Babylonia to the Land of Israel.

148. On the word *nimosot*—in an earlier midrash, Sifra—see Berkowitz 2012, 72, 91–92.

149. Gen. Rabbah 63:6, ed. Theodor and Albeck, 682.

After an additional comment by R. Berekhiah,[150] who emphasizes that Esau had already showed hostility toward Jacob in their mother's womb, the midrash reports an anonymous interpretation of "The children struggled together within her," which holds that when Rebecca passed by a place (lit. "a house") of idolatry, Esau struggled to come out of her womb, whereas when she passed by a synagogue or a *beit midrash*, it was Jacob who struggled to come out. Taken together, these interpretations of Genesis 25:22 depict a strong antagonism between Esau/Rome and Jacob/Israel that involved physical struggle, legal competition, and religious opposition. The discussion between R. Yoḥanan and Resh Laqish is particularly striking: R. Yoḥanan seems to interpret Genesis 25:22 in light of the future physical—that is, military—confrontation between Israel and Rome, whereas Resh Laqish emphasizes the clash between Esau/Rome and Jacob/Israel around the issue of law (lit. "commands" or "commandments"). Matthias Morgenstern interprets Resh Laqish's statement in connection with the Christian context in which the final redaction of Genesis Rabbah took place, arguing that Esau "(like Christianity) shares some kind of spiritual heritage with Judaism but has chosen to deny the binding nature of the prescriptions of the Hebrew Bible." However, Morgenstern quotes the midrash only partially, merely mentioning that "[Esau] will cancel the laws of his brother."[151] He does not explain why Resh Laqish presents both Rome and Israel as canceling the other's laws. This reciprocity—the wording of the midrash is absolutely identical in both cases—may indicate that we are dealing not with a tradition responding to Christian criticism of the law of Moses but rather with an echo of the perceived rivalry in legal matters between Israel and Rome. As for the anonymous interpretation mentioned afterward, which is not directly linked to the discussion between R. Yoḥanan and Resh Laqish, the connection it establishes between Esau and idolatry (*'avodah zarah*) can be interpreted as a reference to either Roman "paganism" or Christianity. There is no element in the text forcing us to choose the latter as the implicit referent.

That Jews (in this case rabbis), especially from the third century CE on,[152] could have perceived Rome as annuling the laws of Israel does indeed make sense. As we saw previously, Jews who became Roman citizens after 212 CE had full access to Roman jurisdiction. There was a risk that they would no longer consider Jewish laws mandatory and perhaps even question their status as valid legislation, despite their partial integration in the Roman legal system as customary laws. Roman policy could thus lead to the obliteration of Jewish

150. According to rabbinic tradition, R. Berekhiah was a fifth-generation Palestinian amora (fourth century).

151. Morgenstern 2016, 209.

152. Although such attributions are open to question (see Introduction), the fact that this discussion is ascribed to R. Yoḥanan and Resh Laqish, both active in the second half of the third century, is interesting.

legal tradition. The question that remains, however, is how Israel could be thought capable of annulling the laws of Rome.

I suggest that the writings of Juvenal and Tacitus, although composed considerably earlier than both the time of Resh Laqish and the period of the final redaction of Genesis Rabbah, can help us grasp the meaning of Resh Laqish's remark (whatever the real origin of the saying might be). In a famous passage from *Satire* 14 that alludes to the differences between a Judaizer and a full convert, Juvenal writes:

> Some happen to have been dealt a father who respects the sabbath. They worship nothing except the clouds and spirit [or: deity] of the sky. They think there is no difference between pork, which their father abstained from, and human flesh. In time, they get rid of their fore-skins. And with their habit of despising the laws of Rome (*Romanas . . . contemnere leges*), they study, observe, and revere the Judaic code (*Iudaicum ius*), as handed down by Moses in his mystic scroll, which tells them not to show the way to anyone except a fellow worshipper and if asked, to take only the circumcised to the fountain. But it is the father who is to blame, taking every seventh day as a day of laziness and separate from ordinary life.[153]

This passage testifies to the Roman perception, at the beginning of the second century CE, of an antagonism between Roman and Jewish laws, which comes to the fore with particular force in the case of converts. Obviously, Juvenal is dealing with proselytes who were Roman citizens and thus were supposed to revere the laws of Rome. Shockingly (from a Roman viewpoint), the persons who have embraced Judaism are depicted as despising Roman laws and, by contrast, as revering the Jewish law code (*Iudaicum ius*). Juvenal's tone in the *Satires* is ironic, but to make sense, his humor must rely on perceptions that were common among his audience. Tacitus' description of the Jews in his *Histories*, in which he also mentions converts, tends to corroborate Juvenal's description: "Those who are converted to their ways follow the same practice (circumcision), and the earliest lesson they receive is to despise the gods, to disown their country (*exuere patriam*), and to regard their parents, children, and brothers as of little account."[154] To be sure, Tacitus does not refer explicitly to Roman laws. However, the notion that converts disown or reject their *patria*—Rome—implies that they reject its laws.

Although the testimonies of Juvenal and Tacitus date to the beginning of the second century CE, they help us make sense of the statement attributed to Resh Laqish that the confrontation between Esau/Rome and Jacob/Israel

---

153. Juvenal, *Satires* 14.96–106, trans. S. Morton Braund, LCL, 465–467 (slightly modified).

154. Tacitus, *Hist.* 5.5.2, trans. Clifford H. Moore, LCL, 183.

was about law. In Jewish sources, beyond the examples from Genesis Rabbah mentioned above, a sense of rivalry between Jewish and Roman laws and judicial institutions surfaces in several ways, which I will now explore further. Philo and Josephus produced apologias for the Mosaic law as the best law ever found among humankind, paralleling and even imitating Roman claims for the superiority of Roman law while refraining from explicitly comparing the Jewish and Roman legal systems. The rabbis' apologetic strategy was different from that of Philo and Josephus in that they celebrated the Torah's superiority by creating imaginary cases of Romans admiring the laws of the Jews, for example by telling stories about Roman emissaries who came to the rabbis to study the Torah and ended by praising its merits. The rabbis' sense of rivalry with Rome was further reflected in their claims that Israel's laws were different from and superior to those of the nations and that Jews should stick to their own laws and avoid turning to non-Jewish tribunals. Although this discourse of differentiation and opposition has biblical roots, it took on a new dimension in the Roman context. Moreover, it could coexist with a degree of imitation of Roman norms. As we saw in previous chapters, the combination of opposition and mimesis can be an expression of rivalry.

3.1 THE TORAH AS THE MOST PERFECT AND THE MOST ANCIENT LAW

The defense or praise of the Torah as excellent and wise legislation did not begin in the Roman period. This perspective is present in the Letter of Aristeas, for example, which includes an apologia for the law of Moses, emphasizing the allegorical and rational meaning of the dietary rules.[155] The Letter does not compare Mosaic legislation with other legal systems, however, but rather with other religious beliefs and cults.[156] In some cases, Jewish authors of the Hellenistic period give Moses a measure of credit for other peoples' cultural achievements. The fragments of Artapanus, which describe Moses as a *Kulturbringer*, and of Aristobulus—which say that Pythagoras, Socrates, and Plato studied and adopted many aspects of the "philosophy" of the Hebrews as known through Greek translations of the Mosaic legislation (*nomothesia*)— testify to this current of thought.[157] Yet we find no explicit statement concerning the influence of Moses on Greek lawgivers. In a Hellenistic context, the challenge to the Jews came from Greek philosophy or wisdom, not Greek laws

---

155. Let. Aris. 140–157; Wright 2015, 266–292.

156. Let. Aris. 130–139; Wright 2015, 248–251.

157. Artapanus: Holladay 1983, 189–243; Borgeaud, Römer, and Volokhine 2010, 3–82. Aristobulus, frags. 3–4: Holladay 1995, 150–163. In frag. 5, Aristobulus also states that Homer and Hesiod took the idea of the number 7's holiness from the law of Moses; see Holladay 1995, 189; Weber 2000, 317; de Vos 2016.

sensu stricto.[158] The main issue for Jews was to defend the rational character of the Mosaic law, not to compare the Torah with the legal systems of the Greek *poleis*—hence the development of a Jewish discourse presenting the law of Moses as conforming to the law of nature.[159] During the Hellenistic period, Jews also had to defend the Mosaic law against accusations of misanthropy, but it is only in the Roman period that we find answers to the charge of misanthropy that are based on a comparison of the laws of the Jews to those of other peoples.[160]

In a Roman context, the issue of the Mosaic law's rationality and conformity to the law of nature remained relevant, be it only in answer to Roman elites interested in philosophy. Cicero, for instance, in his treatise on laws (*De legibus*), tends to look at them from a philosophical viewpoint, rather than from the perspective of a jurist.[161] Philosophically oriented Jewish works of the Roman period, such as Philo's exegetical treatises or 4 Maccabees, still debate the issue of the law's conformity to nature.[162] The main challenge, however, pertained not to the philosophical understanding of the law but rather, as we saw in the previous sections of this chapter, to the Roman claim that theirs were the best laws ever written.

That the nature of the challenge around the law was different in the Roman period is corroborated by the testimonies of Philo and Josephus. Their works exalt the distinctiveness and superiority of the Mosaic law over all other legal systems, in a way that is unheard of in Jewish works of the Hellenistic period.[163] The comparison with Aristobulus, for example, is illuminating. The Alexandrian author writes:

> All philosophers agree that it is necessary to hold devout convictions about God, something which our school prescribes particularly well.

158. In the Letter of Aristeas, the king praises the translators of the Torah, who, "in their conduct and speech, surpassed the philosophers by a lot, since they made God their starting point" (§235, trans. Wright 2015, 368). The challenge is clearly Greek philosophy rather than Greek legislation.

159. See in particular the discussion around the Sabbath in Aristobulus, frag. 5; and Letter of Aristeas 171. Wright 2015, 265, notes: "For our author, the Jewish 'legislation' derives from the rational mind of Moses, who was 'prepared by God for knowledge of all things.'"

160. In Josephus' *Against Apion*; see below. On Jewish answers to charges of misanthropy, see Berthelot 2003.

161. Note in particular *Leg.* 1.57.

162. See in particular 4 Macc 5:22–24, which characterizes the Jewish way of life based on God's law as a philosophy which teaches the four cardinal virtues. The next verse (5:25) states that the law of Moses is in accordance with nature. The whole book is about the rationality of the Mosaic law and how it teaches mastery of the passions.

163. Even as far as the philosophical understanding of the law is concerned, Philo's work displays an evolution. His claim that the law of Moses is the best written expression of the law of nature parallels Cicero's understanding of the laws of Rome, as Carlos Lévy has shown (Lévy 1992, 509–521). By contrast, no Greek author tried to demonstrate the conformity of the particular laws of a given *polis* to the law of nature (Lévy 1992, 519).

And the whole structure of our law has been drawn up with concern for piety, justice, self-control, and other qualities that are truly good.[164]

The claim that the Mosaic law teaches such virtues is also found under the pens of Philo and Josephus, but they argue for much more—namely, that the Mosaic law teaches these virtues better and to a greater extent than the laws of other peoples. The Torah is not only excellent; it is the best.

Moreover, Philo and Josephus' rhetorical and ideological discourse on the superiority of the Mosaic law resembles Cicero's claims for Roman law in *On the Making of an Orator*, quoted at the beginning of this chapter, and puts the Jews in a position vis-à-vis other legal systems that is similar to that of the Romans themselves. Let us first consider Philo's *On the Life of Moses*. At the beginning of book 2, while describing Moses' qualities as king, lawgiver, priest, and prophet, Philo writes:

> 12 That Moses himself was the best (*aristos*) of all lawgivers in all countries, better in fact than any that have ever arisen among either the Greeks or the barbarians, and that his laws are most excellent and truly come from God, since they omit nothing that is needful, is shown most clearly by the following proof. [. . .] 14 Moses is alone in this, that his laws, firm, unshaken, immovable, stamped, as it were, with the seals of nature herself, remain secure from the day when they were first enacted to now, and we may hope that they will remain for all future ages as though immortal, so long as the sun and moon and the whole heaven and universe exist.[165]

In the next paragraph, Philo continues to emphasize the permanence of the Mosaic laws, despite Israel's changes of fortune throughout history. By contrast, the other nations are unable to preserve their laws, which are constantly modified (§18). Beyond the Torah's immutability, another decisive argument for its superiority in Philo's eyes is the universal character of the Mosaic legislation, demonstrated by the fact that peoples from every nation, Greeks and barbarians alike, have adopted it. There is no people, Philo argues, that does not reject the laws of other nations as foreign: the Athenians reject the customs and institutions of the Lacedaemonians and vice versa, and barbarian peoples such as the Egyptians and the Scythians, who respectively represent the southern and northern parts of the inhabited world, reject other peoples' laws as well (§19). However, Philo adds, "it is not so with ours. They attract and win the attention of all, of barbarians, of Greeks, of dwellers on the mainland and islands, of nations of the east and the west, of Europe and Asia, of the whole inhabited world from end to end."[166] I will return to the issue of the

164. Aristobulus, frag. 4, trans. Holladay 1995, 175. See also Letter of Aristeas 131, 278.
165. *Mos.* 2.12–14, trans. F. H. Colson, LCL, 457.
166. *Mos.* 2.20, trans. F. H. Colson, LCL, 459.

Torah's universal dimension below. What needs attention here is the way that Philo places the Mosaic law above all other legislation, including those of the Greek cities associated with the famous lawgivers Solon and Lycurgus and, implicitly, that of Rome.[167]

Josephus' strategy in *Against Apion*, an apologetic work in which he defends the law of Moses against various charges, resembles that of Philo in several respects.[168] Like Philo, he suggests that the Mosaic law is in fact the finest legislation known to mankind, but his formulation is less direct and more cautious.[169] Josephus emphasizes that he does not want to criticize the laws of other peoples but is forced to do so because detractors of the Jews, Apollonius Molon and Apion, have undertaken such a comparison themselves (*C. Ap.* 2.150, 237–238, 287). This remark may have been intended especially for his Roman audience. As a matter of fact, Josephus' criticism focuses essentially on the Greeks, especially the Athenians and the Lacedaemonians, in a way that recalls Cicero's negative comments on their respective legislations, and may have been meant to align the Jews with the Romans.[170] He includes barbarian peoples only occasionally, referring to the Scythians and the Persians in 2.269–270.

Like Philo in *On the Life of Moses* 2.12–16, Josephus highlights the immutability of the Jewish laws—as well as the Jews' exceptional faithfulness to them.[171] This permanence is all the more extraordinary as the Mosaic law is extremely ancient. Josephus in fact claims that it is the most ancient law ever produced by humankind:

> Well, I maintain that our legislator exceeds in antiquity the legislators referred to anywhere else. The Lycurguses, and Solons, and Zaleukos, the legislator of the Locrians, and all those admired by the Greeks seem to have been but "yesterday or the day before" compared to him, which is why not even the term "law" was known among the Greeks of old.[172]

That the antiquity of one's law is a critical issue and arouses competition between nations is clear from the preceding paragraphs: "Of course, each

---

167. See also *Mos.* 2.48–52 and *Opif.* 1–2 for a general comparison between Moses and other lawgivers. For references to Solon and/or Lycurgus, see *Opif.* 104–105; *Probus* 47. Philo rejects the claim that Greek laws had a divine origin, even though he admits that the notion of law, generally speaking, does have a divine origin (*Sacr.* 131). On Israel's cultural competition with the Greeks in Philo's work and how it compares to Rome's relationship to the Greeks, see Niehoff 2001, 142–143; Berthelot 2011a.

168. On Josephus' dependence on Philo in *Against Apion*, see Berthelot 2003, 368–374; Berthelot, forthcoming (with further bibliography).

169. See *C. Ap.* 2.163, 170–175.

170. *C. Ap.* 2.172, 259–268. I do not mean that Josephus had read Cicero, only that he may have been familiar with similar Roman discourses among the Roman elites.

171. *C. Ap.* 2.220–221, 226, 228, 232–233, 277–279.

172. *C. Ap.* 2.154, trans. Barclay 2007, 254–255. See also 2.295.

attempts to trace their legislation back to the most ancient point in time, so as to appear not to imitate others but themselves to have instructed others how to live in a lawful manner."[173] Here Josephus allusively suggests that the Mosaic law inspired other legislators—a point that is explicit in Philo's *On the Special Laws* 4.61.

Josephus also resorts to the second argument put forward by Philo in *On the Life of Moses*—namely, that all kinds of peoples in different parts of the world have adopted and imitated the Mosaic laws. Josephus claims, first, that while remaining faithful to the civic laws of their *poleis*, the Greek philosophers followed the Mosaic law's teachings on the nature of the deity and ethical matters (*C. Ap.* 2.281). Second,

> even among the masses for a long time there has been much emulation of our piety, and there is not one city of the Greeks, nor a single barbarian nation, where the custom of the seventh day, on which we rest, has not permeated, and where our fasts and lighting of lamps and many of our prohibitions with regard to food have not been observed.[174]

The Sabbath ("the seventh day") and the fast(s) are precisely the two "laws" that Philo calls upon in *On the Life of Moses* (2.21–24) to illustrate his claim that Mosaic law enjoys universal recognition. Josephus then adds the argument that the Mosaic law has attained universal popularity in spite of being difficult to follow, a clear demonstration of its excellence (*C. Ap.* 2.284–286). In the conclusion to *Against Apion*, he even seems to suggest that it was Mosaic legislation that taught other peoples the very notion of obedience to law (§293). That he has a Roman audience in mind at this point of his demonstration is indicated by the next paragraph (§294), which looks like a catalogue of Roman values (supposedly promoted by the law of Moses): *homonoia* (*concordia*) between citizens, contempt for death in war, dedication to work (notably agriculture) in time of peace, and piety.

The Mosaic law's superiority is manifest in other ways as well. Josephus argues that it is the only legislation that unites theoretical and practical teachings:

> All education and custom-construction is of two kinds: one instructs by means of words, the other through training in character. 172 Other legislators (*nomothetai*) were divided in their opinions, choosing one kind and omitting the other, as each saw fit: thus, the Lacedaemonians and Cretans used to conduct their education through customs, not words, whereas the Athenians and almost all the rest of the Greeks used to issue instruction on what should or should not be done through

173. *C. Ap.* 2.152, trans. Barclay 2007, 254.

174. *C. Ap.* 2.282, trans. Barclay 2007, 327–328.

laws (*nomoi*), but neglected to accustom people to these through deeds. 173 But our legislator combined both forms with great care: he neither left character-training mute nor allowed the words from the law to go unpracticed.[175]

As in Philo, the Lacedaemonians and the Athenians form a pair of opposites that together represent the totality of the Greek *poleis*. The law of Moses is thus contrasted with the law codes of all the Greek cities, and its superiority becomes all the more impressive.

The way in which both Philo and Josephus exalt the Jewish law's superiority over the legislation of the Greeks, especially the Athenians and the Lacedaemonians, recalls Cicero's stance in *On the Making of an Orator*, mentioned at the beginning of this chapter. By echoing such claims made by Roman elites about Roman laws, Philo and Josephus implicitly point to a similarity and/or a rivalry between the Jewish and the Roman legal systems. They may be suggesting that the Jews and the Romans had similar positions vis-à-vis the other nations. However, they also explicitly state that the Mosaic law is superior to any other law produced by human beings, and this logically includes the legal traditions of the Romans. Although they refrain from mentioning the laws of Rome, let alone explicitly comparing Jewish and Roman laws (for political reasons, obviously), both Philo and Josephus thus affirm the superiority of the laws of Israel not only to those of the Greeks but also to those of Rome.

Another possible line of argument might have claimed Mosaic influence on Greek lawgivers, with the implication of an indirect influence on the XII Tables. From this perspective, Moses would have been the ultimate originator of Roman law. As far as I know, however, such a bold affirmation is not found—at least explicitly—in Jewish authors from the Early Roman period, although Philo does claim that the Mosaic law influenced Greek lawgivers and Josephus comes close to making the same affirmation.[176] Moreover, as we have seen, both argue that numerous peoples have adopted or imitated the Mosaic law, which leaves the door open to the possibility that it influenced Roman jurists too.

The idea that the law of Moses predates the laws of Rome and may have somehow contributed to the latter's formulation seems to lie in the background of the *Collatio Legum Mosaicarum et Romanarum*, which is probably a Jewish work (dating to the fourth century CE). Before examining the *Collatio* and the question of its Jewish or Christian authorship, however, we need to take into account some Christian reflections on the relationship between Roman and Mosaic laws.

---

175. *C. Ap.* 2.171–173, trans. Barclay 2007, 267–268.

176. *Spec.* 4.61 (Greek lawgivers have copied Moses's law that forbids judicial testimonies based on hearsay [Exod 23:1]; cf. *Conf.* 141 and *QE* 2.9, which tackle the same topic but do not claim such a borrowing). Josephus, *C.Ap.* 2.152–154, 291–295.

Roman law aroused ambiguous feelings among Christian authors, because it was perceived as part of Rome's non-Christian legacy. (In the long run, however, classical—i.e., "pagan"—Roman law remained the law of the empire, including under Christian emperors.) Some of them brazenly appropriated the argument concerning the Mosaic law's antiquity and the influence it had on Greek and/or Roman lawgivers. In his *Apology*, Tertullian argues that the laws of the Romans—such as the prohibition of murder—must have derived from the law of Moses, because the latter was more ancient.[177] For Tertullian as for Josephus, the argument of antiquity was crucial, not least because the Romans themselves recognized it as such—as Tertullian notes: "And among you it is almost a superstition to make credit depend on time elapsed."[178] Yet he is more explicit than Josephus in deducing from the antiquity of the Mosaic law that it influenced the laws of the Romans, arguing that "it can be seen that your laws and your studies alike were fertilized from the [Hebrew] law and teaching of God."[179] Ultimately, however, Tertullian emphasizes the Gospel's superiority to Mosaic teachings and, like most Christian authors, distinguishes between the commandments of the Decalogue and the other prescriptions in the Pentateuch.

The idea that the Romans were indebted to the biblical notion of law surfaces again in the *Commentary on Romans* (7.1) of Ambrosiaster (or Pseudo-Ambrose), a Christian author active under Pope Damasius I in the second half of the fourth century:

> Therefore, the Romans know what law is because they are not barbarians, but understand natural justice, in part from themselves, and in part from the Greeks, just as the Greeks do from the Hebrews. Before Moses, while the law (*lex*) was not hidden, neither organization (*ordo*) nor authority (*auctoritas*) existed. For laws (*leges*) were brought to the Romans from Athens.[180]

As Andrew S. Jacobs notes, although Ambrosiaster's context differed greatly from that of Tertullian, and Roman law came to be viewed differently with the Christianization of the empire, in the fourth century "we still find Christians locating their sense of simultaneous identification with and alienation from the Empire (increasingly their Empire) in the decisive sphere of civil jurisprudence."[181] Ambrosiaster is one of the Christian voices that tried to bridge the gap between Roman and biblical laws. In the passage quoted above,

177. Tertullian, *Apology* 19.1, 45.2–4; see also Burrows 1988, 227; Jacobs 2006, 85; Fowler 2021, 430–435.

178. *Apology* 19.1, trans. T. R. Glover and Gerald H. Rendall, LCL, 93.

179. Ibid., 95.

180. Trans. Kimberley Fowler, "Ambrosiaster, *Commentary on Romans* 7.1," http://www.judaism-and-rome.org/ambrosiaster-commentary-romans-71 (slightly modified). See also Ambrosiaster, *Liber quaestionum (appendix novi testamenti)* 75.2.

181. Jacobs 2006, 85.

he builds on the tradition of the Greek origin of the XII Tables while arguing that the Greeks themselves learned law from the Hebrews. As a consequence, Roman laws can at least partly be traced back to those of Moses.[182] As in Tertullian's case, however, Ambrosiaster's relationship to both Roman and Jewish (biblical) law was ambivalent, since for him the higher law of the Gospel had supplanted most of the laws of the Hebrew Bible. It was only the Decalogue that retained legal and spiritual value in his eyes.

The argument that the Mosaic law was a precursor of Roman law is also found in the *Syrian-Roman Law Book*, an anonymous collection of laws in Syriac dating to the fifth century, which may have originated in ecclesiastical circles. The introduction to the work's second recension presents Moses as the most ancient lawgiver on earth, whose legislation influenced all other, subsequent legal systems, including those of the Greeks, Romans, and Egyptians. The *Syrian-Roman Law Book* thus suggests even more clearly than Ambrosiaster that Roman laws got their original inspiration from the law of Moses. However, for this work as well, the coming of Christ led to the "fulfillment" of the Mosaic law and its de facto replacement by "the law of the Messiah," of which the content is not made fully clear.[183]

The *Collatio Legum Mosaicarum et Romanarum* represents another attempt to bridge the gap between Roman and biblical legal traditions, but one that attributes great value to the details of the Mosaic law. The identity of its author, who was probably a contemporary of Ambrosiaster's, remains hotly debated today. Some argue for a Jew, whereas others identify him as a Christian.[184] The *Collatio* juxtaposes biblical and Roman laws arranged according to topic, which would seem to suggest their convergence and compatibility, and maybe the influence of the former on the latter. For each topic, the biblical law comes first (except in 6.7.1), followed by various Roman laws taken from the works of Gaius, Paulus, Ulpian, Papinianus, and Modestinus, as well as from the collections of imperial constitutions called the *Codex Gregorianus* and the *Codex Hermogenianus*. The author does not analyze the laws, which leaves the meaning of the comparison implied by the juxtaposition elusive. Yet one finds an indication at 7.1.1: at the beginning of this section dealing with thieves and the punishments for theft, the author first refers to the distinction that the

---

182. Jacobs 2006, 95–97; Fowler 2021, 441–444. Jacobs concludes that "the twofold gesture of rejection and accommodation—of both Jewish Law and Roman *ius*—can be read, therefore, not as the confused jumble of a failed apologetic, but rather as the deliberate compilation of an authoritative, even imperial, religious self" (97).

183. Sachau 1907, 46–49 (with a German translation); Rutgers 1995, 236–237.

184. See, among others: in favor of a Jewish author, Volterra 1930, esp. 86–123; Rabello 1967; Gaudemet 1979, 96–98; Daube 1991, 107; Barone Adesi 1992, 173–174; Rutgers 1995, 218–253; in favor of a Christian author, Liebs 1987, 162–174; Jacobs 2006; Frakes 2011, 129–140; Fowler 2021. For the history of research on this text, see in particular Rabello 1967; Rutgers 1995, 210–211.

Law of the XII Tables makes between a thief who comes by night and one who comes by day, and then claims, "Know you jurists, that Moses had previously so ordained" (followed by a quotation of Exodus 22:1–2, which makes a similar distinction between theft by night and by day).[185] This statement implies that the author was working under the assumption that the Mosaic law was an antecedent of the Roman law. Leonard Rutgers aptly concludes that "the *Collatio* was composed to stress the primacy of Mosaic law and to show that the injunctions of Mosaic law were not at variance with the ordinances of Roman law." In his view, this goal fits the context of the end of the fourth century CE, when Christian authors were particularly critical of the laws of the Pentateuch.[186] Rutgers' arguments in favor of a Jewish author are: (1) the sharp contrast between the *Collatio*'s interest in and positive treatment of the details of the Mosaic law and the Christian lack of interest in and criticism of them (even by authors who emphasized the Mosaic law's anteriority to the laws of Rome, one may add);[187] and (2) the total absence of references to Christ and other elements of Christian doctrine in the *Collatio*—an argument from silence but nevertheless a striking point in view of overtly Christian texts, such as the *Syrian-Roman Law Book*. Rutgers concludes that "the *Collatio* was the last major Jewish apologetic work to be written in antiquity."[188] Indeed, it exemplifies an apologetic strategy whose inspiration goes back to the beginning of the Roman period. The main difference was that the author was now addressing an audience of Christians—at least in part—who themselves had previously used the argument of the antiquity of Moses' legislation to defend Christianity against Roman accusations of religious innovation. To assert the antiquity of the law of Moses was thus insufficient for the Jewish author of the *Collatio*. What he probably aimed to achieve was to defend Mosaic law against the Christian discourse of substitution, by arguing that the law of Moses was fundamentally in accord with the Roman laws on which the Christian empire was built, and thus remained relevant for Christians. Hence this surprising work juxtaposing discrete legal prescriptions, for which we have no precedent in previous Jewish literature.

3.2 ROMAN ADMIRATION FOR JEWISH LAW?

Contrary to Philo, Josephus, and the Christian authors mentioned above, the rabbis did not use the antiquity of the law of Moses, or its influence on Greek and/or Roman lawgivers as arguments for the Torah's superiority over other

185. Hyamson 1913, 92–93.

186. Rutgers 1995, 247–250, 252–253 (quotation at 247). See also Volterra 1930, 119; Rabello 1967, 343–344, which concludes that the author wanted to emphasize the Mosaic law's anteriority and superiority.

187. See, however, the remarks of Jacobs 2006, 92–93, on the links between the laws mentioned in the *Collatio* and the Decalogue.

188. Rutgers 1995, 253.

legal systems. Nevertheless, they developed apologetic strategies that explicitly involved Roman protagonists. To fully appreciate the rabbis' perspective, we must remember that the Hebrew Bible already expressed the hope that the nations would come to recognize the wisdom of the Torah, which would in turn demonstrate the wisdom of the people of Israel. As Deuteronomy 4:6 states, "You must observe [these laws] diligently, for this will show your wisdom (*ḥokhmah*) and discernment (*binah*) to the peoples, who, when they hear all these statutes (*ḥuqqim*), will say, 'Surely this great nation (*goy gadol*) is a wise and discerning people!'" In addition, Deuteronomy 4:8 asks: "And what other great nation (*goy gadol*) has statutes (*ḥuqqim*) and ordinances (*mishpatim*) as just as this entire law (Torah) that I am setting before you today?"

In rabbinic literature, we encounter numerous non-Jews who quote biblical verses when addressing Jews in imaginary dialogues that, from the redactors' viewpoint, showcase the rabbis' wisdom.[189] For example, there are texts reporting alleged legal discussions between rabbis and Roman legal experts that leave no doubt as to who commands the superior law. Seth Schwartz points to an interesting example in y. Ketubbot 9:10, 33b.[190] The story features a discussion between a certain R. Mana and a (presumably Roman) legal expert called Alexas, which "appears to concern a situation in which the court attempts to force a man to pay off the sum stipulated in his marriage contract."[191] R. Mana explains rabbinic law to the non-Jewish expert and explicitly states that rabbinic legal procedure is superior to the Roman norm, even though in this case the rabbinic and Roman procedures look very similar (they both decree that if the man refuses to come to court, he must receive three letters before his property is expropriated, the only difference being that the rabbinic ruling specifies that there must be thirty days between letters).[192]

Other rabbinic texts stage a scenario in which Roman authorities (the "kingdom," *malkhut*) send emissaries to inquire of the rabbis about Jewish law, and in which the emissaries end up singing its praises. We find such a story in the Jerusalem Talmud:

> It happened that the kingdom (*malkhut*, Rome) sent two officers (*istratiotot*, from the Greek *stratiōtai*) to learn Torah from Rabban Gamaliel. They learned Scripture (*miqra*), the Mishnah, the Talmud, *halakhot*, and *aggadot*. Finally they said to him: "Your whole Torah is beautiful and praiseworthy except for these two things: That you say a Jewish woman should not act as midwife for a non-Jew but a non-Jewish woman may act as midwife for a Jew, and similarly, a Jewish

189. See, e.g., m. Avodah Zarah 3:4, the famous encounter between Proclos and Rabban Gamaliel in Aphrodite's bathhouse.

190. Schwartz 2010a, 125–126.

191. Schwartz 2010a, 126.

192. See also y. Bava Batra 8:1, 16a; Schwartz 2010a, 126–129.

woman may not nurse the child of a non-Jewish woman but a non-Jewish woman may be wet nurse for a Jewish woman, under the latter's control (m. Avodah Zarah 2:1). What is stolen from a Jew is prohibited, but [what is stolen] from a non-Jew (*nokhri*) is permitted." Then and there Rabban Gamaliel decreed that it is forbidden to [use, sell, or buy] what is stolen from a non-Jew, so as not to profane the Divine name. [And they also said:] "'If the ox of a Jew gores the ox of a non-Jew (*nokhri*) [the owner] is not liable [but if the ox of a non-Jew gores the ox of a Jew (the owner) is liable, regardless of whether (the ox) was previously harmless or dangerous]' (m. Bava Qamma 4:3, elaborating on Exod 21:35–36)]. On this matter we do not inform the Roman authorities [lit.: the kingdom]." In spite of this they had not reached the Ladder of Tyre before they had forgotten everything [they had learned].[193]

The redactors of this story seem to have perceived that gentiles, including Roman authorities, could take issue with laws disadvantaging non-Jews with respect to Jews.[194] It must be emphasized, however, that the laws questioned here belong to the Oral Torah—the rabbinic tradition of interpretation—and not to the Hebrew Bible.[195] For example, the laws concerning goring oxen in Exodus 21 do not differentiate between Israelite and gentile owners. Therefore, one could also imagine that Jews who did not belong to the circles of the rabbis might find their interpretations faulty, in which case this talmudic passage could be understood as a response to both external and internal criticism. Finally, it is possible that some rabbis did not feel comfortable with this specific tradition of interpretation either.

The story features Rabban Gamaliel (II), who, according to rabbinic tradition, was the successor of R. Yoḥanan ben Zakkai at Yavne and was thus supposedly active at the end of the first century and the beginning of the second. What we have then is an encounter between the main representative of the emerging rabbinic movement and delegates of the empire, an imaginary encounter, for there is certainly nothing historical in the story.[196] Its ideological significance is important nonetheless: the story suggests that not long after

193. y. Bava Qamma 4:3, 4b; Schäfer and Becker 1991–2001 (1995, *Synopse* IV), 24. Translated according to Oppenheimer 2005a, 173, modified based on MS Leiden. The last sentence, in Aramaic (in contrast to the rest of the text, which is in Hebrew), may be a later addition based on Mekhilta Deuteronomy (see below). See also Rosental 1983, which provides a detailed critical apparatus for the text and compares the versions of this story found in Sifre Deuteronomy, the Yerushalmi, and the Bavli (he did not have access to the fragments of Mekhilta Deuteronomy).

194. On accusations of misanthropy against Jews, see Berthelot 2003.

195. A point rightly stressed by Joshua Burns in connection with the version in Sifre (Burns 2017b, 295–296).

196. See Fraade 1991, 214–215, notes 130, 137; Schwartz 2010a, 124–125; Burns 2017b, 293–294 (on the version found in Sifre).

the First Jewish Revolt and the destruction of the Temple, it was possible for the legal activity of the rabbis to obtain the approval of the Roman authorities. This message would actually fit better in the context of the third century CE, when cooperation between the patriarchs and the Roman authorities had taken a more concrete form and rabbinic law was codified in the Mishnah and the Tosefta, than in that of the first century CE.[197]

As a matter of fact, this talmudic story builds upon previous traditions found in halakhic midrashim—Sifre Deuteronomy 344 and Mekhilta Deuteronomy 33:3—whose final redaction dates to the third century.[198] The Sifre version is the shortest and refers only to the issue of stolen property. Here the officers sent by the Roman authorities are instructed to pretend that they are *gerim* (converts), suggesting that otherwise—had they presented themselves as Roman officers—the rabbis would have rejected their request; however, in the rest of the story their real identity seems to be known.[199] They go to Rabban Gamaliel in Usha, a place in Galilee that, according to rabbinic tradition, became the center of the rabbinic movement after the Bar Kokhba Revolt, under Rabban Shimon ben Gamaliel II, the son of Rabban Gamaliel (II) and father of R. Yehudah ha-Nasi. The reference to Usha seems to indicate that the identity of the Gamaliel involved in the story was uncertain (either Rabban Gamaliel II or Rabban Shimon ben Gamaliel II). The officers are said to learn not only Scripture but also the Mishnah, midrash, *halakhot*, and *aggadot*. When they leave, the Roman emissaries conclude that "your entire Torah is beautiful and praiseworthy" except for the law stating that "what is stolen from a non-Jew (*goy*) is permitted, but what is stolen from a Jew is prohibited," but they promise not to report this point to the authorities. In the Mekhilta, which probably represents a later development of this tradition and certainly reflects a greater sensitivity to the issue of relations with non-Jews, the law is modified to become "What is stolen from a Jew is prohibited, but the lost property of a non-Jew is permitted."[200] Instead of allowing the use of an object stolen from a non-Jew and thus seemingly condoning theft, the Mekhilta permits the use of an object that was merely lost. That it reformulates and softens an existing tradition attested in Sifre and later in the Jerusalem Talmud is apparent from the fact that this is the

197. Joshua Burns interprets this story as reflecting the new context that developed in the wake of the promulgation of the Antonine Constitution, and the integration of the rabbis' laws, as customs, into Roman legislation (Burns 2017b, on the version found in Sifre).

198. On these two midrashic texts, see Yael Wilfand, "Sifre Deuteronomy 344," http://www.judaism-and-rome.org/sifre-deuteronomy-344, and "Mekhilta Deuteronomy 33:3," idem.

199. On the officers' instruction to pretend to be Jews or converts, a detail found only in Sifre, see Fraade 1991, 53; Cohen 1999a, 37–39.

200. On the differences between Sifre and the Mekhilta, including the different approaches to non-Jews that they may reflect, see Kahana 1988, esp. 183–184.

only example in which the nature of the case differs for the Jew and the non-Jew (a stolen object versus a lost object). The Mekhilta mentions other laws—which feature in the Yerushalmi as well—concerning goring oxen, midwives, and wet nurses, but in these cases the action remains the same for the Jew and the non-Jew, the difference being whether it is permitted or prohibited.[201]

Other ways in which the Mekhilta differs from Sifre include the identity of the emissaries, whom the Mekhilta presents as astrologers rather than military officers, and the ending of the story, in which the astrologers declare that "your entire Torah is beautiful and praiseworthy" except for the law of the goring ox (not the law about stolen or lost objects as in Sifre, probably because of the modification mentioned above). As in Sifre, they promise not to report the issue to the authorities. Then the Mekhilta adds that Rabban Gamaliel prayed and the emissaries forgot everything they had learned.

In Sifre Deuteronomy, Mekhilta Deuteronomy, and y. Bava Qamma, we find the same yearning on the part of the rabbis "that the nations praise them and their (rabbinic) Torah, even as the latter provides the basis for Israel's self-understanding as being distinct among the nations as God's especially beloved," to quote Steven Fraade's felicitous formulation.[202] Yet the story's ending in the Mekhilta and the Yerushalmi, which mention in slightly different ways that the Roman emissaries forgot what they had learned from Rabban Gamaliel, indicates anxiety and ambivalence. As Natalie Dohrmann perceptively remarks, in the end,

> the desire to be admired is trumped by the desire to disengage. Forgetting—the great bane of the rabbis, for whom loss of memory is a loss of God's covenant—befalls the Roman (whether by human nature or divine intervention is unclear). This passage is a wishful inversion of their own confrontation with an imperial law they can neither admire nor forget.[203]

The story about the Roman emissaries may in fact embody the essence of the rabbis' ambivalent relationship to Rome and its legal power (at least for most rabbis). On the one hand they wanted to see rabbinic laws and legal

201. According to Rosental 1983, 14–15, the words "two things" in the Jerusalem Talmud ("Your whole Torah is beautiful and praiseworthy except for these two things . . .") refer not to two laws—the passage actually mentions four halakhot—but rather to the fact that two different norms are applied to Jews and non-Jews.

202. Fraade 1991, 53.

203. Dohrmann 2015, 206. See also Schwartz 2010a, 125, which states: "The storyteller wavers between the Deuteronomist's mildly competitive universalism (compare Josephus' introduction to *Antiquities*, where he decides that the Torah is a treasure that should be revealed to admiring gentiles), one that tacitly acknowledges the value of the Romans' approval, and differently anxious resistance."

expertise recognized by the Roman authorities but on the other, they preferred to remain separate and secluded in their own legal realm.[204] We shall examine this logic of differentiation and seclusion—together with the difficulties it entailed—more closely in the next section.

Before turning to this aspect of rabbinic discourse, however, let me add a last remark about the story of the Roman emissaries who come to learn Torah: what it also argues, obliquely, is that Jews can be proud of their laws, since the latter were admired by the Romans themselves. That this interpretation is not farfetched and that some rabbis were indeed anxious lest Jews fail to see in the Torah a legitimate and valuable legal corpus is shown by the following passage from Sifra (found in the section known as Mekhilta de-Arayot):[205]

> Lest you should say: "They have statutes and we have no statutes," Scripture says: *You shall keep my ordinances* (mishpatim), *and my commandments/statutes* (ḥuqqot) *you shall observe, to walk in them. I am the Lord your God* (Lev 18:4).
>
> Still, there is hope for the evil inclination (*yetzer ha-raʿ*) to deliberate on it and say: "Theirs are nicer than ours." [Therefore] Scripture says: *You shall observe and do [my ordinances], for it is your wisdom and your understanding [in the eyes of the nations, who, when they hear all these statutes, will say: "What great nation has such statutes and ordinances such as this entire law* (Torah)*?"]* (Deut 4:6)[206]

This passage indicates that non-Jewish laws or customs might appeal to Jews, who would find them nicer than the Torah's commandments. It also suggests that at the time of the rabbis, some Jews considered Jewish laws to be faulty. Deuteronomy 4:6–8 is here brought as a proof text assuring Israel that if they observe God's commandments, the nations will praise them for their wisdom.[207] Like the previously examined passages that stage Roman officials

204. See also Schwartz 2010a, 128–129.

205. Mekhilta de-Arayot is an addition to Sifra that scholars associate with the school of Rabbi Ishmael (whereas the rest of Sifra is attributed to the school of R. Aqiva). See Yadin 2004, x-xii; Kahana 2006, 17–39, 86–87.

206. Sifra, Aḥarey Mot 9.13.9, ed. Weiss, 86a, on Lev 18:4 (Ma'agarim: parashah 8, chapter 3). Translation in Dohrmann 2003, 89. See also Hirshman 1999, 52; Dohrmann 2015, 201; Hayes 2015, 248–252, which proposes a different reading of this passage: "And lest you say, 'for them they are laws (*ḥuqqim*) but for us they are not laws' Scripture says, '*you shall observe . . .*'" (250). See also Yael Wilfand, "Sifra, Aḥarey Mot parashah 8 chapter 3, 86a–b," http://www .judaism-and-rome.org/sifra-a%E1%B8%A5arey-mot-parashah-8-chapter-3-86a-b.

207. A few lines afterward in Sifra, the midrash mentions the case of a gentile who chooses to practice the commandments of the Torah and is thus said to be equal to the high priest (see the discussion below in §4.1). This may be seen as an illustration of the claim that the nations will admire the Torah's wisdom. See Hayes 2015, 251–252.

praising (most of) the laws of the Jews, this text reflects a sense of rivalry between the laws of Israel and those of non-Jews, encapsulated in the underlying question "Are their laws nicer than ours?"

3.3 THE LAWS OF ISRAEL VERSUS THE LAWS OF THE NATIONS

While the rabbinic texts on Roman officers and Rabban Gamaliel invoke the Romans' appreciation of the Torah, they reveal very little of the rabbis' views on the other camp. Explicit judgment passed by rabbis (or other Jews) on Roman law is quite rare in rabbinic literature. Jewish writers do not quote and discuss specific Roman laws as they portray gentiles doing with, for example, the Jewish law of the goring oxen. As we shall see below, Roman—and, more broadly, non-Jewish—courts are discussed a bit more explicitly. Despite this relative silence, however, it is possible to affirm that rabbinic discourse tends to contrast Israel's legal system with those of non-Jews, in accordance with the religious—or covenantal—rationale behind the Torah, which states that the Torah's laws are God's gift to Israel at Sinai. One must note, however, that when cases involve Jews and non-Jews, the rabbis do consider the possibility of adjudicating for non-Jews as well. We shall return in Section 4 to the question of the Torah's universal character in rabbinic thought, an issue that is closely linked to its applicability to gentiles. In this section I will limit myself to analyzing the rhetoric of opposition at work in rabbinic discourse, and its underlying covenantal rationale.

Not only is "rabbinic religious discourse a legal discourse," as Natalie Dohrmann rightly argues,[208] but conversely, rabbinic legal discourse is a religious discourse. This characterization is to be taken seriously, as is the connection between law and authority or sovereignty. The rabbis were legal experts, but the Torah's authority ultimately derived from its divine origin.[209] Leviticus 18:3–4, which forbids the children of Israel to walk in the ways or the laws (*ḥuqqot*) of other nations, reminds Israel that "I am the Lord your God," thereby indicating that the laws according to which they will live are not a neutral matter but instead divinely prescribed obligations that are an integral part of God's covenant. Ancient Jewish authors could thus interpret Leviticus 18:3–4 as defining two radically separate legal orders, that of the Jews and that of the non-Jews (the diversity of the latter being irrelevant), and as forbidding Jews to participate in the legal systems of other peoples.

The passage from Sifra (Mekhilta de-Arayot) we examined above, on Leviticus 18:4, continues as follows:

208. Dohrmann 2015, 198.
209. Hayes 2015.

[*You shall keep my ordinances* (mishpatim), *and my commandments/ statutes* (huqqot) *you shall observe,*] *to walk in them* (Lev 18:4). Make them the essence [of your conduct] and do not make them ancillary (or: secondary). That your dealings should be conducted only according to them; that you should not mix them with other things (*devarim*); that you should not say: I have learned the wisdom of Israel, [now] I will learn the wisdom of the nations. [Therefore] Scripture says: *to walk in them* (Lev 18:4). [You cannot] abandon them. So it says: *Let them be for yourself alone and not for sharing with strangers* (Prov 5:17).[210]

The association of wisdom and law found here is already present in the midrash's previous passage, which quotes Deuteronomy 4:6. It is characteristic of Jewish writings of various kinds, such as the Wisdom of Ben Sira,[211] for Torah encompasses not only law sensu stricto but also ethical and theological guidance. This passage may reflect the fear that in comparison with Roman laws, rabbinic rulings might appear strange and ill-conceived. What is of particular interest here, in any case, is the strong requirement that Israel's laws be preserved as a separate body and not mixed up with foreign elements—the Hebrew term *devarim*, which has several meanings ("words," "commands," "things," "affairs"), probably refers to foreign laws or customs. Jews are not supposed to import foreign elements into their laws and way of life; the midrash may even be saying that they are not to learn the laws of non-Jews and compare them with the laws of Israel. Finally, the quotation of Proverbs 5:17 at the end of the passage emphasizes that Israel is likewise not to share its own laws with other nations.

This rhetoric of seclusion should logically pertain not only to the laws but also to the tribunals of the nations—that is, to their legal systems as a whole. Beth Berkowitz recalls that there are already examples of such a rejection of non-Jewish courts in the Second Temple period.[212] According to Yonder Gillihan, the *Damascus Document* from Qumran (CD IX 1, with parallels in 4QD[a] and 4QD[e]) forbids the members of the community to appeal to the laws and courts of non-Jews in a capital case.[213] We might also cite here the rejection of pagan tribunals in Paul's First Letter to the Corinthians:

When one of you has a grievance against a brother, does he dare go to law before the unrighteous instead of the saints? Do you not know

---

210. Sifra, Aharey Mot 9.13.11, ed. Weiss, 86a–b (Ma'agarim: parashah 8, chapter 3). My translation is based on Berkowitz 2012, 71; see also Hayes 2015, 250. On the different interpretations of Lev 18:3–4 found in Sifra, see Berkowitz 2012, 77–111, and Berkowitz 2017, 135–141.

211. See especially Ben Sira 24; Burns 2017a.

212. Berkowitz 2017, 132–133.

213. Gillihan 2012, 191–197. The interpretation of this specific passage is difficult, however.

that the saints will judge the world? And if the world is to be judged by you, are you incompetent to try trivial cases? [. . .] I say this to your shame. Can it be that there is no man among you wise enough to decide between members of the brotherhood, but brother goes to law against brother, and that before unbelievers? (1 Cor 6:1–6)

Paul's exhortation to the members of this community shows that they brought cases before the local courts instead of trusting in community-based arbitration. The rationale behind his criticism is both moral—Christians should be united in brotherly love, *agapē*, and should tolerate no strife whatsoever among themselves—and theological: believers should be judged by believers. When Christians submit their case to a pagan tribunal, they submit themselves to the authority of unbelievers and accept being judged by them, whereas in the heavenly kingdom, it is the "saints" who will judge the world.

Although Paul makes this argument on the basis of his faith in Christ, his theological rationale has an equivalent in rabbinic literature, albeit obliquely. Some rabbinic texts reflect an effort to prevent Jews from turning to non-Jewish tribunals, but their argument is less straightforward than Paul's, and the nature of the issue is likely quite different as well.[214] Mishnah Gittin 9:8 thus states: "A bill of divorce given by force, if by Israel, it is valid, if by the nations (*goyim*), it is not valid. But [it is valid if] gentiles force him [the husband] and say to him: 'Do as the Israelite [authorities] tell you.'"[215] This passage shows that the rabbis were particularly keen to control marital and family law and to prevent Jews from turning to non-Jewish courts in this domain. Another case in point is t. Yevamot 12:13, which deals with *ḥalitzah*, the procedure to be followed if a man has declined to marry his childless brother's widow (Deut 25:5–10). The Tosefta asserts that a *ḥalitzah* performed under compulsion is valid at an Israelite court but invalid at a gentile court, unless non-Jews compel the man and say to him: "Do what Rabbi X bids you." This formulation is very similar to that of m. Gittin 9:8, except that here the vague term "Israel" (or "the Israelites") is replaced by the more explicit "Rabbi X" (*rabbi peloni*). The evidence from the Tosefta reveals that what was at stake was not merely Jewish control but rabbinic control.[216]

214. Jackson 1975, 237; Hezser 1997, 476–477; Lapin 2012, 98–111; Berthelot 2021.

215. Trans. Dohrmann 2003, 91 (based on MS Kaufmann). On this passage, see also Furstenberg 2019b, 495–498. Furstenberg remarks: "In this case, the rabbis could reasonably expect Roman cooperation in applying their own laws, since on this point they accorded with the Roman vision of marriage as based on continuing mutual consent" (498). This is another instance of the dialectic of ideological opposition and practical acculturation mentioned above.

216. See Lieberman 1955–1973, 3:44; Lieberman 1955–1988, 6:141–145; Goodman 1983, 156. That there were Jews who turned to non-Jewish courts for matrimonial issues is

Interestingly enough, these passages from the Mishnah and the Tosefta both reject the authority of gentile courts even as they assent to its use in forcing Jews to comply with Jewish (that is, rabbinic) law and legal decisions. In practice, then, the Roman legal system may have been accepted, even in matters of divorce, if it served the rabbinic legal system—if it was, in a way, subservient to the latter. Here the notion of rivalry between Israel (the rabbis) and Rome (gentiles) comes to the surface again, precisely in the realm of jurisdiction and judicial power. On the other hand, the rabbinic rulings in m. Gittin 9:8 and t. Yevamot 12:13 indicate a pragmatic acknowledgment of the fact that Roman jurisdiction could be more effective than rabbinic arbitration. The fact that the Mishnah apparently accepted Roman imperial dating on divorce documents (m. Gittin 8:5) also points to a pragmatic approach and reflects the concern that these documents be considered valid by the Roman authorities.

The rule formulated in m. Gittin 9:8 is echoed in Mekhilta de-Rabbi Ishmael. Commenting on Exodus 21:1—"And these are the ordinances [*mishpatim*] that you [Moses] shall set before them"—the midrash reports the following opinion attributed to Rabbi Eleazar ben Azariah:[217]

> Now whenever the gentiles were to judge according to the laws of Israel, I might think that their decisions are valid. Scripture says: *And these are the ordinances [which you shall set before them]*—You may judge theirs but they may not judge yours. On the basis of this interpretation they [the Sages] say: "A bill of divorce given by force, if by Israel, it is valid, if by the nations, it is not valid. But [it is valid if] gentiles force him [the husband] and say to him: 'Do as the Israelite [authorities] tell you'" [quoting m. Gittin 9:8].[218]

Natalie Dohrmann has analyzed this text in depth,[219] so I will limit myself to two points. First, R. Eleazar ben Azariah here generalizes the prohibition found in m. Gittin. While the Mishnah deals with the very limited case of a bill of divorce given under compulsion, R. Eleazar's statement in the Mekhilta has far-ranging implications. In theory, it means that Jews should never be judged by non-Jewish courts, even if the non-Jewish judges ruled according to the laws of Israel—and all the more so, this statement implies, if they judged according to Roman or any other non-Jewish law. Jewish judges, however, may judge non-Jews, a point one could describe as an imitation of the universal jurisdiction of the Romans within their empire. This passage therefore

shown by papyri from Egypt and the Judean desert. See *CPJ* II, p. 10–12, no. 144 (13 BCE); Cotton 1998 and 1999; and, more generally, §1.2 above.

217. According to rabbinic tradition, Rabbi Eleazar ben Azariah was a tanna active in the late first and early second centuries.

218. MRI Neziqin (Mishpatim) 1, trans. Dohrmann 2003, 85, based on the edition of Horowitz and Rabin, 246. See also Lauterbach 2004, 2:355–356.

219. Dohrmann 2003.

represents something very different from the Mishnah and may be characterized as a fantasy of jurisdiction over non-Jews, including Romans. (We will
return to this issue below.)

Second, it is important to emphasize that it is not the *content* of the laws
that is the issue here. There are at least two ways to understand R. Eleazar's
statement. He may be admitting that in some cases, non-Jewish and Jewish
laws and verdicts agree and may therefore look similar. Alternatively, he may
be saying that in some civil matters, non-Jewish tribunals use the laws of the
Jews (perhaps classified as customs) in trials involving Jews.[220] Whatever the
exact scenario envisaged by Rabbi Eleazar, his point is that a non-Jewish court
lacks legitimacy to judge the people of Israel, even if it should judge according to the laws of Israel. From his perspective, the non-Jewish court is illegitimate per se.[221] Only when it merely enforces a legal decision handed down by
an Israelite court—which may in fact have been an arbitration ruling—can its
intervention be accepted.

A *baraita* in b. Gittin 88b—which discusses the aforementioned m. Gittin
9:8—contains a saying attributed to R. Tarfon that sheds further light on
R. Eleazar ben Azariah's teaching:[222]

> In any place where you find gentile courts (*agorayot*, from the Greek
> *agora*), even though their laws are law like the Israelite laws, it is not
> permitted to resort to them, since it says: *And these are the ordinances
> which you shall set before them* (Exod 21:1). *Before them*, and not before
> gentiles (*goyim*).[223]

Like the Mekhilta de-Rabbi Ishmael, the *baraita* chooses Exodus 21:1 as a
proof text, but it adds the interpretation of the words "before them" at the end
of the verse, explaining them as meaning "not before gentiles." These words
probably refer to non-Jewish courts, implying that the laws of Israel were
not to be brought to ("before") Roman courts. This *baraita* might also imply
that Israel has received laws that are not to be disclosed to gentiles and thus

220. This interpretation is corroborated by the reading *be-diney Israel*, found in one
MS, as opposed to *ke-diney Israel*. On custom in Roman law, see Section 1.2 above.

221. An alternate interpretation of this text would have Rabbi Eleazar prohibit recourse
to non-Jewish courts especially—or only?—when the law being applied was a Jewish law, in
which case the intention behind the prohibition would be to prevent Jews from confusing
the two legal systems. Recourse to Roman courts in matters falling under non-Jewish law
would then be permitted. Yet the rabbis' interpretative work seems to aim to establish the
Torah as a body of rules codifying every aspect of Jewish life, leaving very little room for
the use of non-Jewish laws in cases involving only Jews.

222. According to rabbinic tradition, R. Tarfon was a third-generation tanna (early
second century CE).

223. My translation is based on MS Vaticanus 130, consulted on Ma'agarim.

pertain to Jews alone, as Mekhilta de-Arayot 9.13.11 states. In this case, Jews are not to share their laws with gentiles, just as they are not supposed to turn to non-Jewish laws and jurisdictions.[224]

The problem posed by Roman jurisdiction was political but also religious. It had to do with the nature of the authority involved. That this authority was perceived as ungodly is shown by the designation of Rome as "the evil kingdom" in rabbinic texts and by numerous stories depicting the impious and evil behavior of individual Romans.[225] Besides, the issue of the oaths taken at court and in legal contexts more broadly (for example in contracts) must have troubled the rabbis (though not necessarily all Jews), insofar as these oaths involved swearing by Zeus/Jupiter (or other deities) or by the *tychē/genius* of the emperor.[226] In relation to *CPJ* II, no. 427, in which a Jew swears by the emperor Trajan (rather than by his *tychē*), Victor Tcherikover and Alexander Fuks note that even if the emperor was not a god, the oath implied his superhuman character.[227] According to m. Sanhedrin 7:6, he who takes a vow or swears in the name of an idol—which could be anyone or anything that is worshiped—violates a negative commandment.

Moreover, as the beginning of this chapter mentioned, a mishnah found in tractate Avodah Zarah (1:7) forbids Jews to participate in the building of "a

224. Bernard Jackson mentions a more indirect and implicit example of rabbinic attempts to prevent Jews from using Roman courts. He refers to the rabbinic ruling according to which "one who voluntarily confesses to an offence involving a penalty and a fine is exempt from that fine" and, in the case of theft, "is liable only to restore the stolen property, or its value"—pointing to m. Shevu'ot 5:4, m. Ketubbot 3:9, m. Bava Qamma 7:4, and t. Bava Qamma 8:2—and suggests that it "is one of a series designed to keep disputes within the Jewish community, and thereby prevent them from being taken to alien, i.e. Roman, jurisdiction." He mentions as a possible source "the Roman rule of *lis crescens*, e.g. in the *Lex Aquilia* (*Dig.* 9.2.2.1, Gaius)," and adds: "If this is indeed its background, then the possibility that it was based on a Roman model assumes a somewhat novel and ironic complexion" (Jackson 1975, 237–238).

225. See in particular the texts cited in Chapters Two and Three pertaining to Titus' desecration of the Jerusalem Temple.

226. For oaths by the emperor's *tychē/genius* in private contracts, see the archives of the Sulpicii (*TPSulp* 68); in legal documents involving Jews, see P. Yadin 16, lines 33–34 (*Babtha Simōnos omnumi tychēn kyriou Kaisaros*); XḤev/Se 61, line 2; Czajkowski 2015. An oath by the emperor (rather than by his *tychē*) is found in a papyrus from Egypt dated to 101 CE (*CPJ* II, no. 427, lines 20–24); Tcherikover and Fuks note that "the Roman oath 'by the genius of the Emperor' was not yet familiar in Egypt" (Tcherikover and Fuks 1954–1964, 2:214). On oaths taken by litigants and witnesses at court, see Guérin 2015, 114–117, which states that witnesses could not give evidence without swearing by Jupiter; see also Amirante 1954, 181–183. For oaths by the emperor's *tychē/genius* in trials against Christians, see, e.g., *Martyrdom of Polycarp* 9.2, 10.1; *Acts of the Scillitan Martyrs* 5. Tertullian derided the awe with which pagans swore by the emperor's *genius* (*Apology* 28.3; see also Minucius Felix, *Octavius* 29.5).

227. Tcherikover and Fuks 1954–1964, 2:214; Cotton 1998, 167–168.

basilica, a *gradus* (platform),[228] a stadium,[229] or a tribunal (*bemah*)." The reference to the basilica and the *bemah* alongside the *gradus*, a location for executions, and the stadium (or the arena more generally), where criminals were occasionally killed, indicates that spots at which Roman authorities dispensed justice were associated with bloodshed.[230] Although the text does not explicitly characterize these places as idolatrous, the fact that this prohibition is found in tractate Avodah Zarah, which deals with idolatrous objects and festivals and broadly codifies relationships between Jews and non-Jews, suggests that Roman jurisdiction was perceived as belonging to the realm of what was forbidden to Jews.[231] The underlying argument may have been that Roman jurisdiction substituted itself not only for rabbinic or other Jewish judges but for God himself as the source of true judicial authority and as the ultimate judge of Israel. It seems that among rabbinic views, therefore, there was at least one current of thought that contrasted the jurisdiction of Rome (or the gentiles in general), seen as ungodly, with that of Israel, based on God's revealed law and thus endowed with divine authority.[232]

However, explicit associations of Roman tribunals with idolatry rarely come to the fore in Palestinian rabbinic sources (up to the beginning of the fifth century). This is probably to be explained by the fact that the majority of the rabbis opted for a more accommodationist and pragmatic position, exemplified by their recognition of the role played by public archives, for

228. On the *gradus* as a platform on which the convict was questioned and occasionally tortured or put to death, see Lieberman 1944; Sperber 1984, 76–78; Hayes 1995, esp. 158.

229. In this case *istariah*, which Jastrow 1950, 92, characterizes as "a cacophemistic appellation of all kinds of gentile sports," probably stands for *istadion*; Lapin 2012, 130, says that it was "specifically invoked as a venue for execution of convicts."

230. The exercise of justice was also a kind of spectacle. Clifford Ando emphasizes the visibility of the governors' assizes and trials, which attracted great crowds (Ando 2000, 375–378).

231. On Mishnah Avodah Zarah, see, e.g., Halbertal 1998.

232. That God is the ultimate guarantor of justice in Israel is expressed in, e.g., Sifre Deuteronomy 9 (ed. Finkelstein, 17). For a more detailed presentation of this argument, see Berthelot 2021. Non-Jewish tribunals are explicitly associated with the gods of the nations and idolatry in later sources, such as Midrash Tanḥuma (a collection of homilies on the Pentateuch that may date to the beginning of the fifth century but has a complicated transmission history), Mishpatim 3. This midrash influenced the great medieval commentator Rashi (see Rashi on Exodus 21:1). Beyond Rashi, R. Tarfon's position in b. Gittin 88b enjoyed a wide reception in medieval Judaism—one notable proponent was Rabbi Solomon ibn Adret (the Rashba, d. 1310), who reiterated that Jews "are prohibited by the Torah from showing a preference for the law of the Gentiles and their ordinances. Moreover, it is forbidden to bring litigation into their courts even in matters where their laws are identical to Jewish law" (quotation in Lauer 2016, 115). This position was quite common in medieval rabbinic law, yet it was not put into practice by medieval Jewish communities (Lauer 2016, 115).

example.[233] After all, Jews had no choice but to go before the Roman courts in criminal cases, and it would not necessarily have been possible to settle civil disputes between Jews and non-Jews through rabbinic or other Jewish arbitration. If the views of R. Eleazar ben Azariah and R. Tarfon really are to be associated with these tannaim—who, according to rabbinic tradition, were active before the Bar Kokhba Revolt—then they may reflect a position that went back to a time of severe conflict between Rome and the Jews, which lost part of its intensity after the failure of the last revolt against Rome and gave way to a more realistic perspective. The focus on family issues, such as marriage and divorce, that characterizes the evidence from the Mishnah and the Tosefta may indicate a shift from an absolute to a selective prohibition. In addition, m. Gittin 9:8 and t. Yevamot 12:13 open the door to the possibility of Roman enforcement of rabbinic decisions. One may thus cautiously suggest that there was a diachronic evolution in tannaitic thought on these issues. In any case, when looking at Palestinian rabbinic sources as a whole, it is possible to speak of a dialectic of rejection and accommodation vis-à-vis Roman jurisdiction.

So far, this section has argued that rabbinic rulings concerning Jews and gentile legal systems project a strong opposition or contrast between Israel and the nations. However, this rhetoric of opposition coexists with cases of unconscious absorption or conscious imitation of the Roman models.[234]

A first example has to do with capital punishment. I referred in Chapter Three to the rabbinic debate on execution by the sword, which some rabbis considered an intolerable imitation of the evil kingdom.[235] The issue of capital punishment's cruelty is a crucial one in rabbinic literature, a nodal point of self-definition vis-à-vis the imperial power. Sifre Deuteronomy 323, commenting on Deuteronomy 32:31—"For their rock is not as our Rock [God], that our enemies be judges upon us,"[236] a verse that already contrasts Israel and the nations—explains that Israel does not behave like the nations, because when Jews rule over non-Jews, they judge them (lit. "behave with them") with mercy (*be-middat raḥamim*), whereas the nations treat the Jews with cruelty: they

233. In m. Gittin 1:5, the majority opinion is that documents deposited in such archives are valid, except for writs of divorce and documents related to manumission. This text also mentions the diverging opinion of R. Shimon ben Yoḥai, who argues that all documents deposited in public archives are to be considered valid, except for those made by an individual in a private context. See also t. Gittin 1:4 (with an extended discussion of the same issues); y. Gittin 1:4, 7a; and t. Avodah Zarah 1:5–8, which recommends that Jews register their transactions with non-Jews in public archives to secure their rights of ownership. See Yael Wilfand, "Mishnah Gittin 1:5," http://www.judaism-and-rome.org/mishnah-gittin-15, with bibliography.

234. For examples of rabbinic adoption of Roman legal principles, see Section 2 above.

235. See also Berkowitz 2005.

236. On this translation and the interpretation of this biblical verse in other rabbinic texts, see Berthelot 2021.

burn them, crucify them, and execute them in the most outrageous ways.[237] Yet in another third-century midrash, Sifre Numbers, crucifixion is paradoxically presented as an instruction given to Moses by God! The midrash comments on Numbers 25:4, which recounts God's reaction when the people of Israel committed idolatry and debauchery with Moabite women at Shittim. In the biblical narrative, God tells Moses: "Take all the chiefs of the people, and impale (or: hang, *we-hoqaʿ*) them in the sun before the Lord." In the next verse, Moses requests that "the judges of Israel" (*shoftey Israel*) have those who have worshiped Baal Peor, the deity of the Moabites, put to death (root *h-r-g*). In the midrash, God instructs Moses to appoint judges (*dayanim*) and to order them to crucify (root *tz-l-b*) the sinners "in the sun" (that is, publicly).[238] The midrash follows the biblical text rather closely. The choice of the verb "to crucify" rather than "to hang" to refer to the death penalty inflicted on the rebels may reflect a simple transposition of biblical notions into contemporary reality. Crucifixion was characteristic of Roman rule in the eyes of the Jews (and other provincials) living in the empire.[239] In Sifre Numbers, God can thus be seen as repressing a rebellion among his people just as cruelly as a Roman emperor would. This passage illustrates both the acculturation of the rabbis and their ambivalence toward Roman methods of execution.[240]

We encounter the dialectic of rejection and absorption of Roman norms in other contexts as well, for example in the roles played by prosecutors and advocates in the courts.[241] The Mekhilta de-Rabbi Ishmael interprets the biblical verse "Keep far from a false charge" (Exod 23:7) as a prohibition against the appointment of an advocate (*sanegor*, from the Greek *synēgoros*) by the judge, on the basis of another biblical passage, "The case of both parties shall come before God" (Exod 22:8).[242] The end of Exodus 22:8 ("the one whom God condemns shall pay double to the other") indicates that God is the ultimate judge for Israelites. As a consequence, the Jewish judge acts as God's representative, and nobody is to intervene between him and the plaintiffs: the latter are to come before the judge with no intermediaries—who, the Mekhilta suggests, could bring false charges against the other side. By emphasizing this aspect of the ideal judicial procedure in a Jewish context, the Mekhilta thus

237. Sifre Deuteronomy 323, ed. Finkelstein, 373.

238. Sifre Numbers 131, ed. Kahana 2011–2015, 1:55 [רנ] (cf. Horovitz 1917, 172).

239. Josephus states that King Alexander Jannaeus had some of his opponents crucified at the beginning of the first century BCE, but this may be echoing a biased account of Jannaeus' reign (see *A.J.* 13.380).

240. See Berkowitz 2006, 159–165; Hayes 2020.

241. Riggsby 2010, 47–55, 75, 79, 197.

242. MRI Kaspa (Mishpatim) 20, ed. Horovitz and Rabin, 326–327. On the term *sanegor*, see Sperber 1984, 126–128. See also Yael Wilfand, "Mekhilta de Rabbi Ishmael, Kasfa (Mishpatim) 20," http://www.judaism-and-rome.org/mekhilta-de-rabbi-ishmael-kasfa-mishpatim-20.

builds a strong contrast between Roman and Jewish jurisdiction.[243] According to Richard Hidary, rabbinic literature on the whole tends to reject advocates and foreground the role of judges (in earthly courts). He further argues that the rabbis deliberately attempted to elaborate "a system in opposition to the corruption they saw in the Roman legal system."[244]

However, other texts depict God as a judge who sits in a heavenly court that looks quite Roman. In the Jerusalem Talmud's tractate Rosh ha-Shanah—concerning the new year festival, an event associated in rabbinic tradition with God's judgment of Israel and indeed all of humankind—God is a judge who allows Israel to determine the exact date of the trial (i.e., the festival). The point is that Rosh ha-Shanah takes place on the first day of Tishri, and the beginning of the month is linked to the observation of the moon by a Jewish court, which may be mistaken but nevertheless has full authority to establish the date.[245] The Jerusalem Talmud presents the fact of Israel's setting the date of Rosh ha-Shanah as an illustration of Deuteronomy 4:8: "What other great nation has statutes and ordinances as just as this entire law that I am setting before you today?" The Talmud—quoting a teaching attributed to R. Hoshayah[246]—contrasts these heavenly proceedings with the regular functioning of a royal court, in which it is the king, not the convict, who decides the trial's date. The text thus draws an opposition between the imperial court and that of Israel's God (rather than between Roman and Jewish courts as in MRI). However, on hearing that the date of Rosh ha-Shanah has been declared for the current day, God says to the ministering angels: "Set up the platform (*bemah*), let the advocates (*sanegorin*) stand, let the prosecutors (*qategorin*, from the Greek *katēgoros*) stand." Alternately, on hearing that Rosh ha-Shanah has been postponed to the next day, God declares to the ministering angels: "Remove the platform, let the advocates go away, let the prosecutors go away."[247] The text states that one finds a *bemah*, advocates, and prosecutors at the heavenly court, which therefore appears to be built on a Roman model.[248] As in the previous example (crucifixion), it is God

243. See Hidary 2018, 221–238, which refers to the MRI and to Mekhilta de-Rashbi, Mishpatim 23:1 (on Exod 23:1). Hidary also points to the fact that the Mishnah never refers to advocates, except in Avot 1:8 (in a negative way), and examines further evidence from both Talmuds that confirms the analysis of the tannaitic sources.

244. Hidary 2018, 241.

245. See m. Rosh ha-Shanah 2:1–3:1; t. Rosh ha-Shanah 1:11.

246. According to rabbinic tradition, there were two sages named Hoshayah: a first-generation amora (first half of the third century), and a third-generation amora who was active in the late third and early fourth centuries. Both were from the Land of Israel.

247. y. Rosh ha-Shanah 1:2, 57b (1:2 according to Ma'agarim; 1:3 in Schäfer and Becker 1991–2001 [2001, *Synopse* II/5–12], 188–189); my translation is based on MS Leiden. See also Pesiqta de-Rav Kahana (Ha-Ḥodesh ha-zeh) 5:13, ed. Mandelbaum, 1:102.

248. See Yael Wilfand, "Jerusalem Talmud Rosh Hashanah 1:2, 57b," http://www .judaism-and-rome.org/jerusalem-talmud-rosh-hashanah-12-57b. Two other texts

himself who looks Romanized and who behaves in a way that is forbidden to the judges of Israel. This is all the more surprising as the text emphasizes that Israel and God abide by the same law, quoting Psalms 81:5, "For it is a statute for Israel, an ordinance for the God of Jacob."[249] Like Sifre Numbers 131, this passage of the Jerusalem Talmud highlights the rabbis' familiarity with Roman jurisdiction and their absorption of some of its aspects, despite their oppositional stance. Moreover, as Hidary hypothesizes, they may have "envisioned the heavenly court in terms of Roman courts, not in spite of the corruption of the latter but precisely because of it," in order to suggest that "a heavenly court that followed strict justice [. . .] would issue impossibly harsh, even if justifiable, verdicts." From the perspective of the rabbis, admitting advocates into the heavenly court would allow mercy to prevail.[250]

All in all, the rhetoric of opposition to Roman jurisdiction is thus real but ambiguous, and only partial. Moreover, the remark attributed to R. Eleazar ben Azariah that "you may judge theirs but they may not judge yours," probably meaning that Jews can legitimately be judges or arbitrators in trials involving non-Jews, contradicts the rigid distinction between "our laws" and "their laws." If Jews may judge cases brought by non-Jews, this blurs the distinction between Israel and *goyim* that rabbinic texts attempt to build.[251] It also raises again the question of mimesis vis-à-vis Rome.

From a historical perspective, it is indeed possible that rabbis or other local Jewish arbitrators occasionally had to settle a dispute between a Jew and a non-Jew (for example in business dealings), especially in majority-Jewish areas. Sifre Deuteronomy 16 seems to address such a situation:

> [*I commanded your judges at that time, saying:*] *Hear between your brethren,* [*and judge rightly between one person and another, whether his brother or a resident alien* (ger) (Deut 1:16)]. Such was the ruling of R. Ishmael: When an Israelite and a gentile came to him for adjudication, if [they came to be judged] according to the laws of Israel (*ke-diney Israel*), he favored the Israelite [lit: he made the Israelite win]; and if [they came to be judged] according to the laws of the nations of the world (*ke-diney ummot ha-'olam*), he favored the Israelite. He said: Why should I care? Doesn't the Torah say: *Hear between your brethren*?

---

mention a *qategor* at the heavenly court: m. Avot 4:11 and t. Sotah 6:5. This idea has a biblical basis in the figure of the *satan*. In fact, Exodus Rabbah 18:5 represents Satan as a prosecutor. On the functioning of the heavenly court in rabbinic texts and its similarities with Roman courts, see Hidary 2018, 250–261; and already Lieberman 1944, 31–32.

249. I have modified the NRSV version, which avoids the exegetical difficulty by translating this as "an ordinance *of* the God of Jacob."

250. Hidary 2018, 250–251, 261.

251. On the Israel/*goyim* divide, see Rosen-Zvi and Ophir 2011; Ophir and Rosen-Zvi 2018; and the responses of Hayes 2017a, Furstenberg 2019a, and Irshai 2019, 165–168.

R. Shimon ben Gamaliel[252] says: There is no need [to rule in this way]. If he comes for an adjudication according to the laws of Israel, let him judge according to the laws of Israel. [If he comes for an adjudication] according to the laws of the nations of the world, let him judge according to the laws of the nations of the world.[253]

The biblical verse (Deut 1:16) cited here mentions the obligation to judge rightly between two Israelites or between an Israelite and a *ger*. In the Bible, the term *ger* generally means "foreign resident," but in rabbinic literature it designates a convert. Therefore the verse could be understood as applying only to legal proceedings between fellow Jews (converts being considered members of the people of Israel). R. Ishmael interpreted the verse in such a restrictive way and thus favored the Israelite no matter the laws under which the Israelite and the gentile came for adjudication. What is remarkable in this text is the very suggestion that a Jew and a gentile could ask a rabbinic judge or arbitrator to adjudicate according to the laws of the nations of the world. Moreover, R. Shimon ben Gamaliel's response to R. Ishmael clearly affirms the legitimacy of such an option, in addition to rejecting R. Ishmael's treatment of non-Jews. We have seen above other examples of the rabbis' preoccupation with laws that could appear discriminatory to the Roman authorities, and R. Shimon's response reflects this concern—which, in these midrashim, is attributed to his father, Rabban Gamaliel (II).[254]

The question that must be answered is: "What exactly is meant by "the laws of the nations of the world?" Are we dealing with the different law codes of various peoples, such as Greeks and Romans, or is the text referring to the laws of the children of Noah, despite not using this expression?[255] The first possibility seems more probable to me, although other rabbinic texts that mention the *diney ummot ha-'olam* do so in connection with the prohibition of certain sexual relationships, one of the seven commandments of the children of Noah.[256] I will discuss these commandments in the next section, which deals with the Torah's universal character in rabbinic thought. As far as Sifre Deuteronomy 16 is concerned, two points are critical: First, if we suppose that *diney ummot ha-'olam* refers to the actual laws of various nations— first and foremost those of Rome—then the rabbis are presented as able to

252. Certainly to be identified with Rabban Shimon ben Gamaliel II, a tanna of the third generation, the son of Rabban Gamaliel (II) and father of Yehudah ha-Nasi (see above).

253. Sifre Deuteronomy 16, ed. Finkelstein, 26–27; the translation of the biblical verse is mine.

254. Sifre Deuteronomy 344; Mekhilta Deuteronomy 33:3.

255. According to Furstenberg 2018, the "laws of the nations of the world" are associated with Roman jurisdiction. On the Noahide commandments, see below, § 4.3.

256. See Sifra, Qedoshim 10.1, ed. Weiss, 91b (Ma'agarim: parashah 5, chapter 1); t. Avodah Zarah 9:4; y. Qiddushin 1:1, 58b–c.

adjudicate according to foreign laws and thus as experts both in the law of Israel and in the laws of foreign peoples, including Roman law. Second, if rabbinic judges are able to settle disputes between Jews and non-Jews according to different sets of laws, they are to a certain extent similar to the Roman judges who adjudicated on the basis of both Roman and local laws. If we follow this interpretation, this passage from Sifre becomes an example of Jewish mimesis of imperial jurisdiction.[257]

In sum, this subsection argues that rabbinic literature reflects both rejection of and accommodation to Roman jurisdiction. The rabbis maintained the Bible's covenantal understanding of the Torah and strongly correlated Jewish—or rabbinic—jurisdiction, be it only in the form of arbitration, with God's law and justice. Yet in practice they integrated elements of Roman law (as we saw in Section 2 above) while finding ways to legitimize the enforcement of Jewish law by Roman courts. Some rabbinic texts in fact combine attitudes of opposition and receptivity (either as imitation or unconscious absorption) toward the Roman model. In some cases, a clear sense of rivalry between Israel and Rome comes to the fore, around the underlying question of who had the best laws.

It is probably against the background of this rivalry that we must understand the choice made by the majority of the rabbis to define the Torah as the exclusive law of Israel rather than as the most perfect expression of the universal law of nature, the position favored by philosophically oriented Jewish authors writing in Greek.

4. The Torah as Nonuniversal Law

4.1 FROM A LAW ACCESSIBLE TO ALL TO ISRAEL'S EXCLUSIVE LAW

The notion that the Torah is the most perfect written expression of the law of nature and therefore rational and universal is common among Jewish authors writing in Greek, who were eager to respond to the cultural challenge that Greek philosophical thought on law presented to them.[258] In a Hellenistic world that witnessed the development of Stoic philosophy, which placed nature and rationality at the core of its ethical thinking, reconciling Greek and

---

257. Yair Furstenberg emphasizes the "reciprocity" of the positioning of the rabbis and Roman authorities vis-à-vis local laws according to rabbinic sources. He also highlights chronological evolutions, first from the period of the sages of Yavneh to that of later tannaim, and then from tannaitic to amoraic sources, the latter being more open to legal pluralism—that is, to the recognition of non-Jewish (Roman) courts (Furstenberg 2018, esp. 23, 37).

258. Biblical texts reflect different views of the Torah, including a universalistic one, yet in contrast to Jewish Hellenistic texts, their perspective is mostly eschatological. See, e.g., Isaiah 2:2–3.

biblical notions of law was not an easy task, as Christine Hayes aptly recalls in her book on divine law.[259]

The Torah's universal character is articulated with particular force in Jewish writings in Greek on the commandment of the Sabbath.[260] In the fifth fragment of Aristobulus, quoted in Eusebius' *Praeparatio evangelica* 13.12.9–16, the Sabbath embodies a law of nature (it is *ennomos*) and "serves as a symbol [or: a sign] of the sevenfold principle established all around us through which we have knowledge of things both human and divine" (§12).[261] Cornelis de Vos rightly notes that with his exposure of the Sabbath's universal dimension, Aristobulus "proclaimed the Jewish law as an expression of the logical structure of the world and of knowledge."[262] In Aristobulus' thought, the Torah as a whole was an expression of the law of nature.

We encounter a similar perspective in Philo's writings. For him, the Sabbath is "the festival, not of a single city or country, but of the universe, and it alone strictly deserves to be called 'public' as belonging to all people, and the birthday of the world."[263] Moreover, as we have mentioned, the treatise *On the Life of Moses* contains an explicit statement about the universal dimension of the Mosaic law as a whole, based on the observation that it is followed widely among the nations. Philo claims that all peoples despise laws that are not part of their own legislation. The laws of the Jews, however, "attract and win the attention of all":

> For, who has not shown his high respect for that sacred seventh day, by giving rest and relaxation from labour to himself and his neighbours, freemen and slaves alike, and beyond these to his beasts? [. . .] Again, who does not every year show awe and reverence for the fast, as it is called, which is kept more strictly and solemnly than the "holy month" of the Greeks?[264]

By "the fast," Philo probably means the Day of Atonement (Yom Kippur). His claim that crowds of non-Jews regularly observe both the Sabbath and the fast of Yom Kippur is clearly exaggerated, but not completely without parallel in Greco-Roman sources. The statement that many people honor the Sabbath is found in Seneca's *De superstitione*, known from Augustine's quotation in *De civitate Dei* 6.11, and is alluded to in Juvenal's *Satires* 14. Indeed, Roman

---

259. Hayes 2015, esp. Chapter Three.

260. Yet this is not limited to texts that discuss the Sabbath. See, e.g., Wisdom 18:4, which states that through the children of Israel, "the incorruptible light of the law was to be given to the world."

261. Holladay 1995, 185; cf. de Vos 2016, 153.

262. De Vos 2016, 151. On the Sabbath's universal dimension in Aristobulus, see Doering 1999, 306–315.

263. *Opif.* 89, trans. F. H. Colson and G. H. Whitaker, LCL, 73.

264. *Mos.* 2.21–23, trans. F. H. Colson, LCL, 459–461.

satirists often referred to the practice of the Sabbath in Roman society.[265] It is also noteworthy that Roman authors often associated the sabbatical rest with fasting.[266]

Josephus' *Against Apion* echoes Philo's statements:

> What is more, even among the masses for a long time there has been much emulation of our piety, and there is not one city of the Greeks, nor a single barbarian nation, where the custom of the seventh day, on which we rest, has not permeated, and where our fasts and lighting of lamps and many of our prohibitions with regard to food have not been observed.[267]

Like Philo (in *Mos.* 2.18, 20), Josephus highlights the Mosaic law's universality by dividing humankind into two categories, Greeks and barbarians, and claiming that members of both these groups have unanimously adopted Jewish customs. It seems that, again, these customs are primarily the fast of Kippur and the celebration of the Sabbath. Indeed, the lighting of lamps, which Josephus states was a Jewish practice imitated by non-Jews, is associated by Seneca with the Sabbath (*Epistulae* 95.47) and by Persius with "Herod's day," probably also to be identified as the Sabbath (*Saturae* 5.180–181). It must be emphasized that in Philo's treatise *On the Life of Moses*, as in Josephus' *Against Apion*, the "universality" of the Mosaic law means more than harmony with the law of nature or the structure of the cosmos: it is not merely an idea but also a concrete fact demonstrated by its worldwide reception among the nations, a practical universality that evokes the universal presence and availability of Roman law in the framework of the empire. Indeed, the emphasis laid by Philo and Josephus on the universal acceptance of the Mosaic law by non-Jews has no precedent in Jewish writings of the Hellenistic period. It should probably be understood as a response to the growing sway of Roman law within the empire's provinces, as described in Section 2 above.[268]

Alongside the universalistic vision of the Torah as a law that gives expression to the decrees of nature and is open to non-Jews even absent their proper conversion, one finds in ancient Jewish sources a particularistic understanding of the Torah, according to which it is given to Israel alone. In the Book of Ben

---

265. In *Sermones* 1.9.60–78, Horace features a certain Aristius Fuscus who observes the Sabbath. For other examples, see Berthelot 2020c.

266. See Pompeius Trogus, *apud* Justin, *Epitome* 36.2.14; Petronius, *Fragmenta*, no. 37 (he speaks about "the fasts of Sabbath [*ieiuna sabbata*] imposed by the law"); Martial, *Epig.* 4.4.7; Suetonius, *Life of Augustus* 76.2. See also Goldenberg 1979, 439, which suggests that this association could have stemmed from the fact that Jews refused to light fires or cook on the Sabbath.

267. *C. Ap.* 2.282, trans. Barclay 2007, 327–328. See also Josephus, *B.J.* 2.463, 2.560, 7.45.

268. This response was probably made possible by the growing attention to Judaizers and proselytes in Roman society, as attested in sources from the first century CE.

Sira 24:1–12, Wisdom, which Ben Sira intimately associates with the Torah, originally looked for a dwelling place among "every people and nation" (24:6), but in the end was commanded by God to "encamp in Jacob," apparently in a quite exclusive way (24:8–12). As Joshua Ezra Burns notes, this does not mean that the nations are now completely unable to achieve wisdom.[269] Yet insofar as true wisdom and the Torah are closely intertwined, the nations are in fact deprived of both. The Book of Jubilees, which deals with the period of the patriarchs prior to the revelation of the Torah at Sinai, specifically states that the descendants of Jacob are to be the exclusive beneficiaries and guardians of the Sabbath.[270] Another example of a particularistic understanding of the Torah comes from the Book of Baruch, which states that the Law has been given to Israel alone and that the other nations do not know it. Exhorting Israel to keep and observe "the law that remains forever," the author beseeches: "Do not give your glory to another and your benefits to a foreign nation. Happy are we, O Israel, because what is pleasing to God is known to us."[271]

In rabbinic literature we hear different voices, but a majority speaks quite clearly in support of the particularist view of the Torah as the exclusive inheritance of Israel, within the framework of the covenant between God and his people.[272] The question that arises is whether this orientation, which breaks from the universalist perspective of Jewish literature written in Greek, is merely a matter of resistance to a Greek or Greco-Roman philosophical discourse on law or (and maybe also) a reaction prompted by the specific Roman imperial context that confronted the rabbis.

First, we need to examine more precisely the extent to which the rabbis opted for a particularist view of the Torah, taking stock of early rabbinic texts that may still reflect a universalist understanding of the Torah as a law open to all human beings—in other words, a law that can and should be practiced by non-Jews, even those unconverted. Marc Hirshman has argued that this perspective characterizes the school of R. Ishmael, whereas the particularist trend, associating the Torah with only Jews or full converts, characterizes the school of R. Aqiva.[273] Not all the passages that Hirshman presents as evidence are equally convincing, however. For example, Sifre Numbers 119 states:

> You may say that [there are] three crowns: the crown of priesthood and the crown of royalty and the crown of Torah. The crown of priesthood, Aaron won it and took it. The crown of royalty, David won it and took it.

269. Burns 2017a, 245–246.
270. Jub. 2.19–21; see Doering 1999, 64–65; Oliver 2013, 106, 108.
271. Baruch 4:3–4, trans. Tony S. L. Michael, NETS, 930. See also 3:37.
272. Hirshman 2000, 114, n. 41, and 115.
273. Hirshman 1999 and 2000. On the schools of R. Ishmael and R. Aqiva, see, e.g., Kahana 2006; Yadin 2004 and Yadin-Israel 2014. Rabbinic literature presents both as second-generation tannaim, active during the first half of the second century.

The crown of Torah rests [in place] in order not to give those who come into the world (*baey ha-'olam*) an opportunity to argue: "Had the crowns of priesthood and royalty been in place I could have won them and taken them." The crown of Torah is a reproof for all those who come into the world [and would so argue], for whoever wins it I reckon it as if all three crowns had [remained] in their place and he had won them all.[274]

The phrase "those who come into the world" is admittedly universal in scope, but the aim of the text could simply be to affirm that no matter whether one is born a priest, a descendant of David, or a simple Israelite, the greatest honor one can obtain comes from one's commitment to the Torah rather than from one's birth. Even if the text were meant to include non-Jews, it would still be unclear whether one could acquire the crown of Torah without converting. This possibility seems very unlikely, and Hirshman himself recognizes that "the question remains: Does this call presume conversion or is this avenue of Torah open to the Gentile [i.e., the unconverted non-Jew] also?"[275]

The text that Hirshman puts forward as the decisive proof of the existence of a universalistic outlook in tannaitic literature associated with the school of R. Ishmael comes from the Mekhilta de-Arayot, considered an "Ishmaelian" composition inserted in Sifra, which is otherwise attributed to the school of R. Aqiva.[276] The passage relates to Leviticus 18:5, "You shall keep my statutes and my ordinances; the person (*ha-adam*) who puts them in practice [lit.: does them] shall live by them: I am the Lord."[277] The midrash comments:

R. Yirmiyah[278] was wont to say: "Whence do you say that even a gentile (*goy*) who does (*'oseh*) Torah, behold, he is like the high priest? Scripture teaches: *By doing* (ya'aseh) *them the person* (ha-adam) [*shall live*] (Lev 18:5). Likewise it says: 'This is the Torah of priests, Levites, and Israelites'? This is not said there [in 2 Sam 7:19]; rather [Scripture says]: *This is the Torah of a person* (ha-adam), *Lord God* (2 Sam 7:19). And likewise it says: 'Open the gates and let priests, Levites, and Israelites enter'? This is not said; rather, *Open the gates and let a righteous nation* (goy), *keeper of the faith, enter* (Isa 26:2)."[279]

---

274. Sifre Numbers 119, trans. Hirshman 2000, 106–107. For the Hebrew text, see Kahana 2011–2015, 1:32 [לב]; and the commentary in ibid., 4:939–941. On the "crown of priesthood" and the covenant with Aaron, see Himmelfarb 2017.

275. Hirshman 2000, 107.

276. See Hirshman 1999, 45–60, for a detailed analysis; Hirshman 2000, 107–110. On Mekhilta de-Arayot, see note 205 above.

277. My translation (based on NRSV).

278. Here R. Yirmiyah is probably to be identified as a fifth-generation tanna who bore this name.

279. Sifra, Aḥarey Mot 9.13.13, ed. Weiss, 86b. The following lines (not included in Hirshman 2000) quote biblical verses that refer to "righteous (persons)" (*tzadiqim*) rather

R. Yirmiyah interprets the indefinite term "a person" (*ha-adam*) in Leviticus 18:5 as including the gentile (*goy*) and adds further biblical proof texts that use either *ha-adam* or *goy* instead of referring to "Israel" or a subdivision of the people of Israel. Moreover, the verb "to do" (*'asah*) makes it clear that R. Yirmiyah is speaking about a non-Jew who follows the commandments of the Torah and not merely someone who studies it. However, again the question arises as to whether we are dealing with a non-Jew who adopts some of the commandments without converting or a non-Jew who fully takes up the yoke of the Torah (i.e., a convert).

The second option seems more likely. Hirshman notes that "what precedes R. Yirmiyah's statement is an extensive diatribe against the laws of the nations, which prohibit everything from leisure time activity (theater and circus) to hair styles, and most pointedly the laws and wisdom of the nations."[280] As we saw previously, this diatribe attests to a sharp opposition between the laws of Israel and the laws of the nations.[281] It is thus quite doubtful that a gentile who did not convert, and who thus remained at least to some degree bound to the "ways/laws of the nations" though also practicing some of the laws of the Torah, would be praised by the redactor of the Mekhilta de-Arayot.

The discussions associated with the school of R. Ishmael may in fact reflect a debate between those who disparaged converts and those who saw them in a positive light. If, as is commonly argued, R. Ishmael was of priestly stock and/or was in some respects close to priestly views, the question tackled in the texts quoted above may have to do with the prestige of birth and pedigree. Scholarship often presents priestly circles as conservative and attached to lineage, and the evidence from Qumran certainly corroborates this analysis.[282] By this worldview, converts rank very low in the hierarchy of the people of Israel, if they are accepted at all. Against such a perspective, Sifre Numbers 119 clearly argues that glory stems not from birth but from one's commitment to the Torah (close to Philo's position). The underlying issue in the sources that Hirshman quotes could thus be the very possibility of gentiles' conversion to Judaism and integration into the people of Israel on an equal footing with native Israelites. If read with this concern in mind, R. Yirmiyah's teaching in Mekhilta de-Arayot does not mean that gentiles can access the Torah without converting but rather that a non-Jew who converts—that is, who takes up the yoke of the commandments and "does Torah"—is as righteous as the high priest, who enjoys the most prestigious status among the children of Israel.[283]

---

than to "priests, Levites, and Israelites." This parallel suggests that the *goy* or *adam* who "does Torah" is considered a *tzadiq*, a righteous one.

280. Hirshman 2000, 108.

281. See the end of §3.2 and note 206 above.

282. See Schwartz 1990b and 2007. On *gerim* at Qumran, see Berthelot 1999, and Chapter Five for additional references.

283. See note 279 above.

The message of the text would thus be the equal standing of all—priests, Levites, Israelites, and converts (righteous *goyim*)—with regard to the Torah, and a concomitant drop in the value of lineage or inherited status.

So far, the view that a particular strand of early rabbinic literature was open to the idea that non-Jews who did not convert could and should practice Torah rests on shaky foundations. To complement Hirshman's study, it is illuminating to look at rabbinic texts pertaining to "heaven fearers" (*yirey shamayim*), whom scholars identify as pious non-Jews who worshiped the God of Israel and imitated Jewish practices but did not undergo full conversion.[284] Most scholars believe that rabbis viewed these Judaizing gentiles—often described as "sympathizers"—in a positive light. The issue is quite intricate, however.

First, we must keep in mind that there are very few references to *yirey shamayim* in rabbinic literature from the Land of Israel up to the 5th century CE—no more than a dozen.[285]

Second (and more problematic), the meaning of the expression *yirey shamayim* varies from text to text. Just as Greek texts can characterize Jews, Greeks, and Romans as *theosebeis* (God-fearers), so rabbinic literature can call Jews *yirey shamayim* as well, in which case the phrase refers to Jewish devotion to the God of Israel.[286] In some cases the expression could also refer to converts and thus be synonymous with the term *gerim*. This at least is how Numbers Rabbah 8:2 (an admittedly late midrash) interprets an earlier midrashic text, Mekhilta de-Rabbi Ishmael (Neziqin 18), which mentions both converts and heaven fearers. The reading of Numbers Rabbah makes sense, since the section of the Mekhilta where this passage is found deals with converts (*gerim*) and ends with four categories enumerated on the basis of Isaiah 44:5—those who claim to belong to the Lord; righteous converts (*gerey tzedeq*); sinners who have repented; and the God-fearers (heaven fearers)—which are not distinct but overlapping.[287] Moreover, the God-fearers are associated with the last part of Isaiah 44:5, which mentions those who will "adopt the name of Israel." This is an additional indication that the God-fearers in this passage of MRI are to be identified with converts.[288]

284. See Lévy 1905–1907; Lieberman 1942, 68–90; Siegert 1973, 110–119; Feldman 1993, 353–356; Wander 1998, 45–52; Levinson 2000. On Judaizing and Judaizers more broadly (not only in rabbinic literature but also in the New Testament, the epigraphic evidence, etc.), see Lieu 1995; Cohen 1999a, 175–197; Kraemer 2014; Berthelot 2020c.

285. For the sake of comparison, note that the same corpus has around five hundred occurrences of the term *ger*, "convert." On *gerim*, see Chapter Five.

286. See, e.g., Genesis Rabbah 49:2 (in connection with Abraham) and Leviticus Rabbah 12:2. As far as the Babylonian Talmud is concerned, nearly all the occurrences of *yirey shamayim* refer to pious Jews, not to Judaizers; see Feldman 1993, 353.

287. MRI Neziqin (Mishpatim) 18, ed. Horovitz and Rabin, 312.

288. For the opposite opinion, see Lévy 1905–1907.

Third, even when the *yirey shamayim* are not to be identified with Jews or converts, in most cases the fact that individuals are designated as such does not allow us to determine what Jewish practices they adopted.[289] It looks as though some *yirey shamayim* were gentiles who protected Jews, while others merely expressed admiration for the God of Israel.[290] However, one tradition, found in three parallel passages of the Jerusalem Talmud, tells of heaven fearers wearing only one shoe (a sign of mortification) on the Day of Atonement and thus partaking in Jewish rituals.[291] The issue debated in these passages is whether "Antoninus," an unidentified emperor whom several rabbinic passages describe as a close friend of Rabbi and a righteous gentile, underwent a full conversion or not.[292] The argument that he must have converted because people saw him wear only one shoe on Yom Kippur is refuted by the affirmation that even heaven fearers do so. The tone is not hostile, but neither does it express admiration or praise. These passages from the Jerusalem Talmud recall the testimony of Philo and Josephus concerning the non-Jews who fast on the Day of Atonement. But this is almost everything we are told about the Judaizing practices of the heaven fearers.

Finally, an important aspect of rabbinic traditions concerning the heaven fearers, to which little attention has been paid so far, is that they feature in aggadic texts and not in halakhic ones. Yet several halakhic texts define what the path of righteous non-Jews should be. Some of them state that gentiles should observe the commandments of the descendants of Noah, to which we will return below. In no case do the commandments given to non-Jews prescribe specific Jewish customs, such as the Sabbath, the fast of Yom Kippur, circumcision, or specific dietary prohibitions.

Most rabbis apparently came to see the commandments of the Torah (the Law revealed by God) as the exclusive property of Israel and those who underwent full conversion "for the sake of heaven," as the saying goes.[293] A famous teaching attributed to R. Aqiva and found in m. Avot 3:14 is an example of this stance. The text states that human beings (*adam*) are "beloved"

289. See, e.g., Genesis Rabbah 28:5 and Leviticus Rabbah 3:2.

290. See Deuteronomy Rabbah 2:24, which tells the story of a Roman senator who committed suicide in order to save Jews. The fact that he circumcized himself before dying seems to indicate a desire to convert. On the different ways in which non-Jews could relate positively to Israel, see Cohen 1999a, Chapter 5.

291. y. Megillah 1:10, 72b; 3:1, 74a; Sanhedrin 10:3, 29c.

292. Krauss 1910, 59. See also Leviticus Rabbah 3:2, which interprets Ps 22:24—"You who fear the Lord (*yirey YHWH*), praise him! All you offspring of Jacob, glorify him; stand in awe of him, all you offspring of Israel!"—as referring either to God-fearers (*yirey shamayim*) or to righteous converts (*gerey tzedeq*). The text ends with the claim that among righteous converts, Antoninus comes first, thereby asserting that he did in fact convert. On Antoninus' identity and his relationship with Rabbi more broadly, see Krauss 1910; Jacobs 1995, 125–154; Cohen 1998.

293. On this notion, see, e.g., MRI Amalek (Yithro) 1, ed. Horovitz and Rabin, 193.

because they are created in the image of God (Gen 1:26–27), whereas Israelites are "beloved" because they are called the children of God (Deut 14:1) and because the Torah, through which the world was created, was given to them.[294] This implies that the Torah was bestowed not on human beings in general but on Israel alone.

A passage of Sifre Deuteronomy—a midrash that scholars associate with the school of R. Aqiva—is even more explicit. Commenting on Deuteronomy 33:4—"Torah was commanded to us (*lanu*) by Moses, an inheritance (*morashah*) for the assembly of Jacob"—the Sifre states succinctly: "This command is only for us (*lanu*)."[295] It then suggests another interpretation:

> Do not read *morashah* (inheritance) but *meorasah* (betrothed); this teaches that the Torah is betrothed: [the Torah] is for Israel,[296] and [she is like] a forbidden woman [lit.: (another) man's woman] for the nations of the world (*ummot ha-'olam*), as [Scripture] says: *Can fire be carried in the bosom without burning one's clothes? Or can one walk on hot coals without scorching the feet? So is he who sleeps with his neighbor's wife; no one who touches her will go unpunished* (Proverbs 6:27–29).[297]

The Torah is compared to a woman who is betrothed (or married, according to Proverbs) to a man (Israel) and thus prohibited to all other men (the nations).[298] Non-Jews are thus forbidden from appropriating its commandments. Moreover, the quotation from Proverbs introduces a threatening tone and suggests that God will punish those who ignore the prohibition.[299]

In Genesis Rabbah 11:8, R. Shimon b. Yoḥai—a third-generation tanna and a disciple of R. Aqiva, according to rabbinic tradition—offers specific teaching on the exclusive gift of the Sabbath to Israel. This midrash imagines a

---

294. Hirshman 2000, 105, note 16.

295. Sifre Deuteronomy 345, ed. Finkelstein, 402.

296. In Ma'agarim (based on MS London 341): "Do not read *morashah* ('inheritance'), but *meorasah* ('betrothed'), for the Torah is betrothed to Israel."

297. Sifre Deuteronomy 345, ed. Finkelstein, 402. On the fact that the nations have no share in the Torah, see also Canticles Rabbah 8:7, which states that even if the nations were to offer all their treasures for one commandment of the Torah, their request would still not be accepted.

298. The comparison with b. Pesahim 49b (MS JTS, EMC, 271, consulted on Ma'agarim), which quotes the same verse as Sifre, sheds light on the difference of perspective between the Palestinian and Babylonian sources. In the Bavli, the Torah is the rabbis' betrothed and not to be shared with uneducated Jews, *'ammey ha-aretz*, who are said to hate the rabbis more than the nations hate Israel. The shift of focus from *goyim* to uneducated Jews is characteristic of the Bavli. See Rubenstein 2003, 124–142, esp. 129–131. See also Wasserman 2017, 213–227, on a similar shift at the end of tractate Avodah Zarah in the Bavli.

299. See Ben-Shalom 1993, 163–164.

dialogue between the personified Sabbath, who pleads for a partner, and God, who replies: "The community of Israel (*knesset Israel*) is your partner." Then, as soon as Israel stands at the foot of Mount Sinai, God orders them to remember what he said to the Sabbath and to keep and sanctify the festival.[300]

On the whole, the prohibition against non-Jews observing the Sabbath or following other specific Torah commandments seems to become stronger in the Babylonian Talmud and later sources that were familiar with the Bavli. In particular, they are more explicit about the ensuing punishment. A passage from the Babylonian Talmud attributes to Resh Lakish the teaching that a non-Jew who rests on the Sabbath deserves death (b. Sanhedrin 58b). As for R. Yoḥanan, he is said to have taught that a non-Jew who studies the Torah is subject to the death penalty (b. Sanhedrin 59 a).[301] The talmudic passage then continues with remarks on the apparent contradiction between R. Yoḥanan's teaching and the teaching in Sifra concerning the gentile who does Torah and is equal to the hight priest, which presupposes that the gentile has studied Torah. The Talmud rejects the objection, however, stating that "doing Torah" in this case is limited to studying and observing the seven commandments of the children of Noah (on which see below). Finally, in b. Hagigah 13a, R. Ammi, who according to rabbinic sources was a disciple of R. Yoḥanan, is said to have prohibited the transmission of words of the Torah to a gentile, on the basis of Psalm 147:(19–)20: "He (God) declares his word to Jacob, his statutes and ordinances to Israel; he has not dealt thus with any other nation (*goy*), they do not know his ordinances."[302] Even though these teachings are attributed to third-century Palestinian amoraim, one must emphasize that they are found only in the Babylonian Talmud and may reflect the Bavli's perspective on the issue.[303] Another example is found in the late midrash Deuteronomy Rabbah, which rehearses the prohibitions concerning the Sabbath (1:21) and the commandments of the Law in general, on the grounds that the words of the Torah, like the bee that produces honey but also stings, "are [words of] life to Israel, but a lethal poison to the nations of the world" (1:6).[304]

To sum up: in most rabbinic texts, which in this respect differ from the perspectives of Philo and Josephus, Jewish monotheistic beliefs may be shared by non-Jews, who are expected to renounce idolatry if they are to be considered righteous and who will be praised for this insightful choice, but non-Jews who

---

300. Gen. Rabbah 11:8, ed. Theodor and Albeck, 95–96.

301. Feldman 1993, 356.

302. Some MSS (for example, MS Munich 95) have R. Assi rather than R. Ammi.

303. The Bavli seems to be on the whole more exclusive than the Palestinian sources. For example, Kiel 2015 shows that as far as the Noahide commandments about prohibited sexual relations are concerned, a particularistic and exclusive rhetoric characterizes the Babylonian Talmud, whereas Palestinian rabbinic discourse tends to be more inclusive.

304. My translation is based on MS Parma (Biblioteca Palatina 3122), consulted on Ma'agarim.

do not convert are not to observe the Torah's commandments (*mitzvot*).[305] Even if dissenting voices may occasionally be heard, on the whole, rabbinic Judaism in the first centuries CE soundly rejected the appropriation (without proper conversion) of Jewish laws and customs by non-Jews, though it did not oppose the appropriation of Jewish beliefs.[306]

Yet there is a difference between the teachings from the early rabbinic period, up to the end of the third century and even into the fourth, and the Babylonian Talmud and later works. Among the former, we mainly encounter the notion that the Torah is the exclusive possession of Israel (including converts) and that the gentiles have no share in it, whereas among the latter, we find a more hostile discourse explicitly prohibiting non-Jews who do not convert from following the commandments given to Israel, and threatening them with death (an admittedly theoretical threat that in reality carried no weight and could even have meant heavenly punishment in the authors' minds). This evolution may have to do with the development of Christianity, the issue of the Christian appropriation of the Bible, and the adoption of Judaizing practices by some Christians (especially participation in Jewish religious ceremonies), which the Church Fathers also tried to counter.[307]

4.2 A UNIVERSAL PROMULGATION OF THE TORAH IN RABBINIC SOURCES?

To assess whether the rabbinic rejection of a universalistic view of the Torah has anything to do with the Roman imperial context, we must take into account a set of rabbinic texts that imagine a universal proclamation and/or publication of the Torah. These texts raise two questions: First, do they contradict the conclusion reached in the previous section? Second, how are we to interpret the fact that some of their features resemble those of Roman edicts?

305. On the commandments of the children of Noah and their relationship to the Torah, see below.

306. Interestingly, some fragments from the Cairo Genizah illustrate the fact that in the Middle Ages the discussion about the Torah's universality and binding character for non-Jews was revived in connection with the question of whether the law of Moses had been abrogated by Islam or not, which Haggai Ben-Shammai describes as "the most hotly debated issue between Muslims and Jews in the Middle Ages" (Ben-Shammai 1992, 25).

307. John Chrysostom's homilies in *Against the Jews* (in fact directed at Judaizing Christians), from the late fourth century, are a famous example of this trend among the Church Fathers (1.5, 8.4, 8.8). On Judaizing practices among Christians and the reactions of the Church Fathers, see Simon 1964, 356–393; Goodman 1994a, 143–144; Boyarin 1999, 12–14; Katzoff 2009, 319. On the relationship to Christianity of the Bavli's redactors, see Bar-Asher Siegal 2013, 5–20. Karin Hedner Zetterholm argues that already in the first centuries, the existence of Judaizing Christians and the blurring of the lines between Jews and gentiles that ensued "was one of the factors that contributed to the redefinition of Jewishness in rabbinic terms" (Hedner Zetterholm 2018, 323).

Roman authorities invested a great deal of energy in communicating their rules to the provincials.[308] In Clifford Ando's words, "The government at Rome always paraded its wish that its words should come to the attention of all its subjects."[309] The publication of imperial edicts, ordinances, and letters was duly codified. For example, it was mandatory to post such documents publicly for at least thirty days.[310] Numerous Roman sources testify to the requirement to publish imperial documents in public places and in a way that would make them visible.[311] A papyrus from Egypt, dated to the end of the second or the beginning of the third century CE and consisting of a letter addressed by the prefect of Egypt to the *stratēgoi*, thus specifies that a copy of the letter should be published "in a public place" (*dēmosia*).[312] Moreover, in both inscriptions and papyri, it is sometimes requested that the letters be clearly written: formulas such as "in clear and distinct/visible letters" (*saphesi kai eusēmois grammasi* or *eudēlois grammasin*) are common.[313] Different media were used to communicate information or keep records, among them marble, bronze, and papyrus, but many ancient sources refer also to whitened board or white stones, on which the letters would be more clearly visible. Noteworthy in this respect is a law dating to 100 BCE regulating certain aspects of provincial administration, whose Greek translation is preserved in two copies, one from Delphi and one from Cnidus. It prescribes that "the letters, engraved on a bronze tablet, or, if not, either on a marble slab or even on a whitened board, be openly published in the cities in a sanctuary or agora, in such a way that the people shall be able to read them properly from ground level."[314] Another inscription, found in the bouleuterion of Miletus in Asia Minor, reproduces the instructions given by a Roman governor to the *conventus* of the province of Asia in 51/50 BCE,

in order that each of you might dispatch [copies of this letter] to the cities in your own judiciary district and see to it that the letter is engraved on a pilaster of white stone in the most conspicuous place, so

308. Ando 2000, 79 and Chapter 4 ("The Communicative Actions of the Roman Government") in general; Haensch 2009.

309. Ando 2000, 81, also 96.

310. Ando 2000, 99–100. Copies were also kept in the *tabularia publica*, where they could always be consulted thereafter. On the practical problems raised by illiteracy, Ando writes: "The government's acknowledgment of the logistical difficulties faced by its subjects in fact extended to include the problem of literacy, in two ways: first, the government insisted that published materials should be legible; second, it probably required that all such texts be recited at least once at the time of their posting" (ibid., 101).

311. Ando 2000, 101–102.

312. *BGU* IV 1086, col. 2, line 3; von Schwind 1940, 84, 86.

313. See *Or. Gr. Inscr.* II 665, line 12 (49 CE); P. Oxy. VIII 1100, line 3 (206 CE); von Schwind 1940, 83.

314. Trans. Ando 2000, 82, based on Crawford 1996, 1:254, no. 12. According to Jean-Louis Ferrary, however, such prescriptions remained exceptional at that time; see Ferrary 2009, 67–68.

that justice might be established for all time uniformly for all the province, and in order that all other cities and peoples might do the same thing among themselves.[315]

A passage from the *Digest* (14.3.11.3) demonstrates that the rules regulating the publication of official documents in the empire were matters of concern to the Roman authorities for centuries. We shall see the relevance of these Roman rules in a moment.

Several tannaitic texts claim that God initially wanted to reveal the Torah to all the nations rather than to Israel alone. According to Sifre Deuteronomy 343, God even reached out to Israel's biblical neighbors, such as Edom, Ammon, Moab, and Ishmael, to offer the Torah to them, but they rejected it, thereby provoking God's wrath, as illustrated by Micah 5:14: "And in anger and wrath I will execute vengeance on the nations that did not obey." This passage of Sifre Deuteronomy goes as far as to state that these nations also rejected the seven commandments incumbent on the children of Noah (on which see Section 4.3 below), a quite extreme view in the rabbinic corpus.[316] In this text, even though God's Torah is presented as originally open to all, its universal character actually intensifies the guilt of the nations, who, unlike Israel, were unworthy of and unable to receive it.[317]

In a comparable way, the Mekhilta de-Rabbi Ishmael argues that the Torah was revealed in a desert so that all peoples could come and partake in it:

> *They encamped in the wilderness* (Exod 19:2). The Torah was given publicly (*dēmos*, a transliteration from the Greek), openly (*parrēsia*, another transliteration from the Greek), in a free place (*be-maqom hefqer*). For had the Torah been given in the Land of Israel, [the Israelites] would have said to the nations of the world: "You have no share in it."[318] Therefore it was given in the wilderness publicly, openly, in a free place, [so that] everyone wishing to accept it [may] come and accept it.[319]

315. Sherk 1969, 273–274, no. 52, trans. Ando 2000, 83.

316. On this passage, see Hayes 2015, 335, 351, 367–368, which rightly states that the midrash's polemical rhetoric "serves not to establish the common humanity of Israel and other nations but precisely to differentiate them" (367).

317. Interestingly, the *Epistle of Barnabas* (composed between 70 and 130 CE) states on the basis of Exodus 32 that God's gift was refused by Israel at Sinai and ultimately given to Christ's followers. At first glance, this argument may look similar to that of Sifre Deuteronomy. However, the Christian author refers not to the Law but to the covenant (*diathēkē*). See *Epistle of Barnabas* 14, esp. §§4–5.

318. A small correction to the edition of Horovitz and Rabin, 205, which has "They have no share in it." Yet MS Oxford 151 has "You have no share in it." This is merely an issue of direct versus indirect speech.

319. MRI Baḥodesh 1, ed. Horovitz and Rabin, 205; trans. Lauterbach 2004, 2:293–294 (slightly modified). MS Oxford 151 omits the first occurrence of *dēmos* but not the second.

The midrash comments on the fact that the Torah was not revealed in the land that God gave to Israel, noting that this could have been interpreted as an indication of the "local" character of Israel's law. The midrash thus implicitly affirms the Torah's universal dimension.

Hirshman remarks: "It is striking that the *Mekilta* not only advanced the claim that revelation had been intended for all peoples, but did so in a vocabulary that was the hallmark of Greco-Roman democracy."[320] However, the midrash does not tackle the issue of political regime but rather alludes to the way that laws were made public in the context of the Roman empire. As we have seen, access to legal and administrative documents was a key issue, and this explains the Mekhilta's insistence on the fact that the Law was revealed "publicly, openly, in a free place." That this place was a desert, an area where people normally would not be expected to gather, is irrelevant in this context. The authors of the midrash did not have in mind a realistic, historical scenario; rather, they were addressing the principles underlying the publication process.

It might be argued that, as in the case of Roman legal texts, the issue at stake in the Mekhilta is that people can only be judged—and possibly condemned—if the laws have first been properly promulgated and communicated to them. This is in fact made explicit at the end of this section of the midrash:

> Rabbi Eliezer the son of R. Yose the Galilean[321] used to say: Behold it says: *He declares his word to Jacob* [. . .] *He has not dealt so with any other nation* (Ps 147:19–20). But what had those wretched nations done that he did not want to give them the Torah? *They do not know his ordinances* (ibid.)—they did not want to accept [them], as it is said: *God comes from Teman* [. . .] *and a brightness appears as the light* [. . .] *before him goes the pestilence* [. . .] *He stands, and shakes the earth, he beholds, and makes the nations to tremble*, etc. (Hab 3:3–6).[322]

On the basis of Psalm 147:19–20, which states that God has not declared his word (*davar*) to the nations, R. Eliezer expresses the view that God has not given the Torah to non-Jews. This could be seen as contradicting the idea expressed in the preceding passage, according to which the Torah was given to anyone wishing to accept it. There is no contradiction, however, because according to R. Eliezer, the point is precisely that the nations "did not want to accept" it, a piece of information that he draws from Psalm 147:20, "They

---

The idea that the Torah was given publicly (*dēmos*) and openly (*parrēsia*) is found again in MRI Baḥodesh 5, ed. Horovitz and Rabin, 222.

320. Hirshman 2000, 103.

321. According to rabbinic tradition, Rabbi Eliezer son of R. Yose was a third-generation tanna who lived during the second half of the second century CE.

322. MRI Baḥodesh 1, ed. Horovitz and Rabin, 206, trans. Lauterbach 2004, 2:295 (slightly modified).

do not know his ordinances."[323] This teaching of R. Eliezer sheds light on the previous passage, the one commenting on "They encamped in the wilderness." God indeed made it possible for the nations to receive the Torah, but they were not among those "wishing to accept it," and this is precisely what they are guilty of. This section of the Mekhilta de-Rabbi Ishmael makes clear that the nations cannot complain that God intentionally withheld the Torah from them, or claim that he dealt with them unfairly. The message is ultimately the same as that of Sifre Deuteronomy 343, and the insistence on the fact that the Torah was originally offered to all merely serves to condemn the nations.[324]

Yet there are other rabbinic texts that raise the possibility that the Torah was made known to the nations after Sinai and even translated into their languages. This tradition is based on Deuteronomy 27:2–8 and Joshua 8:30–35 and 4:1–10, which state that after their entrance into the Promised Land, the children of Israel copied the words of the Torah on stones, in accordance with the command given to Moses. Deuteronomy 27:8 states that "you shall write upon the stones all the words of this law very plainly (*baer heytev*)," a detail that the Mishnah interprets as meaning "in seventy languages" (m. Sotah 7:5). In the Tosefta (Sotah 8:6–7), Mekhilta Deuteronomy (on Deut 27:8),[325] and the two Talmuds (y. Sotah 7:5, 21d; b. Sotah 35b–36a), various rabbis discuss how the Torah, in its entirety or in part, was communicated to the nations by being published on whitened stones and then translated into and copied in the seventy languages of the world by scribes inspired by God.[326] Like Sifre Deuteronomy 343 and Mekhilta de-Rabbi Ishmael Baḥodesh 1, however, the tradition about the promulgation and translation of God's law ultimately implies that the nations cannot argue that it was not made available to them and so are themselves to blame for not agreeing to live according to its instruction.

323. The passage from Habakkuk is quoted as further proof that the nations did not accept God's laws: he saw their disobedience and made them tremble. The same verse is quoted in b. Avodah Zarah 2b, in a similar context: the nations appear before God and are condemned not only for not having accepted the Torah but also for not having kept even the seven commandments that the children of Noah had taken upon themselves. The similarity between this talmudic passage and Sifre Deuteronomy 343 is striking.

324. Here the difference of perspective between the schools of R. Ishmael (MRI) and R. Aqiva (Sifre Deuteronomy) is not clear-cut. Menahem Kahana has drawn attention to the fact that their differences are much less significant in the aggadic parts of the midrashim than in the halakhic parts, even though certain nonlegal portions of Mekhilta Deuteronomy (associated with the school of R. Ishmael) are characterized by a more universalistic attitude toward non-Jews than that of the corresponding passages in Sifre Deuteronomy. See Kahana 1988, esp. 180–185, 200–201; and Kahana 2006, 51. On the differences between these schools, see also Yadin 2004 and Yadin-Israel 2014.

325. See Kahana 2005, 345, no. 10, l.5–17.

326. I have analyzed these texts in detail elsewhere and refer the reader to Berthelot 2018b for a full demonstration. See also Lieberman 1950, 200–202; Hirshman 1999, 105–113; Fraade 2011b, 54*–55*; Fraade, forthcoming.

It is significant that the rabbinic texts describing the Torah being copied on stones dwell on the manner in which the letters were to be written and the length of time during which the law was to remain public and accessible to the nations (which determines whether the scribes they sent were able to make copies or translations). These aspects of the rabbinic discussion strongly recall Roman rules relating to the publication of edicts that are attested in inscriptions and Roman legal texts.[327] Awareness of these rules is particularly clear in the passage from the Jerusalem Talmud (y. Sotah 7:5, 21d), which explicitly states that the Torah was translated into the languages of the nations and written on *stēlai* permanently displayed in a public and accessible place, thereby ensuring that the scribes would be provided with suitable working conditions in which to perform the work of transcription.[328] Yet it is not primarily the details of the procedures that matter—there are of course numerous differences between the Roman sources and the rabbinic texts—but above all the reasoning underlying the publication of legal documents in the Roman empire: unless the law was properly communicated to people, they could not be judged liable for breaking it. Hence the Roman evidence provides not just vague parallels but the very context that makes the rabbinic texts concerning the copying of the Torah on stones fully understandable and meaningful.

By connecting the revelation of the Torah with the reasoning behind the prescriptions for the publication of legal documents in the Roman empire, these rabbinic texts implicitly suggest that the God of Israel is in the same position as the Roman emperor, that God makes his law known in accordance with the same principles as are followed in the Roman empire, and that Israel is therefore responsible for acting toward the nations as the imperial administration did toward the provincials. Israel must publish the text of God's law in such a way as to communicate it properly to the nations, who can therefore not claim ignorance of it.[329] This tradition thus appears to be yet another example of the deliberate imitation and subversion of Roman norms. As in other texts analyzed in this volume, the rabbis integrated elements of their Roman environment but simultaneously resisted the ideological message of the empire's judicial and administrative efficiency. Ultimately, what these rabbinic texts

327. On the fact that an edict had to remain posted long enough for people to know what it said, see in particular *Digest* 14.3.11.4.

328. On the rabbis' familiarity with "the contents, the publication, the reception, and the general perception of the Roman edict," see also Tropper 2005, 227.

329. In connection with Exodus Rabbah 30:16, Amram Tropper remarks that "our midrash portrays God as the ultimate emperor and the *mitzvot* (i.e., the divine commandments) as his edicts" (Tropper 2005, 213). Natalie Dohrmann also notes: "In the rabbinic theological imaginary, the rabbis function in relation to their god as do the legal experts in the inner circle of the deified *princeps* who translated and mediated his will" (Dohrmann 2015, 191). In the case examined here, however, it is Israel rather than the rabbis that functions as an intermediary between God and the nations.

attempt to do is demonstrate the guilt of the nations and justify the latter's future punishment at the hands of God in a way that is culturally appropriate in the rabbis' cultural and political context.[330]

According to the rabbinic traditions examined in this section, although the Law was originally offered to the nations, they refused it. It is thus no longer accessible to them and has become Israel's exclusive property. The rabbis used Roman norms and principles to demonstrate the guilt of the non-Jews and thus mimicked the universal promulgation of laws in the empire while reclaiming the Torah as the particular law of Israel.

4.3 THE SIGNIFICANCE OF THE NOAHIDE LAWS

Some scholars have argued that the Torah retained a universal dimension within rabbinic Judaism through the notion of the commandments given to the children of Noah (humanity as a whole).[331] By living in accordance with these laws, gentiles would still be able to participate in the Torah—be it only a minimal, pre-Sinaitic Torah—without having to undergo full conversion.

Before we examine this possibility further, let me briefly review what the Noahide laws are.[332] Their exact number varies in rabbinic sources, but the most common tradition speaks of seven commandments.[333] A passage from Tosefta Avodah Zarah (8[9]:4–9) provides the key list: the children of Noah are commanded to establish tribunals or legal sytems (*dinim* or *dinin*) and to refrain from idolatry, blasphemy, murder, sexual immorality, robbery, and tearing any limb off a living animal. The Tosefta also reports the opinions of various rabbis concerning additional laws, such as the prohibition of castration and of witchcraft.[334]

Scholars have often compared these commandments to those that Noah gave his sons in the Book of Jubilees, as well as to the prescriptions for gentile believers in the Book of Acts in the New Testament and to the ethical teachings of the *Didachē*.[335] In a recent study, Moshe Lavee has definitively shown that whereas

330. See Fraade, forthcoming.

331. Cohen 1944, 420–421; Stone 1990–1991, 1161–1162; Novak 1998 and 2011 (1983); Bockmuehl 2000, 161–162; 2013, 124.

332. The most detailed discussion of the Noahide commandments is found in b. Sanhedrin 56a–60a. For a detailed analysis of each commandment, see Novak 2011 (1983).

333. In y. Avodah Zarah 2:1, 40c, Rav Huna reports in the name of Rav that there will be thirty Noahide laws in the future.

334. Ed. Zuckermandel, 473, based on MS Erfurt. In this manuscript, the reference to the limb torn from a living animal is missing in the first part of the text, but it is mentioned afterward in the discussion of the individual laws. MS Vienna has the complete list to start with. On this passage, see Hayes 2015, 356–359; Hayes 2018, 229–233.

335. Jubilees 7.20 (and 7.30–33 on the prohibition of blood); Acts 15:20, 28–29; *Didachē* 3.1–6. See, e.g., Cohen 1992; Bockmuehl 2000, 156, 159; Vana 2012; Hanneken 2015; Van Zile 2017. On the *Didachē*, see Flusser 1988.

Second Temple Jewish sources—including Acts—do indeed contain some "building blocks" that eventually made their way into the tradition of the Noahide commandments, the latter is nevertheless an original rabbinic concept (whose closest precedent is in fact Acts 15).[336] Undoubtedly, the question of what could make non-Jews acceptable from a religious and ethical perspective occupied Jewish authors before the rabbis. Yet the rabbinic response was sui generis.

Scholars have also argued that the Noahide laws are the rabbinic equivalent of natural law and in some cases have stressed what they see as a significant convergence between rabbinic discourse and Roman legal theory and practice by comparing the Noahide laws with the Roman concept of *ius gentium*.[337] However, in t. Avodah Zarah 8(9):4–9, the Noahide laws differ for Jews and non-Jews. Concerning idolatry and blasphemy, for example, the punishment for Noahides (non-Jews) is decapitation by the sword, the privileged form of execution in the Roman world, whereas according to biblical laws, an Israelite blasphemer is under penalty of stoning (Lev 24:16).[338] In other cases, it is the nature of the prohibition itself that varies. Most important, as Christine Hayes notes,

> in the case of illicit sexual relations, different prohibitions apply to Jews and non-Jews and as regards bloodshed, theft, robbery and the law of the captive woman, a substantively different and discriminatory law applies to non-Jews. Specifically, a Jew is not liable for murder, theft and robbery when the victim is a non-Jew, though a non-Jew in the reverse situation is liable, and a beautiful war captive is permitted to a Jew but not to a non-Jew. The blatantly inequitable application of these basic laws is the single most compelling evidence that the seven Noahide laws featured in talmudic texts are not understood to be invariable ethical norms of universal application, and did not originate or function as a rabbinic version of natural law.[339]

David Sabato has demonstrated that the Tosefta integrates and edits earlier rabbinic traditions and that there are in fact different views in tannaitic

---

336. Lavee 2013. See also Novak 2011 (1983), 11–35; Oliver 2013; Hayes 2015, 354–370; Hayes 2018. *Pace* Finkelstein 1923, 60; Cohen 1992, 55; Vana 2012, 222.

337. On the Noahide laws and natural law, see Cohen 1944, 420–421; Rakover 1994, 151–152; Novak 1998, 149–167. This idea is rejected by Stone 1990–1991; Wilf 2008, 62–63; Morgenstern 2011, 65–66; Hayes 2015 and 2018. On the comparison with *ius gentium*, see in particular Cohen 1944, 420–421; Bockmuehl 2000, 150, 162. Stone recalls that Grotius and Selden considered the Noahide laws "an early model for the Roman 'law of nations'" (Stone 1990–1991, 1162, also 1165).

338. The source of this teaching is the exegesis of Leviticus 24 found in Sifra, Emor 19.1.4; see Hayes 2018, 232, note 12. Hayes refers to David Sabato's unpublished master's thesis, "The Noahide Commandments in Tannaic Literature" (Hebrew University, 2014), which I was not able to access.

339. Hayes 2018, 233.

texts.[340] Some passages reflect the notion of a gradual revelation of the divine law, from the Noahide commandments (or, before that, those given to Adam) through the commandments given to the patriarchs—such as that of circumcision—to the commandments given to Israel at Mara (Exod 15:25) and then on to the full revelation of the Torah at Sinai.[341] Whether the Noahide laws were confirmed at Sinai and integrated into the Torah or remained pre-Sinaitic laws that were now relevant only for gentiles is a matter of debate in rabbinic sources.[342] There are thus several models for understanding the relationship between the Noahide commandments and those of the Torah. Nevertheless, in all cases there are differences in the nature of the prohibitions, so that the identification of the Noahide laws as natural law common to Jews and non-Jews alike does not hold.

Moreover, as Suzanne Stone and Christine Hayes have stressed, the Noahide laws are binding commandments because they are prescribed by God, and not on the basis of reason alone, as the classical theory of natural law would have it.[343] Admittedly, a passage from Sifra (Mekhilta de-Arayot) comments on Leviticus 18:4—"You shall observe my ordinances, and you shall keep my statutes, following them: I am the Lord your God"—in terms that could be interpreted as a reference to natural law:

> You shall observe my ordinances. These are matters written in the Torah which—had they not been written—it would be logical (*din*) to write them, such as robbery, sexual violations, idolatry, blasphemy and bloodshed. If they had not been written [in the Torah] it would be logical to write them.[344]

This passage clearly states that some of the Torah's commandments have a rational basis. However, according to Stone, this should not be interpreted as a reference to the concept of natural law; rather, what is at stake is "the intelligibility of these revealed laws and their suitability for all human nature."[345] Moreover, their rational character does not undermine their being ordered by God.

340. I could access Sabato's MA thesis only through the summary provided by Hayes (see n. 338 above). On the different views of the Noahide commandments among tannaitic sages, see Hirshman 1999, 90–104.

341. See MRI, Vayassaʿ (Beshallaḥ) 1, ed. Horovitz and Rabin, 156 (on the commandments given at Mara); MRI, Baḥodesh (Yithro) 3, ed. Horovitz and Rabin, 211; Seder ʿOlam 5, ed. Milikowsky 2013, 1:235–236 (in connection with Gen 2:16; cf. Gen. Rabbah 16:6). On rabbinic views of normativity before Sinai, see Wilf 2008; Paz 2009; Hayes 2015, 330–354.

342. Sifre Deuteronomy 76; b. Sanhedrin 59a.

343. Stone 1990–1991, 1167–1168; Hayes 2015, 370. Cf. Steinmetz 2008, 31–32.

344. Sifra, Aḥarey Mot 9.13.10, ed. Weiss, 86a, trans. Hayes 2018, 237. The text continues with the identification of the "statutes" or "laws" (*ḥuqqim*) of Lev 18:4 as irrational commandments, such as the prohibitions against eating pork and wearing mixed seeds. Yet it suggests that the most valuable and praiseworthy commandments are in this second category, not the first. See Hayes 2015, 248–252; Hayes 2018, 237–259.

345. Stone 1990–1991, 1168.

For these two reasons, it is not possible to consider the Noahide commandments as the equivalent of the *ius gentium* as defined by Gaius at the beginning of the *Institutes*: "the law that natural reason establishes among all human beings is followed by all peoples alike, and is called *ius gentium*, being, as it were, the law observed by all peoples."[346] Admittedly, in the history of Roman law, the notion of *ius gentium* did not always mean natural law. Boaz Cohen notes:

> About 242 BCE, when intercourse between Romans and foreigners became more frequent, a special magistrate, called the *praetor peregrinus*, was appointed to deal with disputes involving aliens. The principles by which he operated constituted the *ius gentium*, namely a body of rules which the Roman praetor thought worthy to regulate the legal relations of Roman citizens with outsiders.[347]

Yet here too, the notion of Noahide laws found in rabbinic literature does not neatly fit the Roman concept, insofar as the Noahide commandments are not applicable only to relations between Jews and non-Jews. Although the rabbinic texts that deal with the laws of Noah project Jewish judges into a position much like that of Roman judges in the empire—especially before 212 CE, when they frequently adjudicated between citizens and noncitizens—these writings remain very theoretical and are not meant to provide guidelines for concrete cases.[348]

From a theological and ethical viewpoint, conversely, the notion of Noahide commandments prescribed by God to humankind equipped the rabbis with a conceptual tool with which to evaluate the behavior of the nations. The Noahide laws thus served to ground God's judgment of the non-Jews and to justify their condemnation. Hence, Mekhilta de-Rabbi Ishmael, Baḥodesh (Yithro) 5, and Sifre Deuteronomy 343 both convey the idea that the nations have proved unable to keep the Noahide commandments—which demonstrates that they could hardly have taken up the yoke of the Torah.[349]

Ultimately, despite some diverging voices here and there in rabbinic literature, the Noahide laws helped to create a chasm between Israel and the gentiles,

---

346. *Inst.* 1.1, trans. Ando 2011, 115. According to *Digest* 1.1.1.3–4, *ius gentium*, which is common to all human beings, differs not only from *ius civile* but also from *ius naturale*, which is common to all animals.

347. Cohen 1966, 26, also 139.

348. Novak 1998, 149–150.

349. MRI, Baḥodesh (Yithro) 5: ed. Horovitz and Rabin, 221–222; Sifre Deut. 343: ed. Finkelstein, 396–397. For a fine comparative analysis of these two texts, see Wilf 2008, 63–66. In t. Sotah 6:9, in connection with Ezekiel 33:25–26, it is the Israelites who are described as having failed to keep the seven Noahide laws, but the conclusion is that they are unworthy of receiving the Land again (after the Exile), not that they will be deprived of the Torah. Given the exegetical and rhetorical dimensions of the argument, it is difficult to infer from this passage that the Noahide commandments are binding on Israel after Sinai.

rather than building a bridge.[350] Non-Jews who follow the Noahide laws are not to behave like Jews. Thus, a passage from Sifra states that they are not to bring a sin offering as Israelites do when they sin.[351] The fact that this was a theoretical issue after the destruction of the Temple highlights the statement's purpose, which was to distinguish between Noahides and Israelites.[352] Later on, Maimonides, basing his conclusion on b. Sanhedrin 59a, explicitly affirmed: "A gentile who occupies himself with the Torah is liable to the death penalty. He should only occupy himself with the Seven Noahide Commandments" (*Laws of Kings and Wars* 10.9, my translation). Moreover, as David Novak notes,

> One effect of limiting the number of commandments was to eliminate any gradual conversion to Judaism. Gentiles could either practice their own commandments with impunity, or they would have to fully adopt Judaism *in toto* in order to become full members of the Jewish people.[353]

The notion of the Noahide commandments goes hand in hand with the rabbis' judgment of intermediate and ill-defined categories, such as Judaizers, as illegitimate. Its aim—at least in theory—was to establish clear boundaries between those who belong to the people of Israel and those who do not.

In the end, despite the plurality of opinions expressed in rabbinic texts, the Noahide commandments most often perform the same task as the texts that oppose the laws of Israel to the laws of the nations. They serve to maintain a distinction between Jews and non-Jews and to stress that the Torah revealed at Sinai is for Israel alone (and those who join Israel through conversion). As a consequence, they do not contradict the conclusion that the rabbis rejected a universal view of the Torah.

In sum, rabbinic literature tends to reject the universalist understanding of Jewish law commonly held by Jewish authors writing in Greek and to favor a notion of the Torah as the exclusive inheritance of Israel. Admittedly, this particularistic notion has biblical roots, and, as mentioned previously, there were advocates of the idea in the Second Temple period too. Yet there are differences between their views and those of the rabbis. In Jubilees, for example, the exclusive notion of the Torah goes together with a rejection of the possibility for non-Jews to become part of Israel. Not so in rabbinic literature, which on the whole is open to converts, as we have seen in this chapter and will consider at greater length in the next. The question therefore remains as to why the rabbis in the main opted for such an exclusive conception of Jewish law rather than a universalistic one. I argue that the Roman context at least partly explains this rabbinic tendency.

---

350. As rightly emphasized by Hayes 2018, 233, *pace* Morgenstern 2011, 48. See also Hedner Zetterholm 2018, 341.

351. Sifra, Vayiqra 1.1, ed. Weiss, 15b.

352. See also Sifra, Tzav 10.1, ed. Weiss, 38c.

353. Novak 2006, 653.

In her book on divine law, Christine Hayes understands the nonuniversal rabbinic view of the Torah as a deliberate distancing from Greco-Roman notions of divine law. She emphasizes that, in some respects, rabbinic literature considers Torah ordinances as Greeks and Romans would have considered positive laws (in the sense of legal precepts established by the state). Furthermore, she notes that

> the rabbis' construction of Torah did not stem from systematic philosophical commitments, and in this respect the rabbis were like the Roman jurists, whose writings show a general if eclectic familiarity with theoretical accounts of the law but lack a serious engagement with these theories as they work at the jurist's trade.[354]

Building on these crucial insights, I would like to go one step further.

As mentioned at the beginning of this section, it is striking that the emphasis on the Mosaic law's universal character and rationality—its relationship to natural law—stems from Jewish authors who were involved in a "dialogue" with Greco-Roman *philosophical* discourses about law. This is patently the case in Philo's writings, even though they are on the whole exegetical rather than philosophical sensu stricto.

In Josephus' work, by contrast, there is little on the relationship between the law of Moses and the law of nature, the rationality of the Mosaic law, or its harmony with the cosmos. Josephus, however, does pay considerable attention to the universal adoption of Jewish rituals among the nations, as Philo already had. This apologetic discourse found in Philo's *On the Life of Moses* and Josephus' *Against Apion*, respectively, is absent from previous Jewish works written in Greek. It aims to prove the Torah's superiority to other legislation, not to other types of wisdom literature, and represents a different kind of universality than the one linked to the philosophical discourse on law. I have argued above that this understanding of the Mosaic law's universality and the claim for the absolute superiority of the Jewish law among all human legal systems, found under the pens of Philo and Josephus, are innovations of the Roman period that are to be understood as a response to the wide diffusion of Roman law within the empire and to Roman or pro-Roman claims for its perfection. Note that here the law of Moses (that is, the legal system of the Jewish people) is being compared to the legislation of other peoples and cities, and not to philosophical teachings. Although Moses is clearly considered to have been divinely inspired (as were some Greek lawgivers), the apologetic discourse of Philo and Josephus in *On the Life of Moses* and *Against Apion* was a response not to philosophical notions of law but to competing claims as to the excellence of positive laws.

The tendency in rabbinic literature to look on the Torah as a positive law, at least in certain respects—while yet maintaining its divine origin—and to avoid

354. Hayes 2015, 376.

philosophical debates about law is in line with this apologetic approach, which is not attested before the first century CE. As we saw in the previous section, the rabbis struggled with the question of the comparative value of non-Jewish and Jewish legal systems, as did Philo and Josephus. While they all posited that the Torah was superior to all other legal systems, the rabbis took a stance opposite to that of Philo and Josephus on the issue of the Torah's universal reach. Their writings reflect competition with Rome over who had the better laws. Yet they were not concerned to promote the universal diffusion of their laws among the nations, nor to argue over which laws had superior powers of attraction. The Roman context may again help to explain this evolution. The rabbis' emphasis on the Torah as the "national" law of Israel is consistent with the perspective of Roman jurists, who regarded Roman *ius civile*, at least on a theoretical level, as applicable to Roman citizens only. The association between membership in the people of Israel and observance of the Torah's commandments, strongly put forward in rabbinic writings, parallels the correlation between citizenship and law in Roman society, which, as we saw, admitted exceptions but nevertheless remained a central principle of Roman legal theory.

I therefore suggest understanding the shift from a conception of the Mosaic law as universal, rational, and philosophical, to the rabbinic view of the Torah as the exclusive legislation of the Jewish people, as in part a response to the valorization of Roman positive law in Roman culture. It must be emphasized again that Romans boasted not about their philosophical understanding of law but about their actual *ius*, their positive law. It was the activity of Roman jurists and judges that was esteemed and praised, not philosophical treatises on law, even though some members of the Roman elite were quite conversant in philosophy as well, as the examples of Cicero and Seneca illustrate. Within the framework of the Roman empire, one may to a certain extent speak of a reversal of hierarchy between natural law and positive law, with the latter now more highly valued than in the Greek view, not only in practice (as in every human society) but also in theory. The prestige enjoyed by law schools, especially from the second century CE onward in the East, where they competed with more traditional trainings in philosophy and rhetoric, illustrates this reversal. The intellectual challenge for Jews was thus different in a Roman context than in a Hellenistic one. The Torah's conformity to natural law became less of an issue, whereas its qualities as positive law, as the *ius* of the Jewish people, became crucial. Ultimately, in reclaiming the exclusive association between the Torah and Israel, the rabbis not only displayed a strong commitment to the covenantal understanding of the Mosaic law but also accorded with contemporary Roman views of law.

{≈≈✺≈≈}

This chapter has emphasized two phenomena in particular: Jewish rivalry with Rome in the legal sphere, at the ideological level, and the need to protect

Jewish law—considered divinely inspired by the rabbis, even though it now lay in the hands of men—either from falling into disuse as Jews were increasingly able to access Roman jurisdiction or from being integrated into the Roman legal system under the status of mere custom and thus merged with foreign laws. These two factors led the rabbis to produce their codifications of Jewish law, the Mishnah and the Tosefta, and the subsequent commentaries.

Imitation, subversion, and rejection of the Roman model are combined in this rabbinic project. Legal codification may be considered a form of imitation, as this was an activity characteristic of Roman jurists, especially from the second century CE on, whereas it was foreign to Second Temple Judaism. On the other hand, by producing their own code, hardly accessible to the Romans, and including fields, such as criminal law, that were the privilege of Roman judicial authorities, the rabbis *symbolically* challenged the Roman legal order. The fact that this was done in Hebrew and Aramaic rather than Greek—in contrast to the production of the Greek translation of the Pentateuch in Alexandria, which was meant at least in part to communicate the law of Moses to the Ptolemaic authorities—and that the rabbinic codification of the law remained oral for a long time undermine the hypothesis that it was an attempt to integrate Jewish law into Roman law. However, this does not preclude the possibility that on a practical level, some rabbis did try to achieve some accommodation with the Roman legal system. Recent studies have shown that they adopted and adapted some Roman legal principles within their own legal thinking and progressively created more space for "the laws of the nations" within their own jurisdiction, whether real or imagined.

The encounter with Rome thus prompted significant evolutions in Jewish conceptions of the Torah, among which we find the claim of an exclusive connection between the Torah and Israel. In marked contrast to Hellenistic Jewish texts, which were mainly involved in a debate with Greek philosophical views of law and articulated an understanding of the Torah as a universal and rational law, rabbinic texts tend to present the Torah as a law that belongs exclusively to Israel, just as the Roman *ius civile* was conceived of as the law of Roman citizens. Rabbinic discourse matches that of Roman jurists, not philosophers—even though some rabbinic texts feature philosophers as the rabbis' interlocutors. The evolution of the challenge confronted—first cultural and linked to the Jews' exposure to Greek philosophy in the Hellenistic period, then political-religious and linked to the Jews' exposure to Roman law—helps to explain the rabbis' deliberate insistence on the Torah as the particular law of the Jewish people, in which only gentiles who were full converts could participate, a vision still in force in orthodox Judaism nowadays.

CHAPTER FIVE

The Challenge of Roman Citizenship

A people is not every crowd of men, gathered in whatever fashion, but a crowd united by consensual commitment to a particular normative order and common utility.

CICERO, *THE REPUBLIC* 1.39.1[1]

You stand assembled today, all of you, before the Lord your God—the leaders of your tribes, your elders, and your officials, all the men of Israel, your children, your women, and the ger who is in your camp, both those who cut your wood and those who draw your water—to enter into the covenant of the Lord your God, sworn by an oath, which the Lord your God is making with you today; in order that he may establish you today as his people, and that he may be your God, as he promised you and as he swore to your ancestors, to Abraham, to Isaac, and to Jacob.

DEUTERONOMY 29:9–12

THE *CONSTITUTIO ANTONINIANA* of 212 CE transformed most free Jews in the Roman empire into Roman citizens. Beyond its legal consequences, which we examined in the previous chapter, this edict implied that part of the people of Israel was somehow being absorbed into the entity called the *populus Romanus*. Both Roman and pro-Roman discourses praised the Roman people for its willingness to progressively include all humankind, but it is far from certain that all provincials viewed this universalist ideology positively. Moreover, the rhetoric of universalism that was so attractive to some clashed with the persisting differences of social status between citizens and with deep-rooted prejudices.

---

1. Trans. Ando 2000, 48 (slightly modified).

If we keep in mind the issues discussed in Chapter Two—the rivalry between Israel and Rome from a Jewish perspective, and the perception of at least some Jews that Rome was taking Israel's place in the world—the question arises of how Jews regarded their newly granted Roman citizenship. Sadly, no Jewish source documents Jewish reactions to Caracalla's edict (as a matter of fact, there are relatively few documents shedding light on provincials' reception of the edict more broadly). These reactions must have been diverse, ranging from full acceptance of the new conditions of provincial participation in the imperial project, through indifference, to anxiety about Israel's ability to persist as an entity separate from Rome. As far as rabbinic sources are concerned, it is worth noting that they tend to describe the Severan dynasty positively, and the stories about Antoninus, the emperor who had a friendly relationship with Rabbi Yehudah ha-Nasi, certainly fit this picture of a more relaxed relationship between Jews and Romans under the Severans.[2] Yet it is unclear whether this positive assessment was connected in any way to Caracalla's edict.[3]

Roman and Jewish definitions of peoplehood differed. Translating both the Latin *populus* and the Hebrew *'am* (or *ummah*) as "people," as in this chapter's two epigraphs, is common and natural but may be misleading. From the Romans' perspective, a *populus* was characterized by civic institutions, whereas a *natio* or a *gens* (in Greek, an *ethnos*) was not.[4] This explains why Roman texts generally do not characterize the Jews as a *populus*; in the eyes of the Romans, they were merely a *gens*, because they had no civic organization.[5] Conversely, even though some Latin sources describe the Roman people as a *gens* (using phrases such as *gens Romana* and *gens togata*), it was also a *populus*. As we shall see in greater detail below, to be a Roman meant first and foremost to be a citizen.

Admittedly, people who were not Roman citizens could still participate to a certain extent in the political, cultural, and religious dimensions of "Romanness."

2. See Irshai 2019. On Antoninus, see Chapter Four, note 292.

3. On the reception of the Antonine Constitution in rabbinic circles, see also Appelbaum 2010, 10–17; Burns 2017b; Furstenberg 2018 and 2021; and the discussion in Chapter Four.

4. From the second century CE onward, however, there is a growing use of *populus* as a synonym of *gens*.

5. We must remember, however, that the use of vocabulary is never completely consistent, especially in poetic works. Indeed, we find two occurrences of the term *populus* in relation to the Jews in Justin's *Epitome* of Pompeius Trogus' writings (at 36.2.5 and 36.2.14, on ancient Israel at the time of Moses; see Stern 1976–1984, 1:335, no. 137), and another in a fragment of the satirist Petronius (*Fragmenta*, ed. Ernout, no. 37; Stern 1976–1984, 1:444, no. 195). Nonetheless, these passages are too exceptional to disprove the rule. In Roman legal texts up to the end of the 4th century, the terms used in connection with the Jews are *religio*, *superstitio*, *natio*, *universitas*, *ritus*, *secta*, *synagoga*, and *coetus*. The last three appear only in Christian imperial legislative decisions. The term *populus* is very rare and first appears in a prohibition on tax collection by the Jewish patriarch's emissaries dated to 11 April 399, under Arcadius and Honorius (C.Th. 16.8.14). See Linder 1987, no. 30, p. 216.

Being Roman was a matter of legal status, but "feeling Roman" was a different issue altogether, as was one's adhesion to or involvement in the imperial project.[6] In the past two decades, scholars have warned against understanding Roman "identity" in exclusively legal and political terms and have reassessed the role of ethnicity in Roman self-definitions.[7] However, this chapter will focus not on Roman "identity" but on Roman citizenship as a political tool in an imperial context. It will thus concentrate on the Roman practice of enfranchisement, the ideological discourses about Roman citizenship grants, and the impact of these on provincial populations. My purpose is to assess to what extent Roman policies and discourses on citizenship contributed to how Jewish authors conceived of membership in the people of Israel—not at the level of the practical requirements and rituals associated with conversion, however, but rather at the level of the concepts used to reflect on the integration of newcomers.

To clarify in what ways notions of citizenship could be relevant to Jews in antiquity, it is worth recalling that already in biblical texts there are at least two models that define Israel as a people: the family or clan with common ancestors (the Abrahamic covenant), and the group united by common laws (the Sinaitic covenant). As we shall see at greater length in Sections 2 and 3 below, the definition of Israel as a people joined by their commitment to God's commandments, with its corresponding emphasis on the legal realm, opened the way for Jewish writings composed in Greek to use civic terminology to talk about membership in the people of Israel, and to present proselytes as having received a new citizenship. This civic terminology may generally be described as metaphorical, yet it raises questions about the integration of Greek and Roman notions of citizenship into Jewish thought, and these questions extend to rabbinic texts, even though they were not composed in Greek.

On the other hand, genealogical definitions of the people of Israel—as the descendants of Abraham, Isaac, and Jacob—endured in the Hellenistic and Roman periods. This chapter will argue that the centrality of the "family," or genealogical, model among Jews led to yet another way to conceive of the integration of foreigners into Israel: through the legal fiction of adoption. Adoption played a crucial role in Roman society. It was not a legal instrument used to transform peregrines into Romans, because Romans could adopt only fellow citizens, but it was the means to confer a new lineage on a person who was not born with the right pedigree and to put him or her under the authority of a new *pater familias*—as adoptions within the imperial family exemplify.

6. Inglebert 2002 and 2005, 463–482.

7. See in particular Dench 2005; Farney 2007 and 2014. On the importance of kinship in definitions of ethnicity, see the discussions in McInerney 2014. On ethnicity as a social construction, see the influential work of Barth (1969), which highlights the central role played by myths of common origins/ancestors; Smith 1986; Jones 1997. On the difficulty of precisely defining the polysemous "ethnicity," see in particular Malkin and Müller 2012; Müller 2014.

Therefore, it could appear to Jews as an appropriate concept to reflect about the integration of proselytes into Israel's "family" and to solve the problem raised by the converts' non-Israelite ancestors, at least at the theoretical level.

This chapter shall thus explore Roman and Jewish constructions of peoplehood and how they relate to civic definitions of membership on the one hand and ethnicity or common ancestry—be it imagined or real—on the other. It will argue that converts who joined the Jewish people came to be viewed as new citizens in Israel's body politic and/or as new family members, through their adoption by the patriarch Abraham. These two notions are complementary rather than exclusive, since they rely on the two complementary definitions of Israel mentioned above, as a group united by law and as a family. Finally, both resort to Greco-Roman legal concepts, citizenship and adoption. As we shall see below, the evidence suggests that it was more particularly the Roman notions of citizenship and adoption that impacted Jewish thinking.

As in the previous chapters, I will first explain the nature of the challenge. That is to say, this chapter will make clear how the Roman practice of citizenship and the ideological discourse surrounding it differed from those of Greek cities and raised new questions for at least some Jews in the context of the rivalry described in Chapter Two and further explored in Chapters Three and Four. It will then examine how Greek and Roman models of citizenship contributed to Jewish conceptions of membership in the people of Israel and highlight the dialectics of imitation and differentiation at work in certain texts. Finally, pointing to some limits of the citizenship model, it will suggest that Roman adoption, in both theory and practice, represents another important conceptual model that must be taken into account to fully understand the development of the rabbinic view of converts. Ultimately, given the influence of rabbinic notions on modern Judaism, it might be argued that Roman norms and social practice contributed, in the long run, to the elaboration of modern Judaism's view of converts.

One last preliminary remark: it must be emphasized again that the investigation conducted in this chapter pertains mainly to the history of ideas and does not aim to clarify the varied and complex ways in which non-Jews were integrated into Jewish communities in everyday life. We must keep in mind the gap between theory and practice, remembering that social and cultural interactions in ancient societies were far more complex than the norms reflected in literary sources suggest.

1. The Nature of the Challenge

1.1 THE ROMAN "MELTING POT"

The notion that the Roman people emerged from encounters between different ethnic groups and their subsequent merging is a commonplace of both ancient and modern historiography. From the pens of ancient authors we read many accounts of the origins of the Romans, all stressing this feature, which stands in sharp contrast to Greek models (especially the Athenian myth of autochthony).[8] According to Virgil and Livy, Aeneas married Lavinia, the daughter of Latinus, the king of the Aborigeni, and from the union of the Trojans and the Aborigeni the Latins were born, from whom the Romans later stemmed—Livy emphasizes that Aeneas' privileging of the name "Latin" rather than "Trojan" was a political gesture made in the interests of victory and peace.[9]

According to an alternative narrative, found first and foremost in Dionysius of Halicarnassus' *Roman Antiquities*, Latium's original inhabitants were "the barbarian Sicels," who were expelled and replaced by the Aborigeni and the Pelasgians (both of Greek origin), who subsequently adopted the name "Latins" and finally, after Romulus founded his city, were called "Romans."[10] For Dionysius, the Aborigeni were probably of Arcadian stock (1.11.1–2).[11] What he aimed to demonstrate was that the Romans were no barbarians.

In literary accounts of the time following the foundation of Rome, we read about further unions with neighboring peoples, notably in the myths of the abduction of the Sabine women and of Romulus' asylum, which are often found side by side in narratives of the early imperial period.[12] According to the asylum tradition, at the time of Romulus, Rome became a refuge for a mixed crowd of people: political refugees fleeing tyranny (in Dionysius' version), but also slaves and, according to more negative and critical accounts, criminals.[13] In any case, we can see both myths as speaking indirectly about citizenship. Beginning in the first century BCE, Roman and pro-Roman Greek sources state this quite explicitly. After the rape of the Sabine women, Cicero states, Romulus added the Sabines to the *civitas* of the Romans through a treaty with their king, Titus Tatius (*Rep.* 2.13); similarly, Livy attributes to Romulus the promise that the young women seized by the Romans "should be wedded and become co-partners in all the possessions of the Romans, in their

8. See Gruen 1992, 6–51 (esp. on ancient accounts of Rome's Greek origins and the Greek elaboration of the Trojan myth); Moatti 1997, 258–273, esp. 265–266.

9. Virgil, *Aeneid* 6.756–766; Livy, 1.1.1–2, 1.2.4–5; Ando 2000, 53. Cf. Strabo, *Geogr.* 5.3.2.

10. Dionysius, *Rom. Ant.* 1.9.1–11.1. Dionysius describes Rome as having surpassed Greek *poleis* in what were supposedly Greek virtues; see Hartog 1991; 1996, 198–200.

11. Strabo (*Geogr.* 5.3.3) reports a different version of the connection between the Arcadians and Rome, which he deems unreliable. See also Moatti 1997, 261, on the testimonies of Fabius Pictor and Varro.

12. Dench 2005, 20–21.

13. Dionysius, *Rom. Ant.* 2.15.3. Cf. Strabo, *Geogr.* 5.3.2; Juvenal, *Sat.* 8.272–275. Cicero, the first author to clearly attribute the role of asylum giver to Romulus, describes the people who gathered at that time as "shepherds and immigrants" (*On the Making of an Orator* 1.9.37). Livy's account is ambivalent: the asylum's social openness originally contributed to Rome's strength and growth but constituted a potential threat in the long run; see Dench 2005, 15–20, esp. 19; Moatti 1997, 262–263.

citizenship (*civitas*) and, dearest privilege of all to the human race, in their children."[14] As for the asylum, Strabo notes in the passage of the *Geography* on the origins of Rome: "After the founding Romulus set about collecting a promiscuous rabble by designating as an asylum a sacred precinct between the Arx and the Capitol, and by declaring citizens (*politai*) all the neighbours who fled thither for refuge."[15] Here Strabo is to a certain extent projecting the Roman policy of the first century BCE back on to Romulus.

Considering Roman and Greek narratives, Clifford Ando aptly concludes that "the many and varied legends of the foundation of Rome agree on at least two details: Rome's original population had been heterogeneous, to say the least, and it had established and maintained itself in its early years through warfare."[16] Erich Gruen notes in a similar vein: "The idea of autochthony or indigenous origins never made much headway in Rome. [. . .] Romans represented themselves without embarrassment as a composite people who belonged intimately to the broader Mediterranean world."[17] Logically, as Gruen further remarks in another publication, "Roman traditions claimed no purity of lineage. [. . .] Mixed ancestry, in fact, was part of the Roman image from its inception."[18] I will return later to the notions of ancestry and lineage in Roman society, distinguishing between the people as a whole and the individual *gentes* (families or clans), for whom ethnicity and ancestry did matter and who used them as political arguments at least until the early imperial period.[19] For the time being, however, we shall focus on the *populus Romanus* as a whole, keeping in mind that in contrast to Israel, it was not considered to be united by shared ancestors and shared kinship.

The populations of the empire were well aware of this Roman characteristic, which most sources indicate was perceived positively—although in theory, mixed origins were inglorious, even contemptible—because ancient minds closely associated it with the Roman grants of citizenship at the end of the Republic and during the imperial period (more on these grants below).

Interestingly enough, the mixed origins of the Romans could be considered an aspect of self-definition rivaling that of a group that set itself up partly in opposition to Rome: not the Jews in this case, but the Christians (at least in the eyes of some Christian authors writing before 212 CE). It is in light of the mixed origins of the Romans that the author of the *Commentary on Daniel* (Pseudo-Hippolytus), writing at the very beginning of the third century, before the *Constitutio Antoniniana*, explains the vision of the fourth beast in Daniel 7:7. If the beast, which Daniel describes as "terrifying and dreadful and

---

14. Livy, 1.9.14–15, trans. B. O. Foster, LCL, 37.

15. Strabo, *Geogr.* 5.3.2, trans. Horace Leonard Jones, LCL, 383–385.

16. Ando 2000, 52.

17. Gruen 2011, 249.

18. Gruen 2009, 345.

19. Farney 2007. See also Smith 2006.

exceedingly strong" and which Jewish and Christian exegetes had long associated with Rome, has no name, it is because it "is not one people (*ethnos*), but gathers to itself [individuals] from all languages and from the whole human race, and prepares an army in battle array, and all are called Romans, although they are not all from one country."[20] The author is clearly conscious that the Romans are not a people based on ethnicity or common ancestry, and that this applies equally to Christians. In the next paragraph (4.9), he recalls that at the time of Augustus, "the Lord summoned all peoples (*ethnē*) and all languages" in order to form the people (*ethnos*) of the Christians. Romans and Christians thus appear as rival universal groups, the first representing the earthly and warlike kingdom, the second the heavenly and peace-loving kingdom.[21]

In a fourth-century context, the opposition between these two peoples and kingdoms gave way to new models, in which the universality of the empire and that of the Gospel converged. Paradoxically enough, Eusebius also emphasizes similarities between the Romans and "the Hebrews," precisely in relation to the fact that the Roman people is composite, made of peoples stemming from different ethnic groups:

> Just as the procurators and governors appointed in the Roman Empire over nations, their praefects and military chiefs, and their highest kings, are not all drawn from Rome nor from the seed (*spora*) of Remus and Romulus, but from many different peoples (*ethnē*), and yet all their kings and the rulers and governors below them are all called Romans, and their power is named Roman, and the rule of them all generally has this appellation, in the same way we should think of the affairs among the Hebrews, where you have the name of the tribe of Judah applied generally to the whole nation (*ethnos*), though there be kings and governors of divisions from different tribes, but all honoured with the name of Judah.[22]

20. *Comm. Dan.* 4.8, my translation, based on the edition of Bonwetsch and Achelis 1897, 206. A somewhat comparable perspective might be present in Sifre Deuteronomy 320, which comments on Deut 32:21b, "I will make them jealous with what is no people (*be-lo 'am*), provoke them with a foolish nation." The midrash states: "Do not read *be-lo 'am* ['with what is no people'] but *beloyey 'am* ['dregs of [the] people,' lit. 'rags of [the] people']. They are those who come from among the nations (*ummot*) and the kingdoms (*malkhuyot*) and take them [Israel?] out of their houses." The reference seems to be to the Roman army, which comes to take Jews out of their homes either in the context of a revolt or, alternately, in order to conscript them. If this interpretation is correct, it is yet another echo of the perception of the Roman army as composed of people from various nations. Moreover, in view of the biblical verse that the midrash comments on, it may be possible to infer that the midrash's author perceived the Roman people (represented by its army) as not being a real people because of the multiple ethnic origins of its citizens.

21. Inglebert 2016a, 100–102.

22. Eusebius, *Proof of the Gospel* 8.1, trans. Ferrar 1920, 106 (slightly modified).

Eusebius notes that the members of the people of Israel are all called by the name of the tribe of Judah—that is, they are named *Ioudaioi*, Judahites/Judeans/ Jews—even though they do not all belong to this tribe (they are not all descendants of this patriarch). He contends that the situation in the Roman empire— the fact that people of various ethnic origins are all called Romans—sheds light on this phenomenon. The comparison, however, is misleading, because the Hebrews, here described as stemming from different tribes, even if not descended from Judah still shared a common ancestor, Jacob, with the members of that tribe. By contrast, the various ethnic groups that, according to Roman traditions, were integrated into the Roman people at one stage or another did not have ancestors in common with the original inhabitants of the *Urbs*.

1.2 *CIVIS ROMANUS SUM*: THE CHARACTERISTICS OF ROMAN CITIZENSHIP

Membership in the *populus Romanus* was not defined primarily in reference to ethnicity—understood as implying not only a common language and a shared culture but also a common descent, no matter how fictitious. Rather, membership was defined in political and legal terms: being a member of the *populus Romanus* was equivalent to being a Roman citizen.[23]

Obviously, the most common way to be a Roman citizen was to be born to parents who were Roman citizens, which comes close to the transmission of ethnicity. Hereditary transmission of citizenship, however, was not the only way of becoming Roman. As Clifford Ando puts it:

> The Roman community was constituted on premises atypical in the ancient world. The Romans' disinterest in defining themselves as a race and, therefore, in limiting their franchise to the children of citizens stood in stark contrast to practice elsewhere around the Mediterranean.[24]

Roman *civitas* differed in many ways from citizenship in the Greek world. The absence of emphasis on descent and ethnicity, as well as territory, represents a first divergence.[25] Then, there was the fundamental difference in nature between the Greek *poleis* and the Roman *civitas*, which makes

---

23. On Roman self-definition as based on juridical status rather than ethnicity or culture, see in particular Inglebert 2005, 29; Wallace-Hadrill 2008, 41. On Roman citizenship, see Sherwin-White 1973a; Nicolet 1976; Jacques and Scheid 1990, 209–289; Garnsey 2004; Marotta 2009; Heller and Pont 2012; Ando 2016c; Lavan 2019a.

24. Ando 2000, 338.

25. Nicolet 1976, 31–69; Gauthier 1981; Moatti 1997, 270; Ando 1999, 14–15. Obviously, these observations are to be qualified in accordance with the period under study. The connection between Roman citizenship and the city of Rome was stronger under the Republic than in the imperial period.

comparing them problematic to a certain extent.[26] Adopting Philippe Gauthier's terminology, we may broadly characterize Greek *poleis* as structures of participation and Rome as a structure of integration.[27] Participation in political assemblies, magistracies, and the administration of the city's affairs was central to the definition of Greek citizenship. To put it bluntly, the main issue in a Greek context was the functions fulfilled by the citizen, rather than his personal status. Hellenistic *poleis*, it is important to remember, continued to operate as structures of participation until at least the beginning of the first century CE.[28] By contrast, for most Roman citizens, especially from the end of the Republic onward, participation in political assemblies in Rome had little significance.[29] The crucial element of Roman citizenship was instead one's personal status as a subject of Roman law, with a corresponding set of rights and obligations.[30] Cicero thus writes: "A commonwealth (*res publica*) is the property of a people (*res populi*); but a *populus* is not every crowd of men, gathered in whatever fashion, but a crowd united by *consensual commitment to a particular normative order* and common utility."[31] Elsewhere, he explains that Roman citizens are forbidden to hold another citizenship simultaneously because otherwise they would be subject to two different types of law, a remark that illustrates the intimate connection, in his eyes, between *civitas* and *ius*.[32] Livy reports that immediately after organizing the religious rituals of the city, Romulus gave its inhabitants legal institutions (*iura*), "since nothing else but laws (*leges*) could unite them into one body as a single people (*in populi unius corpus*)."[33] Four centuries later, the emperor Julian still asserted that people became Roman citizens "by participating in Rome's constitution, by adopting our customs, and by using our laws."[34]

A third divergence between Roman and Greek citizenship lies in the fact that Roman citizens were far more numerous and spread over an enormously greater expanse of geography than those of any Greek city. In the second century BCE, the number of Roman citizens was already approximately 300,000. By 14 CE, it is said to have exceeded four million, and Myles Lavan suggests that it could even have been six million—women and children included—if the entire Italian peninsula, the Roman colonies, Cisalpine Gaul,

---

26. Gauthier 1974, 207.

27. Gauthier 1974 and 1981.

28. Gauthier 1981, 172–173. See also Heller and Pont 2012, esp. 9–15.

29. Compare Nicolet 1976, which focuses on the Republican period and emphasizes the participation of Roman citizens in the processes of political decision-making then.

30. Ando 2000, Chapter 9; Marotta 2009, 31.

31. Cicero, *Rep.* 1.39.1, trans. Ando 2000, 48 (slightly modified; emphasis added). See also Moatti 1997, 288–291.

32. Cicero, *Pro Balbo* 13.31. See Humbert 2010, 150–152.

33. Livy, 1.8.1–2, my translation.

34. Julian, *Or.* 1.4, trans. Ando 2000, 65.

and individual cities in the provinces are counted.[35] Irrespective of how uncertain these figures are, even in the second century BCE the Romans would have been considered as constituting not a *polis* but rather an *ethnos*, if Aristotle's definition of the *polis* in *Politics* 7.4, 1726a–b is accepted.[36]

The discrepancy in numbers is directly linked to yet another significant difference between Rome and the Greek cities: namely, their policies regarding enfranchisement. In a Greek framework, it was impossible for a citizen to grant citizenship to a slave by manumitting him or her, and more generally for an individual to decide alone on such an important issue as the growth of the civic body.[37] The question of how people became Roman is thus a crucial one for understanding the specificity of the Roman *civitas*.

There were at least five ways one could obtain Roman citizenship if one was not born a Roman citizen: (1) manumission, (2) service in the army, (3) an individual grant, (4) a community grant, or (5) service as a magistrate in a community ruled by Latin law, generally a Latin *municipium*. A slave could become a Roman citizen through manumission, if the master was himself a citizen and if the manumission was performed in accordance with Roman law—by the rod (*vindicta*) before a magistrate, by will, or through the census. Augustus restricted this possibility by requiring that the slave be at least thirty years old, limiting the total number of slaves that a master could manumit, and excluding certain categories of slaves who executed degrading tasks. Slaves who had not been freed in accordance with Roman law or did not fall into the right categories became "Junian Latins," a kind of personal status modeled on Latin law.[38] From the reign of Claudius onward, foreigners who served for at least twenty-five years in the *auxilia* or twenty-six years in the fleets could obtain Roman citizenship, together with their children (after 140 CE children born before the enfranchisement were excluded from the grants), and were given bronze diplomas documenting their enfranchisement.[39] Independent of military service, individuals who displayed exceptional loyalty to Rome or made exceptional contributions to its prosperity also could be granted Roman citizenship, either on a strictly personal basis or together with their wife and children, first through a vote of the Roman people, then through the action of a magistrate, and finally, from Augustus onward, exclusively through an imperial decree.[40]

35. Lavan 2019a, 30; see also Nicolet 1976, 31–32; Lavan 2016.

36. Gauthier 1981, 169; Marotta 2009, 31–32.

37. Mouritsen 2011, 67.

38. Watson 1987, 23–34; Humbert 2010; Lavan 2019a, 23.

39. Waebens 2012; Haynes 2013, 42, 49, 56–58; Lavan 2019b. A military diploma dating to 70 CE (*AE* 1997, 1771) documents an exceptional grant of citizenship to soldiers from the imperial fleet at Ravenna before they had served for twenty-six years. It was a reward for the fleet's support of Vespasian and his troops during the civil war of 68–69 CE.

40. Antipater, Herod's father, received Roman citizenship from Julius Caesar, together with immunity from taxes (*ateleia*, i.e. *immunitas*) (Josephus, *B.J.* 1.194 and *A.J.* 14.137;

In practice, various networks of patronage were instrumental in securing the emperor's grants, as Pliny the Younger's letters and various inscriptions attest. Communities that had been faithful allies of the Roman people or of a given emperor could receive Roman citizenship collectively—for example, by gaining the status of a Roman *municipium* or *colonia*—but these grants were much rarer.[41] Philo writes that some of Caligula's friends obtained citizenship for their home cities, and suggests that Agrippa I, one of the emperor's close friends, could have asked the same for Jerusalem but refrained from doing so.[42] Especially noteworthy is the fact that, in communities under Latin law (considered a privilege in itself), people who were elected to local magistracies would receive Roman citizenship at the end of their term.[43] This policy meant that in practice, noncitizens could choose who would become a Roman citizen, a feature that further distinguished Rome from Greek cities.[44]

Throughout Roman history, the significance of citizenship grants varied considerably in the eyes of both Romans and non-Romans. As Myles Lavan recalls, "In the earliest phases of Roman expansion, naturalisation was employed as a means of organising and controlling conquered populations. It was a status imposed on rebellious, not loyal, aliens—a striking inversion of later practice."[45] Thereafter, especially following the Second Punic War, Rome used citizenship grants not as a punishment but as a reward. Yet this policy, too, was slowly reversed, and in the second half of the second century BCE, several sources testify to the Romans' growing reluctance to grant full citizenship to their Latin allies, leading to some candidates' expulsion from Rome. Ultimately, the allies waged the Social War (91–88 BCE), which, according to ancient historians, was motivated by a desire to obtain Roman citizenship. This was granted to them through the *lex Plautia Papiria*, which considerably increased the number of citizens, up to the Principate. In the imperial period, individual and community grants continued at a varying rate until the turning point of 212 CE, which saw most free individuals become Romans.[46]

Gilboa 1972). Octavian's grant of citizenship to his naval captain Seleucus (also with *immunitas/aneisphoria*) is particularly well documented (*SEG* 54.1625; *IGLS* III.1, no. 718; Raggi 2004 and 2009).

41. See, e.g., under Claudius, *CIL* V, 5050, documenting a grant of citizenship to the Adauni, Tulliasses, and Sunduni, three Alpine tribes; Sherk 1988, 94–96.

42. *Legat.* 285–287.

43. The key document for understanding this policy is the inscription known as the *Lex Irnitana* (§21–23), from Spain in the Flavian period; see González and Crawford 1986; Jacques and Scheid 1990, 232–234; Gardner 2001. On Latin law (*ius Latinum*), see Kremer 2006.

44. Ando 2016c; Lavan 2019a, 36.

45. Lavan 2019a, 24. See also Humbert 1978, 76–81; Humbert 2010, 140.

46. For an overall view of the evolution of Roman enfranchisement policy, see Humbert 2010, 140–147; Lavan 2019a (rightly avoiding a teleological perspective). Against a teleological perspective, see also Marotta 2009, 30.

What did Roman citizenship imply for those who enjoyed it? Beyond active participation in the political institutions of Rome—which presumed presence in the *Urbs*, very much depended upon one's wealth and social status, and progressively came to an end in the imperial period—Roman citizenship meant three things: (1) participation in the *maiestas* (majesty) of the Roman people;[47] (2) specific rights—*conubium* (marriage), *commercium* (commerce), *provocatio* (appeal, first *ad populum*, to the people, and then *ad imperatorem*, to the emperor)—and better judicial protection than *peregrini* enjoyed (from the second century this right gradually became the sole privilege of the *honestiores*, those with higher social status); and (3) administrative, military, fiscal, and religious duties.[48] At the end of the Republic, some grants of citizenship also included freedom from financial duties in the city of origin (*immunitas*, a privilege otherwise granted to faithful allies of Rome who did not become Roman citizens) and in Rome (immunity from imperial taxation), but these benefits saw reductions under Augustus and gradually ended.[49] The inscription of the *Tabula Banasitana* from Mauritania, which documents a grant of citizenship *salvo iure gentis* to prominent members of a local tribe, the Zegrenses, by Marcus Aurelius in 177 CE, demonstrates that—at least in this context—local elites who benefited from such a grant still had to uphold their fiscal and legal obligations to their local community and did not receive *immunitas* in addition to *civitas*; on the other hand, they retained the right to follow their traditional laws in their dealings with their fellow countrymen.[50]

With the passage of time and the growth of the civic body, Roman citizens saw some of their rights lose significance. Conversely, from the Antonine dynasty onward, only the performance of religious duties and the payment of certain taxes—but no military service—were still incumbent upon them. According to Cassius Dio, the aim of Caracalla's decree extending Roman citizenship to all free persons in the empire (with the exception of the *dediticii* [on which see below]) was to increase the number of taxpayers and thus alleviate

47. This aspect is illustrated a contrario by Josephus' recounting of Florus' cruel punishment of the inhabitants of Jerusalem, among whom Josephus claims there were persons belonging to the equestrian order, who were "Jews by birth (*to genos*)" yet of "Roman dignity (*to axiōma Rhōmaikon*)" (*B.J.* 2.308). Here the Greek term *axiōma* seems to echo the notion of *maiestas*. Florus was not supposed to have Roman citizens flogged and crucified without a proper judgment and the possibility of appealing to the emperor, all the more so as these belonged to the upper strata of Roman society. See Mason 2008, 247.

48. Jacques and Scheid 1990, 212–214. Concerning judicial protection, one may recall the famous example of Paul in the Acts of the Apostles (16:37–38, 22:26–29, 25:10–12). On the differences in judicial treatment of *honestiores* and *humiliores*, see Marotta 2009, 40–42.

49. Sherwin-White 1973a, 91–94; Raggi 2009; Blanco Pérez 2019.

50. *CRAI* 1971, 468–490; *IAM* II, no. 94; Seston and Euzennat 1971; Oliver 1972; Sherwin-White 1973a, 274, 312, 336, 393 and Sherwin-White 1973b; Christol 1988; Blanco Pérez 2019.

the fiscal burden connected to the inheritance tax, which was paid by Roman citizens alone.[51] Although the exact relationship of Papyrus Giessen 40 (*P.Giss.* 40) to the edict of 212 CE is still debated, the first column of this document suggests that there was a religious aspect to the emperor's decision as well.[52]

From the Social War to the edict of Caracalla, Roman citizenship was not universally desired by local elites in every city or region, but on the whole it was considered an honor and a privilege, and the Romans themselves presented it as such. According to Cicero, who famously spoke about the two *patriae*, the *patria* of origin and the *communis patria* (Rome), no status or membership could be more prestigious than Roman citizenship.[53] In the second half of the second century CE, Aulus Gellius similarly contended that at the collective level, no status was preferable to or more prestigious for provincial communities than that of a Roman colony—which included Roman citizenship for the inhabitants and the use of all the laws and institutions of Rome—because of "the greatness and majesty of the Roman people (*amplitudinem maiestatemque populi Romani*)."[54] We shall see below that provincial elites were quite unanimous in celebrating individual grants of citizenship.[55] As for collective grants through the transformation of an existing community into a Roman colony, there are several examples, including in the East (and specifically in Palestine), showing that some cities sought this privileged status.[56] Often their coinage would subsequently reflect their Roman character, as on this bronze coin from Neapolis issued under Philip I (247–249 CE), whose reverse displays the she-wolf suckling the twins (Fig. 5.1).

The most important act of enfranchisement was performed by Caracalla, with the promulgation of the *Constitutio Antoniniana* in 212 CE. According

51. Cassius Dio, *Rom. Hist.* 77.9.5.

52. Kuhlmann 1994, 215–255; Buraselis 2007, 10; Bryen 2016. See also the concise presentation and discussion by Aitor Blanco Pérez, "P.Giss. 40 and the Constitutio Antoniniana," http://www.judaism-and-rome.org/pgiss-40-and-constitutio-antoniniana.

53. Cicero, *On Laws* 2.5; Thomas 1996; Ando 2000, 10.

54. Aulus Gellius, *Attic Nights* 16.13.9. The Jews who witnessed the refoundation of Jerusalem as a Roman colony but were excluded from it probably had a different perception of the phenomenon.

55. According to Heller 2019, inscriptions from Greek cities show that citizenship was one coveted honor among many, whose main importance was to enhance the possessor's prestige.

56. For example, Berytus, Ptolemais, and Caesarea (Maritima) became Roman colonies in the first century CE (veterans were settled in the first two, while Caesarea was an instance of transformation into a Roman colony with no addition of veterans), and so did Sebaste (under the name Lucia Septimia Sebaste) at the beginning of the second century. The case of Flavia Neapolis in Samaria (originally founded as a *polis* in 72/73 CE, it became Colonia Iulia Sergia Neapolis in the middle of the third century) shows that even after 212 CE the status of *colonia* remained appealing. See Isaac 1980–81; Belayche 2001, 199–202 (on Neapolis), 209–212 (on Sebaste); Millar 2006. For a late rabbinic echo of the possibility for a city to become a colony by imperial decision, see b. Avodah Zarah 10a.

FIGURE 5.1. Bronze coin of the *colonia* Neapolis, featuring Philip I on the obverse, and the she-wolf suckling the twins on the reverse (247–249 CE). The Israel Museum, Jerusalem, 2012.001.32994. Photograph © The Israel Museum, Jerusalem.

to the text known through *P.Giss.* 40, the emperor declared: "I give to everyone across the world the citizenship (*politeia*) of the Romans, preserving the right of the communities (*menontos* 9 [*tou dikaiou tōn politeum*]*atōn*) [or: without prejudice to local rights (*dikaiōm*]*atōn*)], except for the *dediticii*."[57] The exact identity of the *dediticii*—who may have been either groups that had been defeated by the Romans, or former slaves who were under the jurisdiction of the *lex Aelia Sentia*—is a matter of debate, but it is highly unlikely that the category included Jews, and some scholars even contend that the text contains no clause of exclusion.[58] The reference to the "right of the communities" or the absence of "prejudice to local rights"—depending on the reconstitution of line 9—is probably to be understood in light of the notion of *salvo iure gentis*, as in the *Tabula Banasitana*, which allowed new citizens to continue to follow

57. Greek text according to Kuhlmann 1994, no. 6, col. I, on 222, and http://papyri.info /ddbdp/p.giss;1;40. Trans. Aitor Blanco Pérez, "P.Giss. 40 and the Constitutio Antoniniana," http://www.judaism-and-rome.org/pgiss-40-and-constitutio-antoniniana. Cf. Mitteis 1912, II/2, no. 377 ([*m*]*enontos* 9 [*pantos genous politeum*]*atōn*); Buraselis 2007, 10. For the alternative reconstitution with *dikaiōmatōn*, see Benario 1954, 190; Bryen 2016, 32.

58. See in particular Sherwin-White 1973a, 381–385; Marotta 2009, 112–115; Marotta 2017, 192–194. See also Benario 1954; Kuhlmann 1994, 220–221. On whether the Jews were *dediticii*, see Irshai 2019, 174–175. In view of Cassius Dio's consistent interest in Jewish revolts against Rome and their consequences, had the Jews been excluded from the citizenship grant, he certainly would have mentioned it. Christian authors probably would have emphasized this too.

their local laws; it may also refer to special statutes and privileges accorded to whole communities, especially *poleis*.[59]

The Antonine Constitution's impact on the empire's populations has been varyingly assessed by scholars and is still debated. Some point out that we have very few traces of this decree and its consequences, as if it had passed relatively unnoticed.[60] The only documents informing us about it are the papyrus commonly held to contain the Greek version of the edict, and a passage from the *Digest* (1.5.17). In addition, some Christian literary texts briefly allude to Caracalla's decree.[61] To explain this relative lack of testimony, scholars have argued that Roman citizenship was already widespread. However, recent studies have shown that this was not the case, with only 15% to 30% of the empire's free population enjoying the status of citizen on the eve of 212 CE.[62] The *Constitutio Antoniniana*'s impact has also been reevaluated in light of the growing number of unearthed papyri and inscriptions that illustrate the spread of the *nomen* Aurelius after 212, a consequence of the grant of Roman citizenship by Caracalla (Marcus Aurelius Severus Antoninus Pius).[63] Most important, contrary to what several scholars have long argued, Roman citizenship remained a valuable asset in the eyes of many of the empire's inhabitants after 212.[64] Certainly, it no longer conferred as many benefits upon its recipients as in the first century BCE or CE. From the middle of the second century CE, being a citizen was not enough to escape flogging or to benefit from privileged treatment in criminal trials more generally if one was not part of the *honestiores* as well.[65] Yet Ralph Mathisen contends that "Roman citizenship continued not only to be a factor in how people perceived themselves, but also to entail legal rights that were available only to persons who were identified as 'Roman

---

59. Sherwin-White 1973a, 382, 393; Blanco Pérez 2019. On the use of local laws, see Chapter Four.

60. See Buraselis 2007, 94–120, for a critique of this argument. For a concise description of the paucity of sources, see Marotta 2009, 101–106.

61. John Chrysostom, *Homily 48* on Acts 1 (PG 60, 333) (which wrongly dates it to the time of Hadrian); Augustine, *De civitate Dei* 5.17.1; see also Inglebert 2016a, 106–107, 109–111.

62. Lavan 2016 and 2019a.

63. Jacques and Scheid 1990, 289; Garnsey 2004. On the diffusion of the *nomen* Aurelius, see especially Buraselis 2007, 94–120; Rizakis 2011.

64. For the view that Roman citizenship lost its significance after 212, see Sherwin-White 1973a, 445; Brown 1992, 154; Gardner 1993, 187; additional references in Mathisen 2006, 1014, note 27, and Buraselis 2007, 120–121, note 1. Garnsey 1968 suggests that "the value of citizenship may have declined in the second century, perhaps because of the increase in the number of citizens" (23), and states that the "citizen/alien distinction lost most of its meaning" after 212 (23, note 87).

65. Mathisen 2006, 1015. Lavan even states that "by the later second century peregrine *honestiores* enjoyed privileges denied to lower status citizens" (Lavan 2019a, 47). For the view that all of the citizens' privileges were maintained, see Buraselis 2007, 120–130.

Citizens.'"[66] In the fifth century, Augustine still valued and praised as very "generous" or "humane" (*humanissimus*) the fact that the Romans had shared their citizenship with all.[67]

1.3 ROMAN GRANTS OF CITIZENSHIP: IDEOLOGICAL ASPECTS

On the basis of some ancient accounts concerning the spread of Roman citizenship, modern scholars have tended to believe that the Roman policy of enfranchisement helped to integrate conquered populations into the empire and thus to extend its dominion, especially in the West. In other words, this strategy has traditionally been seen as key to the success of Roman imperialism, especially through the co-opting of provincial elites.[68] However, both Clifford Ando and Myles Lavan have emphasized that citizenship grants were neither necessary nor sufficient to secure provincials' loyalty and the stability of Rome's *imperium*. As a matter of fact, both citizens and noncitizens had complex sets of motivations for supporting the empire, and there were peregrines who were loyal to Rome despite not possessing the *civitas Romana*.[69]

The connection that ancient sources draw between Rome's enfranchisement policy on the one hand and its victories and success as an empire on the other is thus not to be taken as historical reality. Yet its ideological significance is no less important for all that. First, Roman sources themselves regularly put forward this idea. The most famous such statement occurs in Cicero's speech in defense of Balbus, who had received Roman citizenship from Pompey and saw this grant challenged in a prosecution instigated by enemies of the Triumvirate in 56 BCE:

> What undoubtedly has done most to establish our Empire and to increase the renown of the Roman People, is that Romulus, that first founder of this city, taught us by the treaty which he made with the Sabines, that this State ought to be enlarged by the admission even of enemies as citizens. Through his authority and example our forefathers never ceased to grant and to bestow citizenship.[70]

Not only are Romans ready to bestow citizenship on foreigners: they grant it even to former enemies and thus transform them into fellow Romans.

---

66. Mathisen 2006, 1015. See also Garnsey 2004 (which, however, also focuses on "the profound social inequalities that rendered the mass of the population powerless to make citizenship work for them" [133]).

67. Augustine, *De civitate Dei* 5.17.1.

68. See, e.g., Brunt 1976, 166–167 [273–274]; Vittinghoff 1994, 276–277.

69. Ando 2000, 10; Lavan 2019a, 41–47.

70. Cicero, *Pro Balbo* 13.31, trans. R. Gardner, LCL, 665.

The same idea recurs in a speech that Livy attributes to the consul Lucius Furius Camillus, who is described as addressing the Senate after the Roman victories against the Latin peoples in 338 BCE in the following terms:

> You may blot out all Latium, and make vast solitudes of those places where you have often raised a splendid army of allies and used it through many a momentous war. Would you follow the example of your fathers, and augment the Roman state (*augere rem Romanam*) by receiving your conquered enemies (lit.: [your] conquered [enemies], *victos*) as citizens? You have at hand the means of waxing great and supremely glorious.[71]

Again, the ability of the Romans to transform their adversaries into fellow citizens is presented as key to Rome's prosperity and glory.

With the passing of time, foreigners who were granted Roman citizenship were allowed to integrate the upper strata of Roman society and even to enter the Senate. Claudius was particularly active in opening the doors of this venerable *ordo* to newcomers, as the converging testimonies of the Lyon tablet (48 CE) and Tacitus demonstrate.[72] While Claudius' speech as inscribed on the Lyon tablet focuses on opening membership in the Roman Senate to the elite of Gallia Comata, in Tacitus' account it deals with the combined issues of enfranchising and co-opting magistrates and senators of foreign origin:

> 1 [. . .] In my own ancestors, the eldest of whom, Clausus, a Sabine by extraction, was made simultaneously a citizen and the head of a patrician house, I find encouragement to employ the same policy in my administration, by transferring hither all true excellence, let it be found where it will. 2 For I am not unaware that the Julii came to us from Alba, the Coruncanii from Camerium, the Porcii from Tusculum; that—not to scrutinize antiquity—members were drafted into the senate from Etruria, from Lucania, from the whole of Italy; and that finally Italy itself was extended to the Alps, in order that not individuals merely but countries and peoples should form one body under the name of Romans (*ut non modo singuli viritim, sed terrae, gentes in nomen nostrum coalescerent*). [. . .] 4 What else proved fatal to Lacedaemon and Athens, in spite of their power in arms, but their policy of holding the conquered aloof as alien-born? But the sagacity of our own founder Romulus was such that several times he fought and naturalized a people in the course of the same day! Strangers have been kings over us: the conferment of magistracies on the sons of freedmen is not

---

71. Livy, 8.13.15–16, trans. B. O. Foster, LCL, 57.

72. *CIL* XIII, 1668; Tacitus, *Annals* 11.24.1–7. See Fabia 1929, 62–65; Sherwin-White 1973a, 237–244; Chastagnol 1992; Giardina 1994.

the novelty which it is commonly and mistakenly thought, but a frequent practice of the old commonwealth.[73]

In this speech we again encounter the central argument used in discourses praising Rome's policy of enfranchisement: it contributed to the *Urbs'* security and success because it transformed former enemies into fellow citizens (§4). The comparison with Sparta and Athens is noteworthy; it constituted a topos of the encomium of Rome, as the writings of Greek authors also illustrate.[74] The underlying idea was that both Sparta and Athens had experienced a shortage of soldiers which led to their decline, whereas Rome was able to increase the number of its legions by welcoming new citizens (since the latter had military obligations) and thus became all the more powerful. In addition, Tacitus suggests that Romans valued "excellence" (virtue) more than birth (pedigree) (§1), a notion found under Cicero's pen as well. As a consequence, Rome was able to rally the best and most illustrious men, from various ethnic origins, to its cause.[75] Claudius' policy aroused opposition from some senators and from members of ancient Roman families more widely. After the emperor's death, Seneca composed a satirical work titled *Apocolocyntosis*—the "Pumpkinification" of the deceased princeps—in which he mocks Claudius' desire "to see the whole world in the toga, Greeks, Gauls, Spaniards, Britons, and all."[76] His nephew Lucan seems to have shared this derisive view.[77] Clearly, Romans were not unanimously pleased by the openness of their *civitas* to foreigners. Nonetheless this Roman feature was frequently cited as a factor contributing to Rome's superiority over the Greek cities.

Numerous sources testify that the Greeks themselves were aware of this unique Roman openness and connected it with Rome's exceptional military strength. As early as the end of the third century BCE, a letter of Philip V to Larisa (*SIG*³ 543) reproaches the Larisaeans for not having followed his advice to grant citizenship to the Thessalians and other Greeks dwelling among them to compensate for a shortage of manpower, referring to the Romans as an example that all the Greeks should imitate. The Macedonian king notes that

73. Tacitus, *Annals* 11.24.1–2, 4, trans. John Jackson, LCL, 287–289. See also Moatti 1997, 285–286.

74. Griffin 1982, 410. See the quotations of Dionysius and Dio in this section (below).

75. In Tacitus, *Annals* 11.24.3, Claudius mentions the Balbi, from Spain—a reference that recalls Cicero's speech quoted above. Latin sources sometimes describe such illustrious men who became Romans with the metaphor of "the flower of the nations," which rabbinic writings use in a similar way, to designate the righteous proselytes from the nations who joined themselves to Israel. See Roux and Wilfand 2020.

76. Seneca, *Apocolocyntosis* 3, trans. Michael Heseltine (rev. E. H. Warmington), LCL, 443.

77. See Lucan's bitter comment in *The Civil War* 7.535–543, where he addresses a personification of the battle of Pharsalus between Pompey and Caesar, imagining the "original" Romans replaced by new nations (implying that they will receive Roman citizenship).

the Romans even grant citizenship to former slaves and give them a share in the magistracies, and thus they have grown to the point of sending part of their population abroad to found colonies.[78]

In the imperial period, one of the most remarkable commendations of the Roman enfranchisement policy came from Dionysius of Halicarnassus, who bundled together all the themes mentioned above:

> And in the course of time they [the Romans] contrived to raise themselves from the smallest nation to the greatest and from the most obscure to the most illustrious, not only by their humane (*philanthrōpos*) reception of those who sought a home among them, but also by sharing the rights of citizenship (*politeia*) with all who had been conquered by them in war after a brave resistance, by permitting all the slaves, too, who were manumitted among them to become citizens, and by disdaining no condition of men from whom the commonwealth might reap an advantage.[79]

First Dionysius repeats the general argument that Rome's openness to foreigners was key to its success. Second, he mentions both the admission of former enemies and that of freedmen.[80] Third, he suggests that the Romans welcomed worthy men regardless of their origins and thus valued merit over birth. Moreover, this passage shows how the traditions pertaining to Rome's mixed origins (alluded to in the phrase "those who sought a home among them") were associated with the praise of Roman "generosity" in granting citizenship to foreigners. Dionysius' characterization of the asylum as "humane" or hospitable (*philanthrōpos*) is in line with other Roman and pro-Roman discourses on Rome's *philanthrōpia* or *humanitas* as manifested in its openness to foreigners. This attitude marks a critical difference between Romans and Greeks, as Dionysius indicates in another passage:

> When I compare the customs of the Greeks with these [of the Romans], I can find no reason to extol either those of the Lacedaemonians or of the Thebans or of the Athenians, who pride themselves most on their wisdom; all of whom, jealous of their noble birth (*to eugenēs*) and granting citizenship (*politeia*) to none or to very few (I say nothing of the fact that some even expelled foreigners[81]), not only received no advan-

---

78. Marotta 2009, 33–34.

79. *Rom. Ant.* 1.9.4, trans. Earnest Cary, LCL, 31. Dionysius also mentions the importance of their "form of government."

80. On the latter, see also *Rom. Ant.* 4.22.2–23.7.

81. This is an allusion to the Spartan practice of expelling foreigners, called *xenēlasia*, to which Athenian authors referred in order to praise Athens' hospitality to foreigners. See Berthelot 2003, 91.

tage from this haughty attitude, but actually suffered the greatest harm because of it.[82]

Dionysius' allusion to the Greeks' pride in their "noble birth" draws attention to the difference between Greek and Roman valuations of lineage in their models of citizenship. The reference to the Greeks' confidence in their own wisdom (*sophia*) recalls Cicero's discussion of the respective wisdom of the laws of Sparta, Athens, and Rome in *On the Making of an Orator*.[83] In addition, this excerpt anticipates Tacitus' argument in the passage of the *Annals* quoted above (§4).

Dionysius' claim finds a remarkable parallel in Dio of Prusa's forty-first discourse, "To the Apameians, On Concord," dated to 101 CE:

> That city (Rome), while so superior to the rest of mankind in good fortune and power, has proved to be even more superior in fairness (*epi-eikeia*) and benevolence (*philanthrōpia*), bestowing ungrudgingly both citizenship (*politeia*) and laws (*nomoi*) and offices (*archai*), believing no man of worth to be an alien, and at the same time safeguarding justice (*to dikaion*) for all alike.[84]

Like Dionysius, Dio praises Rome's openness to foreigners, its readiness to grant citizenship and magistracies to worthy men regardless of their origin. And again, this policy is presented as a mark of *philanthrōpia* (and *epieikeia*, fairness).

Writing a few years before Dio's speech, Josephus too characterized the Romans' enfranchisement policy as *philanthrōpos*, asking rhetorically,[85]

> Has not the benevolence (*philanthrōpia*) of the Romans ensured that their name has been shared with practically everyone, not only with individuals but with sizeable nations as a whole? Thus, those who were once Iberians, Tyrrhenians, and Sabines are called "Romans."[86]

In this passage of *Against Apion*, Josephus attempts to refute the Alexandrian grammarian's claim that the Jewish inhabitants of Alexandria could not be citizens of the city. Yet, as Sylvie Honigman has aptly demonstrated, Josephus' argument is confusing. He suggests that since the Jews there are called

82. *Rom. Ant.* 2.17.1, trans. Earnest Cary, LCL, 359. In the following paragraphs, Dionysius insists on the role that the Spartans' small number played in Sparta's defeat and Rome's success.

83. See Chapter Four, §1.1.

84. Dio, *To the Apameians, On Concord* 41.9, trans. H. Lamar Crosby, LCL, 159 (slightly modified). On Dio's relationship to Rome and Roman citizenship, see Jones 1978, 124–131; Kemezis 2019, 83–90.

85. On the similarities between Josephus and Dionysius, see Balch 1982, 111, 118; Barclay 2007, 190, note 129; Cowan 2018 (with further bibliography in nn. 5–7).

86. *C. Ap.* 2.40, trans. Barclay 2007, 190.

"Alexandrians," they must be citizens. But as administrative documents show, people residing in the town could designate themselves "Alexandrians" in the loose sense of "inhabitants of Alexandria" rather than according to the word's civic meaning.[87] By contrast, in Rome's case, the appellation "Roman" had to coincide with the bearer's legal and political status. Josephus' reference to Roman grants of citizenship is thus misleading, since it meant different things to share the names "Roman" and "Alexandrian."[88] What is most interesting in this text from our perspective, however, is Josephus' adoption of the pro-Roman topos of Rome's generous enfranchisement policy.[89] I will return to the significance of his familiarity with this topos below.

Praise of Rome's generosity in granting citizenship was a recurring feature of pro-Roman writings up to late antiquity. Aelius Aristides' *Roman Oration*, for instance, includes an account of Roman citizenship policy that aligns with those of his predecessors Dionysius and Dio. Aristides particularly highlights the fact that the Romans disregarded the ethnic origin and the pedigree of the persons whom they promoted to the rank of citizen, looking instead at virtue and merit and transforming strangers into kin (§59–60). Reflecting the perspective of the Greek imperial elite, he celebrates the fact that deserving people of foreign extraction could access magistracies as if they were native Romans (§65). Again following in the footsteps of Dionysius and Dio, he characterizes this policy as a mark of Roman *philanthrōpia* (§66) and contrasts it with the political practice of the Greeks, which lacked this virtue (§57).[90]

In the fourth century, the Greek sophist Libanius, a pagan, still recalled with admiration the Romans' grants of citizenship to their former enemies. In a discourse in defense of the temples of Rome's traditional gods, addressed to the emperor Theodosius, he argues:

> [I]t was with these gods to aid them that the Romans used to march against the foe, engage them in battle, conquer them and, as conquerors, grant the vanquished a condition of life better than that which they had before their defeat, removing their fears and allowing them a share in their own civic life (or: citizenship; *politeia*).[91]

---

87. Barclay 2007, 188–189, note 124. The "Helenos papyrus" (*CPJ* II, no. 151, dated to 5/4 BCE) illustrates this point: to avoid possible confusion, the scribe replaced the word "Alexandrian" in Helenos' declaration with "a Jew from Alexandria."

88. Honigman 1997, 83; Berthelot 2003, 42–43.

89. Berthelot 2003, 37–43.

90. Oliver 1953, 901–902; Nicolet 1976, 32; Kemezis 2019, 90–96. On Aristides' reservations toward Rome, beyond the rhetoric of the encomium, see Pernot 2008.

91. Libanius, *Oration* 30.5, trans. A. F. Norman, LCL, 105. The association of peace, security, and access to citizenship (*politeia*) is also found in Herodian (first half of the third century), *History of the Empire* 8.2.4.

Claudian, a pagan who wrote Latin poetry at the end of the fourth century, originally from Alexandria but later closely associated with the court of Honorius in Milan, similarly celebrates the unity that the Romans achieved thanks to their welcoming attitude toward defeated peoples:

> [Rome] alone received the conquered to her bosom and cherished the human race with a common name, in the fashion of a mother, not of an empress; and she called "citizens" those whom she subdued and bound with her far-reaching and pious embrace. To her pacifying customs we owe everything: [. . .] that we are all of us one people (*gens*).[92]

Claudian then adds that there will never be a limit to Rome's empire, unlike those of the Assyrians, the Medes, and the Macedonians. Rome's policy of enfranchisement had a pacifying effect on her enemies, and it is thus again presented as the crucial factor in the empire's successful and lasting domination.

In the third and especially the fourth century, Christian authors concurred with pagan ones in celebrating Rome's policy. In contrast to the *Commentary on Daniel* (see above), which sharply opposes the citizenship of the earthly kingdom of Rome to that of the heavenly kingdom of Christ, later Christian authors like Prudentius and Augustine praise the unification of different peoples under Rome's sway and name, interpreting it as the result of a divine design to facilitate the spread of the Gospel.[93] Prudentius argues that it was to put an end to wars that "God taught the nations everywhere to bow their heads under the same laws and become Romans."[94] Consequently, "a common law (*ius commune*) made them equals and bound them by a single name, bringing them by conquest into bonds of brotherhood (*fraterna vincla*)."[95] Prudentius articulates the same connection between citizenship and law that we find in Cicero.[96] Moreover, he speaks of the Roman people's unity in terms of brotherhood or kinship, recalling Claudian's description of the Romans as a *gens* related to a common mother, Rome. Yet Prudentius may have had a different type of kinship in mind—namely, brotherhood in Christ—if he was equating being Roman with being Christian.

The question that arises is, how did Rome's enfranchisement policy and the abundant praise it received throughout the empire from the first to the fifth century affect Jews? How did it impact their thinking about their own community, the people of Israel? We may ask in particular: Are there connections between Jewish conceptions of membership in Israel and Roman

---

92. Claudian, *On Stilicho's Consulship* 3.150–155, 159, trans. Ando 2000, 65 (with one modification: I have translated *gens* as "people" rather than "race").

93. Inglebert 2016a.

94. Prudentius, *A Reply to the Address of Symmachus* 2.602–604, trans. H. J. Thomson, LCL, 55.

95. Ibid., 2.608–609.

96. See, e.g., Cicero, *Pro Balbo* 13.31.

notions of citizenship from the first century BCE to the fourth century CE? Do we find in Jewish writings a rival notion of universal peoplehood, as we find in early Christian texts? Or, conversely, do we find a definition of Israel along more "particularist" lines?

2. Judaism as "Citizenship": The Hellenistic Context and the Impact of Rome

To fully appreciate Rome's impact on Jewish conceptions of membership in Israel, we must first understand what notions of peoplehood the ancient Jews held before their encounter with Rome, in biblical times and during the Hellenistic period.

2.1 GENEALOGY VERSUS ADHERENCE TO THE LAW: BIBLICAL AND SECOND TEMPLE FOUNDATIONS

As mentioned in the introduction to this chapter, the Hebrew Bible contains at least two definitions of Israel, associated respectively with the covenant with Abraham and with the covenant at Sinai.[97] First, "Israel" designates the descendants of Abraham via Isaac and Jacob: in Genesis and at the beginning of the book of Exodus, the members of Israel are "sons (or: children) of Israel," *beney Israel*, a family, a clan, or an association of clans that are all supposed to be connected by kinship through their common ancestors. Moreover, every Israelite is also defined by membership in a tribe, each tribe being imagined to descend from one of Jacob's sons. The tribe of Levi has a special status, insofar as its male members are dedicated to the cult of the God of Israel. Among these men, a further distinction is made, between the majority of Levites and a smaller group who are considered the descendants of Aaron: the *kohanim*, or

---

97. A third definition, starting with Exodus 4:22, presents Israel as God's son (or children). While in the Ancient Near East it was the king who was considered God's son—a notion we encounter in biblical texts as well, for example in 2 Samuel 7 and Psalms 2—the Hebrew Bible extends the concept of God's sonship to the people of Israel as a whole. On the respective roles of genealogy and commitment to the Torah in the definition of Israel, see Porton 1994, 195; Stern 1994, 90–95; Levinson 2000, 344–345; Collins 2017, 5–8. According to Levinson, this dual definition emerged only after 70 CE. Prior to the destruction of the Second Temple, there were "various and conflicting models of identity (covenantal, biological, historical, territorial, tribal)" (344). These categories are not neatly distinct, however. For example, what is the difference, from an emic perspective, between biological and tribal? Moreover, history and territory may represent important aspects of identity, but in biblical and Second Temple texts they do not in themselves constitute ways to integrate people into Israel independent of the acceptance of the covenant and the commandments. I therefore contend that as far as the integration of foreigners is concerned, the dual model or paradigm (descent or covenant—i.e., acceptance of the commandments) is already present in biblical texts.

priests. Different commandments and duties are imposed according to one's status as an Israelite, a Levite, or a priest. Genealogy is thus not only what differentiates Israelites from non-Israelites but also what allows an Israelite to define his or her place within the people of Israel.[98]

Alongside this genealogical vision of the people of Israel, is another one based on the revelation of the Torah at Sinai. This alternative definition does not contradict the preceding one but is in tension with it, as it is not based on descent but instead puts emphasis on the acceptance of the Sinaitic covenant. These two definitions of Israel intersect rather than coincide. According to the book of Exodus, at Sinai non-Israelites were included in the covenant on the basis of their willingness to join Israel and to observe its commandments, whatever their lineage. Thus, Exodus 2:21 clearly states that Moses' wife was a Midianite and not an Israelite—and this is only one example of the fact that in most biblical books, foreign women who married Israelite men were supposed to foresake their foreign gods as they were incorporated into Israel. In addition, Leviticus 24:10–16 notes the presence among the children of Israel of a man who was not considered an Israelite, because he was born of an Israelite mother and an Egyptian father—in biblical texts and in Jewish evidence from the Second Temple period, the patrilineal principle prevails. Moreover, both Exodus 12:38 and Numbers 11:4 refer to a "mixed multitude" ('erev rav or asafsuf) of non-Israelites who departed from Egypt with and continued to accompany Israel, hence participating in the Sinai event as well. Although their presence is often alluded to in a negative way, the "fact" remains that "Israel" included non-Israelites already at Sinai.[99]

More generally, the laws of the Torah evoke the presence of gerim, "resident aliens," among the children of Israel, starting with Exodus 12:19 (which forbids leavened bread to both Israelites and gerim during Passover), 12:48 (which states that a ger must be circumcised in order to eat the Passover meal) and 20:10 (which includes the gerim among those who rest on the Sabbath). Scholars have rightly emphasized the diversity of meanings of the term ger in the Bible; in some cases different meanings can even be distinguished in different redactional layers of a given book.[100] In most biblical texts, however,

---

98. The genealogical definition of a person's membership in the people of Israel is found repeatedly in texts from the biblical, Hellenistic, and Roman periods. See § 3 below.

99. Vana 2012, 213.

100. *Ger* is sometimes used to describe the Israelites who were "resident aliens" in Egypt (Exod 22:20, 23:9; Lev 19:34; Ps 105:12; 1 Chr 16:19) or even the Israelites in the land of Israel, to emphasize that only God is the land's rightful owner (Lev 25:23). In the vast majority of occurrences, however, *ger* designates the foreigner who lives permanently among the Israelites and has to follow the laws that God has given to Israel (see below). On *gerim* in biblical books, see van Houten 1991, esp. 159–165; Ramírez Kidd 1999; Enger 2006; Na'aman 2008; Achenbach, Albertz, and Wöhrle 2011 (esp. Albertz 2011); Awabdy 2014; Glanville 2018b.

the term *ger* refers to a non-Israelite who resides in the Land and is integrated in a permanent way into the people of Israel—that is, a non-Israelite who is expected to follow the same laws and the same way of life as Israel.[101] The *ger* is distinct from both the *toshav*, who lives in the Land but is not integrated into Israel, and the *nokhri* or *zar*, the complete foreigner or stranger.[102]

If one looks at the biblical texts from a synchronic perspective, as Jewish authors in the Hellenistic and Roman periods did when interpreting them, three main aspects of the *ger* are worth emphasizing. First, what distinguishes *gerim* from Israelites is lineage: a *ger* cannot claim to be a descendant of Jacob/Israel.[103] This genealogical aspect has important consequences for the possession of the Land of Israel: since it was allotted according to one's ancestral tribe, in most texts the *ger* has no share in the Land.[104] Second, this category has a strong social connotation (even though it cannot be reduced to this aspect): *gerim* are often associated with the poor and the destitute[105]—in part this is a consequence of the fact that they do not own land. Several texts define their economic rights within Israelite society, as well as the protections they are entitled to, or, conversely, denounce

101. The *ger* must celebrate Shavuot (Deut 16:11), Sukkot (Deut 16:14, 31:12), Yom Kippur (Lev 16:29), and Pessaḥ (Exod 12:19), yet male *gerim* eat of the Passover meal only if they have been circumcised (Exod 12:48). Deuteronomy 14:21 forbids the Israelite to eat the carcass of a dead animal that was not ritually killed (*nevelah*) but allows the *ger* to do so. Conversely, Leviticus 17:15 forbids this to both categories. Admittedly, priestly and Deuteronomic views of Israel (and of the *ger*) differ in some respects; see, e.g., Weinfeld 1972, 225–232; Rendtorff 1996; Joosten 1996, 54–73; Awabdy 2014.

102. Joosten 1996, 54–76 (in the Holiness Code); Achenbach 2011.

103. The book of Leviticus (17:8, 10, 13; 20:2) makes clear that the *ger* does not belong to the "house of Israel" or "the children of Israel," two concepts with a genealogical dimension. Nadav Na'aman contends that in Deuteronomy, the word *gerim* refers to Judahites who were displaced during Sennacherib's campaign against Judah at the end of the eighth century BCE (Na'aman 2008). This may be the background of some of the texts that mention *gerim*. However, Deut 1:16 clearly distinguishes bweeen "brothers" (*aḥim*) and "strangers" (*gerim*), and it seems doubtful that *aḥim* in this verse should be understood as designating a subgroup among the Judahites. Moreover, passages like Deut 14:21 and 28:43–45 do not fit Na'aman's interpretation either. On *gerim* in Deuteronomy, see also, e.g., Awabdy 2014 (which understands *ger* to refer to a displaced person from outside the kingdoms of Israel and Judah); Glanville 2018a (for which Deuteronomy's *ger* means "a vulnerable person who is from outside the core family," from any ethnic background, including Judahites [604]) and 2018b (with the same conclusion). There is no room to discuss these theories in depth in the framework of this book.

104. It is only in the book of Ezekiel that one perceives an evolution on this point (Ezek 47:22–23).

105. According to Lev 25:39–54, an Israelite may sell himself (to repay his debts) to either a fellow Israelite or a *ger*, which indicates that *gerim* were not categorically seen as poor. In Deut 28:43, becoming the slaves of *gerim* is one of the curses that will befall Israel if they do not remain faithful to the covenant.

their oppression.[106] Third, the *ger* forms a pair with the *ezraḥ* (native), and most biblical texts emphasize their equality before the law.[107] Numbers 15:26 and Deuteronomy 29:9–12 and 31:10–13 describe the *ger* as part of the "people of Israel" (*'am Israel*), a notion that seems to be more covenantal than genealogical; in Deuteronomy 29:9–12, the *ger* explicitly takes part in the covenant.

Yet, even though *gerim* are sometimes described as belonging to the people of Israel and are expected to follow the law together with native Israelites, according to biblical evidence they will never become *beney Israel* themselves, and thus hold a separate, lower status. People cannot change their pedigree or lineage. A priest is necessarily the son of a priest, a Levite the son of a Levite, and a regular Israelite the son of a regular Israelite. The children of male *gerim* were certainly considered *gerim* too. Interestingly, Leviticus 17:8 LXX uses the expression "sons of proselytes"—*prosēlytos* is the term used to translate *ger*—as a parallel to "sons of Israel," as if it too were a status transmitted genealogically.[108] Historically, some kind of assimilation or at least blurring of the lines probably happened through intermarriage, and in practice descendants of *gerim* may have been considered Israelites at a certain stage in history. The point is that we do not really know how Israelite society integrated foreigners during the biblical period. According to biblical evidence, it was common for foreign women to join Israel through marriage to Israelite men; the presupposition seems to have been that they would adopt the cult of the god of their husbands (although Solomon's wives were perceived as a threat to the king's religious integrity). According to the patrilinear principle, their offspring were considered Israelite. But what about male *gerim* who married Israelite women? Would their descendants have been considered Israelites? These remain open questions.

What is striking in the biblical corpus is the absence of a procedure for conversion. In fact, even the concept seems to be lacking.[109] First, however, the notion of conversion requires definition.[110] As Shaye Cohen argues, ancient

---

106. Exod 22:20; Lev 19:10, 19:34, 23:22; Deut 10:18–19, 24:14, 24:17, 24:19–21, 26:12–13, 27:19; Ezek 22:7, 22:29; Zech 7:10; Mal 3:5.

107. See, e.g., Exod 12:49; Lev 16:29, 24:22; Num 15:15–16; Josh 8:33; Rendtorff 1996. The Septuagint translators generally rendered *ezraḥ* as *autochtōn*, even though the Hebrew term refers not primarily to the land but rather to the fact of being a native Israelite, of belonging to one of the tribes of Israel. They also use the term *enchōrios*, whose etymology also includes the idea of territory.

108. On the term *prosēlytos* and its original Greek meaning of "newcomer" or "resident alien," see Moffitt and Butera 2013; Thiessen 2013.

109. As already noted in Cohen 1983.

110. The word "conversion" has no precise equivalent in ancient Hebrew or Greek until Late Antiquity. The Greek term *metanoia* refers to an inner change and possibly a change of lifestyle but not to a change of affiliation. The Hebrew *giyyur* (conversion), corresponding to the biblical term *ger*, is late. The *piel* form of the verb *g-w-r*, "to convert (someone)," "to make a convert," is attested for the first time in the Mekhilta de-Rabbi Ishmael, Amalek

Jewish texts differ in what they consider critical: some point to a change of religious belief, while others insist on adhesion to the Jewish way of life and even on political loyalty to the Jewish *ethnos*.[111] In all cases, however, the newcomer is described as joining the people of Israel. Some scholars therefore define conversion to Judaism as a change of ethnicity.[112] But this does not solve the problem, as there are also various definitions assigned to the notion of ethnicity. It may be preferable to formulate a definition that eschews reference to either "religion" or "ethnicity," both of these being debated concepts. In the context of ancient Judaism, I would suggest that "conversion" refers to someone's acceptance of the laws and lifestyle of the Jews—including circumcision for males—and a concomitant affiliation with the people of Israel, a group that Jewish, Greek, and Roman sources define in both ethnic and religious terms.[113] Yet the details of the conversion procedure continue to elude us to a great extent. The conditions probably varied from place to place and from one Jewish community to another. It is unclear, for example, how and when the ritual immersion of converts became mandatory. Tannaitic sources show that rabbinic circles considered immersion obligatory in the third century, but the ritual and the discussions surrounding it may go back to the first century CE.[114] It seems, however, that the conversion procedure was not fully codified before late antiquity.[115]

The following pages will deal not with the conversion process or the ritual procedure but with the status of the newcomer. The *ger* in biblical sources is not identical to the *ger* in rabbinic literature. Whereas the latter can be considered a convert, the former cannot be labeled in this way. What distinguishes biblical from rabbinic *gerim* is their degree of "naturalization." As mentioned above, according to biblical sources, the *ger* never becomes an Israelite. In

---

(Yithro) 2, and in other third-century rabbinic sources. In spite of the lack of a specific conceptual Hebrew, Greek, or Latin term to refer to conversion to Judaism, the latter is described, especially in Jewish and Roman sources from the end of the first century CE onward, as the fact of becoming a Jew, implying the acceptance of the Jewish (or Mosaic) laws, including circumcision for men.

111. Cohen 1999a, Chapter 5.

112. Mason 2007, esp. 491, 508; Palmer 2017, 40 ("a notion of mutable ethnicity is involved in conversions"); Fredriksen 2019, 136.

113. On Judaism as an ethno-religion (rather than simply an *ethnos*) already in the Bible, see Schwartz 2011, contra Cohen 1999a and Mason 2007. On circumcision's mandatory character from at least the first century CE, see Nolland 1981.

114. On the immersion ritual, see Cohen 1999a, 207–211. Tosefta Pesahim 7:14 discusses when a proselyte who has been immersed becomes fit to eat of Passover sacrifice, attributing differing opinions to Hillel and Shammai and hence putting the debate in a first-century context. See also the anecdote about Valoria's female slaves in Mekhilta de-Rabbi Ishmael Pisḥa (Bo) 15, ed. Horovitz and Rabin, 57.

115. Cohen 1999a, Chapter 7; Lavee 2011 and 2017. It is mainly in the Babylonian Talmud (Yevamot 47a–b) that we find information on the conversion procedure, which is also described in the tractate Gerim, although this is post-talmudic and thus even later.

rabbinic sources, we hear different voices and diverging opinions, but at least the children of *gerim* are generally considered Israelites, and some rabbis deem the *ger* equal in every respect to a native Israelite.[116] Clearly, a shift occurred between the biblical and the rabbinic texts.

The evidence from Qumran, where the word *ger(im)* features in a limited number of compositions dated to the second and first centuries BCE, suggests a meaning consonant with biblical uses of the term. Thus, in the Damascus Document (CD col. VI, line 21), the *ger* appears alongside the poor and the needy, as in numerous biblical texts (the background of this passage may be Leviticus 19:9–10). Moreover, CD XIV, lines 4–6 (// 4Q267 frag. 9, col. v, line 10)—a passage dealing with how a *moshav*, an assembly or session of the community, is to be organized in each "camp"—mentions *gerim* alongside priests, Levites, and Israelites. All the participants are listed in a given order: the priests first, then the Levites, next the Israelites, and finally the *gerim*. They are also supposed to sit and ask questions in that precise order. This text shows that, from the perspective of the redactors of CD, *gerim* are part of the people of Israel (the true Israel, represented by the community) but with a distinct and inferior status, based on lineage—which means that, as in the biblical texts, they cannot become Israelites (let alone priests or Levites).[117] This is in line with the priestly worldview that is dominant in the sectarian scrolls from Qumran, as I have explained elsewhere.[118]

The word *ger* and its Greek and Latin equivalents, *prosēlytos* and *proselytus*, appear in yet another set of documents dating from the end of the Hellenistic through the Roman period—namely, inscriptions (but as far as I know, there are no references to *prosēlytoi* in Jewish papyri).[119] A detailed discussion

116. See §3 below.

117. *Pace* Palmer 2017, which takes the word "brother" in CD literally and speaks of "ethnic mutability" (130–132). Among the Dead Sea Scrolls, note also 4Q169 (pesher Nahum) frag. 3–4, col. ii, line 9, which mentions the *ger* "who has been joined to the people (of Israel)," probably an echo of Isaiah 14:1 ("the resident alien [*ger*] will join them [Israel] and they will attach themselves to the house of Jacob"). Achior in the book of Judith (14:10) also falls into the category of a *ger* added to Israel: he is said to have believed in the God of Israel and to have been circumcised and "added to the house of Israel" (the Greek verb is *prostithēmi*, which generally translates the verb *nilwah*, "to be joined," used in Isa 14:1 and 4Q169). For a different interpretation of Achior's story, suggesting that he may be considered the first convert in the history of Israel, see Levine Gera 2014, 418.

118. Berthelot 1999. Several studies dealing with the *ger* at Qumran have come out more recently; see in particular Gillihan 2011; Jokiranta 2014; Akiyama 2016a and 2016b; Palmer 2017 (the first monograph on the topic). In the framework of this book I cannot discuss the arguments put forward by these scholars, but I hope to do so in a future publication.

119. Van der Horst 1991, 72, counted fourteen or fifteen Jewish inscriptions referring to *gerim*, *prosēlytoi*, or *proselyti*; cf. Donaldson 2007, 437, which refers to nineteen. See *CIJ* I, nos. 21, 68, 202, 222, 256, 462, 523, 576(?) (*JIWE* II, nos. 489, 491, 392, 224, 218, 62, 577; *JIWE* I, no. 52, from Venosa); *CIJ* II, nos. 1385 (the ossuary of Ioudas (?), son of

of this epigraphic corpus is not possible in this book, but the fact that someone was buried as a *ger/giyoret, prosēlytos,* or *proselytus/a* may indicate that at least first-generation converts retained a distinct status within Jewish communities (see Section 3 below). However, we cannot determine whether this status would have been passed on to the *ger*'s children—that is, whether it was an inherited status. Moreover, calling someone "X the proselyte" may well have been just a simple method of identification rather than an insistence on their status.

While it may be impossible to pinpoint a precise moment and context in which the evolution from the biblical to the rabbinic *ger* took place, for this was no doubt a gradual and differentiated process, we can nevertheless look at what the ancient sources reveal concerning the concepts used to think about the integration of new members into the people of Israel: we can examine when new notions appear and what might be the implications of these conceptual shifts.

2.2 JUDAISM AS "CITIZENSHIP" IN THE HELLENISTIC PERIOD

In the Bible, the main political model is kingship, conferred first by divine election and then, in most cases, through hereditary transmission.[120] Civic institutions, as known to us from the Greek or Roman context, are absent from the world of the Bible. It is therefore not surprising that we cannot identify any single Hebrew term equivalent to "citizen" in the biblical books—the word *ezraḥ*, used for "citizen" in modern Hebrew, did not have this meaning in biblical Hebrew. That the translators of the Septuagint were well aware of this discrepancy between the political institutions of biblical Israel and those of the Greek cities is demonstrated by the fact that Greek civic vocabulary such as *politēs, politeia, politeuma,* and *politeuomai* is only very rarely used in the Septuagint books that were translated from Hebrew. In Genesis 23:11, the term *politai* translates the expression *beney 'ami,* "sons of my people," used by Ephron the Hittite. In Proverbs 11:9, 12 and 24:28, as well as in Jeremiah 36:23 LXX (MT 29:23) and 38:34 LXX (MT 31:34), the term *politēs* is used to translate the Hebrew *re'a,* "neighbor." Finally, Zechariah 13:7 uses *politēs* for

---

Laganion the *prosēlytos*), 1390 ("Mariah the *giyoret*") (*CIIP* I [Jerusalem], nos. 551 and 238, respectively); *CIIP* I (Jerusalem), nos. 6, 174, 181, 190, 304; *CIIP* II, no. 1456 (from Caesarea); Lüderitz 1983, p. 26, no. 12 (from Cyrene); *IJO* II, no. 14 = *I.Aphr.2007* 11.55 (on which see Reynolds and Tannenbaum 1987; Aitor Blanco Pérez, "The Jews, Proselytes and God-Fearers of Aphrodisias," http://www.judaism-and-rome.org/jews-proselytes-and-god-fearers-aphrodisias); Naveh 1978, p. 127, no. 88 (from Dura-Europos).

120. I put the term "citizenship" in quotation marks because in most Jewish texts in Greek that use it to speak about membership in Israel, the word has a metaphorical meaning; see below.

'amit, "fellow." The Jewish translators thus used Greek civic vocabulary only marginally. Similarly, 1 Maccabees, a Hebrew composition that was translated into Greek probably shortly after its original redaction, does not contain a single occurrence of *politēs*, *politeia*, *politeuma*, or *politeuomai*. The translator did not consider these terms appropriate to describe Judea's political organization.

In Jewish literature written originally in Greek during the Hellenistic and Roman periods, the situation is very different: the Greek civic lexicon is used repeatedly to describe not only the institutions of the Greeks and the Romans, but also the Jewish people and their laws.[121] This use of Greek political vocabulary can be traced back to at least the second century BCE. In the fragments of Aristobulus, the Letter of Aristeas, and 2 Maccabees, for instance, the members of the Jewish *ethnos* are described as fellow citizens, *politai*.[122] The term *politeia* is used as well and generally refers to the Law of Moses, considered the ancestral constitution of the Jewish *ethnos*: the Jews are fellow *politai* to one another, no matter where they dwell, insofar as they live under the same laws.[123]

We must be aware, however, that the use of the term *politēs* in connection with membership in the people of Israel is often metaphorical or analogical, and does not prove the existence of Jewish civic institutions in Judea or elsewhere. There was no such thing as Jewish or Judean citizenship, in the institutional meaning of the term.[124] Most important, Jerusalem was not a *polis*, in relation to which Jews could have defined their citizenship.[125] Victor Tcherikover has decisively demonstrated that the vocabulary used in the sources from the beginning of the Roman period cannot be taken at face value:

121. Troiani 1994; Rajak 1998; Carlier 2008.

122. See Aristobulus, frag. 3.1 (Holladay 1995, 154); Let. Aris. 3, 126; 2 Macc 5:6, 5:23, 9:19, 15:30. In the Letter of Aristeas, the Egyptian Jews are the fellow "citizens" of the high priest in Jerusalem (Let. Aris. 36, 44). In 2 Maccabees, the *politai* are not the citizens of Jerusalem but the members of the *ethnos* as a whole.

123. See, e.g., 2 Macc 4:11, 8:17; Carlier 2008, 77–126. In 2 Maccabees 13:14, *politeia* (probably with the meaning of "constitution") is listed alongside the Jews' laws, temple, city, and *patris*; see Schwartz 2008, 446.

124. Shaye Cohen has argued that the Judaization of the Idumeans, the Itureans, and other groups by the Hasmoneans at the end of the second and the beginning of the first century BCE was tantamount to naturalization and that these groups received Judean citizenship (Cohen 1999a, 70, 118, 127). The Hasmoneans would have embraced a Hellenistic definition of political membership and invested the term *Ioudaios* with a new, political meaning—or rather, a political-religious meaning, insofar as political communities were also united through cult. However, Cohen's analysis confuses representations and institutions. For a full discussion of this issue, see Berthelot 2018a, 298–304; Berthelot 2019a, 108–116.

125. See Bernett 2004, which raises the question of a possible Greek influence on the institutions of Yehud in the Persian period but answers negatively.

It follows that under the procurators 'archons', a 'boule', and a 'demos' did exist in Jerusalem, but the archons were not *archons* in the Greek sense, nor was the boule a *boule*, nor the demos a *demos*. *Throughout, the Greek names, borrowed from the Hellenistic world, reflected ancient Jewish institutions—the product of the evolution of the Jewish people through the ages.*[126]

If we look back at the Hellenistic period, the only moment when Jerusalem may have enjoyed the status of a *polis* was under the high priest Jason, with the foundation of "Antiocheia in Jerusalem" (2 Macc 4:9–10, 19).[127] The Maccabean uprising put an end to that experiment.[128]

The fact that Jews tended to describe membership in the Jewish *ethnos* in terms of citizenship, despite Jerusalem's not being a *polis* and despite there being nothing like Judean citizenship, says a lot about the Greek model's power of attraction. In their places of residence in the diaspora, Jews enjoyed various statuses and were sometimes citizens of the *poleis* in which they dwelt.[129] From the first century BCE onward, some Jews also received Roman citizenship.[130] Diasporic Jews therefore had quite extensive knowledge of the way that Greek and Roman civic institutions worked.

In addition, another institution, the *politeuma*, may help to explain the adoption of Greek civic vocabulary by Jews, at least in Egypt and Cyrenaica. Papyri from Herakleopolis dating between 144/3 and 133/2 BCE have demonstrated that in some places in Egypt, Jews were organized in *politeumata*.[131]

---

126. Tcherikover 1964, 74 (italics in the original).

127. 1 Maccabees 1:11–15 interprets this episode as a betrayal of the covenant and a result of a desire to join the nations.

128. The events preceding the Maccabean revolt have recently been examined anew by John Ma (see esp. Ma 2012) and Sylvie Honigman (Honigman 2014, 387–404). Particularly illuminating for understanding the foundation of Antiocheia in Jerusalem is the contemporary case of Tyriaion, or Toriaion, in the Pergamene kingdom, a *katoikia* that Eumenes II granted the status of *polis* (*SEG* 47.1745; Kennell 2005, 12–14; Honigman 2014, 29–30, 212, 277–278, 363–364, 375).

129. Ritter 2011, 198–240.

130. *A.J.* 14.228, 232, 234, etc.

131. Cowey and Maresh 2001; Honigman 2002 and 2003 (Honigman argues strongly in favor of the existence of a Jewish *politeuma* in Alexandria, mentioned only in Letter of Aristeas 310); Sänger 2014, 2016, and 2019. It would not make sense to consider the Herakleopolis *politeuma* unique. Yet the view of Arieh Kasher (1985) that Jews in the diaspora preferred to be citizens of their own civic structures, the *politeumata*, rather than citizens of Greek *poleis* has rightly been refuted by Constantine Zuckerman (1985–1988), and the papyri from Herakleopolis further demonstrate the inadequacy of this theory. For a concise history of research on Jewish *politeumata*, see Ritter 2015, 1–11; for a detailed study, Sänger 2019. Bradley Ritter is the only scholar who rejects the interpretation of the papyri from Herakleopolis as referring to a Jewish *politeuma*, arguing that the *politeuma* in P. Polit. Iud. no. 8, lines 4–5, is the civic body of Herakleopolis (Ritter 2011).

According to this documentation, the members of the Jewish *politeuma* at Herakleopolis were called *politai*, even though membership in a *politeuma* was not equivalent to citizenship in a *polis*.[132] Admittedly, in Greek literary and epigraphical sources, the term *politeuma* has various meanings and may designate the community of citizens in a given *polis*.[133] The Jewish *politeuma* in Herakleopolis, however, is to be understood in the context of the ethnic *politeumata* found in Ptolemaic Egypt, which seem to have originated as groups of mercenaries who shared a common origin—Boeotians, Cilicians, Cretans, Lycians, Phrygians, or Idumaeans—and were settled together. Around the middle of the second century BCE, a fort was built in the harbor of Herakleopolis, and part of the Jewish *politeuma* may have been Jewish soldiers who lived near this military base.[134] According to Patrick Sänger, the *politeuma* was an institution found only in the Ptolemaic kingdom and in areas that had been under Ptolemaic rule for a while. He thus doubts that Jewish communities were organized as *politeumata* elsewhere in the diaspora.[135]

Politeumata had to be approved by the king and his administration, but once approved they enjoyed a great deal of autonomy: "Unlike private associations, a community constituted as a *politeuma* can be considered as an institutionalized part of the kingdom's administrative structure which—similar to a *polis*—carried responsibility for itself."[136] The *archontes* (leaders) of the *politeuma* played administrative and judicial roles but did not infringe on the jurisdiction of the *dikastēria* (the tribunals for the Hellenes).[137] The Herakleopolis papyri mainly document legal cases concerning contracts. These disputes involved Jews, but also non-Jews. It must be emphasized that not all Jews who lived in the area and turned to the archons were members of the *politeuma*. Nor was every Jewish settlement organized in this fashion.[138]

In the Roman period, *politeumata* no longer had a military dimension.[139] They seem also to have been deprived of their legal power and to have become mainly cultic associations. Two honorary inscriptions tell us something about one Jewish *politeuma* in Berenikē (in Cyrenaica) under Augustus and

---

132. P. Polit. Iud. no. 1, line 18. On the difference between membership in a *politeuma* and citizenship, see Zuckerman 1985–1988, 184; Sänger 2016, 1686; Oakes 2019, 163.

133. As shown by the case of Tyriaion, mentioned above (n. 128). In his first letter to this community, Eumenes II granted its members the right "to organize together into a single citizen body (*politeuma*) and to use their own laws" (*SEG* 47.1745, lines 27–28, trans. Kennel 2005, 13). On the various meanings of *politeuma*, see Zuckerman 1985–1988, 174; Sänger 2014, 52; Sänger 2016.

134. Sänger 2014, 60.

135. Sänger 2016, 1682–1683.

136. Sänger 2014, 63.

137. Cowey and Maresh 2001, 11–17; Honigman 2003, 63–64.

138. Honigman 2002, 254.

139. Zuckerman 1985–1988, 178; Honigman 2002, 263.

Tiberius.[140] They indicate that the members made their decisions by democratic vote, by casting black or white stones in accordance with Greek custom. Constantine Zuckerman notes that the decrees (*psēphismata*) of this *politeuma* were "formulated in perfect accord with the protocol of civic decrees (under magistrates so-and-so [. . .]), and were displayed in the municipal amphitheater."[141] This example shows how Jews integrated Greek civic norms not only when they were citizens of Greek cities but also in the framework of their own ethnic *politeumata*.

Some Greek and Roman literary sources refer to the autonomy of Jewish communities in the diaspora, to the point of describing a kind of self-administration. For instance, Josephus attributes the following statement to Strabo:

> And it has come about that Cyrene, which had the same rulers as Egypt, has imitated it in many respects, particularly in notably encouraging and aiding the expansion of the organized groups (*syntagmata*) of Jews, which observe the ancestral Jewish laws. In Egypt, for example, territory has been set apart for a Jewish settlement, and in Alexandria a great part of the city has been allocated to this people (*ethnos*). And an ethnarch of their own has been installed, who governs the people (*ethnos*) and adjudicates suits and supervises contracts and ordinances, just as if he were the head of an autonomous *politeia*.[142]

Interestingly, in this case as well the connection with the Ptolemaic kingdom is explicit. The fact that Strabo describes the Jewish communities in Cyrene (or Cyrenaica more widely) and Alexandria as partly autonomous may be related to the existence of *politeumata* in these cities, even though Strabo does not use this term.[143] Noteworthy is the fact—if Josephus quotes Strabo accurately—that the Greek geographer only compares the Jewish *ethnos* to an autonomous civic community. The Jewish ethnarch behaves *as if* (*ōs* in Greek) he were the *archōn* (head) of a sovereign *politeia*. Strabo does not state that the Jewish group was in fact a *politeia*; he still describes it as an *ethnos*. Nonetheless, this text sheds light on the use of the term *politai* by diaspora Jews.

The impact of Hellenistic civic models on Jewish communities was thus not limited to linguistic borrowings and metaphorical representations. Through the adoption of the *politeuma*'s structure, Jews integrated some aspects of

---

140. Lüderitz 1983, 148–155, nos. 70 (*SEG* 16.931; in honor of Decimus Valerius Dionysius, who was a member of the *politeuma*), 71 (in honor of Marcus Tittius, son of Sextus). This *politeuma* had its own archons, mentioned in an inscription from 24/5 CE (*IGR* I, 1024), and a synagogue is attested in 56 CE (*SEG* 17.823).

141. Zuckerman 1985–1988, 179.

142. Josephus, *Ant.* 14.116, trans. Ralph Marcus, LCL, 509 (slightly modified).

143. On the existence of a Jewish *politeuma* in Alexandria, see Honigman 2003; Sänger 2016, 1688; Sänger 2019, 43–72, which reaches a negative conclusion.

Greek civic organization into their community life, at least in the case of those living in the Ptolemaic orbit.

Now the following questions arise: How were new members integrated into these communities? Did the use of the word *politai* to designate fellow Jews, or fellow members of a given *politeuma*, impact the way that newcomers who wanted to join the *ethnos* of the Jews were seen? Were they described as new "citizens"? Did such terminology affect their status?

The use of *politēs* to designate converts is hardly attested in texts dating to the Hellenistic period. The only possible example that I am aware of comes from 2 Maccabees, in connection with the death of Antiochus IV. When the king falls ill—to the point that "worms came bubbling up out of the villain's eyes"—he repents and, to obtain divine mercy, vows to become a Jew and to proclaim God's power worldwide. Then he writes a letter to the Jews, which opens with the following words: "To the respected Jews, fellow citizens (*politai*), many greetings, health and success (from) the King and Governor Antiochus."[144] However, it is clear that the author of 2 Maccabees does not consider the king's intention to become a Jew sincere and presents Antiochus as merely imitating the Jews' way of speaking. Daniel R. Schwartz rightly notes in his commentary: "The king speaks like a Jew (as promised in v.17 and exemplified in v.20), denoting the Jews as his 'fellow citizens.' . . . This too is part of the joke."[145] This text in itself does not allow us to conclude that native Jews would have considered proselytes as "fellow citizens."

As a matter of fact, it is only in the Roman period that Jewish authors start to refer explicitly to proselytes as new citizens in the *politeia* of the Jews.

2.3 JUDAISM AS "CITIZENSHIP" IN NONRABBINIC JEWISH SOURCES OF THE ROMAN PERIOD

The two main authors whom we need to consider when it comes to Judaism as "citizenship" in the Roman period are obviously Philo and Josephus, together with a few additional sources, such as 4 Maccabees—possibly 3 Maccabees too, if it is dated to the first century CE—and some inscriptions. In the works of Philo and Josephus we encounter various meanings for the words *politeia*, *politeuma*, *politēs*, and *politeuomai*. Josephus often uses *politēs* in the loose sense of "inhabitant" rather than in the technical sense of "citizen."[146] The only occurrence of this term in 3 Maccabees (1:22) might have this meaning too.[147] In the Testament of Job 29:1, it is likewise unclear whether *politai*

144. 2 Macc 9:19, trans. Schwartz 2008, 350.

145. Schwartz 2008, 361.

146. See, e.g., *A.J.* 7.291, 8.361, 8.370, 9.80, 10.126, 10.129, 12.252, 15.3 (the inhabitants of Jerusalem); *Vita* 42–43 (the inhabitants of Tiberias), 135 (the inhabitants of Tarichea).

147. Mélèze Modrzejewski 2008, 82. The scene of 3 Macc 1:22 takes place in Jerusalem, and it is unclear whether *politēs* refers to the inhabitants of the city or, metaphorically, to

refers to fellow citizens or merely to inhabitants; in any case, this work does not present Job and his neighbors as Jewish.

Overall, *politēs* frequently has a civic meaning in the works of Philo and Josephus, which also use *politeia* with the meaning of "citizenship," alongside the notion of a "constitution."[148] The New Testament too employs citizenship as a metaphor to speak about membership in the people of Israel, but this use remains marginal. Ephesians 2:12—part of an epistle attributed to a disciple of Paul—states that before hearing and accepting the Gospel, non-Jews were deprived of "citizenship of/in Israel" (*politeia tou Israēl*), which means that they had no share in Israel's covenant with God. From the perspective of the author of Ephesians, the non-Jews who now received this "citizenship of Israel" were those who had joined the community of the new covenant established in Christ, not those who became Jews. In a different vein, the *Letter to Diognetus*, written in the second century CE, states that Christians are citizens of Heaven.[149] There are thus different meanings of *politeia*, concrete and political as well as metaphorical or spiritual, in Jewish and Christian writings of the Roman period.

Although Philo was steeped in Greek philosophical thought, his Roman context influenced his conception of the Jewish *politeia* in many ways. Let me start by mentioning a passage in the *Legatio* which reveals that he could present being a Jew as a form of citizenship comparable to Roman citizenship, the two being eminently compatible (even though in his eyes Jewish "citizenship" was far more important). Speaking of Augustus' policy toward the Jews of Rome, Philo emphasizes that the princeps knew of their synagogues and was perfectly aware that they sent money to the Jerusalem Temple (§156). Yet, Philo argues,

> nevertheless he neither ejected them from Rome nor deprived them of their Roman citizenship (*tēn Rhōmaïkēn autōn politeian*) because they also cared about their Jewish [citizenship] (*tēn Ioudaïkēn*), nor took any violent measures against the houses of prayer, nor prevented them from meeting to receive instructions in the laws, nor opposed their offerings of the firstfruits.[150]

Even though the word *politeia* is not repeated twice, the adjective *Ioudaïkos* clearly parallels *Rhōmaïkos*. There is thus no doubt that *politeia* is the implied

---

Jews as fellow citizens. Yet in 3 Maccabees the Jews in Alexandria are not described as *politai* of one another or of the Judean Jews.

148. Troiani 1994; Rajak 1998; Carlier 2008. In 3 Macc 3:21, 23, *politeia* refers to Alexandrian citizenship. In 4 Macc 3:20, *politeia* refers to a "constitution," or set of ancestral laws; see also 8:7 and 17:9.

149. *Letter to Diognetus* 5.4, 9; Troiani 1994, 21; Dorival 2019, 277, 279–280. Whether this is also the meaning of Philippians 3:20 is debated among scholars; see Oakes 2019.

150. *Legat.* 157, trans. F. H. Colson, LCL, 81 (modified).

noun that *Ioudaïkos* characterizes. In Philo's discourse, not only is "Jewish-ness" (the fact of belonging to the people of Israel) a "citizenship," but it is even comparable to Roman citizenship, and the two can be put on an equal footing. The claim was quite bold.[151]

Moreover, Philo's understanding of the Jewish *politeia* shares several features with the Roman definition of *civitas*. As Clifford Ando explains, in Roman political thought,

> a political collectivity, a *populus*, is formed through the consensual commitment of its members to a particular normative order. [. . .] The distinctiveness and pervasiveness of this Roman commitment to contractarianism is visible above all in the common use of *civitas*, citizenship, as a metonym for both city and political community. The corresponding term in Greek, *politeia*, which can mean citizenship or governing order, interanimates no such cluster of concepts. The ability of *civitas* to serve as a metonym for political community rests upon the assumption that it is individual possession of membership, and indi-vidual commitment to the entailments of membership, that bind one to the community.[152]

In Philo—particularly his treatise *On the Special Laws*—*politeia* can in fact refer to a political community (that is, the people of Israel linked together by the laws of Moses).[153] This usage, which differs from previous ones in clas-sical and Hellenistic Greek (even though some passages in Aristotle's *Politics* may point in this direction), probably resulted from Philo's exposure to the Roman notion of *civitas*.[154] Indeed, both Philo's discourse on the Mosaic *politeia* and Cicero's writings about the Roman *civitas* highlight the supreme importance that common laws and the citizens' commitment to the law play in the definition of the political community (see below).[155] The insistance

151. See also Honigman 1997, 75–78, which argues that for Philo, Roman citizenship plays the role of local citizenship, comparable to that of Alexandria, Ephesus, or Antioch, whereas "Jewish citizenship" is a universal one.

152. Ando 2011, 3.

153. See, e.g., *Her.* 169; *Mos.* 2.211; *Spec.* 1.51, 1.60, 1.63, 1.314, 1.319, 3.51, 3.181, 4.100, 4.105. Birnbaum 1996, 214–215.

154. On *politeia*'s meanings in classical and Hellenistic texts, see Bordes 1980 (on Aris-totle); Bordes 1982 (on Greek sources up to Aristotle); Lévy 1990 (on *politeia* and *politeuma* in Polybius); Casevitz 1990 (on Diodorus); Murray 1993 (on Aristotle, *Politics* 3.3, 1276b, whose *politeia* Murray translates as "constitution"). The original meaning of the term *polis* may have been equivalent to that of *civitas*, as it referred to both the city and the political community (Lévy 1990, 15).

155. In addition to their respective traditions, the Stoic notion of the true city as a group of human beings administered by law may have inspired both writers; see Schofield 1991, 61, 63–64, which refers to Dio Chrysostom's 36th discourse (§20) and Clement of Alexan-dria, *Stromata* 4.26.

on the legal dimension of membership in the Mosaic *politeia* is in fact a logical outcome of the Torah's centrality in the self-definition of the Jews in both biblical and Second Temple sources. In this respect, the apparent convergence between the Roman conception of citizenship and Jewish notions of peoplehood is understandable.

To the notion that Jews are *politai* united by their ancestral laws, Philo adds that adhesion to these laws also joins native Israelites and proselytes. In *Questions on Exodus* 2.2, he explains that the term *prosēlytos* in Exodus 22:20—"you were strangers (*gerim, prosēlytoi*) in Egypt"—might mean different things, depending on the context: it can designate a person who settles in a foreign land, a "newcomer to the land," or a proselyte, a "(newcomer) to laws and customs."[156] What characterizes these proselytes is their adhesion to the law of Moses. Defining them as new citizens was thus a logical next step.

Philo seems to be the first author to formulate the idea that proselytes who convert to Judaism become citizens of the Mosaic *politeia*, understood as the community of Jewish citizens.[157] Clearly, in Philo's work, the integration of new "citizens" into the *politeia* of Moses is a metaphor, not a political reality, but some of his remarks probably reflect the changed social reality that conversion would have wrought for a proselyte in Alexandria.

In *On the Special Laws*, while commenting on the first commandment of the Decalogue, the recognition of the one true God, Philo reflects on the condition of the proselytes within the people of Israel. He distinguishes between people who have been trained in the truth since childhood (native Jews) and those from a pagan background who have discovered it (converts):

> 51 [. . .] These last he [Moses] calls "proselytes" (or: newly-joined), because they have joined a new and god-loving civic community (*politeia*). They disregard mythical inventions and seize the unaltered truth. 52 Thus, while giving equal honour (*isotimia*) to all in-comers (*epēlytai*) with all the privileges which he gives to the native-born (*autochthōnes*), he exhorts the old nobility to honour them not only with marks of respect but with special friendship and with more than ordinary goodwill. And surely there is good reason for this; they have left, he says, their country (*patris*), their relatives (*syngeneis*) and their friends (*philoi*) for the sake of virtue and holiness. Let them not be deprived of other cities (*poleis*), parents (*oikeioi*), and friends (*philoi*),

---

156. *Q.E.* 2.2, trans. Ralph Marcus, LCL, 37. The term *prosēlytos* also retains the meaning "stranger" in *Cher.* 108, 119.

157. *Spec.* 1.51; Berthelot 2003, 272–279; cf. Carlier 2008, 183–184. According to Joseph Mélèze Modrzejewski, the Jewish *politeia* in this case is Jewishness itself or the Jewish way of life (Mélèze Modrzejewski 2011, 157–158). See also Ritter 2015, 79. However, Birnbaum 1996, 214–217 and Carlier 2008, 171–173 argue that it is actually the community of Jewish citizens—that is, the Jewish people.

and let them find places of shelter standing ready for refugees to (the camp of) piety. For the most effectual love-charm, the chain which binds indissolubly the goodwill which makes us one, is to honour the one God. 53 Yet he counsels them that they must not, presuming on the equality before the laws (*isonomia*) and the tributes (*isoteleia*) which he grants them because they have denounced the vain imaginings of their fathers and ancestors, deal in idle talk or revile with an unbridled tongue the gods whom others acknowledge, lest they on their part be moved to utter profane words against Him Who truly is.[158]

Paragraph 53 makes clear that the newcomers were born and raised in a polytheistic context and have rejected what Philo considers to be the false gods of their ancestors. Moreover, the words *prosēlytos/epēlytēs* (newcomer) and *autochtōn* (native) indicate that Philo is dealing with the biblical categories of the *ger* and the *ezraḥ*.[159] Yet to describe the status of the newcomers—the fact that, as new citizens in the *politeia* of Israel (§51), they have the same rights as native citizens—Philo uses three Greek terms, *isotimia* (§52), *isonomia*, and *isoteleia* (§53), which emphasize equality of rights and status rather than political participation, and thus indicate that he tends to define the Mosaic *politeia* as a "structure of integration" rather than a "structure of participation," to use Philippe Gauthier's terminology again.[160]

In ancient Greek literature, the word *isotimia*—literally "equality of honors"—is not common.[161] The sole occurrence of the term in Strabo's *Geography*, where it is part of a criticism of Sparta, potentially sheds light on its use by Philo:

Though the neighbouring peoples, one and all, were subject to the Spartans, still they had equal rights (*isonomoi*), sharing both in the

---

158. *Spec.* 1.51–53, trans. F. H. Colson, LCL, 127–129 (slightly modified).

159. See n. 107 above. The term *epēlytēs* is not found in the LXX but is equivalent to *prosēlytos* in Philo's work (Birnbaum 1996, 195).

160. Gauthier 1981, 169, 171.

161. The term *isotimia* appears once in Dionysius' *Roman Antiquities* (10.30.4), in the context of the tensions between plebeians and patricians under the Republic. The notion figures prominently in the writings of Lucian, the satirist from the second century CE, in connection with the divide between the rich and the poor (Baldwin 1961). Epigraphic testimony demonstrates rare use too: the word is found in eight inscriptions from Thessaly, dated to the third and second centuries BCE. *SEG* 36.548 concerns a *syngeneia* composed of four families that excluded people who were not members of these families from the *taga* (a kind of magistracy) and the *isotimia* (lines 5–7), here the equal rights of the *syngeneis*, mainly in cultic matters (Zelnick-Abramovitz 2000, 114). Other inscriptions associate *isotimia* and *politeia* or *isopoliteia* (*SEG* 33.448, 48.660; *Gonnoi* II, 30, 31). *SEG* 33.448 also mentions *isoteleia* and *proxenia* (privileges associated with the function of *proxenos*). *IG* IX.2, 461b, associates *isotimia* with *ateleia* (exemption from taxes) and *asylia* (right of asylum). In most cases, these are individual grants to benefactors (and their descendants).

rights of citizenship (*politeia*) and in the offices of state (*archai*), and they were called Helots; but Agis, the son of Eurysthenes, deprived them of the equality of rights [or: honors] (*isotimia*) and ordered them to pay tribute to Sparta; now all obeyed except the Heleians, the occupants of Helus, who, because they revolted, were forcibly reduced in a war, and were condemned to slavery.[162]

Strabo's description of the initial relations between the Spartans and their neighbors sounds like an allusion to Rome's policy after the Social War. (Although perhaps here implicit, the comparison is explicit in the passages of Dionysius' work that deal with the Roman practice of enfranchising former enemies.) Despite having an originally fair policy, the Spartans later chose a discriminatory system of domination, depriving subjected populations of *isotimia*, which Horace Jones rightly understands as equality of political rights in this case. It is possible that in characterizing the *politeia* of Israel as one in which newcomers receive *isotimia*, *isonomia*, and *isoteleia*, Philo is implicitly contrasting the Jewish model with that of the Spartans and suggesting that it is similar to the Roman pattern.[163]

Philo may imply that there are similarities between the Roman and Jewish enfranchisement policies in yet another passage dealing with the integration of newcomers, *On the Virtues* 102–108. In this treatise, Philo returns to the issue of proselytes and the benevolence toward them that the Law of Moses prescribes. As in *On the Special Laws*, Philo exhorts native Jews to receive those who have rejected polytheistic ideas (proselytes) as their closest friends and their most intimate relatives, since they have "displayed a character friendly to God, the greatest route to friendship (*philia*) and kinship (*oikeiotēs*)."[164] In the section *Peri Philanthrōpias* (*On Humanity/Benevolence*), Philo describes proselytes (*epēlytai*) as having left behind "their family by blood, their homeland, their customs, the temples and images of their gods and the gifts and honors offered to them" (*Virt.* 102; this description recalls the story of Abraham in Genesis 12:1–5). The attitude that Philo recommends is based on Leviticus 19:34—"you shall love the *ger/prosēlytos* as yourself": "(Moses) commands those of the nation to love the proselytes, not only as friends (*philoi*) and relatives (*syngeneis*), but as themselves in both body and soul" (*Virt.* 103).[165]

---

162. *Geogr.* 8.5.4, trans. Horace Leonard Jones, LCL, 135. Cf. Isocrates, *Discourses* 12.178 (*Panathenaicus*).

163. This is also Josephus' strategy in *Against Apion*; see below. According to him, *isonomia* and *isoteleia* are precisely what Augustus restored to the Jews living in Greek cities in Cyrenaica (*A.J.* 16.160–161).

164. *Virt.* 179, trans. Wilson 2011, 79. This paragraph is at the beginning of the section on repentance (*metanoia*).

165. Trans. Wilson 2011, 64. See also Deut 10:18–19; Borgen 1997, 249, 252.

Philo continues his demonstration of the humanity of the Mosaic commandments concerning non-Jews by tackling the case of *metoikoi*, foreign residents.[166] Rather than talking about the *metoikoi* living among the Israelites, however, he reminds the Israelites that they were themselves once foreigners in Egypt and must be grateful to those who welcomed them in the past.[167] Philo admits that the Egyptians did not treat the Israelites who had settled among them well, and by means of this reproach casts a contrasting positive light on Mosaic law's generosity, quoting Deuteronomy 23:8, "You shall not abhor any of the Egyptians, because you were a foreigner residing in their land." Maybe alluding to the events of his own time, especially the attacks against Jews by Alexandrians and Egyptians,[168] he then adds:

> 107 And yet what evil was there that the Egyptians neglected to inflict upon our nation, ever adding new evils to old with schemes contrived for the sake of cruelty? Nevertheless, since they initially welcomed them, neither closing off their cities nor making the countryside inaccessible to those who came, he [Moses] says that, because of this acceptance, they should be granted as a privilege terms of peace. 108 And if any of them should want to cross over to the Jewish civic community (*pros tēn Ioudaiōn politeian*), they are not to be scorned unyieldingly like the children of enemies, but are to be treated in such a manner that the third generation is invited into the congregation (*eis ekklēsian*) and granted that share of the divine oracles into which the native- and noble-born are also rightfully initiated.[169]

Philo here depends on Deuteronomy 23:9, which prescribes letting Edomites and Egyptians enter the assembly of the Lord (*qehal YHWH, ekklēsia Kyriou*) in the third generation. He interprets this verse as allowing Egyptians to become members of "the *politeia* of the Jews"—that is, the Jewish people. The choice of a biblical passage in which favors are granted to former enemies—or, more precisely, their descendants—may be understood as a deliberate echo of the Roman or pro-Roman discourses celebrating Rome's grants of citizenship to its former enemies, which are analyzed in the first section of this chapter. Moreover, Philo sees the Mosaic *politeia*'s openness to the Egyptians as an expression of *philanthrōpia* (§105). As we saw above, Rome was praised for its *philanthrōpia* precisely because it granted citizenship to foreigners, including former enemies. That Philo uses a term that was characteristic of pro-Roman discourses can hardly be a coincidence.[170]

---

166. Birnbaum 1996, 204.
167. Wilson 2011, 256–257.
168. Wilson 2011, 261.
169. *Virt.* 107–108, trans. Wilson 2011, 65, very slightly modified (I have translated *politeia* by "civic community" rather than "polity").
170. Berthelot 2019, 126–127.

The Romans, however, did not grant citizenship to Egyptians who were not already Greek citizens of one of the three *poleis* of Egypt—Alexandria, Naucratis, and Ptolemais. Josephus, who claims that Apion was originally an Egyptian, emphasizes that "it is only to Egyptians that the Romans, who are now rulers of the world, have refused to grant any form of citizenship."[171] The question arises as to whether Philo, who shared the contempt and hostility of some Romans toward the Egyptians, used the example of Deuteronomy 23:8b–9 with an implicit a fortiori argument in mind: if the Jews were ready to go further than the Romans and grant citizenship even to Egyptians, then their *philanthrōpia* was greater than that of Rome. Whatever the case, it seems clear that the Roman notion of citizenship and the ideological discourse surrounding it influenced Philo's presentation of the Jewish *politeia*.

Josephus took over Philo's line of argument, especially in *Against Apion*, where he counters the accusation of misanthropy leveled at the Jews by Apollonius Molon and Apion.[172] What was partly allusive in Philo becomes more explicit in Josephus. Hence, when he describes the Jews as cheerfully welcoming and granting citizenship to those who want to live under their laws, he explicitly contrasts them with the Spartans:

> 256 [. . .] Plato says that no other poet should be admitted into citizenship, and he dismisses Homer in laudatory terms, once he has crowned him and anointed him with perfume, lest he obscure the correct conception of God with myths. 257 Plato in particular imitated our legislator [Moses] both in prescribing for citizens no education on a par with universal learning of the laws, thoroughly and in detail, and further in prohibiting outsiders from mixing with them on a casual basis; rather, he took care that the state [or: civic body, *politeuma*][173] should be pure, consisting of those who remain faithful to the laws. 258 Without taking any of this into account, Molon Apollonius accused us [Jews] of not admitting those who are in the grip of other opinions about God, and of not wishing to share fellowship with those who choose to live according to a different way of life. 259 But even this practice is not unique to us, but generally common, not just to Greeks, but to the most illustrious among Greeks: the Lacedaemonians used to conduct "deportations of foreigners" (*xenēlasia*) repeatedly, and also did not allow their own citizens to go abroad, suspecting in both cases that their laws would be corrupted. 260 They perhaps might reasonably be criticized for their churlishness (*dyskolia*): for they would not grant anyone the

---

171. *C. Ap.* 2.41, trans. Barclay 2007, 191. See Marotta 2017, esp. 175–181.

172. *C. Ap.* 2.121, 148; Schäfer 1997, 21–22, 28–29; Berthelot 2003, 144–153.

173. Here it is preferable to translate *politeuma* as "civic body" or "community of the citizens." See Carlier 2008, 109.

right of citizenship (*politeia*) or of residence among them.[174] 261 We, on the other hand, are not inclined to emulate other people's customs, but gladly welcome those who wish to share ours; and that would be evidence, I take it, of both benevolence (*philanthrōpia*) and generosity (*megalopsychia*).[175]

Here Josephus uses *politeia* in the sense of "citizenship."[176] He shares several ideas with Philo, such as that Jewish "citizenship" mainly implies a life in accordance with the Mosaic laws and that the openness of the Mosaic *politeia* to new citizens is proof of its benevolent character (*philanthrōpia*).[177] Moreover, in an earlier passage, Josephus had already praised the Romans for their generosity in granting citizenship, which he calls an act of *philanthrōpia* (2.40), just as Greek pro-Roman authors did. His underlying argument is that Jews and Romans share common values.[178] Here his strategy is similar to that of Dionysius of Halicarnassus, who refers to well-known stereotypes about the Spartans—for instance their *xenēlasia*, their practice of expelling foreigners to avoid the corruption of their ancestral laws—and criticizes the Athenians' timorousness in granting citizenship in order to highlight the Romans' openness and generosity.[179] Tacitus' account of Claudius' speech to the Senate plays with a similar opposition of both the Spartans and the Athenians to the Romans (*Annals* 11.24). When Josephus compares the Jews with the Spartans (and the Athenians), he aims to achieve a similar goal, and this rhetorical strategy is yet another way to align the Jews with the Romans.[180]

The testimony of the two main Jewish authors writing in Greek in the Roman empire thus shows that Roman and pro-Roman discourses about the generosity that Romans displayed in granting citizenship influenced their presentation of the integration of foreigners (converts) into the Jewish community. Their discourse also echoes the argument that this had contributed to Rome's superiority and success, and the Roman notion of citizenship as status, based first and foremost on a common commitment to the laws of the *civitas*. While

---

174. Lit. "they would not share with anybody either their citizenship or their lifestyle."

175. *C. Ap.* 2.256–261, trans. Barclay 2005, 314–318. See also Berthelot 2003, 359–368.

176. Josephus also uses *politeia* (*tōn*) *Rhōmaiōn* to speak of Roman citizenship, as in *Vita* 423.

177. *C. Ap.* 2.210, 261.

178. Goodman 1999, 55–58; Haaland 1999; Barclay 2000.

179. Dionysius of Halicarnassus, *Rom. Ant.* 2.17.1, 14.6.1–6. Many stereotypes of Spartans had an Athenian origin; see Plato, *Laws* XII, 949e; Thucydides, 1.144.2, 2.39.1–2; Ollier 1933–1943, a detailed study of Sparta's image in Greek literature.

180. Josephus also takes into account positive Roman stereotypes of the Lacedaemonians: their endurance, their simplicity, and their faithfulness to their ancestral laws, which were likewise perceived as Roman characteristics. He argues that the Jews surpassed the Spartans (and, implicitly, the Romans) in these virtues while keeping their *politeia* open to newcomers. See Berthelot 2003, 363–365.

not completely denying the privileges of birth and ancestry (especially Josephus, who was a priest and valued aristocratic genealogies), they minimized the importance of pedigree and celebrated virtue and piety (linked to the observance of the laws) as central to the definition of what they called Jewish "citizenship."

From the second century CE onward, we have no Jewish literary works in Greek (or Latin) that document the evolution of Jewish thought on these issues tackled by Philo and Josephus. We do, however, have a few inscriptions that attest the continued use of civic vocabulary in Jewish communities. A well-known example is the inscription of Claudius Tiberius Polycharmus from the synagogue of Stobi in Macedonia, probably dating to the second half of the second century CE.[181] It records a donation of several rooms to the Jewish community, built at Polycharmus' expense as the fulfillment of a vow, and thus as an act of piety. Polycharmus was a Roman citizen, as his *nomen* (Claudius) and *praenomen* (Tiberius) indicate (the names' order in the inscription is unusual, as Habas [Rubin] observes), but he had a Greek *cognomen* (Polycharmos) and a surname of uncertain origin, Achyrius.[182] He could have been a non-Jewish benefactor of the synagogue—other inscriptions document several of these[183]—but was probably a Jew, because he presents himself in the first lines as the *patēr* (father) of the *synagogē* (Jewish community) in Stobi and as *poleiteusamenos* (or: *politeusamenos*) *pasan poleiteian* (or: *politeian*) *kata ton Ioudaïsmon* (lines 6–9).[184] This phrase has been translated and interpreted in various ways. According to Lucio Troiani, "The expression means that the donor has conformed his entire conduct during his life to the laws and customs of the fathers, i.e., has been a practicing Jew."[185] Similarly, David Noy, Alexander Panayotov, and Hanswulf Bloedhom understand *politeuomai* here in its fairly common sense of "to behave, to lead one's life (according to certain norms)" and *politeia* as "(way of) life," a usage attested in literary sources; therefore they propose the translation "having lived my whole life according to

---

181. *I.Stobi* 19; *IJO* I, Mac1. The second-century date is based on N. Vulić's epigraphic and palaeographical observations (Vulić 1932). Martin Hengel has proposed dating the inscription to the third century, mainly because of the reference to the patriarch (Hengel 1966). Lifshitz suggests the second half of the third century, based on the amount of the fine mentioned in lines 26–27 (Lifshitz 1967, 19). For a detailed discussion of the date and other aspects of this inscription, see Habas (Rubin) 2001; Noy, Panayotov, and Bloedhom 2004 (*IJO* I), 62–71.

182. Habas (Rubin) 2001, 45.

183. See Van der Horst 2015, 31–32; Kraemer 2014, 73–79. There are also women among these benefactors; see *IJO* II, 140–143, no. 27; II, 348–355, no. 168.

184. On the use of *patēr* in Jewish inscriptions, see also *IJO* I, Mac3 and Mac4. This epigraphic use is reminiscent of parental references in civic communities and associations of the Greek East more broadly (Harland 2007, 64–73).

185. Troiani 1994, 17.

the (prescriptions of) Judaism."[186] Yet the parallel that they present to justify this, an epitaph from Rome or Portus stating that a certain Cattia Ammias lived a good life in Judaism, *kalōs biōsasa en tō Ioudaïsmō* (*JIWE* II, no. 584), in fact demonstrates that there was a more straightforward way to express the idea that one had conducted one's life in accordance with the precepts of Judaism. They also point to the use of *pasan politeian politeusamenos* in non-Jewish inscriptions, where it seems to indicate that people had performed a public service for their city.[187] Ephrat Habas (Rubin) suggests the translation "having conducted himself (throughout) all (his) public career according to Judaism."[188] Aitor Blanco Pérez proposes "after having always conducted his life in community according to Judaism," inspired by *politeia*'s meaning of "community of citizens."[189] Arthur Marmorstein formulated yet another interpretation: in his opinion, *pasan politeian* is a reference to Jewish "citizenship" by birth—full citizenship, so to speak—in contrast to Jewish "citizenship" obtained through conversion.[190] This interpretation, however, is doubtful from a syntactical viewpoint and remains speculative.

All in all, it seems unlikeky that *politeia* referred to local citizenship or a municipal office in Stobi, which would have been disconnected from the Jewish community.[191] The phrase *politeusamenos pasan politeian* is closely associated with *kata ton Ioudaïsmon*. Maybe it is possible to understand *pasan politeian* as a reference to the constitution (that is, the laws) of the Jews—even though this meaning does not seem to be frequent in an epigraphic context—and translate "having conducted his life (according to) the whole constitution (or: all the laws) of Judaism," which in the end is equivalent to the interpretations of Troiani and Noy, Panayotov, and Bloedhom. Alternately, we may render the debated expression as "having conducted himself (in) all (his) community life according to Judaism." In this case, *politeia* would relate to the donor's public life and commitments, but in the framework of the Jewish community.[192] In other words, Polycharmus would have been an active member of the Jewish community, performing "civic" duties such as offering it benefactions. Maybe he also represented the community in front of the Roman authorities—though this must remain a hypothesis. This interpretation of *politeia* as relating to the Jewish community would imply that the metaphor in the writings of Philo and others was widespread and still retained force in the second (or third)

186. Noy, Panayotov, and Bloedhom 2004 (*IJO* I), 64. On *politeia* as "(way of) life," see also Habas (Rubin) 2001, 47.

187. Noy, Panayotov, and Bloedhom 2004 (*IJO* I), 67.

188. Habas (Rubin) 2001, 44.

189. Blanco Pérez, "Donation of Claudius Tiberius Polycharmus to the Synagogue of Stobi," http://www.judaism-and-rome.org/donation-claudius-tiberius-polycharmus-synagogue-stobi.

190. Marmorstein 1937, 382.

191. The possibility is raised in passing by Habas (Rubin) 2001, 47.

192. Habas seems to favor this interpretation; Habas (Rubin) 2001, 47.

century CE. However, we cannot exclude the possibility that in this context, in association with *politeuomai*, the meaning of *politeia* was simply "life." The interpretation of this inscription therefore remains an open question.

Finally, it is worth mentioning an inscription from Venosa (Italy) that refers to the Jewish community as a *civitas*, even though its date, in the fifth or sixth century CE, places it beyond the chronological boundaries of the present investigation.[193] The inscription is an epitaph for Faustina, the daughter of an apparently important member of Venosa's Jewish community. She is also presented as the granddaughter of Vitus and Asellus, "who were the leaders (*maiures*) of the community (*cibitas*)."[194] The inscription has aroused much scholarly interest because it refers to the visit of two *apostuli* (apostles or envoys) and two *rebbites* (rabbis), who, on the occasion of Fautina's funeral, "spoke dirges for her." It further records that "she made great enough grief for her parents and tears for the community (*lagrimas cibitati*)."[195] It is therefore clear that the word *civitas* refers not to the civic community of Venosa as a whole but to the local Jewish community. This epitaph suggests that the description of the Jewish people as a civic community may have been as common in the western part of the empire as it was among Greek-speaking Jews in the east, and may have remained so for a very long time. Unfortunately, the paucity of documents prevents us from reaching firmer conclusions about the weight of Greco-Roman notions of citizenship in Greek- and Latin-speaking late antique Jewish communities. For complementary insights, we must now turn to rabbinic texts.

2.4 JUDAISM AS "CITIZENSHIP" IN RABBINIC LITERATURE

As Chapter Four mentions, the question of the Roman citizenship model's impact on the rabbis has received growing attention in the past few years.[196] Two methodological issues make its resolution particularly complex: First, the rabbis did not write in Greek or Latin; even though rabbinic texts include many Greek and Latin loanwords, we do not find civic vocabulary in this literature, as we did in the writings of Philo and Josephus, and in inscriptions.[197]

193. *CIJ* I, no. 611; *JIWE* I, no. 86.
194. Ed. and trans. Noy in *JIWE* I, 114–115. Spelling as in *JIWE*.
195. Trans. Noy, *JIWE* I, 115.
196. See Cohen 1999a, 293–298; Hayes 2017b, 71–72; Furstenberg 2019a (which argues that the ambiguous status of the Samaritans in rabbinic law must be interpreted in light of the Roman notion of citizenship); Malka and Paz 2019 and 2021; Wilfand 2019b, 2020b, and 2021. Moshe Lavee has hinted at the possible impact of Greco-Roman models of citizenship on Palestinian rabbinic views of conversion, but only in passing, since his focus is on the Bavli (Lavee 2003, 275–280; Lavee 2014, 100; Lavee 2017, 1, 68–69 [following Cohen 1999a]).
197. See Sperber 1984.

Second, the issue of Roman citizenship must have been different before and after the *Constitutio Antoniniana* of 212 CE. The new status that it granted to most free persons, including Jews, cannot have left the rabbis indifferent. At the very least they must have reacted to the legal consequences of Caracalla's decree: as Chapter Four discusses, the new citizens gained full access to Roman tribunals and laws. Since most, if not all, rabbinic works were completed after 212, we must take into account the possibility that the rabbis responsible for the final composition of this literature were themselves Roman citizens, together with most of the Jews around them.

Did the quasi-universal character of Roman citizenship after 212 trouble the rabbis? In an article on early rabbinic views of the joining of non-Jews to Israel through conversion, Oded Irshai raises the question: "What prompted some rabbinic circles to try to devise a social and ritual *modus operandi* for accommodating interested gentiles, and how did this approach develop?"[198] He rejects the traditional interpretation of rabbinic openness to converts as motivated by competition with Christianity and suggests that the inner evolutions of the Roman empire from the mid-second to the early third century—such as the inclusion of the Jews in the universal grant of citizenship under Caracalla—may be more illuminating.[199] Irshai hypothesizes that "equality of legal identity, albeit allowing for ethnic differences, perhaps enabled or stimulated the rabbis to conceptualize a similar situation of non-Jews wanting to become a part of the *gens Iudaeorum*, forging new links, social and religious, with Jews."[200]

Irshai's formulation is cautious and he raises many interesting points, yet one may wonder whether the link between the Roman policy of enfranchisement and rabbinic attitudes toward converts can be as straightforward as he suggests. First, as we saw above, proselytes were a well-known phenomenon in the Roman world already in the first century CE and much discussed in Jewish sources. Indeed, the ritual of conversion may have taken shape during that century, even though its full description appears only in much later sources. Openness to converts could also go back to this period, together with more negative opinions of proselytes. Second, asserting that rabbinic attitudes toward converts evolved from the period of the Severans onward would require a more in-depth analysis of the rabbinic sources than Irshai could undertake in the framework of his essay. And even if these sources did attest a more welcoming attitude from the beginning of the third century, the question would remain as to whether this evolution was due primarily to the *Constitutio Antoniniana* or to other factors, alone or in

198. Irshai 2019, 169.
199. Irshai 2019, 169–170.
200. Irshai 2019, 177.

addition.[201] Finally, despite their acceptance of converts, rabbinic texts display a consistent view of Israel as a separate people that is not supposed to encompass humankind as a whole, an attitude that contrasts sharply with the Roman model of quasi-universal citizenship. It does not seem that this view was modified in any significant way from the third century onward. It is therefore doubtful that the impact of Roman policies on the rabbis can be located at such a general level as global willingness or reluctance to accept proselytes.

The Roman policy of granting citizenship irrespective of the beneficiary's ethnic background (which does not mean that Romans did not have ethnic prejudices or subscribe to a hierarchy of peoples, only that from a legal point of view, people of different ethnic origins could become Roman citizens) may nevertheless have impacted the rabbis in a general way, pushing them to rethink the respective roles of ethnicity and commitment—or lineage and observance of the commandments—in the definition of membership in the people of Israel. The pressure may have been both direct (part of the general Zeitgeist, so to speak) and indirect, as a result of the impact of Roman policies on Jews more broadly. Some Jews may have been as impressed as other provincials by the Roman practice of enfranchisement. Philo and Josephus are to a certain extent examples of this positive reception of Roman practice and ideology. The rabbis may thus have needed to respond to internal evolutions within Jewish communities, prompted by Roman policies, long before 212 CE.

To identify the possible impact of Roman citizenship policies and ideology on rabbinic halakhah, we must ultimately consider specific issues concerning not only converts but also manumitted slaves and captives.

The Manumission of Slaves

As mentioned at the beginning of this chapter, in the ancient world only Roman law prescribed that a slave could, under certain conditions, become a citizen through manumission. The rabbinic texts on non-Jewish slaves owned by Jews suggest that rabbinic halakhah created a similar process.[202] In opposition to biblical rules, which contemplate neither the manumission of foreign slaves nor the possibility that a non-Israelite slave might become an Isralite during the period of slavery (see, e.g., Leviticus 25:39–46), rabbinic halakhah prescribes that the foreign slave be circumcised (in the case of men) and immersed in a ritual bath, transforming him or her into a "Jew(ess) in the making."[203] As Catherine Hezser notes,

201. Whether the "Antoninus" whom rabbinic sources describe as a friend of Rabbi who converts to Judaism (in the Jerusalem Talmud) is to be identified with Caracalla is irrelevant here. On this issue, see Cohen 1998, which carefully distinguishes between the rabbinic tradition's stages.

202. Dohrmann 2008, 56.

203. For the combination of both injunctions, see t. Avodah Zarah 3:11. There are, however, some debates on the issue of circumcision. In t. Pisḥa 8:18, R. Eliezer ben Yaʻaqov

The circumcision and immersion of gentile slaves function as symbolic purification rites supposed to cleanse the slaves from their former contact with idolatry then. They do not render the gentile slaves Israelites [. . .]. Through these rites the slave becomes an [*'eved Israel*] ('slave of Israel').[204]

In rabbinic halakhah, slaves living in a Jewish household thus receive an intermediate status: they belong to the Jewish family that owns them and in a sense are part of the Jewish community more broadly, and yet their servile status prevents them from being considered "citizens" in Israel.[205] After manumission and a final immersion, they become Jewish and can thus be considered "citizens" within the Jewish people by analogy with the Roman model. According to rabbinic halakhah, freedpersons have a distinct status within the people of Israel, for instance as far as matrimonial possibilities are concerned, just as freedmen or freedwomen who had received Roman citizenship were barred from marrying into senatorial families.[206] Several aspects of the condition of slaves in rabbinic halakhah thus have parallels

---

seems to allow uncircumcised slaves in a Jewish household; see also Mekhilta de-Rabbi Ishmael, Pisha (Bo) 15. In the Jerusalem Talmud, some rabbis allow the master to wait up to a year before circumcising the slave, who may be sold to a gentile if he refuses to undergo circumcision after twelve months (y. Yevamot 8:1, 8d). As mentioned above, a full discussion of the conversion process is found only in the Babylonian Talmud (b. Yevamot 46a–48b) and in the later, extratalmudic tractate Gerim; see Cohen 1999a, 198–238; Lavee 2017, 27–45. The issue of circumcision became problematic in the second century CE when a rescript of Antoninus Pius (*Dig.* 48.8.11, quoting Modestinus' *Legal Rules*, a compilation dating to the first half of the third century CE) allowed the Jews to circumcise their sons but not non-Jews (Linder 1987, 99–102; see also Abusch [Boustan] 2003). However, the fact that this prohibition was repeated again and again in imperial legislation in the following centuries indicates that the law was not necessarily applied (Hezser 2005, 42). Kulp 2006 argues that in tannaitic texts, the divergent opinions attributed to rabbis about the mandatory character of the slave's circumcision reflect ideological differences rather than changing historical circumstances.

204. Hezser 2005, 36.

205. Novak 2006, 657, speaking of "quasi-Judaism"; Dohrmann 2008, 59–60; Furstenberg 2019a, 187, which states that the slave's legal (halakhic) obligations "were comparable to those of a Jewish woman." The idea that gentile slaves acquired by Jewish masters somehow enter the covenant may already be found in the Damascus Document (CD), which forbids the master to sell his male or female slave to gentiles (*goyim*) because the former has "entered with him into Abraham's covenant" (CD XII 11). This expression seems to indicate that the text does not deal with Israelite slaves. In the Mishnah and the Tosefta, if a master sells his slave to a gentile, the slave is considered freed; the Tosefta specifies that the former master must give the slave a certificate of emancipation (*get shiḥrur*) in such a case (m. Gittin 4:6; t. Avodah Zarah 3:16).

206. See m. Qiddushin 4:1; t. Qiddushin 4:15. See also m. Qiddushin 4:6–7 and y. Bikkurim 1:5, 64a, which discuss the possibility for the daughter of converts to marry a priest; Wilfand 2019b and 2020b. On the "stain of slavery" in Roman society, see Mouritsen 2011, 10–35.

in Roman laws and social practice. There are differences in certain areas, such as duties owed toward the former master, but the parallels or similarities witness to the impact of the Roman citizenship model on rabbinic thinking.[207]

Can the comparison be pushed further? In Roman legal sources, a Roman citizen—a member of the *populus Romanus*—was necessarily free. Once enslaved, a Roman citizen lost his or her citizenship. Moreover, slaves were considered as having no ethnic background and no relatives. Children born to slave parents belonged to their master, and after manumission, a freedman or freedwoman would not have been considered the father or mother of his or her children born in slavery. Slavery thus entailed the complete suppression of kinship ties. Henrik Mouritsen emphasizes that "this convention was more than a legal fiction, and can be traced in popular perceptions of the freedman, who was frequently taunted for his lack of parentage."[208]

Both Paul Virgil McCraken Flesher and Catherine Hezser have suggested that the rabbis developed a similar view of slaves, even of slaves who were originally Jewish.[209] To quote Hezser, who explicitly emphasizes the analogous stance of the Romans and the rabbis (but interprets it as "an intercultural commonplace in the ancient world"):

> Enslavement constituted a total uprooting from one's family, religion, and society of origin. In rabbinic sources, slaves were seen as devoid of relatives and ancestry. Without parents and ancestors their claim to Jewishness could hardly be maintained. While Romans considered slavery incompatible with Roman citizenship, rabbis considered it incompatible with Jewishness: to be the slave of a human master was a reversal of the Exodus experience and a transgression of Jewish monotheistic beliefs.[210]

Some rabbinic texts do indeed describe slaves as deprived of ancestors and more generally of all family ties whatsoever, as well as the capacity to form

---

207. Dohrmann 2008, 53, 56; Furstenberg 2019a, 187–189. In Roman society, the relationship between a freedperson and the former owner was in many respects a client-patron relationship, because the former still had duties vis-à-vis the latter (Mouritsen 2011, 36–42). Rabbinic sources about manumitted slaves do not mention this subject and generally tend to view patronage as foreign to their values (Schwartz 2010, 161–165; Wilfand 2014, 233–239, 266–268 [in relation to charity]). Some Jewish manumission inscriptions from the Bosporan kingdom, a client kingdom of Rome in the first century CE, seem to indicate that in this context, manumitted slaves of Jewish masters retained obligations to the synagogue—that is, the Jewish community—but not to their former masters (*CIRB* 70, 71, 73; *SEG* 43.510; Gibson 1999, 134–150).

208. Mouritsen 2011, 37.

209. McCraken Flesher 1988, 35–36; Hezser 2005, 21–22, 28, 33–34.

210. Hezser 2005, 28, 21–22.

legal marriages.[211] In this respect, they reproduce the Roman view of slavery described above.[212]

Yet rabbinic texts rarely discuss the possibility of a Jew serving as a slave in a Jewish house, although instances of this are codified at length in biblical sources, which clearly distinguish between Hebrew and foreign slaves—the most important difference being that the Israelite owner is obliged to free his Hebrew slave after seven years, whereas no such commandment exists for non-Israelite slaves.[213] Admittedly, m. Qiddushin 1:2–3 differentiates between Hebrew and Canaanite slaves, both in how they are acquired and how they obtain their freedom. Yet McCraken Flesher notes that of 129 passages in the Mishnah that relate to bondmen, only six mention the distinction between Hebrew and Canaanite slaves, whereas in all other cases there is no reference at all to the slave's ethnic background.[214] He further remarks that these six passages use the category "Canaanite slave" to illustrate a principle that does not apply to the bondman as defined elsewhere in the Mishnah. According to him, these six passages thus represent residual traces of an alternative system, anchored in biblical texts.[215] Since the rabbinic texts that blur ethnic distinctions between slaves run against explicit biblical commandments, it seems that the evolution of the concept of slavery from the Bible to the Mishnah is to be explained by growing familiarity with the Roman definition of servile status.

McCraken Flesher further states that in the Mishnah, "if the bondman was originally an Israelite, enslavement affects him just as it affects the enslaved

---

211. See, e.g., Sifre Deuteronomy 292. The tendency to depict slaves as deprived of family ties is even more pronounced in the Bavli; see, e.g., b. Yevamot 62a (the opinion attributed to Rav); b. Sanhedrin 58b.

212. Dohrmann 2008, 60, 63–64.

213. According to Boaz Cohen, in both biblical and rabbinic law, the Hebrew 'eved is not a slave but a bondman, whose status and duration of service differed from those of a slave (Cohen 1945, 114–115). Josephus testifies to the reluctance among Jews to let convicted Jewish thieves be sold into slavery to gentiles, echoing the view that they must instead be sold to fellow Jews and freed after six years of bondage, in accordance with biblical law (A.J. 16.1–5). Josephus attributes the practice of selling Jewish thieves to gentiles to Herod, who, according to Cohen, may have been partly inspired by a Roman rule concerning housebreakers, reproduced in Digest 47.18.2 (Cohen 1945, 118). Mekhilta de-Rabbi Ishmael, Neziqin (Mishpatim) 1 (ed. Horovitz and Rabin, 247–250), which comments on Exodus 21:2, "When you buy a male Hebrew slave, he shall serve for six years, but in the seventh he shall go out a free person, without debt," also discusses the case of a Jew sold into slavery by the court for stealing. In opposition to the plain meaning of the biblical verse, the midrash states that in such a case, the slave must serve not only his master but also his master's son after him (ed. Horovitz and Rabin, 247).

214. McCraken Flesher 1988, 36. The biblical expression "Hebrew slave" does occur in rabbinic literature (see, e.g., y. Mo'ed Qatan 1:2, 80b), but rabbinic halakhah is not built upon the distinction between Hebrew and non-Hebrew slaves, as biblical law is.

215. McCraken Flesher 1988, 54–59.

gentile; it cuts him off from his membership and position in his former society."[216] Once manumitted, he will be considered a freedman, not an Israelite. However, there is another possible interpretation of the evidence found in the Mishnah and in rabbinic literature more generally: we could equally consider that, from a rabbinic perspective, Jews were enslaved by gentiles but not by fellow Jews (that this view is unrealistic—i.e., that there were Jews who owned Jewish slaves—is irrelevant to the argument that the rabbis developed such a theoretical notion of slavery).[217] In other words, a slave in a Jewish household may have been considered a gentile by default—or, after the initial ritual, a Jew in the making, but not yet quite a Jew; in which case there no longer would have been a practical necessity to differentiate between Hebrew and Canaanite slaves. The rabbis may thus have embraced the view of slaves as deprived of family ties and ethnic background, while resisting the idea that an enslaved Jew lost his or her genealogical and ethnic connection to Israel and identity as a Jew. If this interpretation is correct, then we may have reached the point where adoption of the Roman citizenship model by the rabbis could go no further: they did not adopt the view that citizens (i.e., Jews), once enslaved, lost their citizenship. Similarly, if we consider the evidence found in Mekhilta de-Rabbi Ishmael, Neziqin (Mishpatim) 1 (ed. Horovitz and Rabin, 247–250), which is exceptional in discussing at length the case of the "Hebrew slave" in Exodus 21:2–3, we see that the Hebrew (Jewish) slave retains his ethnic identity and is treated differently from the Canaanite (non-Jewish) slave. In both cases, whether the rabbis discuss the Hebrew slave or pass over this category in silence, there is no proof that in their eyes an enslaved Jew lost his or her identity as a Jew. This resistance may have been motivated by the rabbis' fidelity toward an ethnic/genealogical notion of membership. I will return to this issue below.

Captives

Another realm where we can see an impact of the Roman citizenship model on rabbinic halakhah is that of captivity, which overlaps with slavery. According to Roman law, a citizen who was captured by enemies of Rome lost his citizenship and its corresponding rights. His marriage was dissolved (*Dig.* 24.2.21, 24.3.56, 49.15.12.4), his *patria potestas* over his children was suspended until his return (Gaius, *Inst.* 1.129), and his property rights were greatly undermined.[218] Most of his rights could be reestablished upon his return through the law of *postliminium*, but not his marriage, unless the couple explicitly wished to renew their marital bond (*Dig.* 49.15.14.1). These legal prescriptions were valid if a Roman

216. McCraken Flesher 1988, 40.
217. Novak 2006, 656–657.
218. On the property rights of the captive, see the discussion in Malka and Paz 2021, Section 4. In the opinion of some jurists, captives were considered dead (*Dig.* 49.15.18), so captivity triggered an immediate and automatic intestate succession. Yet captives could also be considered enslaved (*Inst.* 1.3.4). See also *Dig.* 9.2.43, 42.5.39.1, 50.4.1.4.

citizen was captured by a state hostile to Rome but not if he was abducted by bandits, in which case he was not a captive from a legal point of view. The person taken prisoner by bandits thus retained his or her rights as a citizen.[219]

Orit Malka and Yakir Paz have convincingly argued that these Roman laws are behind the distinction made in t. Ketubbot 4:5 between two types of captives, the "captive of a kingdom" and the "captive of banditry."[220] This rabbinic text, about the obligations of a husband to his wife who has been taken prisoner, argues that he must ransom her if she is a "captive of banditry" but not if she is a "captive of a kingdom." Moreover, if the husband divorces his wife after having ransomed her, she will receive only half of the monetary amount to which she was entitled according to the marriage contract (*ketubbah*), as if she had not been a virgin when they married. Malka and Paz state that "the distinction between two types of captors is a direct adoption of Roman law" and "the reduced *ketubbah* should be understood in light of the legal consequences of captivity for a citizen, which, according to the Roman law, entail suspension or dissolution of the citizen's legal bonds, including marriage."[221] The Roman legal rationale implicitly underlying the Tosefta's statement views the captive woman's marriage as dissolved, and she is considered to have remarried on her return (albeit to the same husband). Hence, the amount paid to her in a case of divorce corresponds to that of a woman who was not a virgin when she got married.[222]

Malka and Paz further argue that according to t. Ketubbot 4:5,

> The legal bond of Jewish marriage is dissolved (or at least suspended) upon captivity, as a result of the change in civil status. In an analogy to the Roman parallel, Jewish law is no longer fully applicable to the captive woman. In other words, she is no longer a Jewish "citizen," that is, a full subject of Jewish law.[223]

Malka and Paz presume that the rabbis' adoption of the Roman laws concerning captives is consistent and includes not only these specific laws but also the legal rationale behind them—that is, the loss of citizenship. This would

---

219. For a more detailed presentation of the Roman laws on captives, see D'Amati 2004; Malka and Paz 2019, 153–156.

220. They also refer to a *baraita* in b. Ketubbot 51b that states: "Captives of a kingdom are regarded as captives; captives of bandits are not regarded as captives" (Malka and Paz 2019, 145; see also Lieberman 1955–1988, 6:236). In a later article, they argue that t. Ketubbot 8:3 contains a stratum reflecting the Roman view that captives regain their rights of property only once they have returned from captivity, in conformity with the Roman law of *postliminium* (Malka and Paz 2021). On t. Ketubbot 4:5 and the distinction between "captives of a kingdom" and "captives of banditry," see also Mor 2019, 60–62, 115–119.

221. Malka and Paz 2019, 141; Mor 2019, 118.

222. Malka and Paz 2019, 158–161.

223. Malka and Paz 2019, 166.

mean that the woman was no longer considered Jewish and that the laws of the Torah no longer applied to her. However, the only thing that the Tosefta clearly implies is dissolved when a married woman becomes "a captive of a kingdom" is the marital bond. That this also involved the loss of "Jewishness" remains to be demonstrated.

Even if we were to conclude that the woman is considered to have lost her Jewish "citizenship" in this specific instance, it would still represent an exceptional statement. As David Novak asserts, "Jews were expected to go to extraordinary lengths to redeem Jews who had been sold into captivity to Gentiles because, if unredeemed, they would no doubt be lost to the Jewish people."[224] Jewish communities throughout history dedicated great efforts to redeeming Jewish captives, including those taken prisoner by hostile powers, thus demonstrating that they were still considered Jews. Admittedly, Jewish communities do not necessarily behave according to rabbinic rulings, so this does not prove that rabbinic halakhah (or particular strata of the halakhic compilations) does not consider "captives of a kingdom" to have lost their "Jewishness." However, other rabbinic texts contradict the view that Malka and Paz identify in the Tosefta—namely, that a Jewish captive of a foreign power loses his or her "citizenship" and is no longer considered a Jew. Mishnah Ketubbot 4:8–9 states that a man is obliged to redeem his wife who has been taken captive and to take her back as his wife, even if this is not written explicitly in her *ketubbah*. In other words, he is forbidden to divorce her while she is in captivity. This means that, contrary to the view expressed in t. Ketubbot 4:5, the legal bond of marriage is not dissolved upon captivity.[225] Other texts suggest that redeeming captives was a normal activity, which needed merely to be regulated. Mishnah Gittin 4:6 thus states that captives should not be redeemed at a higher price than is customary, so as not to encourage the kidnapping of Jews. This ruling does not distinguish among types of captivity, however, and kidnapping may be considered a common practice of brigands rather than of foreign powers. Similarly, a passage in the Jerusalem Talmud declares that in the seventh year, one must perform all sorts of actions that serve the public need, such as redeeming captives, but again, this text does not make a distinction between kinds (y. Mo'ed Qatan 1:2, 80b).[226] The rarity of the opposition between "captives of a kingdom" and "captives of bandits" in rabbinic literature may actually indicate that the adoption of these Roman notions was limited. Finally, the Jerusalem Talmud

---

224. Novak 2006, 657. On the duty to redeem captives, see Rotman 2012; Mor 2019, 69–106.

225. See Rotman 2012, 228–229, which also refers to Babatha's *ketubbah*.

226. See also, e.g., t. Pe'ah 4:16, t. Terumot 1:10, t. Shevi'it 7:9, which refer to the types of funds people may or may not use to redeem captives.

stories about rabbis who were taken prisoner and brought to the kingdom of Queen Zenobia in Palmyra—a kingdom hostile to Rome, thus qualifying as an enemy state from both a Roman and a rabbinic perspective—and the subsequent efforts of Resh Laqish and others to free them are further indications that the status of "captive of a kingdom" did not deprive one of one's Jewishness—that is, one's "citizenship."[227]

As a consequence, with captives we may be facing the same stopping point that we tentatively identified in the case of slaves, beyond which the rabbis could go no further in adopting the Roman citizenship model: namely, that Jews could not lose their "citizenship." As Robert Brody aptly notes,

> It is not at all clear that anyone once a member of the Jewish collective can be considered to have left it. [. . .] It seems more likely that for classical rabbinic Judaism, as for other monotheistic religions, the boundary enclosing the religious collective was conceived to be permeable in one direction only: outsiders could join, but insiders—even those who had joined from the outside—could never leave.[228]

In their second article on captives, Malka and Paz argue that t. Ketubbot 8:3 has two redactional layers: an early one that adopts the Roman notion of *postliminium*, and a later one that rejects it. In the end they conclude that "the conditional relation between law and its subjects" involved in the legal definition of Roman citizenship "stands in contradiction to the dominant rabbinic view that Jewish law has a permanent and indissoluble hold over its Jewish subjects." In other words, while "status under Jewish law may change, ceasing to be subject to Jewish law is regarded as impossible." The fact remains, as they rightly stress, that the very existence of such a debate among the redactors of the Tosefta shows the rabbis' "deep engagement, whether affirmatory or dissenting, with Roman concepts of citizenship."[229]

Converts

Another crucial case study for evaluating the Roman citizenship model's impact on the rabbis is that of converts, including to what extent they were viewed as "new citizens" of Israel. Christine Hayes has argued that the rabbinic invention of conversion is based on the rabbis' rejection of ontological notions of identity in favor of legally constructed identities; and, moreover, that it owes much to the Roman idea of citizenship through participation in the law.

---

227. See Chapter Three, referring to y. Terumot 8:11, 46b (numbers according to Ma'agarim). For a detailed account of the issue of captivity in rabbinic literature, see Mor 2019.

228. Brody 2017, 282–283.

229. Malka and Paz 2021, 340.

She aptly remarks that "conversion is by definition a legal fiction—a nominalist strategy that assigns Israelite identity to an individual who, prior to the
moment of conversion, had no naturally grounded (no physically or biologically based) Israelite identity."[230] According to Hayes, the legal fiction of conversion is analogous to the Roman legal fiction that allowed for the treatment
of "non-Roman litigants in a given case as though they were Roman citizens
and subject to Roman civil law."[231]

I suggest a related but nevertheless different understanding of the evidence: an analogy between the rabbinic notion of conversion as attested in
a number of Palestinian rabbinic sources and Roman grants of citizenship.
This idea differs from Hayes's because grants of citizenship are no legal fictions. These are two distinct phenomena. In particular, grants of citizenship
were not legal fictions in the common sense in which Hayes and other scholars use this phrase, namely a reasoning that suspends natural and empirical
facts (such as birth, biological ties, or even death) by treating something as
if it did not exist or were something else (in the case of conversion, by treating someone not born a Jew as a Jew).[232] Because Roman citizenship was in
no way reducible to a status inherited at birth and was thus never "naturally
grounded," as membership in Israel originally was, Roman grants of citizenship did not suspend natural or biological facts. Moreover, they must be carefully distinguished from the Roman legal fiction that implied the treatment of
"non-Roman litigants in a given case as though they were Roman citizens."[233]
Grants of citizenship were political and legal decisions and acts—by a magistrate, by the people, or later by the emperor—that genuinely conferred Roman
citizenship on someone; there was no element of fiction in them. They did not
treat the person "as though" he or she were a Roman citizen. It is precisely
because such an "as though" clause does not exist in a grant that it cannot be
equated with a legal fiction. The grant could have been considered a legal fiction if it had implied that the person was becoming a Roman citizen as though
he or she had been born of Roman parents, for example. But Roman grants of
citizenship carried no such implication. (I will argue below that, on the other
hand, there is an analogy between the rabbinic legal fiction of conversion and
the Roman legal fiction of *adoptio*.)

230. Hayes 2015, 214.
231. Hayes 2017b, 71 for the quotation, and 72. Hayes refers to Ando 2011.
232. This definition is narrower than how specialists of Roman law understand legal
fictions to have functioned in a Roman context. See Ando 2011, 1–18, 117–122 (pp. 117–118
consider the example of Cicero, *Contra Rullum* 2.29, which shows that a legal fiction could
imply the suspension of legal rather than natural or empirical facts). Furthermore, modern
definitions of legal fictions do not necessarily refer to "nature." Lon Fuller, for example,
writes: "A fiction is either (1) a statement propounded with a complete or partial consciousness of its falsity, or (2) a false statement recognized as having utility" (Fuller 1967, 9).
233. Hayes 2017b, 71.

As the examples from Philo and Josephus analyzed above show, even though grants of citizenship are not legal fictions, they nevertheless shed light on how ancient Jews conceptualized conversion in a Roman context. To assess the impact of the Roman citizenship model on rabbinic views of converts, we must look at the details of rabbinic halakhah. Yael Wilfand has fruitfully investigated the legal links between a new citizen (in Roman law) or a convert (in rabbinic halakhah) and the children born prior to this change in status. Her study reveals striking similarities that cannot be considered coincidental, especially since this issue is absent from biblical law.[234] According to some tannaitic sources, even if both the father and the children underwent proper conversion (thus becoming "citizens" in Israel), their kinship ties would be severed; as a consequence, the children would no longer be considered their father's heirs.[235] This ruling is comparable to Roman laws—notably Gaius, *Institutes* 1.93 and 3.19–20—which state that if Roman citizenship is granted to a man and to his children (which was not automatic), he will nevertheless have no *patria potestas* over them, unless an explicit imperial decree establishes his *potestas*. Similarly, if a man's wife is pregnant before she receives Roman citizenship together with her husband, the child, who will be born a Roman citizen, will nevertheless not be placed under the father's *patria potestas*, unless the emperor so orders (1.94).[236] Most important, the absence of *patria potestas* affected children's inheritance rights, just as the severing of kinship ties did in rabbinic halakhah. Up to the time of Nerva, new Roman citizens, in contrast to "native" Roman citizens, were thus subject to the *vicesima hereditatium* (a 5% tax on inheritances and legacies), even on the inheritances of first-degree heirs. According to Pliny the Younger, Nerva exempted children's inheritance from their mother from the tax and even made the legal recognition of cognatic relationships automatic for those living under Latin law who had obtained Roman citizenship.[237] Although the two sets of laws, Roman and rabbinic, are not a perfect match (Roman law is more complex), their similarities are nevertheless striking.

We may refine this analysis a bit further. A free person who became Roman, for example through an imperial grant or after having held a magistracy in a community ruled under Latin law, was not a second-rank citizen from a

---

234. Wilfand 2021.

235. Thus, if the father dies, his debtors are not obliged to repay the debts to his children—but although there is no legal obligation, it is nevertheless praiseworthy to give them the money (m. Shevi'it 10:9).

236. According to Gaius, *Inst.* 1.95–96, however, this does not apply to fathers under Latin law who receive Roman citizenship: they do have *patria potestas* over their children.

237. Pliny, *Panegyricus* 37.4–7, 39.2. See Gardner 2001; Marie Roux, "Pliny the Younger, *Panegyric of Trajan* 37," http://www.judaism-and-rome.org/pliny-younger -panegyric-trajan%C2%A0A037.

legal point of view (prejudices are a different matter). By contrast, freedmen who had been manumitted in the appropriate way and had received Roman citizenship remained barred from accessing certain functions and honors and from marrying members of senatorial families. In rabbinic texts, converts are in many respects comparable to freedpersons in a Roman context. Numerous tannaitic sources do not view them as equal to native Israelites ("full citizens" of the people of Israel), especially when it comes to their marriage prospects.[238] Another parallel between freedmen in Roman society and converts in a Jewish setting relates to the severing of kinship ties. Just as a former slave was deprived of family connections upon manumission, even if he or she had engendered children while enslaved (or before), a convert was considered childless even if he or she had begotten sons or daughters before converting. This case differs from that of a new Roman citizen who did not have *patria potestas* over his sons even though they had become citizens too. Those children could still be recognized as his and even be placed under his *patria potestas* by imperial decree, whereas this was not possible with the children of a former slave. In this respect at least, the convert (*ger*) in rabbinic literature, especially in tannaitic texts, appears to be closer to the Roman freedman than to the new citizen who was born a free person.

The Roman citizenship model's impact on rabbinic views of converts may thus extend to the association between freedmen and converts (*gerim*) in rabbinic literature. As Natalie Dohrmann notes, "Tannaitic law shows an insistent and frequent pairing and comparison of proselyte to freedman."[239] Slaves freed by their Jewish masters were considered to have converted to Judaism, even though they were still in a different category from freeborn converts (*gerim*), at least in certain respects.[240] Conversion could thus be perceived

---

238. Until recently, rabbinic rulings on the marriage possibilities of converts (especially women) had not been studied in connection with Roman laws concerning freedmen and freedwomen; see Porton 1994, 155–165; Hayes 2002a, 164–192. But see now Wilfand 2019b and 2020b (referring to m. Qiddushin 4:6–7 in particular).

239. Dohrmann 2008, 59 (referring to m. Horayot 3:8, t. Horayot 2:10, to which we may add m. Ma'aser Sheni 5:14; m. Bikkurim 1:5; m. Ketubbot 1:2, 4; m. Yevamot 6:5; t. Yevamot 6:6; t. Qiddushin 5:2; t. Bava Qamma 4:6, 9:20; t. Bava Batra 7:1). The two categories remain distinct, however: see, e.g., m. Qiddushin 4:1; m. Horayot 3:8; t. Rosh haShanah 2:5; t. Megillah 2:7; t. Horayot 2:10). See also Cohen 1966, 1:146.

240. Several epitaphs from Rome seem to indicate that freed slaves were called "proselytes" after manumission. See, e.g., *JIWE* II, 54, no. 62 (*CIJ* I, no. 462): "Felicitas, a proselyte for 6 (?) years, named (?) Peregrina, who lived 47 years. Her (male) patron for the well-deserving woman" (trans. David Noy); *JIWE* II, 194, no. 218 (*CIJ* I, no. 256): "For Nicetas the proselyte, worthy and well-deserving, Dionysias his patroness (had this) made" (trans. David Noy). Both inscriptions date to the third or fourth century CE. On former masters as *patroni*, see Mouritsen 2011, 36–42.

as the common denominator between the two categories. This association between freedpersons and converts in rabbinic halakhah could then explain why, as Wilfand in particular has shown, several tannaitic rulings concerning proselytes and their descendants make sense in light of Roman laws on freedmen and freedwomen.[241]

On the whole, it seems undeniable that Roman notions of citizenship, especially rulings concerning new citizens and laws related to partial or total loss of citizenship, impacted rabbinic definitions of membership in Israel. However, there were some limits to this model's influence, as the rabbis apparently resisted the idea that a Jew could lose his or her "citizenship," even in the cases of converts and freedpersons. In particular, the fact that a Roman citizen could be deprived of citizenship (partially or completely) because of criminal behavior has no parallel in rabbinic rulings on membership in Israel, even for manumitted slaves and *gerim*.[242] Once these people had become Jews, if they transgressed the laws of the Torah they were considered bad or even criminal Jews, but they would not revert to their former gentile status. As t. Demai 2:4 states: "A convert who took upon himself all the commandments of the Torah and is suspected on account of one— even on account of the whole Torah—behold, he is like [an] apostate [or: renegade] Israelite (*ke-Israel meshummad*)."[243] In the end, the citizenship model or paradigm leaves unsolved many issues that the rabbinic texts raise concerning new members of the people of Israel, be they freedpersons or converts. We must take into account other models as well, especially the legal fiction of adoption.

241. Wilfand 2019b and 2020b.

242. On partial and total loss of citizenship in Roman law, see Gaius, *Inst.* 1.159–161; Girard 1929, 119 (highlighting the difference between *capitis deminutio media* and *capitis deminutio maxima*).

243. My translation is based on MS Vienna. MS Erfurt has *goy* (non-Jew) instead of *ger* (convert), but the meaning is the same (the text speaks about a non-Jew who has converted) (ed. Zuckermandel, 47). See also Bamberger 1939, 60; Brody 2017, 284–285. Admittedly, the notion of *meshummad* is complex, and its exact meaning may vary. In some rabbinic texts, *meshummadim* seem to have ceased to be bound by the covenant, as if they were not considered Israelites anymore; see Schremer 2012, 258–265, which discusses Sifra, Nedava 2 (ed. Finkelstein, 2:20–21), and Mekhilta de-Rabbi Ishmael, Pisḥa 15 (ed. Horovitz and Rabin, 53). Yet *meshummadim* are not *goyim*. In t. Demai, the important point is that the sinful *ger* is considered not a *goy* but *ke-Israel meshummad*. Compare with Mekhilta de-Rabbi Ishmael, Kaspa 20 (ed. Horovitz and Rabin, 324), where R. Eliezer interprets the "enemy" in Exodus 23:4 as a *ger* who has returned to his evil nature—i.e., probably his former condition as an idolater (Schremer 2012, 266). This interpretation seems to be a minority opinion.

3. Beyond Citizenship: The Enduring Significance of Lineage and the Legal Fiction of Adoption

3.1 CONVERTS AS CHILDREN OF ABRAHAM IN Y. BIKKURIM: A LEGAL FICTION RELATED TO THE ROMAN NOTION AND PRACTICE OF ADOPTION

Applying the citizenship paradigm to the children of Israel presupposes that they are a people united by common laws, an idea that goes back to the biblical model associated with the covenant at Sinai (discussed at the beginning of the previous section). The growing popularity of the citizenship model, with roots in Hellenistic and Roman notions of citizenship, did not, however, make the other biblical model used to define Israel, that of the family or clan, disappear. For many Jews, including the rabbis, the genealogical model remained central. Lineage and pedigree continued to matter, and the definition of Jews as the descendants of Abraham, Isaac, and Jacob endured.[244] What did this mean for the integration of newcomers?

Within the framework of the family or genealogical model, we find different views of the inclusion of foreigners both in the Bible and in Second Temple Jewish literature. The book of Ezra develops an essentialist notion of Israel as "holy seed," which we encounter again in Jubilees and some sectarian compositions from Qumran.[245] According to this perspective, intermarriage results in a profanation of Israel's holy seed that can never be undone and that disqualifies the children of such unions from marriage with another Israelite.[246] Even marrying a convert is completely prohibited, since he or she remains "biologically" distinct from Israel. This attitude amounts to a firm rejection of conversion in the modern sense of the term (a non-Jew becoming a Jew). The borders were not permeable and could not be crossed.[247]

By contrast, other Jewish sources attest the integration of foreigners through marriage (at least women) and, later on, through conversion. Yet this does not mean that proselytes did not remain distinct from native Israelites, at

244. See, e.g., 3 Macc 6:3 (which uses the expression "seed (*sperma*) of Abraham"); 4 Macc 6:17, 6:22, 18:1: "O Israelite children, offspring of the seeds (*spermata*) of Abraham, obey this law, and act piously in every way" (trans. Stephen Westerholm, NETS, 540 [slightly modified]). According to Erich Gruen, Josephus did not have a genealogical notion of the people of Israel (Gruen 2017). Yet lineage mattered for Josephus as far as priestly—that is, elite—status was concerned (Berthelot 2020e). The bibliography on lineage and pedigree in Second Temple and rabbinic Judaism is vast. See, e.g., Porton 1994, 28–29; Cohen 1999a, 308–340; Hayes 2002a, esp. 164–192; Hayes 2002b; Himmelfarb 2006, 174–181; Thiessen 2011; Koren 2018; Wilfand 2020b; further bibliography in n. 322 below.

245. Hayes 2002a, 68–91; Himmelfarb 2006, 79–80.

246. Hayes 1999.

247. Hayes 2002a, 89–91; Thiessen 2011, 67–86 (on Jubilees), 87–110.

least as far as the first generation was concerned. Converts could be integrated into Israel but nevertheless might retain a distinct status based on genealogy.

Hence, the epigraphic documents—generally epitaphs—that refer to individuals as "proselytes" rather than "Jews" or "Israelites" prompt a question. If the person had become Jewish through conversion, why was he or she remembered as a proselyte rather than a Jew?[248] Interestingly enough, some inscriptions even refer to the length of time spent as a proselyte. A sarcophagus from Rome, dated to the third or fourth century, thus bears the mention: "Veturia Paula, placed in her eternal home, who lived 86 years 6 months, a proselyte (*proselyta*) for 16 years under the name of Sarah, mother of the synagogues of Campus and Volumnius. In peace her sleep."[249] More striking still is the Greek epitaph of Irene (Eirēnē), also from third- or fourth-century Rome, tentatively translated by David Noy as "Irene, foster-child (?), proselyte, of father and mother, Jewess, Israelite (?) (*Eirēnē trezptē* [read *threptē*] *prosēlytos patros kai mētros Eioudea Isdraēlitēs*). She lived 3 years 7 months 1 day."[250] The translation and interpretation of this inscription vary greatly from scholar to scholar, and it is not possible to rehearse the debate here.[251] One possible interpretation is that the girl's parents were both proselytes and wanted to state that even though she was the child of two converts, Irene herself was fully Jewish and could be considered an Israelite in all respects.[252] Yet the fact that she is called a *threptē* (foster child) raises questions about her status and the exact nature of her relationship with those designated as her parents (she might have been adopted and/or raised by people who considered her their own child).[253] This inscription therefore remains open to interpretation.

The exact status and rights of proselytes and their offspring was of considerable concern to the rabbis. Rabbinic literature on the whole clearly favored the acceptance of converts, but it nonetheless cleaved to the enduring significance of lineage. As Shaye Cohen aptly notes:

> The ambiguity of the convert's status is clear in rabbinic legislation. The rabbis declare that a proselyte is a Jew (*yisrael*) in all respects, but this ideology cannot mask the fact that the proselyte remains, in some matters at least, a non-Israelite. [. . .] In sum, the convert is not an Israelite, but he is a Jew.[254]

248. See n. 119 above.

249. *JIWE* II, 457, no. 577 (*CIJ* I, no. 523).

250. *JIWE* II, 390, no. 489 (*CIJ* I, no. 21).

251. See the summary of the discussion in *JIWE* II, 391; Van der Horst 1991, 110–111.

252. For a similar view attributed to R. Yose (the daughter of two converts is to be considered a native Israelite), see m. Qiddushin 4:6–7; y. Qiddushin 4:6, 66a. See further below.

253. On *threptoi* and *alumni* ("foster children" in Greek and Latin, respectively), see further below.

254. Cohen 1983, 33.

In his study of *gerim* in rabbinic literature, Gary Porton too insists on the enduring significance of lineage, concluding that "according to some sages, in specific contexts converts could not be fully equated with native-born Israelites."[255] On the other hand, Christine Hayes notes that even though "the rabbis were restricted in their ability to subvert privileges based on genealogical descent [. . .] there was much that the rabbis could, and did, do to overcome the claims of genealogy and the blemish of foreign descent in various areas of law."[256]

Genealogical thinking particularly comes to the fore in rabbinic texts that discuss marriage issues, such as m. Qiddushin 4:1:

> Ten genealogical classes came up from Babylonia: priests, Levites, Israelites, *ḥalalim* [impaired or profaned priests], converts (*gerim*), freed slaves, mamzers, *netinim* [foreign temple servants], hush-children and foundlings.[257]
>
> Priests, Levites, Israelites are permitted to intermarry.
>
> Levites, Israelites, *ḥalalim*, converts and freed slaves are permitted to marry among one another.
>
> Converts, freed slaves, mamzers, *netinim*, hush-children and foundlings are permitted to intermarry.[258]

This text, together with many others, shows that the rabbinic worldview recognized different statuses within Israel. Although all these groups could be deemed "citizens" of the people of Israel, they were not equal, and the rationale for their differentiated rights (according to the rabbinic interpretation of the law) was grounded in their pedigree. Furthermore, other rabbinic texts discuss the status of children of *gerim* and report the opinion of some (but not all) rabbis that the inferior standing of converts extended to their children as well.[259]

255. Porton 1994, 29 (on the Mishnah), 86, 155–165.

256. Hayes 2002a, 190. An interesting example is found in t. Yadaim 2:17–18, which tells the fictitious story of an Ammonite convert who goes to the rabbinic study house and asks the rabbis whether he is allowed to enter the congregation (*qahal*). According to Deuteronomy 23:4 he is prohibited from becoming part of the "congregation of the Lord" (*qehal YHWH*), and Rabban Gamaliel's response follows this ruling. Yet R. Joshua is of the opposite opinion and argues that since the Assyrian king Sennacherib deported and mixed up all nations, it is not possible to identify Ammonites (or other ancient ethnic groups) any longer. At the end of the story, the Ammonite convert is thus allowed to enter the congregation.

257. Hush-children (*shtuqim*, lit. "silenced ones") are children whose father's identity is unknown. Foundlings (*asufim*) are children whose parents are both unknown.

258. Trans. Hayes 2002a, 167. See also t. Qiddushin 5:1; y. Qiddushin 4:1, 65b; Hayes 2002a, 168–169; Hayes 2015, 216–217; Koren 2018, 419; Yael Wilfand, "Tosefta Qiddushin 5:1–2," http://www.judaism-and-rome.org/tosefta-qiddushin-51-2.

259. At least as long as they did not have one Israelite parent. See, e.g., m. Bikkurim 1:5; m. Qiddushin 4:6–7; y. Qiddushin 4:6, 66a; Hayes 2002a, 173–176; Wilfand 2020b.

Admittedly, several rabbinic passages forbid native Israelites to express derogatory opinions about converts and their descendants, especially concerning their foreign origins. Mishnah Bava Metzi'a 4:10 thus states: "If he was a child of converts (*ben gerim*), one will not say to him: 'Remember what the practice of your ancestors was!' For it is said: *You shall not wrong or oppress a resident alien* (ger), *for you were* gerim *in the land of Egypt* (Exod 22:20)."[260] Note that although the biblical text mentions the *ger* (a word that the rabbis understood to refer to a convert), the prohibition in the Mishnah refers to a descendant of *gerim*, showing that the issue could also arise with the following generation (or generations).

According to m. Bikkurim 1:4, however, converts were reminded of their non-Israelite lineage on certain ritual occasions. This mishnah deals with the commandment of Deuteronomy 26:1–11 to bring the firstfruits and recite to a priest: "Today I declare to the Lord your God that I have come into the land that the Lord swore to our ancestors (or: fathers) to give us" (26:3). The mishnaic text states:

> These [people must] bring [the firstfruits] but do not recite [the declaration prescribed in Deut 26:3]: the convert (*ger*) brings [them] but he does not recite, since he cannot say *That the Lord swore to our fathers to give us*. But if his mother was an Israelite, he brings [them] and recites.
>
> And when he prays in private (lit.: between him and himself) he says: "God of the fathers of Israel"; but when he is in the synagogue [with the community] he says: "God of your fathers." If his mother was an Israelite he says: "God of our fathers."[261]

According to the anonymous teaching in this mishnah, the *gerim*, who do not have Israelite ancestors and thus have no share in the Land of Israel, are not allowed to recite "I have come into the land which the Lord swore to our fathers to give us" nor to say "God of our fathers" in private or public prayers.[262] In t. Bikkurim 1:2, the same opinion about the offering of the firstfruits and the recitation is attributed to R. Yehudah, who, according to rabbinic tradition, was a third-generation tanna living in the second century CE. After the destruction of the Temple, the prohibition on recitation became largely irrelevant. The second prohibition, however, if put into practice would

---

260. My translation is based on MS Kaufmann. See also t. Bava Metzi'a 3:25; Mekhilta de-Rabbi Ishmael Neziqin (Mishpatim) 18, ed. Horovitz and Rabin, 311; Sifra, Qedoshim 8.2, ed. Weiss, 91a.

261. My translation is based on MS Kaufmann. See Cohen 1999a, Chapter 10; Yael Wilfand, "Mishnah Bikkurim 1:4–5," http://www.judaism-and-rome.org/mishnah -bikkurim-14-5.

262. See also m. Ma'aser Sheni 5:14 (converts have no share in the Land); Mekhilta de-Rabbi Ishmael, Kaspa (Mishpatim) 20 (ed. Horovitz and Rabin, 335) (converts and slaves do not recite); Sifre Deuteronomy 299 (converts do not recite).

have publicly set apart converts in synagogues by constantly reminding them (and others) of their non-Israelite lineage. It was a logical consequence of the genealogical model, but it could well have been perceived as demeaning.

An additional point worthy of attention in this passage is the role attributed to a mother of Israelite lineage. How are we supposed to understand that a *ger* may have an Israelite mother? According to other rabbinic texts, the child of an Israelite woman and a non-Israelite man is either an Israelite or a mamzer.[263] Yet m. Bikkurim 1:4 states that a *ger* could have an Israelite mother. The implied situation may be that the father is a *ger* and the child inherits his status, in accordance with the biblical worldview (in which case the text deals with two generations of converts).[264] Another possible interpretation is that this *ger*, the son of an Israelite woman and a non-Jew, was himself originally considered a non-Jew (*goy*) before converting (y. Bikkurim 1:4, 64a, discusses this possibility).[265] In both interpretations, the prohibition implies a patrilineal model (the child of an Israelite woman takes on the father's status), which is challenged by the statement (based on a matrilineal Israelite lineage) that a Jewish mother is sufficient grounds for a person to claim Israelite ancestry and to recite "God of our fathers." The case of the offspring of a convert mother and an Israelite father is not addressed, because in a patrilineal model it poses no problem: the child of an Israelite father is able to recite "God of our fathers." Ultimately, however, the text suggests that it is necessary for a convert to have one Israelite parent—more specifically, a Jewish mother—to be considered of Israelite lineage (see also R. Eliezer b. Jacob's statement in the following mishnah, m. Bikkurim 1:5, and in m. Qiddushin 4:7[266]). Still other opinions come to the fore in rabbinic texts, especially in connection with R. Yose, who is said to have considered the child of two converts an Israelite in all respects (m. Qiddushin 4:7). In the end, however, the first-generation convert remains problematic, for he or she cannot claim to have Israelite ancestors.

In the section of the Jerusalem Talmud that discusses m. Bikkurim 1:4, we encounter a revolutionary approach to this issue:

263. See the discussion in Chapter Four.

264. Cohen 1992; Cohen 1999a, 310–312.

265. Cohen points out that no other rabbinic source sees the child of a Jewish mother and a gentile father as a non-Jew (Cohen 1992, 24–25). A third way to understand the text is that this *ger*, as the son of an Israelite woman and a non-Jew, originally had the status of mamzer or was considered like a mamzer and was allowed to convert; see Sifra, Emor 14.1 (ed. Weiss, 104c), on Leviticus 24:10. Yet the most common opinion on *mamzerim* in rabbinic literature is that they cannot gain a "normal" status through conversion—that is, a status that would allow their children to be Israelites. M. Qiddushin 3:13 discusses whether the offspring of a mamzer and a female slave, who would be born a slave, would receive the status of freedperson if manumitted and thus be able to have children who would be considered Israelites, yet no solution is offered for the mamzer himself or herself.

266. According to rabbinic tradition, R. Eliezer b. Jacob (II) was another third-generation tanna.

It was taught [on tannaitic authority] in the name of R. Yehudah: [The] convert himself brings [the firstfruits] and recites [the declaration prescribed in Deut 26:3]. What is the reason [i.e., the scriptural basis for this ruling]? [*No longer shall your name be Abram, but your name shall be Abraham,*] *for I have made you the father of a multitude of nations* (Gen 17:5). In the past you were a father to Aram, but from now on you are a father to all the nations (*goyim*).

R. Yehoshua b. Levi said: The law (halakhah) accords with R. Yehudah.

A case came before R. Abbahu and he rendered a decision in accordance with [the position of] R. Yehudah.[267]

The redactors of the Yerushalmi attribute to R. Yehudah a halakhic position that is diametrically opposed to the one that is associated with him in t. Bikkurim 1:2 and presented as an anonymous teaching in the Mishnah.[268] In the Jerusalem Talmud, R. Yehudah regards even a first-generation convert as obligated to bring the firstfruits and recite the declaration prescribed in Deuteronomy, because he has become a descendant of Abraham and can thus claim Israelite ancestry (at least in connection to Abraham).[269] Because this ruling contradicts the teaching of the Mishnah (as well as those of the Tosefta and the Babylonian Talmud, to which I will return), a scriptural basis had to be provided, which was found in God's promise to Abram in Genesis 17:5: "No longer shall your name be Abram, but your name shall be Abraham, for I have made you the father of a multitude of nations/peoples (*goyim*)." This reference involves a pun: the name Abram is read *av-ram*, which could be understood as "high [or exalted] father" (as Philo, *On Abraham* 82, indicates), whereas "Abraham" is interpreted as *av hamon goyim*, "father of a multitude of nations/peoples/non-Jews." In t. Berakhot 1:12, this phrase is quoted to explain that by being called Abraham, the patriarch became a father for the whole world (*av le-khol ha-'olam kulo*), meaning in fact: a father for all the non-Jews who convert.[270]

---

267. y. Bikkurim 1:4, 64a; my translation is based on MS Leiden, consulted on Ma'agarim; see also Schäfer and Becker 1992 (*Synopse* I/6–11), 446. See Cohen 1992, 22; Cohen 1999a, 328. According to rabbinic tradition, R. Yehoshua b. Levi was a first-generation amora (first half of the third century CE) and R. Abbahu a third-generation amora (end of the third century), both from the Land of Israel.

268. In this case, it is worth considering the possibility that the attribution to R. Yehudah in the Tosefta was original and was deliberately erased in the Mishnah in order not to conflict with amoraic views like those reflected in y. Bikkurim 1:4, 64a. On the relationship between the Tosefta and the Mishnah, see Friedman 1999 and Hauptman 2005, which argue for the Tosefta's primacy in some cases. Whatever the case, my point here is not that the attribution to R. Yehudah is historically accurate (or inaccurate). The issue is the transmission of textual traditions.

269. See Lieberman 1955–1988, 2:824.

270. t. Berakhot 1:12, MS Vienna, consulted on Ma'agarim.

In the Jerusalem Talmud, the fact that the biblical verse is interpreted to signify that Abraham can be considered the father or the ancestor of converts is even more explicit. As Joshua Levinson notes of this passage from the Yerushalmi, "The conversion process enables the gentile to acquire the necessary patriarchal pedigree, which is literally reinvented for this purpose."[271] He further observes: "By displacing the biological father with a mythological one, he [R. Yehudah] gains inclusiveness at the price of relinquishing the grounding of ethnicity in a common genealogical origin."[272] Levinson thus considers Abraham a "mythological" father and believes that the solution of the Yerushalmi implies the relinquishment of the genealogical model. In relation to the same text, Moshe Lavee speaks of Abraham as a "spiritual father" for converts.[273]

Levinson's analysis, especially the conclusion that Abraham is only a "mythological" (or "spiritual") father in this text, is not entirely convincing. Admittedly, the notion of spiritual fatherhood appears in rabbinic sources dealing with converts: t. Horayot 2:7 states that "every person who brings one creature under the wings of the Shekhinah [the divine presence—meaning: whoever makes a convert], it is accounted to him as if he [had] created him [the convert] and formed him and brought him into the world."[274] Sifre Deuteronomy reports a similar tradition, this time about Abraham himself: the verse "Abram took his wife Sarai and his brother's son Lot, and all the possessions that they had gathered, and the persons (lit.: souls) whom they had acquired (lit.: made, 'asu) in Ḥaran" (Gen 12:5) is interpreted as referring not to the acquisition of slaves, as most modern translators understand it, but to the "making" of converts. The midrash explains that the "souls" were "made" by Abraham because he brought them under the wings of the Shekhinah (i.e., he converted them).[275] A later commentary on this verse found in Genesis Rabbah interprets the phrase "they had made" ('asu) as "they had made converts" (giyyeru): Abraham and Sarah are said to have "made converts," and the reason for the use of the verb "to make" in the biblical verse is "to teach

271. Levinson 2000, 346. Christine Hayes also observes that "R. Yehudah shows his notion of lineage to be statutory and nominalist rather than historical or realist" (Hayes 2002a, 167).

272. Levinson 2000, 346. See also Levinson 2014, 125–126.

273. Lavee 2017, 218: "The notion of Abraham as the spiritual father of all nations is used here to support the inclusive law. This is a legal expression of the concept of the spiritual paternity of Abraham implied in Palestinian missionary traditions." In connection with these sources, Lavee also mentions "concepts of spiritual or alternative paternity, making converts into metaphorical offspring of Abraham, who initiated their conversion" (217). Yet in y. Bikkurim 1:4, 64a, the fictive kinship is not merely a metaphor.

274. My translation is based on MS Vienna, consulted on Ma'agarim.

275. Sifre Deuteronomy 32, ed. Finkelstein, 54. On Abraham as "proselytizing" in rabbinic texts, see, e.g., Goodman 1994a, 144–145; Lavee 2010 (on this text, 204–206); Levenson 2012, 133–138; in the Targums of the Pentateuch, Hayward 1998.

you that whoever brings the non-Jew (*goy*) closer to [God—meaning: converts him or her], [it is] as if he had created him."[276] The idea of creation is expressed with the verb *bara'*, which is used to describe the creation of the world in Genesis and specifically that of human beings in Genesis 1:27 (while Gen 1:26 uses *'asah*). In these midrashic traditions, the convert is seen as a new being, and the agent of the conversion may be seen as spiritually giving birth to him or her. Yet these texts do not refer to the creation of a kinship relation between the proselyte and the person who was responsible for his or her conversion of the sort that would have had legal implications.

By contrast, the fictive kinship put forward in y. Bikkurim 1:4, 64a, is not merely a spiritual kinship based on the exegesis of a given biblical verse or an aggadic development: it has halakhic consequences.[277] R. Yehudah's argument casts aside the very serious objection raised in the Mishnah and other sources to the possibility that a *ger* may recite the declaration of Deuteronomy 26:3 or say "God of our fathers" more broadly. As noted above, the stakes were particularly high in the case of prayers that took place in a community setting. The solution attributed to R. Yehudah in the Yerushalmi is not a metaphor or an allegory but a legal fiction that creates a new reality from a halakhic, social, and psychological point of view. The convert's kinship with Abraham is obviously fictive, in the sense that no actual biological link with the patriarch is thereby established, but the legal consequences are real. In particular, claiming that the convert can bring the firstfruits and recite means that the (male) convert has come to have a share in the Land of Israel. This results from his being now genealogically linked to Abraham and thus heir to the promises made to the chosen descendants of the patriarch, including those concerning the Land. To understand how this fictive kinship helps to resolve the tension between genealogical (kinship-based) and covenantal (Law-based) definitions of Israel, let us look at the Roman notion and practice of adoption and consider the possibility that the creative step taken by the Yerushalmi was a consequence of the rabbis' exposure to this Roman legal concept.

Before developing this idea, however, I will first deal with two factors that might shed light on the innovation in the Jerusalem Talmud. Speaking more generally about the rabbinic trend "toward leniency and an increasing discomfort with genealogical purity," Christine Hayes has highlighted a "shift toward a more merit-based society in which Torah learning began to outweigh lineage as a criterion for authority, leadership, and personal value."[278] The emphasis on

---

276. Gen. Rabbah 39:14, ed. Theodor and Albeck, 378–379. Note also the tradition about Sarah suckling the children of noblewomen in Gen. Rabbah 53:9, with the gloss that "whoever came for the sake of heaven became a God-fearer" (ed. Theodor and Albeck, 564; see also Levinson 2000, 352–356; Lavee 2010, 211–213; Lavee 2017, 109–112).

277. As Cohen emphasizes, "A piece of fanciful exegesis with homiletical intent [...] has become an important proof in a legal discussion" (Cohen 1999a, 329).

278. Hayes 2002a, 188, 191.

Torah learning over genealogy, Hayes further notes, "is most prevalent among Palestinian authorities"[279] and can be found already in the Mishnah, as m. Horayot 3:8, for example, illustrates. This text establishes a pedigree-based hierarchy of the groups that constitute Israel but concludes that a mamzer who is versed in the laws of the Torah ranks above a high priest who is ignorant. The dialectic between Torah learning and genealogy is an important aspect of the Palestinian rabbis' worldview and sheds light on many discussions found in rabbinic literature. Yet it does not explain how converts could be considered *children* of Abraham—by its terms they would instead have been presented as *disciples* of the patriarch.

Alternately, Yael Wilfand interprets R. Yehudah's position in the Yerushalmi in light of the Roman citizenship model, emphasizing the disconnection between citizenship and genealogical or ethnic origin that was characteristic of the Roman definition.[280] But again, this background provides only a general context for the debate in rabbinic sources, between those who stuck with the genealogical model (though not in an absolute way) and those who opted for a more open, less lineage-based definition of Israel. In the case of y. Bikkurim 1:4, 64a, the model of citizenship is not helpful. A grant of citizenship did not confer a new ancestry on the new citizen and thus cannot explain the position attributed to R. Yehudah. The case of the freedman is potentially more relevant, if we follow the analysis of Mouritsen, who notes, comparing the relationship between the freedman and his former master to other types of patron-client relationships:

> In the case of the freedman the paternal element went beyond the purely symbolic. For, unlike clients, the former slave's position did in many respects come close to that of a quasi-son, just as the position of the former master commonly was associated with that of the father.[281]

The freedman, who, as a former slave, had no kinship ties, may have seen his former master, his *patronus*, as a kind of father (*pater*). It is noteworthy that the former often took the latter's name. However, no less important is the fact that the freedman did not enter into the *gens* of his *patronus*.[282] Neither did he become his former master's heir—as Mouritsen remarks: "The patron was a statutory heir of the freedman but not vice versa."[283] Even though a freedman could sometimes look like an adopted child, in Roman law his status was by no means that of an adopted son, who would fully inherit from his adoptive father.[284]

279. Hayes 2002a, 188.
280. Wilfand 2020b.
281. Mouritsen 2011, 37.
282. Mouritsen 2011, 39, n. 18. See also Smith 2006, 15.
283. Mouritsen 2011, 41.
284. Mouritsen 2011, 38–42.

Conversely, the status of the convert in y. Bikkurim 1:4, 64a, is analogous to that of an adopted son, as shown by his right of inheritance, implied by the fact that he recites the declaration of Deuteronomy 26:3 like a native Israelite.[285] I contend that it is the notion of adoption, widely practiced in Roman society, including by prominent emperors (see below), that provided the redactors of y. Bikkurim with the appropriate model to fully conceptualize the integration of converts into Israel. The reason is very simple (so simple that previous scholarship has overlooked it):[286] the legal fiction of adoption is precisely what makes it possible to confer on a person a new lineage (different ancestors), along with the corresponding legal and religious duties and inheritance rights, as if this person really had been born into his or her family of adoption. These features are similar to central aspects of conversion as conceptualized in Palestinian rabbinic sources (see below).

The crucial point of the legal fiction of adoption lies in the fact that it does not minimize the importance of genealogy. Although it circumvents the notion of biological lineage, at the same time it reaffirms the relevance of lineage as such—by creating a fictive genealogy that has legal implications just like a biological one. The importance of this point can hardly be overstated. The rabbis were jurists and fond of legal fictions, and adoption was exactly the legal tool that they needed to solve the issues raised by the problematic lineage of converts, at least at the conceptual level (they did not integrate adoption as a legal tool to solve problems of inheritance or to help childless parents, and in that respect did not modify biblical law).

That adoption went together with due care for lineage is shown by the Roman nobility's use of this legal fiction. It is essential to understand that even though the Romans had a rather inclusive notion of citizenship, lineage and ethnicity nevertheless retained their relevance among the elite.[287] Aristocratic families proudly referred to their ancestors, whose memories they used to

285. That adoption was closely associated with inheritance rights is also clear in Philo, *Congr.* 23. On adoption in Philo's writings, see below, section 3.2.

286. Although scholars such as Cohen, Levinson, Hayes, and Lavee have noted the creation of fictive kinship in y. Bikkurim 1:4, 64a (see, e.g., Cohen 1999a; Levinson 2000; Hayes 2002a; Levinson 2014; Lavee 2017), the idea that the conceptual model behind this passage relates to the Roman notion and practice of adoption has never been explored before. Binyamin Katzoff observes in passing that converts may be considered fictive biological descendants of the patriarchs and simply states in a note: "By means of a rigorous process governed by halakhah a fiction of biological descent may perhaps be created, analogous to the Roman notions of adoption" (Katzoff 2009, 317, n. 30).

287. This was true not only for the old patrician families but also for the *homines novi* (new members of the elite) like Cicero, who wrote: "We are descended from a very ancient family of this district; here are our ancestral sacred rites (*sacra*) and the origin of our race (*genus*); here are many memorials of our forefathers (*maiores*)" (*Leg.* 2.3, trans. Clinton W. Keyes, LCL, 373). On the connections between aristocratic families and ethnic origins in the Republican period, see Farney 2007; Lee-Stecum 2014.

consolidate their hold on power. (The *gens Iulia*, which claimed Aeneas—and his mother, Venus—among its ancestors, and into which Octavian was adopted, is a famous example; later on, the Julio-Claudian dynasty made extensive use of its alleged connections to Aeneas and Venus.)[288] These families had a keen sense of their genealogy, as shown by the stemmata exhibited in the halls of their houses and the masks of illustrious ancestors (*imagines*) which were kept in their *armaria* (cupboards) and processed at funerals.[289] By providing an heir to a *pater familias*, adoption made it possible to keep alive the name, the patrimony, and the *sacra* (family cults) of the family. Moreover, adoption served to create kinship ties between families, as marriage strategies did. Roman elites thus used it to serve the interests, preserve the name, and continue the lineage of their families.[290] Put succinctly, adoption did not undermine lineage; rather, it consolidated it.

This is particularly obvious in the case of imperial adoptions. From Augustus onward, emperors with no son whom they could designate as their successor resorted to adoption.[291] If lineage had been irrelevant to political legitimacy, there would have been no need for Augustus, Claudius, Nerva, Trajan, Hadrian, and others to adopt their anticipated successors, for they could have simply nominated them. But joining the *gens* of the living emperor and being designated as his son was crucial.[292] This insistence on lineage might be compared in a way to the dynastic principle in the Hellenistic kingdoms.[293] Yet the comparison with the Hellenistic monarchies simultaneously reveals how distinct Roman imperial practice was, for Hellenistic kings did not designate their successors through adoption and never chose someone outside the family. Finally, we must keep in mind that the Roman emperors' frequent use of adoption to name successors, and the advertisement that these decrees received through inscriptions and coinage, made the notion widely known among the populations of the empire—including, of course, the Jews[294] (Fig. 5.2).

Admittedly, a possible objection to my reading of y. Bikkurim 1:4, 64a, is that adoption was not a legal tool meant to integrate foreigners into the

288. On the relationship between the modern noun "family" and the Roman notions of *familia* and *gens*, see Hekster 2015, 23–25; on the Roman *gens*, see also Smith 2006. In some Palestinian rabbinic texts, the rabbis seem to conceive of Israel as an aristocratic *gens*. On the genealogical claims of the Julian *gens* and the Julio-Claudian dynasty, see Hekster 2015, 240–250. Note that Hadrian wrote a poem for his adoptive father in which he presents Trajan as "the descendant of Aeneas" (*Anth. Pal.* 6.332; Arrian, *Parthica*, frag. 36; Ando 2000, 37).

289. See Polybius, 6.53.4; Cassius Dio, *Rom. Hist.* 74.4; Badel 2005, esp. 30–39, 106–155; Corbier 2007, 71, 74–76; Hekster 2015, 13–14.

290. Gardner 1998, 202; Kunst 2005, 48–51; Hekster 2015, 24.

291. Ando 2000, 34; Hekster 2015.

292. On the dynastic principle, see Hekster 2015, 2–25.

293. Hekster 2015, 17–21.

294. Peppard 2011, 67–70.

FIGURE 5.2. Denarius featuring Hadrian on the obverse, and Trajan and Hadrian
clasping hands, with the legend ADOPTIO on the reverse
(117 CE, minted in Syria, probably in Antioch).
Harold Mattingly, *Coins of the Roman Empire in the British Museum*,
vol.III: Nerva to Hadrian, London: BMP, 1976, no. 1021, p. 372.
Photograph © The Trustees of the British Museum.

populus Romanus. It did not serve as an instrument to create new citizens,
because a Roman citizen could adopt only another citizen. Laws of adoption
pertained to people under the same *ius civile*.[295] In view of this objection,
we must keep in mind that the analogy between adoption and conversion is
based on the representation of Israel not as a civic body but as a family group
(the descendants of common ancestors). The convert is to be seen not as a
new citizen in this case but as a new child or as some new family member. The
important question, then, is whether one could adopt a person from outside
the family in Roman society. In practice, most Roman adoptees were members
of the extended family who did not belong to the agnatic line (the legal family
connections on the father's side) of the adoptive father but were nevertheless
related to him by blood, such as sons of a sister or another female relative.[296]
It was possible, however, to adopt someone from a different *gens*, as Nerva's
choice of Trajan (from entirely outside the imperial house) shows.[297] From a
functional perspective, the analogy between adoption and conversion is thus
operational (converts come from a different "family" than Israel and are integrated into it).[298]

295. Moreau 1992, 21.
296. Moreau 1992, 24–25; Gardner 1998, 116; Kunst 2005, 131–149.
297. Hekster 2015, 78.
298. We must also recall that after 212 CE, most free persons in the empire were
Roman citizens, which means that from a legal viewpoint, they could be adopted; the distinction that had prevailed in the past had lost its significance.

Another objection that could be raised relates to the fact that adoption was apparently less practiced from the third century onward.[299] Literary and epigraphic evidence shows a decrease in adoptions beginning in the period of the Severan dynasty, at least within aristocratic circles. Christophe Badel suggests that this decline may have resulted from changes in Roman law that led to a revaluation of cognatic family ties: since adoption was meant primarily to shape the agnatic line, it thus became less important.[300] Badel nevertheless notes that sources from late antiquity document the continued practice of adoption by people of several social layers, including the very poor, up to the early Middle Ages. Moreover, this observation is not problematic for our study of y. Bikkurim 1:4, 64a, because we do not know when this particular halakhic view developed. It is ascribed to R. Yehudah, who was active in the middle of the second century CE, according to rabbinic tradition, a time when adoptions were the rule within the imperial *domus*. Although this attribution is not necessarily trustworthy, it may indicate that the debate among the rabbis originated in this period, while other sources may lead us to date it even earlier (see the discussion about Paul in Section 3.2 below).

Finally, a third possible objection is that Jews had been exposed to adoption in other cultural contexts prior to their encounter with Rome. I will return below to the question of references to adoption in Jewish texts composed before the Roman period. For the time being, let us look more closely at the characteristics of Roman adoption. What made it different from the types of adoption practiced in Mesopotamia or Greece was first and foremost the notion of *patria potestas*, the legal power that a man had over every person in his household who was legally placed under his *potestas*. *Patria potestas* was a Roman concept, foreign to Jewish legal tradition, just as the notion of adoption originally was (see Section 3.2 below). Since women had no *potestas*, only males could adopt. From the adoptee's viewpoint, adoption meant the extinction of his or her agnatic connections with the natal family—the *familia* rather than the *gens*; the *familia* being "a group headed by a *paterfamilias* and consisting of the persons and property under his control," to quote Jane Gardner's definition[301]—and placement under the *potestas* of the adoptive father. Roman law made a distinction between *adoptio*, the adoption of someone who was still under the *patria potestas* of another person (a father or grandfather), and *adrogatio*, the adoption of someone who was *sui iuris*, which implied that his property and all the persons under his *patria potestas* (his children, grandchildren, etc.) passed with him under the *patria potestas* of his adoptive father. *Adrogatio* meant putting an end to an existing family and its *sacra* and was thus originally supervised by the pontiffs in the assembly

299. Badel 2012.
300. Badel 2012, 98–99, 101.
301. Gardner 1999, 63.

of the *comitia curiata*, which would issue a *lex curiata* to ratify this decision; after the first century CE, it was accomplished by imperial rescript. *Adoptio*, on the other hand, occurred in two stages: first the *mancipatio*, to put an end to the *postestas* of the biological father, in the presence of the adoptee, the natural and the adoptive fathers, and witnesses; and then the adoption itself, which required the presence of a magistrate in addition to the fathers and the adoptee.[302] Two aspects of both *adrogatio* and *adoptio* are especially noteworthy for the present investigation: the adoptee lost his agnatic inheritance rights and abandoned the *sacra* of his natal family (in a case of *adrogatio*, this happened in a public renunciation known as *detestatio sacrorum*) while passing under the *patria potestas* of his adopting father, with the same inheritance rights and duties toward the family deities as a natural child.[303]

Roman law nevertheless granted the original kinship ties a certain relevance after the adoption had occurred. The adoptee took the name of his adoptive father while retaining his former *nomen* as a *cognomen*.[304] In contrast to *agnatio* (legal parenthood based on *patria potestas*), *cognatio* (natural, biological kinship) mattered for marriage: to avoid incest, the law forbade unions between an adoptee and his biological kin.[305] Moreover, he could still inherit from his biological mother (provided she left a valid will), as the connection with her was not legally cut.[306] The adoptee could even inherit a part of his biological father's patrimony (not as a son, but as a cognate).[307] Under the Severi, Ulpian ruled that for the sake of generosity, a son who remained under the *potestas* of his grandfather when his father was adopted by another *pater* should still be able to inherit from his biological father, even though they were no longer in the same *familia*.[308]

The provisions of Roman law concerning the severing of the adoptee's natural kinship ties, including the preservation of certain aspects of these ties, have analogies in rabbinic halakhah on proselytes. In theory, according to tannaitic rulings, a convert who did not beget children after conversion was

302. On adoption in Roman law and society, see, e.g., Gaius, *Inst.* 1.99–107; *Dig.* 1.7; Buckland 1975, 121–128; Moreau 1992, esp. 15–16 for the procedural details; Gardner 1998, 114–208; Gardner 1999; Kunst 2005; Lindsay 2009.

303. The distinction between *adrogatio* and *adoptio* does not really matter to understand the analogy with conversion. Taking into account the fact that conversion is supposed to be an individual's free decision, *adrogatio* appears to be a better model. However, in rabbinic sources a convert does not bring the members of his household with him "into Judaism" (as the model of *adrogatio* would imply). Even when a parent and children convert together, their kinship ties are considered severed (see m. Yevamot 11:2; t. Yevamot 12:2; m. Ketubbot 4:3; m. Shevi'it 10:9).

304. Moreau 1992, 19.

305. Humbert 2005, 19–20.

306. On women's transmission of property to their children, see Gardner 1999, 65–66.

307. Moreau 1992, 19–20; Gardner 1998, 118, 221–222.

308. *Dig.* 37.4.3.9; Gardner 1998, 191.

considered childless regardless of whether he or she had had children before conversion—but as Moshe Lavee notes, in Palestinian rabbinic sources "it seems that the actual practice was that converts did bequeath their property to their children, even if this was not considered as an inheritance according to biblical law."[309] In the Mishnah we encounter the idea that although it is not a halakhic obligation for debtors of a deceased convert to pay his sons (born before his conversion) the money owed to their father, because they are not legally his sons anymore, it is fairer and thus praiseworthy to do so (m. Shevi'it 10:9). This mishnah recalls the just-mentioned ruling by Ulpian.[310] Moreover, the notion that a convert can partly inherit from a biological parent, especially a father, despite the severing of their kinship ties, is found in m. Demai 6:10. As for matrimony, despite the abolition of the convert's natural kinship ties, Palestinian rabbinic halakhah nevertheless forbade marriage with biological parents and siblings.[311] Rabbinic texts thus display a degree of flexibility that is comparable to what we find in Roman law.

A central feature of Roman adoption was the renunciation of the *sacra* of one's original family and the adoption of those of the new family. This is clearly an important similarity between adoption and conversion, given the definition of Israel as a family: the worship of the God of Israel and the observance of his commandments (especially cultic ones) can be considered analogous to the *sacra* of the adoptive family in a Roman context. Note that Greco-Roman family and civic cults differed here: the latter were not exclusive, while the former were. As a consequence, citizenship grants did not imply a religious shift comparable to that involved in adoption: for example, Greeks from Asia Minor who received Roman citizenship on an individual basis before 212 CE were not required to abandon the deities of their city of origin; they would worship both their traditional gods and those of Rome. By contrast, in Roman family law, one could be placed under the *patria potestas* of only one man and thus attached to the *sacra* of one *familia* alone. In this regard, conversion to Judaism was closer to a case of adoption than to a citizenship grant.

Mesopotamian, Greek, and Roman notions of adoption differed in certain respects, and some of these differences are relevant to understanding the analogy between Roman adoption and conversion in y. Bikkurim. In contrast to classical Athens, in Rome a man who already had a son (or several sons) could nevertheless adopt.[312] The idea that Abraham, who was the father of several

---

309. Lavee 2017, 162.

310. In m. Shevi'it 10:9, the sons are said to have converted too, but the fact that they were born prior to their father's conversion invalidates the kinship ties (see n. 303 above and Wilfand 2021).

311. See the discussion in y. Yevamot 11:2, 12a; cf. b. Yevamot 98a–b; Lavee 2017, 163–164.

312. See Demosthenes 46.14–15; Gardner 1999, 64; Walters 2003, 46; Vélissaropoulos-Karakostas 2005.

sons (Ishmael, Isaac, and the ones he had with Keturah [Gen 25:1–2]), could also be the adoptive father of additional children (converts) was compatible with Roman but not Athenian practice.

A comparison between Roman and Mesopotamian evidence is also illuminating. Mesopotamian sources indicate that adoption could be ended relatively easily: the adopted person (generally a child) could be sent away or, conversely, could decide to leave the adoptive father (in both cases, with a compensatory payment).[313] In Roman law, the legal link created by adoption was much more difficult to sever. The adoptee had no possibility of escaping from the *potestas* of his or her adoptive father, to cease being considered his son or daughter. Conversely, the *pater* could emancipate his adoptive offspring (freeing the adoptee from his *potestas* but not annulling the filiation or all the inheritance rights) or, more radically, give him or her in adoption to someone else (but this would have been rare). The first aspect is relevant to the analogy between conversion and adoption. As previously mentioned, once converted, the *ger* cannot revert to the status of *goy*—at worst he or she can only be a bad Jew, or, quoting the Tosefta, *ke-Israel meshummad* (renegade/apostate). Hence, converts cannot leave the people of Israel.[314] This aspect of conversion is similar to the status of a Roman adoptee, who could not put an end to his or her membership in the new *familia*, even had he or she wished too, but could of course behave badly, as an unworthy son or daughter, and bring shame on the adoptive family.

Another original feature of Roman adoption, absent from Mesopotamian and Greek practice and worth exploring in light of the analogy with conversion in y. Bikkurim, is its creative use to modify the shape of the family. For example, a man with a son and a grandson by that son might emancipate the grandson and adopt him as a son alongside his father (Ulpian, *Dig.* 37.8.31.9). Conversely, through adoption a man could give a son to his son who was still under his *patria potestas*. He could also emancipate a grandson born to one of his sons and then give him as son to another son of his (*Dig.* 1.7.15.1). Or he could emancipate his son and then adopt him as a grandson, placing the latter alongside his own children (Ulpian, *Dig.* 38.6.1.7).[315] The possibilities for reshaping the family and inheritance rights were thus considerable. In theory, the analogy between conversion and adoption in a Roman context might lead one to imagine Abraham adopting converts and giving them as children to Isaac, or even to Jacob (had Abraham lived long enough).

Admittedly, it would have been quite impossible for Abraham to adopt converts who lived centuries after his death. In the Yerushalmi's construction, the reasoning is thoroughly nominalist and the fiction is twofold. The first

---

313. Yaron 1965, 179; Prévost 1967, 73; Bord 1997, 181–182, 189; Paul 2005b, 114–115.
314. Sagi and Zohar 2007, 269.
315. Gardner 1998, 190–199, esp. 195, 198.

fiction consists in the conferring of a new lineage on a person who was born with different ancestors, as in any case of adoption. The second fiction consists in proceeding as if Abraham were still alive.

There is no equivalent to this situation in Roman law, but some cases among the Roman elite raise the issue of the validity of testamentary adoption and indicate that some adoptions were organized posthumously, after the death of the adoptive father, despite the illegality of the procedure. The first example that comes to mind is obviously that of Octavian, who discovered that he had been chosen as Julius Caesar's heir only after the latter's death. This seems to have been a testamentary adoption, implying that Octavian would only receive part of Caesar's patrimony and take his name. It did not mean that he would join Caesar's *gens*, that he would receive a new filiation or lineage.[316] However, Octavian, who understood the political benefits that he could gain from a direct filiation with Caesar, seems to have organized a kind of postmortem *adrogatio*, which resulted in the publication of a *lex curiata* registering a change of filiation for him. Although this proceeding was highly unusual, he could from then on be called *divi Iulii filius*, "son of the deified Julius."[317]

Even more problematic was Hadrian's situation, since Trajan left no official will and was said to have adopted Hadrian orally on his deathbed in a military camp, in front of a few witnesses. Some doubted the veracity of this event, but in the end Hadrian was recognized as Trajan's legitimate successor, with all the titles gained through adoption, as illustrated, for example, by the dedication on the Arch of Hadrian in Gerasa: "For the salvation of the Emperor Caesar, son of the god Trajan Parthicus, grandson of the god Nerva, Trajan Hadrian Augustus [. . .]."[318]

The most interesting example, however, is that of Septimius Severus, who, after defeating his rival Clodius Albius, presented himself in an address to the Senate in 197 CE as the son of the emperor Marcus Aurelius and the brother of Aurelius' natural son, the emperor Commodus.[319] As John Richardson aptly notes,

> Aurelius had been dead for seventeen years, and certainly had had no intention of adopting the then somewhat obscure senator from the province of Africa. At one level, Severus' assertion was simply absurd, and recognised as such at the time. A notorious wit of the period,

316. Corbier 2007, 78.

317. Prévost 1949, 29–34; Richardson 1995, 127, which speaks of a "doubly fictive form of testamentary adoption" in this case; Lindsay 2009, 182–189; Hekster 2015, 162.

318. Welles 1938, 401–402, no. 58; Prévost 1949, 50–52. See also Aitor Blanco Pérez, "The Inscription of the Arch of Hadrian in Gerasa," http://www.judaism-and-rome.org /inscription-arch-hadrian-gerasa.

319. See the detailed analysis of this episode in Hekster 2015, 205–221.

Pollienus Auspex, is recorded as saying to the emperor, "I congratulate you, Caesar, on finding a father". On another level, it is a sign of the continuing significance of a completely artificial conception of a family tie: artificial not only in that Severus was not the son of Marcus Aurelius, which is the fiction common to all adoptions; nor that he could not be transferred into the *patria potestas* of a dead man, which was the further fiction implicit in testamentary *adrogatio*, but that he could claim to be the son of a man who had not indicated in any way, either in the face of the *comitia curiata*, or in a will or even in his last words, uttered in a military camp, that he wished to make Severus his son. Although there is no evidence what form of procedure, if any, Severus employed in order to establish his claim, the matter is, in such a case, of no significance.[320]

These situations provide a general context in which to interpret the claim made in y. Bikkurim. It seems that the details of the procedure through which converts became the adopted children of Abraham did not matter much in the eyes of the rabbis, since the claim that *gerim* were descendants of the patriarch was first and foremost a conceptual-legal construction.

Obviously, there are numerous differences between the social phenomenon of adoption in Roman society and conversion to Judaism. *Gerim* were not adopted into Jewish families (which would have been another way, in theory, to solve the lineage problem of converts). More generally, the rabbis did not introduce adoption into Jewish law and in that respect remained faithful to the biblical legal tradition. Nevertheless, some of them found in the legal fiction of adoption a useful intellectual tool—that is, a useful analogy—for conceptualizing the integration of converts into the people of Israel as far as inheritance rights were concerned. It also enabled converts to blend more thoroughly into the congregation at public prayers.

That the notion of adoption behind y. Bikkurim 1:4 stems from the Roman context in which this rabbinic tradition developed is corroborated by a comparison with rabbinic Babylonian texts, in which such a notion does not surface at all. The Babylonian Talmud lacks a Bikkurim tractate, but in b. Makkot 19a, Rav Ashi reiterates the anonymous ruling of the Mishnah that a convert brings the firstfruits but does not recite. The Bavli thus completely disregards the teaching attributed to R. Yehudah in the Jerusalem Talmud. More generally and fundamentally, the Bavli "does not formulate an alternative paternity."[321] Analysis of the Bavli's discourse of converts as "newborn children," which insists on the severing of kinship ties in a way that might at first look similar to what we find in Palestinian sources, in fact reveals a

---

320. Richardson 1995, 129–130, referring to Cassius Dio, *Rom. Hist.* 75.7.5, 76.9.4.
321. Lavee 2017, 218.

remarkable difference from the position attributed to R. Yehudah. Here Moshe Lavee's in-depth study of conversion in the Babylonian Talmud is of invaluable help:

> Newborn imagery in the Bavli is [. . .] embedded within a genealogical context. The phrase "A convert is like a newborn infant" proclaims the severing of kinship. While converts are separated outright from their family, however, they are not absorbed into the "family of Israel". [. . .] The newborn image thus becomes a marker, if not an accelerator, of legal distinctions between converts and Israelites. In fact, it sharpens the legal reality of a convert not being "an Israelite in every respect".[322]

This is exactly the opposite of what is achieved in y. Bikkurim 1:4, 64a, which makes the first-generation convert equal to a native Israelite (at least concerning the inheritance of the Land and prayers in private and public contexts). Even though the Palestinian rabbis were concerned about lineage and did not dismiss it in favor of a purely egalitarian ethos or a hierarchy based solely on Torah learning, they nevertheless tended to promote an open conception of Israel as family, which contrasts with Babylonian constructions of Jewish identity that emphasize the purity of Israelite lineage and the inferiority of converts.[323]

To further corroborate my claim that it is the Roman notion and practice of adoption that lie in the background of y. Bikkurim 1:4, 64a, I will now look at how the notion of adoption is used (if at all) in Jewish sources from before the Roman period and in pre-rabbinic works produced in the Roman context.

3.2 ADOPTION IN PRE-RABBINIC JEWISH TEXTS

Adoption does not exist in biblical or classical Jewish law.[324] Its absence from the biblical legal corpus is all the more conspicuous as legal codes and documents from the ancient Near East, such as the Code of Hammurabi, the adoption contracts from Old Babylonian Nippur, and the Nuzi tablets, attest

---

322. Lavee 2017, 217. On converts as newborn infants, see, e.g., b. Yevamot 22a, 62a, 97b. On the importance of lineage in Babylonian rabbinic sources, see, e.g., Gafni 1990, 121–122, 147; Gafni 1997, 54; Kalmin 1999, 51–60; Levinson 2000, 347; Hayes 2002a, 176–178, 191; Rubenstein 2003, 80–101; Oppenheimer 2009; Lavee 2017, Chapter 12; Koren 2018 (which questions "the accepted distinction between the Palestinian and Babylonian Amoraic discussions of genealogy" and proposes a more refined analysis, based on the different terminology in Palestinian and Babylonian sources [418]).

323. Lavee 2017, 84–101, 220–224, provides a few examples of derogatory Babylonian views of converts.

324. See, e.g., Lyall 1969; Lavee 2003, 278; Yarden 2012. For a modern perspective on this issue, see Gold 1987.

the widespread use of adoption in these societies.[325] Although biblical laws include several prescriptions meant to protect orphans, they do not consider the possibility that a child—let alone an adult—may receive a new filiation.[326] Scholars have tried to explain this phenomenon either by pointing to the high number of children in ancient Israelite families, which would have made adoption useless from the father's perspective, or to the institution of the levirate, which was a way to provide a deceased man with a succession by marrying his widow to one of his brothers, but such suggestions are not convincing.[327] It might be argued that the emphasis laid on birth and lineage in ancient Israel, and their importance in determining people's status, made adoption problematic and led to its omission from biblical (and later rabbinic) law.[328]

However, while Mesopotamian rulings on adoption did not influence biblical law, they seem to have left a mark on some biblical narratives. The story of Moses' adoption by Pharaoh's daughter in Exodus is well known, but it is there described as an Egyptian practice. Jacob's choice to promote Joseph's children, Ephraim and Manasseh—Jacob's grandsons—to the rank of direct sons, alongside his natural children (Gen 48:3–12), is not strictly speaking an adoption but rather a reordering of the degrees of kinship, with the aim of granting a share of the Promised Land to the tribes of Ephraim and Manasseh, together with the tribes of Judah, Benjamin, and Jacob's other sons. (Interestingly enough, from a functional perspective this is comparable to some Roman uses of adoption, as mentioned above.) Esther is an ambiguous case as well: the Masoretic text presents her as the daughter of Mordecai's uncle and states that she was an orphan; her cousin "took her [to be] a daughter (*bat*) for him" (Esth 2:7). According to Shalom Paul, the Hebrew phrase in Esther 2:7 is similar to Akkadian formulas used in the context of adoption, but ancient Jewish interpreters understood the verse in various ways.[329] The LXX also describes Esther as the daughter of Mordecai's uncle and calls her a *pais threptē*, a child raised by foster parents, but the Greek text further states that Mordecai took her to himself as a *gunē* (woman or wife), which seems to depart from the meaning of the Hebrew word *bat* (the translator may have read *bayt*, "house," and understood it as a reference to a wife, as in b. Megillah

---

325. Yaron 1965; Prévost 1967; Lyall 1984, 77–78 (Nuzi); Stone and Owen 1991 (Nippur); Bord 1997; Paul 2005b.

326. On care for orphans in the Bible, see, e.g., Exod 22:22; Deut 14:29, 16:11, 16:14, 24:19–21. For later Jewish practice, see, e.g., P. Yadin 12 (125 CE); m. Pesahim 8:1; m. Gittin 5:4 (which uses the term *epitropos* to designate a guardian of orphans); and the epitaph of "the foster-mother Helene, a Jewess (*Ioudaia*) who loved the orphans," from the second to the fourth century CE (Blumell 2016; trans. Van der Horst 2017, 265).

327. Feigin 1931, esp. 192–194; Prévost 1967; Bord 1997, 191–193.

328. See Lyall 1969, 459–460. *Pace* Feigin 1931, who thought adoption was practiced in ancient Israel.

329. Paul 2005b, 116–117; see also Bord 1997, 179.

13a later on).[330] Josephus has yet another version of the story, since he refers to Mordecai as Esther's uncle and simply says that Mordecai loved her as if she were his daughter (*A.J.* 11.204). By contrast, the late midrash Genesis Rabbah (30:8) gives a vivid picture of Mordecai as an adoptive father, describing him as miraculously breastfeeding baby Esther because he could not find a wet nurse.[331]

What is clearly present in the Bible, however, is the notion of the king as God's son and the people of Israel as God's children.[332] Paul argues that this "father-son imagery can [. . .] be traced back to the nomenclature of adoption."[333] He adds that the promise expressed in 2 Samuel 7:14, "I will be a father to him [David's descendant], and he shall be a son to me," "is generally acknowledged to be an adoption formula, which serves to provide the legal basis for the grant of eternal dynasty to the Davidic line." Similarly, "on a national level, these metaphors are employed to express the bond which exists between God and Israel," and "as a father bequeaths his inheritance to his son (as above, eternal dynasty and gift of nations to the Davidic king), so God allots and validates his gift of the land of Israel to His 'sons,' the children of Israel," as Jeremiah 3:19 clearly articulates: "I thought how I would set you among my children, and give you a pleasant land, the most beautiful inheritance of all the nations. And I thought you would call me 'my Father,' and would not turn from following me."[334] The God of Israel (unlike pagan deities and human beings) does not beget children but establishes a filial relationship with Israel through the covenant, which has legal aspects. There is indeed an analogy with adoption. The fact that the discourse of inheritance is an integral part of the covenant corroborates this conclusion (as noted above, adoptions always involve inheritance issues).[335]

Beyond the biblical evidence, some Jewish inscriptions mention *threptoi* and *alumni*, some of whom might have been adopted children, in which case we would have evidence for the practice of adoption at least in the diaspora (especially in Rome in the third and fourth centuries CE).[336] Most epigraphic testimonies are ambiguous, however, as these words generally refer to foster

330. Walfish 2002, 307; Yarden 2012, 277.

331. Bregman 2017.

332. 2 Sam 7:14; 1 Chr 17:13, 22:10; Ps 2:7–8; Exod 4:22; Deut 14:1, 32:18–20; Jer 3:19, 31:9.

333. Paul 2005b, 112. See also Melnyk 1993; Bord 1997, 194.

334. Paul 2005b, 113.

335. As noted by Bord 1997, 194.

336. See *CIJ* I, nos. 3 (*threptos*), 21 (*threptē* [Irene, see supra]), 144 (*threptos*), 358 (which mentions a foster father, *tropheus*) (=*JIWE* II, nos. 531, 489, 246, 25); *CIIP* I, no. 363 (unclear); Leon 1960, 232–233. The reading in *JIWE* II, no. 360, is very uncertain. An epitaph from Leontopolis in Egypt (*JIGRE*, no. 34, uncertain dating) addresses a certain Dositheus with the phrase "You are my child, for I departed childless," thereby indicating that Dositheus was the foster child of the deceased, yet the word *threptos* is not used.

children, who may have been freeborn orphans, slaves, or freed slaves.[337] The word *threptos* may also have designated slaves who were born in the house of their master but were not considered foster children, or it might simply have applied to domestic slaves.[338] Some papyri refer to cases of adoption, but none of them can be shown to involve a Jewish family.[339]

Both the epigraphic evidence that we have for the practice of adoption by Jews and explicit Jewish literary references to adoption date mainly from the first century CE onward—that is, none can be shown to predate the Roman period. Two first-century Jewish authors in particular provide an illuminating background to y. Bikkurim 1:4, 64a: Philo and Paul.

As we saw above, in *On the Special Laws* Philo exhorts native Israelites to offer new cities, new friendships, and new kinships to proselytes, to make them feel as if they were natives (*Spec.* 1.51–52). For Philo, the citizenship, friendship, and kinship that unite Israelites and proselytes are based on their common worship of the one true God. In other words, the kinship between Israelites and proselytes is spiritual. Elsewhere in his work, Philo states that the true kinship ties between native Israelites are also spiritual—that is, grounded in shared piety and the observance of the commandments.[340] Logically enough, he harshly condemns apostate Jews and affirms that natural family ties with them must be set aside if these conflict with the duties of piety. From Philo's perspective, in certain cases descent must therefore be dismissed as unimportant, because the true bond between Jews is piety and not blood.[341]

Now, for Philo, the fact that Abraham was the first to leave his homeland and family to take refuge in God and become his worshipper implies that the patriarch is a model for proselytes, an idea with parallels in rabbinic literature.[342] Moreover, in *On the Virtues* 218, Philo writes that Abraham left

337. On *threptoi*, see Cameron 1939 (for examples of *threptoi* as freedmen or slaves, 42–43). On *alumni* (who were generally young children), see Nielsen 1987; Moreau 1992, 14; Kunst 2005, 257–265. On fosterage and adoption, see Corbier 1999.

338. The term *threptos* is used in nearly all the Jewish inscriptions related to manumission from the Bosporus kingdom. See, e.g., *IJO* I, no. BS5 (the manumission of a home-bred slave called Heraclas, in 81 CE); *IJO* I, 272–273; Gibson 1999, 104–105. See also the inscription praising "Severos the *threptos* of the most illustrious patriarchs" in the synagogue at Hammat Tiberias (trans. Price and Misgav 2006, 478; Naveh 1978, no. 26), which could refer to a slave born in the house of the patriarchs or to a freedman.

339. See Corley 2004, 110–114. The only exception may be a Jewish papyrus from Elephantine, which seems to refer to the adoption of a manumitted slave, yet this may reflect non-Jewish customs in Egypt rather than a traditional Jewish practice (Yaron 1961, 40).

340. See, e.g., *QE* 2.36; *Virt.* 179. On the different types of kinship in Philo's work, see Berthelot 2004, 140–148, 192–199.

341. See *Mos.* 2.171; *Spec.* 1.317, 3.126, 3.155; *Virt.* 195; Berthelot 2004, 144–146; Carlier 2008, 307.

342. See Gen 12:1; *Abr.* 67; *Virt.* 214, 219; Borgen 1997, 220–223; Wilson 2011, 409–410. According to Mekhilta de-Rabbi Ishmael, Neziqin 18 (ed. Horovitz and Rabin, 312), God gave Abraham the commandment of circumcision when he was old to teach that it is

because he was looking for kinship (*syngeneia*) with God, which he clearly obtained. This suggests that proselytes, who follow Abraham's example, also receive kinship with God. A passage in *On the Preliminary Studies* (*Congr.* 177) states that this is true of virtuous men in general, and *On the Confusion of Tongues* 144–145 asserts that those who know the one true God and Creator are appropriately called "sons of God" (*huioi theou*) (based on Deut 14:1).[343] In Philo's eyes then, proselytes, who have abandoned their ancestral gods to worship the God of Israel, clearly qualify to be named children of God (which is one of the definitions of Israel in the Bible, as we saw above).

Moreover, Philo describes Abraham as the *adopted* son of God at least once, in relation to Genesis 18:17, where God says to himself: "Shall I hide from Abraham what I am about to do?" (Masoretic text). In the Septuagint, this question becomes "Shall I hide from Abraham, my *pais*, what I am about to do?" The word *pais* means both "child" (son or daughter) and "young servant." Since Abraham is already a mature man in Genesis 18, *pais* in this case probably means "son," which is the foundation for Philo's presentation of Abraham as God's adopted son. Philo quotes the Septuagint version of Genesis 18:17 in his *Allegorical Interpretation* (*Leg.* 3.27). In *On Sobriety* 56, however, he gives a slightly modified form of the verse:

> For wisdom is rather God's friend than His servant. And therefore He says plainly of Abraham, "Shall I hide anything from Abraham my friend (*philos*)?" (Gen 18:17). But he who has this portion has passed beyond the bounds of human happiness. He alone is nobly born, for he has registered God as his father (*patēr*) and become by adoption His only son (*gegonōs eispoiētos autō monos huios*).[344]

Philo substitutes "friend" (*philos*) for "son" (*pais*) in the biblical verse, because *pais* could be understood as "servant" and in this text he wants to emphasize that God is not a master of the wise human being (embodied by Abraham) but rather a friend. However, Philo keeps the Septuagint version in mind. His comment that Abraham has become the adopted son (*eispoiētos huios*) of God relies on the reading of *pais* with the meaning of "son."

Philo was familiar with the notion of adoption, as his references to adoptions in a Roman imperial context reveal.[345] He never uses the words *huiothesia* or *teknothesia* (lit.: the adoption of a son/of a child) but instead employs *eispoieō* (to give in adoption), *huion poieō* (lit.: to make a son), *thesis* (placing),

---

possible for a man to convert at any stage in life. See also Genesis Rabbah 39:3 (ed. Theodor and Albeck, 367); Lavee 2010, 213.

343. See also *Spec.* 1.318, where Philo again quotes Deut 14:1; Sandmel 1971, 178–179, n. 348.

344. Philo, *Sobr.* 56, trans. F. H. Colson and G. H. Whitaker, LCL, 472. On this text, see Scott 1992, 88–96.

345. See *Flacc.* 9; *Legat.* 23.

and various forms of the verb *tithēmi*.[346] Philo occasionally uses this vocabulary when discussing certain biblical passages. He thus refers to Moses' adoption by Pharaoh's daughter with the words *huion poieō* (*Mos.* 1.19) and *eispoieō* (1.32–33) and describes Moses' adoptive family as *themenoi* (1.149).[347] In *On Abraham* 250, Sarah tells Abraham that the children he will have with Hagar will be hers too, by adoption (*thesis*). When discussing proselytes, however, Philo never uses the vocabulary of adoption and never describes them as adopted children of God or Abraham. While the idea that proselytes become adopted children of God, as Abraham did, may be implicit in his work, the notion that they are to be seen as Abraham's descendants in the more literal sense is conspicuously absent. Philo speaks of spiritual kinship ties between proselytes and native Israelites, but nowhere of a new lineage.[348]

I believe that this distinction is significant and has a twofold explanation. First, the main metaphor with which Philo reflects on Israel is the civic metaphor, and there is no need to assign a new lineage to those who have become new citizens. Second, insofar as spiritual kinship is superior to natural kinship in Philo's eyes, proselytes' ethnic origins simply become irrelevant in view of these higher ties that conversion creates between them and Israel. Although Philo did not necessarily consider birth and ancestry unimportant, the non-Israelite lineage of proselytes was not an issue for him.[349]

Paul's statements about gentiles who turn to God (through Christ, in this case) share some characteristics with Philo's thought. In particular, Paul too describes the relationship between God and gentile believers with kinship language.[350] In contrast to Philo, however, he does not merely formulate the idea that non-Jews who turn to God become his children; Paul explicitly describes this filiation as a case of adoption, using the term *huiothesia*, which is not found in the Septuagint or in Jewish literature in the Greek language prior to Paul's writings.[351] Numerous scholars have written about "the metaphor of adoption" in Paul, but the term *metaphor* may not be fully appropriate, because from Paul's perspective this is not merely a way of speaking by analogy: the phenomenon he describes is real and has

346. There are numerous parallels in non-Jewish sources; see Scott 1992, 13–57; on the papyrological evidence, see Corley 2004, 110–117.

347. Cf. Josephus, *A.J.* 2.232–237, which uses the word *eispoiēsis* (§237) and describes Moses as Pharaoh's heir.

348. Analysis of Josephus' work leads to the same conclusion for him. In *C. Ap.* 2.210 he speaks of kinship (*oikeiotēs*) between converts and native Jews, based on common laws and a common way of life, but he never refers to proselytes as children of God or Abraham.

349. Noteworthy in this respect is the declaration he attributes to Sarah, speaking of her servant Hagar, that although the latter was an Egyptian by birth or lineage (*genos*), she had become a Hebrew by choice (*hairesis*) (*Abr.* 251).

350. See, e.g., 2 Cor 6:18; Gal 4:5–7; Rom 8:15–16; see also Johnson Hodge 2007.

351. The most detailed study remains Scott 1992.

effective implications.[352] In Galatians 4:5–7, he asserts that God has sent his Son

> so that we might receive adoption (*huiothesia*) as children. And because you are children, God has sent the Spirit of his Son into our hearts, crying, "Abba! Father!" So you are no longer a slave but a child (*huios*), and if a child then also an heir (*klēronomos*), through God.

Similarly, Paul writes in Romans 8:15: "For you did not receive a spirit of slavery to fall back into fear, but you have received a spirit of adoption (*pneuma huiothesias*), when we cry, 'Abba! Father!'" The audiences of these two epistles are different—gentile believers who were tempted to judaize in Galatians, versus Jewish believers (or a mixed crowd) in Romans—but in both cases Paul states that gentile believers are adopted by God and thus become his "sons" (*huioi*)[353] through the gift of God's spirit, which in Galatians is specifically Christ's spirit.[354] Note that in accordance with biblical tradition, Paul describes Israel too as God's adopted child, as in Romans 9:4, which states that to the Israelites belong "the adoption (*huiothesia*), the glory, the covenants, the giving of the law, the worship, and the promises." Contrary to gentiles, Israel does not depend on Christ for adoption—i.e., for their status as God's children.[355] Here Paul simply builds upon the biblical notion of the people of Israel as God's (adopted) child or children.[356] As many scholars have emphasized, the idea and the terminology of adoption in Paul's letters derive from both biblical tradition and Paul's Roman context.[357] The fact that he uses

352. See, e.g., Lyall 1969, 466; Walters 2003, 55; Corley 2004; Burke 2006; Johnson Hodge 2007, 69; Burke 2008 (although at p. 266 he notes that "perhaps more than a metaphor is involved here"); Peppard 2011, 135. Filtvedt 2016 argues that Paul used ethnic terminology in a metaphorical way, but redefines *metaphor*, emphasizing that "use of metaphorical language does not suggest a departure from reality; it is rather a way of using language to describe, interpret and discover the nature of reality, as this reality is experienced by specific people" (108). My argument in the following pages rests on the more common understanding of a metaphor as a figure of speech that is partly disconnected from reality and is devoid of concrete implications.

353. On the gendered dimension of the notion of adoption in Paul, see Corley 2004; Johnson Hodge 2007, 69–70.

354. On the differences between the two epistles' audiences and perspectives, see Chance 1993. On gentile believers as "pneumatic adoptees," see Fredriksen 2006, 237; Johnson Hodge 2007, 72–76; Fredriksen 2018, 206–209. On the role of the pneuma, see further Thiessen 2016, 105–160.

355. Fredriksen 2018, 208.

356. See, e.g., Exod 4:22; Jer 31:9; see also Byrne 1979; Scott 1992; Jewett 2007, 561–563.

357. Lyall 1969; Lyall 1984, 95–99; Corley 2004, 108–109; Fredriksen 2006, 237; Burke 2006, esp. 264, n. 18, and 266; Kim 2014; Fredriksen 2017, 148; Fredriksen 2018, esp. 206. Walters 2003, 55, instead sees adoption as a Greco-Roman notion, as does Peppard 2011, 135–137, even though he notes several parallels between Paul's writings and Roman

the notion of adoption most extensively in the epistle written to the believers who were in Rome is a further indication of its Roman cultural relevance.[358]

The role that adoption plays in Paul's epistles does not end with divine adoption through Christ, however. In both Galatians 3 and Romans 4, he states that through their faith, gentile believers have become Abraham's descendants (lit.: seed, *sperma*) and can thus be considered adopted children of this ancestor of Israel (even though neither *huiothesia* nor any other phrase related to adoption terminology is employed in these chapters).[359] For Paul (especially in Romans), the children of Abraham are defined not by lineage alone but also by *pistis* (*emunah*)—that is, trust in the messiah; as a consequence, both Jews and non-Jews may be considered children and heirs of Abraham. Like y. Bikkurim 1:4, 64a, Romans 4:17 uses Genesis 17:5 as its biblical proof text: "No longer shall your name be Abram, but your name shall be Abraham, for I have made you the father of a multitude of nations/gentiles (*patera pollōn ethnōn*)."[360] For Paul as for the redactors of y. Bikkurim 1:4, 64a, the main problem that needed to be solved was the identity of those who could be included among Abraham's legitimate heirs—that is, those able to inherit God's blessings and promises to Abraham, including the inheritance of the Land of Canaan and even, according to some Jewish traditions, the whole world; note that Paul refers to the (eschatological?) inheritance of the world (*kosmos*) in Romans 4:13.[361] From a Jewish perspective, not all of Abraham's biological descendants were supposed to inherit God's promises: Ishmael and the children of Keturah were his natural sons, yet they had no share in Israel's inheritance (nor did Esau). In Genesis 21:12, God promises Abraham that "it is through Isaac that offspring shall be named for you."[362] In Romans 9:6–8, Paul echoes the view that not all of Abraham's genealogical descendants were God's promised posterity. In a rather original way, both he and the rabbis responsible for the tradition found in y. Bikkurim 1:4, 64a, asserted that beyond the genealogical descendants of Jacob/Israel, Abraham

---

practice. Johnson Hodge 2007 considers adoption "an integral part of the patrilineal cultures of the ancient Mediterranean" (68).

358. Kim 2014.

359. Johnson Hodge 2007 argues that Paul uses the ideology of patrilineal descent to "craft a new genealogy for gentile believers, one that links them to Israel through Christ" (20). Note, however, that Christ does not adopt these gentiles but is instead their brother, as the firstborn son of God. On the incorporation of gentiles into the lineage of Abraham, see also Eisenbaum 2004; Fredriksen 2010, 243–244; Levenson 2011, 46–47; Thiessen 2016, esp. 105–128; Rosen-Zvi 2017c.

360. On Paul's understanding of *ethnē* as (individual) gentiles, see, e.g., Rosen-Zvi and Ophir 2015; Rosen-Zvi 2017c, 187, n. 90. In Gal 3:8, Paul's proof text is either Gen 12:3 or 22:18 (the second is more probable).

361. Johnson Hodge 2007, 70; Forman 2011, 6, 58–101; Thiessen 2016, 157–158. Ishay Rosen-Zvi also notes the proximity of Paul and y. Bikkurim (Rosen-Zvi 2017c, 187, n. 90).

362. See also Jub. 16.17–18; Rosen-Zvi 2017c, 186.

could have other legitimate heirs as well: converts to Judaism, in the eyes of these rabbis, and gentile believers in Christ who had received the latter's spirit, according to Paul.

Paul's writings raise the question of whether the notion that converts to Judaism could be seen as children of Abraham already existed in his time.[363] Although we lack precise evidence from contemporaneous Jewish sources, there is reason to suppose that the idea was rooted in contemporary Jewish debates. It is true that the echoes of such debates appear only much later in rabbinic literature, but Paul's reasoning makes sense only if the possibility of integrating proselytes into Israel as children of Abraham was already being discussed in some circles. If converts had been unanimously considered as not related to Abraham because of their pagan ancestors, Paul would not have argued that gentile believers did not need to observe the law and undergo circumcision to become children of Abraham (after all, identifying gentile believers as God's adopted children alongside Israel was already sufficient to guarantee their status in the eschatological age).[364] Paul's argument makes sense only if there were people who claimed that only those proselytes who had committed themselves to observing all the commandments, including circumcision, could be considered children of Abraham alongside native Israelites. In other words, Paul's statement on gentile believers being children of Abraham through faith and Christ's spirit alone was almost certainly a response to his opponents, Jewish Christ followers who preached a different gospel to the gentiles, which required that converts obverse the law and undergo circumcision if they were to be considered part of Abraham's seed and entitled to inherit God's promises.[365] Both Paul and his adversaries valued lineage and filiation from Abraham, but they disagreed on the conditions governing whether non-Jews could be inserted into this filiation and become heirs alongside Israel.[366]

363. See also 1 Peter 3:5-6, which describes female believers as daughters of Sarah.

364. Paul's argument allows only an indirect reconstruction of his opponents' discourse. See, e.g., Gal 3:2-3, 4:17, 4:21, 5:10-12; Rom 4:13-17; also Barclay 1987, esp. 88; Dunn 1993, 15-17, 159; van der Lans 2010, 313-314.

365. See, e.g., Chance 1993, esp. 395-398; Fredriksen 2018, 207.

366. For Paul, the gentiles who become children of Abraham do not also become Israel—they remain distinct; see Fredriksen 2006, 238; Johnson Hodge 2007, 77; Fredriksen 2010, 243-244; Hayes 2015, 150; Thiessen 2016, 162-163. For a dissenting voice, see Rosen-Zvi 2017c, 186, which argues that Paul's view is supersessionist. That Paul took lineage seriously (even though his new identity as an apostle of Christ was probably the most important component of his self-definition) is shown by some of his declarations about his own pedigree. In Philippians 3:5, he emphasizes that he was "circumcised on the eighth day, (is) a member of the people of Israel, of the tribe of Benjamin, a Hebrew born of Hebrews," which means that he is not a convert but a native Jew. This insistence on his Israelite lineage may be compared to the pride with which the Paul of the Book of Acts claims to be a Roman by birth, in contrast to those who acquired this citizenship at some later point in their life (Acts 22:28).

The description of gentile believers as God's adopted children is at least in part based on the biblical notion of Israel as God's child and has a parallel in Philo's depiction of Abraham as God's adopted son. In contrast, the notion that they are Abraham's children and share his inheritance with native Israelites in spite of their foreign origins and improper genealogical background has no biblical precedent and should instead be understood as inspired by the Roman practice of adoption in the cases of both Paul and his opponents. Finally, if it is correct to consider that this idea was not Paul's invention but was in fact already being debated in some Jewish circles in his time, this implies that the idea existed from at least the first century CE, long before the composition of the Jerusalem Talmud.

The view of converts that y. Bikkurim 1:4, 64a attributes to R. Yehudah is quite exceptional in the rabbinic corpus, and it might well have remained marginal in Jewish thought. It is not found in the Babylonian Talmud, which has been much more influential than the Jerusalem Talmud in Jewish history, and that absence could have proved fatal to it. In modern Judaism, however, the notion that converts are to be seen as children of Abraham is common.[367] As Ophir Yarden notes, one of the reasons for the surprising popularity of this idea is probably the influence of Maimonides' rulings.[368] In his letter to Obadiah the convert, who was wondering whether he was allowed to recite the blessings mentioning "our fathers," Maimonides wrote:

> Abraham our Father, peace be with him, is the father of his pious prosperity who keeps his ways, and the father of his disciples and of all the converts who adopt Judaism. Therefore you shall pray "Our God and God of our fathers," because Abraham, peace be with him, is your father. And you shall say "You who have given to our fathers to inherit (a pleasant, good, and spacious land)," for the land has been given to Abraham.[369]

Maimonides then quotes the opinion of R. Yehudah in y. Bikkurim as the authority undergirding his statement. Similarly, in *Mishneh Torah*, Bikkurim 4:3, Maimonides asserts that the convert should bring the firstfruits offering and recite, in agreement with R. Yehudah, because Abraham is the father of all those who gather under the wings of the Shekhinah. Yarden concludes:

> The force of Maimonides' authority—and perhaps his compassion for the converts in their capacity as orphans—overcame previous objections and led to the adoption of his position throughout the Jewish world. This trend reached its pinnacle in the consenting ruling in the Shulhan Arukh.[370]

---

367. Yarden 2012, 279.

368. Yarden 2012, 281. See also Cohen 1999a, 331–336, which provides further evidence of how Jewish religious authorities widely came to accept this position.

369. Trans. Cohen 1999a, 331.

370. Yarden 2012, 281, referring to *Shulhan Arukh, Orah Hayyim* 53:19. See also Cohen 1999a, 336, which adds *Orah Hayyim* 199:4.

Paradoxically enough, an idea that was originally formulated by Jews in a Roman cultural context came to play a significant role in the life of Jewish communities, and continues to do so even to the present, in part through the influence of a medieval Jewish thinker who lived in a Muslim world where adoption in the Roman sense was nonexistent. On the other hand, the fact that adherence to Islam is disconnected from ethnic origins and lineage may have played a role in Maimonides' agreement with the position attributed to R. Yehudah in the Yerushalmi.[371]

◊═══◊

In conclusion, Jewish literary sources from the Roman period attest that the ways in which the *populus Romanus* expanded to include a growing number of people, to the point of potentially including all free individuals (since the empire claimed to be universal), impacted how some Jews thought about the people of Israel. Philo and Josephus, writing at a time when most Jews were not yet Roman citizens, integrated Roman notions of citizenship into their descriptions of the people of Israel as a civic body and emphasized the openness of the Jewish *politeia* to new citizens—an openness comparable to that of the Roman *civitas*. Their works, written in a context where Jews faced accusations of misanthropy, display a dialectic of imitation and differentiation that also has a distinct apologetic dimension.[372] In certain matters, such as the observance of ancestral laws, Philo and Josephus suggest that Jews not only do as well as the Romans but even surpass them (see Chapter Four). As far as grants of citizenship are concerned, however, they do not hint at Jewish superiority. No matter how deeply Jews in the Roman world were impacted by Roman notions of citizenship, these authors nurtured no rival project of universal citizenship.[373]

This is true of rabbinic literature as well. On the one hand, as a growing number of scholarly works show, Roman citizenship laws and social practices did have an impact on rabbinic halakhah, especially those concerning slaves, captives, and new citizens (converts, in a Jewish setting). The Roman model of peoplehood may have made it easier to think of Israel as a people that integrates new "citizens" who were not born Jews, in accordance with the Sinaitic paradigm, which defines Israel as a people united by covenant and law. Yet it

371. On Maimonides' attitude toward converts and his emphasis on belief and faith rather than descent, see Diamond 2007, Chapter 1, esp. 12–21, 28–31; Kellner 2019. In the documents from the Cairo Genizah and other medieval sources we find further evidence for proselytes' connection with Abraham; see Yagur 2017, 123–126.

372. Berthelot 2003.

373. Even though, as argued in Chapter Two, Philo and Josephus occasionally state that the Jewish people is a truly universal people, spread from one extremity of the earth to the other (not only throughout the Roman empire, but also further east), in a way that exceeds the Romans' territorial expansion.

remains difficult to prove that the general tendency of rabbinic texts to welcome converts was a response to Roman enfranchisement policies.

On the other hand, numerous rabbinic texts testify to the permanence of the ethnic or genealogical model of peoplehood and to the difficulty of fully integrating people with different ancestors. It was the importance attributed to lineage that led some Jewish circles, probably as early as the first century CE, to conceive of converts as adopted children of Abraham, who were thus able to inherit God's promises to his people together with native Jews. This idea appears only partially in tannaitic texts (t. Berakhot 1:12) but comes fully to the fore in y. Bikkurim, while remaining conspicuously absent from the Babylonian Talmud. The analogy between conversion and adoption was particularly effective for establishing the inheritance rights of proselytes in relation to the Land and the converts' ability to fully participate in Jewish liturgy. Shalom Paul notes that already in Jeremiah 3:19, the notion that God adopts Israel as his child is connected to the divine plan that they should inherit the Promised Land.[374] In y. Bikkurim, R. Yehudah's teaching is an ad hoc solution to a specific problem involving the firstfruits of the Land, which explains why references to *gerim* as adopted children of Abraham are not common even in the rest of the Jerusalem Talmud.

I have argued that the Palestinian rabbis who embraced this view of converts did so because they were exposed to the practice of adoption in Roman society—especially in the imperial house and in aristocratic families—and this legal fiction was precisely the tool they needed to conceptualize conversion as full integration into the Jewish people while yet preserving the genealogical model of peoplehood. In short, to properly understand the Palestinian rabbinic conceptualization of Israel's incorporation of foreigners, we need both the citizenship and the adoption models.

Scholars who have investigated the rabbis' exposure to Christianity have sometimes emphasized another conceptual dichotomy, that of "ethnicity" and "religion." (While "ethnicity" and the genealogical paradigm described above overlap to some extent, "religion" corresponds in part to the covenantal, or "civic," paradigm.) Some have understood the rabbis' retention of an ethnic or genealogical definition of Israel (alongside characterizations related to law observance or beliefs) as a rejection of the Christian categorization of Judaism as a religion and of Christian descriptions of the Church as a spiritual people contrasted with "carnal Israel."[375] While there is no doubt that Christian legislation (from the fourth century onward) and Christian discourses on

---

374. Paul 2005b, 118–119.

375. See Boyarin 2004a, 202–225; Boyarin 2004b, esp. 43–47; Himmelfarb 2006, 165; Schremer 2010 (whose lens is rabbinic discourse about *minut*). On "the cultivation of ethnic otherness" by the rabbis independently of polemics with Christians, see Lapin 2013 (quotation at 80).

Judaism impacted the rabbis, this chapter suggests that the encounter with the pagan Roman empire had already strongly shaped rabbinic definitions of Israel as a people. Indeed, the rabbis' multifaceted conception of Israel makes sense in relation to both the Roman civic definition of peoplehood and the Roman aristocratic discourse on ethnicity and lineage.[376]

However, while it is clear that some rabbis borrowed conceptual and legal tools from Rome to reflect on Israel as a people, they did not imitate all aspects of the Roman model, and, in contrast to the Church, they strongly resisted the universalist vision of peoplehood that came to characterize the Roman empire. This may in fact have been a position of resistance to both pagan Rome and Christendom (or at least to Christian discourses of universality).

376. Yedidah Koren has highlighted the use of the word *mishpaḥah* ("family" or "clan") in Palestinian rabbinic texts dealing with lineage issues, in contrast to the use of *yoḥasin* (genealogical records) in Babylonian sources (Koren 2018, esp. 444). I wonder whether *mishpaḥah*, which refers to an extended family of several households, is not conceptually analogous to the Roman *gens*.

Conclusion

ROME WAS NOT the first empire that the people of Israel had confronted in the course of its history. The first chapter of this book investigated how from early on, biblical traditions emerged partly as responses to imperial domination and ideology, leading to the suggestion that Jewish attitudes toward Roman imperialism were to some extent a continuation of previous trends. Moreover, as early as the Book of Isaiah or Deuteronomy, we encounter a dialectic of opposition and rejection on the one hand and imitation or mimesis on the other hand. Thus, in response to imperial claims of universal hegemony—a central motif of imperial powers—ancient authors elaborated fantasies of Israel's (or the messiah's) universal rule over the nations at the end of days. Such projections run from the writings of the prophets through apocalyptic texts and late talmudic accounts. While some cases of mimesis are in fact examples of mimicry, implying derision or subversion of the dominant model, others are instances of acculturation and, at times, even of the unintended reproduction of the dominant power's norms. A recurring feature of Israelite/Judean/Jewish attitudes toward empires is their complexity: they cannot be reduced to a dichotomous, oppositional discourse but generally reveal some degree of hybridity.

The fact that ancient empires shared certain characteristics should not obscure the very specific ways in which each imperial state ruled and conceived of its rule. While facing the Roman empire, Jews could find useful models in biblical and Second Temple traditions that had been formulated in previous imperial contexts, but the texts they produced in the Roman period also belie their awareness of specific aspects of Roman policies and ideology. When the Mishnah (Avodah Zarah 3:1) forbids Jews to profit from images or statues with a staff, a bird, or a globe, it targets not merely idolatrous practices but crucial and widespread visual symbols of Roman power. Confronted with Roman claims to universality, Josephus appropriates the Roman notion of victory and rule over "land and sea" and applies it to the dispersion of the Jewish people, suggesting that the truly universal people is Israel rather than the Romans. As for the Roman claim to bring peace and prosperity to the world, some rabbinic sources affirm that Rome's success ultimately stemmed from Israel's presence within the empire and that Rome in fact harmed itself by ill-treating the Jews. This is quite an original response in the repertoire of reactions to imperial power, which contrasts for instance with the Deuteronomist claim that victorious empires are tools in God's hands to chastise Israel (a position also found in some Jewish sources from the Roman period).

Beyond the analysis of Jewish authors' perception of specific features of Roman imperial rule and discourse, Chapter Two argued that Rome represented a unique challenge for at least some Jews because of the combined operation of two factors: (1) the Romans' self-definition as the people who had the best laws ever written and were the most pious on earth, elected by the gods to rule the world for an indefinite lapse of time and bring it peace and order—a description that comes surprisingly close to Israel's self-image, or at least to its self-ideal in the messianic era; and (2) Roman policies that led to the lasting erasure of the Jerusalem Temple and the city itself, which could be interpreted as a desire to substitute Rome for Israel as the elected people and its city, long before Rome became Christian. The incredible efforts and sacrifices that some Jews made to shake Rome's domination—both in Judea and in the diaspora—cannot be fully understood without taking this devastating challenge into consideration. Moreover, the paradoxical similarities between the self-definitions of Rome and Israel explain the surprising choice of some Jewish authors (especially in rabbinic literature) to identify Rome with Esau, Jacob/Israel's twin brother.

This identification reflects a sense of rivalry between Israel and Rome, as two peoples competing for "election" and indeed for the leading role in history. In the narrative of the Book of Genesis, the conflict between the two brothers revolves not only around birthright and the associated paternal blessing, but also power and domination. Chapters Two through Five explored various aspects of the rivalry between Israel and Esau/Rome, as perceived by Jews. Another important issue associated with the identification of Rome with Esau, already highlighted by previous scholars and further illustrated by some of the examples analyzed in this book, was the perception that Israel might be or become similar to its twin brother and enemy. Because rivalry may lead to imitation of the Other, even when meant as a form of subversion and opposition, it risked blurring the distinction between Israel and Rome.

This risk's perception is particularly acute in the texts discussing military power and values such as courage and manliness that are examined in Chapter Three. Against the scholarly trend, exemplified by Daniel Boyarin, of considering rabbinic views of masculinity and the use of force, including military activity, as opposing Roman norms and ideals, this chapter argued that Jewish sources composed in a Roman context—mainly the works of Philo and Josephus and Palestinian rabbinic literature—do not necessarily reject courage in battle and military valor as pointless or exclusively associate these with Rome (or gentiles more broadly). On the contrary, they occasionally display a sense of rivalry with Rome precisely in the realm of combat, celebrating both the bravery and the military skills of Jews.

This sense of rivalry is also clearly perceptible in Jewish discussions of law, even though the comparison with Rome is often only implicit. Some Jews perceived Roman jurisdiction and claims of superior laws as challenges and even threats to the law of Israel. It is no coincidence that Philo, Josephus, and Palestinian rabbinic literature insist with unprecedented vigor (when compared with previous Jewish texts) on the superiority and the perfection of the laws of the Torah and the recognition that these enjoy among the nations. Some rabbinic passages even explicitly feature Roman officials who praise the law of the Jews (and its rabbinic interpretation).

The Roman notion of citizenship, together with Roman and pro-Roman discourses praising Roman "generosity" in granting citizen status to both individuals and groups, represented yet another challenge for Jews. Philo and Josephus describe the integration of proselytes into the people of Israel as a grant of citizenship and a mark of Jewish benevolence quite comparable to the generosity of the Romans. In doing so they reveal an eagerness to locate the Jews vis-à-vis Greek and Roman models, and at the same time signal their sense of rivalry with Rome. In Palestinian rabbinic writings, by contrast, there is no such trend. Rabbinic discussions of the people of Israel make no attempt to compete with Rome in the generosity displayed in grants of citizenship, even though the rabbis generally welcomed converts. Neither did the rabbis compete with Rome's universalistic definition of peoplehood. The absence of a sense of rivalry with Rome in this area is probably due to the fact that the rabbis did not consider Israel a people who would ultimately coincide with humankind as a whole. (In this respect, it was the Church that competed with Rome, before the two universalisms merged in Christendom.)

Rivalry may be accompanied by mimesis, but also by opposition and rejection. These contrary phenomena can partner in the writings of a single author, sometimes even in the same text. Chapters Three through Five examined several examples of this dynamic, emphasizing the inventiveness deployed in both the adoption of Roman motifs, which were transformed or subverted, and the rejection of Roman norms, which led to the elaboration of countermodels. Whatever the nature of the reaction, the encounter with Roman standards resulted in significant changes to Jewish discourses and self-definitions.

Two particularly significant evolutions in rabbinic thought may have sources in Roman models. First, the rabbinic trend of regarding the Torah as the civil law of Israel rather than a universal law engraved in nature and open to all human beings, as was common among Hellenistic Jewish authors, is probably at least partly a consequence of the shift from a Hellenistic to a Roman context. Whereas Hellenistic Jews needed to situate themselves vis-à-vis Greek philosophy, especially discussions of the universal and unwritten character of natural/divine law, the rabbis adopted the perspective of Roman jurists in viewing the Torah as the particular law, or *ius civile*, of Israel, meant to be observed by its members only.

Second, the idea found in the Jerusalem Talmud that people who convert become adopted children of the patriarch Abraham—which probably originates in first-century CE debates about converts in Jewish communities—in all likelihood drew upon the Roman legal fiction of adoption, whose practice became particularly visible with the imperial adoptions that occurred in the Julio-Claudian and Antonine dynasties.

This book has thus argued that the pagan Roman empire had an enduring impact not only on Jewish history but also on Jewish thought, especially as far as notions of power, law, and peoplehood are concerned. In the end, however, Rome's impact proved more significant for the conception of the Torah and the integration of proselytes than for reflections on military power and the use of force, even though the encounter with Rome contributed to the development of Jewish thinking on the true nature of strength and power and raised bold questions about the silence and powerlessness of God.

Interestingly enough, these issues are still relevant in a contemporary context. The problem of God's silence and passivity in the face of Jewish suffering became more acute than ever with the Shoah, while the valorization of bravery, physical strength, and the military and the question of their relation to Torah study gained new prominence with the development of Zionism and the creation of the modern State of Israel.[1] The issue of Jewish law's universal and particular dimensions, including whether and how non-Jews may access it and practice its commandments, continues to have intellectual, legal, and sociological implications, as illustrated, for example, by the creation of the Noahide movement in the US and the Noahide Academy of Jerusalem.[2] Finally, the status of proselytes within the people of Israel and the dialectic of genealogy and adhesion to the covenant remain to this day hotly debated topics in both Israel and the diaspora.

1. See, e.g., Presner 2007.
2. See https://www.noahide-academy.com.

BIBLIOGRAPHY

Digital Resources

Non-exhaustive list of ancient sources relevant to this book that can be found on www
.judaism-and-rome.org

INSCRIPTIONS AND PAPYRI

- Caroline Barron, Dedication of Octavian's victory monument at Nicopolis (29 BCE)
  http://judaism-and-rome.org/dedication-octavian%E2%80%99s-victory
  -monument-nicopolis
- Caroline Barron, Shield of Augustus (AE 1952, 165) (26 BCE)
  http://judaism-and-rome.org/shield-augustus-ae-1952-165
- Caroline Barron, Citizenship grant to the Adauni, Tulliasses and Sunduni tribes
  (CIL V, 5050) (46 CE)
  http://www.judaism-and-rome.org/citizenship-grant-adauni-tulliasses-and
  -sunduni-tribes-cil-v-5050
- Caroline Barron, Tombstone of the Governor of Moesia (CIL XIV, 3608) (74–79 CE)
  http://judaism-and-rome.org/tombstone-governor-moesia-cil-xiv-3608
- Caroline Barron, The Temple of Peace (Rome) (75 CE)
  http://www.judaism-and-rome.org/temple-peace-rome
- Caroline Barron, The Arch of Titus in the Circus Maximus (81 CE)
  http://judaism-and-rome.org/arch-titus-circus-maximus
- Caroline Barron, Dedication for the rebuilding of the Basilica of Cyrene (AE 1974,
  672) (119 CE)
  http://judaism-and-rome.org/dedication-rebuilding-basilica-cyrene-ae-1974-672
- Caroline Barron, Dedication to Sextus Julius Severus, consular legate of Judea
  (CIL III, 2830) (135 CE to 138 CE)
  http://judaism-and-rome.org/dedication-sextus-julius-severus-consular-legate
  -judea-cil-iii-2830
- Caroline Barron, Imperial rescript from Antoninus Pius (CIL III, 411) (139 CE)
  http://judaism-and-rome.org/imperial-rescript-antoninus-pius-cil-iii-411
- Caroline Barron, Citizenship for an African headsman. The Tabula Banasitana
  (IAM II, 94) (168 CE to 177 CE)
  http://www.judaism-and-rome.org/citizenship-african-headsman-tabula
  -banasitana-iam-ii-94
- Caroline Barron, Feriale Duranum (PDura 54) (222 CE to 227 CE)
  http://www.judaism-and-rome.org/feriale-duranum-pdura-54
- Caroline Barron, Jewish dedication to Alexander Severus (CIL III, 3327) (222 CE
  to 235 CE)
  http://judaism-and-rome.org/jewish-dedication-alexander-severus-cil-iii-3327
- Caroline Barron, Philip the Arab as the 'restorer of the whole world' (CIL III, 8031)
  (248 CE)
  http://judaism-and-rome.org/philip-arab-%E2%80%98restorer-whole-world%E2%80
  %99-cil-iii-8031

- Caroline Barron, Dedication to Mars and the founders of Rome (CIL VI, 33856) (306 CE to 312 CE)
  http://judaism-and-rome.org/dedication-mars-and-founders-rome-cil-vi-33856
- Aitor Blanco Pérez, Octavian and the Roman citizenship of Seleukos of Rhosos (42 BCE to 30 BCE)
  http://judaism-and-rome.org/octavian-and-roman-citizenship-seleukos-rhosos
- Aitor Blanco Pérez, All-Ruling Rome, let your power never vanish (SEG 55.1204; I.Eph. 599) (1 CE to 256 CE)
  http://judaism-and-rome.org/all-ruling-rome-let-your-power-never-vanish-seg
  -551204-ieph-599
- Aitor Blanco Pérez, Decree of Halicarnassus celebrating the arrival of Caesar Augustus (between 2 and 14 CE)
  http://judaism-and-rome.org/decree-halicarnassus-celebrating-arrival-caesar
  -augustus
- Aitor Blanco Pérez, A Cypriot Oath of Allegiance to Tiberius (14 CE)
  http://judaism-and-rome.org/cypriot-oath-allegiance-tiberius
- Aitor Blanco Pérez, Honours for Claudius in the Stadiasmus Patarensis (46 CE)
  http://judaism-and-rome.org/honours-claudius-stadiasmus-patarensis
- Aitor Blanco Pérez, Funerary Foundation of Titus Praxias and the Eternal Rule of the Romans (85 CE)
  http://judaism-and-rome.org/funerary-foundation-titus-praxias-and-eternal-rule
  -romans
- Aitor Blanco Pérez, Donation of Claudius Tiberius Polycharmus to the synagogue of Stobi (100 CE to 350 CE)
  http://judaism-and-rome.org/donation-claudius-tiberius-polycharmus-synagogue
  -stobi
- Aitor Blanco Pérez, The Salutaris Foundation and the Roman Representations in Ephesus (104 CE)
  http://judaism-and-rome.org/salutaris-foundation-and-roman-representations
  -ephesus
- Aitor Blanco Pérez, The Inscription of the Arch of Hadrian in Gerasa (130 CE)
  http://www.judaism-and-rome.org/inscription-arch-hadrian-gerasa
- Aitor Blanco Pérez, The Temple of Zeus in Cyrene under Marcus Aurelius (172 CE to 175 CE)
  http://judaism-and-rome.org/temple-zeus-cyrene-under-marcus-aurelius
- Aitor Blanco Pérez, P.Giss. 40 and the *Constitutio Antoniniana* (212 CE)
  http://www.judaism-and-rome.org/pgiss-40-and-constitutio-antoniniana
- Aitor Blanco Pérez, Valerius Statilius Castus, Oinoanda and the arrival of imperial statues under Valerian (255–257 CE)
  http://judaism-and-rome.org/valerius-statilius-castus-oinoanda-and-arrival
  -imperial-statues-under-valerian
- Aitor Blanco Pérez, Maximinus Daia and the Christians in Lycia-Pamphylia (312 CE)
  http://judaism-and-rome.org/maximinus-daia-and-christians-lycia-pamphylia
- Aitor Blanco Pérez, The Jews, Proselytes and God-fearers of Aphrodisias (300 CE to 500 CE)
  http://www.judaism-and-rome.org/jews-proselytes-and-god-fearers-aphrodisias
- Marie Roux, Lyon Tablet (CIL XIII, 1668) (48 CE)
  http://judaism-and-rome.org/lyon-tablet-cil-xiii-1668
- Marie Roux, Imperial dedication of the Flavian amphitheatre (CIL VI, 40454a) (78 CE to 80 CE)
  http://judaism-and-rome.org/imperial-dedication-flavian-amphitheatre-cil-vi-40454a

MONUMENTS, SARCOPHAGI, AND RELIEFS

- Caroline Barron, The Temple of Peace (Rome) (75 CE)
  http://www.judaism-and-rome.org/temple-peace-rome
- Caroline Barron, Arch of Titus, Roman Forum (81–82 CE)_Reliefs
  http://judaism-and-rome.org/arch-titus-roman-forum-81-82-cereliefs
- Caroline Barron, Arch of Galerius, Thessaloniki (298–299 CE)
  http://judaism-and-rome.org/arch-galerius-thessaloniki-298-299-ce
- Samuele Rocca, Sebasteion from Aphrodisias (20–60 CE)
  http://judaism-and-rome.org/sebasteion-aphrodisias-20-60-ce
- Samuele Rocca, Arch of Titus, Roman Forum (81–82 CE)_Architecture
  http://judaism-and-rome.org/arch-titus-roman-forum-81-82-cearchitecture
- Samuele Rocca, Cancelleria reliefs (93–95 CE)
  http://judaism-and-rome.org/cancelleria%E2%80%99s-reliefs-depicting-adventus
  -vespasian-and-profectio-domitian-93-95-ce
- Samuele Rocca, Relief of the Adventus of Hadrian (125–150 CE)
  http://www.judaism-and-rome.org/
  adventus-hadrian-second-quarter-second-century-ce
- Samuele Rocca, Arch of Hadrian at Gerasa (129–130 CE)
  http://www.judaism-and-rome.org/arch-hadrian-gerasa-129-130-ce
- Samuele Rocca, Temple of Venus and Rome (135 CE)
  http://judaism-and-rome.org/temple-venus-and-roma-135-ce
- Samuele Rocca, Ludovisi Sarcophagus (255 CE)
  http://www.judaism-and-rome.org/ludovisi-sarcophagus

WALL PAINTINGS

- Marie Roux, A Painted Parody of Aeneas and Romulus as Dog-Headed Apes
  http://judaism-and-rome.org/painted-parody-aeneas-and-romulus-dog-headed-apes

NUMISMATIC ITEMS

- Kimberley Fowler and Samuele Rocca, Sestertius depicting the head of Hadrian
  and the same raising a kneeling personification of the Orbis Terrarum, or the entire
  world (119–121 CE)
  http://judaism-and-rome.org/sestertius-depicting-head-hadrian-and-same-raising
  -kneeling-personification-orbis-terrarum-or-entire
- Samuele Rocca, Nummus depicting the head of Constantine
  http://judaism-and-rome.org/nummus-depicting-head-constantine-and-two
  -captives-flanking-labarum-319-320-ce
- Marie Roux, Denarius minted by P. Cornelius Lentulus Spinther, representing the
  Genius of the Roman people seated in a curule chair and crowned by Victory (74 BCE)
  http://judaism-and-rome.org/denarius-minted-p-cornelius-lentulus-spinther
  -representing-genius-roman-people-seated-curule-chair
- Marie Roux, Aureus depicting the head of Augustus and the Clipeus Virtutis (19 BCE)
  http://judaism-and-rome.org/aureus-depicting-head-augustus-and-clipeus
  -virtutis-19-bce
- Marie Roux, Cistophorus of Domitian representing the temple of Capitoline Jupiter (82 CE)
  http://judaism-and-rome.org/cistophorus-domitian-representing-temple-capitoline
  -jupiter-82%C2%A0ce

- Marie Roux, Sestertius depicting the head of Antoninus Pius and Aeneas's flight from Troy (140–144 CE)
  http://judaism-and-rome.org/sestertius-depicting-head-antoninus-pius-and
  -aeneas%E2%80%99s-flight-troy-140-144%C2%A0ce
- Marie Roux, Antoninianus depicting Valerian, restitutor generis humani, walking and holding the globe (254–255 CE)
  http://judaism-and-rome.org/antoninianus-depicting-valerian-restitutor-generis
  -humani-walking-and-holding-globe-254-255-ce
- Marie Roux, Aurelianus depicting the head of Aurelian and a woman presenting a wreath to Aurelian restitutor orbis (274–275 CE)
  http://judaism-and-rome.org/aurelianus-depicting-head-aurelian-and-woman
  -presenting-wreath-aurelian-restitutor-orbis-274-275%C2%A0ce
- Marie Roux, Bronze depicting Diocletian and the Genius of the Roman people (mint of Antioch, 294 CE)
  http://judaism-and-rome.org/bronze-depicting-diocletian-and-genius-roman
  -people-mint-antioch-294%C2%A0ce
- Marie Roux, Bronze depicting the head of Constantius I and the Genius of the Roman people (296–297 CE)
  http://judaism-and-rome.org/bronze-depicting-head-constantius-i-and-genius
  -roman-people-296-297-ce
- Marie Roux, Bronze depicting the head of Maxentius and the emperor together with Roma (307 CE)
  http://judaism-and-rome.org/bronze-depicting-head-maxentius-and-emperor
  -together-roma-307-ce

LITERARY SOURCES

- Katell Berthelot, Philo, On Abraham 209–216
  http://www.judaism-and-rome.org/philo-abraham-209-216
- Katell Berthelot, Philo, On the Life of Moses II.17–25
  http://www.judaism-and-rome.org/philo-life-moses-ii12-17-24
- Katell Berthelot, Philo, On the Special Laws I.51–53
  http://www.judaism-and-rome.org/philo-special-laws-i51-53
- Katell Berthelot, Philo, On Virtues 105–108
  http://www.judaism-and-rome.org/philo-virtues-105-108
- Katell Berthelot, On the Embassy to Gaius 8–10
  http://www.judaism-and-rome.org/philo-embassy-gaius-8-10
- Katell Berthelot, On the Embassy to Gaius 143–147
  http://www.judaism-and-rome.org/philo-embassy-gaius-143-147
- Katell Berthelot, On the Embassy to Gaius 153–158
  http://www.judaism-and-rome.org/philo-embassy-gaius-153-158
- Katell Berthelot, On the Embassy to Gaius 278–289
  http://www.judaism-and-rome.org/philo-embassy-gaius-278-289
- Katell Berthelot, On the Embassy to Gaius 311–313
  http://www.judaism-and-rome.org/philo-embassy-gaius-311–313
- Kimberley Fowler, Virgil, Aeneid I.257–296
  http://www.judaism-and-rome.org/virgil-aeneid-i257-296
- Kimberley Fowler, Virgil, Aeneid VI.756–853
  http://www.judaism-and-rome.org/virgil-aeneid-vi756-853
- Kimberley Fowler, Horace, Odes IV.5.1–40
  http://judaism-and-rome.org/horace-odes-iv51-40

- Kimberley Fowler, Horace, Carmen Saeculare 1–75
  http://judaism-and-rome.org/horace-carmen-saeculare-1-75
- Kimberley Fowler, Ovid, Fasti 3.59–78
  http://www.judaism-and-rome.org/ovid-fasti-iii59-78
- Kimberley Fowler, Tertullian, Apology XLV.2–4
  http://judaism-and-rome.org/tertullian-apology-xlv-2-4
- Kimberley Fowler, Tertullian, On Idolatry XIX
  http://judaism-and-rome.org/tertullian-idolatry-xix
- Kimberley Fowler, Tertullian, On the Military Garland XI.1–4
  http://judaism-and-rome.org/tertullian-military-garland-xi1-4
- Kimberley Fowler, Cyprian, On the Vanity of Idols V
  http://judaism-and-rome.org/cyprian-vanity-idols-v
- Kimberley Fowler, Gregory Thaumaturgus, Address of Thanksgiving to Origen I
  http://judaism-and-rome.org/gregory-thaumaturgus-address-thanksgiving-origen-i
- Kimberley Fowler, Arnobius, Against the Pagans I.5
  http://judaism-and-rome.org/arnobius-against-pagans-i5
- Kimberley Fowler, Eusebius of Caesarea, Demonstration of the Gospel VIII.1
  http://judaism-and-rome.org/eusebius-caesarea-demonstration-gospel-viii1
- Kimberley Fowler, Aphrahat, Demonstration V, On Wars XXIV
  http://www.judaism-and-rome.org/aphrahat-demonstration-v-wars-xxiv
- Kimberley Fowler, Collatio Legum Mosaicarum et Romanarum (Comparison of
  Mosaic and Roman Laws), extracts
  http://judaism-and-rome.org/collatio-legum-mosaicarum-et-romanarum
  -comparison-mosaic-and-roman-laws-extracts
- Kimberley Fowler, Chromatius of Aquileia, Sermon 32.1
  http://judaism-and-rome.org/chromatius-aquileia-sermon-321
- Kimberley Fowler, Ambrosiaster, Commentary on Romans 7.1
  http://judaism-and-rome.org/ambrosiaster-commentary-romans-71
- Kimberley Fowler, Prudentius, Against Symmachus Preface 80–89, I.1–8
  http://judaism-and-rome.org/prudentius-against-symmachus-preface-80-89-i1-8
- Kimberley Fowler, Prudentius, Against Symmachus I.455–466
  http://judaism-and-rome.org/prudentius-against-symmachus-i455-466
- Samuele Rocca and Kimberley Fowler, Aelius Aristides, The Roman Oration
  (extracts)
  http://judaism-and-rome.org/aelius-aristides-roman-oration-extracts
- Marie Roux, Livy, History of Rome, Preface 6–9
  http://www.judaism-and-rome.org/livy-history-rome-preface%C2%A06-9
- Marie Roux, Livy, History of Rome XXI.62
  http://judaism-and-rome.org/livy-history-rome%C2%A0xxi62
- Marie Roux, Tibullus, Elegies II.5.19–26
  http://www.judaism-and-rome.org/tibullus-elegies-ii519-26
- Marie Roux, Seneca, Apocolocyntosis III
  http://judaism-and-rome.org/seneca-apocolocyntosis-iii
- Marie Roux, Lucan, The Civil War VII.535–543
  http://judaism-and-rome.org/lucan-civil-war-vii535-543
- Marie Roux, Tacitus, Histories V.4–5
  http://www.judaism-and-rome.org/tacitus-histories%C2%A0v4-5
- Marie Roux, Tacitus, Annals XI.23–24
  http://judaism-and-rome.org/tacitus-annals-xi23-24
- Marie Roux, Pliny the Younger, *Panegyric of Trajan* 37
  http://judaism-and-rome.org/pliny-younger-panegyric-trajan%C2%A037

- Marie Roux, Florus, Epitome Taken from Titus Livius, Preface
  http://judaism-and-rome.org/florus-epitome-roman-history-titus-livius-preface
- Marie Roux, Cassius Dio, Roman History LXV.7.2
  http://judaism-and-rome.org/cassius-dio-roman-history%C2%Aolxv72
- Marie Roux, Cassius Dio, Roman History LXVIII.32.1-3
  http://judaism-and-rome.org/cassius-dio-roman-history%C2%Aolxviii321-3
- Marie Roux, Cassius Dio, Rom. Hist. LXIX.12-14
  http://www.judaism-and-rome.org/cassius-dio-roman-history%C2%Aolxix12-14
- Marie Roux, Ammianus Marcellinus, Res Gestae XIV.6.3-6
  http://judaism-and-rome.org/ammianus-marcellinus-res-gestae%C2%Aoxiv63-6
- Yael Wilfand, Mishnah Avodah Zarah 3:1-2
  http://www.judaism-and-rome.org/mishnah-avodah-zarah-31-2
- Yael Wilfand, Mishnah Bikkurim 1:4-5
  http://www.judaism-and-rome.org/mishnah-bikkurim-14-5
- Yael Wilfand, Mishnah Eruvin 1:10
  http://www.judaism-and-rome.org/mishnah-eruvin-110
- Yael Wilfand, Mishnah Gittin 1:5
  http://www.judaism-and-rome.org/mishnah-gittin-15
- Yael Wilfand, Mishnah Gittin 9:8
  http://www.judaism-and-rome.org/mishnah-gittin-98
- Yael Wilfand, Tosefta Eruvin 2:6
  http://www.judaism-and-rome.org/tosefta-eruvin-26
- Yael Wilfand, Tosefta Eruvin 3:7
  http://www.judaism-and-rome.org/tosefta-eruvin-37
- Yael Wilfand, Tosefta Pisḥa 8:18
  http://www.judaism-and-rome.org/tosefta-pis%E1%B8%A5a-818
- Yael Wilfand, Tosefta Qiddushin 5:1-2
  http://www.judaism-and-rome.org/tosefta-qiddushin-51-2
- Yael Wilfand, Tosefta Sanhedrin 9:10-11
  http://www.judaism-and-rome.org/tosefta-sanhedrin-911
- Yael Wilfand, Tosefta Yevamot 12:13
  http://www.judaism-and-rome.org/tosefta-yevamot-1213
- Yael Wilfand, Mekhilta de Rabbi Ishmael Kasfa (Mishpatim) 20
  http://www.judaism-and-rome.org/mekhilta-de-rabbi-ishmael-kasfa-mishpatim-20
- Yael Wilfand, Sifra 'Aḥarey Mot, parasha 8 chapter 3, 86a–b
  http://www.judaism-and-rome.org/
  sifra-%E2%80%99a%E1%B8%A5arey-mot-parasha-8-chapter-3-86a-b
- Yael Wilfand, Sifre Numbers 42
  http://www.judaism-and-rome.org/sifre-numbers-42-part-one (and -part-two)
- Yael Wilfand, Sifre Numbers 131
  http://www.judaism-and-rome.org/sifre-numbers-131
- Yael Wilfand, Sifre Deuteronomy 16
  http://www.judaism-and-rome.org/sifre-deuteronomy-16
- Yael Wilfand, Sifre Deuteronomy 344
  http://judaism-and-rome.org/sifre-deuteronomy-344
- Yael Wilfand, Mekhilta Deuteronomy 33:3
  http://judaism-and-rome.org/mekhilta-deuteronomy-333
- Yael Wilfand, Jerusalem Talmud Avodah Zarah 3:1, 42c (part one)
  http://www.judaism-and-rome.org/jerusalem-talmud-avodah-zarah-31-42c-part-one
- Yael Wilfand, Jerusalem Talmud Rosh Hashanah 1:2, 57b
  http://www.judaism-and-rome.org/jerusalem-talmud-rosh-hashanah-12-57b

- Yael Wilfand, Genesis Rabbah 9:13
  http://www.judaism-and-rome.org/genesis-rabbah-913
- Yael Wilfand, Genesis Rabbah 63:7
  http://www.judaism-and-rome.org/genesis-rabbah-637
- Yael Wilfand, Genesis Rabbah 66:2
  http://www.judaism-and-rome.org/genesis-rabbah-662
- Yael Wilfand, Leviticus Rabbah 13:5
  http://www.judaism-and-rome.org/leviticus-rabbah-135-part-one (/two / three / four)

Editions of Rabbinic Texts

Epstein and Melamed = J. N. Epstein and E. Z. Melamed (eds.), *Mekhilta d'Rabbi Sim'on b. Jochai*. Jerusalem: Mekitse Nirdamim, 1955.

Finkelstein = Louis Finkelstein (ed.), *Siphre ad Deuteronomium/Sifre on Deuteronomy*. Berlin: Jüdischer Kulturbund in Deutschland, 1939.

Horovitz = Haïm S. Horovitz (ed.), *Siphre ad Numeros adjecto Siphre zutta*. Lipsia: Gustav Fock, 1917.

Horovitz and Rabin = Haïm S. Horovitz and Israel A. Rabin (eds.), *Mechilta d'Rabbi Ismael*. Frankfurt: J. Kauffmann, 1928–1931.

Kahana 2005 = Menahem I. Kahana (ed.), *The Genizah Fragments of the Halakhic Midrashim, Part I. Mekhilta d'Rabbi Ishma'el, Mekhilta d'Rabbi Shim'on ben Yohay, Sifre Numbers, Sifre Zuta Numbers, Sifre Deuteronomy, Mekhilta Deuteronomy*. Jerusalem: Magnes Press, 2005.

Kahana 2011–2015 = Menahem I. Kahana (ed.), *Sifre on Numbers: An Annotated Edition*. 5 vols. Jerusalem: Magnes Press, 2011–2015.

Lieberman 1955–1973 = Saul Lieberman (ed.), *The Tosefta, According to Codex Vienna, with Variants from Codices Erfurt, London, Genizah Mss. and Editio Princeps (Venice 1521)*. 4 vols. New York: The Jewish Theological Seminary of America, 1955–1973.

Mandelbaum = Bernard Mandelbaum (ed.), *Pesikta de-Rav Kahana, according to an Oxford Manuscript with Variants from All Known Manuscripts and Genizoth Fragments and Parallel Passages*. 2 vols. Second, augmented edition. New York: The Jewish Theological Seminary of America, 1987.

Margulies = Mordecai Margulies (ed.), *Midrash Wayyikra Rabbah: A Critical Edition Based on Manuscripts and Genizah Fragments with Variants and Notes*. 3 vols. Jerusalem: Wahrmann, 1953–1960.

Milikowsky 2013 = Chaim Milikowsky (ed.), *Seder Olam: Critical Edition, Commentary, and Introduction*. 2 vols. Jerusalem: Yad Ben-Zvi Press, 2013.

Schäfer and Becker 1991–2001 = Peter Schäfer and Adam Becker (eds.), *Synopse zum Talmud Yerushalmi*. 7 vols. Tübingen: Mohr Siebeck, 1991–2001.

Theodor and Albeck = Julius Theodor and Chanokh Albeck (eds.), *Midrash Bereschit Rabba mit kritischem Apparat und Kommentar*. 3 vols. Berlin: M. Poppelauer, 1903–1935.

Weiss = Isaac H. Weiss (ed.), *Sipra de-be rab hu' seper torat kohanim*. Vienna: Jacob Schlossberg, 1862.

Zuckermandel = Moses S. Zuckermandel (ed.), *Tosephta based on the Erfurt and Vienna Codices, with Parallels and Variants*. Jerusalem: Wahrmann Books, 1963.

Secondary Sources

Abel, Félix-Marie. 1949. *Les livres des Maccabées*. Paris: Gabalda.

Aberbach, David. 1993. *Imperialism and Biblical Prophecy 750–500 BCE*. London: Routledge.

Achenbach, Reinhard. 2011. "*Gêr—Nåkhrî—Tôshav—Zâr*: Legal and Sacral Distinctions Regarding Foreigners in the Pentateuch." In Achenbach, Albertz, and Wöhrle 2011, 29–51.

Achenbach, Reinhard, Rainer Albertz, and Jakob Wöhrle (eds.). 2011. *The Foreigner and the Law: Perspectives from the Hebrew Bible and the Ancient Near East.* Wiesbaden: Harrassowitz Verlag.

Ackerman, Susan. 2010. "Assyria in the Bible." In *Assyrian Reliefs from the Palace of Ashurnasirpal II: A Cultural Biography,* edited by Ada Cohen and Steven E. Kangas, 124–142. Hanover: University of New England.

Adams, James N. 2003. *Bilingualism and the Latin Language.* New York: CUP.

Akiyama, Kengo. 2016a. "The רג and interpretive integration in the Damascus Document 6,20–21 and 14,3–6." *JJS* 67.2: 249–266.

———. 2016b. "The *gēr* in the Damascus Document: A Rejoinder." *Revue de Qumrân* 28.107: 117–126.

Albertz, Rainer. 2011. "From Aliens to Proselytes: Non-Priestly and Priestly Legislation concerning Strangers." In Achenbach, Albertz, and Wöhrle 2011, 53–70.

Alföldy, Géza. 1995. "Eine Bauinschrift aus dem Colosseum." *ZPE* 109: 195–226.

Alon, Gedalyahu. 1980. *The Jews in Their Land in the Talmudic Age.* Translated and edited by Gershon Levi. Jerusalem: Magnes.

Alonso, José L. 2016. "The Status of Peregrine Law in Egypt: 'Customary Law' and Legal Pluralism in the Roman Empire." In *Proceedings of the 27th International Congress of Papyrology,* edited by Tomasz Derda, Adam Łajtar, and Jakub Urbanik, 351–404. Warsaw: University of Warsaw.

Alonso-Núnez, José M. 1983. "Die Abfolge der Weltreiche bei Polybios und Dionysios von Halikarnassos." *Historia* 32: 411–426.

Amandry, Michel (ed.). 2017. *La monnaie antique: Grèce et Rome, VIIe siècle av. J.-C.-Ve siècle apr. J.-C.* Paris: Ellipses.

Aminoff, Irit. 1981. *The Figures of Esau and the Kingdom of Edom in Palestinian Midrashic-Talmudic Literature in the Tannaic and Amoraic Period.* Unpublished PhD, Melbourne University.

Amirante, Luigi. 1954. *Il giuramento prestato prima della litis contestatio nelle legis actiones e nelle formulae.* Naples: Jovene.

Ando, Clifford. 1999. "Was Rome a Polis?" *Classical Antiquity* 18.1: 5–34.

———. 2000. *Imperial Ideology and Provincial Loyalty in the Roman Empire.* Berkeley: University of California Press.

———. 2011. *Law, Language, and Empire in the Roman Tradition.* Philadelphia: University of Pennsylvania Press.

———. (ed.). 2016a. *Citizenship and Empire in Europe 200–1900: The Antonine Constitution after 1800 Years.* Stuttgart: Franz Steiner Verlag.

———. 2016b. "Legal Pluralism in Practice." In Ando, du Plessis, and Tuori 2016, 283–293.

———. 2016c. "Making Romans: Citizens, Subjects and Subjectivity in Republican Empire." In Lavan, Payne, and Weisweiler 2016, 169–185.

———. 2018. "Roman Law." In *The Oxford Handbook of Legal History,* edited by Markus Dubber and Christopher Tomlins, 663–679. Oxford: OUP.

Ando, Clifford, Paul du Plessis, and Kaius Tuori (eds.). 2016. *The Oxford Handbook of Roman Law and Society.* Oxford: OUP.

Andrade, Nathanael. 2020. "Romans and Iranians: Experiences of Imperial Governance in Roman Mesopotamia." In Berthelot 2020a, 361–384.

Appelbaum, Alan. 2009. "'The Idumaeans' in Josephus' *The Jewish War.*" *JSJ* 40.1: 1–22.

———. 2010. *The Rabbis' King-Parables: Midrash from the Third-Century Roman Empire.* Piscataway: Gorgias Press.

———. 2012. "Rabbi's Successors: The Later Jewish Patriarchs of the Third Century." *JJS* 63.1: 1–21.

———. 2018. "A Fresh Look at Philo's Family." *The Studia Philonica Annual* 30: 93–113.

Applebaum, Shimon. 1971. "Jews and Service in the Roman Army." In *Roman Frontier Studies 1967: The Proceedings of the Seventh International Congress Held at Tel Aviv*, 181–184. Tel Aviv: Students' Organization of Tel Aviv University.

———. 1979. *Jews and Greeks in Ancient Cyrene*. Leiden: Brill.

Artzi, Pinḥas. 2008. "'All Nations and Many Peoples': The Answer of Isaiah and Micah to Assyrian Imperial Policies." In *Treasures on Camels' Humps: Historical and Literary Studies from the Ancient Near East Presented to Israel Eph'al*, edited by Mordechai Cogan and Dan'el Kahn, 41–53. Jerusalem: Magnes Press.

Ashkroft, Bill, Gareth Griffiths, and Helen Tiffin. 1989. *The Empire Writes Back: Theory and Practice in Post-Colonial Literatures*. London: Routledge.

Assan-Dhôte, Isabelle, and Jacqueline Moatti-Fine. 2014. "Le vocabulaire de la guerre dans le premier livre des Maccabées. Étude lexicale." In *La mémoire des persécutions: autour des livres des Maccabées*, edited by Marie-Françoise Baslez and Olivier Munnich, 91–106. Louvain: Peeters.

Assenmaker, Pierre. 2010. "La place du Palladium dans l'idéologie augustéenne: entre mythologie, religion et politique." In *Storia delle Religioni e Archeologia: Discipline a confronto*, edited by Igor Baglioni, 35–64. Rome: Alpes Italia.

Assis, Elie. 2006. "Why Edom? On the Hostility Towards Jacob's Brother in Prophetic Sources." *Vetus Testamentum* 56.1: 1–20.

———. 2016. *Identity in Conflict: The Struggle between Esau and Jacob, Edom and Israel*. Winona Lake: Eisenbrauns.

Aster, Shawn Zelig. 2017. *Reflections of Empire in Isaiah 1–39: Responses to Assyrian Ideology*. Atlanta: SBL Press.

Austin, Michel M. 1986. "Hellenistic Kings, War, and the Economy." *The Classical Quarterly* 36.2: 450–466.

Avemarie, Friedrich. 1994. "Esaus Hände, Jakobs Stimme: Edom als Sinnbild Roms in der frühen rabbinischen Literatur." In *Die Heiden*, edited by Reinhard Feldmeier, 177–208. Tübingen: Mohr Siebeck.

Avidov, Avi. 2009. *Not Reckoned among Nations: The Origins of the So-Called "Jewish Question" in Roman Antiquity*. Tübingen: Mohr Siebeck.

Awabdy, Mark A. 2014. *Immigrants and Innovative Law: Deuteronomy's Theological and Social Vision for the גר*. Tübingen: Mohr Siebeck.

Bacher, Wilhelm. 1889. *Die Agada der Tannaiten. Zweiter Band: Von Akiba's Tod bis zum Abschluss der Mischna (135 bis 220 nach der gew. Zeitrechnung)*. Strassburg: Karl J. Trübner.

———. 1892. *Die Agada der Palästinensischen Amoräer. Erster Band. Vom Abschluss der Mischna bis zum Tode Jochanans (220 bis 279 nach der gew. Zeitrechnung)*. Strassburg: Karl J. Trübner.

Badel, Christophe. 2005. *La noblesse de l'empire romain. Les masques et la vertu*. Seyssel: Champ Vallon.

———. 2011. "Les modèles impériaux dans l'Antiquité." *DHA* Supp. 5: 9–25.

———. 2012. "L'adoption, un modèle dépassé ?" In *Les stratégies familiales dans l'Antiquité tardive*, edited by Christophe Badel and Christian Settipani, 81–108. Paris: de Boccard.

Bagnall, Roger. 1997. "Decolonizing Ptolemaic Egypt." In *Hellenistic Constructs: Essays in Culture, History and Historiography*, edited by Paul Cartledge, Peter Garnsey and Erich Gruen, 225–441. Berkeley: University of California Press.

Baker, Cynthia M. 2002. *Rebuilding the House of Israel: Architectures of Gender in Jewish Antiquity*. Stanford: Stanford University Press.

Bakhos, Carol. 2007. "Figuring (out) Esau: The Rabbis and Their Others." *JJS* 58.2: 250–262.

Balch, David L. 1982. "Two Apologetic Encomia: Dionysius on Rome and Josephus on the Jews." *JSJ* 13.1–2: 102–122.

Baldwin, B. 1961. "Lucian as Social Satirist." *The Classical Quarterly* 11.2: 199–208.

Baltrusch, Ernst. 2002. *Die Juden und das Römische Reich. Geschichte einer konfliktreichen Beziehung.* Darmstadt: Wissenschaftliche Buchgesellschaft.

Bamberger, Bernard J. 1939. *Proselytism in the Talmudic Period.* Cincinatti: Hebrew Union College Press.

Bar-Asher Siegal, Michal. 2013. *Early Christian Monastic Literature and the Babylonian Talmud.* Cambridge: CUP.

———. 2015. "Ethics and Identity Formation: Resh Lakish and the Monastic Repentant Robber." In *L'identité à travers l'éthique. Nouvelles perspectives sur la formation des identités collectives dans le monde gréco-romain,* edited by Katell Berthelot, Ron Naiweld, and Daniel Stökl Ben Ezra, 53–72. Turnhout: Brepols.

———. 2019. *Jewish–Christian Dialogues on Scripture in Late Antiquity: Heretic Narratives of the Babylonian Talmud.* Cambridge: CUP.

Bar-Asher Siegal, Michal, Wolfgang Grünstäudl, and Matthew Thiessen (eds.). 2017. *Perceiving the Other in Ancient Judaism and Christianity.* Tübingen: Mohr Siebeck.

Bar-Asher Siegal, Michal, Tzvi Novick, and Christine Hayes (eds.). 2017. *The Faces of Torah: Studies in the Texts and Contexts of Ancient Judaism in Honor of Steven Fraade.* Göttingen: Vandenhoek & Ruprecht.

Bar-Kochva, Bezalel. 2010. *The Image of the Jews in Greek Literature: The Hellenistic Period.* Berkeley: University of California Press.

Barclay, John M. G. 1987. "Mirror-Reading a Polemical Letter: Galatians as a Test-Case." *JSNT* 31: 73–93.

———. 2000. "Judaism in Roman Dress: Josephus' Tactics in the *Contra Apionem.*" In *Internationales Josephus-Kolloquium Aarhus 1999,* edited by Jürgen U. Kalms, 231–245. Münster: LIT Verlag.

———. 2005. "The Empire Writes Back: Josephan Rhetoric in Flavian Rome." In Edmondson, Mason and Rives 2005, 315–332.

———. 2007. *Flavius Josephus, Against Apion: Translation and Commentary.* Leiden: Brill.

Barnes, Timothy D. 1985. "Constantine and the Christians of Persia." *JRS* 75: 126–136.

Baroin, Catherine. 2010. *Se souvenir à Rome. Formes, représentations et pratiques de la mémoire.* Paris: Belin.

Barone Adesi, Giorgio. 1992. *L'età della Lex Dei.* Naples: Jovene.

Barraclough, Ray. 1984. "Philo's Politics: Roman Rule and Hellenistic Judaism." In *Aufstieg und Niedergang der Römischen Welt* II.21.2, edited by Wolfgang Haase, 417–553. Berlin: De Gruyter.

Barron, Caroline. 2020. "The (Lost) Arch of Titus: The Visibility and Prominence of Victory in Flavian Rome." In Berthelot 2020a, 157–177.

Barth, Fredrik. 1969. *Ethnic Groups and Boundaries.* Boston: Little, Brown and Company.

Barton, Carlin A., and Daniel Boyarin. 2016. *Imagine No Religion: How Modern Abstractions Hide Ancient Realities.* New York: Fordham University Press.

Baruch, Eyal. 2018. "Adapted Roman Rituals in Second Century CE Jewish Houses." In *Jews and Christians in the First and Second Centuries: The Interbellum 70–132 CE,* edited by Joshua Schwartz and Peter J. Tomson, 50–74. Leiden: Brill.

Baslez, Marie-Françoise. 2007. *Les persécutions dans l'Antiquité. Victimes, héros, martyrs.* Paris: Fayard.

Beard, Mary. 2007. *The Roman Triumph.* Cambridge: The Belknap Press of Harvard University Press.

Beard Mary, John North, and Simon Price. 1998. *Religions of Rome*. Cambridge: CUP. (2 vol.)

Beaulieu, Paul-Alain. 2007. "Nabonidus the Mad King: A Reconsideration of his Stelas from Harran and Babylon." In *Representation of Political Power: Case Histories from Times of Change and Dissolving Order in the Ancient Near East*, edited by Marlies Heinz and Marian H. Feldman, 137–166. Winona Lake: Eisenbrauns.

Becker, Adam H., and Annette Yoshiko Reed (eds.). 2003. *The Ways that Never Parted: Jews and Christians in Late Antiquity and the Early Middle Ages*. Tübingen: Mohr Siebeck.

Bedford, Peter R. 2009. "The Neo-Assyrian Empire." In Morris and Scheidel 2009, 30–65.

Belayche, Nicole. 1997. "Du Mont du Temple au Golgotha: le Capitole de la colonie d'Aelia Capitolina." *RHR* 214.4: 387–413.

———. 1999. "Dimenticare . . . Gerusalemme. Les paganismes à Aelia Capitolina du IIᵉ au IVᵉ siècle de notre ère." *REJ* 158.3–4: 287–348.

———. 2001. Iudaea-Palaestina: *The Pagan Cults in Roman Palestine (Second to Fourth Century)*. Tübingen: Mohr Siebeck.

———. 2009. "Foundation Myths in Roman Palestine: Traditions and Reworkings." In *Ethnic Constructs in Antiquity: The Role of Power and Tradition*, edited by Ton Derks and Nico Roymans, 167–188. Amsterdam: Archaeological Studies.

Belser, Julia W. 2014. "Sex in the Shadow of Rome: Sexual Violence and Theological Lament in Talmudic Disaster Tales." *Journal of Feminist Studies in Religion* 30.1: 5–24.

———. 2018. *Rabbinic Tales of Destruction: Gender, Sex, and Disability in the Ruins of Jerusalem*. New York: OUP.

Ben-Shalom, Israel. 1984. "Rabbi Judah b. Ilai's Attitude towards Rome." *Zion* 49: 9–24. (Heb.)

———. 1993. *The School of Shammai and the Zealots' Struggle against Rome*. Jerusalem: Yad Izhak Ben-Zvi. (Heb.)

Ben-Shammai, Haggai. 1992. "Some Genizah Fragments on the Duty of the Nations to Keep the Mosaic Law." In *Genizah Research after Ninety Years: The Case of Judaeo-Arabic*, edited by Joshua Blau and Stefan Reif, 22–30. Cambridge: CUP.

Benario, Herbert W. 1954. "The Dediticii of the Constitutio Antoniniana." *Transactions and Proceedings of the American Philological Association* 85: 188–196.

Benoist, Stéphane. 2005. *Rome, le prince et la Cité: pouvoir impérial et cérémonies publiques (Iᵉʳ siècle av.-début du IVᵉ siècle apr. J.-C.)*. Paris: PUF.

Béranger, Jean, in collaboration with François Paschoud and Pierre Ducrey. 1973. *Principatus. Études de notions et d'histoire politiques dans l'Antiquité gréco-romaine*. Genève: Droz.

Berger, Adolf. 1991. *Encyclopedic Dictionary of Roman Law, vol. 43*. Philadelphia: American Philosophical Society.

Berkowitz, Beth A. 2006. *Execution and Invention: Death Penalty Discourse in Early Rabbinic and Christian Cultures*. New York: OUP.

———. 2009. "The Limits of 'Their Laws': Ancient Rabbinic Controversies about Jewishness (and non-Jewishness)." *JQR* 99.1: 121–157.

———. 2012. *Defining Jewish Difference from Antiquity to the Present*. New York: CUP.

———. 2017. "Approaches to Foreign Law in Biblical Israel and Classical Judaism." In *The Cambridge Companion to Judaism and Law*, edited by Christine Hayes, 128–156. Cambridge: CUP.

Berlejung, Angelika. 2017. "Social Climbing in the Babylonian Exile." In *Wandering Arameans: Arameans Outside Syria. Textual and Archaeological Perspectives*, edited by Angelika Berlejung, Aren M. Maeir, and Andreas Schüle, 101–124. Wiesbaden: Harrassowitz Verlag.

Berlin, Andrea. 2005. "Jewish Life before the Revolt: The Archaeological Evidence." *JSJ* 36.4: 417–470.

Berlin, Andrea, and J. Andrew Overman (eds.). 2002. *The First Jewish Revolt: Archaeology, History, and Ideology*. New York: Routledge.

Bernard, Jacques-Emmanuel. 2000. "Philosophie politique et antijudaïsme chez Cicéron." *SCI* 19: 113–131.

Berner, Christoph. 2015. "Abraham amidst Kings, Coalitions and Military Campaigns: Reflections on the Redaction History of Gen 14 and its Early Rewritings." In *The Reception of Biblical War Legislation in Narrative Contexts: Proceedings of the EABS Research Group "Law and Narrative,"* edited by Christoph Berner and Harald Samuel, 23–60. Berlin: De Gruyter.

Bernett, Monika. 2004. "Polis und Politeia. Zur politischen Organisation Jerusalems und Jehuds in der Perserzeit." In *Die Griechen und das antike Israel*, edited by Stefan Alkier, 73–129. Fribourg: Academic Press Fribourg.

Bernhardt, Johannes C. 2017. *Die Jüdische Revolution. Untersuchungen zu Ursachen, Verlauf und Folgen der hasmonäischen Erhebung*. Berlin: W. de Gruyter.

Berthelot, Katell. 1999. "La notion de גר dans les textes de Qumrân." *Revue de Qumrân* 19.74: 171–216.

———. 2003. Philanthrôpia judaica: *Le débat autour de la "misanthropie" des lois juives dans l'Antiquité*. Leiden: Brill.

———. 2004. *"L'humanité de l'autre homme" dans la pensée juive ancienne*. Leiden: Brill.

———. 2006. "L'idéologie maccabéenne: entre idéologie de la résistance armée et idéologie du martyre." *REJ* 165.1–2: 99–122.

———. 2011a. "Grecs, Barbares et Juifs dans l'œuvre de Philon." In *Philon d'Alexandrie. Un penseur à l'intersection des cultures gréco-romaine, orientale, juive et chrétienne*, edited by Baudoin Decharneux and Sabrina Inowlocki, 47–62. Turnhout, Brepols.

———. 2011b. "Philo's Perception of the Roman Empire." *JSJ* 42.2: 166–187.

———. 2016. *"The Rabbis Write Back!* L'enjeu de la "parenté" entre Israël et Rome-Ésaü-Édom." *RHR* 233.2: 165–192.

———. 2017a. "The Paradoxical Similarities between the Jews and the Roman Other." In Bar-Asher Siegal, Grünstäudl, and Thiessen 2017, 95–109.

———. 2017b. "Entre octroi de la citoyenneté et adoption: les modèles pour penser la conversion au judaïsme à l'époque romaine." *Pallas* 104: 37–50.

———. 2018a. *In Search of the Promised Land? The Hasmonean Dynasty between Biblical Models and Hellenistic Diplomacy*. Göttingen: Vandenhoeck & Ruprecht.

———. 2018b. "Rabbinic Universalism Reconsidered: The Roman Context of some Rabbinic Traditions Pertaining to the Revelation of the Torah in Different Languages." *JQR* 108.4: 393–421.

———. 2019. "Judaism as 'Citizenship' and the Question of the Impact of Rome." In Berthelot and Price 2019, 107–129.

——— (ed.). 2020a. *Reconsidering Roman Power: Roman, Greek, Jewish and Christian Perceptions and Reactions*. Rome: École Française de Rome.

———. 2020b. "Power and Piety: Roman and Jewish Perspectives." In Berthelot 2020a, 269–289.

———. 2020c. "To Convert or Not to Convert: The Appropriation of Jewish Rituals, Customs and Beliefs by Non-Jews." In *Lived Religion in the Ancient Mediterranean World: Approaching Religious Transformations from Archaeology, History and Classics*, edited by Valentino Gasparini et al., 493–515. Berlin: De Gruyter.

———. 2020d. "Philo on the Impermanence of Empires." In Price and Berthelot 2020, 112–129.

———. 2020e. "Lineage and Virtue in Josephus: The Respective Roles of Priestly Views and Roman Culture." *JAJ* 11.1: 26–44.

———. 2021. "'Not like Our Rock Is Their Rock' (Deut 32:31): Rabbinic Perceptions of Roman Courts and Jurisdiction." In Berthelot, Dohrmann, and Nemo-Pekelman 2021, 389–408.

———. Forthcoming. "Flavius Josephus as Reader of Philo." In *The Reception of Philo of Alexandria*, edited by Courtney Friesen, David Lincicum, and David T. Runia. Oxford: OUP.

Berthelot, Katell, Natalie B. Dohrmann, and Capucine Nemo-Pekelman (eds.). 2021. *Legal Engagement: The Reception of Roman Law and Tribunals by Jews and Other Inhabitants of the Empire*. Rome: École Française de Rome.

Berthelot, Katell, and Jonathan Price (eds.). 2019. *In the Crucible of Empire: The Impact of Roman Citizenship upon Greeks, Jews and Christians*. Leuven: Peeters.

Bhabha, Homi K. 1994. *The Location of Culture*. London: Routledge.

Bianco, Elisabetta. 1968. "Indirizzi programmatici e propagandistici nella monetazione di Vespasiano." *Rivista Italiana di Numismatica* 70[16]: 145–224.

Bickerman, Elias. 1932. "Bellum Antiochicum." *Hermes* 67.1: 47–76.

———. 1935. "La Charte séleucide de Jérusalem." *REJ* 100: 4–35.

———. 1945. "The Date of Fourth Maccabees." In *Louis Ginzberg Jubilee Volume*, 105–112. New York: The American Academy for Jewish Research.

Bilde, Per. 1998. "Josephus and Jewish Apocalypticism." In *Understanding Josephus: Seven Perspectives*, edited by Steve Mason, 35–61. Sheffield: Sheffield Academic Press.

———. 2009. "Philo as a Polemist and a Political Apologist: An Investigation of his Two Historical Treatises *Against Flaccus* and *The Embassy to Gaius*." In *Alexandria: A Cultural and Religious Melting Pot*, edited by George Hinge and Jens A. Krasilnikoff, 97–115. Aarhus: Aarhus University Press.

Birnbaum, Ellen. 1996. *The Place of Judaism in Philo's Thought: Israel, Jews, and Proselytes*. Atlanta: Scholars Press.

———. 2015. "The Bible's First War: Philo's Interpretation of the Struggle for Power in Genesis 14." In Calabi et al. 2015, 111–127.

Blanco Pérez, Aitor. 2019. "*Salvo Iure Gentium*: Roman Citizenship and Civic Life Before and After the *Constitutio Antoniniana*." *Al-Masāq: Journal of the Medieval Mediterranean*. https://doi.org/10.1080/09503110.2019.1675028

———. 2021. "Appealing for the Emperor's Justice: Provincial Petitions and Imperial Responses Prior to Late Antiquity." In Berthelot, Dohrmann, and Nemo-Pekelman 2021, 159–173.

Blanton, Thomas R. 2019. "The Expressive Prepuce: Philo's Defense of Judaic Circumcision in Greek and Roman Contexts." *The Studia Philonica Annual* 31: 127–162.

Blenkinsopp, Joseph. 2001. "Was the Pentateuch the Constitution of the Jewish Ethnos in the Persian Period?" In Watts 2001, 41–62.

———. 2011. "The Cosmological and Protological Language of Deutero-Isaiah." *CBQ* 73: 493–510. Republished as: "Deutero-Isaiah and the Creator God: Yahweh, Ahuramazda, Marduk." In *Essays on Judaism in the Pre-Hellenistic Period*, 15–29. Berlin: De Gruyter, 2017.

Bloch, René. 2006. "*Di neglecti*. La politique augustéenne d'Hérode le Grand." *RHR* 223.2: 123–147.

Bloom, James J. 2010. *The Jewish Revolts Against Rome, A.D. 66–135: A Military Analysis*. Jefferson: McFarland & Company.

Blumell, Lincoln H. 2016. "A New Jewish Epitaph Commemorating Care for Orphans." *JSJ* 47.3: 310–329.

Bockmuehl, Markus N. A. 2000. *Jewish Law in Gentile Churches: Halakhah and the Beginning of Christian Public Ethics*. Edinburgh: T&T Clark.

Boer, Roland (ed.). 2013. *Postcolonialism and the Hebrew Bible: The Next Step*. Atlanta: Society of Biblical Literature.

Bonesho, Catherine E. 2018. *Foreign Holidays and Festivals as Representative of Identity in Rabbinic Literature*. PhD, University of Wisconsin-Madison.

Bonwetsch, Georg Nathanel, and Hans Achelis. 1897. *Hippolytus Werke. 1 Kommentar zum Buche Daniel und die Fragmente des Kommentars zum Hohenliede*. Leipzig: J.C. Hinrich.

Bord, Lucien-Jean. 1997. "L'adoption dans la Bible et dans le droit cunéiforme." *Zeitschrift für Altorientalische und Biblische Rechtsgeschichte* 3: 174–194.

Bordes, Jacqueline. 1980. "La place d'Aristote dans l'évolution de la notion de *politeia*." *Ktema* 5: 249–256.

———. 1982. *Politeia dans la pensée grecque jusqu'à Aristote*. Paris: Les Belles Lettres.

Borgeaud, Philippe, Thomas Römer, and Youri Volokhine (eds.). 2010. *Interprétations de Moïse: Égypte, Judée, Grèce et Rome*. Leiden: Brill.

Borgen, Peter. 1992. "There Shall Come Forth a Man: Reflections on Messianic Ideas in Philo." In *The Messiah: Developments in Earliest Judaism and Christianity*, edited by James H. Charlesworth, 341–361. Minneapolis: Fortress.

———. 1997. *Philo of Alexandria: An Exegete for His Time*. Leiden: Brill.

Borger, Rykle. 1956. *Die Inschriften Asarhaddons Königs von Assyrien*. Graz: E. Weidner.

Boustan (Abusch), Ra'anan S. 2003. "Negotiating Difference: Genital Mutilation in Roman Slave Law and the History of the Bar Kokhba Revolt." In Schäfer 2003a, 71–91.

———. 2006. "Review of Daniel Boyarin, Border Lines." *JQR* 96.3: 441–446.

Boyancé, Pierre. 1964. "Les Romains, peuple de la *fides*." *Bulletin de l'Association Guillaume Budé* 23.4: 419–435.

Boyarin, Daniel. 1995. "Homotopia: The Feminized Jewish Man and the Lives of Women in Late Antiquity." *Differences: A Journal of Feminist Cultural Studies* 7.2: 41–81.

———. 1997. *Unheroic Conduct: The Rise of Heterosexuality and the Invention of the Jewish Man*. Berkeley: University of California Press.

———. 1999. *Dying for God: Martyrdom and the Making of Christianity and Judaism*. Stanford: Stanford University Press.

———. 2004a. *Border Lines: The Partition of Judaeo-Christianity*. Philadelphia: University of Pennsylvania Press.

———. 2004b. "The Christian Invention of Judaism: The Theodosian Empire and the Rabbinic Refusal of Religion." *Representations* 85: 21–57.

———. 2007. "Semantic Differences; or, 'Judaism'/'Christianity.'" In *The Ways that Never Parted: Jews and Christians in Late Antiquity and the Early Middle Ages*, edited by Adam H. Becker and Annette Yoshiko Reed, 65–85. Minneapolis: Fortress Press.

———. 2009. "Rethinking Jewish Christianity: An Argument for Dismantling a Dubious Category (to which is Appended a Correction of my Border Lines)." *JQR* 99.1: 7–36.

———. 2015. "Friends without Benefits: Or, Academic Love." In *Sex in Antiquity: Exploring Gender and Sexuality in the Ancient World*, edited by Mark Masterson, Nancy Sorkin Rabinowitz and James Robson, 517–535. London: Routledge.

———. 2019. *Judaism: The Genealogy of a Modern Notion*. New Brunswick: Rutgers University Press.

Braund, David C. 1985. *Augustus to Nero: A Sourcebook on Roman History 31 BC–AD 68*. London: Croom Helm.

———. 1993. "Piracy under the Principate and the Ideology of Imperial Eradication." In *War and Society in the Roman World*, edited by John Rich and Graham Shipley, 195–212. London: Routledge.

Bregman, Marc. 2017. "Mordecai Breastfed Esther: Male Lactation in Midrash, Medicine, and Myth." In Bar-Asher Siegal, Novick, and Hayes 2017, 258–274.

Brénot, Claude. 1980. "Les monnaies au nom de *Populus Romanus* à Constantinople." *Quaderni ticinesi di numismatica e antichità classiche* 9: 299–313.

Brettler, Marc Zvi, and Michael Poliakov. 1990. "Rabbi Simeon ben Lakish at the Gladiator's Banquet: Rabbinic Observations on the Roman Arena." *HTR* 83.1: 93–98.

Briant, Pierre. 1979. "Des Achéménides aux rois hellénistiques: continuités et ruptures (Bilan et propositions)." *Annali della Scuola Normale Superiore di Pisa. Classe di Lettere e Filosofia, Serie III* 9.4: 1375–1414.

———. 1982. "Conquête territoriale et stratégie idéologique: Alexandre le Grand et l'idéologie monarchique achéménide." In *Rois, tributs et paysans. Etudes sur les formations tributaires du Moyen-Orient ancien*, 357–404. Besançon: Université de Franche-Comté.

———. 2002. *From Cyrus to Alexander: A History of the Persian Empire*. Trans. Peter T. Daniels. Winona Lake: Eisenbrauns.

Brinkman, John A. 1984. *Prelude to Empire: Babylonian Society and Politics, 747–626 B.C.* Philadelphia: University Museum, Babylonian Fund.

Britt, Karen, and Ra'anan Boustan. 2017. *The Elephant Mosaic Panel in the Synagogue at Huqoq: Official Publication and Initial Interpretations*. Portsmouth: Journal of Roman Archaeology.

Brody, Robert. 2017. "'Rabbinic' and 'Nonrabbinic' Jews in Mishnah and Tosefta." In Bar-Asher Siegal, Novick and Hayes 2017, 275–293.

Brooke, George J. 1991. "The Kittim in the Qumran Pesharim." In *Images of Empire*, edited by Alexander Loveday, 135–159. Sheffield: JSOT Press.

Brown, John Pairman. 2001. *Israel and Hellas. Vol.3: The Legacy of Iranian Imperialism and the Individual*. Berlin: De Gruyter.

Brown, Peter. 1992. *Power and Persuasion in Late Antiquity: Towards a Christian Empire*. Madison: The University of Wisconsin Press.

———. 1999. "Pagan." In *Late Antiquity: A Guide to the Postclassical World*, edited by Glen W. Bowersock, Peter Brown, and Oleg Grabar, 625. Cambridge: The Belknap Press of Harvard University Press.

Brunt, Peter A. 1976. "The Romanization of the Local Ruling Classes in the Roman Empire." In *Assimilation et résistance à la culture gréco-romaine dans le monde ancien*, edited by Dionisie M. Pippidi, 161–173. Paris: Les Belles Lettres. Repr. in *Roman Imperial Themes*, 267–281. Oxford: Clarendon Press, 1990.

———. 1978. "*Laus Imperii.*" In *Imperialism in the Ancient World*, edited by Peter Garnsey and C. R. Whittaker, 159–191. Cambridge: CUP. Repr. in: *Roman Imperial Themes*, 288–323. Oxford: Clarendon Press, 1990.

Bryen, Ari Z. 2008. "Visibility and Violence in Petitions from Roman Egypt." *Greek, Roman, and Byzantine Studies* 48: 181–200.

———. 2012. "Judging Empire: Courts and Culture in Rome's Eastern Provinces." *Law and History Review* 30.3: 771–811.

———. 2014. "Martyrdom, Rhetoric, and the Politics of Procedure." *Classical Antiquity* 33.2: 243–280.

———. 2016. "Reading the Citizenship Papyrus (P.Giss. 40)." In Ando 2016a, 29–43.

———. 2017. "Dionysia's Complaint: Finding Emotions in the Courtroom." *Greek, Roman, and Byzantine Studies* 57: 1010–1031.

———. 2021. "A Frenzy of Sovereignty: Punishment in P.Aktenbuch." In Berthelot, Dohrmann, and Nemo-Pekelman 2021, 89–108.

Buckland, W. W. 1975. *A Text-Book of Roman Law*. Cambridge: CUP. (3rd ed., revised by Peter Stein; originally published in 1921).

Buraselis, Kostas. 2007. Θεῖα δωρεά: *das göttlich-kaiserliche Geschenk. Studien zur Politik der Severer und zur Constitutio Antoniniana*. Vienna: Verlag der Österreichischen Akademie der Wissenschaften. (Trans. of *THEIA DÔREA: Meletes pano stin politiki tis dynastias ton Severon kai tin Constitutio Antoniniana*. Athens: 1989).

Burbank, Jane, and Frederick Cooper. 2010. *Empires in World History: Power and the Politics of Difference*. Princeton: PUP.

Burke, Trevor J. 2006. *Adopted into God's Family: Exploring a Pauline Metaphor*. Downers Grove: InterVarsity Press; Nottingham: Apollos.

Burns, Joshua Ezra. 2017a. "The Wisdom of the Nations and the Law of Israel: Genealogies of Ethnic Difference in Ben Sira and the *Mekhilta*." In *Sibyls, Scriptures, and Scrolls: John Collins at Seventy*, edited by Joel Baden, Hindy Najman, and Eibert Tigchelaar, 241–260. Leiden: Brill.

———. 2017b. "Roman Law in the Jewish House of Study: Constructing Rabbinic Authority after the Constitutio Antoniniana." In Bar-Asher Siegal, Novick, and Hayes 2017, 293–308.

Burrows, Mark S. 1988. "Christianity in the Roman Forum: Tertullian and the Apologetic Use of History." *Vigiliae Christianae* 42: 209–235.

Byrne, Brendan. 1979. *"Sons of God"—"Seed of Abraham": A Study of the Idea of the Sonship of God of All Christians in Paul against the Jewish Background*. Roma: Biblical Institute Press.

Calabi, Francesca, et al. (eds.). 2015. *Pouvoir et puissances chez Philon d'Alexandrie*. Turnhout: Brepols.

Callu, Jean-Pierre. 1960. Genio Populi Romani *(296–316). Contribution à une histoire numismatique de la Tétrarchie*. Paris: Honoré Champion.

Cameron, A. 1939. "Θρεπτός and Related Terms in the Inscriptions from Asia Minor." In *Anatolian Studies Presented to W. H. Buckler*, edited by William M. Calder and Josef Keil, 27–62. Manchester: Manchester University Press.

Campbell, John B. 1994. *The Roman Army, 31 BC–AD 337: A Sourcebook*. London: Routledge.

Capdetrey, Laurent. 2007. *Le pouvoir séleucide. Territoire, administration, finances d'un royaume hellénistique (312-129 avant J.-C.)*. Rennes: Presses Universitaires de Rennes.

———. 2008. "Le royaume séleucide: un empire impossible ?" In Hurlet 2008, 57–80.

———. 2017. "Les chemins de l'État antique: l'exemple des royaumes hellénistiques." *Les Cahiers d'Histoire. Revue d'histoire critique* 134: 21–40.

Cappelletti, Silvia. 2006. *The Jewish Community of Rome: From the Second Century B.C. to the Third Century C.E.* Leiden: Brill.

Carlebach, A. 1975. "Rabbinic References to Fiscus Judaicus." *JQR* 66.1: 57–61.

Carlier, Caroline. 2008. *La cité de Moïse: le peuple juif chez Philon d'Alexandrie*. Turnhout: Brepols.

Carmignac, Jean. 1955. *La Règle de la Guerre*. Paris: Letouzey et Ané.

Carr, David M. 2007. "The Rise of Torah." In Knoppers and Levinson 2007, 39–76.

Carradice, Ian. 2012. "Flavian Coinage." In *The Oxford Handbook of Greek and Roman Coinage*, edited by William E. Metcalf, 375–390. Oxford: OUP.

Carrié, Jean-Michel. 2005. "Developments in Provincial and Local Administration." In *The Cambridge Ancient History*, edited by Alan K. Bowman, Averil Cameron, and Peter Garnsey, 12: 269–312. Cambridge: CUP. (2nd ed.).

Carter, Charles E. 2003. "Ideology and Archaeology in the Neo-Babylonian Period: Excavating Text and Tell." In Lipschits et al. 2003, 301–322.

Carter, George W. 1970. *Zoroastrianism and Judaism*. New York: AMS.

Casevitz, Michel. 1990. "Le vocabulaire politique de Diodore de Sicile: πολιτεία, πολίτευμα et leur famille." *Ktema* 15: 27–33.

Castritius, Helmut. 2002. "Military Service and Militancy Among the Jews of Late Antiquity." *Jewish Studies* 41: 57–65.

Chajes, H.-P. 1899. "Les juges juifs en Palestine." *REJ* 39: 39–52.

Champeaux, Jacqueline. 2008. "Images célestes de Rome: la Ville et ses incarnations divines." In *Roma illustrata: représentations de la ville. Actes du colloque international de Caen,*

6–8 octobre 2005, edited by Philippe Fleury and Olivier Desbordes, 85–95. Caen: Presses Universitaires de Caen.

Chance, J. Bradley. 1993. "The Seed of Abraham and the People of God: A Study of Two Pauls." In *Society of Biblical Literature 1993 Seminar Papers,* edited by Eugene H. Lovering, 384–411. Atlanta: Scholars Press.

Chaniotis, Angelos. 2003. "The Divinity of Hellenistic Rulers." In Erskine 2003, 431–445.

———. 2004. "Justifying Territorial Claims in Classical and Hellenistic Greece." In *The Law and the Courts in Ancient Greece,* edited by Edward M. Harris and Lene Rubenstein, 185–213. London: Duckworth.

Chapman, Honora Howell. 2009. "What Josephus Sees: The Temple of Peace and the Jerusalem Temple as Spectacle in Text and Art." *Phoenix* 63.1–2: 107–130.

Charlesworth, M. P. 1943. "Pietas and Victoria: The Emperor and the Citizen." *JRS* 33.1–2: 1–10.

Chastagnol, André. 1992. "La table claudienne de Lyon." In *Le Sénat romain à l'époque impériale. Recherches sur la composition de l'Assemblée et le statut de ses membres,* edited by André Chastagnol, 79–96. Paris: Les Belles Lettres.

Christol, Michel. 1988. "Rome et les tribus indigènes en Maurétanie Tingitane." In *L'Africa romana. Atti del V convegno di studio. Sassari, 11–13 dicembre 1987,* edited by Attilio Mastino, 305–337. Sassari: Università degli Studi di Sassari.

———. 1999. "Le métier d'empereur et ses représentations à la fin du IIIᵉ et au début du IVᵉ siècle." *Cahiers du Centre Gustave Glotz* 10: 355–368.

———. 2001. "Rome et le peuple romain à la transition entre le Haut et le Bas Empire: identité et tensions." In *Identità e valori fattori di aggregazione e fattori di crisi nell'esperienza politica antica. Vol. 3: Alle radici della casa comune europea,* edited by Alberto Barzanò et al., 209–225. Rome: L'Erma di Bretscheinder.

Chrubasik, Boris. 2016. *Kings and Usurpers in the Seleukid Empire: The Men Who Would Be King.* Oxford: OUP.

Cody, Jane N. 2003. "Conquerors and Conquered on Flavian Coins." In *Flavian Rome: Culture, Image, Text,* edited by Anthony J. Boyle and William J. Dominik, 103–123. Leiden: Brill.

Cogan, Mordechai. 1993. "Judah under Assyrian Hegemony: A Reexamination of Imperialism and Religion." *JBL* 112.3: 403–414.

Cogan, Morton. 1974. *Imperialism and Religion: Assyria, Judah and Israel in the Eighth and Seventh Centuries B.C.E.* Missoula: SBL Scholars Press.

Cohen, Boaz. 1944. "The Relationship of Jewish to Roman Law." *JQR* N.S. 34: 267–280 and 409–424.

———. 1945. "Civil Bondage in Jewish and Roman Law." In *Louis Ginzberg Jubilee Volume,* edited by Solomon Goldman, 113–132. New York: The American Academy for Jewish Research.

———. 1946–1947. "Some Remarks on the Law of Persons in Jewish and Roman Jurisprudence." *Proceedings of the American Academy for Jewish Research* 16: 1–37.

———. 1966. *Jewish and Roman Law: A Comparative Study.* 2 vols. New York: Jewish Theological Seminary.

Cohen, Gerson. 1967. "Esau as Symbol in Early Medieval Thought." In *Jewish Medieval and Renaissance Studies,* edited by Alexander Altman, 19–48. Cambridge: HUP.

Cohen, Naomi G. 1992. "Taryag and the Noahide Commandments." *JJS* 43.1: 46–57.

Cohen, Shaye J. D. 1982. "Josephus, Jeremiah, and Polybius." *History and Theory* 21.3: 366–381.

———. 1983. "Conversion to Judaism in Historical Perspective: From Biblical Israel to Post-biblical Judaism." *Conservative Judaism* 36.4: 31–45.

———. 1992. "Can a Convert to Judaism have a Jewish Mother?" In *Torah and Wisdom: Studies in Jewish Philosophy, Kabbalah and Halacha. Essays in Honor of Arthur Hyman,* edited by Ruth Link-Salinger, 19–31. New York: Shengold.

———. 1998. "The Conversion of Antoninus." In Schäfer 1998, 141–171.

———. 1999a. *The Beginnings of Jewishness: Boundaries, Varieties, Uncertainties.* Berkeley: University of California Press.

———. 1999b. "The Rabbi in Second-Century Jewish Society." In *The Cambridge History of Judaism vol. 3: The Early Roman Period,* edited by William Horbury, William D. Davies, and John Sturdy, 922–990. Cambridge: CUP.

———. 2005. *Why Aren't Jewish Women Circumcised? Gender and Covenant in Judaism.* Berkeley: University of California Press.

Collins, John J. 2002. "Temporality and Politics in Jewish Apocalyptic Literature." In *Apocalyptic in History and Tradition,* edited by Christopher Rowland and John Barton, 26–43. Sheffield: Sheffield Academic Press.

———. 2010. *The Scepter and the Star: Messianism in Light of the Dead Sea Scrolls.* Grand Rapids: Eerdmans. (First edition 1995.)

———. 2011a. "Apocalypse and Empire." *Svensk Exegetisk Årsbok* 76: 1–19.

———. 2011b. "King and Messiah as Son of God." In *Reconsidering the Concept of Revolutionary Monotheism,* edited by Beate Pongratz-Leisten, 291–315. Winona Lake: Eisenbrauns.

———. 2017. *The Invention of Judaism: Torah and Jewish Identity from Deuteronomy to Paul.* Oakland: University of California Press.

Cooley, Alison E. 2009. *Res gestae divi Augusti: Text, Translation, and Commentary.* Cambridge: CUP.

Corbier, Mireille (ed.). 1999. *Adoption et fosterage.* Paris: De Boccard.

———. 2007. "Painting and Familial and Genealogical Memory (Pliny, Natural History 35, 1–14)." In *Vita Vigilia Est: Essays in Honour of Barbara Levick,* edited by Edward Bispham and Greg Rowe, with Elaine Matthews, 69–83. London: Institute of Classical Studies.

Corcoran, Simon. 2017. "Maxentius: A Roman Emperor in Rome." *Antiquité tardive* 25: 59–74.

Cordier, Pierre. 2001. "Les Romains et la circoncision." *REJ* 160.3–4: 337–355.

Coriat, Jean-Pierre. 1997. *Le prince législateur: la technique législative des Sévères et les méthodes de création du droit impérial à la fin du principat.* Rome: École Française de Rome.

Corley, Kathleen E. 2004. "Women's Inheritance Rights in Antiquity and Paul's Metaphor of Adoption." In *A Feminist Companion to Paul,* edited by Amy-Jill Levine with Marianne Blickenstaff, 98–121. London: T&T Clark.

Cornwell, Hannah. 2017. *Pax and the Politics of Peace: Republic to Principate.* Oxford: OUP.

Coşkun, Altay. 2018. "'Friendship and Alliance' between the Judaeans under Judas Maccabee and the Romans (*1Macc* 8: 17–32): A Response to Linda Zollschan's *Rome and Judaea.*" *Electrum* 25: 85–125.

Cotton, Hannah M. 1993. "The Guardianship of Jesus Son of Babatha: Roman and Local Law in the Province of Arabia." *JRS* 83: 94–108.

———. 1998. "The Rabbis and the Documents." In *Jews in a Graeco-Roman World,* edited by Martin Goodman, 167–179. London: Clarendon Press.

———. 1999. "The Languages of the Legal and Administrative Documents from the Judaean Desert." *ZPE* 125: 219–231.

———. 2002. "Jewish Jurisdiction under Roman Rule: Prolegomena." In *Zwischen den Reichen: Neues Testament und Römische Herrschaft,* edited by Michael Labahn, 13–28. Tübingen: Francke Verlag.

Cotton, Hannah M., and Werner Eck. 2005a. "Josephus' Roman Audience: Josephus and the Roman Elites." In Edmondson, Mason, and Rives 2005, 37–52.

——. 2005b. "Roman Officials in Judaea and Arabia and Civil Jurisdiction." In *Law in the Documents of the Judaean Desert*, edited by Ranon Katzoff and David Schaps, 23–44. Leiden: Brill.

Cowan, J. Andrew. 2018. "A Tale of Two Antiquities: A Fresh Evaluation of the Relationship between the Ancient Histories of T. Flavius Josephus and Dionysius of Halicarnassus." *JSJ* 49.4–5: 475–497.

Cowey, James M. S., and Klaus Maresh. 2001. *Urkunden des Politeuma der Juden von Herakleopolis (144/3–133/2 v.Chr.) (P. Polit. Iud.)*. Wiesbaden: Springer Fachmedien.

Crawford, Michael H. 1974. *Roman Republican Coinage*. Cambridge: CUP.

—— (ed.). 1996. *Roman Statutes*. London: Institute of Classical Studies.

Crouch, Carly L. 2009. *War and Ethics in the Ancient Near East: Military Violence in Light of Cosmology and History*. Berlin: De Gruyter.

——. 2014. *Israel and the Assyrians: Deuteronomy, the Succession Treaty of Esarhaddon, and the Nature of Subversion*. Atlanta: SBL.

Cullhed, Mats. 1994. Conservator Urbis Suae: *Studies in the Politics and Propaganda of the Emperor Maxentius*. Stockholm: P. Åströms.

Curran, John. 2014. "*Philorhomaioi*: The Herods between Rome and Jerusalem." *JSJ* 45.4–5: 493–522.

Czajkowski, Kimberley. 2015. "Jewish Attitudes towards the Imperial Cult." *SCI* 34: 181–194.

——. 2017. *Localized Law: The Babatha and Salome Komaise Archives*. Oxford: OUP.

D'Amati, Laura. 2004. Civis ab hostibus captus: *profili di regime classico*. Milano: A. Giuffrè.

Damgaard, Finn. 2008. "Brothers in Arms: Josephus' Portrait of Moses in the 'Jewish Antiquities' in the Light of his Own Self-Portraits in the 'Jewish War' and the 'Life'." *JJS* 59: 218–235.

Danby, Herbert. 1933. *The Mishnah, translated from the Hebrew with introduction and brief explanatory notes*. Oxford: OUP.

Darwal-Smith, Robin H. 1996. *Emperors and Architecture: A Study of Flavian Rome*. Brussels: Latomus.

Daube, David. 1944. "The Civil Law of the Mishnah: The Arrangement of the Three Gates." *Tulane Law Review* 18.3: 351–407.

——. 1991. "Collatio 2.6.5." In Daube, *Collected Studies in Roman Law I*, edited by David Cohen and Dieter Simon, 107–122. Frankfurt am Main: Klostermann.

Davidson, Steed V. 2011. *Empire and Exile: Postcolonial Readings of the Book of Jeremiah*. London: T&T Clark.

De Lange, Nicolas. 1978. "Jewish Attitudes to the Roman Empire." In *Imperialism in the Ancient World*, edited by Peter Garnsey and Charles R. Whittaker, 255–281. Cambridge: CUP.

De Souza, Philip. 1999. *Piracy in the Graeco-Roman World*. Cambridge: CUP.

——. 2008. "*Parta victoriis pax*: Roman Emperors as Peacemakers." In *War and Peace in Ancient and Medieval History*, edited by Philip de Souza and John France, 76–106. Cambridge: CUP.

Dench, Emma. 2005. *Romulus' Asylum: Roman Identities from the Age of Alexander to the Age of Hadrian*. Oxford: OUP.

Di Filippo Balestrazzi, Elena. 1997. "Roma." In *LIMC* VIII.1, 1048–1068. Zürich: Artemis Verlag.

Diamond, James A. 2007. *Converts, Heretics, and Lepers: Maimonides and the Outsider*. Notre Dame: University of Notre Dame Press.

DiTommaso, Lorenzo. 2007a. "Apocalypses and Apocalypticism in Antiquity (Part I)." *CBR* 5.2: 235–286.

——. 2007b. "Apocalypses and Apocalypticism in Antiquity (Part II)." *CBR* 5.3: 367–432.

Dihle, Albrecht. 1994. *Greek and Latin Literature of the Roman Empire: From Augustus to Justinian*, transl. by Manfred Malzahn. London: Routledge.

Doering, Lutz. 1999. *Schabbat: Sabbathalacha und -praxis im antiken Judentum und Urchristentum*. Tübingen: Mohr Siebeck.

Dohrmann, Natalie B. 2002. "Analogy, Empire and Political Conflict in a Rabbinic Midrash." *JJS* 53.2: 273–297.

——. 2003. "The Boundaries of the Law and the Problem of Jurisdiction in an Early Palestinian Midrash." In Hezser 2003a, 83–103.

——. 2008. "Manumission and Transformation in Jewish and Roman Law." In *Jewish Biblical Interpretation and Cultural Exchange: Comparative Exegesis in Context*, edited by Natalie B. Dohrmann and David Stern, 51–65. Philadelphia: University of Pennsylvania Press.

——. 2013. "Law and Imperial Idioms: Rabbinic Legalism in a Roman World." In Dohrmann and Reed 2013, 63–78.

——. 2015. "Can 'Law' Be Private? The Mixed Message of Rabbinic Oral Law." In *Public and Private in Ancient Mediterranean Law and Religion*, edited by Clifford Ando and Jörg Rüpke, 187–216. Berlin: De Gruyter.

——. 2020. "Jewish Books and Roman Readers: Censorship, Authorship, and the Rabbinic Library." In Berthelot 2020a, 417–441.

——. 2021. "*Ad similitudinem arbitrorum*: On the Perils of Commensurability & Comparison in Roman and Rabbinic Law." In Berthelot, Dohrmann, and Nemo-Pekelman 2021, 365–385.

Dohrmann, Natalie B., and Annette Y. Reed (eds.). 2013. *Jews, Christians, and the Roman Empire: The Poetics of Power in Late Antiquity*. Philadelphia: Pennsylvania University Press.

Dolganov, Anna. 2019. "Reichsrecht and Volksrecht in Theory and Practice: Roman Justice in the Province of Egypt (P. Oxy. II 237, P. Oxy. IV 706, SB XII 10929)." *Tyche* 34: 27–60.

Donaldson, Terence L. 2007. *Judaism and the Gentiles: Jewish Patterns of Universalism (to 135 CE)*. Waco: Baylor University Press.

Doran, Robert. 2011. "The Persecution of Judeans by Antiochus IV: The Significance of 'Ancestral Laws.'" In *The Other in Second Temple Judaism: Essays in Honor of John J. Collins*, edited by Daniel C. Harlow et al., 423–433. Grand Rapids: Michigan.

——. 2012. *2 Maccabees: A Critical Commentary*. Minneapolis: Fortress Press.

Dorival, Gilles. 1996. "'Dire en grec les choses juives'. Quelques choix lexicaux du Pentateuque de la Septante." *REG* 109.2: 527–547.

——. 2019. "Christian Redefinitions of Citizenship." In Berthelot and Price 2019, 267–282.

Dubouloz, Julien. 2021. "Accommodating Former Legal Systems and Roman Law: Cicero's Rhetorical and Legal Perspective in the Verrine Orations." In Berthelot, Dohrmann, and Nemo-Pekelman 2021, 47–67.

Duhaime, Jean. 1988. "The War Scroll from Qumran and the Greco-Roman Tactical Treatises." *Revue de Qumrân* 13: 133–151.

Duncan, Thomas S. 1948. "The Aeneas Legend on Coins." *The Classical Journal* 44.1: 15–29.

Dunn, James D.G. 1993. *The Epistle to the Galatians*. Peabody: Hendrickson Publishers.

Dupont, Florence. 2005. *Façons de parler grec à Rome*. Paris: Belin.

Duverger, Maurice (ed.). 1980. *Le concept d'Empire*. Paris: PUF.

Dyson, Stephen L. 1971. "Native Revolts in the Roman Empire." *Historia* 20: 239–274.

Eck, Werner. 1999. "The Bar Kokhba Revolt: The Roman Point of View." *JRS* 89: 76–89.

——. 2003. "Hadrian, the Bar Kokhba Revolt, and the Epigraphic Transmission." In Schäfer 2003a, 153–170.

——. 2007. *Rom und Judaea: Fünf Vorträge zur römischen Herrschaft in Palaestina*. Tübingen: Mohr Siebeck.

Eddy, Samuel K. 1961. *The King is Dead: Studies in Near Eastern Resistance to Hellenism, 334–31 B.C.* Lincoln: University of Nebraska.

Edmonson, Jonathan. 2015. "Making a Request to the Emperor: Rescripts in the Roman Empire." In *Il princeps romano: autocrate o magistrato? Fattori giuridici e fattori sociali del potere imperiale da Augusto a Commodo*, edited by Jean-Louis Ferrary and John Scheid, 127–155. Pavia: IUSS Press.

Edmondson, Jonathan, Steve Mason, and James Rives (eds.). 2005. *Flavius Josephus and Flavian Rome*. Oxford: OUP.

Edrei, Aryeh. 2006. "Divine Spirit and Physical Power: Rabbi Shlomo Goren and the Military Ethic of the Israel Defense Forces." *Theoretical Inquiries in Law* 7.1: 255–297.

Edwell, Peter. 2013. "Definition of Roman Imperialism." In Hoyos 2013, 39–52.

Eisenbaum, Pamela. 2004. "A Remedy for Having Been Born of Woman: Jesus, Gentiles, and Genealogy in Romans." *JBL* 123.4: 671–702.

Elledge, Casey D. 2017. *Resurrection of the Dead in Early Judaism 200 BCE–CE 200*. Oxford: OUP.

Elman, Yaakov, and Shai Secunda. 2015. "Judaism." in *The Wiley Blackwell Companion to Zoroastrianism*, edited by Michael Stausberg, Yuhan Sohrab-Dinshaw Vevaina, and Anna Tessmann, 423–435. Chichester: Wiley.

Enger, Philipp A. 2006. *Die Adoptivkinder Abrahams: eine exegetische Spurensuche zur Vorgeschichte des Proselytentums*. Frankfurt am Main: P. Lang.

Erdkamp, Paul (ed.). 2007. *A Companion to the Roman Army*. Malden: Blackwell.

Errington, R. M. 1980. "Rom, Antiochos der Große und die Asylie von Teos." *ZPE* 39: 279–284.

Erskine, Andrew. 1995. "Rome in the Greek World: The Significance of a Name." In *The Greek World*, edited by Anton Powell, 368–383. London: Routledge.

——— (ed.). 2003. *A Companion to the Hellenistic World*. Malden: Blackwell.

———. 2010. *Roman Imperialism*. Edinburgh: Edinburgh University Press.

Eshel, Hanan. 2000. "The Date of the Founding of Aelia Capitolina." In *The Dead Sea Scrolls Fifty Years after their Discovery*, edited by Lawrence H. Schiffman, Emanuel Tov, and James C. VanderKam, 637–643. Jerusalem: Israel Exploration Society in cooperation with the Shrine of the Book, Israel Museum.

———. 2001. "The Kittim in the War Scroll and in the Pesharim." In *Historical Perspectives: From the Hasmoneans to Bar Kokhba in Light of the Dead Sea Scrolls*, edited by David M. Goodblatt, 29–44. Leiden: Brill.

———. 2008. *The Dead Sea Scrolls and the Hasmonean State*. Grand Rapids: Eerdmans; Jerusalem: Yad Izhak Ben-Zvi.

Fabia, Philippe. 1929. *La table claudienne de Lyon*. Lyon: Impression de M. Audin.

Farney, Gary D. 2007. *Ethnic Identity and Aristocratic Competition in Republican Rome*. New York: CUP.

———. 2014. "Romans and Italians." In McInerney 2014, 437–454.

Fears, J. Rufus. 1978. "Ο ΔΗΜΟΣ Ο ΡΩΜΑΙΩΝ Genius Populi Romani: A Note on the Origin of Dea Roma." *Mnemosyne* 31.3: 274–286.

———. 1981. "The Theology of Victory at Rome: Approaches and Problems." In *Aufstieg und Niedergang der Römischen Welt* II.17.2, edited by Wolfgang Haase, 736–826. Berlin: De Gruyter.

Feigin, Samuel I. 1931. "Some Cases of Adoption in Israel." *JBL* 50: 186–200.

Feldman, Louis H. 1990–91. "Abba Kolon and the Founding of Rome." *JQR* 81.3–4: 449–482.

———. 1992a. "Some Observations on Rabbinic Reaction to Roman Rule in Third Century Palestine." *Hebrew Union College Annual* 63: 39–81. Reprint in: *Studies in Hellenistic Judaism*, 438–483. Leiden: Brill, 1996.

———. 1992b. "Josephus' Portrait of Moses: Part Two." *JQR* 83.1–2: 7–50.

——. 1993. *Jew and Gentile in the Ancient World: Attitudes and Interactions from Alexander to Justinian*. Princeton: PUP.

——. 2000. *Flavius Josephus, Judean Antiquities 1–4*. Leiden: Brill.

——. 2004. *"Remember Amalek!": Vengeance, Zealotry, and Group Destruction in the Bible according to Philo, Pseudo-Philo, and Josephus*. Cincinnati: Hebrew Union College Press.

Ferrar, William J. 1920. *The Proof of the Gospel being the Demonstratio Evangelica of Eusebius of Caesarea, Vol. II*. London: SPCK.

Ferrary, Jean-Louis. 1988. *Philhellénisme et impérialisme. Aspects idéologiques de la conquête romaine du monde hellénistique, de la seconde guerre de Macédoine à la guerre contre Mithridate*. Rome: École Française de Rome.

——. 2009. "La gravure de documents publics de la Rome républicaine et ses motivations." In Haensch 2009, 59–74.

Ferris, Iain. 2003. "The Hanged Men Dance: Barbarians in Trajanic Art." In *Roman Imperialism and Provincial Art*, edited by Sarah Scott and Jane Webster, 53–68. Cambridge: CUP.

Fibiger Bang, Peter, and Dariusz Kołodziejczyk (eds.). 2012. *Universal Empire: A Comparative Approach to Imperial Culture and Representation in Eurasian History*. Cambridge: CUP.

Filtvedt, Ole J. 2016. "A 'Non-Ethnic' People?" *Biblica* 97.1: 101–120.

Fink, Robert O. 1971. *Roman Military Records on Papyrus*. Cleveland: Press of Case Western Reserve University.

Finkelstein, Israel. 2018. *Hasmonean Realities behind Ezra, Nehemiah, and Chronicles: Archaeological and Historical Perspectives*. Atlanta: SBL Press.

Finkelstein, Louis. 1923. "The Book of Jubilees and the Rabbinic Halaka." *HTR* 16: 39–61.

Fischer-Bovet, Christelle, and Sitta von Reden (eds.). Forthcoming. *Comparing the Ptolemaic and Seleucid Empires: Integration, Communication and Resistance*. Cambridge: CUP.

Fishwick, Duncan. 1987–2005. *The Imperial Cult in the Latin West*. 3 vols. Leiden: Brill.

——. 1988. "Dated Inscriptions and the Feriale Duranum." *Syria* 65: 349–361.

Fitzpatrick-McKinley, Anne. 2016. "Continuity between Assyrian and Persian Policies toward the Cults of their Subjects." In *Religion in the Achaemenid Persian Empire: Emerging Judaisms and Trends*, edited by Diana Edelman, Anne Fitzpatrick-McKinley, and Philippe Guillaume, 137–171. Tübingen: Mohr Siebeck.

Flusser, David. 1956 [2009]. "Januvris—Janus." In *Zion* 21: 100–102 (Heb.). English translation by Azzan Yadin in *Judaism of the Second Temple Period, Volume 2: The Jewish Sages and Their Literature*, 305–308. Jerusalem: Magnes; Grand Rapids: Eerdmans, 2009.

——. 1972. "The Four Empires in the Fourth Sybil and in the Book of Daniel." *Israel Oriental Studies* 2: 148–175.

——. 1983 [2007]. "The Roman Empire in Hasmonean and Essene Eyes." *Zion* 48: 149–176. English translation by Azzan Yadin in *Judaism of the Second Temple Period, Volume 1: Qumran and Apocalypticism*, 175–206. Jerusalem: Magnes; Grand Rapids: Eerdmans, 2007.

——. 1988. "The Didache and the Noachic Commandements." In *Judaism and the Origins of Christianity*, 508. Jerusalem: Magnes.

Flynn, Shawn W. 2014. *YHWH is King: The Development of Divine Kingship in Ancient Israel*. Leiden: Brill.

Fournier, Julien. 2010. *Entre tutelle romaine et autonomie civique: l'administration judiciaire dans les provinces hellénophones de l'Empire romain, 129 av. J.-C.–235 apr. J.-C.* Athènes: École française d'Athènes.

——. 2021. "Representing the Rights of a City: *Ekdikoi* in Roman Courts." In Berthelot, Dohrmann, and Nemo-Pekelman 2021, 175–194.

Fowler, Kimberley. 2021. "Early Christian Perspectives on Roman Law and Mosaic Law." In Berthelot, Dohrmann, and Nemo-Pekelman 2021, 429–453.

Fowler, Richard, and Olivier Hekster. 2005. "Imagining Kings: From Persia to Rome." In *Imaginary Kings: Royal Images in the Ancient Near East, Greece and Rome*, edited by Richard Fowler and Olivier Hekster, 9–38. Stuttgart: Franz Steiner Verlag.

Fraade, Steven D. 1991. *From Tradition to Commentary: Torah and Its Interpretation in the Midrash*. Albany: State University of New York Press.

———. 2003. "'The Torah of the King' (Deut 17:14–20) in the Temple Scroll and Early Rabbinic Law." In *The Dead Sea Scrolls as Background to Postbiblical Judaism and Early Christianity: Papers from an International Conference at St. Andrews in 2001*, edited by James R. Davila, 25–60. Leiden: Brill.

———. 2011a. *Legal Fictions: Studies of Law and Narrative in the Discursive Worlds of Ancient Jewish Sectarians and Sages*. Leiden: Brill.

———. 2011b. "Before and After Babel: Linguistic Exceptionalism and Pluralism in Early Rabbinic Literature and Jewish Antiquity." *Diné Israel* 28: 31*–68*.

———. Forthcoming. "The Torah Inscribed/Transcribed in Seventy Languages." In *Hebrew Between Jews and Christians*, edited by Daniel Stein Kokin, forthcoming. Berlin: De Gruyter.

Fraenkel, Yonah. 1981. *'Iyunim ba-'Olamo ha-Ruḥani shel Sippur ha-Aggadah*. Tel Aviv: Ha-Kibbutz ha-Meuḥad. (Heb.)

Frahm, Eckart (ed.). 2017. *A Companion to Assyria*. Hoboken: John Wiley & Sons.

Frakes, Robert M. 2011. *Compiling the Collatio Legum Mosaicarum et Romanarum in Late Antiquity*. Oxford: OUP.

Frankena, Robert. 1965. "The Vassal-Treaties of Esarhaddon and the Dating of Deuteronomy." *Oudtestamentische Studiën* 14 (הכ): 122–154.

Fredriksen, Paula. 2006. "Mandatory Retirement: Ideas in the Study of Christian Origins Whose Time Has Come to Go." *Studies in Religion / Sciences Religieuses* 35: 231–246.

———. 2010. "Judaizing the Nations: The Ritual Demands of Paul's Gospel." *NTS* 56: 232–252.

———. 2017. *Paul, the Pagans' Apostle*. New Haven: Yale University Press.

———. 2018. "How Jewish is God? Divine Ethnicity in Paul's Theology." *JBL* 137.1: 193–212.

———. 2019. "How Do the Nations Relate to Israel? Family, Ethnicity, and Eschatological Inclusion in the Apostle Paul." In Berthelot and Price 2019, 131–140.

Frei, Peter, and Klaus Koch. 1996. *Reichsidee und Reichsorganisation im Perserreich*. Freiburg: Universitätsverlag; Göttingen: Vandenhoek & Ruprecht. (First edition 1984.)

Friedheim, Emmanuel. 2006. *Rabbinisme et paganisme en Palestine romaine: étude historique des Realia talmudiques (Ier–IVème siècles)*. Leiden: Brill.

Friedman, Shamma. 1999. "The Primacy of Tosefta to Mishnah in Synoptic Parallels." In *Introducing Tosefta: Textual, Intertextual and Intertextual Studies*, edited by Harry Fox and Tirzah Meacham, 99–121. Hoboken: Ktav.

Frisch, Alexandria. 2017. *The Danielic Discourse on Empire in Second Temple Literature*. Leiden: Brill.

Fuchs, Harald. 1938. *Der geistige Widerstand gegen Rom in der antiken Welt*. Berlin: De Gruyter.

Fuhrmann, Christopher J. 2012. *Policing the Roman Empire: Soldiers, Administration, and Public Order*. Oxford: OUP.

Fuks, Alexander. 1953. "The Jewish Revolt in Egypt (A.D. 115–117) in the Light of the Papyri." *Aegyptus* 33.1: 131–158.

———. 1961. "Aspects of the Jewish Revolt in A.D. 115–117." *JRS* 51: 98–104.

Fuller, Lon L. 1967. *Legal Fictions*. Stanford: Stanford University Press.

Furstenberg, Yair. 2018. "From Competition to Integration: The Laws of the Nations in Early Rabbinic Literature within its Roman Context." *Diné Israel* 32: 21–58. (Heb.)

———. 2019a. "The Rabbis and the Roman Citizenship Model: The Case of the Samaritans." In Berthelot and Price 2019, 181–216.

———. 2019b. "Provincial Rabbis: Shaping Rabbinic Divorce Procedure in a Roman Legal Environment." *JQR* 109.4: 471–499.

———. 2021. "Imperialism and the Creation of Local Law: The Case of Rabbinic Law." In Berthelot, Dohrmann, and Nemo-Pekelman 2021, 271–300.

Gafni, Isaiah. 1990. *The Jews of Babylonia in the Talmudic Era: A Social and Cultural History*. Jerusalem: Zalman Shazar Center. (Heb.)

———. 1997. *Land, Center and Diaspora: Jewish Constructs in Late Antiquity*. Sheffield: Sheffield Academic Press.

Galinsky, Karl. 1969. *Aeneas, Sicily and Rome*. Princeton: PUP.

———. 1996. *Augustan Culture: An Interpretive Introduction*. Princeton: PUP.

Gambash, Gil. 2013. "Foreign Enemies of the Empire: The Great Jewish Revolt and the Roman Perception of the Jews." *SCI* 32: 173–194.

———. 2015. *Rome and Provincial Resistance*. London: Routledge.

Gambash, Gil, and Haim Gitler (eds.). 2017. *Faces of Power: Roman Gold Coins from the Victor A. Adda Collection*. Jerusalem: The Israel Museum.

Gardner, Andrew. 2013. "Thinking about Roman Imperialism: Postcolonialism, Globalisation and Beyond?" *Britannia* 44: 1–25.

Gardner, Gregg E. 2007. "Jewish Leadership and Hellenistic Civic Benefaction in the Second Century B.C.E." *JBL* 126: 327–343.

Gardner, Jane F. 1993. *Being a Roman Citizen*. London: Routledge.

———. 1998. *Family and Familia in Roman Law and Life*. Oxford: Clarendon Press.

———. 1999. "Status, Sentiment and Strategy in Roman Adoption." In Corbier 1999, 63–79.

———. 2001. "Making Citizens: The Operation of the Lex Irnitana." In *Administration, Prosopography and Appointment Policies in the Roman Empire*, edited by Lukas de Blois, 215–229. Amsterdam: J.C. Gieben.

Garelli, Paul. 1979. "L'Etat et la légitimité royale sous l'empire assyrien." In *Power and Propaganda: A Symposium on Ancient Empires*, edited by Mogens Trolle Larsen, 319–329. Copenhagen: Akademisk Forlag.

———. 1981. "La conception de la royauté en Assyrie." In *Assyrian Royal Inscriptions: New Horizons in Literary, Ideological, and Historical Analysis*, edited by Frederick Mario Fales, 1–11. Rome: Istituto per l'Oriente.

Garnsey, Peter. 1968. "Legal Privilege in the Roman Empire." *Past and Present* 41: 3–24.

———. 1970. *Social Status and Legal Privilege in the Roman Empire*. Oxford: Clarendon Press.

———. 2004. "Roman Citizenship and Roman Law in the Late Empire." In *Approaching Late Antiquity: The Transformation from Early to Late Empire*, edited by Simon Swain and Mark Edwards, 133–155. Oxford: OUP.

Gary, Gilbert. 2004. "Jews in Imperial Administration and Its Significance for Dating the Jewish Donor Inscription from Aphrodisias." *JSJ* 35: 169–184.

Gaudemet, Jean. 1979. *La formation du droit séculier et du droit de l'Église aux IVe et Ve siècles*. Paris: Sirey. (First edition 1957.)

Gauthier, Philippe. 1974. "'Générosité' romaine et 'avarice' grecque: sur l'octroi du droit de cité." In *Mélanges d'histoire ancienne offerts à William Seston*, edited by Pierre Courcelle, 207–215. Paris: De Boccard.

———. 1981. "La citoyenneté en Grèce et à Rome: participation et intégration," *Ktema* 6: 167–179.

———. 1984. "A propos de *politeia*." *REG* 97: 523–530.

———. 1985. *Les cités grecques et leurs bienfaiteurs, IVe-Ier siècle avant J.-C. Contribution à l'histoire des institutions*. Athènes: École française d'Athènes.

Gehler, Michael, and Robert Rollinger. 2014. "Imperien und Reiche in der Weltgeschichte: Epochenübergreifende und globalhistorische Vergleiche (Einleitung)." In *Imperien und*

Reiche in der Weltgeschichte: Epochenübergreifende und globalhistorische Vergleiche, edited by Michael Gehler and Robert Rollinger, 1–32. Wiesbaden: Harrassowitz.

Geiger, Joseph. 1997. "Herodes philorhomaios." *Ancient Society* 28: 75–88.

Giardina, Andrea. 1994. "L'identità incompiuta dell' Italia romana." In *L'Italie d'Auguste à Dioclétien: Actes du colloque international, Rome, 25–28 mars 1992*, 1–89. Rome: École Française de Rome.

Gibbon, Edward. 1972. *The English Essays of Edward Gibbon*, edited by Patricia B. Craddock. Oxford: Clarendon Press.

Gibson, E. Leigh. 1999. *The Jewish Manumission Inscriptions of the Bosporus Kingdom*. Tübingen: Mohr Siebeck.

Gilboa, A. 1972. "L'octroi de la citoyenneté romaine et de l'immunité à Antipater, père d'Hérode." *Revue historique de droit français et étranger* Quatrième série, 50.4: 609–614.

Gillihan, Yonder M. 2011. "The ר who wasn't there: fictional aliens in the Damascus Rule." *Revue de Qumrân* 25.98: 257–305.

———. 2012. *Civic Ideology, Organization, and Law in the Rule Scrolls: A Comparative Study of the Covenanters' Sect and Contemporary Voluntary Associations in Political Context*. Leiden: Brill.

Girard, Paul F. 1929. *Manuel élémentaire de droit romain*. Paris: A. Rousseau.

Glanville, Mark. 2018a. "The Gēr (Stranger) in Deuteronomy: Family for the Displaced." *JBL* 137.3: 599–623.

———. 2018b. *Adopting the Stranger as Kindred in Deuteronomy*. Atlanta: SBL Press.

Gold, Michael. 1987. "Adoption: A New Problem for Jewish Law." *Judaism* 36: 443–450.

Goldenberg, Robert. 1979. "The Jewish Sabbath in the Roman World up to the Time of Constantine the Great." *Aufstieg und Niedergang der Römischen Welt* II.19.1, edited by Wolfgang Haase, 414–447. Berlin: De Gruyter.

Goldstone, Jack A., and John F. Haldon. 2009. "Ancient States Empires and Exploitation: Problems and Perspectives." In Morris and Scheidel 2009, 3–29.

González, Julián, and Michael H. Crawford. 1986. "The Lex Irnitana: A New Copy of the Flavian Municipal Law." *JRS* 76: 147–243.

Goodenough, Erwin R. 1938. *The Politics of Philo Judaeus: Practice and Theory*. New Haven: Yale University Press.

Goodman, Martin. 1983. *State and Society in Roman Galilee, A.D. 132–212*. London: Vallentine Mitchell.

———. 1987. *The Ruling Class of Judaea: The Origins of the Jewish Revolt against Rome A.D. 66–70*. New York: CUP.

———. 1989. "Nerva, the Fiscus Judaicus and Jewish Identity." *JRS* 79: 40–44.

———. 1991. "Opponents of Rome: Jews and Others." In *Images of Empire*, edited by Alexander Loveday, 222–238. Sheffield: JSOT Press.

———. 1992. "The Roman State and the Jewish Patriarch." In *Galilee in Late Antiquity*, edited by Lee I. Levine, 127–139. New York: Jewish Theological Seminary.

———. 1994a. *Mission and Conversion: Proselytizing in the Religious History of the Roman Empire*. Oxford: Clarendon Press.

———. 1994b. "Josephus as Roman Citizen." In *Josephus and the History of the Greco-Roman Period*, edited by Fausto Parente, 329–338. Leiden: Brill.

———. 1999. "Josephus' Treatise *Against Apion*." In *Apologetics in the Roman Empire*, edited by Mark Edwards, Martin Goodman, and Simon Price, 45–58. London: OUP.

———. 2003. "Trajan and the Origins of the Bar Kokhba War." In Schäfer 2003a, 23–29.

———. 2004. "Trajan and the Origins of Roman Hostility to the Jews." *Past & Present* 182: 3–29.

———. 2005. "The *Fiscus Iudaicus* and Gentile Attitudes to Judaism in Flavian Rome." In Edmondson, Mason, and Rives 2005, 167–177.

————. 2007. *Rome and Jerusalem: The Clash of Ancient Civilizations*. New York: Alfred A. Knopf.

Gotter, Ulrich. 2008. "Cultural Differences and Cross-Cultural Contact: Greek and Roman Concepts of Power." *Harvard Studies in Classical Philology* 104: 179–230.

Grabbe, Lester L. 2004. *A History of the Jews and Judaism in the Second Temple Period. Volume 1: Yehud. A History of the Persian Province of Judah*. Edinburgh: T&T Clark.

Graf, Fritz. 2002. "Roman Festivals in Syria Palaestina." In Schäfer 2002a, 435–451.

————. 2015. *Roman Festivals in the Greek East: From the Early Empire to the Middle Byzantine Era*. Cambridge: CUP.

Granerød, Gard. 2013. "'By the Favour of Ahuramazda I Am King': On the Promulgation of a Persian Propaganda Text among Babylonians and Judaeans." *JSJ* 44: 455–480.

Green, William S. 1978. "What's in a Name? The Problematic of Rabbinic 'Biography.'" In *Approaches to Ancient Judaism: Theory and Practice*, edited by William S. Green, 77–96. Missoula: Scholars Press.

Gregerman, Adam. 2016. "From Theodicy to Anti-theodicy: Midrashic Accusations of God's Disobedience to Biblical Law." In *Crossing Boundaries in Early Judaism and Christianity: Ambiguities, Complexities, and Half-forgotten Adversaries: Essays in Honor of Alan F. Segal*, edited by Kimberly B. Stratton and Andrea Lieber, 344–359. Leiden: Brill.

Grenet, Frantz. 2013. "Y a-t-il une composante iranienne dans l'apocalyptique judéo-chrétienne? Retour sur un vieux problème." In *Aux origines des messianismes juifs: actes du colloque international tenu en Sorbonne, à Paris, les 8 et 9 juin 2010*, edited by David Hamidović, 121–144. Leiden: Brill.

Griffin, Miriam T. 1982. "The Lyons Tablet and the Tacitean Hindsight." *Classical Quarterly* 32.2: 404–418.

Gruen, Erich S. 1984. *The Hellenistic World and the Coming of Rome*. Berkeley: University of California Press.

————. 1985. "Augustus and the Ideology of War and Peace." In *The Age of Augustus*, edited by Rolf Winke, 51–72. Providence: Brown University.

————. 1992. *Culture and National Identity in Republican Rome*. Ithaca: Cornell University Press.

————. 1999. "Seleucid Royal Ideology." *SBL Seminar Papers* 38: 24–47.

————. 2002. "Roman Perspectives on the Jews in the Age of the Great Revolt." In *The First Jewish Revolt: Archaeology, History, and Ideology*, edited by Andrea M. Berlin and J. Andrew Overman, 27–42. London: Routledge.

————. 2009. "Kinship Relations and Jewish Identity." In *Jewish Identities in Antiquity: Studies in Memory of Menahem Stern*, edited by Lee I. Levine and Daniel R. Schwartz, 101–116. Tübingen: Mohr Siebeck.

————. 2011. *Rethinking the Other in Antiquity*. Princeton: PUP.

————. 2016. "Was There Judeophobia in Classical Antiquity?" In Erich S. Gruen, *Constructs of Identity in Hellenistic Judaism: Essays on Early Jewish Literature and History*, 313–332. Berlin: De Gruyter.

————. 2017. "Josephus and Jewish Ethnicity." In *Sibyls, Scriptures, and Scrolls: John Collins at Seventy*, edited by Joel Baden et al., 489–508. Leiden: Brill.

————. 2020. "The Sibylline Oracles and Resistance to Rome." In Price and Berthelot 2020, 189–205.

Guérin, Charles. 2015. *La voix de la vérité. Témoin et témoignage dans les tribunaux romains du Ier siècle av. J.-C.* Paris: Les Belles Lettres.

Guggenheimer, Heinrich W. 1999. *The Jerusalem Talmud, First Order: Zeraïm. Tractate Berakhot*. Berlin: De Gruyter.

Gulak, Alexander. 1935. *Das Urkundenwesen im Talmud im Lichte der griechisch-aegyptischen Papyri und des griechischen und roemischen Rechts*. Jerusalem: R. Mass.

Gunderson, Erik. 2000. *Staging Masculinity: The Rhetoric of Performance in the Roman World*. Ann Arbor: The University of Michigan Press.

Haaland, Gunnar. 1999. "Jewish Laws for a Roman Audience: Toward an Understanding of *Contra Apionem*." In *Internationales Josephus-Kolloquium Brüssel 1998*, edited by Jürgen U. Kalms, 282–304. Münster: LIT Verlag.

Habas (Rubin), Ephrat. 2001. "The Dedication of Polycharmos from Stobi: Problems of Dating and Interpretation." *JQR* 92.1–2: 41–78.

Hadas-Lebel, Mireille. 1984a. "Jacob et Esaü ou Israël et Rome dans le Talmud et le Midrash." *RHR* 201.4: 369–392.

——. 1984b. "La fiscalité romaine dans la littérature rabbinique jusqu'à la fin du IIIe siècle." *REJ* 143: 5–29.

——. 1990. *Jérusalem contre Rome*. Paris: Éditions du Cerf. English translation: *Jerusalem against Rome*. Leuven: Peeters, 2006.

Haensch, Rudolph (ed.). 2009. *Selbstdarstellung und Kommunikation: die Veröffentlichung staatlicher Urkunden auf Stein und Bronze in der römischen Welt. Internationales Kolloquium an der Kommission für Alte Geschichte und Epigraphik in München*. Munich: C. H. Beck.

Hagedorn, Anselm C. 2007. "Local Law in an Imperial Context: The Role of Torah in the (Imagined) Persian Period." In Knoppers and Levinson 2007, 57–76.

Halbertal, Moshe. 1998. "Coexisting with the Enemy: Jews and Pagans in the Mishna." In *Tolerance and Intolerance in Early Judaism and Christianity*, edited by Graham Stanton and Guy G. Stroumsa, 159–172. Cambridge: CUP.

——. 2013. "The History of Halakhah and the Emergence of Halakhah." *Diné Israel* 29: 1–23.

Hall, Edith. 1993. "Asia Unmanned: Images of Victory in Classical Athens." In *War and Society in the Greek World*, edited by John Rich and Graham Shipley, 108–133. London: Routledge.

Hanneken, Todd R. 2015. "Moses Has His Interpreters: Understanding the Legal Exegesis in Acts 15 from the Precedent in Jubilees." *CBQ* 77.4: 686–706.

Har-Peled, Misgav. 2013. *The Dialogical Beast: The Identification of Rome with the Pig in Early Rabbinic Literature*. Unpublished PhD thesis, John Hopkins University.

Harding, Brian. 2008. *Augustine and Roman Virtue*. London: Continuum.

Harland, Philip A. 2007. "Familial Dimensions of Group Identity (II): "Mothers" and "Fathers" in Associations and Synagogues of the Greek World." *JSJ* 38.1: 57–79.

Harries, Jill. 2003. "Creating Legal Space: Resolving Disputes in the Roman Empire." In Hezser 2003a, 63–81.

——. 2010. "Courts and the Judicial System." In Hezser 2010, 85–101.

——. 2013. "Roman Law from City State to World Empire." In *Law and Empire: Ideas, Practices, Actors*, edited by Jeroen Duindam et al., 45–61. Leiden: Brill.

Hartog, François. 1991. "Rome et la Grèce: les choix de Denys d'Halicarnasse." In *ΕΛΛΗΝΙΣΜΟΣ: quelques jalons pour une histoire de l'identité grecque*, edited by Suzanne Saïd, 149–167. Leiden: Brill.

——. 1996. *Mémoire d'Ulysse: récits sur la frontière en Grèce ancienne*. Paris: Gallimard.

Hartog, Pieter B. 2019. "Contesting *Oikoumenē*: Resistance and Locality in Philo's *Legatio ad Gaium*." In *Intolerance, Polemics, and Debate in Antiquity: Politico-Cultural, Philosophical, and Religious Forms of Critical Conversation*, edited by George van Kooten and Jacques van Ruiten, 205–231. Leiden: Brill.

Hasan-Rokem, Galit. 1993. "Within Limits and Beyond: History and Body in Midrashic Texts." *International Folklore Review* 9: 5–12.

——. 1998. "Narratives in Dialogue: A Folk Literary Perspective on Interreligious Contacts in the Holy Land in Rabbinic Literature of Late Antiquity." In *Sharing the Sacred: Religious Contacts and Conflicts in the Holy Land*, edited by Aryeh Kofsky and Guy G. Stroumsa, 109–129. Jerusalem: Yad Izhak Ben Zvi.

Haspels, Emilie C. H. 1971. *The Highlands of Phrygia: Sites and Monuments*. 2 vols. Princeton: PUP.

Hauptman, Judith. 2005. *Rereading the Mishnah: A New Approach to Ancient Jewish Texts*. Tübingen: Mohr Siebeck.

Hayes, Christine E. 1995. "Amoraic Interpretation and Halakhic Development: The Case of the Prohibited Basilica." *JSJ* 26.2: 156–168.

———. 1998. "The Abrogation of Torah Law: Rabbinic *Taqqanah* and Praetorian Edict." In Schäfer 1998, 643–674.

———. 1999. "Intermarriage and Impurity in Ancient Jewish Sources." *HTR* 92.1: 3–36.

———. 2000. "Halakhah le-Moshe mi-Sinai in Rabbinic Sources: A Methodological Case Study." In *The Synoptic Problem in Rabbinic Literature*, edited by Shaye J. D. Cohen, 61–117. Providence: Brown University Press.

———. 2002a. *Gentile Impurities and Jewish Identities: Intermarriage and Conversion from the Bible to the Talmud*. Oxford: OUP.

———. 2002b. "Genealogy, Illegitimacy, and Personal Status: The Yerushalmi in Comparative Perspective." In Schäfer 2002a, 73–90.

———. 2015. *What's Divine about Divine Law? Early Perspectives*. Princeton: PUP.

———. 2017a. "The Complicated Goy in Classical Rabbinic Sources." In Bar-Asher Siegal, Grünstäudl, and Thiessen 2017, 147–167.

———. 2017b. "Thiessen and Kaden on Paul and the Gentiles." *Journal for the Study of Paul and His Letters* 7.1–2: 68–79.

——— (ed.). 2017c. *The Cambridge Companion to Judaism and Law*. New York: CUP.

———. 2017d. "Law in Classical Rabbinic Judaism." In Hayes 2017c, 76–127.

———. 2018. "Were the Noahide Commandments Formulated at Yavne? Tosefta Avoda Zara 8:4–9 in Cultural and Historical Context." In *Jews and Christians in the First and Second Centuries: The Interbellum 70–132 CE*, edited by Joshua Schwartz and Peter J. Tomson, 225–264. Leiden: Brill.

———. 2020. "Roman Power through Rabbinic Eyes: Tragedy or Comedy." In Berthelot 2020a, 443–471.

———. 2021. "'Barbarians' Judge the Law: The Rabbis on the Uncivil Law of Rome." In Berthelot, Dohrmann, and Nemo-Pekelman 2021, 455–498.

Haynes, Ian. 2013. *Blood of the Provinces: The Roman Auxilia and the Making of Provincial Society from Augustus to the Severans*. Oxford: OUP.

Hayward, Robert. 1998. "Abraham as Proselytizer at Beer-Sheba in the Targums of the Pentateuch." *JJS* 49: 24–37.

Hedner Zetterholm, Karin. 2018. "Jewishly-Behaving Gentiles and the Emergence of a Jewish Rabbinic Identity." *JSQ* 25: 321–344.

Heemstra, Marius. 2010. *The Fiscus Judaicus and the Parting of the Way*. Tübingen: Mohr Siebeck.

Hekster, Olivier. 1999. "The City of Rome in Late Imperial Ideology: The Tetrarchs, Maxentius, and Constantine." *Mediterraneo Antico* 2.2: 717–748.

———. 2015. *Emperors and Ancestors: Roman Rulers and the Constraints of Tradition*. Oxford: OUP.

Hekster, Olivier, and Koenraad Verboven (eds.). 2019. *The Impact of Justice on the Roman Empire: Proceedings of the Thirteenth Workshop of the International Network Impact of Empire (Gent, June 21–24, 2017)*. Leiden: Brill.

Heller, Anna. 2019. "Greek Citizenship in the Roman Empire: Political Participation, Social Status and Identities." In Berthelot and Price 2019, 55–72.

Heller, Anna, and Valérie Pont (eds.). 2012. *Patrie d'origine et patries électives: les citoyennetés multiples dans le monde grec d'époque romaine: actes du colloque international de Tours, 6–7 novembre 2009*. Bordeaux: Ausonius.

Hengel, Martin. 1966. "Die Synagogeninschrift von Stobi." *ZNW* 57: 145–183.

Herr, Moshe D. 1970. *Roman Rule in Tannaitic Literature*. Unpublished PhD, Hebrew University of Jerusalem. (Heb.)

———. 1972. "Persecutions and Martyrdom in Hadrian's Days." *Scripta Hierosolymitana* 23: 85–125.

Herrenschmidt, Clarisse. 1976. "Désignation de l'empire et concepts politiques de Darius Ier d'après ses inscriptions en vieux-perse." *Studia Iranica* 5.1: 33–65.

———. 1980. "L'Empire perse achéménide." In Duverger 1980, 69–102.

Hevroni, 'Ido. 2008. "A Tale of Two Sinners." *Azure* 33: 93–112.

Hezser, Catherine. 1997. *The Social Structure of the Rabbinic Movement in Roman Palestine*. Tübingen: Mohr Siebeck.

———. 1998. "The Codification of Legal Knowledge in Late Antiquity: The Talmud Yerushalmi and Roman Law Codes." In Schäfer 1998, 581–641.

——— (ed.). 2003a. *Rabbinic Law in Its Roman and Near Eastern Context*. Tübingen: Mohr Siebeck.

———. 2003b. "Slaves and Slavery in Rabbinic and Roman Law." In Hezser 2003a, 133–176.

———. 2005. *Jewish Slavery in Antiquity*. Oxford: OUP.

———. 2007. "Roman Law and Rabbinic Legal Composition." In *The Cambridge Companion to the Talmud and Rabbinic Literature*, edited by Charlotte E. Fonrobert and Martin S. Jaffee, 144–163. Cambridge: CUP.

——— (ed.). 2010. *The Oxford Handbook of Jewish Daily Life in Roman Palestine*. Oxford: OUP.

———. 2013. "Seduced by the Enemy or Wise Strategy? The Presentation of Non-Violence and Accommodation with Foreign Powers in Ancient Jewish Literary Sources." In *Between Cooperation and Hostility: Multiple Identities in Ancient Judaism and the Interaction with Foreign Powers*, edited by Albertz Rainer and Jacob Wöhrle, 221–250. Göttingen: Vandenhoeck & Ruprecht.

———. 2021. "Did Palestinian Rabbis Know Roman Law? Methodological Considerations and Case Studies." In Berthelot, Dohrmann, and Nemo-Pekelman 2021, 303–322.

———. Forthcoming. "Physical Strength and Weakness as Means of Social Stratification in Palestinian Rabbinic Discourse of Late Antiquity." In *Judaism and Health: Tradition, History, and Practice*, ed. by Catherine Hezser, forthcoming. Leiden: Brill.

Hidary, Richard. 2018. *Rabbis and Classical Rhetoric: Sophistic Education and Oratory in the Talmud and Midrash*. Cambridge: CUP.

Himmelfarb, Martha. 2006. *A Kingdom of Priests: Ancestry and Merit in Ancient Judaism*. Philadelphia: University of Pennsylvania Press.

———. 2017. "'Greater Is the Covenant with Aaron' (Sifre Numbers 119): Rabbis, Priests, and Kings Revisited." In Bar-Asher Siegal, Novick, and Hayes 2017, 339–350.

Hirschfeld, Gustav. 1916. *Greek Inscriptions of the British Museum. Part IV: Knidos, Halikarnassos and Branchidae*. Oxford: Clarendon Press.

Hirshman, Menahem (Marc). 1999. *Torah le-kol ba'ei ha'olam: Zerem universali be-sifrut ha-tannaim we-yeraso le-ḥokhmat ha-'amim*. Tel Aviv: Ha-Kibbutz ha-Mehuḥad. (Heb.)

———. 2000. "Rabbinic Universalism in the Second and Third Centuries." *HTR* 93.2: 101–115.

Hodkin, Bernie. 2014. "Theologies of Resistance: A Re-examination of Rabbinic Traditions about Rome." In *Reactions to Empire: Sacred Texts in Their Socio-Political Contexts*, edited by John Anthony Dunne and Dan Batovici, 163–177. Tübingen: Mohr Siebeck.

Holladay, Carl R. 1983. *Fragments from Hellenistic Jewish Authors. Volume I, Historians*. Atlanta: Scholars Press.

———. 1995. *Fragments from Hellenistic Jewish Authors. Volume III, Aristobulus*. Atlanta: Scholars Press.

Honigman, Sylvie. 1997. "Philon, Flavius Josèphe, et la citoyenneté alexandrine: vers une utopie politique." *JJS* 48: 62–90.

———. 2002. "The Jewish Politeuma at Heracleopolis." *SCI* 21: 251–266.

———. 2003. "'Politeumata' and Ethnicity in Ptolemaic and Roman Egypt." *Ancient Society* 33: 61–102.

———. 2014. *Tales of High Priests and Taxes: The Books of the Maccabees and the Judean Rebellion against Antiochos IV*. Berkeley: University of California Press.

Horbury, William. 2014. *Jewish War under Trajan and Hadrian*. Cambridge: CUP.

Horbury, William, and David Noy. 1992. *Jewish Inscriptions of Graeco-Roman Egypt*. Cambridge: CUP.

Horsfall, Nicholas M. 2013. *Virgil, "Aeneid" 6: A commentary*. Berlin: De Gruyter.

Horsley, Richard A. (ed.). 2004. *Hidden Transcripts and the Arts of Resistance: Applying the Work of James C. Scott to Jesus and Paul*. Atlanta: SBL Press.

——— (ed.). 2008. *In the Shadow of Empire: Reclaiming the Bible as a History of Faithful Resistance*. Louisville: Westminster John Knox.

Howard-Brook, Wes. 2010. *"Come Out My People!": God's Call Out of Empire in the Bible and Beyond*. Maryknoll: Orbis.

Howgego, Christopher. 2005. "Coinage and Identity in the Roman Provinces." In *Coinage and Identity in the Roman Provinces*, edited by Christopher Howgego, Volker Heuchert, and Andrew Burnett, 1–27. Oxford: OUP.

Humbert, Michel. 1978. "Municipium" et "civitas sine suffragio": *l'organisation de la conquête jusqu'à la guerre sociale*. Rome: École Française de Rome.

———. 2005. "Adoption (Droit romain)." In *Dictionnaire de l'Antiquité*, edited by Jean Leclant, 19–20. Paris: PUF.

———. 2010. "Le *status civitatis*. Identité et identification du *civis Romanus*." In *Homo, caput, persona: la costruzione giuridica dell'identità nell'esperienza romana, dall'epoca di Plauto a Ulpiano*, edited by Alessandro Corbino, Michel Humbert, and Giovanni Negri, 139–173. Pavia: IUSS Press.

Humfress, Caroline. 2011. "Law and Custom under Rome." In *Law, Custom, and Justice in Late Antiquity and the Early Middle Ages: Proceedings of the 2008 Byzantine Colloquium*, edited by Alice Rio, 23–47. London: Centre for Hellenic Studies.

———. 2013a. "Thinking through Legal Pluralism: 'Forum shopping' in the Later Roman Empire." In *Law and Empire: Ideas, Practices, Actors*, edited by Jeroen Duindam et al., 225–250. Leiden: Brill.

———. 2013b. "'Laws' Empire: Roman Universalism and the Legal Practice." In *New Frontiers: Law and Society in the Roman World*, edited by Paul J. du Plessis, 73–101. Edinburgh: Edinburgh University Press.

———. Forthcoming. *Multilegalism in Late Antiquity*. Oxford: OUP.

Hurlet, Frédéric (ed.). 2008. *Les Empires, Antiquité et Moyen Âge. Analyse comparée*. Rennes: Presses Universitaires de Rennes.

———. 2011. "(Re)penser l'Empire romain. Le défi de la comparaison historique." *DHA* Suppl. 5: 107–140.

———. 2019. "Justice, *Res Publica* and Empire: Subsidiarity and Hierarchy in the Roman Empire." In Hekster and Verboven 2019, 122–137.

Hurlet, Frédéric, and Bernard Mineo (eds.). 2009. *Le principat d'Auguste: réalités et représentations du pouvoir autour de la* Res publica restituta. Rennes: Presses universitaires de Rennes.

Hurlet, Frédéric, and John Tolan. 2008. "Conclusion. Vertus et limites du comparatisme." In Hurlet 2008, 239–250.

Hyamson, Moses. 1913. *Mosaicarum et Romanarum legum collatio*. Oxford: OUP.

Ilan, Tal. 1998. "King David, King Herod and Nicolaus of Damascus." *JSQ* 5: 195–240.

Inglebert, Hervé. 1996. *Les Romains chrétiens face à l'histoire de Rome: histoire, christianisme et romanités en Occident dans l'Antiquité tardive, IIIe-Ve siècles.* Paris: Institut d'études augustiniennes.

———. 2001. Interpretatio Christiana. *Les mutations des savoirs (cosmographie, géographie, ethnographie, histoire) dans l'Antiquité chrétienne (30–630 après J.-C.).* Paris: Institut d'études augustiniennes.

———. 2002. "Citoyenneté romaine, romanités et identités romaines sous l'Empire." In *Idéologies et valeurs civiques dans le monde romain: Hommage à Claude Lepelley,* edited by Hervé Inglebert, 241–260. Paris: Picard.

———. (ed). 2005. *Histoire de la civilisation romaine.* Paris: PUF.

———. 2014. *Le monde, l'histoire: essai sur les histoires universelles.* Paris: PUF.

———. 2016a. "Christian Reflections on Roman Citizenship (200–430)." In Ando 2016a, 99–112.

———. 2016b. "Les images bibliques de Rome dans les textes juifs et chrétiens: Les Kittim, Babylone, Tyr et Ésaü-Édom." *RHR* 233.2: 223–254.

Irshai, Oded. 2019. "How Do the Nations Relate to Israel? Rabbis, the Conversion of *Goyim,* and the *Constitutio Antoniniana.*" In Berthelot and Price 2019, 165–180.

Isaac, Benjamin. 1980–81. "Roman Colonies in Judaea: The Foundation of Aelia Capitolina." *Talanta* 12–13: 31–54. Reprint in Isaac, *The Near East under Roman Rule: Selected Papers,* 87–109. Leiden: Brill, 1998.

———. 1983. "Cassius Dio on the Revolt of Bar Kokhba." *SCI* 7: 68–76.

———. 1984. "Bandits in Judaea and Arabia." *Harvard Studies in Classical Philology* 88: 171–203.

———. 1990. *The Limits of Empire: The Roman Army in the East.* Rev. ed. Oxford: Clarendon Press.

———. 2004. *The Invention of Racism in Classical Antiquity.* Princeton: PUP.

———. 2017. *Empire and Ideology in the Graeco-Roman World: Selected Papers.* Cambridge: CUP.

Jackson, Bernard S. 1975. *Essays in Jewish and Comparative Legal History.* Leiden: Brill.

———. 1980. "History, Dogmatics, and *Halakhah.*" In *Jewish Law in Legal History and the Modern World,* edited by Bernard S. Jackson, 1–26. Leiden: Brill.

———. 1981. "On the Problem of Roman Influence on the Halakah and Normative Self-Definition in Judaism." In *Jewish and Christian Self-Definition, vol. 2: Aspects of Judaism in the Graeco-Roman Period,* edited by Ed P. Sanders et al., 157–203, 352–379. Philadelphia: SCM Press.

Jacobs, Andrew S. 2006. " 'Papinian Commands One Thing, Our Paul Another': Roman Christians and Jewish Law in the *Collatio Legum Mosaicarum et Romanarum.*" In *Religion and Law in Classical and Christian Rome,* edited by Clifford Ando and Jörg Rüpke, 85–99. Stuttgart: Franz Steiner Verlag.

Jacobs, Martin. 1995. *Die Institution des jüdischen Patriarchen: Eine quellen- und traditionskritische Studie zur Geschichte der Juden in der Spätantike.* Tübingen: Mohr Siebeck.

———. 1998. "Römische Thermenkultur im Spiegel des Talmud Yerushalmi." In Schäfer 1998, 219–311.

———. 2000. "Theatres and Performances as Reflected in the Talmud Yerushalmi." In Schäfer and Hezser 2000, 327–347.

Jacobson, David M. 1994. "King Herod, Roman Citizen and Benefactor of Kos." *Bulletin of the Anglo-Israel Archaeological Society* 13: 31–35.

———. 2000. "The Anchor on the Coins of Judaea." *Bulletin of the Anglo-Israel Archaeological Society* 18: 73–81.

———. 2001. "Three Roman Client Kings: Herod of Judaea, Archelaus of Cappadocia and Juba of Mauretania." *PEQ* 133: 22–38.

———. 2007. "The Jerusalem Temple of Herod the Great." In *The World of the Herods: Volume 1 of the International Conference The World of the Herods and the Nabataeans held at the British Museum, 17–19 April 2001*, edited by Nikos Kokkinos, 145–176. Stuttgart: Franz Steiner Verlag.

———. 2015. "Herod the Great, Augustus Caesar and Herod's 'Year 3' coins." *Strata: Bulletin of the Anglo-Israel Archaeological Society* 33: 89–118.

Jacobson, David M., and Nikos Kokkinos (eds.). 2009. *Herod and Augustus: Papers Presented at the IJS Conference, 21st–23rd June 2005*. Leiden: Brill.

Jacques, François, and John Scheid (eds.). 1990. *Rome et l'intégration de l'empire, 44 av. J.-C.–260 ap. J.-C.: Tome 1, Les Structures de l'empire romain*. Paris: PUF.

Janssen, L. F. 1979. "'*Superstitio*' and the Persecution of the Christians." *Vigiliae Christianae* 33.2: 131–159.

Jastrow, Marcus. 1950. *A Dictionary of the Targumim, the Talmud Babli and Yerushalmi, and the Midrashic Literature*. New York: Pardes.

Jaubert, Annie. 1964. "Les sources de la conception militaire de l'église en 1 Clément 37." *Vigiliae Christianae* 18: 74–84.

Jewett, Robert. 2007. *Romans: A Commentary*. Minneapolis: Fortress Press.

Joannès, Francis. 2011. "Assyriens, Babyloniens, Perses achéménides: la matrice impériale." *DHA* Suppl. 5: 27–47.

Johnson Hodge, Caroline. 2007. *If Sons, Then Heirs: A Study of Kinship and Ethnicity in the Letters of Paul*. New York: OUP.

Jokiranta, Jutta. 2014. "Conceptualizing *ger* in the Dead Sea Scrolls." In *In the Footsteps of Sherlock Holmes*, edited by Kristin De Troyer, Timothy M. Law, and Marketta Liljeström, 659–677. Leuven: Peeters.

Jones, Christopher M. 2018. "Embedded Written Documents as Colonial Mimicry in Ezra-Nehemiah." *Biblical Interpretation* 26.2: 158–181.

Jones, Christopher P. 1978. *The Roman World of Dio Chrysostom*. Cambridge: HUP.

———. 2001a. "The Claudian Monument at Patara." *ZPE* 137: 161–168.

———. 2001b. "Diplomatie et liens de parenté: Ilion, Aphrodisias et Rome." In *Origines Gentium*, edited by Valérie Fromentin and Sophie Gotteland, 179–185. Bordeaux: Ausonius.

———. 2007. "Juristes romains dans l'Orient grec." *Comptes-rendus des séances de l'Académie des Inscriptions et Belles-Lettres* 151.3: 1331–1359.

Jones, Kenneth R. 2011. *Jewish Reactions to the Destruction of Jerusalem in A.D. 70: Apocalypses and Related Pseudepigrapha*. Leiden: Brill.

Jones, Siân. 1997. *The Archaeology of Ethnicity: Constructing Identities in the Past and Present*. London: Routledge.

Joosten, Jan. 1996. *People and Land in the Holiness Code: An Exegetical Study of the Ideational Framework of the Law in Leviticus 17–26*. Leiden: Brill.

Jursa, Michael. 2014. "The Neo-Babylonian Empire." In *Imperien und Reiche in der Weltgeschichte: Epochenübergreifende und globalhistorische Vergleiche*, edited by Michael Gehler and Robert Rollinger, 1:121–148. Wiesbaden: Harrassowitz.

Juster, Jean. 1914. *Les Juifs dans l'Empire romain, leur condition juridique, économique et sociale*. 2 vols. Paris: Librairie orientaliste Paul Geuthner.

Kaden, David A. 2011. "Flavius Josephus and the *Gentes Devictae* in Roman Imperial Discourse: Hybridity, Mimicry, and Irony in the Agrippa II Speech (*Judean War* 2.345–402)." *JSJ* 42.4–5: 481–507.

Kahana, Menahem I. 1988. "Pages of the Deuteronomy Mekhilta on *Ha'azinu* and *Wezot ha-Berakhah*." *Tarbiz* 57: 165–201. (Heb.)

———. 2006. "The Halakhic Midrashim." In Safrai et al. 2006, 3–105.

Kallet-Marx, Robert M. 1995. *Hegemony to Empire: The Development of the Roman Imperium in the East from 148 to 62 B.C.* Berkeley: University of California Press.

Kalmin, Richard L. 1999. *The Sage in Jewish Society of Late Antiquity.* New York: Routledge.

——. 2003. "Rabbinic Traditions about Roman Persecutions of the Jews: A Reconsideration." *JJS* 54.1: 21–50.

Kantor, Georgy. 2009. "Knowledge of Law in Roman Asia Minor." In Haensch 2009, 249–265.

Kasher, Aryeh. 1985. *The Jews in Hellenistic and Roman Egypt: The Struggle for Equal Rights.* Tübingen: Mohr Siebeck.

Kattan Gribetz, Sarit. 2016. "A Matter of Time: Writing Jewish Memory into Roman History." *AJS Review* 40.1: 57–86.

——. 2020. *Time and Difference in Rabbinic Judaism.* Princeton: PUP.

Katzoff, Binyamin. 2009. "'God of our Fathers': Rabbinic Liturgy and Jewish-Christian Engagement." *JQR* 99.3: 303–322.

Katzoff, Ranon. 2003. "Children of Intermarriage: Roman and Jewish Conceptions." In Hezser 2003a, 277–286.

Keddie, G. Anthony. 2018. *Revelations of Ideology: Apocalyptic Class Politics in Early Roman Palestine.* Leiden: Brill.

Keenan, James G., John G. Manning, and Uri Yiftach-Firanko (eds.). 2014. *Law and Legal Practice in Egypt from Alexander to the Arab Conquest: A Selection of Papyrological Sources in Translation, with Introductions and Commentary.* Cambridge: CUP.

Kelle, Brad E., Frank Ritchel Ames, and Jacob L. Wright (eds.). 2014. *Warfare, Ritual, and Symbol in Biblical and Modern Contexts.* Altlanta: SBL.

Kellner, Menahem. 2019. "The Convert as the Most Jewish of Jews? On the Centrality of Belief (the Opposite of Heresy) in Maimonidean Judaism." *Jewish Thought* 1: 33–52.

Kellum, Barbara. 1997. "Concealing-Revealing: Gender and the Play of Meaning in the Monuments of Augustan Rome." In *The Roman Cultural Revolution*, edited by T. Habinek and A. Schiesaro, 158–181. Cambridge: CUP.

Kemezis, Adam M. 2019. "Beyond City Limits: Citizenship and Authorship in Imperial Greek Literature." In Berthelot and Price 2019, 73–103.

Kennell, Nigel M. 2005. "New Light on 2 Maccabees 4:7–15." *JJS* 56: 10–25.

Kiel, Yishai. 2015. "Noahide Law and the Inclusiveness of Sexual Ethics: Between Roman Palestine and Sasanian Babylonia." *Jewish Law Annual* 21: 59–109.

——. 2017. "Reinventing Mosaic Torah in Ezra-Nehemiah in the Light of the Law (*dāta*) of Ahura Mazda and Zarathustra." *JBL* 136.2: 323–345.

Klawans, Jonathan. 2006. *Purity, Sacrifice, and the Temple: Symbolism and Supersessionism in the Study of Ancient Judaism.* Oxford: OUP.

——. 2010. "Josephus, the Rabbis, and Responses to Catastrophes Ancient and Modern." *JQR* 100.2: 278–309.

——. 2016. "Maccabees, Martyrs, Murders, and Masada: Noble Deaths and Suicides in 1 and 2 Maccabees and Josephus." In *Crossing Boundaries in Early Judaism and Christianity: Ambiguities, Complexities, and Half-Forgotten Adversaries: Essays in Honor of Alan F. Segal*, edited by Kimberly B. Stratton and Andrea Lieber, 279–299. Leiden: Brill.

Kloner, Amos. 2006. "The Dating of the Southern Decumanus of Aelia Capitolina and Wilson's Arch." In *New Studies on Jerusalem*, edited by Eyal Baruch, Zvi Greenhut and Avraham Faust, 2:239–247. Ramat-Gan: Ingeborg Rennert Center for Jerusalem Studies. (Heb.)

Knoppers, Gary N., and Bernard M. Levinson (eds.). 2007. *The Pentateuch as Torah: New Models for Understanding Its Promulgation and Acceptance.* Winona Lake: Eisenbrauns.

Koren, Yedidah. 2018. "'Look through Your Book and Make Me a Perfect Match': Talking about Genealogy in Amoraic Palestine and Babylonia." *JSJ* 49: 417–448.

Kosman, Admiel. 2010. "R. Johanan and Resh Lakish: The Image of God in the Study Hall: 'Masculinity' versus 'Feminity.'" *European Judaism* 43.1: 128–145.

Kosmin, Paul J. 2014. *The Land of the Elephant Kings: Space, Territory, and Ideology in the Seleucid Empire*. Cambridge: HUP.

———. 2018. *Time and Its Adversaries in the Seleucid Empire*. Cambridge: Belknap Press.

Kraemer, David. 1995. *Responses to Suffering in Classical Rabbinic Literature*. Oxford: OUP.

———. 2013. "Adornment and Gender in Rabbinic Judaism." In *Envisioning Judaism: Studies in Honor of Peter Schäfer on the Occasion of his Seventieth Birthday*, edited by Ra'anan S. Boustan et al., 1:217–234. Tübingen: Mohr Siebeck.

Kraemer, Ross S. 2014. "Giving up the Godfearers." *JAJ* 5: 61–87.

Krause, Joachim. 2008. "Tradition, History, and Our Story: Some Observations on Jacob and Esau in the Books of Obadiah and Malachi." *JSOT* 32.4: 475–486.

Krauss, Samuel. 1910. *Antoninus und Rabbi*. Vienna: Israelitisch-theologischen Lehranstalt.

———. 1947. *Persia and Rome in the Talmud and the Midrashim*. Jerusalem: Mossad haRav Kook. (Heb.)

Kremer, David. 2006. *Ius latinum, le concept de droit latin sous la République et l'Empire*. Paris: De Boccard.

Kreuzsaler, Claudia, and Jakub Urbanik. 2008. "Humanity and Inhumanity of Law: The Case of Dionysia." *Journal of Juristic Papyrology* 38: 119–155.

Kuhlmann, Peter Alois. 1994. *Die Giessener literarischen papyri und die Caracalla-Erlasse: Edition, Übersetzung und Kommentar*. Giessen: Universitätsbibliothek.

Kuhrt, Amélie. 2001. "The Persian Kings and their Subjects: A Unique Relationship?" *Orientalistische Literaturzeitung* 96: 165–173.

———. 2007. "The Problem of Achaemenid 'Religious Policy.'" In *Die Welt der Götterbilder*, edited by Brigitte Groneberg and Hermann Spieckermann, 117–142. Berlin: De Gruyter.

———. 2010. *The Persian Empire: A Corpus of Sources from the Achaemenid Period*. London: Routledge.

Kuhrt, Amélie, and Susan Sherwin-White. 1991. "Aspects of Seleucid Royal Ideology: The Cylinder of Antiochus I from Borsippa." *Journal of Hellenic Studies* 111: 71–86.

Kulp, Joshua. 2006. "History, Exegesis or Doctrine: Framing the Tannaitic Debates on the Circumcision of Slaves." *JJS* 57.1: 56–79.

Kunckel, Hille. 1974. *Der Römische Genius*. Heidelberg: F. H. Kale Verlag.

Kunst, Christiane. 2005. *Römische Adoption: Zur Strategie einer Familienorganisation*. Hennef: Clauss.

Kyle, Donald J. 1998. *Spectacles of Death in Ancient Rome*. London: Routledge.

Laconi, Sonia. 1988. *Virtus: studio semantico e religioso dalle origini al Basso Impero*. Cagliari: Centro Stampa della Facoltà di Magistero.

Lapin, Hayim. 2010. "The Rabbinic Class Revisited: Rabbis as Judges in Later Roman Palestine." In *"Follow the Wise": Studies in Jewish History and Culture in Honor of Lee I. Levine*, 255–273. Winona Lake: Eisenbrauns.

———. 2012. *Rabbis as Romans: The Rabbinic Movement in Palestine, 100–400 CE*. New York: OUP.

———. 2013. "The Law of Moses and the Jews: Rabbis, Ethnic Marking, and Romanization." In Dohrmann and Reed 2013, 79–97.

———. 2021. "Pappus and Julianus, the Maccabaean Martyrs, and Rabbinic Martyrdom History in Late Antiquity." In Berthelot, Dohrmann, and Nemo-Pekelman 2021, 133–155.

Lauer, Rena N. 2016. "Jewish Law and Litigation in the Secular Courts of the Late Medieval Mediterranean." *Critical Analysis of Law* 3.1: 114–132.

Lauinger, Jacob. 2015. "Neo-Assyrian Scribes, 'Esarhaddon's Succession Treaty,' and the Dynamics of Textual Mass Production." In *Texts and Contexts: The Circulation and Transmission of Cuneiform Texts in Social Space*, edited by Paul Delnero and Jacob Lauinger, 285–314. Berlin: De Gruyter.

Lauterbach, Jacob Z. 2004. *Mekhilta de-Rabbi Ishmael: A Critical Edition, Based on the Manuscripts and Early Editions, with an English Translation, Introduction, and Notes.* 2 vols. Philadelphia: The Jewish Publication Society. (First edition 1976.)

Lavan, Myles. 2013. *Slaves to Rome: Paradigms of Empire in Roman Culture.* Cambridge: CUP.

———. 2016. "The Spread of Roman Citizenship, 14–212 CE: Quantification in the Face of High Uncertainty." *Past and Present* 230: 3–46.

———. 2017. "Peace and Empire: *pacare, pacatus* and the Language of Roman Imperialism." In *Peace and Reconciliation in the Classical World*, edited by E. P. Moloney and Michael S. Williams, 102–114. London: Routledge.

———. 2019a. "The Foundation of Empire? The Spread of Roman Citizenship from the Fourth Century BCE to the Third Century CE." In Berthelot and Price 2019, 21–54.

———. 2019b. "The Army and the Spread of Roman Citizenship." *JRS* 109: 1–43.

Lavan, Myles, Richard E. Payne, and John Weisweiler (eds.). 2016. *Cosmopolitanism and Empire: Universal Rulers, Local Elites, and Cultural Integration in the Ancient Near East and Mediterranean.* Oxford: OUP.

Lavee, Moshe. 2003. *'A Convert is Like a Newborn Child'—The Concept and its Implications in Rabbinic Literature.* PhD, Ben-Gurion University of the Negev. (Heb.)

———. 2010. "Converting the Missionary Image of Abraham: Rabbinic Traditions Migrating from the Land of Israel to Babylon." In *Abraham, the Nations, and the Hagarites: Jewish, Christian, and Islamic Perspectives on Kinship with Abraham*, edited by Martin Goodman et al., 203–222. Leiden: Brill.

———. 2011. "The 'Tractate' of Conversion—BT Yeb. 46–48 and the Evolution of Conversion Procedure." *European Journal of Jewish Studies* 4.2: 169–213.

———. 2013. "The Noachide Laws: The Building Blocks of a Rabbinic Conceptual Framework in Qumran and the Book of Acts." *Meghillot: Studies in the Dead Sea Scrolls* 10: 73–114. (Heb.)

———. 2014. "No Boundaries for the Construction of Boundaries: The Babylonian Talmud's Emphasis on Demarcation of Identity." In *Rabbinic Traditions between Palestine and Babylonia*, edited by Ronit Nikolsky and Tal Ilan, 84–116. Leiden: Brill.

———. 2017. *The Rabbinic Conversion of Judaism: The Unique Perspective of the Bavli on Conversion and the Construction of Jewish Identity.* Leiden: Brill.

Le Bohec, Yann. 2015. "Jews." In *The Encyclopedia of the Roman Army*, edited by Yann Le Bohec, 559. Chichester: Wiley Blackwell.

Lee-Stecum, Parshia. 2014. "Roman Elite Ethnicity." In McInerney 2014, 455–469.

Leon, Harry J. 1960. *The Jews of Ancient Rome.* Philadelphia: The Jewish Publication Society of America.

Lepelley, Claude. 2002. "Le nivellement juridique du monde romain à partir du IIIᵉ siècle et la marginalisation des droits locaux." *Mélanges de l'Ecole Française de Rome, Moyen Âge* 113: 839–856.

Levenson, Jon D. 2011. *Abraham between Torah and Gospel.* Milwaukee: Marquette University Press.

———. 2012. *Inheriting Abraham: The Legacy of the Patriarch in Judaism, Christianity, and Islam.* Princeton: PUP.

Lévêque, Pierre. 1980. "Empire d'Alexandre et empires hellénistiques." In Duverger 1980, 103–120.

Levi, Mario Attilio. 1985. "'Pax Romana' e imperialismo." In Sordi 1985, 203–210.

Levick, Barbara. 1982. "Propaganda and the Imperial Coinage." *Antichthon* 16: 104–116.

Levine, Baruch A. 2005. "Assyrian Ideology and Israelite Monotheism." *Iraq* 67.1: 411–427.

Levine, Lee I. 1979. "The Jewish Patriarch (Nasi) in Third Century Palestine." In *Aufstieg und Niedergang der Römischen Welt* II.19.2, edited by Wolfgang Haase, 649–688. Berlin: De Gruyter.

———. 2000. *The Ancient Synagogue: The First Thousand Years.* New Haven: Yale University Press.

Levine Gera, Deborah. 2014. *Judith.* Berlin: De Gruyter.

Levinson, Bernard M. 2010. "Esarhaddon's Succession Treaty as the Source for the Canon Formula in Deuteronomy 13:1." *Journal of the American Oriental Society* 130.3: 337–347.

Levinson, Bernard M., and Jeffrey Stackert. 2012. "Between the Covenant Code and Esarhaddon's Succession Treaty." *JAJ* 3.2: 123–140.

Levinson, Joshua. 2000. "Bodies and Bo(a)rders: Emerging Fictions of Identity in Late Antiquity." *HTR* 93.4: 343–372.

———. 2003. "Tragedies Naturally Performed: Fatal Charades, Parodia Sacra, and the Death of Titus." In *Jewish Culture and Society under the Christian Roman Empire*, edited by Richard Kalmin and Seth Schwartz, 349–382. Leuven: Peeters.

———. 2014. "Changing Minds–Changing Bodies: The Gendered Subject of Conversion." In *Religious Conversion: History, Experience and Meaning*, edited by Ira Katznelson and Miri Rubin, 123–149. London: Routledge.

Lévy, Carlos. 1992. *Cicero Academicus: recherches sur les* Académiques *et sur la philosophie cicéronienne.* Rome: École Française de Rome.

———. 2021. "Cicero, Law, and the Barbarians." In Berthelot, Dohrmann, and Nemo-Pekelman 2021, 29–45.

Lévy, Edmond. 1990. "*Politeia* et *politeuma* chez Polybe." *Ktema* 15: 15–26.

Lévy, Israël. 1905–1907. "Le prosélytisme juif." *REJ* 50: 1–9; 51: 1–31; 53: 56–61.

Lewy, Johanan (Yohanan). 1941–1942. "Cicero's Remarks on the Jews in the *Pro Flacco*." *Zion* 7: 109–134. (Heb.)

Lieberman, Saul. 1942. *Greek in Jewish Palestine: Studies in the Life and Manners of Jewish Palestine in the II–IV Centuries C.E.* New York: The Jewish Theological Seminary of America.

———. 1944. "Roman Legal Institutions in Early Rabbinics and in the Acta Martyrum." *JQR* N.S. 35: 1–57.

———. 1950. *Hellenism in Jewish Palestine: Studies in the Literary Transmission, Beliefs and Manners of Palestine in the I Century B.C.E.–IV Century C.E.* New York: The Jewish Theological Seminary of America.

———. 1955–1988. *Tosefta Ki-fshuṭah: A Comprehensive Commentary on the Tosefta.* 10 vols. New York: The Jewish Theological Seminary of America. (Heb.)

Liebs, Detlef. 1987. *Die Jurisprudenz im spätantiken Italien (260–640 n. Chr.).* Berlin: Dunker and Humbolt.

Lieu, Judith M. 1995. "The Race of the God-Fearers." *Journal of Theological Studies* 46: 483–501.

Lifshitz, Baruch. 1967. *Donateurs et fondateurs dans les synagogues juives: répertoire des dédicaces grecques relatives à la construction et à la réfection des synagogues.* Paris: Gabalda.

Lincoln, Bruce. 2007. *Religion, Empire, and Torture: The Case of Achaemenian Persia, with a Postscript on Abu Ghraib.* Chicago: The University of Chicago Press.

———. 2012. "Sacred Kingship?" In *"Happiness for Mankind": Achaemenian Religion and the Imperial Project* (collected papers by Bruce Lincoln), 167–186. Leuven: Peeters.

Lind, L. R. 1972. "Concept, Action, and Character: The Reasons for Rome's Greatness." *TAPhA* 103: 235–283.

Linder, Amnon. 1987. *The Jews in Roman Imperial Legislation*. Detroit: Wayne State University Press.

———. 2006. "The Legal Status of the Jews in the Roman Empire." In *The Cambridge History of Judaism 4: The Late Roman-Rabbinic Period*, edited by Steven T. Katz, 128–173. Cambridge: CUP.

Lindsay, Hugh. 2009. *Adoption in the Roman World*. Cambridge: CUP.

Lintott, Andrew W. 1993. Imperium Romanum: *Politics and Administration*. London: Routledge.

Lipschits, Oded, Gary N. Knoppers, and Manfred Oeming (eds.). 2003. *Judah and the Judeans in the Neo-Babylonian Period*. Winona Lake: Eisenbrauns.

Liverani, Mario. 1979. "The Ideology of the Assyrian Empire." In *Power and Propaganda: A Symposium on Ancient Empires*, edited by Mogens Trolle Larsen, 297–317. Copenhagen: Akademisk Forlag.

———. 2017a. *Assyria: The Imperial Mission*, translated by Andrea Trameri and Jonathan Valk. Winona Lake: Eisenbrauns.

———. 2017b. "Thoughts on the Assyrian Empire and Assyrian Kingship." In Frahm 2017, 534–546.

Lobur, John A. 2008. Consensus, Concordia, *and the Formation of Roman Imperial Ideology*. New York: Routledge.

Long, Anthony A. 1993. "Hellenistic Ethics and Philosophical Power." In *Hellenistic History and Culture*, edited by Peter Green, 138–167. Berkeley: University of California Press.

Long, Anthony A., and David N. Sedley. 1987. *The Hellenistic Philosophers*. Cambridge: CUP.

Lorberbaum, Yair. 2015. *In God's Image: Myth, Theology, and Law in Classical Judaism*. New York: CUP.

Lüderitz, Gert, with Joyce M. Reynolds. 1983. *Corpus jüdischer Zeugnisse aus der Cyrenaika*. Wiesbaden: Ludwig Reichert Verlag.

Lukes, Steven. 2005. *Power: A Radical View*. New York: Palgrave Macmillan. (First edition 1974.)

Lyall, Francis. 1969. "Roman Law in the Writings of Paul: Adoption." *JBL* 88.4: 458–466.

———. 1984. *Slaves, Citizens, Sons: Legal Metaphors in the Epistles*. Grand Rapids: Zondervan Press.

Ma, John. 1999. *Antiochos III and the Cities of Western Asia Minor*. Oxford: OUP.

———. 2003. "Kings." In Erskine 2003, 177–195.

———. 2012. "Relire les Institutions des Séleucides de Bikerman." In *Rome, a City and Its Empire in Perspective: The Impact of the Roman World Through Fergus Millar's Research*, edited by Stéphane Benoist, 59–84. Leiden: Brill.

Machinist, Peter. 1983. "Assyria and Its Image in the First Isaiah." *Journal of the American Oriental Society* 103.4: 719–737.

———. 2003. "Mesopotamian Imperialism and Israelite Religion: A Case Study from the Second Isaiah." In *Symbiosis, Symbolism, and the Power of the Past*, edited by William G. Dever, 237–264. Winona Lake: Eisenbrauns.

———. 2006. "Kingship and Divinity in Imperial Assyria." In *Text, Artifact, and Image: Revealing Ancient Israelite Religion*, edited by Gary Beckman and Theodore J. Lewis, 152–188. Providence: Brown Judaic Studies.

Machinist, Peter, and Hayim Tadmor. 1993. "Heavenly Wisdom." In *The Tablet and the Scroll*, edited by William W. Hallo, 146–151. Bethesda: CDL Press.

Magness, Jodi. 2008. "The Arch of Titus at Rome and the Fate of the God of Israel." *JJS* 59.2: 201–217.

Mahieu, Bieke. 2012. *Between Rome and Jerusalem. Herod the Great and His Sons in Their Struggle for Recognition: A Chronological Investigation of the Period 40 BC–39 AD with a Time Setting of New Testament Events*. Leuven: Peeters.

Makhlaiuk, Aleksandr V. 2015. "Memory and Images of Achaemenid Persia in the Roman Empire." In *Political Memory in and after the Persian Empire*, edited by Jason M. Silverman and Caroline Waerzeggers, 299–324. Atlanta: SBL Press.

Malka, Orit, and Yakir Paz. 2019. *"Ab hostibus captus et a latronibus captus*: The Impact of the Roman Model of Citizenship on Rabbinic Law." *JQR* 109.2: 141–172.

———. 2021. "A Rabbinic *Postliminium*: The Property of Captives in Tannaitic Halakha in Light of Roman Law." In Berthelot, Dohrmann, and Nemo-Pekelman 2021, 323–344.

Malkin, Irad, and Christel Müller. 2012. "Vingt ans d'ethnicité: bilan historiographique et application du concept aux études anciennes." In *Mobilités grecques. Mouvements, réseaux, contacts en Méditerranée, de l'époque archaïque à l'époque hellénistique*, edited by Laurent Capdetrey and Julien Zurbach, 25–37. Bordeaux: Ausonius.

Manders, Erika. 2012. *Coining Images of Power: Pattern in the Representation of Roman Emperors on Imperial coinage, AD 193–283.* Leiden: Brill.

Marienberg, Evyatar. 2003. *Niddah: lorsque les juifs conceptualisent la menstruation.* Paris: Les Belles Lettres.

Markl, Dominik. 2018. "Deuteronomy's "Anti-King": Historicized Etiology or Political Program?" In *Changing Faces of Kingship in Syria-Palestine 1500–500 BC*, edited by Agustinus Gianto and Peter Dubovský, 165–186. Münster: Ugarit-Verlag.

Marmorstein, A. 1937. "The Synagogue of Claudius Tiberius Polycharmus in Stobi." *JQR* N.S. 27.4: 373–384.

Marotta, Valerio. 2009. *La cittadinanza romana in età imperiale, secoli I-III d.C.: una sintesi.* Torino: G. Giappichelli.

———. 2014. "Populus e Princeps Nel Diritto Pubblico d'età Imperiale. Storici, Biografi e Giuristi." *Studia et Documenta Historiae et Iuris* 80: 599–622.

———. 2016. *Esercizio e trasmissione del potere imperiale (secoli I-IV d.C.): studi di diritto pubblico romano.* Torino: Giappichelli.

———. 2017. "Egyptians and Citizenship from the First Century AD to the *Constitutio Antoniniana*." In *Citizens in the Graeco-Roman World: Aspects of Citizenship from the Archaic Period to AD 212*, edited by Lucia Cecchet and Anna Busetto, 172–198. Leiden: Brill.

Marshak, Adam K. 2015. *The Many Faces of Herod the Great.* Grand Rapids: Eerdmans.

Martens, John W. 2003. *One God, One Law: Philo of Alexandria on the Mosaic and Greco-Roman Law.* Leiden: Brill.

Martinez-Sève, Laurianne. 2011. "Le renouveau des études séleucides." *DHA* Suppl. 5: 89–106.

Mason, Steve. 1998. "'Should Any Wish to Enquire Further' (*ANT.* 1.25): The Aim and Audience of Josephus's *Judean Antiquities/Life*." In *Understanding Josephus: Seven Perspectives*, edited by Steve Mason, 64–103. Sheffield: Sheffield Academic Press.

———. 2005a. "Of Audience and Meaning: Reading Josephus' *Bellum Judaicum* in the Context of a Flavian Audience." In *Josephus and Jewish History in Flavian Rome and Beyond*, edited by Joseph Sievers and Gaia Lembi, 71–100. Leiden: Brill.

———. 2005b. "Figured Speech and Irony in T. Flavius Josephus." In Edmondson, Mason, and Rives 2005, 244–288.

———. 2007. "Jews, Judeans, Judaizing, Judaism: Problems of Categorization in Ancient History." *JSJ* 38.4–5: 457–512.

———. 2008. *Josephus. Judean War 2.* Leiden: Brill.

———. 2014. "Why Did Judaeans Go to War with Rome in 66–67 CE? Realist-Regional Perspectives." In *Jews and Christians in the First and Second Centuries: How to Write Their History*, edited by Peter J. Tomson and Joshua Schwartz, 126–206. Leiden: Brill.

———. 2016. *A History of the Jewish War: A.D. 66–74.* New York: CUP.

Mathisen, Ralph W. 2006. "*Peregrini, Barbari*, and *Cives Romani*: Concepts of Citizenship and the Legal Identity of Barbarians in the Later Roman Empire." *American Historical Review* 111.4: 1011–1040.

Mattingly, David J. (ed.). 1997. *Dialogues in Roman Imperialism: Power, Discourse, and Discrepant Experience in the Roman Empire.* Portsmouth: Journal of Roman Archaelogy.

——. 2011. *Imperialism, Power, and Identity: Experiencing the Roman Empire.* Princeton: PUP.

Mattingly, Harold. 1930. *Coins of the Roman Empire in the British Museum. II. Vespasian to Domitian.* London: OUP.

McCraken Flesher, Paul V. 1988. *Oxen, Women, or Citizens? Slaves in the System of the Mishnah.* Atlanta: Scholars Press.

McDonnell, Myles. 2006. *Roman Manliness: Virtus and the Roman Republic.* Cambridge: CUP.

McInerney, Jeremy (ed.). 2014. *A Companion to Ethnicity in the Ancient Mediterranean.* Chichester: Wiley Blackwell.

Mélèze Modrzejewski, Joseph. 1970. "La règle de droit dans l'Égypte romaine. État des questions et perspectives de recherche." In *Proceedings of the XIIth International Congress of Papyrology*, edited by Deborah H. Samuel, 317–378. Toronto: A. M. Hakkert.

——. 1971. "Grégoire le Thaumaturge et le droit romain." *Revue historique de droit français et étranger* 49: 313–324.

——. 1995. *The Jews of Egypt From Rameses II to Emperor Hadrian*, translated by Robert Cornman, preface by Shaye J. D. Cohen. Philadelphia: Jewish Publication Society.

——. 2008. *Troisième Livre des Maccabées.* Paris: Cerf.

——. 2011. *"Un peuple de philosophes": Aux origines de la condition juive.* Paris: Fayard.

——. 2014. *Loi et Coutume dans l'Égypte grecque et romaine.* Warsaw: University of Warsaw.

Mellor, Ronald. 1975. *ΘΕΑ ΡΩΜΗ: The Worship of the Goddess Rome in the Greek World.* Göttingen: Vandenhoeck & Ruprecht.

——. 1981. "The Goddess Roma." In *Aufstieg und Niedergang der Römischen Welt* XVII.2.2, edited by Wolfgang Haase, 950–1030. Berlin: De Gruyter.

Melnyk, Janet L. R. 1993. "When Israel Was a Child: Ancient Near Eastern Adoption Formulas and the Relationship between God and Israel." In *History and Interpretation*, edited by M. Patrick Graham, 245–259. Sheffield: JSOT Press.

Mendels, Doron. 1981. "The Five Empires: A Note on a Propagandistic Topos." *AJPh* 102: 330–337.

Meshorer, Yaʿakov. 1982. *Ancient Jewish Coinage. Volume II: Herod the Great through Bar Cochba.* Jerusalem: Israel Museum; New York: Amphora Books.

——. 1985. *City-Coins of Eretz-Israel and the Decapolis in the Roman Period.* Jerusalem: The Israel Museum.

Methy, N. 1992. "La représentation des provinces dans le monnayage romain de l'époque impériale (70–235 après J.C.)." *Numismatica e Antichita classiche* 21: 267–289.

Milgram, Jonathan S. 2019. *From Mesopotamia to the Mishnah: Tannaitic Inheritance Law in its Legal and Social Contexts.* Brighton: Academic Studies Press. (First edition Tübingen: Mohr Siebeck, 2016).

Millar, Fergus. 1964. *A Study of Cassius Dio.* Oxford: Clarendon Press.

——. 1977. *The Emperor in the Roman World, 31 BC–AD 337.* London: Duckworth.

——. 1993a. *The Roman Near East, 31 B.C.–A.D. 337.* Cambridge: HUP.

——. 1993b. "Hagar, Ishmael, Josephus and the Origins of Islam." *JJS* 44.1: 23–45.

——. 2004. *Rome, the Greek World, and the East. Volume 2, Government, Society, and Culture in the Roman Empire*, edited by Hannah M. Cotton and Guy M. Rogers. Chapel Hill: University of North Carolina Press.

——. 2005. "Last Year in Jerusalem: Monuments of the Jewish War in Rome." In Edmonson, Mason, and Rives 2005, 101–128.

——. 2006. "The Roman Coloniae of the Near East." In *Rome, the Greek World, and the East. Volume 3, The Greek World, the Jews, and the East*, edited by Hannah M. Cotton and Guy M. Rogers, 164–222. Chapel Hill: University of North Carolina Press.

——. 2015. "Transformations of Judaism under Greco-Roman Rule: Responses to Seth Schwartz's *Imperialism and Jewish Society.*" In *Empire, Church and Society in the Late Roman Near East: Greeks, Jews, Syrians and Saracens, Collected Studies, 2004–2014*, 313–337. Leuven: Peeters.

Miller, David M. 2010. "The Meaning of *Ioudaios* and Its Relationship to Other Group Labels in Ancient 'Judaism.'" *CBR* 9.1: 98–126.

——. 2012. "Ethnicity Comes of Age: An Overview of Twentieth-Century Terms for *Ioudaios.*" *CBR* 10.2: 293–311.

——. 2014. "Ethnicity, Religion and the Meaning of *Ioudaios* in Ancient 'Judaism.'" *CBR* 12.2: 216–265.

Miller, Stuart S. 2017. "The Study of Talmudic Israel and/or Roman Palestine: Where Matters Stand." In Bar-Asher Siegal, Novick, and Hayes 2017, 433–454.

Mitchell, Christine. 2014. "A Note on the Creation Formula in Zechariah 12:1–8; Isaiah 42:5–6; and Old Persian Inscriptions." *JBL* 133.2: 305–308.

Mitford, Terence Bruce. 1960. "A Cypriot Oath of Allegiance to Tiberius." *JRS* 50.1–2: 75–79.

Mittag, Achim, and Fritz-Heiner Mutschler (eds.). 2008. *Conceiving the Empire: China and Rome Compared.* Oxford: OUP.

Mitteis, Ludwig. 1891. *Reichsrecht und Volksrecht in der östlischen Provinzen des Römischen Kaiserreichs.* Leipzig: Teubner.

Mitteis, Ludwig, and Ulrich Wilcken. 1912. *Grundzüge und Chrestomathie der Papyruskunde. II. Juristischer Teil, 2. Chrestomathie.* Leipzig: Teubner.

Moatti, Claudia. 1997. *La raison de Rome: naissance de l'esprit critique à la fin de la République, IIᵉ-Iᵉʳ siècle avant Jésus-Christ.* Paris: Seuil.

Moffitt, David M., and C. Jacob Butera. 2013. "P.Duk. inv. 727r: New Evidence for the Meaning and Provenance of the Word Προσήλυτος." *JBL* 132: 159–178.

Momigliano, Arnaldo. 1942a. "Terra Marique." *JRS* 32.1–2: 53–64.

——. 1942b. "The Peace of the Ara Pacis." *Journal of the Warburg and Courtauld Institutes* 5: 228–231.

——. 1980. "Daniele e la teoria greca della successione degli imperi." *RAL* 35: 157–162. Reprint in *Settimo contributo alla storia degli studi classici e del mondo antico*, 297–304. Rome: Edizioni di Storia e Letteratura, 1984.

——. 1982. "The Origins of Universal History." *Annali della Scuola Normale Superiore di Pisa. Classe di Lettere e Filosofia, Serie III* 12.2: 533–560.

——. 1987. "Some Preliminary Remarks on the 'Religious Opposition' to the Roman Empire." In *Opposition et résistances à l'Empire d'Auguste à Trajan*, edited by Adalberto Giovannini, 103–129. Geneva: Fondation Hardt.

Moore, F. G. 1894. "On Urbs Aeterna and Urbs Sacra." *Transactions of the American Philological Association* 25: 34–60.

Moore, George F. 1927–1930. *Judaism in the First Centuries of the Christian Era: The Age of the Tannaim.* 3 vols. Cambridge: HUP.

Mor, Menahem. 2016. *The Second Jewish Revolt: the Bar Kokhba War, 132–136 CE.* Leiden: Brill.

Mor, Sagit. 2019. *"Captivity Is Harder Than All": Captives, Captivity and the Discourse of Captivity in the Rabbinic Literature.* Tel Aviv: Ha-Kibbutz ha-Meuḥad. (Heb.)

More, Jonathan. 2012. "On Kingship in Philo and the Wisdom of Solomon." In *Text-critical and Hermeneutical Studies in the Septuagint*, edited by Johann Cook and Hermann-Josef Stipp, 409–425. Leiden: Brill.

Moreau, Philippe. 1992. "Les adoptions romaines." *Droit et cultures* 23: 13–35.

Morgenstern, Matthias. 2011. "The Quest for a Rabbinic Perception of a Common Humanity." In *The Quest for a Common Humanity: Human Dignity and Otherness in the Religious*

Traditions of the Mediterranean, edited by Katell Berthelot and Matthias Morgenstern, 42–66. Leiden, Brill.

———. 2016. "The Image of Edom in Midrash Bereshit Rabbah." *RHR* 233.2: 193–222.

Morris, Ian, and Walter Scheidel. 2009. *The Dynamics of Ancient Empires: State Power from Assyria to Byzantium*. Oxford: OUP.

Moscovitz, Leib. 2003. "Legal Fictions in Rabbinic Law and Roman Law: Some Comparative Observations," in Hezser 2003a, 105–132.

———. 2006. "The Formation and Character of the Jerusalem Talmud." In *The Cambridge History of Judaism: Volume Four: The Late Roman Period*, edited by Steven T. Katz, 663–677. Cambridge: CUP.

Mouritsen, Henrik. 2011. *The Freedman in the Roman World*. Cambridge: CUP.

Muffs, Yohanan. 1982. "Abraham the Noble Warrior: Patriarchal Politics and Laws of War in Ancient Israel." *JJS* 33: 81–107.

Müller, Christel. 2014. "Introduction: La fin de l'ethnicité ?" *DHA* Suppl. 10: 15–33.

Murray, Oswyn. 1993. "*Polis* and *Politeia* in Aristotle." In *The Ancient Greek City-State*, edited by Mogens Herman Hansen, 197–210. Copenhagen: Munksgaard.

Musurillo, Herbert (ed.). 1972. *The Acts of the Christian Martyrs*. Oxford: Clarendon Press.

Na'aman, Nadav. 2008. "Sojourners and Levites in the Kingdom of Judah in the Seventh Century BCE." *Zeitschrift für Altorientalische und Biblische Rechtsgeschichte* 14: 237–279.

Naiweld, Ron. 2016. "The Use of Rabbinic Traditions about Rome in the Babylonian Talmud." *RHR* 233.2: 255–285.

———. 2021. "The Rabbinic Model of Sovereignty in Biblical and Imperial Contexts." In Berthelot, Dohrmann, and Nemo-Pekelman 2021, 409–427.

Naveh, Joseph. 1978. *On Stone and Mosaic: The Aramaic and Hebrew Inscriptions from Ancient Synagogues*. Tel Aviv: Ha-Hevrah le-Hakirat Eretz Israel ve-Atikotenah.

Neis, Rachel. 2016. "Religious Lives of Image-things, 'Avodah Zarah', and Rabbis in Late Antique Palestine." *Archiv für Religionsgeschichte* 17.1: 91–122.

Nemo-Pekelman, Capucine. 2010. *Rome et ses citoyens juifs, IVe-Ve siècle*. Paris: Champion.

———. 2014. "Pouvoir et réseaux des juges juifs dans les provinces orientales de l'Empire romain. À propos de la constitution XVI, 8, 9 du Code Théodosien (17 avril 392)." In *Réseaux sociaux et contraintes dans l'Antiquité Tardive*, edited by Ariane Bodin and Tiphaine Moreau, 289–304. Paris: Association THAT.

Netzer, Ehud. 2006. *The Architecture of Herod, the Great Builder*. Tübingen: Mohr Siebeck.

Neusner, Jacob. (ed.). 1983–1994. *The Talmud of the Land of Israel: A Preliminary Translation and Explanation*. 35 vols. Chicago: The University of Chicago Press.

———. 1995. "Evaluating the Attributions of Sayings to Named Sages in the Rabbinic Literature." *JSJ* 26.1: 93–111.

———. 1996. *Judaism in the Matrix of Christianity*. Philadelphia: Fortress.

———. 2006. *How Important was the Destruction of the Second Temple in the Formation of Rabbinic Judaism?* Lanham: University Press of America.

———. 2008. *Persia and Rome in Classical Judaism*. Lanham: University Press of America. (First edition 1984.)

Newman, Hillel. 2014. "The Temple Mount of Jerusalem and the Capitolium of Aelia Capitolina." In *Knowledge and Wisdom: Archaeological and Historical Essays in Honour of Leah Di Segni*, edited by Giovanni C. Bottini, L. Daniel Chrupcała, and Joseph Patrich, 35–42. Milano: Edizioni Terra Santa.

Nicolet, Claude. 1976. *Le métier de citoyen dans la Rome républicaine*. Paris: Gallimard.

———. 1983. "L'Empire romain: espace, temps et politique." *Ktema* 8: 163–173.

———. 1988. *L'inventaire du monde. Géographie et politique aux origines de l'Empire romain*. Paris: Fayard. English translation: *Space, Geography, and Politics in the Early Roman Empire*. Ann Arbor: University of Michigan Press, 1991.

Niditch, Susan. 1993. *War in the Hebrew Bible: A Study in the Ethics of Violence*. New York: OUP.

Niehoff, Maren R. 2001. *Philo on Jewish Identity and Culture*. Tübingen: Mohr Siebeck.

——. 2011. "Philo's Exposition in a Roman context." *The Studia Philonica Annual* 23: 1–21.

——. 2015. "'The Power of Ares' in Philo's *Legatio*." In Calabi et al. 2015, 129–139.

——. 2018. *Philo of Alexandria: An Intellectual Biography*. New Haven: Yale University Press.

——. 2019. "A Hybrid Self: Rabbi Abbahu in Legal Debates in Caesarea." In *Self, Self-Fashioning, and Individuality in Late Antiquity: New Perspectives*, edited by Maren R. Niehoff and Joshua Levinson, 293–329. Tübingen: Mohr Siebeck.

Nielsen, Hanne S. 1987. "Alumnus: A Term of Relation Denoting Quasi-Adoption." *Classica et Medievalia* 38: 141–187.

Nikiprowetzky, Valentin. 1971. "La mort d'Éleazar fils de Jaïre et les courants apologétiques dans le *De Bello Judaico* de Flavius Josèphe." In *Hommages à André Dupont-Sommer*, edited by André Caquot and Marc Philonenko, 461–490. Paris: Adrien Maisonneuve.

Noam, Vered. 2010. *From Qumran to the Rabbinic Revolution: Conceptions of Impurity*. Jerusalem: Yad Ben-Zvi. (Heb.)

——. 2020. "'Will This One Never Be Brought Down?': Reflections of Jewish Hopes for the Downfall of the Roman Empire in Biblical Exegesis." In Price and Berthelot 2020, 169–188.

Nolland, John L. 1981. "Uncircumcised Proselytes?" *JSJ* 12.2: 173–194.

Nongbri, Brent. 2013. *Before Religion: A History of a Modern Concept*. New Haven: Yale University Press.

Noreña, Carlos F. 2003. "Medium and Message in Vespasian's *Templum Pacis*." *Memoirs of the American Academy in Rome* 48: 25–43.

——. 2011. *Imperial Ideals in the Roman West: Representation, Circulation, Power*. Cambridge: CUP.

North, John. 1993. "Roman Reactions to Empire." *SCI* 12: 127–138.

Novak, David. 1998. *Natural Law in Judaism*. Cambridge: CUP.

——. 2006. "Gentiles in Rabbinic Thought." In *The Cambridge History of Judaism. 4. The Late Roman-Rabbinic Period*, edited by Steven T. Katz, 647–662. Cambridge: CUP.

——. 2011. *The Image of the Non-Jew in Judaism: The Idea of Noahide Law*, edited by Matthew Lagrone. Portland: The Littman library of Jewish civilization. (First edition 1983.)

Novenson, Matthew V. 2009. "Why Does R. Akiba Acclaim Bar Kokhba as Messiah?" *JSJ* 40.4–5: 551–572.

O'Brien, Julia. 2007. "From Exile to Empire: A Response." In *Approaching Yehud: New Approaches to the Study of the Persian Period*, edited by Jon L. Berquist, 209–214. Atlanta: SBL Press.

Oakes, Peter. 2019. "The Christians and their *Politeuma* in Heaven: Philippians 3:20 and the Herakleopolis Papyri." In Berthelot and Price 2019, 141–163.

Oded, Bustanay. 1979. *Mass Deportations and Deportees in the Neo-Assyrian Empire*. Wiesbaden: Reichert.

——. 1992. *War, Peace and Empire: Justification for War in Assyrian Royal Inscriptions*. Wiesbaden: Reichert.

Oliver, Isaac W. 2013. "Forming Jewish Identity by Formulating Legislation for Gentiles." *JAJ* 4: 105–132.

Oliver, James H. 1941. *The Sacred Gerusia*. Athens: American School of Classical Studies at Athens.

——. 1953. *The Ruling Power: A Study of the Roman Empire in the Second Century after Christ through the Roman Oration of Aelius Aristides*. Philadelphia: American Philosophical Society.

————. 1972. "Text of the Tabula Banasitana, A.D. 177." *The American Journal of Philology* 93.2: 336–340.

————. 1989. *Greek Constitutions of Early Roman Emperors from Inscriptions and Papyri*. Philadelphia: American Philosophical Society.

Ollier, François. 1933–1943. *Le mirage spartiate*. 2 vols. Paris: E. de Boccard.

Ophir, Adi, and Ishay Rosen-Zvi. 2018. *Goy: Israel's Multiple Others and the Birth of the Gentile*. Oxford: OUP.

Oppenheimer, Aharon. 2005a. "Jewish Penal Authority in Roman Judaea." In *Between Rome and Babylon: Studies in Jewish Leadership and Society*, edited by Nili Oppenheimer, 173–182. Tübingen: Mohr Siebeck.

————. 2005b. "Jewish Conscripts in the Roman Army?" In *ibid.*, 183–191.

————. 2005c. "The Ban on Circumcision as a Cause of the Revolt: A Reconsideration." In *ibid.*, 243–255.

————. 2009. "Purity of Lineage in Talmudic Babylonia." In *Manières de penser dans l'Antiquité méditerranéenne et orientale*, edited by Christophe Batsch and Madalina Vârtejanu-Joubert, 145–156. Leiden: Brill.

————. 2017. *Rabbi Judah ha-Nasi: Statesman, Reformer, and Redactor of the Mishnah*. Tübingen: Mohr Siebeck.

Östenberg, Ida. 2009. *Staging the World: Spoils, Captives and Representations in the Roman Triumphal Procession*. Oxford: OUP.

Otto, Eckart. 1999a. *Das Deuteronomium: Politische Theologie und Rechtsreform in Juda und Assyrien*. Berlin: De Gruyter.

————. 1999b. *Krieg und Frieden in der Hebräischen Bibel: Aspekte für eine Friedensordnung in der Moderne*. Stuttgart: Kohlhammer.

————. 2002. *Gottes Recht als Menschenrecht: Rechts- und literaturhistorische Studien zum Deuteronomium*. Wiesbaden: Otto Harrassowitz Verlag.

————. 2003. "Psalm 2 in neuassyrischer Zeit: Assyrische Motive in der judäischen Königsideologie." In *Textarbeit: Studien zu Texten und ihrer Rezeption aus dem Alten Testament und der Umwelt Israels*, edited by Peter Weimar, 335–349. Münster: Ugarit-Verlag.

————. 2005. "Die Rechtshermeneutik des Pentateuch und die achämenidische Rechtsideologie in ihren altorientalischen Kontexten." In *Kodifizierung und Legitimierung des Rechts in der Antike und im Alten Orient*, edited by Markus Witte and Marie Theres Fögen, 71–116. Wiesbaden: Harrassowitz Verlag.

————. 2009. "Anti-Achaemenid Propaganda in Deuteronomy." In *Homeland and Exile: Biblical and Ancient Near Eastern Studies in Honour of Bustenay Oded*, edited by Gershon Galil, Mark Geller and Alan Millard, 547–558. Leiden: Brill.

————. 2013. "The Book of Deuteronomy and Its Answer to the Persian State Ideology: The Legal Implications." In *Loi et justice dans la littérature du Proche-Orient ancien*, edited by Olivier Artus, 112–122. Wiesbaden: Harrassowitz Verlag.

————. 2016. *Deuteronomium 12–34, Erster Teilband: 12, 1–23, 15*. Freiburg: Herder.

————. 2017. *Deuteronomium 12–34, Zweiter Teilband: 23, 16–34, 12*. Freiburg: Herder.

Otzen, Benedikt. 1990. "Crisis and Religious Reaction: Jewish Apocalypticism." In *Religion and Religious Practice in the Seleucid Kingdom*, edited by Per Bilde, 224–236. Aarhus: Aarhus University Press.

Pairman Brown, John. 2001. *Israel and Hellas. Vol. III: The Legacy of Iranian Imperialism and the Individual*. Berlin: De Gruyter.

Paladini, Maria Luisa. 1985. "A proposito di 'pax Flavia.'" In Sordi 1985, 223–229.

Palmer, Carmen. 2017. *Converts in the Dead Sea Scrolls: The Gēr and Mutable Ethnicity*. Leiden: Brill.

Parpola, Simo. 1997. *Assyrian Prophecies*. Helsinki: Helsinki University.

——. 2003. "Assyria's Expansion in the 8th and 7th Centuries and Its Long-Term Repercussions in the West." In *Symbiosis, Symbolism, and the Power of the Past: Canaan, Ancient Israel, and Their Neighbors from the Late Bronze Age through Roman Palaestina*, edited by William G. Dever and Seymour Gitin, 99–111. Winona Lake: Eisenbrauns.

Paul, Shalom M. 1991. *Amos: A Commentary on the Book of Amos*. Minneapolis: Fortress Press.

——. 2005a. "Deutero-Isaiah and Cuneiform Royal Inscriptions." In *Divrei Shalom: Collected Studies of Shalom M. Paul on the Bible and the Ancient Near East 1967–2005*, 11–22. Leiden: Brill. Originally published in *Essays in Memory of E. A. Speiser*, edited by William W. Hallo, 180–186. New Haven: American Oriental Society, 1968.

——. 2005b. "Adoption Formulae: A Study of Cuneiform and Biblical Legal Clauses." In *Divrei Shalom: Collected Studies of Shalom M. Paul on the Bible and the Ancient Near East 1967–2005*, 109–119. Originally published in *Maarav* 2.2 (1979–80): 173–185.

——. 2012. *Isaiah 40–66: Translation and Commentary*. Grand Rapids: Eerdmans.

Paz, Yakir. 2009. "Prior to Sinai: The Patriarchs and the Mosaic Law in Rabbinic Literature in View of Second Temple and Christian Literature." Unpublished MA thesis, Hebrew University of Jerusalem.

Pearce, Laurie E., and Cornelia Wunsch. 2014. *Documents of Judean Exiles and West Semites in Babylonia in the Collection of David Sofer*. Bethesda: CDL Press.

Pekáry, Thomas. 1987. "'Seditio'. Unruhen und Revolten im Römischen Reich von Augustus bis Commodus." *Ancient Society* 18: 133–150.

Peppard, Michael. 2011. *The Son of God in the Roman World: Divine Sonship in its Social and Political Context*. New York: OUP.

Perani, Mauro. 2005. "*Yhwh iš milḥamah* (Es 15,3). L'espressione 'Yhwh è un uomo di guerra' nell'esegesi ebraica." In *Guerra santa, guerra e pace dal Vicino Oriente antico alle tradizioni ebraica, cristiana e islamica*, edited by Mauro Perani, 141–150. Florence: La Giuntina.

Perdue, Leo G., and Warren Carter. 2015. *Israel and Empire: A Postcolonial History of Israel and Early Judaism*. London: Bloomsbury.

Pernot, Laurent. 2008. "Aelius Aristides and Rome." In *Aelius Aristides between Rome, Greece, and the Gods*, edited by W. V. Harris and Brooke Holmes, 175–201. Leiden: Brill.

Petitfils, James M. 2014. "Martial Moses in Flavian Rome: Josephus's *Antiquities* 2–4 and Exemplary Roman Leadership." *Journal of Greco-Roman Christianity and Judaism* 10: 194–208.

Phang, Sara E. 2007. "Military Documents, Languages, and Literacy." In Erdkamp 2007, 286–305.

Pongratz-Leisten, Beate. 2015. *Religion and Ideology in Assyria*. Berlin: De Gruyter.

Popović, Mladen (ed.). 2011. *The Jewish Revolt Against Rome: Interdisciplinary Perspectives*. Leiden: Brill.

Porten, Bezalel, and Ada Yardeni. 1986. *Textbook of Aramaic Documents from Ancient Egypt. Volume 1, Letters. Appendix, Aramaic Letters from the Bible*. Jerusalem: Hebrew University Department of the History of the Jewish People.

Portier-Young, Anathea E. 2011. *Apocalypse Against Empire: Theologies of Resistance in Early Judaism*. Grand Rapids: Eerdmans.

——. 2014. "Jewish Apocalyptic Literature as Resistance Literature." In *The Oxford Handbook of Apocalyptic Literature*, edited by John J. Collins, 145–162. New York: OUP.

Porton, Gary G. 1994. *The Stranger within Your Gates*. Chicago: University of Chicago Press.

Postgate, Nicholas. 2007. *The Land of Assur & the Yoke of Assur: Studies on Assyria, 1971–2005*. Oxford: Oxbow Books.

Pratt, Kenneth J. 1965. "Rome as Eternal." *Journal of the History of Ideas* 26.1: 25–44.

Presner, Todd S. 2007. *Muscular Judaism: The Jewish Body and the Politics of Regeneration*. Abingdon: Routledge.

Prévost, Marcel-Henri. 1949. *Les adoptions politiques à Rome sous la République et le Principat*. Paris: Sirey.

———. 1967. "Remarques sur l'adoption dans la Bible." *Revue internationale des droits de l'antiquité* 14: 67–77.

Price, Jonathan J. 2005. "The Provincial Historian in Rome." In *Josephus and Jewish History in Flavian Rome and Beyond*, edited by Joseph Sievers and Gaia Lembi, 101–118. Leiden: Brill.

———. 2020a. "Structural Weaknesses in Rome's Power? Greek Historians' Views on Roman Stasis." In Berthelot 2020a, 255–267.

———. 2020b. "The Future of Rome in Three Greek Historians of Rome." In Price and Berthelot 2020, 85–111.

Price, Jonathan J., and Katell Berthelot (eds.). 2020. *The Future of Rome: Roman, Greek, Jewish and Christian Visions*. Cambridge: CUP.

Price, Jonathan J., and Haggai Misgav. 2006. "Jewish Inscriptions and Their Use." In Safrai et al. 2006, 461–483.

Price, Simon. 1984. *Rituals and Power: The Roman Imperial Cult in Asia Minor*. Cambridge: CUP.

Pucci Ben Zeev, Miriam. 1998. *Jewish Rights in the Roman World: The Greek and Roman Documents Quoted by Josephus Flavius*. Tübingen: Mohr Siebeck.

———. 2005. *Diaspora Judaism in Turmoil, 116/117 CE: Ancient Sources and Modern Insights*. Leuven: Peeters.

———. 2018. "New Insights into Roman Policy in Judea on the Eve of the Bar Kokhba Revolt." *JSJ* 49.1: 84–107.

Rabello, Alfredo M. 1967. "Sul l'ebraicità dell'autore della 'Collatio Legum Mosaicarum et Romanarum'." *La Rassegna Mensile di Israel* 33: 339–349.

———. 1980. "The Legal Condition of the Jews in the Roman Empire." *Aufstieg und Niedergang der Römischen Welt* II.13, edited by Wolfgang Haase, 662–762. Berlin: De Gruyter.

———. 1995. "The Ban on Circumcision as a Cause of Bar Kokhba's Rebellion." *Israel Law Review* 29: 176–214.

Radner, Karen. 2015. "High Visibility Punishment and Deterrent: Impalement in Assyrian Warfare and Legal Practice." *Zeitschrift für Altorientalische und Biblische Rechtsgeschichte* 21: 103–128.

Raggi, Andrea. 2004. "The Epigraphic Dossier of Seleucus of Rhosus: A Revised Edition." *ZPE* 147: 123–138.

———. 2009. "*Cives Romani optimo iure optimaque lege immunes*. Cittadinanza romana e immunità in Oriente nella tarda repubblica." In *Transforming Historical Landscapes in the Ancient Empires*, edited by Toni Ñaco del Hoyo and Borja Antela-Bernárdez, 131–136. Oxford: B.A.R.

Rajak, Tessa. 1991. "Friends, Romans, Subjects: Agrippa II's Speech in Josephus's *Jewish War*." In *Images of Empire*, edited by Loveday Alexander, 122–134. Sheffield: JSOT Press.

———. 1998. "The *Against Apion* and the Continuities in Josephus's Political Thought." In *Understanding Josephus: Seven Perspectives*, edited by Steve Mason, 222–246. Sheffield: Sheffield Academic Press.

———. 2001. "Dying for the Law: The Martyr's Portrait in Jewish-Greek Literature." In Rajak, *The Jewish Dialogue with Greece and Rome: Studies in Cultural and Social Interaction*, 99–133. Leiden: Brill.

———. 2012. "Reflections on Jewish Resistance and the Discourse of Martyrdom in Josephus." In *Judaea-Palaestina, Babylon and Rome: Jews in Antiquity*, edited by Benjamin Isaac and Yuval Shahar, 166–180. Tübingen: Mohr Siebeck.

——. 2013. "Josephus in Rome: The Outsiders' Insider and Insiders' Outsider." *SCI* 33: 191–208.

Rakover, Nahum. 1994. "The 'Law' and the Noahides." In *Politics and Theopolitics in the Bible and Postbiblical Literature*, edited by Henning Graf Reventlow, 148–159. Sheffield: JSOT Press.

Ramírez Kidd, José E. 1999. *Alterity and Identity in Israel: The גר in the Old Testament*. Berlin: De Gruyter.

Rappaport, Uriel. 2004. *The First Book of Maccabees: Introduction, Hebrew Translation, and Commentary*. Jerusalem: Yad Izhak Ben-Zvi. (Heb.)

Regev, Eyal. 2010. "Herod's Jewish Ideology Facing Romanization: On Intermarriage, Ritual Baths, and Speeches." *JQR* 100.2: 197–222.

Reinhartz, Adele. 1989. "Rabbinic Perceptions of Simeon bar Kosiba." *JSJ* 20.2: 171–194.

Rendtorff, Rolf. 1996. "The *Ger* in the Priestly Laws of the Pentateuch." In *Ethnicity and the Bible*, edited by Mark G. Brett, 77–87. Leiden: Brill.

Resnick, Irven M. 2000. "Medieval Roots of the Myth of Jewish Male Menses." *HTR* 93.3: 241–263.

Reynolds, Joyce. 1982. *Aphrodisias and Rome: Documents from the excavation of the theatre at Aphrodisias conducted by Professor Kenan T. Erim, together with some related texts*. London: Society for the Promotion of Roman Studies.

Reynolds, Joyce, and Robert Tannenbaum. 1987. *Jews and Godfearers at Aphrodisias*. Cambridge: Cambridge Philological Society.

Richardson, John S. 1991. "*Imperium Romanum*: Empire and the Language of Power." *JRS* 81: 1–9.

——. 1995. "The Roman Mind and the Power of Fiction." In *The Passionate Intellect: Essays on the Transformation of Classical Traditions, presented to Professor I. G. Kidd*, edited by Lewis Ayres, 117–130. New Brunswick: Transaction Publishers.

——. 2008. *The Language of Empire: Rome and the Idea of Empire from the Third Century BC to the Second Century AD*. Cambridge: CUP.

——. 2015. "Roman Law in the Provinces." In *The Cambridge Companion to Roman Law*, edited by David Johnston, 45–58. Cambridge: CUP.

Richardson, Peter. 1996. *Herod, King of the Jews and Friend of the Romans*. Columbia: University of South Carolina Press.

Rieger, Paul. 1926. "The Foundation of Rome in the Talmud: A Contribution to the Folklore of Antiquity." *JQR* N.S. 16.3: 227–235.

Riggsby, Andrew M. 2010. *Roman Law and the Legal World of the Romans*. Cambridge: CUP.

Ritter, Bradley. 2011. "On the 'Politeuma' in Heracleopolis." *SCI* 30: 9–37.

——. 2015. *Judeans in the Greek Cities of the Roman Empire: Rights, Citizenship and Civil Discord*. Leiden: Brill.

Rives, James. 2005. "Flavian Religious Policy and the Destruction of the Jerusalem Temple." In Edmondson, Mason, and Rives 2005, 145–166.

Rizakis, Athanasios. 2011. "La diffusion des processus d'adaptation onomastique: les Aurelii dans les provinces orientales de l'Empire." In *Les noms de personnes dans l'Empire romain. Transformations, adaptation, évolution*, edited by Monique Dondin-Payre, 253–262. Bordeaux: Ausonius.

Roberts, Alexander, and James Donaldson (eds.). 1886–1905. *The Ante-Nicene Fathers: Translations of the Writings of the Fathers Down to A.D. 325, volume III*. New York: Scribner.

Roberts, Alexander, James Donaldson, and A. Cleveland Coxe (eds.). 1886. *Ante-Nicene Fathers, volume VI*. Buffalo: Christian Literature Publishing Company.

Rocca, Samuel. 2008. *Herod's Judaea: A Mediterranean State in the Classical World*. Tübingen: Mohr Siebeck.

———. 2010. "Josephus, Suetonius, and Tacitus on Military Service of the Jews of Rome." *Italia* 20: 7–30.

Rochette, Bruno. 1997. "Vrbis—Orbis. Ovide, *Fastes* II, 684: *Romanae spatium est Vrbis et orbis idem.*" *Latomus* 56.3: 551–553.

———. 2001. "Juifs et Romains: Y a-t-il eu un antijudaïsme romain ?" *REJ* 160: 1–31.

Rodgers, René. 2003. "Female Representations in Roman Art: Feminising the Provincial 'Other.'" In *Roman Imperialism and Provincial Art*, edited by Sarah Scott and Jane Webster, 69–93. Cambridge: CUP.

Rogers, Guy M. 1991. *The Sacred Identity of Ephesos: Foundation Myths of a Roman City*. London: Routledge.

Römer, Thomas. 2005. *The So-Called Deuteronomistic History: A Sociological, Historical and Literary Introduction*. London: T&T Clark.

———. 2015. *The Invention of God*, translated by Raymond Geuss. Cambridge: HUP.

Ronen, Israel. 1988. "Formation of Jewish Nationalism Among the Idumeans." In Arieh Kasher, *Jews, Idumaeans, and Ancient Arabs: Relations of the Jews in Eretz-Israel with the Nations of the Frontier and the Desert during the Hellenistic and Roman Era (332 BCE–70 CE)*, 214–239. Tübingen: Mohr Siebeck.

Root, Margaret Cool. 1979. *The King and Kingship in Achaemenid Art: Essays on the Creation of an Iconography of Empire*. Leiden: Brill.

———. 2000. "Imperial Ideology in Achaemenid Persian Art: Transforming the Mesopotamian Legacy." *Bulletin of the Canadian Society for Mesopotamian Studies* 35: 19–27.

Rosen-Zvi, Ishay. 2011. *Demonic Desires: Yetzer hara and the Problem of Evil in Late Antiquity*. Philadelphia: University of Pennsylvania Press.

———. 2013. "The Rise and Fall of Rabbinic Masculinity." *JSIJ* 12: 1–22.

———. 2017a. "Rabbis and Romanization: A Review Essay." In *Jewish Cultural Encounters in the Ancient Mediterranean and Near Eastern World*, edited by Mladen Popović et al., 218–245. Leiden: Brill.

———. 2017b. "Is the Mishnah a Roman Composition?" In Bar-Asher Siegal, Novick, and Hayes 2017, 487–508.

———. 2017c. "Pauline Traditions and the Rabbis: Three Case Studies." *HTR* 110.2: 169–194.

Rosen-Zvi, Ishay, and Adi Ophir. 2011. "*Goy*: Toward a Genealogy." *Diné Israel* 28: 69–122.

———. 2015. "Paul and the Invention of the Gentiles." *JQR* 105.1: 1–41.

Rosental, Eliezer S. 1983. "Two Things." In *Essays on the Bible and the Ancient World: Isaac Leo Seeligmann Volume*, edited by Alexander Rofé and Yair Zakovitch, 463–481. Jerusalem: E. Rubinstein's Publishing House. (Heb.)

Rosso, Emmanuelle. 2005. *Idéologie impériale et art officiel sous les Flaviens: formulation, diffusion et réception dans les provinces occidentales de l'Empire romain (69–96 ap. J.-C.)*. Unpublished PhD, Paris 4 Sorbonne University.

———. 2009. "Le thème de la *Res publica restituta* dans le monnayage de Vespasien: pérennité du « modèle augustéen » entre citations, réinterprétations et dévoiements." In Hurlet and Mineo 2009, 205–238.

——— (Rosso Caponio). 2020. "Personnifications de Rome et du pouvoir romain en Asie Mineure: quelques exemples." In Berthelot 2020a, 127–155.

Roth, Jonathan. 2007. "Jews and the Roman Army: Perceptions and Realities." In *The Impact of the Roman Army (200 BC–AD 476)*, edited by Lukas de Blois and Elio Lo Cascio, 409–420. Leiden: Brill.

Rotman, Yuval. 2012. "Captives and Redeeming Captives: The Law and the Community." In *Judaea-Palaestina, Babylon and Rome: Jews in Antiquity*, edited by Benjamin Isaac and Yuval Shahar, 227–247. Tübingen: Mohr Siebeck.

Roux, Marie. 2017. "A Re-Interpretation of Martial, Epigram XI.94." *SCI* 36: 1–24.

Roux, Marie, and Yael Wilfand. 2020. "'The Flower of the Whole World': A Jerusalem Talmud's Homily on Converts in the Light of Greco-Roman Floral Motives." *REJ* 179.3–4: 315–331.

Rubenstein, Jeffrey L. 2003. *The Culture of the Babylonian Talmud*. Baltimore: Johns Hopkins University Press.

Russell, Donald A., and Nigel G. Wilson. 1981. *Menander Rhetor, Edited with Translation and Commentary*. Oxford: Clarendon Press.

Rutgers, Leonard V. 1995. *The Jews in Late Ancient Rome: Evidence of Cultural Interaction in the Roman Diaspora*. Leiden: Brill.

Sachau, Eduard. 1907. *Syrische Rechtsbücher*. Band I. Berlin: Reimer.

Safrai, Shmuel, et al. (eds.). 2006. *The Literature of the Sages. Second Part: Midrash and Targum, Liturgy, Poetry, Mysticism, Contracts, Inscriptions, Ancient Science and the Languages of Rabbinic Literature*. Assen: Van Gorcum; Minneapolis: Fortress Press.

Sagi, Avi, and Zvi Zohar. 2007. *Transforming Identity: The Ritual Transition from Gentile to Jew—Structure and Meaning*. New York: Continuum.

Said, Edward. 1993. *Culture and Imperialism*. New York: Knopf.

Sandmel, Samuel. 1962. "Parallelomania." *JBL* 81: 1–13.

———. 1971. *Philo's Place in Judaism: A Study of Conceptions of Abraham in Jewish Literature*. Hoboken: Ktav Publishing House.

Sänger, Patrick. 2014. "The *Politeuma* in the Hellenistic World (Third to First Century BC): A Form of Organization to Integrate Minorities." In *Migration und Integration—wissenschaftliche Perspektiven aus Österreich. Jahrbuch 2/2013*, edited by Julia Dahlvik, Christoph Reinprecht, and Wiebke Sievers, 51–68. Göttingen: V&R Unipress.

———. 2016. "The Meaning of the Word πολίτευμα in the Light of the Judaeo-Hellenistic Literature." In *Proceedings of the 27th International Congress of Papyrology, Warsaw, 29 July–3 August 2013*, edited by Tomasz Derda, Adam Lajtar, and Jakub Urbanik, 1679–1693. Warsaw: University of Warsaw.

———. 2019. *Die ptolemäische Organisationsform* politeuma. *Ein Herrschaftsinstrument zugunsten jüdischer und anderer hellenischer Gemeinschaften*. Tübingen: Mohr Siebeck.

Satlow, Michael L. 1996. "'Try to Be a Man': The Rabbinic Construction of Masculinity." *HTR* 89.1: 19–40.

———. 2006. "Defining Judaism: Accounting for 'Religions' in the Study of Religion." *Journal of the American Academy of Religion* 74.4: 837–860.

———. 2008. "Beyond Influence: Toward a New Historiographic Paradigm." In *Jewish Literatures and Cultures: Context and Intertext*, edited by Anita Norich and Yaron Z. Eliav, 37–53. Providence: Brown University.

Schäfer, Peter. 1980. "Rabbi Aqiva and Bar Kokhba." In *Approaches to Ancient Judaism*, edited by William Scott Green, 113–130. Atlanta: Scholars Press.

———. 1981. "The Causes of the Bar Kokhba Revolt." In *Studies in Aggadah, Targum and Jewish Liturgy in Memory of Joseph Heinemann*, edited by Jakob J. Petuchowski, 74–94. Jerusalem: Magnes.

———. 1990. "Hadrian's Policy in Judaea and the Bar Kokhba Revolt: A Reassessment." In *A Tribute to Geza Vermes: Essays on Jewish and Christian Literature and History*, edited by Philip R. Davies and Richard T. White, 281–303. Sheffield: JSOT Press.

———. 1997. *Judeophobia: Attitudes toward the Jews in the Ancient World*. Cambridge: HUP.

——— (ed.). 1998. *The Talmud Yerushalmi and Graeco-Roman Culture*. Vol. I. Tübingen: Mohr Siebeck.

——— (ed.). 2002a. *The Talmud Yerushalmi and Graeco-Roman Culture*. Vol. III. Tübingen: Mohr Siebeck.

———. 2002b. "Jews and Gentiles in Yerushalmi Avodah Zarah." In Schäfer 2002a, 335–352.

——— (ed.). 2003a. *The Bar Kokhba War Reconsidered: New Perspectives on the Second Jewish Revolt against Rome*. Tübingen: Mohr Siebeck.

———. 2003b. "Bar Kokhba and the Rabbis." In Schäfer 2003a, 1–22.

———. 2007. *Jesus in the Talmud*. Princeton: PUP.

Schäfer, Peter, and Catherine Hezser (eds.). 2000. *The Talmud Yerushalmi and Graeco-Roman Culture*. Vol. II. Tübingen: Mohr Siebeck.

Schaff, Philip, and Henry Wace (eds.). 1890. *Nicene and Post-Nicene Fathers, Second Series, Volume 13*. Buffalo: Christian Literature Publishing Co.

———. 1904. *Nicene and Post-Nicene Fathers, Second Series, Volume 14*. New York: Scribner.

Schalit, Abraham. 1960. "The Letter of Antiochus III to Zeuxis regarding the Establishment of Jewish Military Colonies in Phrygia and Lydia." *JQR* 50.4: 289–318.

Scharf, Ralf. 1997. "*Regii Emeseni Iudaei*: Bemerkungen zur einer spätantiken Truppe." *Latomus* 56.2: 343–359.

Scheid, John. 2001. *Religion et piété à Rome*. Paris: Albin Michel. (First edition 1985.)

———. 2005. *Quand faire, c'est croire: les rites sacrificiels des Romains*. Paris: Aubier.

———. 2007a. Res Gestae Divi Augusti: *Hauts faits du divin Auguste*. Paris: Les Belles Lettres.

———. 2007b. "Sacrifier pour l'Empereur, sacrifier à l'Empereur. Le culte des Empereurs sous le Haut-Empire romain." *Cours du Collège de France, Religion, institutions et société de la Rome antique, 2006–2007*, 663–681. Available at https://www.college-de-france.fr /site/john-scheid/resumes.htm

Scheidel, Walter (ed.). 2009. *Rome and China: Comparative Perspectives on Ancient World Empires*. Oxford: OUP.

Schmid, Konrad. 2007. "The Persian Imperial Authorization as a Historical Problem and as a Biblical Construct: A Plea for Distinctions in the Current Debate." In Knoppers and Levinson 2007, 23–38.

Schmitt, Rüdiger. 2009. *Die altpersischen Inschriften der Achaimeniden. Editio Minor mit deutscher Übersetzung*. Wiesbaden: Reichert Verlag.

Schoenfeld, Andrew J. 2006. "Sons of Israel in Caesar's Service: Jewish Soldiers in the Roman Military." *Shofar: An Interdisciplinary Journal of Jewish Studies* 24.3: 115–126.

Schofield, Malcolm. 1999. *The Stoic Idea of the City*. Chicago: University of Chicago Press.

Schremer, Adiel. 2008. "'The Lord Has Forsaken the Land': Radical Explanations of the Military and Political Defeat of the Jews in Tannaitic Literature." *JJS* 59.2: 183–200.

———. 2009. "The Christianization of the Roman Empire and Rabbinic Literature." In *Jewish Identities in Antiquity: Studies in Memory of Menahem Stern*, edited by Lee I. Levine and Daniel R. Schwartz, 349–366. Tübingen: Mohr Siebeck.

———. 2010. *Brothers Estranged: Heresy, Christianity, and Jewish Identity in Late Antiquity*. New York: OUP.

———. 2012. "Thinking about Belonging in Early Rabbinic Literature: Proselytes, Apostates, and 'Children of Israel,' or: Does It Make Sense to Speak of Early Rabbinic Orthodoxy?" *JSJ* 43.2: 249–275.

Schultz, Brian. 2009. *Conquering the World: The War Scroll (1QM) Reconsidered*. Leiden: Brill.

Schürer, Emil. 1973. *The History of the Jewish People in the Age of Jesus Christ (175 B.C.–A.D. 135). Volume I: A New English Version*, revised and edited by Géza Vermes, Fergus Millar, and Matthew Black. Edinburgh: T&T Clark.

Schwartz, Daniel R. 1990a. *Agrippa I: The Last King of Judaea*. Tübingen: Mohr Siebeck.

———. 1990b. "On Two Aspects of a Priestly View of Descent at Qumran." In *Archaeology and History in the Dead Sea Scrolls*, edited by Lawrence H. Schiffman, 157–179. Sheffield: Sheffield Academic Press.

———. 2007. "Doing like Jews or Becoming a Jew? Josephus on Women Converts to Judaism." In *Jewish Identity in the Greco-Roman World / Jüdische Identität in der griechisch-römischen Welt*, edited by Jörg Frey, Daniel R. Schwartz, and Stephanie Gripentrog, 93–109. Leiden: Brill.

———. 2008. *2 Maccabees*. Berlin: De Gruyter.

———. 2014. *Judeans and Jews: Four Faces of Dichotomy in Ancient Jewish History.* Toronto: University of Toronto Press.

Schwartz, Daniel R., and Zeev Weiss, in collaboration with Ruth A. Clements (eds.). 2012. *Was 70 CE a Watershed in Jewish History? On Jews and Judaism before and after the Destruction of the Second Temple.* Leiden: Brill.

Schwartz, Seth. 1999. "The Patriarchs and the Diaspora." *JJS* 50: 208–222.

———. 2001. *Imperialism and Jewish Society, 200 B.C.E. to 640 C.E.* Princeton: PUP.

———. 2010a. *Were the Jews a Mediterranean Society? Reciprocity and Solidarity in Ancient Judaism.* Princeton: PUP.

———. 2010b. "'Rabbinic culture' and Roman culture." In *Rabbinic Texts and the History of Late-Roman Palestine*, edited by Martin Goodman and Philip Alexander, 283–299. Oxford: OUP.

———. 2011. "How Many Judaisms Were There?: A Critique of Neusner and Smith on Definition and Mason and Boyarin on Categorization." *JAJ* 2.2: 208–238.

———. 2014. *The Ancient Jews from Alexander to Muhammad.* Cambridge: CUP.

———. 2016. "The Impact of the Jewish Rebellions, 66–135 CE: Destruction or Provincialization?" In *Revolt and Resistance in the Ancient Classical World and the Near East: In the Crucible of Empire*, edited by John J. Collins and Joseph G. Manning, 234–252. Leiden: Brill.

———. 2020. "The Mishnah and the Limits of Roman Power." In Berthelot 2020a, 387–415.

Scott, James C. 1990. *Domination and the Arts of Resistance: Hidden Transcripts.* New Haven: Yale University Press.

Scott, James M. 1992. *Adoption as Sons of God: An Exegetical Investigation into the Background of ΥΙΟΘΕΣΙΑ in the Pauline Corpus.* Tübingen: Mohr Siebeck.

———. 1995. "Philo and the Restoration of Israel." In *SBL 1995 Seminar Papers*, edited by Eugene H. Lovering, 553–575. Atlanta: SBL Press.

Seeman, Chris. 2013. *Rome and Judea in Transition: Hasmonean Relations with the Roman Republic and the Evolution of the High Priesthood.* New York: P. Lang.

Seland, Torrey. 2010. "'Colony' and 'Metropolis' in Philo: Examples of Mimicry and Hybridity in Philo's Writing Back from the Empire?" *Etudes Platoniciennes* 7: 11–33.

Seston, William, and Maurice Euzennat. 1971. "Un dossier de la chancellerie romaine, la *Tabula Banasitana*: étude de diplomatique." *Comptes rendus des séances de l'Académie des Inscriptions et Belles-Lettres* 115.3: 468–490.

Shahar, Yuval. 2003. "Rabbi Akiba and the Destruction of the Temple: The Establishment of the Fast Days." *Zion* 68: 145–165. (Heb.)

Shaked, Shaul. 1984. "Iranian Influence on Judaism: First Century B.C.E. to Second Century C.E." In *The Cambridge History of Judaism. Volume One, Introduction: The Persian Period*, edited by William D. Davies et al., 308–325. Cambridge: CUP.

———. 1998. "Eschatology. I. In Zoroastrianism and Zoroastrian Influence." In *Encyclopœdia Iranica* VIII.6: 565–569. Available at iranicaonline.org.

Sharon, Nadav. 2017. *Judea under Roman Domination: The First Generation of Statelessness and Its Legacy.* Atlanta: SBL Press.

———. 2020. "Rome and the Four-Empires Scheme in Pre-Rabbinic Jewish Literature." In Berthelot 2020a, 37–60.

Shatzman, Israel. 1999. "The Integration of Judaea into the Roman Empire." *SCI* 18: 49–84.

Shaw, Brent D. 1984. "Bandits in the Roman Empire." *Past and Present* 105: 3–52.

Shemesh, Aharon. 2009. *Halakhah in the Making: The Development of Jewish Law from Qumran to the Rabbis*. Berkeley: University of California Press.

Sherk, Robert K. 1969. *Roman Documents from the Greek East*. Baltimore: John Hopkins Press.

———. 1988. *The Roman Empire: Augustus to Hadrian*. Cambridge: CUP.

Sherwin-White, Adrian N. 1973a. *The Roman Citizenship*. Oxford: Clarendon Press. (First edition 1939.)

———. 1973b. "The *Tabula* of Banasa and the *Constitutio Antoniniana*." *JRS* 63: 86–98.

Sherwin-White, Susan, and Amélie Kuhrt. 1993. *From Samarkhand to Sardis: A New Approach to the Seleucid Empire*. Berkeley: University of California Press.

Sicker, Martin. 2001. *Between Rome and Jerusalem: 300 Years of Roman-Judaean Relations*. Westport: Praeger.

Siegert, Folker. 1973. "Gottesfürchtige und Sympathisanten." *JSJ* 4: 107–164.

Silverman, Jason M. 2009. "Persian Influence on Jewish Apocalyptic." *Proceedings of the Irish Biblical Association* 32: 49–59.

———. 2011. "Iranian-Judaean Interaction in the Achaemenid Period." In *Text, Theology, and Trowel: New Investigations in the Biblical World*, edited by Lidia D. Matassa and Jason M. Silverman, 133–168. Eugene: Pickwick Publications.

———. 2012. *Persepolis and Jerusalem: Iranian Influence on the Apocalyptic Hermeneutic*. London: T&T Clark.

———. 2013. "Iranian Details in the Book of Heavenly Luminaries (1 Enoch 72–82)." *Journal of Near Eastern Studies* 72.2: 195–208.

———. 2016. "Was There an Achaemenid 'Theology' of Kingship? The Intersections of Mythology, Religion, and Imperial Religious Policy." In *Religion in the Achaemenid Persian Empire: Emerging Judaisms and Trends*, edited by Diana Edelman, Anne Fitzpatrick-McKinley, and Philippe Guillaume, 172–196. Tübingen: Mohr Siebeck.

———. 2017. "Achaemenid Creation and Second Isaiah." *Journal of Persianate Studies* 10.1: 26–48.

Simon, Marcel. 1964. *Verus Israel: Étude sur les relations entre chrétiens et Juifs dans l'empire romain (135–425)*. Paris: E. de Boccard. (First edition 1948.)

Simon, Maurice. 1936. *The Babylonian Talmud. Seder Nashim IV*, edited by Isidore Epstein. London: The Soncino Press.

Simon-Shoshan, Moshe. 2012. *Stories of the Law: Narrative Discourse and the Construction of Authority in the Mishnah*. Oxford: OUP.

———. 2018. "Did the Rabbis Believe in Agreus Pan? Patriarchs, Emperors, and Gods in Bereshit Rabba 63." *HTR* 111.3: 425–450.

Sivertsev, Alexei M. 2011. *Judaism and Imperial Ideology in Late Antiquity*. Cambridge: CUP.

Smallwood, Mary E. 1976. *The Jews Under Roman Rule from Pompey to Diocletian*. Leiden: Brill.

Smith, Anthony D. 1986. *The Ethnic Origins of Nations*. Oxford: Basil Blackwell.

Smith, Christopher J. 2006. *The Roman Clan: The Gens from Ancient Ideology to Modern Anthropology*. Cambridge: CUP.

Smith, Morton. 1963. "II Isaiah and the Persians." *Journal of the American Oriental Society* 83.4: 415–421.

———. 1996. "The Common Theology of the Ancient Near East." In Morton Smith, *Studies in the Cult of Yahweh*, 15–27. Leiden: Brill.

———. 1999. "The Gentiles in Judaism, 125 BCE—CE 66." In *The Cambridge History of Judaism. III. The Early Roman Period*, edited by William Horbury, William D. Davies, and John Sturdy, 192–249. Cambridge: CUP.

Smith, Roland R. R. 1988. *"Simulacra Gentium*: The Ethne from the Sebasteion at Aphrodisias." *JRS* 78: 50–77.

———. 2013. *The Marble Reliefs from the Julio-Claudian Sebasteion.* Damstadt–Mainz: Verlag P. von Zabern.

Smith-Christopher, Daniel L. 2014. "A Postcolonial Reading of Apocalyptic Literature." In *The Oxford Handbook of Apocalyptic Literature*, edited by John J. Collins, 180–198. New York: OUP.

Sokoloff, Michael. 2017. *A Dictionary of Jewish Palestinian Aramaic of the Byzantine Period.* Ramat-Gan: Bar Ilan University Press. (First edition 1990.)

Sordi, Martha (ed.). 1985. *La pace nel mondo antico.* Milano: Vita e pensiero.

Spannagel, Martin. 1999. *Exemplaria Principis: Untersuchungen zu Entstehung und Ausstattung des Augustusforums.* Heidelberg: Verlag Archäologie und Geschichte.

Sperber, Daniel. 1984. *A Dictionary of Greek and Latin Legal Terms in Rabbinic Literature.* Ramat-Gan: Bar-Ilan University Press.

Spieckermann, Hermann. 2013. "Historiography, 'Rod of My Anger', and Covenant: The Impact of Asshur on the Old Testament." In *Uomini e profeti. Scritti in onore di Horacio Simian-Yofre SJ*, edited by Elżbieta Obara and Giovanni P. D. Succu, 319–342. Rome: Gregorian Biblical Press.

Spilsbury, Paul. 2002. "Josephus on the Burning of the Temple, the Flavian Triumph, and the Providence of God." *SBL Seminar Papers* 41: 306–327.

———. 2003. "Flavius Josephus on the Rise and Fall of the Roman Empire." *JTS* 54: 1–24.

Steinmetz, Devora. 2008. *Punishment and Freedom: The Rabbinic Construction of Criminal Law.* Philadelphia: University of Pennsylvania Press.

Stemberger, Günter. 1983. *Die römische Herrschaft im Urteil der Juden.* Darmstadt: Wissenschaftliche Buchgesellschaft.

———. 2000. *Jews and Christians in the Holy Land: Palestine in the Fourth Century*, translation by Ruth Tuschling. Edinburgh: T&T Clark.

———. 2005. "La guerra nella *Mišnah* e nei *Midrašim* halakici." In *Guerra santa, guerra e pace dal Vicino Oriente antico alle tradizioni ebraica, cristiana e islamica*, edited by Mauro Perani, 131–139. Florence: La Giuntina.

———. 2010. "Halakhic Midrashim as Historical Sources." In *Rabbinic Texts and the History of Late-Roman Palestine*, edited by Martin Goodman and Philip Alexander, 129–142. Oxford: OUP.

Stern, Karen. 2018. *Writing on the Wall: Graffiti and the Forgotten Jews of Antiquity.* Princeton: PUP.

Stern, Menahem. 1976–1984. *Greek and Latin Authors on Jews and Judaism.* 3 vols. Jerusalem: Israel Academy of Sciences and Humanities.

Stern, Sacha. 1994. *Jewish Identity in Early Rabbinic Writings.* Leiden: Brill.

———. 2001. *Calendar and Community: A History of the Jewish Calendar, 2nd Century BCE to 10th Century CE.* Oxford: OUP.

———. 2003. "Rabbi and the Origins of the Patriarchate." *JJS* 54.2: 193–215.

———. 2017. "Subversion and Subculture: Jewish Time-Keeping in the Roman Empire." In *Jewish Cultural Encounters in the Ancient Mediterranean and Near Eastern World*, edited by Mladen Popović, Myles Schoonover, and Marijn Vandenberghe, 246–264. Leiden: Brill.

Stevens, Kathryn. 2014. "The Antiochus Cylinder, Babylonian Scholarship and Seleucid Imperial Ideology." *The Journal of Hellenic Studies* 134: 66–88.

Steymans, Hans Ulrich. 1995a. *Deuteronomium 28 und die adê zur Thronfolgeregelung Asarhaddons: Segen und Fluch im Alten Orient und in Israel.* Göttingen: Vandenhoeck & Ruprecht.

———. 1995b. "Eine assyrische Vorlage für Deuteronomium 28,20–44". In *Bundesdokument und Gesetz: Studien zum Deuteronomium*, edited by G. Braulik, 119–141. Freiburg i.B.: Herder.

———. 2013. "Deuteronomy 28 and Tell Tayinat." *Verbum et Ecclesia* 34: Art. #870, 13 p. http://dx.doi.org/10.4102/ve.v34i2.870

Stone, Elizabeth C., and David I. Owen. 1991. *Adoption in Old Babylonian Nippur and the Archive of Mannum-mesu-lissur*. Winona Lake: Eisenbrauns.

Stone, Michael E. 1990. *Fourth Ezra: A Commentary on the Book of Fourth Ezra*. Minneapolis: Fortress Press.

Stone, Suzanne L. 1990–1991. "Sinaitic and Noahide Law: Legal Pluralism in Jewish Law." *Cardozo Law Review* 12: 1157–1214.

Strack, Herman L., and Günter Stemberger. 1996. *An Introduction to the Talmud and Midrash*, translated by Markus Bockmuehl. Minneapolis: Fortress Press. (First edition 1991.)

Stratton, Kimberly B. 2010. "The Eschatological Arena: Reinscribing Roman Violence in Fantasies of the End Times." *Biblical Interpretation* 17: 45–76.

Strawn, Brent A. 2007. "'A World under Control': Isaiah 60 and the Apadana Reliefs from Persepolis." In *Approaching Yehud: New Approaches to the Study of the Persian Period*, edited by Jon L. Berquist, 85–116. Atlanta: SBL Press.

Strootman, Rolf. 2013. "Babylonian, Macedonian, King of the World: The Antiochos Cylinder from Borsippa and Seleukid Imperial Integration." In *Shifting Social Imaginaries in the Hellenistic Period: Narrations, Practices, and Images*, edited by Eftychia Stavrianopoulou, 67–97. Leiden: Brill.

———. 2014a. "Hellenistic Imperialism and the Ideal of World Unity." In *The City in the Classical and Post-Classical World: Changing Contexts of Power and Identity*, edited by Claudia Rapp and H. A. Drake, 38–61. Cambridge: CUP.

———. 2014b. *Courts and Elites in the Hellenistic Empires: The Near East after the Achaemenids, c. 330 to 30 BCE*. Edinburgh: Edinburgh University Press.

Sugirtharajah, Rasiah S. 2002. *Postcolonial Criticism and Biblical Interpretation*. Oxford: OUP.

Suspène, Arnaud. 2009. "Les rois amis et alliés face au principat: rapports personnels, représentations du pouvoir et nouvelles stratégies diplomatiques en Méditerranée orientale." In *L'Expression du pouvoir au début de l'Empire. Autour de la Maison Carrée à Nîmes*, edited by Michel Christol and Dominique Darde, 45–51. Paris: Errance.

Sutherland, C. H. V. 1963. "Some Political Notions in Coin Types between 294 and 313." *JRS* 53: 14–20.

Swain, Joseph Ward. 1940. "The Theory of the Four Monarchies: Opposition History under the Roman Empire." *Classical Philology* 35: 1–21.

Sysling, Harry. 1996. Tehiyyat Ha-Metim: *The Resurrection of the Dead in the Palestinian Targums of the Pentateuch and Parallel Traditions in Classical Rabbinic Literature*. Tübingen: Mohr Siebeck.

Tcherikover, Victor A. 1964. "Was Jerusalem a 'Polis'?" *IEJ* 14.1–2: 61–78.

Tcherikover, Victor A., and Alexander Fuks. 1957–1964. *Corpus Papyrorum Judaicarum*. 3 vols. Cambridge: HUP.

Thiessen, Matthew. 2011. *Contesting Conversion: Genealogy, Circumcision, and Identity in Ancient Judaism and Christianity*. New York: OUP.

———. 2013. "Revisiting the προσήλυτος in 'the LXX.'" *JBL* 132: 333–350.

———. 2016. *Paul and the Gentile Problem*. New York: OUP.

Thomas, Yan. 1996. *"Origine" et "commune patrie": étude de droit public romain, 89 av. J.-C.-212 ap. J.-C.* Rome: École française de Rome.

Thompson, Richard J. 2013. *Terror of the Radiance: Assur Covenant to YHWH Covenant.* Göttingen: Vandenhoeck & Ruprecht.

Thraede, Klaus. 1991–1994. "Jakob und Esau." In *Reallexikon für Antike und Christentum: Sachwörterbuch zur Auseinandersetzung des Christentums mit der antiken Welt. Band XVI, Hofzeremoniell—Ianus*, edited by Ernst Dassmann et al., 1118–1207. Stuttgart: Anton Hiersemann.

Toynbee, Jocelyne. 1925. "Some 'Programme' Coin-types of Antoninus Pius." *Classical Review* 39: 170–173.

Treggiari, Susan. 1991. *Roman Marriage: "Iusti Coniuges" from the Time of Cicero to the Time of Ulpian.* Oxford: OUP.

Trimm, Charles. 2012. "Recent Research on Warfare in the Old Testament." *CBR* 10.2: 171–216.

Troiani, Lucio. 1994. "The Πολιτεία of Israel in the Graeco-Roman Age." In *Josephus and the History of the Greco-Roman Period: Essays in Memory of Morton Smith*, edited by Fausto Parente and Joseph Sievers, 11–22. Leiden: Brill.

Tropper, Amram. 2004. *Wisdom, Politics, and Historiography: Tractate Avot in the Context of the Graeco-Roman Near East.* Oxford, OUP.

———. 2005. "Roman Contexts in Jewish Texts: On *Diatagma* and *Prostagma* in Rabbinic Literature." *JQR* 95.2: 207–227.

Tuck, Steven L. 2016. "Imperial Image-Making." In Zissos 2016, 109–128.

Tuori, Kaius. 2016. *The Emperor of Law: The Emergence of Roman Imperial Adjudication.* Oxford: OUP.

Turcan, Robert. 1964. "La 'fondation' du temple de Vénus et de Rome." *Latomus* 23.1: 42–55.

Turner, E. G. 1954. "Tiberius Iulius Alexander." *JRS* 44: 54–64.

Tuval, Michael. 2013. *From Jerusalem Priest to Roman Jew: On Josephus and the Paradigms of Ancient Judaism.* Tübingen: Mohr Siebeck.

Ulrich, Theodor. 1930. Pietas (pius) *als politischer Begriff im römischen Staate bis zum Tode des Kaisers Commodus.* Breslau: M. H. Marcus.

Umemoto, Naoto. 1994. "Juden, 'Heiden' und das Menschengeschlecht in der Sicht Philons von Alexandrien." In *Die Heiden. Juden, Christen und das Problem des Fremden*, edited by Reinhard Feldmeier, 22–51. Tübingen: Mohr Siebeck.

Urbach, Ephraim E. 1959. "The Rabbinical Laws of Idolatry in the Second and Third Centuries in the Light of Archaeological and Historical Facts." *IEJ* 9: 149–165, 229–245.

Uusimäki, Elisa. 2018. "The Rise of the Sage in Greek and Jewish Antiquity." *JSJ* 49.1: 1–29.

Van der Horst, Peter W. 1991. *Ancient Jewish Epitaphs: An Introductory Survey of a Millennium of Jewish Funerary Epigraphy (300 BCE–700 CE).* Kampen: Kok Pharos Publishing House.

———. 2003. Philo's Flaccus, *The First Pogrom: Introduction, Translation and Commentary.* Leiden: Brill.

———. 2015. Saxa Iudaica Loquuntur: *Lessons from Early Jewish Inscriptions.* Leiden: Brill.

———. 2017. "A Short Note on the Epitaph of Ama Helenê Ioudaia." *JSJ* 48.2: 261–265.

Van der Lans, Birgit. 2010. "Belonging to Abraham's Kin: Genealogical Appeals to Abraham as a Possible Background for Paul's Abrahamic Argument." In *Abraham, the Nations, and the Hagarites: Jewish, Christian, and Islamic Perspectives on Kinship with Abraham*, edited by Martin Goodman et al., 307–318. Leiden: Brill.

Van Henten, Jan Willem. 1997. *The Maccabean Martyrs as Saviours of the Jewish People: A Study of 2 and 4 Maccabees.* Leiden: Brill.

———. 1999. "Martyrion and Martyrdom: Some Remarks about Noble Death in Josephus." In *Internationales Josephus-Kolloquium Brüssel 1998*, edited by Jürgen U. Kalms and Folker Siegert, 124–141. Münster: LIT.

Van Henten, Jan Willem, and Friedrich Avemarie. 2002. *Martyrdom and Noble Death: Selected Texts from Graeco-Roman, Jewish and Christian Antiquity*. London: Routledge.

Van Houten, Christiana. 1991. *The Alien in Israelite Law*. Sheffield: JSOT Press.

Van Nijf, Onno M., with Sam van Dijk. 2020. "Experiencing Roman Power at Greek Contests: Romaia in the Greek Festival Network." In Berthelot 2020a, 101–125.

Van Zile, Matthew P. 2017. "The Sons of Noah and the Sons of Abraham: The Origins of Noahide Law." *JSJ* 48: 386–417.

Vana, Liliane. 2012. "Les lois noaḥides: Une mini-Torah pré-sinaïtique pour l'humanité et pour Israël." *Pardès* 52.2: 211–236.

Vanderhooft, David S. 1999. *The Neo-Babylonian Empire and Babylon in the Latter Prophets*. Atlanta: Scholars Press.

Vélissaropoulos-Karakostas, Julie. 2005. "Adoption (Grèce)." In *Dictionnaire de l'Antiquité*, edited by Jean Leclant, 20. Paris: PUF.

Veyne, Paul. 1975. "'Y a-t-il eu un impérialisme romain?' *Mélanges de l'École Française à Rome: Antiquité* 87: 793–855.

———. 1980. "L'Empire romain." In Duverger 1980, 121–130.

———. 2002. "Lisibilité des images, propagande et apparat monarchique dans l'Empire romain." *Revue Historique* 304.1 (621): 3–30.

———. 2005. *L'empire gréco-romain*. Paris: Seuil.

Victor, Royce M. 2010. *Colonial Education and Class Formation in Early Judaism: A Postcolonial Reading*. London: T&T Clark.

Vismara, Cinzia. 1991. *Il supplizio come spettacolo*. Rome: Quasar.

Visotzky, Burton L. 2003. *Golden Bells and Pomegranates: Studies in Midrash Leviticus Rabbah*. Tübingen: Mohr Siebeck.

Vittinghoff, Friedrich. 1994. *Civitas romana: Stadt und politisch-soziale Integration im Imperium Romanum der Kaiserzeit*, edited by Werner Eck. Stuttgart: Klett-Cotta.

Vogt, Joseph. 1960. "*Orbis romanus*. Ein Beitrag zum Sprachgebrauch und zur Vorstellungswelt des römischen Imperialismus." In *Orbis: Ausgewählte Schriften zur Geschichte des Altertums*, 151–198. Freiburg: Herder.

Volterra, Edoardo. 1930. *Collatio Legum Mosaicarum et Romanarum*. Rome: G. Dardi.

Von Ehrenkrook, Jason. 2011. "Effeminacy in the Shadow of Empire: The Politics of Transgressive Gender in Josephus's 'Bellum Judaicum.'" *JQR* 101.2: 145–163.

Von Rad, Gerhard. 1951. *Der Heilige Krieg im alten Israel*. Göttingen: Vandenhoeck & Ruprecht.

Von Schwind, Fritz F. 1940. *Zur Frage der Publikation im römischen Recht*. Munich: C. H. Beck.

de Vos, Jacobus Cornelis. 2016. "Aristobulus and the Universal Sabbath." In *Goochem in Mokum / Wisdom in Amsterdam*, edited by George J. Brooke and Pierre Van Hecke, 138–154. Leiden: Brill.

Vulić, N. 1932. "Inscription grecque de Stobi." *BCH* 56: 291–298 and pl. XIX.

Waebens, Sofie. 2012. "Imperial Policy and Changed Composition of the Auxilia: The 'Change in A.D. 140' Revisited." *Chiron* 42: 1–23.

Waerzeggers, Caroline. 2015. "Babylonian Kingship in the Persian Period: Performance and Reception." In *Exile and Return: The Babylonian Context*, edited by Jonathan Stökl and Caroline Waerzeggers, 181–222. Berlin: De Gruyter.

Walbank, Frank W. 1984. "Monarchy and Monarchic Ideas." In *The Cambridge Ancient History. Volume 7, Part 1: The Hellenistic World*, edited by F. W. Walbank et al., 62–100. Cambridge: CUP.

Walfish, Barry D. 2002. "Kosher Adultery? The Mordecai-Esther-Ahasuerus Triangle in Midrash and Exegesis." *Prooftexts* 22.3: 305–333.

Wallace-Hadrill, Andrew. 1982. "Civilis Princeps: Between Citizen and King." *JRS* 72: 32–48.

———. 2008. *Rome's Cultural Revolution.* Cambridge: CUP.

Walters, James C. 2003. "Paul, Adoption, and Inheritance." In *Paul in the Greco-Roman World: A Handbook,* edited by J. Paul Sampley, 42–76. Harrisburg: Trinity Press International.

Walters, Jonathan. 1997. "Invading the Roman Body: Manliness and Impenetrability in Roman Thought." In *Roman Sexualities,* edited by Judith P. Hallett and Marilyn B. Skinner, 29–43. Princeton: PUP.

Walzer, Michael. 2006. "Commanded and Permitted Wars." In *Law, Politics, and Morality in Judaism,* edited by Michael Walzer, 149–168. Princeton: PUP.

Wander, Bernd. 1998. *Gottesfürchtige und Sympathisanten: Studien zum heidnischen Umfeld von Diasporasynagogen.* Tübingen: Mohr Siebeck.

Wasserman, Mira B. 2017. *Jews, Gentiles, and Other Animals: The Talmud after the Humanities.* Philadelphia: University of Pennsylvania Press.

Watson, Alan. 1987. *Roman Slave Law.* Baltimore: Johns Hopkins University Press.

Watts, James W. 2001. *Persia and Torah: The Theory of Imperial Authorization of the Pentateuch.* Atlanta: SBL Press.

Wazana, Nili. 2008. "Are Trees of the Field Human? A Biblical War Law (Deuteronomy 20:19–20) and Neo-Assyrian Propaganda." In *Treasures on Camels' Humps: Historical and Literary Studies from the Ancient Near East Presented to Israel Eph'al,* edited by Mordechai Cogan and Dan'el Kahn, 274–295. Jerusalem: Magnes.

———. 2012. "'For an impaled body is a curse of God' (Deut 21:23): Impaled Bodies in Biblical Law and Conquest Narratives." In *Law and Narrative in the Bible and in Neighbouring Ancient Cultures,* edited by Klaus-Peter Adam, Friedrich Avemarie, and Nili Wazana, 69–98. Tübingen: Mohr Siebeck.

———. 2016. "The Law of the King (Deuteronomy 17,14–20) in the Light of Empire and Destruction." In *The Fall of Jerusalem and the Rise of the Torah,* edited by Peter Dubovský, Dominik Markl, and Jean-Pierre Sonnet, 169–194. Tübingen: Mohr Siebeck.

Weber, Max. 1972. *Wirtschaft und Gesellschaft. Grundriss der verstehenden Soziologie,* edited by J. Winckelmann. Fifth edition. Tübingen: Mohr Siebeck.

Weber, Reinhard. 2000. *Das Gesetz im hellenistischen Judentum. Studien zum Verständnis und zur Funktion der Thora von Demetrios bis Pseudo-Phokylides.* Frankfurt: P. Lang.

Weinfeld, Moshe. 1972. *Deuteronomy and the Deuteronomic School.* Oxford: Clarendon Press.

———. 1986. "The Protest Against Imperialism in Ancient Israelite Prophecy." In *The Origins and Diversity of Axial Age Civilizations,* edited by Shmuel N. Eisenstadt, 169–182. Albany: State University of New York Press.

———. 1993. *The Promise of the Land: The Inheritance of the Land of Canaan by the Israelites.* Berkeley: University of California Press.

———. 1998. "Jerusalem: A Political and Spiritual Capital." In *Capital Cities: Urban Planning and Spiritual Dimensions,* edited by J. Goodnick Westenholz, 15–40. Jerusalem: Bible Lands Museum.

Weinstock, Stefan. 1960. "Pax and the 'Ara Pacis.'" *JRS* 50: 44–58.

Weiss, Daniel H. 2018. "The Christianization of Rome and the Edomization of Christianity: Avodah Zarah and Political Power." *JSQ* 25.4: 394–422.

Weiss, Zeev. 2014. *Public Spectacles in Roman and Late Antique Palestine.* Cambridge: HUP.

Weisweiler, John. 2016. "From Empire to World-State: Ecumenical Language and Cosmopolitan Consciousness in the Later Roman Aristocracy." In Lavan, Payne, and Weisweiler 2016, 187–208.

Weitzman, Steven. 2009. "Mimic Jews and Jewish Mimics in Antiquity: A Non-Girardian Approach to Mimetic Rivalry." *Journal of the American Academy of Religion* 77.4: 922–940.

Weksler-Bdolah, Shlomit. 2014. "The Foundation of Aelia Capitolina in Light of New Excavations along the Eastern Cardo." *IEJ* 64.1: 38–62.

———. 2015. "The Role of the Temple Mount in the Layout of Aelia Capitolina: The Capitolium after all." In *Ehud Netzer Volume*, edited by Zeev Weiss, 126–137. Jerusalem: Israel Exploration Society. (Heb.)

———. 2020. *Aelia Capitolina—Jerusalem in the Roman Period in Light of Archaeological Research.* Leiden: Brill.

Weksler-Bdolah, Shlomit, and Renate Rosenthal-Heginbottom. 2014. "Two Aspects of the Transformation of Jerusalem into the Roman Colony of Aelia Capitolina." In *Knowledge and Wisdom: Archaeological and Historical Essays in Honour of Leah Di Segni*, edited by Giovanni Claudio Bottini, L. Daniel Chrupcala, and Joseph Patrich, 43–61. Milano: Edizioni Terra Santa.

Welles, Charles B. 1938. *The Inscriptions: Gerasa City of the Decapolis.* New Haven: American Schools of Oriental Research.

Whitmarsh, Timothy. 2001. *Greek Literature and the Roman Empire: The Politics of Imitation.* Oxford: OUP.

———. 2013. "Resistance is Futile?: Greek Literary Tactics in the Face of Rome." In *Les Grecs héritiers des Romains*, edited by Luc van der Stockt et al., 57–78. Geneva: Fondation Hardt.

Wiesehöfer, Josef. 2009. "The Achaemenid Empire." In Morris and Scheidel 2009, 66–98.

———. 2013. "Polybios und die Entstehung des römischen Weltreichsschemas." In *Polybios und seine Historien*, edited by Volker Grieb and Clemens Koehn, 59–69. Stuttgart: F. Steiner.

Wilf, Steven. 2008. *The Law before the Law.* Lanham: Lexington Books.

Wilfand, Yael. 2014. *Poverty, Charity and the Image of the Poor in Rabbinic Texts from the Land of Israel.* Sheffield: Sheffield Phoenix Press.

———. 2017. "The Roman Context for the Rabbinic Ban on Teaching Greek to Sons." *JAJ* 8: 365–387.

———. 2019a. "'How Great Is Peace': Tannaitic Thinking on Shalom and the *Pax Romana*." *JSJ* 50: 223–251.

———. 2019b. "Did Roman Treatment of Freedwomen Influence Rabbinic Halakhah on the Status of Female Converts in Marriage?" *Journal of Legal History*, https://doi.org/10 .1080/01440365.2019.1625216 (Published online: 11 June 2019).

———. 2020a. "Alexander the Great in the Jerusalem Talmud and Genesis Rabbah: A Critique of Roman Power, Greed and Cruelty." In Berthelot 2020a, 338–360.

———. 2020b. "Roman Concepts of Citizenship, and Rabbinic Approaches to the Lineage of Converts and the Integration of their Descendants into Israel." *JAJ* 11.1: 45–75.

———. 2021. "'A Proselyte Whose Sons Converted with Him': Roman Laws on New Citizens' Authority Over Their Children and Tannaitic Rulings on Converts to Judaism and Their Offspring." In Berthelot, Dohrmann, and Nemo-Pekelman 2021, 345–364.

Wilker, Julia. 2005. "Herodes der Große—Herrschaftslegitimation zwischen jüdischer Identität und römischer Freundschaft." In *Roms auswärtige Freunde in später Republik und frühem Prinzipat*, edited by Altay Coşkun, 201–223. Göttingen: Duehrkopp & Radicke.

———. 2007. *Für Rom und Jerusalem. Die herodianische Dynastie im 1. Jahrhundert n.Chr.* Frankfurt: Verlag Antike.

———. 2012. "'God is with Italy Now': Pro-Roman Jews in the First Century CE." In *Groups, Normativity, and Rituals: Jewish Identity and Politics between the Maccabees and Bar Kokhba*, edited by Benedikt Eckhardt, 157–187. Leiden: Brill.

Will, Edouard. 1985. "Pour une 'anthropologie coloniale' du monde hellénistique." In *The Craft of the Ancient Historian*, edited by John W. Eadie and Josiah Ober, 273–301. Lanham: Rowman & Littlefield.

Williams, Craig A. 1999. *Roman Homosexuality: Ideologies of Masculinity in Classical Antiquity*. Oxford: OUP.

Wilson, Walter T. 2011. *Philo of Alexandria. On Virtues: Introduction, Translation, and Commentary*. Leiden: Brill.

Wilson-Wright, Aren M. 2015. "From Persepolis to Jerusalem: A Reevaluation of the Old-Persian–Hebrew Contact in the Achaemenid Period." *Vetus Testamentum* 65.1: 152–167.

Winston, David. 1995. "Sage and Super-Sage in Philo of Alexandria." In *Pomegranates and Golden Bells*, edited by David P. Wright, 815–824. Winona Lake: Eisenbrauns.

Wiseman, Donald J. 1958. "The Vassal-Treaties of Esarhaddon." *Iraq* 20: 1–99.

Wolf, Eric R. 1999. *Envisioning Power: Ideologies of Dominance and Crisis*. Berkeley: University of California Press.

Woolf, Greg. 1993. "Roman Peace." In *War and Society in the Roman World*, edited by John Rich and Graham Shipley, 171–194. London: Routledge.

———. 1994. "Becoming Roman, Staying Greek: Culture, Identity and the Civilizing Process in the Roman East." *Proceedings of the Cambridge Philological Society* 40: 116–143.

———. 1997. "Beyond Romans and Natives." *World Archaeology* 28.3: 339–350.

———. 1998. *Becoming Roman: The Origins of Provincial Civilization in Gaul*. Cambridge: CUP.

———. 2011. "Provincial Revolts in the Early Roman Empire." In Popović 2011, 27–44.

———. 2015. "Rome and Imperialism." In *Palgrave Encyclopedia of Imperialism and Anti-Imperialism*, edited by Immanuel Ness and Zak Cope, 725–739. London: Palgrave MacMillan.

———. 2020. "The Rulers Ruled." In Berthelot 2020a, 85–100.

Wright, Benjamin G. 2015. *The Letter of Aristeas: "Aristeas to Philocrates" or "On the Translation of the Law of the Jews."* Berlin: De Gruyter.

Wright, Jacob L. 2008. "Military Valor and Kingship: A Book-Oriented Approach to the Study of a Major War Theme." In *Writing and Reading War: Rhetoric, Gender, and Ethics in Biblical and Modern Contexts*, edited by Brad E. Kelle and Frank Ritchel Ames, 33–56. Atlanta: SBL.

———. 2011. "Surviving in an Imperial Context: Foreign Military Service and Judean Identity." In *Judah and the Judeans in the Achaemenid Period: Negotiating Identity in an International Context*, edited by Oded Lipschits, Gary N. Knoppers, and Manfred Oeming, 505–528. Winona Lake: Eisenbrauns.

Yadin, Azzan. 2004. *Scripture as Logos: Rabbi Ishmael and the Origins of Midrash*. Philadelphia: University of Pennsylvania Press.

Yadin-Israel, Azzan. 2014. *Scripture and Tradition: Rabbi Akiva and the Triumph of Midrash*. Philadelphia: University of Pennsylvania Press.

Yagur, Moshe. 2017. "The Donor and the Gravedigger: Converts to Judaism in the Cairo Geniza Documents." In *Contesting Inter-Religious Conversion in the Medieval World*, edited by Yaniv Fox and Yosi Yisraeli, 115–134. London: Routledge.

Yarden, Ofir. 2012. "Adoption in Judaism." *Dialog: A Journal of Theology* 51.4: 276–283.

Yaron, Reuven. 1960. *Gifts in Contemplation of Death in Jewish and Roman Law*. Oxford: Clarendon Press.

———. 1961. *Introduction to the Law of the Aramaic Papyri*. Oxford: Clarendon Press.

———. 1965. "Varia on Adoption." *Journal of Juristic Papyrology* 15: 171–183.

Yavetz, Zvi. 1998. "Latin Authors on Jews and Dacians." *Historia: Zeitschrift für Alte Geschichte* 47.1: 77–107.

Yuval, Israel J. 2002. "Rabbinical Perspectives on the Bearing of Weapons by the Jews." *Jewish Studies* 41: 51*–55*.

———. 2006. *Two Nations in Your Womb: Perceptions of Jews and Christians in Late Antiquity and the Middle Ages*, translated by Barbara Harshav and Jonathan Chipman. Berkeley: University of California Press.

——. 2011. "The Orality of Early Jewish Law: From Pedagogy to Ideology." In *Judaism, Christianity, and Islam in the Course of History: Exchange and Conflicts*, edited by Lothar Gall and Dietmar Willoweit, 237–260. München: R. Oldenbourg Verlag.

Zadok, Ran. 2014. "Judeans in Babylonia–Updating the Dossier." In *Encounters by the Rivers of Babylon: Scholarly Conversations Between Jews, Iranians and Babylonians in Antiquity*, edited by Uri Gabbay and Shai Secunda, 109–129. Tübingen: Mohr Siebeck.

Zalkah, Y. 2013. *"Gilgulo shel Sippur: Beyn Metziyut le-Ideologya."* *Asufot* 4: 87–104. (Heb.)

Zanker, Paul. 1988. *The Power of Images in the Age of Augustus*, translated by Alan Shapiro. Ann Arbor: University of Michigan Press.

Zarrow, Edward M. 2006. "Imposing Romanisation: Flavian Coins and Jewish Identity." *JJS* 57.1: 44–55.

Zeichmann, Christopher B. 2015. "Martial and the *fiscus Iudaicus* Once More." *JSP* 25.2: 111–117.

Zellentin, Holger. 2016. "The Rabbis on (the Christianisation of) the Imperial Cult: Mishnah and Yerushalmi Avodah Zarah 3:1 (42b, 54–42c, 61)." In *Jewish Art in Its Late Antique Context*, edited by Catherine Hezser and Uzi Leibner, 321–357. Tübingen: Mohr Siebeck.

Zelnick-Abramovitz, Rachel. 2000. "The *Xenodokoi* of Thessaly." *ZPE* 130: 109–120.

Zissu, Boaz, and Hanan Eshel. 2016. "Religious Aspects of the Bar Kokhba Revolt: The Founding of Aelia Capitolina on the Ruins of Jerusalem." In *The Religious Aspects of War in the Ancient Near East, Greece and Rome. Ancient Warfare, volume I*, edited by Krzysztof Ulanowski, 387–405. Leiden: Brill.

Zollschan, Linda. 2017. *Rome and Judaea: International Law Relations, 162–100 BCE*. London: Routledge.

Zuckerman, Constantine. 1985–1988. "Hellenistic *Politeumata* and the Jews. A Reconsideration." *SCI* 8–9: 171–185.

Zunz, Leopold. 1845. *Zur Geschichte und Literatur*. Berlin: Veit & Comp.

INDEX OF ANCIENT SOURCES